Jon E. Lewis is a writer and historian. He is author of the best-selling *The Mammoth Book of Eyewitness History* and *The Mammoth Book of Eyewitness Britain*.

The Mammoth Book of
EYEWITNESS AMERICA

The history of the world's most powerful nation

CARROLL & GRAF PUBLISHERS
New York

Carroll & Graf Publishers
An imprint of Avalon Publishing Group, Inc.
161 William Street
NY 10038–2607
www.carrollandgraf.com

First published in the UK by Robinson,
an imprint of Constable & Robinson Ltd 2003

First Carroll & Graf edition 2003

Collection and editorial material
copyright J. Lewis-Stempel 2003

ISBN 0–7867–1167–1

Printed and bound in the EU

For Penny, Tristram and Freda.

Contents

Part Three: Destiny, America 1816–1900   145

Part Four: Century, America 1901–2001   **305**

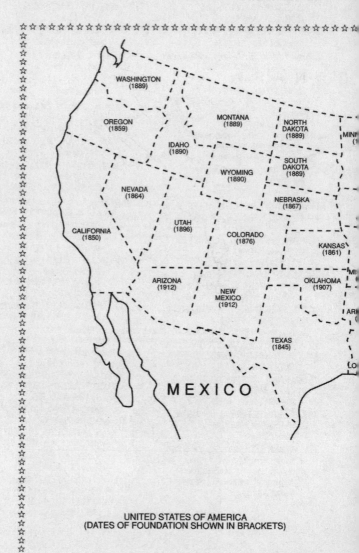

WASHINGTON
(1889)

OREGON
(1859)

MONTANA
(1889)

NORTH
DAKOTA
(1889)

MINN
(1

IDAHO
(1890)

SOUTH
DAKOTA
(1889)

WYOMING
(1890)

NEVADA
(1864)

NEBRASKA
(1867)

CALIFORNIA
(1850)

UTAH
(1896)

COLORADO
(1876)

KANSAS
(1861)

MI

ARIZONA
(1912)

NEW
MEXICO
(1912)

OKLAHOMA
(1907)

ARI

TEXAS
(1845)

LO

MEXICO

UNITED STATES OF AMERICA
(DATES OF FOUNDATION SHOWN IN BRACKETS)

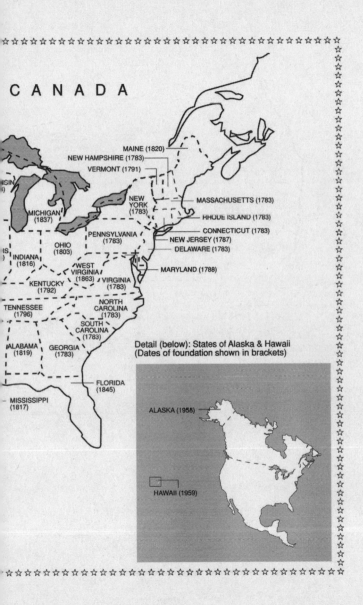

CANADA

MAINE (1820)
NEW HAMPSHIRE (1783)
VERMONT (1791)

SIN
)

MICHIGAN
(1837)

NEW
YORK
(1783)

MASSACHUSETTS (1783)

RHODE ISLAND (1783)

CONNECTICUT (1783)

NEW JERSEY (1787)

DELAWARE (1783)

PENNSYLVANIA
(1783)

IS
)

OHIO
(1803)

INDIANA
(1816)

MARYLAND (1788)

WEST
VIRGINIA
(1863)

VIRGINIA
(1783)

KENTUCKY
(1792)

NORTH
CAROLINA
(1783)

TENNESSEE
(1796)

SOUTH
CAROLINA
(1783)

ALABAMA
(1819)

GEORGIA
(1783)

Detail (below): States of Alaska & Hawaii
(Dates of foundation shown in brackets)

FLORIDA
(1845)

MISSISSIPPI
(1817)

ALASKA (1958)

HAWAII (1959)

CHRONOLOGY

KEY DATES	HISTORY, POLITICS, WAR	RELIGION, SCIENCE, CULTURE	SOCIAL LIFE
1492	Columbus discovers Watling Island, Bahamas		
1497	Cabots reach east coast of N. America		
1524	Da Verrazano discovers New York Bay		
1538		Mercator uses term America	
1541	Coranado leads expedition from Mexico to Texas, Oklahoma, Kansas; de Soto sights Mississippi		
1607	Founding of Jamestown, Va.		
1608		Capt. John Smith *A True Relation of Virginia*	
1612			Tobacco planted Virginia
1619			African slaves introduced into Virginia

KEY DATES	HISTORY, POLITICS, WAR	RELIGION, SCIENCE, CULTURE	SOCIAL LIFE
1620	Pilgrim Fathers land at Plymouth, Mass.		
1626	Dutch found New Amsterdam		
1630	Puritan John Winthrop founds Boston		
1636		Founding of Harvard College	
1639		First printing press in America	
1643	Confederation of New England		
1682	La Salle claims Lousiana for France		
1683			German settlers begin arriving. N. America
1692	Salem trials for witchcraft		
1704			*Boston News-Letter* founded
1711	Tucarora (Indian) war in N. Carolina		
1721			Rifles introduced N. America
1729			Franklin bros. publish *The Pennsylvania Gazette*

KEY DATES	HISTORY, POLITICS, WAR	RELIGION, SCIENCE, CULTURE	SOCIAL LIFE
1732	George Washington born		
1750			First theater New York
1754	Anglo-French War		
1765	Britain passes Stamp Act		
1766	Mason-Dixon Line drawn between Pennsylvania and Maryland		
1768	Boston refuses to quarter British troops		
1773	Boston Tea Party protest		
1775	Skirmish at Lexington begins American Revolution against British rule (until 1783)		
1776	Congress votes for Declaration of Independence		
1777			Importation of slaves into US prohibited
1781	British capitulate at Yorktown		
1783	Britain recognizes US independence		
1786	Shay's rebellion, Mass.		

KEY DATES	HISTORY, POLITICS, WAR	RELIGION, SCIENCE, CULTURE	SOCIAL LIFE
1787	Constitution of US signed	Fitch launches mechanical steamboat, Delaware River	Dollar currency introduced
1789	George Washington becomes first President of US		
1790			Washington D.C. founded
1791	Bill of Rights ratified		
1803	US purchases Louisiana from France		
1804–6	Lewis and Clark's *Voyage of Discovery*		
1812	US declares war on Britain (until 1815)		
1818	US and Canada agrees 49th Parallel as border		
1821			Population of US approx. 10 million
1831	Nat Turner leads slave revolt, Va.		Horse-drawn buses New York
1836	Battle of the Alamo; Texas wins independence from Mexico		
1843	1000 pioneers travel overland from Missouri to Pacific Coasts		

KEY DATES	HISTORY, POLITICS, WAR	RELIGION, SCIENCE, CULTURE	SOCIAL LIFE
1846	US-Mexican War (Until 1848)	Smithsonian founded	
1850–60			424,000 English and 914,000 Irish emigrate to US
1854	Republican Party founded		
1860	Abraham Lincoln elected 16th President of US		
1861	Confederate States of America formed; Confederates take Fort Sumpter; US Civil War inaugurated		
1862	*Emancipation Proclamation* declares all slaves in rebel territory free		
1864	Gen. Sherman defeats Confederates at Savanah		
1865	Confederate States of America surrenders at Appomattox Courthouse. Slavery abolished by 13th Amendment to Constitution		Ku Klux Klan founded
1867	US buys Alaska from Russia for $7,200,000		
1868			Cincinnati Redstockings becomes first pro baseball club

KEY DATES	HISTORY, POLITICS, WAR	RELIGION, SCIENCE, CULTURE	SOCIAL LIFE
1875			Mark Twain *Adventures of Tom Sawyer*
1876	Battle of Little Big Horn (Custer's Last Stand)		
1881	Billy the Kid shot dead		
1883			Chicago site of first skyscraper
1886	American Federation of Labor founded		
1890	Battle of Wounded Knee ends Indian Wars		
1898	US declares war on Spain; Guam and Philippines among territories ceded by Madrid in Peace Treaty of Paris		
1902	US gains control of Panama Canal		
1903		First manned flight by Wright bros. N. Carolina	
1905	International Workers of the World founded		
1906	San Francisco earthquake		
1908–28			Henry Ford's "assembly-line" mass-produces 15 million Model T cars

KEY DATES	HISTORY, POLITICS, WAR	RELIGION, SCIENCE, CULTURE	SOCIAL LIFE
1909	Peary reaches N. Pole		
1917	US enters WW I (Until 1918)		
1927	Lindbergh flies the Atlantic		
1929	Wall Street Crash; St Valentine's Day Massacre in Chicago		
1932	Depression results in 14 million unemployed in US		
1933	F.D. Roosevelt inaugurated as 32nd president; "New Deal" National Recovery Act and Farm Credit Act passed		
1934	Gangster John Dillinger shot dead by FBI		
1939		Aaron Copland *Billy the Kid*; John Steinbeck *Grapes of Wrath*	
1941	Japan bombs Pearl Harbor; US enters WWII (Until 1945)		
1942	Battle of Midway	Fermi splits the atom	
1944	D-Day Landings (France)		
1945	Atom bomb dropped on Hiroshima and Nagasaki; Japan sues for peace		

KEY DATES	HISTORY, POLITICS, WAR	RELIGION, SCIENCE, CULTURE	SOCIAL LIFE
1950	Korean War (until 1953); Senator McCarthy begins anti-Communist witch-hunt		Approx 10,000 TV sets sold
1957	School integration crisis at Little Rock		
1960	John F. Kennedy elected President		
1961	Abortive Bay of Pigs invasion of Castro's Cuba		
1962	Cuban missile crisis		
1963	Civil rights March on Washington; assassination of JFK at Dallas		
1964	US destroyer allegedly attacked off Vietnam; US involvement in Vietnam (against Communist forces) escalates		
1965	Race riots in Watts, Los Angeles		
1967	Boxing champion Muhammad Ali (Cassius Clay) refuses to fight in Vietnam		
1968	My Lai massacre, Vietnam; assassination of Martin Luther King	Tom Wolfe *Electric Kool-Aid Acid Test*	
1969	Armstrong and Aldrin land on moon		Woodstock rock festival

KEY DATES	HISTORY, POLITICS, WAR	RELIGION, SCIENCE, CULTURE	SOCIAL LIFE
1970	Four students shot dead in anti-war protest, Kent State Univ.		
1974	President Nixon resigns over Watergate bugging scandal		
1975	Last American forces evacuated from Saigon		
1979	Siege of US embassy in Iran		
1980	Ronald Reagan elected president		
1987	Stock market crash		
1991	Persian Gulf War		
1992	Riots in Los Angeles		
1999	President Clinton acquitted in "Zippergate" scandal		
2000	George W. Bush elected President		
2001	"9/11" terrorist attacks on New York and Washington DC		
2003	Gulf War II		

Part One

DISCOVERY

America 1492–1763

INTRODUCTION

In 1492 Columbus sailed the ocean blue and landed in the Bahamas. Believing he had reached an outpost of India, he termed the people he found "indios". He wrote to his patrons, the King and Queen of Spain: "So tractable, so peaceable, are these people, that I swear to your majesties there is not in the world a better nation . . . and although it is true that they are naked, yet their manner are decorous and praiseworthy".

Columbus' mistake in navigation aside, his voyage re-discovered the American continent for the Europeans. On his heels came the conquistadors, hard-fighting Spanish noblemen who overran the Carribbean, Mexico and Peru before venturing northward. Always the lure was gold. In 1513 Ponce de León landed in Florida. It is with de León that the history of what would become the USA really begins.

Ponce de Léon found no gold, only flowers (hence the nomenclature *Florida*). Nothing daunted, another conquistador, de Soto, landed in Florida in 1541 and staggered westwards, fighting repeated skirmishes with Indians, until he reached Arkansas (discovering the Mississippi en route); in the same year, de Coronado rode up out of Mexico in search of the fabled golden cities of Cibola and Quivira, penetrating as far north as present-day Kansas.

Disappointed by the lack of yellow ore, the Spanish took little interest in the northern New World. They had no coherent colonization policy. Neither did their rivals the French, whose explorers probed the Atlantic coast from 1524 onwards, but mainly with an eye to get-rich-quick grabs of the continent's cod and fur. This left the whole of the Eastern seaboard from Canada to Florida unclaimed.

It was the fortune and fate of Britain that when she came to build an empire that this rich and temperate land remained free. The British were as keen on plunder and geopolitical advantage as the next nation, but they were also desirous of settling people in the New World. Under Sir Walter Raleigh's sponsorship, the English founded their first colony at Roanoke in 1585. This failed – the colonists asked to be removed in 1587 – but the settlement founded at Jamestown, Virginia, in 1607 did not.

More British immigrants arrived; settlements and farms spread along the James River, and then to Maryland and the Carolinas. In 1620 a group of religious dissenters, the Pilgrims, landed in Massachusets after their vessel the *Mayflower* was blown off its course for Virginia. The Pilgrims decided to build their homes at Plymouth, where luck had washed them up. With them they brought their "compact", drawn up and agreed in the cabin of the *Mayflower*, which called for political self-rule; and so was the idea of government by consent planted early in the English New World.

Despite the hardships suffered by the new "plantations", notably the "Starving Time" at Jamestown, they endured, then prospered, and soon stable British colonies, fuelled by waves of emigration, stretched along the Atlantic seaboard from New Hampshire to Georgia. (The colonies included New York and New Jersey, seized from the Dutch, who had much of the mindset of the British, but not the might). As the white population of America grew, so the native population declined inexorably. War took its toil, so did land snatching, which deprived the Eastern agrarian tribes of their means of subsistence. But nothing killed the natives of America like the white man's disease. Microbes, especially of the smallpox variety, wiped out nearly 90% of some Algonquin. There were sporadic Indian resistances to Caucasian expansion – the Wampanoags of King Philip killed 600 New Englanders in 1675 – but still the whites came.

And eventually, when the coastal strip was used up, the whites began to venture westwards. By the turn of the 1700s, hard-scrabble farmers were entering into the Great Appalachian Valley, hewing through the wilderness. As these immigrants, many of them rugged Scotch-Irish, laboured on the frontier in the backwoods they transformed themselves just as they transformed their environment. They became less European. The mentality of the woodlanders was that of future America: pragmatic, wary of government, and inclined to optimism.

That said, there were meaningful divides in the new society of America. If the colonies of New England and the "Middle" were inclined to religious toleration (excepting for the moment the Puritan Congregationalists of Massachusetts) and populated by free people on small farms, the South was different almost from the beginning. In Virginia, Maryland and North Carolina it was the practice to grant Englishmen large tracts of fertile land, which encouraged large-scale agriculture (tobacco was the favoured crop; by 1639 Virginia was producing 1,500,000 pounds of the "weed" per annum). These plantations were worked by slaves shipped in from Africa.

One day the dispute over slavery would rip America apart, but long before that there were the vexed problems of the French and self-government to face. The massive expansion of British colonies in America irked the French, who tried to make good their imperial status by settling in eastern Canada ("New France") and then, after Robert Cavalier descended the Illinois and Mississippi, claiming all the lands that the latter drained. The British colonialists were not inclined to heed France's staked claim, and the matter came to a head in 1753 when the French tried to seal off the Ohio Valley. Virginia's British governor, Robert Dinwiddie, sent the young George Washington to tell the French to vamoose. They refused, and so began the Seven Years War. Initially, the British proved serially inept in combatting the French, until a change of ministry in London removed the army's dusty leaders and replaced them with shiny new ones. One of these, James Wolfe, destroyed the French at Quebec on 13 September 1759. There was four more years of warfare, but the war was already won. By the Treaty of Paris of 1763, the French lost all their possessions on the continent. Canada and all lands east of the Mississippi went to Britain. The land west of the Mississippi France sold to its ally Spain.

Britain more than doubled its territorial holdings in North America as a result of the Treaty of Paris. It also doubled its trouble. Fearing unrest among its new French Catholic subjects, the British determined to build a new defence system in North America – and determined equally that the colonialists should pay for it. Britain's attempts to raise money and tighten imperial administration in America would soon spark another war. A war of colonial independence from Britain itself.

COLUMBUS REACHES THE AMERICAS, BAHAMAS, 12 October 1492

Christopher Columbus

Seeking a new trade route to the East on behalf of Imperial Spain, the explorer sailed west, reaching the Bahamas two months later. He was not the first European to reach the New World (the Viking Bjarni Herjolfsson had explored the coast of Labrador as early as AD 985), but he did unveil the continent's existence to Europe.

I was on the poop deck at ten o'clock in the evening when I saw a light. It was so indistinct that I could not be sure it was land, but I called Gutiérrez, the Butler of the King's Table and told him to look at what I thought was a light.

He looked and saw it. I also told Rodrigo Sánchez de Segovia, Your Majesties' observer on board, but he saw nothing because he was standing in the wrong place. After I had told them, the light appeared once or twice more, like a wax candle rising and falling. Only a few people thought it was a sign of land, but I was sure we were close to a landfall.

Then the *Pinta*, being faster and in the lead, sighted land and made the signal as I had ordered. The first man to sight land was called Rodrigo de Triana. The land appeared two hours after midnight, about two leagues away. We furled all sail except the *treo*, the mainsail with no bonnets, and we jogged off and on until Friday morning, when we came to an island. We saw naked people, and I went ashore in a boat with armed men, taking Martín Alonso Pinzón and his brother Vicente Yáñez, captain of the *Nina*. I took the royal standard, and the captains each took a banner with the Green Cross, which each of my ships carries as a device, with the letters F and Y, surmounted by a crown, at each end of the cross.

When we stepped ashore we saw fine green trees, streams everywhere and different kinds of fruit. I called to the two captains to jump ashore with the rest, who included Rodrigo de Escobedo, secretary of the fleet, and Rodrigo Sánchez de Segovia, asking them to bear solemn witness that in the presence of them all I was taking possession of this island for their Lord and Lady the King and Queen, and I made the necessary declaration which are set down at greater length in the written testimonies.

Soon many of the islanders gathered round us. I could see that they were people who would be more easily converted to our Holy Faith by love than by coercion, and wishing them to look on us with friendship I gave some of them red bonnets and glass beads which they hung round their necks, and many other things of small value, at which they were so delighted and so eager to please us that we could not believe it. Later they swam out to the boats to bring us parrots and balls of cotton thread and darts, and many other things, exchanging them for such objects as glass beads and hawk bells. They took anything, and gave willingly whatever they had.

However, they appeared to me to be a very poor people in all respects. They go about as naked as the day they were born, even the women, though I saw only one, who was quite young. All the men I saw were quite young, none older than thirty, all well built, finely bodied and handsome in the face. Their hair is coarse, almost like a horse's tail, and short; they wear it short, cut over the brow, except a few strands of hair hanging down uncut at the back.

Some paint themselves with black, some with the colour of the Canary islanders, neither black nor white, others with white, others with red, others with whatever they can find. Some have only their face painted, others their whole body, others just their eyes or nose. They carry no weapons, and are ignorant of them; when I showed them some swords they took them by the blade and cut themselves. They have no iron; their darts are just sticks without an iron head, though some of them have a fish tooth or something else at the tip.

They are all the same size, of good stature; dignified and well formed. I saw some with scars on their bodies, and made signs to ask about them, and they indicated to me that people from other islands nearby came to capture them and they defended themselves. I thought, and still think, that people from the mainland come here to take them prisoner. They must be good servants, and intelligent, for I can see that they quickly repeat everything said to them. I believe they would readily become Christians; it appeared to me that they have no religion. With God's will, I will take six of them with me for Your Majesties when I leave this place, so that they may learn Spanish.

I saw no animals on the island, only parrots.

THE DISCOVERY OF FLORIDA, April 1513

Juan Ponce de León

A Spanish conquistador, de León (1460–1521) both discovered and named Florida.

Juan Ponce de León, finding himself without office . . . and seeing himself rich, determined to do something by which to gain honour and increase his estate; and as he had news that there were lands to the northward, he resolved to go to explore toward that part; for which he armed three vessels, well provided with food, men, and mariners, which for the purpose of discovery are most necessary. He sailed from the island Thursday, in the afternoon, the 3rd of March, setting out from the harbour of San German. He went to Aguada, in order to set from there his course. The night following he went out to sea, north-west a quarter by north, and the vessels went eight leagues of a day's run, before the sun rose. They sailed on until on Tuesday, the 8th of the said month, they came to anchor at the banks of Babueca, at an island that they call El Viejo, which is in 22.5° [latitude]. Next day they anchored in an islet of the Lucayos called Caycos. Soon they anchored in another called La Yaguna, in 24°. On the 11th of the same month they reached another island called Amaguayo, and there they remained for repairs. They passed on to the island called Manegua, which is in 24.5°. On the 14th they reached Guanahani, which is in 25°40′, where they made ready one ship to cross the Windward gulf of the islands of the Lucayos. This island, Guanahani, was the first that the admiral Don Christoval Colon discovered, and where, in his first voyage, he went ashore and named it San Salvador. They set out from here, running north-west, and on Sunday, the 27th, which was the day of the Feast of the Resurrection, which commonly they call [the feast] "of Flowers", they saw an island but did not examine it.

And Monday, the 28th, they ran fifteen leagues in the same direction, and Wednesday went on in the same manner, and afterward, with bad weather, until the 2nd of April, running west-north-west, the water diminishing to nine fathoms, at one league from land, which was in 30° 8′, they ran along beside the coast seeking harbour, and at night anchored near the land in eight fathoms of water. And believing that this land was an island, they named it La Florida, because it had a very beautiful view of many and cool woodlands, and it was level and uniform; and because, moreover, they discovered it in the time of the Feast of Flowers [Pascua Florida], Juan Ponce wished to conform in the name to these two reasons. He went ashore to get information, and take possession.

On Friday, the 8th, they set sail, running in the same direction: and Saturday they sailed to the south a quarter by south-east; and keeping the same course until the 20th of April, they discovered some huts of Indians, where they anchored: the day following, all three vessels following the sea-coast, they saw such a current that, although they had a strong wind, they could not go forward, but rather backward, and it seemed that they were going on well; and finally it was seen that the current was so great it was more powerful than the wind. The two vessels that found themselves nearest the land anchored, but the current was so strong that the cables twisted: and the third vessel, which was a brigantine, which was farther out to sea, could find no bottom, or did not know of the current, and it was drawn away from land, and lost to their sight, though the day was clear with fair weather.

BISON, Kansas, 1540

Francisco Vasquez de Coronado

De Coronado (1510–1554) led an expedition out of Mexico in search of cities paved with gold. He reached as far north as present day Kansas. There was no gold, but there were bison.

I want to tell, also, about the appearance of the bulls, which is likewise remarkable. At first there was not a horse that did not run away on seeing them, for their faces are short and narrow between the eyes, the forehead two spans wide. Their eyes bulge on the sides, so that, when they run, they can see those who follow them. They are bearded like very large he-goats. When they run they carry their heads low, their beards touching the ground. From the middle of the body back they are covered with very woolly hair like that of fine sheep. From the belly to the front they have very heavy hair like the mane of a wild lion. They have a hump larger than that of a camel. Their horns, which show a little through the hair, are short and heavy. During May they shed the hair on the rear half of their body and look exactly like lions. To remove this hair they lean against some small trees found in some small barrancas and rub against them until they shed their wool as a snake sheds its skin. They have short tails with a small bunch of hair at the end. When they run they carry their tails erect like the scorpion. One peculiar thing about them is that when they are calves they are reddish like ours, and with time, as they become older, they change in colour and appearance . . . .

[The Indians] go together in companies, and move from one place to another . . . following the seasons and the pasture after their oxen.

These oxen are of the bigness and colour of our bulls, but their horns are not so great. They have a great bunch upon their fore-shoulders, and more hair on their fore part than on their hinder part: and it is like wool. They have as it were a horse-mane upon their backbone, and much hair and very long from the knees downward. They have great tufts of hair hanging down their foreheads, and it seems that they have beards, because of the great store of hair hanging down at their chins and throats. The males have very long tails, and a great knob or flock at the end: so that in some respect they resemble the lion, and in some other the camel. They push with their horns, they run, they overtake and kill a horse when they are in their rage and anger. Finally, it is a foul and fierce beast of countenance and form of body. The horses fled from them, either because of their deformed shape or else because they had never seen them. Their masters have no other riches nor substance: of them they eat, they drink, they apparel, they shoe themselves; and of their hides they make many things, as houses, shoes, apparel, and ropes; of their bones they make bodkins: of their sinews and hair, thread; of their horns, maws, and bladders, vessels; of their dung, fire; and of their calves' skins, budgets [pouches], wherein they draw and keep water. To be short, they make so many things of them as they have need of, or as many as suffice them in the use of this life.

SIGHTING THE MISSISSIPPI, 1541

Hernando de Soto

De Soto (1496–1542) led an expedition which stumbled westwards from Florida, fighting repeated skirmishes with Indians, until he reached Arkansas. He "took to his pallet" and died in 1542 and was buried in the great river he had discovered: the Mississippi.

Three days having passed since they had looked for some maize (and it was little that was found in proportion to what was needed), and for this reason, even though rest was needed because of the wounded, on account of the great need of finding a place where there was maize, the governor was obliged to set out immediately for Quizquiz. He marched seven days through an unpopulated region of many swamps and thick woods, but all passable on horseback except several marshes or swamps which were crossed by swimming. He reached the town of Quizquiz without being perceived. He seized all the people of the town before they got out of their houses. The cacique's mother was captured there, and then he sent to him one of the Indians who had been seized there, bidding him come to see him and that he would give him his mother and all the other people who had been taken there. For reply, he said that his lordship should order them released and sent and that he would come to visit and serve him. Inasmuch as his men were ill and weary for lack of maize and the horses were also weak, he determined to pleasure him, in order to see whether he could have peace with him. So he ordered the mother and all the others released and dispatched them and sent them with words of kindness.

Next day when the governor was awaiting the cacique, many Indians came with their bows and arrows with the intention of attacking the Christians. The governor ordered all the horsemen to be armed and mounted and all in readiness. When the Indians saw that they were on guard, they stopped a crossbow-flight from the spot where the governor was, near a stream, and after they had stayed there for a half-hour, six of the principal Indians came to the camp and said that they were come to see what people they were and that they had learned from their ancestors that a white race would inevitably subdue them; and that they were about to return to the cacique to tell him to come immediately to render obedience and service to the governor. And after offering him six or seven skins and blankets which they brought they took leave of him and together with the others, who were waiting on the shore, returned. The cacique did not again come nor did he send another message.

Inasmuch as there was little maize in the town where the governor was, he moved to another town located a half-league from the large river, where maize was found in abundance. He went to see the river, and found there was an abundance of timber near it from which piraguas could be constructed and an excellently situated land for establishing the camp. He immediately moved thither, houses were built, and the camp was established on a level place, a crossbow-flight from the river. All the maize of all the towns behind was collected there and the men set to work immediately to cut timber and square the planks for canoes. Immediately the Indians came down the river, landed, and told the governor that they were vassals of a great lord called Aquiro, who was lord of many towns and people on the other side of the river. On his behalf they informed him that he would come the next day with all his men to see what his lordship would command him.

Then next day, the cacique came with 200 canoes full of Indians with their bows and arrows, painted with red ochre and having great plumes of white and many-coloured feathers on either side and holding shields in their hands with which they covered the paddlers, while the warriors were standing from prow to stern with their bows and arrows in their hands. The canoe in which the cacique came had an awning spread in the stern and he was seated under the canopy. Also other canoes came bearing other Indian notables. The chief, from his position under the canopy, controlled and gave orders to the other men. All the canoes were together and came to within a stone's throw from the bluff. From there, the cacique told the governor, who was walking along the river with others whom he had brought with him, that he had come to visit him and to serve and obey him, for he had heard that he was the greatest and most powerful lord of all the earth and that he should bethink him in what to command him.

The governor thanked him and asked him to land so that they might better be able to talk, but without answering this, he ordered three canoes to come up in which he brought a quantity of fish and loaves made of the pulp of plums in the shape of bricks. All having been received, he thanked him and again asked him to land. But since his intent was to see whether he might do some damage by means of that pretence, upon seeing that the governor and his men were on their guard, they began to withdraw from land. With loud cries, the crossbowmen, who were ready, shot at them and struck five or six. They withdrew in splendid order; no one abandoned his paddle even though the one near him fell. Flaunting themselves, they retired.

Afterward they came frequently and landed, and when they

went toward them, they would return to their canoes. Those canoes were very pleasing to see, for they were very large and well built; and together with the awnings, the plumes of feathers, the shields and banners, and the many men in them, they had the appearance of a beautiful fleet of galleys. During the thirty days the governor was there, they made four piraguas, in three of which, one early morning three hours before it became light, he ordered a dozen horse to enter four to each one – men who he was confident would succeed in gaining the land in spite of the Indians and assure the crossing or die in doing it – and with them some of foot – crossbowmen and rowers – to place them on the other side. In the other piragua, he ordered Juan de Guzman to cross with men of foot, he having become captain in place of Francisco Maldonado.

And because the current was strong, they went upstream along the shore for a quarter of a league, and in crossing they were carried down with the current of the river and went to land opposite the place where the camp was. At a distance of two stones' throw before reaching shore, the men of horse went from the piraguas on horseback to a sandy place of hard sand and clear ground, where all the men landed without any accident. As soon as those who crossed first were on the other side, the piraguas returned immediately to where the governor was and, in two hours after the sun was up, all the men finished crossing. It was nearly a half league wide, and if a man stood still on the other side, one could not tell whether he were a man or something else. It was of great depth and of very strong current. Its water was always turgid and continually many trees and wood came down it, borne along by the force of the water and current. It had abundance of fish of various kinds, and most of them different from those of the fresh waters of Spain.

DRAKE CLAIMS CALIFORNIA FOR QUEEN ELIZABETH, June 1579

Sir Francis Drake

In 38° 30′ we fell with a convenient and fit harbour and 17 June came to anchor therein, where we continued till the 23rd day of July following. During all which time, notwithstanding it was in the height of summer and so near the sun, yet were we continually visited with like nipping colds as we had felt before; insomuch that

if violent exercises of our bodies and busy employment about our
necessary labours had not sometimes compelled us to the contrary,
we could very well have been contented to have kept about us still
our winter clothes; yea (had our necessities suffered us), to have
kept our beds; neither could we at any time, in whole 14 days
together, find the air so clear as to be able to take the height of sun
or star. . . .

The next day after our coming to anchor in the aforesaid
harbour the people of the country showed themselves, sending
off a man with great expedition [very speedily] to us in a canoe
who, being yet but a little from the shore and a great way from our
ship, spoke to us continually as he came rowing on. And at last, at a
reasonable distance staying himself, he began more solemnly a
long and tedious [slow] oration after his manner, using in the
delivery thereof many gestures and signs, moving his hands,
turning his head and body many ways, and after his oration
ended, with great show of reverence and submission, returned
back to shore again. He shortly came again the second time in like
manner, and so the third time, when he brought with him (as a
present from the rest) a bunch of feathers, much like the feathers of
a black crow, very neatly and artificially gathered upon a string
and drawn together into a round bundle, being very clean and
finely cut and bearing in length an equal proportion one with
another, a special cognizance (as we afterwards observed) which
they that guard their king's person wear on their heads. With this
also he brought a little basket made of rushes and filled with an
herb which they called *tabah*, both which, being tied to a short rod,
he cast into our boat. Our general intended to have recompensed
him immediately with many good things he would have bestowed
on him, but, entering into the boat to deliver the same, he could
not be drawn to receive them by any means, save one hat which,
being cast into the water out of the ship, he took up (refusing
utterly to meddle with any other thing, though it were upon a
board put off unto him), and so presently made his return. After
which time our boat could row no way but, wondering at us as at
gods, they would follow the same with admiration.

The third day following, the 21st, our ship, having received a
leak at sea, was brought to anchor nearer the shore that, her goods
being landed, she might be repaired; but for that we were to
prevent any danger that might chance against our safety, our
general first of all landed his men with all necessary provision to

build tents and make a fort for the defence of ourselves and goods, and that we might under the shelter of it with more safety (whatever should befall) end our business. Which when the people of the country perceived us doing, as men set on fire to war in defence of their country, in great haste and companies, with such weapons as they had, they came down into us, and yet with no hostile meaning or intent to hurt us, standing, when they drew near, as men ravished in their minds with the sight of such things as they never had seen or heard of before that time, their errand being rather with submission and fear to worship us as gods than to have any war with us as with mortal men. Which thing, as it did partly show itself at that instant, so did it more and more manifest itself afterward during the whole time of our abode amongst them. At this time, being willed by signs to lay from them their bows and arrows, they did as they were directed, and so did all the rest, as they came more and more by companies unto them, growing in a little while to a great number, both of men and women.

To the intent, therefore, that this peace which they themselves so willingly sought might, without any cause of the breach thereof on our part given, be continued, and that we might with more safety and expedition end our business in quiet, our general with all his company used all means possible gently to entreat them, bestowing upon each of them liberally good and necessary things to cover their nakedness, withal signifying unto them we were no gods but men and had need of such things to cover our own shame; teaching them to use them to the same ends, for which cause also we did eat and drink in their presence, giving them to understand that without that we could not live and therefore were but men as well as they.

Notwithstanding, nothing could persuade them nor remove that opinion which they had conceived of us that we should be gods.

In recompense of those things which they had received of us, as shirts, linen cloth, etc., they bestowed upon our general and divers of our company divers things, as feathers, cauls of network, the quivers of their arrows made of fawn-skins, and the very skins of beasts that their women wore upon their bodies. Having thus had their fill of this time's visiting and beholding of us, they departed with joy to their houses, which houses are digged round within the earth and have from the uppermost brims of the circle clefts of wood set up and joined close together at the top like our spires on the steeple of a church, which, being covered with earth, suffer no water to enter and are very warm. The door in the most part of them performs the office also of a chimney to let out the smoke; it is made in bigness and fashion like to an ordinary scuttle in a ship, and standing slopewise. Their beds are the hard ground, only with rushes strewed upon it, and lying round about the house have their fire in the midst, which, by reason that the house is but low vaulted, round, and close, gives a marvellous reflection to their bodies to heat the same.

Their men for the most part go naked; the women take a kind of bulrush and, combing it after the manner of hemp, make themselves thereof a loose garment which, being knit about their middles, hangs down about their hips and so affords to them a covering of that which Nature teaches should be hidden; about their shoulders they wear also the skin of a deer with the hair upon it. They are very obedient to their husbands and exceedingly ready in all service, yet of themselves offering to do nothing without the consents or being called of the men . . . .

Against the end of three days more (the news having the while spread itself further and, as it seemed, a great way up into the country) were assembled the greatest number of people which we could reasonably imagine to dwell within any convenient distance round about. Amongst the rest, the king himself, a man of a goodly stature and comely personage, attended with his guard of about 100 tall and warlike men, this day, June 26 came down to see us . . . .

They made signs to our general to have him sit down, unto whom both the king and divers others made several orations, or rather, indeed, if we had understood them, supplications, that he would take the province and kingdom into his hand and become their king and patron, making signs that they would resign unto him their right and title to the whole land and become his vassals in themselves and their posterities; which that they might make us indeed believe that it was their true meaning and intent, the king himself, with all the rest, with one consent and with great reverence, joyfully singing a song, set the crown upon his head, enriched his neck with all their chains, and offering unto him many other things, honoured him by the name of *hioh*. Adding thereunto (as it might seem) a song and dance of triumph, because they were not only visited of the gods (for so they still judged us to be), but the great and chief God was now become their God, their king and patron, and themselves were become the only happy and blessed people in the world.

These things being so freely offered, our general thought not meet to reject or refuse the same, both for that he would not give them any cause of mistrust or disliking of him (that being the only place wherein at this present we were of necessity enforced to seek relief of many things), and chiefly for that he knew not to what good end God had brought this to pass or what honour and profit it might bring to our country in time to come.

Wherefore, in the name and to the use of Her Most Excellent Majesty, he took the sceptre, crown, and dignity of the said country into his hand, wishing nothing more than that it had lain so fitly for Her Majesty to enjoy as it was now her proper own, and that the riches and treasures thereof (wherewith in the upland countries it abounds) might with as great convenience be transported, to the enriching of her kingdom here at home, as it is in plenty to be attained there; and especially that so tractable and loving a people as they showed themselves to be might have means to have manifested their most willing obedience the more unto her, and by her means, as a mother and nurse of the Church of Christ, might by the preaching of the Gospel be brought to the right knowledge and obedience of the true and ever-living God.

The ceremonies of this resigning and receiving of the kingdom being thus performed, the common sort, both of men and women, leaving the king and his guard about him with our general, dispersed themselves among our people, taking a diligent view or survey of every man; and finding such as pleased their fancies (which commonly were the youngest of us), they, presently enclosing them about, offered their sacrifices unto them, crying out with lamentable shrieks and moans, weeping and scratching and tearing their very flesh off their faces with their nails; neither were it the women alone which did this, but even old men, roaring and crying out, were as violent as the women were . . . .

After that our necessary businesses were well dispatched, our general, with his gentlemen and many of his company, made a journey up into the land to see the manner of their dwelling and to be the better acquainted with the nature and commodities of the country. Their houses were all such as we have formerly described and, being many of them in one place, made several villages here and there. The inland we found to be far different from the shore, a goodly country and fruitful soil, stored with many blessings fit for the use of man. Infinite was the company of very large and fat deer which there we saw by thousands, as we supposed, in a herd;

besides a multitude of a strange kind of conies by far exceeding them in number. Their heads and bodies, in which they resemble other conies, are but small, his tail, like the tail of a rat, exceeding long, and his feet like the paws of a want or mole. Under his chin, on either side, he hath a bag into which he gathereth his meat when he hath filled his belly abroad, that he may with it either feed his young or feed himself when he lists not to travel from his burrow. The people eat their bodies and make great account of their skins, for their king's holiday's coat was made of them.

This country our general named Albion, and that for two causes: the one in respect of the white banks and cliffs which lie toward the sea; the other that it might have some affinity, even in name also, with our own country, which was sometime so called.

Before we went from thence, our general caused to be set up a monument of our being there, as also of Her Majesty's and successors' right and title to that kingdom; namely, a plate of brass, fast nailed to a great and firm post, whereon is engraven Her Grace's name and the day and year of our arrival there and of the free giving up of the province and kingdom, both by the king and people, into Her Majesty's hands, together with Her Highness's picture and arms in a piece of sixpence current English money, showing itself by a hole made of purpose through the plate. Underneath was likewise engraved the name of our general, etc.

The Spaniards never had any dealing or so much as set a foot in this country, the utmost of their discoveries reaching only to many degrees southward of this place . . . .

VOYAGE TO VIRGINIA, 1584

Arthur Barlowe

Barlowe co-captained the first voyage to Virginia equipped by Raleigh after he had been granted a patent by Elizabeth I. Roanoke Island, which Barlowe describes here, was to become, in the ensuing year, the site of the first English colony in America.

The 27 day of April, in the year of our redemption, 1584 we departed the West of England, with two barkes well furnished with men and victuals, having received our last and perfect directions by your letters, confirming the former instructions, and commandments delivered by yourself at our leaving the river of Thames . . . .

The second of July, . . . we entered, though not without some difficulty, & cast anchor about three harquebuz-shot within the havens mouth, on the left hand of the same: and after thanks given to God for our safe arrival thither, we manned our boats, and went to view the land next adjoining, and to take possession of the same, in the right of the Queen's most excellent Majesty, as rightful Queen, and Princess of the same, and after delivered the same over to your use, according to her Majesty's grant, and letters patent, under her Highness great Seal. Which being performed according to the ceremonies used in such enterprises, we viewed the land about us being, whereas we first land, very sandy and low towards the waters side, but so full of grapes, as the very beating and surge of the Sea overflowed them . . . .

This Island had many goodly woods full of Deer, Conies [rabbits], Hares, and Fowl, even in the midst of Summer in incredible abundance. The woods are not such as you find in Bohemia, Moscovia, or Hercynia, barren and fruitless, but the highest and reddest Cedars in the world, far bettering the Ceders of the Azores . . . We remained by the side of this Island two whole days before we saw any people of the Country: the third day we espied one small boat rowing towards; us, having in it three persons: this boat came to the Island side, four harquebuz-shot from our ships, and there two of the people remaining, the third came along the shoreside towards us, and we being then all within board, he walked up and down upon the point of the land next unto us: then the Master and the Pilot of the Admiral, Simon Ferdinando, and the Captain Philip Amadas, myself, and others rowed to the land, whose coming this fellow attended, never making any show of fear or doubt. And after he had spoken of many things not understood by us, we brought him with his own good liking, aboard the ships, and gave him a shirt, a hat, & some other things, and made him taste of our wine, and our meat, which he liked very well: and having viewed both barks, he departed, and went to his own boat again, which he had left in a little Cove or Creek adjoining: as soon as he was two bow shot into the water, he fell to fishing, and in less then half an hour, he had laden his boat as deep, as it could swim, . . . after he had (as much as he might) requited the former benefits received, departed out of our sight.

The next day there came unto us divers boats, and in one of them the Kings brother, accompanied with forty or fifty men, very handsome and goodly people, and in their behavior as mannerly and civil as any in Europe. His name was Granganimeo, and the

king is called Wingina, the country Wingandacoa and now by her
Maiesty Virginia . . . .

The King is greatly obeyed, and his brothers and children
reverenced: the King himself in person was at our being there,
sore wounded in a fight which he had with the King of the next
country. . . . A day or two after this, we fell to trading with them,
exchanging some things that we had, for Chamoys, Buffe, and
Deer skins: when we showed him all our packet of merchandise, of
all things that he saw, a bright tin dish most pleased him, which he
presently took up and clapt it before his breast, and after made a
hole in the brim thereof and hung it about his neck, making signs
that it would defend him against his enemies arrows: for those
people maintain a deadly and terrible warr, with the people and
King adjoining. We exchanged our tin dish for twenty skins, worth
twenty Crowns, or twenty Nobles: and a copper kettle for fifty skins
worth fifty Crowns. They offered us good exchange for our
hatchets, and axes, and for knives, and would have given anything
for swords: but we would not depart with any. After two or three
days the Kings brother came aboard the ships and drank wine, and
eat of our meat and of our bread, and liked exceedingly thereof:
and after a few days overpassed, he brought his wife with him to
the ships, his daughter and two or three children: his wife was very
well favoured, of mean stature and very bashful she had on her
back a long cloak of leather, with the fur side next to her body, and
before her a piece of the same: about her forehead she had a band
of white Coral, and so had her husband many times: in her ears she
had bracelets of pearls hanging down to her middle, (whereof we
delivered your worship a little bracelet) and those were of the
bignes [bigness?] of good peace. The rest of her women of the
better sort had pendants of copper hanging in either ear, and some
of the children of the king's brother and other noble men, have five
or six in either ear: he himself had upon his head a broad plate of
gold, or copper, for being unpolished we knew not what metal it
should be, neither would he by any means suffer us to take it of his
head, but feeling it, it would bow very easily. His apparel was as his
wives, only the women wear their hair long on both sides, and the
men but on one. They are of colour yellowish, and their hair black
for the most part, and yet we saw children that had very fine
auburn, and chestnut coloured hair.

. . . Their boats are made of one tree, either of Pine, or of Pitch
trees: a wood not commonly known to our people, nor found

growing in England. They have no edge-tools to make them withall: if they have any they are very few, and those it seems they had twenty years since, which, as those two men declared, was out of a wreak which happened upon their coast of some Christian ship, . . . The manner of making their boats is thus: they burn down some great tree, or take such as are wind fallen, and putting gum and rosin upon one side thereof, they set fire into it, and when it hath burnt it hollow, they cut out the coal with their shells, and everywhere they would burn it deeper or wider they lay on gums, which burn away the timber, and by this means they fashion very fine boats, and such as will transport twenty men. Their oars are like scoops, and many times they set with long poles, as the depth serveth.

The Kings brother had great liking of our armour, a sword, and divers other things which we had: and offered to lay a great box of pearl engage for them: but we refused it for this time, because we would not make them know, that we esteemed thereof, until we had understood in what places of the country the pearl grew: which now your Worship doeth very well understand . . . .

The soil is the most plentiful, sweet, fruitful and wholesome of all the world: there are above fourteen several sweet smelling timber trees, and the most part of their underwoods are Bays, and such like: they have those Oaks that we have, but far greater and better. After they had been divers times aboard our ships, myself, with seven more went twenty mile into the River, that runneth toward the City of Skicoak, which River they call Occam: and the evening following, we came to an Island, which they call Raonoak [Roanoke], distant from the harbour by which we entered, seven leagues: and at the North end thereof was a village of nine houses, built of Cedar, and fortified round about with sharp trees, to keep out their enemies, and the entrance into it made like a turn pike very artificially: when we came towards it, standing near unto the waters side, the wife of Granganimo, the kings brother came running out to meet us very cheerfully and friendly . . . .

After we had thus dried ourselves, she brought us into the inner room, where she set on the board standing along the house, some wheat like fermenty, sodden Venison, and roasted, fish sodden, boiled and roasted, Melons raw, and sodden, roots of divers kinds, and divers fruits: their drink is commonly water, but while the grape lasteth, they drink wine, and for want of casks to keep it, all the year after they drink water, but it is sodden with Ginger in it, and black Cinnamon, and sometimes Sassaphras, and divers other wholesome, and medicinable herbs and trees. We were entertained with all love and kindness, and with as much bounty (after their manner) as they could possibly devise. We found the people most gentle, loving, and faithful, void of all guile and treason, and such as live after the manner of the golden age. The people only care how to defend themselves from the cold in their short winter, and to feed themselves with such meat as the soil affordeth: their meat is very well sodden and they make broth very sweet and savory: their vessels are earthen pots, large, white and sweet, their dishes are wooden platters of sweet timber: within the place where they feed their lodging, and within that their Idol, which they worship, of whom they speak incredible things . . . .

Into this river falleth another great river, called Cipo, in which there is found great store of Muscles in which there are pearls: likewise there descendth into this Ocean, another river, called Nomopana. . . . Towards the Southwest, four days journey is situate a town called Sequotan, which is the Southernmost town of Wingandacoa, near unto which, six and twenty years past, there was a ship cast away, whereof some of the people were saved, and those were white people, whom the country people preserved . . . .

. . .other than these, there was never any people appareled, or white of colour, either seen, or heard of amongst these people, and these aforesaid were seen only by the inhabitants of Sequotan, which appeared to be very true, for they wondered marvelously when we were amongst them at the whiteness of our skins, ever coveting to touch our breasts, and to view the same. Besides they had our ships in marvelous admiration, & all things else were so strange unto them, as it appeared that none of them had ever seen the like. When we discharged any piece, were it but an hargubuz, they would tremble thereat for very fear, and for the strangeness of the same: for the weapons which themselves use are bows and arrows: the arrows are but of small canes, headed with a sharp shell or tooth of a fish sufficient enough to kill a naked man. Their swords be of wood hardened: likewise they use wooden breastplates for their defense. They have beside a kind of club, in the end whereof they fasten the sharp horns of a stag, or other beast. When they go to Wars they carry about with them their idol, of whom they ask counsel, as the Romans were wont of the Oracle of Apollo. They sing songs as they march towards the battle instead of drums and trumpets: their wars are very cruel and bloody, by reason whereof, and of their civil dissentions which have happened of late years amongst them, the people are marvelously wasted, and in some places the country left Desolate.

Beyond this Island called Roanoak, are main Islands very plentiful of fruits and other natural increases, together with many towns, and villages, along the side of the continent, some bounding upon the Islands, and some stretching up further into the land.

When we first had sight of this country, some thought the first land we saw to be the continent: but after we entered into the Haven, we saw before us another mighty long Sea: for there lieth along the coast a tract of Islands, two hundreth miles in length, adjoining to the Ocean sea, and between the Islands, two or three entrances: when you are entered between them (these Islands being very narrow for the most part, as in most places six miles broad, in some places less, in few more) then there appeareth another great Sea, containing in breadth in some places, forty, and in some fifty, in some twenty miles over, before you come unto the continent: and in this enclosed Sea there are above an hundreth Islands of divers bignesses, whereof one is sixteen miles long, at which we were, finding it a most pleasant and fertile ground, replenished with goodly Cedars, and divers other sweet woods, full of Currants, of flax, and many other notable commodities, which we at that time had no leisure to view . . . .

Thus Sir, we have acquainted you with the particulars of our discovery made this present voyage, as far forth as the shortness of the time we there continued would afford us to take view of: and so contenting ourselves with this service at this time, which we hope hereafter to enlarge, as occasion and assistance shall be given, we resolved to leave the country, and to apply ourselves to return for England, which we did accordingly, and arrived safely in the West of England about the midst of September.

And whereas we have above certified you of the country taken in possession by us, to her Majesty's use, and so to yours by her Majesty's grant, we thought good for the better assurance thereof, to record some of the particular Gentlemen, & men of account, who then were present, as witnesses of the same . . . .

We brought home also two of the Savages being lusty men, whose names were Wanchese and Manteo.

THE VIRTUES OF TOBACCO, Virginia, 1585

Thomas Hariot

The writer was a member of Sir Richard Grenville's unsuccessful attempt
to establish an English colony at Roanoke.

There is an herbe which is sowed apart by itselfe, and is called by
the inhabitants Uppowoc; in the West Indies it hath divers names,
according to the severall places and countreys where it groweth
and is used; the Spanyards generally call it Tabacco. The leaves
thereof being dried and brought into pouder, they use to take the
fume or smoake thereof, by sucking it thorow pipes made of clay,
into their stomacke and head; from whence it purgeth superfluous
fleame and other grosse humours, and openeth all the pores and
passages of the body: by which meanes the use thereof not onely
preserveth the body from obstructions, but also (if any be, so that
they have not bene of too long continuance) in short time breaketh
them; whereby their bodies are notably preserved in health, and
know not many grievous diseases, wherewithall we in England are
often times afflicted.

This Uppowoc is of so precious estimation amongst them, that
they thinke their gods are marvellously delighted therewith:
whereupon sometime they make hallowed fires, and cast some
of the pouder therin for a sacrifice: being in a storme upon the
waters, to pacifie their gods, they cast some up into the aire and
into the water: so a weare for fish being newly set up, they cast
some therein and into the aire: after an escape from danger, they
cast some into the aire likewise: but all done with strange gestures,
stamping, sometime dancing, clapping of hands, holding up of
hands, and staring up into the heavens, uttering therewithall, and
chattering strange words and noises.

We ourselves, during the time we were there, used to sucke it
after their manner, as also since our return, and have found many
rare and woonderfull experiments of the vertues thereof: of which
the relation would require a volume by it selfe: the use of it by so
many of late, men and women of great calling, as els, and some
learned Physicians also, is of sufficient witnesse.

"STARVING TIME": THE COLONISTS AT JAMESTOWN, 1607

Captain John Smith

In May 1607 105 colonists of the Virgina Company disembarked in Virginia to found Jamestown. Among them was John Smith (1579–1631), a soldier of fortune. Resourceful and self-confident, Smith became the plantation's leader; it was Smith who saved the colonists from starvation in their first year.

1607. Being thus left to our fortunes, it fortuned that within ten days scarce ten among us could either go or well stand, such extreme weakness and sickness oppressed us. And thereat none need marvel if they consider the cause and reason, which was this. While the ships stayed, our allowance was somewhat bettered by a daily proportion of biscuits, which the sailors would pilfer to sell, give, or exchange with us for money, sassafras, furs, or love. But when they departed, there remained neither tavern, beer, house, nor place of relief, but the common kettle. Had we been as free from all sins as gluttony and drunkenness, we might have been canonized for saints; but our president [Wingfield] would never have been admitted for engrossing to his private [use] oatmeal, sack, aquavitae, beèf, eggs, or what not, but the kettle; that indeed he allowed equally to be distributed, and that was half a pint of wheat, and as much barley boiled with water for a man a day, and this having fried some twenty-six weeks in the ship's hold, contained as many worms as grains; so that we might truly call it rather so much bran than corn, our drink was water, our lodgings castles in the air.

With this lodging and diet, our extreme toil in bearing and planting palisades so strained and bruised and our continual labour in the extremity of the heat had so weakened us, as were cause sufficient to have made us as miserable in our native country, or any other place in the world.

From May to September, those that escaped lived upon sturgeon, and sea crabs. Fifty in this time we buried, the rest seeing the president's projects to escape these miseries in our pinnace by flight (who at this time had neither felt want nor sickness) so moved our dead spirits, as we deposed him, and established Ratcliffe in his place (Gosnoll being dead), Kendall deposed. Smith newly recovered, Martin and Ratcliffe was by his care preserved and relieved, and the most of the soldiers recovered with the skillful diligence of Master Thomas Wolton, our chirurgeon [surgeon] general.

But now was all our provision spent, the sturgeon gone, all helps abandoned, each hour expecting the fury of the savages; when God, the Patron of all good endeavors in that desperate extremity so changed the hearts of the savages that they brought such plenty of their fruits and provision as no man wanted.

And now where some affirmed it was ill done of the Council to send forth men so badly provided, this incontradictable reason will show them plainly they are too ill advised to nourish such ill conceits. First, the fault of our going was our own; what could be thought fitting or necessary we had; but what we should find, or want, or where we should be, we were all ignorant, and supposing to make our passage in two months, with victual to live and the advantage of the spring to work. We were at sea five months, where we both spent our victual and lost the opportunity of the time and season to plant, by the unskillful presumption of our ignorant transporters, that understood not at all what they undertook . . . .

And now, the winter approaching, the rivers became so covered with swans, geese, ducks, and cranes that we daily feasted with good bread, Virginia peas, pumpions [pumpkins], and putcha-mins [persimmons], fish, fowl, and diverse sorts of wild beasts as fat as we could eat them; so that none of our tuftaffety humourists desired to go for England.

Conditions among the settlers actually worsened over the next two years; by the winter of 1609–10 the surviving Virginians had been driven to eat "the flesh and excrements of man as well as our own nation as of the Indian".

POCAHONTAS SAVES THE LIFE OF JOHN SMITH, Virginia, 1607

Captain John Smith

Smith was taken prisoner by Indians on a hunting expedition. The letter below, recounting his adventures and the life of Princess Pocohontas, was written to Queen Anne, the wife of James I of England.

Most admired queene,
    The love I beare my God, my King and Countrie, hath so of

emboldened mee in the worst of extreme dangers, that now honestie doth constraine mee [to] presume thus farre beyond myselfe, [as] to present your Majestie [with] this short discourse.

Some ten yeeres agoe, being in Virginia, and taken prisoner by the power of Powhatan their chiefe King, I received from this great Salvage exceeding great courtesie, especially from his sonne, Nantaquans, the most manliest, comeliest, boldest spirit I ever saw in a Salvage, and his sister Pocahontas, the Kings most deare and welbeloved daughter, being but a childe of twelve or thirteene yeeres of age, whose compassionate pitifull heart, of my desperate estate, gave me much cause to respect her. I being the first Christian this proud King and his grim attendants ever saw, and thus inthralled in their barbarous power, I cannot say I felt the least occasion of want that was in the power of those, my mortall foes, to prevent, notwithstanding all their threats.

After some six weeks fatting amongst those Salvage Courtiers, at the minute of my Execution, she hazarded the beating out of her owne braines to save mine; and not only that, but so prevailed with her father, that I was safely conducted to James Towne, where I found about eight and thirtie miserable, poore and sicke creatures to keepe possession of all those large territories of Virginia: such was the weaknesse of this poore Commonwealth as, had the Salvages not fed us, we directly had starved. And this reliefe, most gracious queene, was commonly brought us by this Lady Pocahontas: notwithstanding all these passages when inconstant Fortune turned our peace to warre, this tender Virgin would still not spare to dare to visit us, and by her our jarres have beene oft appeased and our wants still supplyed. Were it the policie of her father thus to imploy her, or the ordinance of God thus to make her his instrument, or her extraordinarie affection to our Nation, I know not: but of this I am sure – when her father, with the utmost of his policie and power, sought to surprize mee, having but eighteene with mee, the darke night could not affright her from comming through the irkesome woods, and with watered eies gave me intelligence, with her best advice [how] to escape his furie; which had hee knowne, hee had surely slaine her.

James Towne, with her wild traine, she as freely frequented as her fathers habitation, and during the time of two or three yeeres, she next, under God, was still the instrument to preserve this

Colonie from death, famine and utter confusion, which, if in those times had once beene dissolved, Virginia might have lain as it was at our first arrivall to this day.

Since then, this businesse having beene turned and varied by many accidents, it is most certaine [that] after a long and troublesome warre, after my departure, betwixt her father and our Colonie – all which time shee was not heard of – about two yeeres after, shee herselfe was taken prisoner, being so detained neere two yeeres, and, at last, rejecting her barbarous condition, was maried to an English Gentleman with whom at this present she is in England; the first Christian ever of that Nation, the first Virginian ever spake English, or had a childe in mariage by an Englishman, a matter surely, if my meaning bee truly considered and well understood, worthy a Princes understanding.

Thus, most gracious Lady, I have related to your Majestie, what, at your best leisure, our approved Histories will account you at large, and however this might bee presented [to] you from a more worthy pen, it cannot from a more honest heart, [for] as yet I never begged any thing of the state or any; and it is my want of abilitie, and her exceeding desert; your birth, meanes and authoritie; her birth, vertue, want and simplicitie, doth make mee thus bold, humbly to beseech your Majestie to take this knowledge of her, though it be from one so unworthy as my selfe, her husbands estate not being able to make her fit to attend your Majestie. If she should not be well received, seeing this Kingdome may rightly have a Kingdome by her meanes, her present love to us might turne to such scorne and furie as to divert all this good to the worst of evill; where [as] finding so great a Queene should doe her some honour would so ravish her with content as endeare her dearest bloud to effect that [which] your Majestie and all the Kings honest subjects most earnestly desire. And so I humbly kisse your gracious hands.

Hearing she was at Branford with divers of my friends, I went to see her. After a modest salutation, without any word, she turned about, as not seeming well contented. But not long after, she began to talke and remembered mee well what courtesies shee had done; saying:

"You did promise Powhatan what was yours should bee his, and he the like to you. You called him father, being in his land a stranger, and by the same reason so must I doe you."

Which though I would have excused, I durst not allow of that title, because she was a Kings daughter. With a well set countenance she said:

"Were you not afraid to come into my fathers Countrie, and caused feare in him and all his people but mee, and feare you here I should call you father. I tell you then I will, and you shall call mee childe, and so I will bee for ever and ever your Countrieman. They did tell us alwaies you were dead, and I knew no other till I came to Plimoth; yet Powhatan did command Uttamatomakkin to seeke you, and know the truth, because your Countriemen will lie much."

This Salvage, one of Powhatans Councell, being an understanding fellow, the King purposely sent him, as they say, to number the people here and informe him well what wee were and our state. Arriving at Plimoth, according to his directions, he got a long sticke, whereon by notches hee did thinke to have kept the number of all the men hee could see, but hee was quickly wearie of that taske. Comming to London, where by chance I met him, having renewed our acquaintance, he told mee Powhatan did bid him to finde me out, to shew him our God, the King, Queene and Prince, I so much had told them of. Concerning God, I told him the best I could; the King, I heard he had seene, and the rest hee should see when he would. He denied ever to have seene the King, till by circumstances he was satisfied he had. Then he replyed very sadly:

"You gave Powhatan a white Dog, which Powhatan fed as himselfe, but your King gave me nothing, and I am better than your white Dog."

The small time I staid in London, divers Courtiers and others, my acquaintances, hath gone with mee to see her, that did thinke God had a great hand in her conversion, and they have seene many English Ladies worse favoured, proportioned and behavioured: and it pleased both the King and Queenes Majestie honourably to esteeme her, accompanied with that honourable Lady, the Lady De la Ware, and that honourable Lord, her husband, and divers other persons of good qualities, both publikely at the maskes and otherwise, to her great satisfaction and content: which, doubtlesse, she would have deserved, had she lived to arrive in Virginia.*

---

* Pocahontas (aka Rebecca) died in 1617 of smallpox off Gravesend.

KILLING IROQUOIS INDIANS, 1609

Samuel de Champlain

The French explorer de Champlain (1567–1635) was the founder of
Quebec and sometime lieutenant of Canada. The incident below occurred
during an exploration of Lake Champlain, the majority of which lies in
modern Vermont.

When it was evening, we embarked in our canoes to continue our
course; and, as we advanced very quietly and without making any
noise, we met on the 29th of the month the Iroquois, about ten
o'clock at evening, at the extremity of a cape which extends into
the lake on the western bank. They had come to fight. We both
began to utter loud cries, all getting their arms in readiness. We
withdrew out on the water, and the Iroquois went on shore, where
they drew up all their canoes close to each other and began to fell
trees with poor axes, which they acquire in war sometimes, using
also others of stone. Thus they barricaded themselves very well.

Our forces also passed the entire night, their canoes being drawn
up close to each other and fastened to poles, so that they might not
get separated and that they might be all in readiness to fight, if
occasion required. We were out upon the water, within arrow
range of their barricades. When they were armed and in array,
they dispatched two canoes by themselves to the enemy to enquire
if they wished to fight, to which the latter replied that they wanted
nothing else; but they said that, at present, there was not much
light and that it would be necessary to wait for daylight, so as to be
able to recognize each other; and that, as soon as the sun rose, they
would offer us battle. This was agreed to by our side. Meanwhile,
the entire night was spent in dancing and singing, on both sides,
with endless insults and other talk; as, how little courage we had,
how feeble a resistance we should make against their arms, and
that, when day came, we should realize it to our ruin. Ours also
were not slow in retorting, telling them they would see such
execution of arms as never before, together with an abundance
of such talk as is not unusual in the siege of a town. After this
singing, dancing, and bandying words on both sides to the fill,
when day came, my companions and myself continued under
cover, for fear that the enemy would see us. We arranged our
arms in the best manner possible, being, however, separated, each
in one of the canoes of the savage Montagnais. After arming

ourselves with light armour, we each took an arquebus and went on shore. I saw the enemy go out of their barricade, nearly 200 in number, stout and rugged in appearance. They came at a slow pace toward us, with a dignity and assurance which greatly amused me, having three chiefs at their head. Our men also advanced in the same order, telling me that those who had three large plumes were the chiefs, and that they had only these three, and that they could be distinguished by these plumes, which were much larger than those of their companions, and that I should do that I could to kill them. I promised to do all in my power . . .

Our men began to call me with loud cries; and, in order to give me a passageway, they opened in two parts, and put me at their head, where I marched some 20 paces in advance of the rest until I was within about 30 paces of the enemy, who at once noticed me, and, halting, gazed at me, as I did also at them. When I saw them making a move to fire at us, I rested my musket against my cheek, and aimed directly at one of the three chiefs. With the same shot, two fell to the ground; and one of their men was so wounded that he died some time after. I had loaded my musket with four balls. When our side saw this shot so favourable for them, they began to raise such loud cries that one could not have heard it thunder. Meanwhile, the arrows flew on both sides. The Iroquois were greatly astonished that two men had been so quickly killed, although they were equipped with armour woven from cotton thread and with wood which was proof against their arrows. This caused great alarm among them. As I was loading again, one of my companions fired a shot from the woods, which astonished them anew to such a degree that, seeing their chiefs dead, they lost courage and took to flight, abandoning their camp and fort, and fleeing into the woods, whither I pursued them, killing still more of them. Our savages also killed several of them, and took ten or twelve prisoners. The remainder escaped with the wounded. Fifteen or sixteen were wounded on our side with arrow shots; but they were soon healed.

After gaining the victory, our men amused themselves by taking a great quantity of Indian corn and some meal from their enemies, also their armour, which they had left behind that they might run better. After feasting sumptuously, dancing and singing, we returned three hours after with the prisoners. The spot where this attack took place is . . . Lake Champlain.

THE "PILGRIM FATHERS" LAND IN NEW ENGLAND, November 1620

William Bradford

Bradford was one of the leaders of the Pilgrim Fathers, a group of religious non-conformists who sailed in the *Mayflower* to America to escape the religious intolerance of James I of England. Although New England was named and explored by John Smith, the Pilgrims founded the first permanent settlement there, at Plymouth, in what would become the state of Massachusetts.

About ten a clocke we came into a deepe Valley, full of brush, wood-gaile, and long grasse, through which wee found little paths or tracts, and there we saw a Deere, and found Springs of fresh Water, of which we were hartily glad, and sat us downe and drunke our first New England Water, with as much delight as ever we drunke drinke in all our lives.

When we had refreshed ourselves, we directed our course full South, that wee might come to the shoare, which within a short while after we did, and there made a fire, that they in the Ship might see where we were (as wee had direction) and so marched on towards this supposed River: and as we went in another Valley, we found a fine cleere Pond of fresh water, being about a Musket shot broad, and twice as long: there grew also many small Vines, and Fowle and Deere haunted there; there grew much Sassafras: from thence we went on and found much plain ground about fiftie Acres, fit for the Plow, and some signes where the Indians had formerly planted their Corne: after this, some thought it best for nearnesse of the River to goe downe and travaile on the Sea sands, by which meanes some of our men were tired, and lagged behinde, so we stayed and gathered them up, and strucke into the Land againe; where we found a little path to certaine heapes of Sand, one whereof was covered with old Mats, and had a wooden thing like a Morter whelmed on the top of it, and an earthen pot laid in a little hole at the end thereof; we musing what it might be, digged and found a Bowe, and as we thought, Arrowes, but they were rotten; We supposed there were many other things, but because we deemed them graves, we put in the Bow againe and made it up as it was, and left the rest untouched, because we thought it would be odious unto them to ransacke their Sepulchers. We went on further and found new stubble of which they had gotten Corne this yeare,

and many Walnut trees full of Nuts, and great store of Strawber-
ries, and some Vines; passing thus a field or two, which were not
great, we came to another, which had also bin new gotten, and
there wee found where an house had beene, and foure or five old
Plankes laied together; also we found a great Kettle, which had
beene some Ships kettle and brought out of Europe; there was also
an heape of sand, made like the former, but it was newly done, wee
might see how they had padled it with their hands, which we
digged up, and in it we found a little old Basket full of faire Indian
Corne, and digged further, and found a fine great new Basket full
of very faire Corne of this yeare, with some sixe and thirty goodly
eares of Corne, some yellow, and some red, and others mixt with
blew, which was a very goodly sight: the Basket was round, and
narrow at the top, it held about three or foure bushels, which was
as much as two of us could lift up from the ground, and was very
handsomely and cunningly made: But whilst we were busie about
these things, we set our men Sentinell in a round ring, all but two
or three which digged up the Corne. Wee were in suspense, what to
doe with it, and the Kettle, and at length after much consultation,
we concluded to take the Kettle, and as much of the Corne as wee
could carry away with us: and when our Shallop came if we could
finde any of the people, and came to parley with them, wee would
give them the Kettle againe, and satisfie them for their Corne . . .

When wee had marched five or six miles into the Woods, and
could find no signes of any people, wee returned againe another
way, and as we came into the plaine ground, wee found a place like
a grave, but it was much bigger and longer than any wee had yet
seene. It was also covered with boords, so as wee mused what it
should be, and resolved to dig it up; where we found, first a Mat,
and under that a faire Bow, and there another Mat, and under
that a Boord about three quarters long, finely carved and painted,
with three Tynes, or broches on the top, like a Crown; also
betweene the Mats we found Bowles, Trayes, Dishes, and such
like Trinkets; at length wee came to a faire new Mat, and under
that two Bundles, the one bigger, the other lesse, we opened the
greater and found in it a great quantitie of fine and perfect Red
Powder, and in it the bones and skull of a man. The skull had fine
yellow haire still on it, and some of the flesh unconsumed; there
was bound up with a Knife, a Packneedle, and two or three old
Iron things. It was bound up in a Saylers Canvas Casacke, and a
payre of Cloth Breeches; the Red Powder was a kind of Embaul-

ment, and yielded a strong, but not offensive smell; It was as fine as any Flower. We opened the lesse bundle like wise, and found of the same Powder in it, and the bones and head of a little childe, about the legges, and other parts of it was Bound strings, and Bracelets of fine white Beads; there was also by it a little Bow, about three quarters long, and some other odde knackes: we brought sundry of the prettiest things away with us, and covered the Corps up againe . . .

We went ranging up and downe till the Sunne began to draw low, and then we hasted out of the Woods, that we might come to our Shallop. By that time we had done, and our Shallop come to us it was within night, and we fed upon such victualls as we had, and betooke us to our rest after we had set out our watch. About midnight we heard a great and hideous cry, and our Sentinell called, "Arme, Arme." So we bestirred our selves and shot off a couple of Muskets and noise ceased: we concluded, that it was a company of Wolves & Foxes, for one told us he had heard such a noise in New-found-land. About five a clocke in the morning we began to be stirring . . . upon a sudden wee heard a great & strange cry which we knew to be the same voices, though they varied their notes; one of the company being abroad came running in, and cried, "They are men, Indians, Indians"; and withall, their Arrowes came flying amongst us, our men ran out with all speed to recover their Armes . . . The cry of our enemies was dreadfull, especially, when our men ran out to recover their Armes, their note was after this manner, "Woath woach ha ha hach woach": our men were no sooner come to their Armes, but the enemy was readie to assault them.

There was a lustie man, and no whit lesse valiant, who was thought to be their Captain, stood behind a Tree within halfe a Musket shot of us, and there let his Arrowes flie at us; hee stood three shots off a Musket, at length one tooke as he said full ayme at him, after which he gave an extraordinarie cry and away they went all, wee followed them about a quarter of a mile, but wee left sixe to keepe our Shallop, for wee were carefull of our businesse . . . We tooke up eighteene of their Arrowes, which wee had sent to England by Master Jones, some whereof were headed with brasse, others with Harts horne, and others with Eagles clawes; many more no doubt were shot, for these wee found were almost covered with leaves: yet by the speciall providence of God, none of them either hit or hurt us . . . On Monday we found a very good

Harbour for our shipping, we marched also into the Land, and found divers corne Fields and little running Brookes, a place verie good for scituation, so we returned to our Ship againe with good newes to the rest of our people, which did much comfort their hearts.

OPECHANCANOUGH ENTRAPS AND MASSACRES VIRGINIA COLONISTS, 22 May 1622

Anthony Chester

Opechancanough's carefully planned massacre killed a quarter of Virginia's 1200 English settlers.

Several days before this bloodthirsty people put their plan into execution, they led some of our people through very dangerous woods into a place from which they could not extricate themselves without the aid of a guide, others of us who were among them to learn their language were in a friendly way persuaded to return to our colony, while new comers were treated in an exceedingly friendly manner.

On Friday before the day appointed by them for the attack they visited, entirely unarmed, some of our people in their dwellings, offering to exchange skins, fish and other things, while our people entirely ignorant of their plans received them in a friendly manner.

When the day appointed for the massacre had arrived, a number of the savages visited many of our people in their dwellings, and while partaking with them of their meal the savages, at a given signal, drew their weapons and fell upon us murdering and killing everybody they could reach sparing neither women nor children, as well inside as outside the dwellings. In this attack 347 of the English of both sexes and all ages were killed. Simply killing our people did not satisfy their inhuman nature, they dragged the dead bodies all over the country, tearing them limb from limb, and carrying the pieces in triumph around.

When the occurrence of this massacre became known in the mother country, the English were ordered to take revenge by destroying with fire and sword everything of the Indians; consequently they set out for Pamunkey, destroyed both the houses and crops of the Indians, took Opechancanough prisoner and shot him on the very place where his house stood before it was burned down. On this spot the English then built a new town. By these means the

Indians became very much subdued and lived in constant dread of the English.

The English in the meantime became thereafter more prudent in their dealings with the Indians. Moreover, the King of England sent from his arsenals all sort of weapons and ammunition and ordered his subjects to more and more cultivate the land and bring the Indians into submission.

SHIPWRECKED BY A HURRICANE, New England, 16 August 1635

Anthony Thacher

But now with the leaf I must alter my matter and subject and turn my drowned pen with my shaking hand to write other news and to rouse up my heavy heart and sadded spirits to indite the story of such sad news as never before this happened in New England and been lamented both in the public on the pulpit and concourse of the people and in private in the closet and in the same places hath God's name been magnified for his great mercy and wonderful deliverance of me out of the bottom of the angry sea.

The story is thus. First there was a league of perennial friendship solemnly made between my cousin Avary and myself made in Mr Graves his ship never to forsake each other to the death but to be partaker each of other's misery or welfare as also of habitation in one place. Now it pleased God immediately on our arrival unto New England there was an offer made unto us, and my cousin Avary was invited to Marblehed by the men of that place to be their pastor, there being as yet no church there planted but there a town appointed by the whole country to be planted there, intended for the good of the whole country to set up the trade of fishing. Now because that many there (the most being fishers) were something loose and remiss in their carriage and behavior, my cousin was unwilling to go thither, and so refusing it we went to Newberry to Mr Parker and others of his acquaintance, intending there to sit down and plant, but being solicited so often both by the men of the place and by the magistrates, and counselled to it by Mr Cotten and most of the ministers in the patent, alleging what a benefit we might do both to the people there and also unto the country and commonweal to settle there a plantation, at length we embraced it and there consented to go. The men of Marblehed

forthwith sent a pinnace for us and our goods, and we were at
Ipswich on Tuesday the twelfth of August, 1635, embarked
ourselves and all and every one of our families with all our goods
and substance for Marblehed, we being in all twenty-three souls, to
wit eleven in my cousin's family and seven in mine and one Master
William Elliott and four mariners. Whence the next morning
having recommended ourselves unto the Lord with cheerful and
contented hearts we hoisted sail for Marblehed.

But the Lord suddenly turned our cheerfulness into mourning
and sad lamentation. Thus on Friday the fourteenth of August
1635 in the evening about ten of the clock our sails being old and
torn, we, having a fine fresh gale of wind, were split. Our sailors,
because it was something dark would not put on new sails presently
but determined to cast their sheet anchor and so to ride at anchor
until the next morning and then to put [them] on. But before
daylight it pleased God to send so mighty a storm as the like was
never felt in New England since the English came there nor in the
memory of any of the Indeans. It was [so] furious that our anchor
came home, whereupon our mariners let slip more cable, yea, even
to the utmost end thereof, and so made it fast only about the bit,
whence it slipped away end for end. Then our sailors knew not
what to do but were driven as pleased the storm and waves. My
cousin and we, perceiving our danger, solemnly recommended
ourselves to God, the Lord both of earth and seas, expecting with
every wave to be swallowed up and drenched in the deeps. And as
my cousin, his wife and children and maid servant, my wife and
my tender babes sat comforting and cheering on the other in the
Lord against ghastly death, which every moment stares us in the
face and sat triumphingly on each other's forehead, we were by the
violence of the waves and fury of the winds by the Lord's permission lifted up upon a rock between two high rocks yet all was but
one rock but ragged, with the stroke whereof the water came into
the pinnace. So as we were presently up to the middle in water as
wet, the waters came furiously and violently over us and against us
but by reason of the rock's proportion could not lift us off but beat
her all to pieces. Now look with me upon our distresses and
consider of my misery, who beheld the ship broken, the water
in her and violently overwhelming us, my goods and provision
swimming in the seas, my friends almost drowned and mine own
poor children so untimely (if I may so term it without offence)
before mine eyes half drowned and ready to be swallowed up and

dashed to pieces against the rocks by the merciless waves and myself ready to accompany them.

But I must go on to an end of this woeful relation. In the same room with us sat he that went master of the pinnace, not knowing what to do. Our foremast was cut down, our mainmast broken in three pieces, the forepart of our pinnace beaten away, our goods swimming about the seas, my children bewailing me as not pitying themselves, and myself bemoaning them, poor souls whom I had occasioned to such an end in their tender years whenas they could scarce be sensible of death. And so likewise my cousin, his wife and his children and both of us bewailing each other in Our Lord and only Savior Jesus Christ, in whom only we had comfort and cheerfulness, insomuch that from the greatest to the least of us there was not one screech or outcry made, but all as silent sheep were contentedly resolved to die together lovingly as since our acquaintance we had lived together friendly.

Now as I was sitting in the cabinroom door, lo, one of the sailors by a wave being washed out of the pinnace was gotten in again, and coming into the cabinroom over my back, cried out, "oh, we are all cast away. Lord, have mercy on us. I have been washed overboard into the sea and am gotten in again." His speeches made me look forth, and looking toward the sea and seeing how we were, I turned myself toward my cousin and the rest and these words, 'Oh, cousin, it hath pleased God here to cast us between two rocks, and the shore not far off from us, for I saw the top of trees when I looked forth." Whereupon the said master of the pinnace, looking up at the s[c]uttle hole of the half deck went out of it, but I never saw him afterward. Then he that had been in the sea went out again by me and leaped overboard toward the rock, whom afterward also I could never see.

Now none were left in the bark that I knew or saw, but my cousin and his wife and children, myself and mine and his maidservant. I put [on] my great coat, a waistcoat of cotton but had neither sleeves nor skirts, a thin pair of breeches, a pair of boots without stockings. My coat I put off me and laid it under my poor babe's feet to raise it out of the water (a poor supporter), but my cousin thought I would have fled from him and said unto me, "Oh, cousin, leave us not. Let us die together," and reached forth his hand unto me. Then I, letting go my son Peter's hand, took him by the hand and said to him, "I purpose it not whither shall I go. I am willing and ready here to die with you. And my poor children, God be merciful to us," adding these words, "The Lord is able to help and to deliver us." He replied, saying, "True, cousin, but what His pleasure is, we know not; I fear we have been too unthankful for former mercies. But He hath promised to deliver us from sin and condemnation, through the all-sufficient satisfaction of Jesus Christ. This, therefore, we may challenge of him." To which I, replying, said, "That is all the deliverance I now desire and expect," which words I had no sooner spoken but by a mighty wave I was with a piece of the bark washed out upon part of the rock, where the wave left me almost drowned. But recovering my feet, [I] saw above me on the rock my daughter Mary, to whom I was no sooner gotten but my cousin Avary and his eldest son came to us, being all four of us washed out with one and the same wave. We went all into a small hole on the top of the rock, whence we called to those in the pinnace to come unto us. Supposing we had been in more safety than they were in, my wife, seeing us there, was crept into the scuttle of the half deck to come unto us, but presently another wave dashing the pinnace all to pieces carried away my wife in the scuttle as she was with the greater part of the half deck [carried] to the shore, where she was safely cast, but her legs were something bruised, and much timber of the vessel being there also cast, she was some time before she could get away, washed with the waves. All the rest that were in the bark were drowned in the merciless seas.

We four by that wave were clean swept away from off the rock also into the sea, the Lord in one instant of time disposing of the souls of us to his good pleasure and will. His wonderful mercy to me was thus. Standing on the rock as before you heard with my eldest daughter, my cousin, and his eldest son, [I was] looking upon and talking unto them in the bark when as we were by that cruel wave washed off the rock as before you heard. God in his mercy caused me to fall by the stroke of the wave flat on my face, for my face was toward the sea insomuch that I was sliding down the rock into the sea. The Lord directed my toes into a joint in the rock's side as also the tops of some of my fingers with my right hand by means whereof, the waves leaving me, I remained so, having only my head above the water. On my left hand I espied a board or plank of the pinnace, and as I was reaching out my left hand to lay hold on it, by another wave coming on the top of the rock I was washed away from the rock and by the violence of the waves was driven hither and thither in the sea a great while and had many dashes against the rocks. At length past hope of life and wearied both in body and spirit I even gave out to nature, and being ready to receive in the waters of death I lifted up both my heart and hands to the God of heaven (for, note, I had my senses remaining and perfect with me all the time I was under and in the water), who at that instant lifted my head clean above the top of waters that so I might breathe without hindrance by the waters. I stood bolt upright as if I stood upon my feet but I felt no bottom nor had any footing for to stand upon but the waters. While I was thus above the waters I saw a piece of the mast as I supposed about three foot long which I laboured to catch into my arms, but suddenly I was overwhelmed with water and driven to and fro again and at last I felt the ground with my right foot. Immediately I was violently thrown grovelling on my face. When presently I recovered my feet [I] was in the water up to my breast and through God's great mercy had my face to the shore and not to the sea. I made haste to get out but was thrown down on my hands with the waves and so with safety crept forth to the dry shore, where, blessing God, I turned about to look for my children and friends but saw neither them nor any part of the pinnace where I left them as I supposed, but I saw my wife about a butt-length from me, getting herself forth from amongst the timber of the broken bark, but before I could get unto her she was gotten to the shore. When we were come each to other we went up into the land and sat us down under a cedar tree, which the winds had thrown down, where we sat about an hour, even dead with cold, for I was glad to put off my breeches, they being rent all to pieces in the rocks.

But now the storm was broken up and the wind was calm, but the sea remained rough and fearful to us. My legs was much bruised and so was my heart, and other hurt had I none, neither had I taken in much water. But my heart would not suffer me to sit still any longer, but I would go to see if any more was gotten to the land in safety, especially hoping to have met with some of mine own poor children, but I could find none, neither dead nor yet living. You condole with me my further miseries, who now began to consider of my losses. Now [I] called to my remembrance the time and manner how and when I last saw and left my children and friends. One was severed from me sitting on the rock at my feet, the other three in the pinnace, my little babe (ah, poor Peter) sitting in his sister Edith's arms, who to the utmost of her power sheltered him out of the waters, my poor William standing close unto her, all three of them looking ruefully on me on the rock, their very countenance calling unto me to help them, whom I could not go unto, neither could they come unto me, neither could the merciless waves afford me space or time to use any means at all, either to help them or myself.

Oh I yet see their cheeks, poor, silent lambs, pleading pity and help at my hands. Then on the other side to consider the loss of my dear friends with the spoil and loss of all our goods and provisions, myself cast upon an unknown land in a wilderness, I know not where, and how to get there we did not know. Then it came into my mind how I had occasioned the death of my children, who had occasioned them out of their native land, who might have left them there, yea and might have sent some of them back again and cost me nothing. These and many such thoughts do press down my heavy heart very much, but I leave, this till I see your face, before which time I fear I shall never attain comfort. Now having no friend to whom I can freely impart myself, Mr Cotten is now my chiefest friend to whom I have free welcome and access, as also Mr Mavericke, Mr Warde, Mr Ward, Mr Hocker, Mr Weles, Mr Warhad, and Mr Parker also, Mr Noyes, who use me friendly. This is God's goodness to me, as also to set the eyes of all the country on me, especially of the magistrates who much favour and comfort me.

But I let this pass and will proceed on in the relation of God's goodness unto me. While I was in that desolate island on which I was cast, I and my wife were almost naked, both of us, and wet and cold even unto death. When going down to the shore as before I said I found cast on the shore a snapsack in which I had a steel and a flint and a powder horn. Going further I found a drowned goat. Then I found a hat and my son Will's coat, both which I put on. My wife found one of her own petticoats which she put on. I found also two cheeses and some butter driven ashore. Thus the Lord sent us some clothes to put on and food to sustain our new lives which he had given lately unto us, and means also to make fire, for in my horn I had some gunpowder, which to my own and other men's admiration was dry. So, taking a piece of my wife's neckcloth, which I dried in the sun, I struck fire and so dried and warmed our wet bodies, and then skinned the goat, and having found a small brass pot we boiled some of it. Our drink was brackish water. Bread we had none. There we remained until the Monday following, where about three o'clock in the afternoon in a boat that came that way, we went off that desolate island, which I named after my own name, "Thacher's Woe," and the rock I named "Avary his Fall," to the end their fall and loss and mine own might be had in perpetual remembrance. In the island lieth buried the body of my cousin's eldest daughter, whom I found dead on the shore. On the Tuesday following in the afternoon we arrived at Marblehed, where I am now remaining in health and good respect though very poor, and thus you have heard such relation as never before happened in New England, and as much bewailed as it was strange. What I shall do or what course I shall take I know not. The Lord in his mercy direct me that I may so lead the new life which he hath given me as may be most to his own glory.

Praise God and pray to God for me.

MANNERS AND CUSTOMS OF THE INDIANS, New England, 1637

Thomas Morton

Of Their Houses and Habitations: The Natives of New England are accustomed to build themselves houses much like the wild Irish; they gather poles in the woods and put the great end of them in the ground, placing them in form of a circle or circumference, and, bending the tops of them in form of an arch, they bind them together with the bark of walnut trees, which is wondrous tough, so that they make the same round on the top for the smoke of their fire to ascend and pass through; these they cover with mats, some made of reeds and some of long flags, or sedge, finely sewed together with needles made of the splinter bones of a crane's leg, with threads made of their Indian hemp, which there grows naturally, leaving several places for doors, which are covered with mats, which may be rolled up and let down again at their pleasure, making use of the several doors, according as the wind sits. The fire is always made in the middle of the house, with windfall commonly, yet sometimes they fell a tree that grows near the house, and, by drawing in the end thereof, maintain the fire on both sides, burning the tree by degrees shorter and shorter, until it be all consumed, for it burns night and day.

Their lodging is made in three places of the house about the fire; they lie upon blankets, commonly about a foot or 18 inches above the ground, raised upon rails that are borne upon forks; they lay mats under them, and coats of deer skins, otters, beavers, racoons, and of bears' hides, all which they have dressed and converted into good leather, with the hair on, for their coverings, and in this manner they lie as warm as they desire. In the night they take their rest; in the day time either the kettle is on with fish or flesh, by no allowance, or else the fire is employed in the roasting of fishes, which they delight in. The air does beget good stomachs, and they feed continually and are no niggards of their victuals, and they are willing that any one shall eat with them. Nay, if any one that shall come into their houses and there fall asleep, when they see him disposed to lie down, they will spread a mat for him of their own accord, and lay a roll of skins for a bolster, and let him lie. If he sleep until their meat be dished up, they will set a wooden bowl of meat by him that sleeps, and wake him, saying, "Cattup keene Meckin." That is, "If you be hungry, there is meat for you, whereof if you will eat you may." Such is their humanity.

Likewise, when they are minded to remove, they carry away the mats with them; other materials the place adjoining will yield. They use not to winter and summer in one place, for that would be a reason to make fuel scarce; but, after the manner of the gentry of civilized natives, remove for their pleasures; sometimes to their hunting places, where they remain keeping good hospitality for that season; and sometimes to their fishing places, where they abide for that season likewise; and at the spring, when fish comes in plentifully, they have meetings from several places, where they exercise themselves in gaming and playing of juggling tricks and all manner of revelries which they are delighted in; so that it is admirable to behold what pastime they use of several kinds, every one striving to surpass each other. After this manner they spend their time.

Of the Indians' Apparel: The Indians in these parts do make their apparel of the skins of several sorts of beasts, and commonly of those that do frequent those parts where they do live; yet some of them, for variety, will have the skins of such beasts that frequent the parts of their neighbors, which they purchase of them by commerce and trade. Their skins they convert into very good leather, making the same plume and soft. Some of these skins they dress with the hair on, and some with the hair off; the hairy side in winter time they wear next their bodies, and in warm weather they wear the hair outwards. They make likewise some coats of the feathers of turkeys, which they weave together with twine of their own making, very prettily. These garments they wear like mantels knit over their shoulders, and put under their arms. They have likewise another sort of mantel, made of moose skins, which beast is a great large deer, so big as a horse. These skins they commonly dress bare, and make them wondrous white, and stripe them with furs round about the borders, in form like lace set on by a tailor, and some they stripe with fur in works of fantasies of the workmen, wherein they strive to excel one another. And mantels made of bears' skins is a usual wearing among the natives that live where the bears do haunt.

They make shoes of moose skins, which is the principal leather used to that purpose; and for want of such leather (which is the strongest) they make shoes of deer skins, as they dress bare, they make stockings that comes within their shoes, like a stirrup stocking, and is fastened above at their belt, which is about their middle. Every male, after he attains unto age which they call Puberty, wears a belt about his middle, and a broad peace of leather that goes between his legs and is tucked up both before and behind under that belt; those garments they always put on, when they go a hunting, to keep their skins from the brush of the shrubs, and when they have their apparel on they look like Irish in their trousers, the stockings join so to their breeches. A good well grown deer skin is of great account with them, and it must have the tail on, or else they account it defaced; the tail being three times as long as the tails of our English deer, yea four times so long, this when they travel is wrapped round their body and, with a girdle of their making, bound round about their middles, to which girdle is fastened a bag, in which his instruments be with which he can strike fire upon any occasion. Thus with their bow in their left hand, and their quiver of arrows at their back, hanging on their left shoulder with the lower end of it in their right hand, they will run away on a dog trot until they come to their journey's end; and, in this kind of ornament, they do seem to me to be handsomer than when they are in English apparel, their gesture being answerable to their own habit and not unto ours.

Their women have shoes and stockings to wear likewise when they please, such as the men have, but the mantle they use to cover their nakedness with is much longer than that which the men use, for, as the men have one deer skin, the women have two sewed together at the full length, and it is so large that it trails after them like a great lady's train; and in time I think they may have their pages to bear them up; and where the men use but one bear skin for a mantle, the women have two sewed together, and if any of their women would at any time shift one, they take that which they intend to make use of, and cast it over them round, before they shift away the other, for modesty, which is to be noted in people uncivilized; therein they seem to have as much modesty as civilized people, and deserve to be applauded for it.

Of Their Custom in Burning the Country, and the Reason Thereof: The savages are accustomed to set fire of the country in all places where they come, and to burn it twice a year, viz.: at the spring, and the fall of the leaves. The reason that moves them to do so, is because it would otherwise be so overgrown with underweeds that it would be all a coppice wood, and the people would not be able in any wise to pass through the country out of a beaten path. The means that they do it with, is with certain mineral stones, that they carry about them in bags made for that purpose of the skins of little beasts, which they convert into good leather, carrying in the same a piece of touch wood, very excellent for that purpose, of their own making. These mineral stones they have from the Piquenteenes (which is to the southward of all the plantations in New England), by trade and traffic with those people.

The burning of the grass destroys the underwoods, and so scorches the elder trees that it shrinks them, and hinders their growth very much; so that he that will look to find large trees and good timber, must not depend upon the help of a wooden prospect to find them on the upland ground; but must seek for them (as I and others have done), in the lower grounds, where the grounds are wet, when the country is fired, by reason of the snow water that remains there for a time, until the sun by continuance of that has exhaled the vapors of the earth, and dried up those places where the fire (by reason of the moisture) can have no power to do them any harm; and if he would endeavor to find out any goodly cedars, he must not seek for them on the higher grounds, but make his inquest for them in the valleys, for the savages, by this custom of theirs, have spoiled all the rest; for this custom has been continued from the beginning.

And lest their firing of the country in this manner should be an occasion of damnifying us, and endangering our habitations, we ourselves have used carefully about the same time to observe the winds, and fire the grounds about our own habitations; to prevent the damage that might happen by any neglect thereof, if the fire should come near those houses in our absence. For, when the fire is once kindled, it dilates and spreads itself as well against, as with the wind; burning continually night and day, until a shower of rain falls to quench it. And this custom of firing the country is the means to make it passable; and by that means the trees grow here and there as in our parks; and make the country very beautiful and commodious.

Of Their Inclination to Drunkenness: Although drunkenness be justly termed a vice which the savages are ignorant of, yet the benefit is very great that comes to the planters by the sale of strong liquor to the savages, who are much taken with the delight of it; for they will pawn their wits, to purchase the acquaintance of it. Yet in all the commerce that I had with them, I never proffered them any such thing; nay, I would hardly let any of them have a dram, unless he were a sachem, or a *winnaytue*, that is a rich man, or a man of estimation next in degree to a sachem or sagamore. I always told them it was amongst us the sachems drink. But they say if I come to the northern parts of the country I shall have no trade, if I will not supply them with lusty liquors; it is the life of the trade in all those parts; for it so happened that thus a savage desperately killed himself; when he was drunk, a gun being charged and the cock up, he sets the mouth to his breast, and, pulling back the trigger with his foot, shot himself dead.

That the Savages Live a Contented Life: A gentleman and a traveller, that had been in the parts of New England for a time, when he returned again, in his discourse of the country, wondered (as he said) that the natives of the land lived so poorly in so rich a country, like to our beggars in England. Surely, that gentleman had not time or leisure while he was there truly to inform himself of the state of that country, and the happy life the savages would lead were they once brought to Christianity. I must confess they want the use and benefit of navigation (which is the very finest of a flourishing commonwealth), yet are they supplied with all manner of needful things for the maintenance of life and livelihood. Food and raiment are the chief of all that we make the use of; and of these they find no want, but have, and may have them, in most plentiful manner.

EXECUTION OF REBELS, Virginia, 1676
Sir William Berkeley

Berkeley was the British governor who suppressed the popular rebellion led by Nathaniel Bacon against Indians and white aristocrats. Bacon himself died of fever, but many of his close associates were caught and hanged. They were:

1. One Johnson, a stirer up of the people to sedition but no fighter.
2. One Barlow, one of Cromwell's soldiers, very active in this rebellion, and taken with forty men coming to surprise me at Accomack.
3. One Carver, a valiant man, and stout seaman, taken miraculously, who came with Bland, with equal com'n and 200 men to take me and some other gentlemen that assisted me, with the help of 200 soldiers; miraculously delivered into my hand.
4. One Wilford, an interpreter, that frighted the Queen of Pamunkey from ye lands she had granted her by the Assembly, a month after peace was concluded with her.
5. One Hartford, a valiant stout man, and a most resolved rebel.

All these at Accomack.

AT YORK WHILST I LAY THERE.

1. One Young, commissionated by Genl. Monck long before he declared for ye King.
2. One Page, a carpenter, formerly my servant, but for his violence used against the Royal Party, made a Colonel.
3. One Harris, that shot to death a valiant loyalist prisoner.
4. One Hall, a Clerk of a County but more useful to the rebels than 40 army men – that died very penitent confessing his rebellion against his King and his ingratitude to me.

AT THE MIDDLE PLANTATION.

One Drummond, a Scotchman that we all suppose was the original cause of the whole rebellion, with a common Frenchman, that had been very bloody.

CONDEMNED AT MY HOUSE, AND EXECUTED WHEN BACON LAY BEFORE JAMESTOWN.

1. One Coll'l Crewe, Bacon's parasyte, that continually went about ye country, extolling all Bacon's actions, and (justifying) his rebellion.
2. One Cookson, taken in rebellion.
3. One Darby, from a servant made a Captain.

WILLM. BERKELEY.

SALEM: THE TRIAL OF MARTHA COREY, 21 March 1692

Deodat Lawson

In January 1692 a group of young girls in the Massachusetts village of Salem began to evidence bizarre behaviour. With no physical cause obvious, it was deduced that the maladies were the work of Satan. Further, the afflicted girls accused a number of women of conspiring with Satan: Martha Corey (Goodwife Corey), a member of the Puritan congregation, was implicated in March. Deodat Lawson was a visiting minister.

On, Monday, the 21st of March, the magistrates of Salem appointed to come to examination of Goodwife Corey. And about twelve of the clock they went into the meeting house, which was thronged with spectators. Mr Noyes began with a very pertinent and pathetic prayer, and Goodwife Corey being called to answer to what was alleged against her, she desired to go to prayer, which was much wondered at, in the presence of so many hundred people. The magistrates told her they would not admit it; they came not there to hear her pray, but to examine her in what was alleged against her. The worshipful Mr Hathorne asked her why she afflicted those children. She said she did not afflict them. He asked her, "Who did then?" She said, "I do not know; how should I know?"

The number of the afflicted persons were about that time ten, viz. four married women: Mrs Pope, Mrs Putnam, Goodwife Bibber, and an ancient woman named Goodall; three maids-. Mary Walcut, Mercy Lewes, at Thomas Putnam's, and a maid at Dr Griggs's; there were three girls from nine to twelve years of age, each of them, or thereabouts, viz. Elizabeth Parris, Abigail Williams, and Ann Putnam.

These were most of them at Goodwife Corey's examination, and did vehemently accuse her in the assembly of afflicting them, by biting, pinching, strangling, etc.; and that they did in their fit see her likeness coming to them, and bringing a book to them. She said she had no book. They affirmed she had a yellow bird that used to suck betwixt her fingers; and being asked about it, if she had any familiar spirit that attended her, she said she had no familiarity with any such thing, she was a gospel woman, which title she called herself by. And the afflicted persons told her ah, she was a gospel witch. Ann Putnam did there affirm that one day when Lieutenant Fuller was at prayer at her father's house she saw the shape of Goodwife Corey and she thought Goodwife N, praying at the same time to the Devil. She was not sure it was Goodwife N., she thought it was, but very sure she saw the shape, of Goodwife Corey. The said Corey said they were poor, distracted children, and no heed to be given to what they said. Mr Hathorne and Mr Noyes replied it was the judgment of all present they were bewitched, and only she, the accused person, said they were distracted.

It was observed several times that if she did but bite her underlip in time of examination, the persons afflicted were bitten on their arms and wrists and produced the marks before the magistrates, ministers, and others. And being watched for that, if she did but pinch her fingers, or grasp one hand hard in another, they were pinched, and produced the marks before the magistrates and spectators. After that, it was observed that if she did but lean her breast against the seat in the meeting house (being the bar at which she stood), they were afflicted. Particularly Mrs Pope complained of grievous torment in her bowels as if they were torn out. She vehemently accused said Corey as the instrument, and first threw her muff at her, but that not flying home, she got off her shoe, and hit Goodwife Corey on the head with it. After these postures were watched, if said Corey did but stir her feet, they were afflicted in their feet, and stamped fearfully.

The afflicted persons asked her why she did not go to the company of witches which were before the meeting house mustering. Did she not hear the drum beat? They accused her of having familiarity with the Devil, in the time of examination, in the shape of a black man whispering in her ear; they affirmed that her yellow bird sucked betwixt her fingers in the assembly; and, order being given to see if there were any sign, the girl that saw it said it was too late now; she had removed a pin, and put it on her head, which was found there sticking upright.

. . . she denied all that was charged upon her, and said they could not prove her a witch. She was that afternoon committed to Salem prison; and after she was in custody, she did not so appear to them and afflict them as before.

Martha Corey was hanged on 22 September, 1692. Her husband, also accused of witchcraft, was executed by having heavy rocks placed upon him two days previously.

SALEM: THE OPINION OF COTTON MATHER, 1692

Cotton Mather

The Puritan clergyman Cotton Mather (1663–1728) published 382 books, among them *Memorable Providences Relating to Witchcraft and Possessions*, which did much to instigate the Salem witch hunt. He writes below to his great uncle, John Cotton Mather

5 August 1692

Reverend Sir,
Our good God is working of miracles. Five witches were lately executed, impudently demanding of God a miraculous vindication of their innocency. Immediately upon this, our God miraculously sent in five Andover witches, who made a most ample, surprising, amazing confession of all their villainies, and declared the five newly executed to have been of their company, discovering many more, but all agreeing in Burroughs being their ringleader, who, I suppose, this day receives his trial at Salem, whither a vast concourse of people is gone, my father this morning among the rest. Since those, there have come in other confessors; yea, they come in daily. About this prodigious matter my soul has been refreshed with some little short of miraculous answers of prayer, which are not to be written; but they comfort me with a prospect of a hopeful issue.

DOMESTIC ECONOMY, New England, 1717

Wait Winthrop

Winthrop (1643–1717), a former general and judge, writes to his son.

BOSTON, Oct. 22d, 1717

DEAR SON:
I have your letter and what you sent by Wilson. There was but nine fish: there was some maggots in them, it being hot weather. We had one of them at dinner today, which eat well. I hear nothing of Parker yet; if I cannot get away this winter, I know not what we shall do. A little butter and cheese will not do, nor 100 sheep. If I were shure of good weather, I would com in Mr. Pickets sloop. Shall send some gallons of

Palm wine for present occation; its farr beyond Canary, and shall look out for strong locks. You say nothing about the fashion of the britches: the bucks skin you brought is drest with very good yellow lether of the ordinary color. Our Genll. Court sits in a few days: I would fain do something about the Tantiusque land before I leave this place, or we shall lose it all. I hear not of your letter by the Indian. Capt Sewalls wife died last Saturday. Mary sends duty, love, and thanks for the nutts, she is now at scoole. All friends well. They are to try pirates here tomorrow, I think. I pray God to bless and keep you all, and send your wife a good time.

Your loving father,
W. WINTHROP

SLAVERY: KIDNAPPING IN GUINEA, c. 1734

Venture Smith

Smith was kidnapped at the age of six in Guinea, Africa, and sold to the steward of a slave ship and brought to Connecticut. By 1800 10–15 million Africans had been transported as slaves to the Americas.

I was born in Dukandarra, in Guinea, about the year 1729. My father's name was Saungm Furro, Prince of the tribe of Dukandarra. My father had three wives. Polygamy was not uncommon in that country, especially among the rich, as every man was allowed to keep as many wives as he could maintain . . . .

The first thing worthy of notice which I remember was, a contention between my father and mother, on account of my father marrying his third wife without the consent of his first and eldest, which was contrary to the custom generally observed among my countrymen. In consequence of this rupture, my mother left her husband and country, and travelled away with her three children to the eastward. I was then five years old. . . . After five days travel . . . my mother was pleased to stop and seek a refuge for me. She left me at the house of a very rich farmer. I was then, as I should judge, not less than one hundred and forty miles from my native place, separated from all my relations and acquaintance . . . .

My father sent a man and horse after me. After settling with my guardian for keeping me, he took me away and went for home. It was then about one year since my mother brought me here.

Nothing remarkable occurred to us on our journey until we arrived safe home.

I found then that the difference between my parents had been made up previous to their sending for me. On my return, I was received both by my father and mother with great joy and affection, and was once more restored to my paternal dwelling in peace and happiness. I was then about six years old.

Not more than six weeks had passed after my return before a message was brought by an inhabitant of the place where I lived the preceding year to my father, that that place had been invaded by a numerous army from a nation not far distant, furnished with musical instrument, and all kinds of arms then in use; that they were instigated by some white nation who equipped and sent them to subdue and possess the country; that his nation had made no preparation for war, having been for a long time in profound peace; that they could not defend themselves against such a formidable train of invaders, and must therefore necessarily evacuate their lands to the fierce enemy, and fly to the protection of some chief; and that if he would permit them they would come under his rule and protection when they had to retreat from their own possessions. He was a kind and merciful prince, and therefore consented to these proposals . . . .

He gave them every privilege and all the protection his government could afford. But they had not been there longer than four days before news came to them that the invaders had laid waste their country, and were coming speedily to destroy them in my father's territories. This affrighted them, and therefore they immediately pushed off to the southward, into the unknown countries there, and were never more heard of.

Two days after their retreat, the report turned out to be but too true. A detachment from the enemy came to my father and informed him, that the whole army was encamped not far out of his dominions, and would invade the territory and deprive his people of their liberties and rights, if he did not comply with the following terms. These were to pay them a large sum of money, three hundred fat cattle, and a great number of goats, sheep, asses, etc.

My father told the messenger he would comply rather than that his subjects should be deprived of their rights and privileges, which he was not then in circumstances to defend from so sudden an invasion. Upon turning out those articles, the enemy pledged their faith and honor that they would not attack him. On these he relied and therefore thought it unnecessary to be on his guard against the enemy. But their pledges of faith and honour proved no better than those of other unprincipled hostile nations; for a few days after a certain relation of the king came and informed him, that the enemy who sent terms of accommodation to him and received tribute to their satisfaction, yet meditated an attack upon his subjects by surprise and that probably they would commence their attack in less than one day, and concluded with advising him, as he was not prepared for war, to order a speedy retreat of his family and subjects. He complied with this advice.

The same night which was fixed upon to retreat, my father and his family set off about the break of day. The king and his two younger wives went in one company, and my mother and her children in another. We left our dwellings in succession, and my father's company went on first. We directed our course for a large shrub plain, some distance off, where we intended to conceal ourselves from the approaching enemy, until we could refresh ourselves a little. But we presently found that our retreat was not secure. For having struck up a little fire for the purpose of cooking victuals, the enemy who happened to be encamped a little distance off, had sent out a scouting party who discovered us by the smoke of the fire, just as we were extinguishing it, and about to eat. As soon as we had finished eating, my father discovered the party, and immediately began to discharge arrows at them. This was what I first saw, and it alarmed both me and the women, who being unable to make any resistance, immediately betook ourselves to the tall thick reeds not far off, and left the old king to fight alone. For some time I beheld him from the reeds defending himself with great courage and firmness, till at last he was obliged to surrender himself into their hands.

They then came to us in the reeds, and the very first salute I had from them was a violent blow on the back part of the head with the fore part of a gun, and at the same time a grasp round the neck. I then had a rope put about my neck, as had all the women in the thicket with me, and were immediately led to my father, who was likewise pinioned and haltered for leading. In this condition we were all led to the camp. The women and myself being pretty submissive, had tolerable treatment from the enemy, while my father was closely interrogated respecting his money which they knew he must have. But as he gave them no account of it, he was instantly cut and pounded on his body with great inhumanity, that he might be induced by the torture he suffered to make the discovery. All this availed not in the least to make him give up his money, but he despised all the tortures which they inflicted, until the continued exercise and increase of torment, obliged him to sink and expire. He thus died without informing his enemies where his money lay. I saw him while he was thus tortured to death. The shocking scene is to this day fresh in my mind, and I have often been overcome while thinking on it . . . .

The army of the enemy was large, I should suppose consisting of about six thousand men. Their leader was called Baukurre. After destroying the old prince, they decamped and immediately marched toward the sea, lying to the west, taking with them myself and the women prisoners. In the march a scouting party was detached from the main army. To the leader of this party I was made waiter, having to carry his gun, etc. As we were scouting we came across a herd of fat cattle, consisting of about thirty in number. These we set upon, and immediately wrested from their keepers, and afterwards converted them into food for the army. The enemy had remarkable success in destroying the country wherever they went. For as far as they had penetrated, they laid the habitations waste and captured the people. The distance they had now brought me was about four hundred miles. All the march I had very hard tasks imposed on me, which I must perform on pain of punishment. I was obliged to carry on my head a large flat stone used for grinding our corn, weighing as I should suppose, as much as twenty-five pounds; besides victuals, mat and cooking utensils. Though I was pretty large and stout at my age, yet these burdens were very grievous to me, being only six years and a half old.

We were then come to a place called Malagasco. When we entered the place we could not see the least appearance of either houses or inhabitants, but upon stricter search found, that instead of houses above ground they had dens in the sides of hillocks, contiguous to ponds and streams of water. In these we perceived they had all hid themselves, as I supposed they usually did on such occasions. In order to compel them to surrender, the enemy contrived to smoke them out with faggots. These they put to the entrance of the caves and set them on fire. While they were engaged in this business, to their great surprise some of them were desperately wounded with arrows which fell from above on them. This mystery they soon found out. They perceived that the enemy discharged these arrows through holes on top of the dens, directly into the air. Their weight brought them back, point downwards on their enemies heads, whilst they were smoking the inhabitants out. The points of their arrows were poisoned, but their enemy had an antidote for it, which they instantly applied to the wounded part. The smoke at last obliged the people to give themselves up. They came out of their caves, first putting the palms of their hands together, and immediately after extended their arms, crossed at their wrists, ready to be bound and pinioned . . . .

The invaders then pinioned the prisoners of all ages and sexes indiscriminately, took their flocks and all their effects, and moved on their way towards the sea. On the march the prisoners were treated with clemency, on account of their being submissive and humble. Having come to the next tribe, the enemy laid siege and immediately took men, women, children, flocks, and all their valuable effects. They then went on to the next district which was contiguous to the sea, called in Africa, Anamaboo. The enemies provisions were then almost spent, as well as their strength. The inhabitants knowing what conduct they had pursued, and what were their present intentions, improve the favourable opportunity, attacked them, and took enemy, prisoners, flocks and all their effects. I was then taken a second time. All of us were then put into the castle [a European slave trading post], and kept for market. On a certain time I and other prisoners were put on board a canoe, under our master, and rowed away to a vessel belonging to Rhode Island, commanded by Captain Collingwood, and the mate Thomas Mumford. While we were going to the vessel, our master told us all to appear to the best possible advantage for sale. I was bought on board by one Robert Mumford, steward of said vessel, for four gallons of rum, and a piece of calico, and called Venture, on account of his having purchased me with his own private venture. Thus I came by my name. All the slaves that were bought for that vessel's cargo, were two hundred and sixty.

"FEW OF THIS CLASS ESCAPE WITH THEIR LIVES": PASSAGE TO AMERICA, 1750

Gottlieb Mittelberger

The 18th century witnessed a tremendous surge in emigration to America; some 250,000 Africans and and a similar number of Europeans reached the colonies in the fifty years before the Revolutionary War. Mittelberger was a German schoolmaster bound for Philadelphia.

. . . during the voyage there is on board these ships terrible misery, stench, fumes, horror, vomiting, many kinds of seasickness, fever, dysentery, headache, heat, constipation, boils, scurvy, cancer, mouth rot, and the like, all of which come from old and sharply-salted food and meat, also from very bad and foul water, so that many die miserably.

Add to this want of provisions, hunger, thirst, frost, heat, dampness, anxiety, want, afflictions and lamentations, together with other trouble, as e.g., the lice abound so frightfully, especially on sick people, that they can be scraped off the body. The misery reaches a climax when a gale rages for two or three nights and days, so that every one believes that the ship will go to the bottom with all human beings on board. In such a visitation the people cry and pray most piteously.

No one can have an idea of the sufferings which women in confinement have to bear with their innocent children on board these ships. Few of this class escape with their lives; many a mother is cast into the water with her child as soon as she is dead. One day, just as we had a heavy gale, a woman in our ship, who was to give birth and could not give birth under the circumstances, was pushed through a loophole (porthole) in the ship and dropped into the sea, because she was far in the rear of the ship and could not be brought forward.

Children from one to seven years rarely survive the voyage; and many a time parents are compelled to see their children miserably suffer and die from hunger, thirst, and sickness, and then to see them cast into the water. I witnessed such misery in no less than thirty-two children in our ship, all of whom were thrown into the sea. The parents grieve all the more since their children find no resting place in the earth, but are devoured by the monsters of the sea. It is a notable fact that children who have not yet had the measles or smallpox generally get them on board the ship, and mostly die of them.

When the ships have landed at Philadelphia after their long voyage, no one is permitted to leave them except those who pay for their passage or can give good security; the others, who cannot pay, must remain on board the ships till they are purchased and are released from the ships by their purchasers. The sick always fare the worst, for the healthy are naturally preferred and purchased first; and so the sick and wretched must often remain on board in front of the city for two or three weeks, and frequently die, whereas many a one, if he could pay his debt and were permitted to leave the ship immediately, might recover and remain alive.

The sale of human beings in the market on board the ship is carried on thus: Every day Englishmen, Dutchmen, and High German people come from the city of Philadelphia and other places, in part from a great distance, say twenty, thirty, or forty hours away, and go on board the newly-arrived ship that has brought and offers for sale passengers from Europe, and select among the healthy persons such as they deem suitable for their business, and bargain with them how long they will serve for their passage money, which most of them are still in debt for. When they have come to an agreement, it happens that adult persons bind themselves in writing to serve three, four, five, or six years for the amount due by them, according to their age and strength. But very young people, from ten to fifteen years, must serve till they are twenty-one years old.

Many parents must sell and trade away their children like so many head of cattle, for if their children take the debt upon themselves, the parents can leave the ship free and unrestrained; but as the parents often do not know where and to what people their children are going, it often happens that such parents and children, after leaving the ship, do not see each other again for many years, perhaps no more in all their lives.

It often happens that whole families, husband, wife, and children, are separated by being sold to different purchasers, especially when they have not paid any part of their passage money.

When a husband or wife has died at sea, when the ship has made more than half of her trip, the survivor must pay or serve not only for himself or herself, but also for the deceased. When both parents have died over halfway at sea, their children, especially when they are young and have nothing to pawn or to pay, must stand for their own and their parents' passage, and serve till they are twenty-one years old. When one has served his or her term, he or she is entitled to a new suit of clothes at parting; and if it has been so stipulated, a man gets in addition a horse, a woman, a cow.

GEORGE WASHINGTON CROSSES THE ALLEGANYS, 31 October 1753–16 January 1754

George Washington

On receiving intelligence that the French were encroaching on British territory beyond the Alleganys, Governor Dinwiddie of Virginia determined to warn the intruders off. The officer chosen for the mission was Major George Washington. He was then aged twenty-one.

I was commissioned and appointed by the Hon. Robert Dinwiddie, Esq., Governor of Virginia, to visit and deliver a letter to the commandant of the French forces on the Ohio, and set out on the intended journey on the same day; the next I arrived at Fredericksburg, and engaged Mr Jacob Vanbraam to be my French interpreter, and proceeded with him to Alexandria, where we provided necessaries. From thence we went to Winchester, and got baggage, horses, etc., and from thence we pursued the new road to Will's Creek, where we arrived on the 14th of November.

Here I engaged Mr Gist to pilot us out, and also hired four others as servitors, Barnaby Currin, and John M'Quire, Indian traders, Henry Steward and William Jenkins; and in company with those persons, left the inhabitants the next day.

The excessive rains and vast quantity of snow which had fallen prevented our reaching Mr Frazier's, an Indian trader, at the mouth of Turtle Creek, on Monongahela River, until Thursday, the 22nd. We were informed here that expresses had been sent a few days before to the traders down the river, to acquaint them with the French general's death, and the return of the major part of the French army into winter quarters.

The waters were quite impassable without swimming our horses, which obliged us to get the loan of a canoe from Frazier, and to send Barnaby Currin and Henry Steward down the Monongahela, with our baggage, to meet us at the Fork of the Ohio, about ten miles; there to cross the Allegany.

As I got down before the canoe I spent some time in viewing the rivers, and the land in the Fork, which I think extremely well situated for a fort, as it has the absolute command of both rivers. The land at the point is twenty or twenty-five feet above the common surface of the water; and a considerable bottom of flat, welltimbered land all around it, very convenient for building. The rivers are each a quarter of a mile or more across, and run here very nearly at right angles, Allegany bearing north-east, and Monongahela south-east. The former of these two is a very rapid and swift running river, the other deep and still, without any perceptible fall.

About two miles from this, on the south-east side of the river, at the place where the Ohio Company intended to erect a fort, lives Shingiss, King of the Delawares. We called upon him, to invite him to counsel at the Logstown.

Shingiss attended us to the Logstown, where we arrived between sun-setting and dark, the twenty-fifth day after I left Williamsburg. We travelled over some extremely good and bad land to get to this place.

As soon as I came into town, I went to Monacatoocha (as the Half-King was out at his hunting-cabin on Little Beaver Creek, about fifteen miles off), and informed him by John Davidson, my Indian interpreter, that I was sent a messenger to the French general, and was ordered to call upon the sachems of the Six Nations to acquaint them with it. I gave him a string of wampum and a twist of tobacco, and desired him to send for the Half-King, which he promised to do by a runner in the morning, and for other sachems. I invited him and the other great men present to my tent, where they stayed about an hour, and returned.

According to the best observations I could make, Mr Gist's new settlement (which we passed by) bears about west-north-west seventy miles from Will's Creek; Shannopins, or the Fork, north by west, or north-north-west, about fifty miles from that; and from thence to the Logstown the course is nearly west about eighteen or twenty miles; so that the whole distance, as we went and computed it, is at least one hundred and thirty-five or one hundred and forty miles from our back inhabitants.

25th. Came to town, four of ten Frenchmen who had deserted from a company at the Kuskuskas, which lies at the mouth of the river. I got the following account from them. They were sent from New Orleans with a hundred men, and eight canoe loads of provisions to this place, where they expected to have met the same number of men from the forts on this side of Lake Erie, to convoy them and the stores up, who were not arrived when they ran off.

I inquired into the situation of the French on the Mississippi, their numbers, and what forts they had built. They informed me that there were four small forts between New Orleans and the

Black Islands, garrisoned with about thirty or forty men, and a few small pieces in each. That at New Orleans, which is near the mouth of the Mississippi, there are thirty-five companies of forty men each, with a pretty strong fort mounting eight carriage guns; and at the Black Islands there are several companies, and a fort with six guns. The Black Islands are about a hundred and thirty leagues above the mouth of the Ohio, which is about three hundred and fifty above New Orleans. They also acquainted me that there was a small palisadoed fort on the Ohio, at the mouth of the Obaish, about sixty leagues from the Mississippi. The Obaish heads near the west end of Lake Erie, and affords the communication between the French on the Mississippi and those on the lakes. These deserters came up from the lower Shannoah town with one Brown, an Indian trader, and were going to Philadelphia.

About three o'clock this evening the Half-King came to town. I went up and invited him, with Davidson, privately, to my tent, and desired him to relate some of the particulars of his journey to the French commandant, and of his reception there; also, to give me an account of the ways and distance. He told me that the nearest and levelest way was now impassable, by reason of many large, miry savannas; that we must be obliged to go by Venango, and should not get to the near fort in less than five or six nights' sleep, good travelling. When he went to the fort, he said he was received in a very stern manner by the late commander, who asked him very abruptly what he had come about, and to declare his business, which he said he did in the following speech:

"Fathers, I am come to tell you your own speeches, what your own mouths have declared. Fathers, you, in former days, set a silver basin before us, wherein there was the leg of a beaver, and desired all the nations to come and eat of it, to eat in peace and plenty, and not to be churlish to one another; and that if any such person should be found to be a disturber I here lay down by the edge of the dish a rod, which you must scourge them with; and if your father should get foolish, in my old days, I desire you may use it upon me as well as others.

"Now, fathers, it is you who are the disturbers of this land, by coming and building your towns, and by taking it away unknown to us, and by force.

"Fathers, we kindled a fire a long time ago at a place called Montreal, where we desired you to stay, and not to come and intrude upon our land. I now desire you may dispatch to that place for be it known to you, fathers, that this is our land, and not yours.

"Fathers, I desire you may hear me in civilness; if not, we must handle that rod which was laid down for the use of the obstreperous. If you had come in a peaceable manner, like our brothers the English, we would not have been against your trading with us as they do; but to come, fathers, and build houses upon our land, and to take it by force, is what we cannot submit to.

"Fathers, both you and the English are white, we live in a country between; therefore, the land belongs to neither one nor the other. But the Great Being above allowed it to be a place of residence for us; so, fathers, I desire you to withdraw, as I have done our brothers the English; for I will keep you at arm's length. I lay this down as a trial for both, to see which will have the greatest regard to it, and that side we will stand by, and make equal sharers with us. Our brothers, the English, have heard this, and I come now to tell it to you; for I am not afraid to discharge you off this land."

This, he said, was the substance of what he spoke to the general, who made this reply:

"Now, my child, I have heard your speech; you spoke first, but it is my time to speak now. Where is my wampum that you took away with the marks of towns on it? This wampum I do not know, which you have discharged me off the land with; but you need not put yourself to the trouble of speaking, for I will not hear you. I am not afraid of flies or musquitoes, for Indians are such as those; I tell you down that river I will go, and build upon it, according to my command. If the river was blocked up, I have forces sufficient to burst it open, and tread under my feet all that stand in opposition, together with their alliances; for my force is as the sand upon the sea shore; therefore, here is your wampum; I sling it at you. Child, you talk foolish; you say this land belongs to you, but there is not the black of my nail yours. I saw that land sooner than you did; before the Shannoahs and you were at war. Lead was the man who went down and took possession of that river. It is my land, and I will have it, let who will stand up for, or say against it. I will buy and sell with the English [mockingly]. If people will be ruled by me, they may expect kindness, but not else."

The Half-King told me he had inquired of the general after two Englishmen who were made prisoners, and received this answer:

"Child, you think it a very great hardship that I made prisoners of those two people at Venango. Don't you concern yourself with it; we took and carried them to Canada, to get intelligence of what the English were doing in Virginia."

He informed me that they had built two forts, one on Lake Erie, and another on French Creek, near a small lake, about fifteen miles asunder, and a large wagon-road between. He gave me a plan of them of his own drawing.

26th. We met in council at the long-house about nine o'clock, where I spoke to them as follows:

"Brothers, I have called you together in council, by order of your brother, the Governor of Virginia, to acquaint you that I am sent with all possible dispatch to visit and deliver a letter to the French commandant, of very great importance to your brothers the English; and I dare say to you, their friends and allies.

"I was desired, brothers, by your brother, the Governor, to call upon you, the sachems of the nations, to inform you of it, and to ask your advice and assistance to proceed the nearest and best road to the French. You see, brothers, I have gotten thus far on my journey.

"His Honour likewise desired me to apply to you for some of your young men to conduct and provide provisions for us on our way, and be a safeguard against those French Indians who have taken up the hatchet against us. I have spoken thus particularly to you, brothers, because his Honour, our Governor, treats you as good friends and allies, and holds you in great esteem. To confirm what I have said, I give you this string of wampum."

After they had considered for some time on the above discourse, the Half-King got up and spoke:

"Now, my brother, in regard to what my brother the Governor has desired of me, I return you this answer:

"I rely upon you as a brother ought to do, as you say we are brothers, and one people. We shall put heart in hand and speak to our fathers, the French, concerning the speech they made to me; and you may depend that we will endeavour to be your guard.

"Brother, as you have asked my advice, I hope you will be ruled by it, and stay until I can provide a company to go with you. The French speech-belt is not here; I have to go for it to my hunting-cabin. Likewise, the people whom I have ordered in are not yet come, and cannot until the third night from this; until which time, brother, I must beg you to stay.

"I intend to send the guard of Mongoes, Shannoahs, and

Delawares, that our brothers may see the love and loyalty we bear them."

As I had orders to make all possible dispatch, and waiting here was very contrary to my inclination, I thanked him in the most suitable manner I could, and told him that my business required the greatest expedition, and would not admit of that delay. He was not well pleased that I should offer to go before the time he had appointed, and told me that he could not consent to our going without a guard, for fear some accident should befall us, and draw a reflection upon him. Besides, said he, this is a matter of no small moment, and must not be entered into without due consideration; for I intend to deliver up the French speech-belt, and make the Shannoahs and Delawares do the same. And accordingly he gave orders to King Shingiss, who was present, to attend on Wednesday night with the wampum; and two men of their nation to be in readiness to set out with us the next morning. As I found it was impossible to get off without affronting them in the most egregious manner, I consented to stay.

I gave them back a string of wampum which I met with at Mr Frazier's, and which they sent with a speech to his Honour the Governor, to inform him that three nations of French Indians – namely, Chippewas, Ottowas, and Orundaks, had taken up the hatchet against the English; and desired them to repeat it over again. But this they postponed doing until they met in full council with the Shannoah and Delaware chiefs.

27th. Runners were dispatched very early for the Shannoah chiefs. The Half-King set out himself to fetch the French speech-belt from his hunting cabin.

28th. He returned this evening, and came with Monacatoocha and two other sachems to my tent, and begged (as they had complied with his Honour the Governor's request, in providing men, etc.) to know on what business we were going to the French. This was a question I had all along expected, and had provided as satisfactory answers as I could; which allayed their curiosity a little.

Monacatoocha informed me that an Indian from Venango brought news a few days ago that the French had called all the Mingoes, Delawares, etc., together at that place; and told them that they intended to have been down the river this fall, but the waters were growing cold, and the winter advancing, which obliged them to go into quarters; but that they might assuredly

64   DISCOVERY

expect them in the spring with a far greater number; and desired
that they might be quite passive, and not intermeddle unless they
had a mind to draw all their force upon them; for that they
expected to fight the English three years (as they supposed there
would be some attempts made to stop them), in which time they
should conquer. But that if they should prove equally strong, they
and the English would join to cut them all off, and divide the land
between them; that though they had lost their general and some
few of their soldiers, yet there were men enough to reinforce them,
and make them masters of the Ohio.

This speech, he said, was delivered to them by one Captain
Joncaire, their interpreter-in-chief, living at Venango, and a man
of note in the army.

29th. The Half-King and Monacatoocha came very early, and
begged me to stay one day more; for notwithstanding they had
used all the diligence in their power, the Shannoah chiefs had not
brought the wampum they ordered, but would certainly be in tonight; if not, they would delay me no longer, but would send it
after us as soon as they arrived. When I found them so pressing in
their request, and knew that the returning of wampum was the
abolishing of agreements, and giving this up was shaking off all
dependence upon the French, I consented to stay, as I believed an
offence offered at this crisis might be attended with greater ill
consequence than another day's delay. They also informed me that
Shingiss could not get in his men, and was prevented from coming
himself by his wife's sickness (I believe by fear of the French), but
that the wampum of that nation was lodged with Kustalogo, one of
their chiefs, at Venango.

In the evening, late, they came again, and acquainted me that
the Shannoahs were not yet arrived, but that it should not retard
the prosecution of our journey. He delivered in my hearing the
speech that was to be made to the French by Jeskakake, one of
their old chiefs, which was giving up the belt the late commandant
had asked for, and repeating nearly the same speech he himself had
done before.

He also delivered a string of wampum to this chief, which was
sent by King Shingiss, to be given to Kustalogo, with orders to
repair to the French, and deliver up the wampum.

He likewise gave a very large string of black and white wampum, which was to be sent up immediately to the Six Nations, if
the French refused to quit the land at this warning, which was the

third and last time, and was the right of this Jeskakake to deliver.

30th. Last night, the great men assembled at their council house, to consult further about this journey, and who were to go; the result of which was, that only three of their chiefs, with one of their best hunters, should be our convoy. The reason they gave for not sending more, after what had been proposed at council the 26th, was, that a greater number might give the French suspicions of some bad design, and cause them to be treated rudely; but I rather think they could not get their hunters in.

We set out about nine o'clock with the Half-King, Jeskakake, White Thunder, and the Hunter; and travelled on the road to Venango, where we arrived the 4th of December, without anything remarkable happening but a continued series of bad weather.

This is an old Indian town, situated at the mouth of French Creek, on the Ohio; and lies near north about sixty miles from the Logstown, but more than seventy the way we were obliged to go.

We found the French colours hoisted at a house from which they had driven Mr John Frazier, an English subject. I immediately repaired to it, to know where the commander resided. There were three officers, one of whom, Captain Joncaire, informed me that he had the command of the Ohio; but that there was a general officer at the near fort, where he advised me to apply for an answer. He invited us to sup with them, and treated us with the greatest complaisance.

The wine, as they dosed themselves pretty plentifully with it, soon banished the restraint which at first appeared in their conversation, and gave a licence to their tongues to reveal their sentiments more freely.

They told me that it was their absolute design to take possession of the Ohio, and by G – they would do it; for that, although they were sensible the English could raise two men for their one, yet they knew their motions were too slow and dilatory to prevent any undertaking of theirs. They pretend to have an undoubted right to the river from a discovery made by one LaSalle, sixty years ago; and the rise of this expedition is, to prevent our settling on the river or waters of it, as they heard of some families moving out in order thereto. From the best intelligence I could get, there have been fifteen hundred men on this side Ontario Lake. But upon the death of the general, all were recalled, to about six or seven hundred, who were left to garrison four forts, one hundred and fifty, or thereabouts, in each. The first of them is on French Creek, near a small lake, about sixty miles from Venango, near north northwest;

the next lies on Lake Erie, where the greater part of their stores are kept, about fifteen miles from the other; from this it is one hundred and twenty miles to the carrying-place, at the Falls of Lake Erie, where there is a small fort, at which they lodge their goods in bringing them from Montreal, the place from whence all their stores are brought. The next fort lies about twenty miles from this, on Ontario Lake. Between this fort and Montreal, there are three others, the first of which is nearly opposite to the English fort Oswego. From the fort on Lake Erie to Montreal is about six hundred miles, which, they say, requires no more (if good weather) than four weeks' voyage, if they go in barks or large vessels, so that they may cross the lake; but if they come in canoes, it will require five or six weeks, for they are obliged to keep under the shore.

December 5th. Rained excessively all day, which prevented our travelling. Captain Joncaire sent for the Half-King, as he had but just heard that he came with me. He affected to be much concerned that I did not make free to bring them in before. I excused it in the best manner of which I was capable, and told him, I did not think their company agreeable, as I had heard him say a good deal in dispraise of Indians in general; but another motive prevented me from bringing them into his company; I knew that he was an interpreter, and a person of very great influence among the Indians, and had lately used all possible means to draw them over to his interest; therefore I was desirous of giving him no opportunity that could be avoided.

When they came in there was great pleasure expressed at seeing them. He wondered how they could be so near without coming to visit him, made several trifling presents, and applied liquor so fast that they were soon rendered incapable of the business they came about, notwithstanding the caution which was given.

6th. The Half-King came to my tent quite sober, and insisted very much that I should stay and hear what he had to say to the French. I fain would have prevented him from speaking anything until he came to the commandant, but could not prevail. He told me that at this place a council-fire was kindled, where all their business with these people was to be transacted, and that the management of the Indian affairs was left solely to Monsieur Joncaire. As I was desirous of knowing the issue of this, I agreed to stay; but sent our horses a little way up French Creek, to raft over and encamp, which I knew would make it near night.

About ten o'clock they met in council. The King spoke much the same as he had before done to the general; and offered the French speech-belt which had before been demanded, with the marks of four towns on it, which Monsieur Joncaire refused to receive, but desired him to carry it to the fort to the commander.

7th. Monsieur La Force, commissary of the French stores, and three other soldiers, came over to accompany us up. We found it extremely difficult to get the Indians off to-day, as every stratagem had been used to prevent their going up with me. I had last night left John Davidson (the Indian interpreter), whom I brought with me from town, and strictly charged him not to be out of their company, as I could not get them over to my tent; for they had some business with Kustalogo chiefly to know why he did not deliver up the French speech-belt which he had in keeping; but I was obliged to send Mr Gist over to-day to fetch them, which he did with great persuasion.

At twelve o'clock, we set out for the fort, and were prevented arriving there until the 11th by excessive rains, snows, and bad travelling through many mires and swamps; these we were obliged to pass to avoid crossing the creek, which was impassable, either by fording or rafting, the water was so high and rapid.

We passed over much good land since we left Venango, and through several extensive and very rich meadows, one of which, I believe, was nearly four miles in length, and considerably wide in some places.

12th. I prepared early to wait upon the commander, and was received and conducted to him by the second officer in command. I acquainted him with my business, and offered my commission and letter; both of which he desired me to keep until the arrival of Monsieur Reparti, captain of the next fort, who was sent for and expected every hour.

This commander is a knight of the military order of St Louis, and named Legardeur de St Pierre. He is an elderly gentleman, and has much the air of a soldier. He was sent over to take the command immediately upon the death of the late general, and arrived here about seven days before me.

At two o'clock the gentleman who was sent for arrived, when I offered the letter, etc., again, which they received, and adjourned into a private apartment for the captain to translate, who understood a little English. After he had done it the commander desired I would walk in and bring my interpreter to peruse and correct it; which I did.

13th. The chief officers retired to hold a council of war, which gave me an opportunity of taking the dimensions of the fort, and making what observations I could.

It is situated on the south or west fork of French Creek, near the water; and is almost surrounded by the creek, and a small branch of it, which form a kind of island. Four houses compose the side. The bastions are made of piles driven into the ground, standing more than twelve feet above it, and sharp at top, with portholes cut for cannon, and loopholes for the small arms to fire through. There are eight six-pounds pieces mounted in each bastion, and one piece of four pounds before the gate. In the bastions are a guard-house, chapel, doctor's lodging, and the commander's private store; round which are laid platforms for the cannon and men to stand on. There are several barracks without the fort, for the soldiers' dwellings, covered, some with bark and some with boards made chiefly of logs. There are also several other houses, such as stables, smith's shop, etc.

I could get no certain account of the number of men here; but, according to the best judgment I could form, there are a hundred, exclusive of officers, of whom there are many. I also gave orders to the people who were with me to take an exact account of the canoes, which were hauled up to convey their forces down in the spring. This they did, and told fifty of birch bark, and a hundred and seventy of pine; besides many others, which were blocked out, in readiness for being made.

14th. As the snow increased very fast, and our horses daily became weaker, I sent them off unloaded, under the care of Barnaby Currin and two others, to make all convenient dispatch to Venango, and there to wait our arrival, if there was a prospect of the river's freezing; if not, then to continue down to Shannopin's Town, at the Fork of the Ohio, and there to wait until we came to cross the Allegany, intending myself to go down by water, as I had the offer of a canoe or two.

As I found many plots concerted to retard the Indians' business, and prevent their returning with me, I endeavoured all that lay in my power to frustrate their schemes, and hurried them on to execute their intended design. They accordingly pressed for admittance this evening, which at length was granted them, privately, to the commander and one or two other officers. The Half-King told me that he offered the wampum to the commander, who evaded taking it, and made many fair promises of love and friendship; said he wanted to live in peace, and trade amicably with them, as a proof of which, he would send some goods immediately down to the Logstown for them. But I rather think the design of that is to bring away all our straggling traders they meet with, as I privately understand they intended to carry an officer with them. And what rather confirms this opinion, I was inquiring of the commander by what authority he had made prisoners of several of our English subjects. He told me that the country belonged to them; that no Englishman had a right to trade upon those waters; and that he had orders to make every person prisoner who attempted it on the Ohio, or the waters of it.

This evening I received an answer to his Honour the Governor's letter from the commandant.

15th. The commandant ordered a plentiful store of liquor and provision to be put on board our canoes, and appeared to be extremely complaisant, though he was exerting every artifice which he could invent to set our Indians at variance with us, to prevent their going until after our departure; presents, rewards, and everything which could be suggested by him or his officers. I cannot say that ever in my life I suffered so much anxiety as I did in this affair. I saw that every stratagem which the most fruitful brain could invent was practised to win the Half-King to their interest; and that leaving him there was giving them the opportunity they aimed at. I went to the Half-King and pressed him in the strongest terms to go; he told me that the commandant would not discharge him until the morning. I then went to the commandant, and desired him to do their business, and complained of ill treatment; for keeping them, as they were part of my company, was detaining me. This he promised not to do, but to forward my journey as much as he could. He protested he did not keep them, but was ignorant of the cause of their stay; though I soon found it out. He had promised them a present of guns, if they would wait until the morning. As I was very much pressed by the Indians to wait this day for them, I consented, on a promise that nothing should hinder them in the morning.

16th. The French were not slack in their inventions to keep the Indians this day also. But as they were obliged, according to promise, to give the present, they then endeavoured to try the power of liquor, which I doubt not would have prevailed at any other time than this; but I urged and insisted with the King so closely upon his word that he refrained, and set off with us as he had engaged.

We had a tedious and very fatiguing passage down the creek. Several times we had liked to have been staved against rocks; and many times were obliged all hands to get out and remain in the water half an hour or more, getting over the shoals. At one place, the ice had lodged and made it impassable by water; we were therefore obliged to carry our canoe across the neck of land, a quarter of a mile over. We did not reach Venango until the 22nd, where we met with our horses.

This creek is extremely crooked. I dare say the distance between the fort and Venango cannot be less than one hundred and thirty miles, to follow the meanders.

23rd. When I got things ready to set off, I sent for the Half-King to know whether he intended to go with us or by water. He told me that White Thunder had hurt himself much, and was sick and unable to walk; therefore he was obliged to carry him down in a canoe. As I found he intended to stay here a day or two, and knew that Monsieur Joncaire would employ every scheme to set him against the English, as he had before done, I told him I hoped he would guard against his flattery, and let no fine speeches influence him in their favour. He desired I might not be concerned, for he knew the French too well for anything to engage him in their favour; and that though he could not go down with us, he yet would endeavour to meet at the Fork with Joseph Campbell, to deliver a speech for me to carry to his Honour the Governor. He told me he would order the Young Hunter to attend us, and get provisions, etc., if wanted.

Our horses were now so weak and feeble, and the baggage so heavy (as we were obliged to provide all the necessaries which the journey would require), that we doubted much their performing it. Therefore, myself and others, except the drivers, who were obliged to ride, gave up our horses for packs, to assist along with the baggage. I put myself in an Indian walking dress, and continued with them three days, until I found there was no probability of their getting home in any reasonable time. The horses became less able to travel every day; the cold increased very fast; and the roads were becoming much worse by a deep snow, continually freezing; therefore, as I was uneasy to get back to make report of my proceedings to his Honour the Governor, I determined to prosecute my journey the nearest way through the woods on foot.

Accordingly, I left Mr Vanbraam in charge of our baggage, with money and directions to provide necessaries from place to place for themselves and horses, and to make the most convenient dispatch in travelling.

I took my necessary papers, pulled off my clothes, and tied myself up in a watch-coat. Then, with gun in hand and pack on my back, in which were my papers and provisions, I set out with Mr Gist, fitted in the same manner, on Wednesday, the 26th. The day following, just after we had passed a place called Murdering Town (where we intended to quit the path and steer across the country for Shannopin's Town), we fell in with a party of French Indians, who had lain in wait for us. One of them fired at Mr Gist or me, not fifteen steps off, but fortunately missed. We took this fellow into custody, and kept him till about nine o'clock at night, then let him go, and walked all the remaining part of the night without making any stop, that we might get the start so far as to be out of the reach of their pursuit the next day, since we were well assured they would follow our track as soon as it was light. The next day we continued travelling until quite dark, and got to the river about two miles above Shannopin's. We expected to have found the river frozen, but it was not, only about fifty yards from each shore. The ice, I suppose, had broken up above, for it was driving in vast quantities.

There was no way for getting over but on a raft, which we set about with but one poor hatchet, and finished just after sun-setting. This was a whole day's work; we next got it launched, then went on board of it and set off; but before we were half way over, we were jammed in the ice in such a manner that we expected every moment our raft to sink, and ourselves to perish. I put out my setting-pole to try to stop the raft, that the ice might pass by, when the rapidity of the stream threw it with so much violence against the pole that it jerked me out into ten feet of water; but I fortunately saved myself by catching hold of one of the raft logs. Notwithstanding all our efforts, we could not get to either shore, but were obliged, as we were near an island, to quit our raft and make to it.

The cold was so extremely severe that Mr Gist had all his fingers and some of his toes frozen; and the water was shut up so hard that we found no difficulty in getting off the island on the ice in the morning, and went to Mr Frazier's. We met here with twenty warriors, who were going to the southward to war; but coming to a place on the head of the Great Kenhawa, where they found seven people killed and scalped (all but one woman with very light hair), they turned about and ran back, for fear the inhabitants should rise and take them as the authors of the murder. They report that the bodies were lying about the house, and some of them much torn and eaten by the hogs. By the marks which were left, they say they were French Indians of the Ottoway nation who did it.

As we intended to take horses here, and it required some time to find them, I went up about three miles to the mouth of Youghiogany, to visit Queen Aliquippa, who had expressed great concern that we passed her in going to the fort. I made her a present of a watchcoat and a bottle of rum, which latter was thought much the better present of the two.

Tuesday, the 1st of January, we left Mr Frazier's house, and arrived at Mr Gist's, at Monongahela, the 2nd, where I bought a horse and saddle. The 6th, we met seventeen horses loaded with materials and stores for a fort at the Fork of the Ohio, and the day after, some families going out to settle. This day we arrived at Will's Creek, after as fatiguing a journey as it is possible to conceive, rendered so by excessive bad weather. From the 1st day of December to the 15th, there was but one day on which it did not rain or snow incessantly; and throughout the whole journey we met with nothing but one continued series of cold, wet weather, which occasioned very uncomfortable lodgings, especially after we had quitted our tent, which was some screen from the inclemency of it.

On the 11th I got to Belvoir, where I stopped one day to take necessary rest, and then set out and arrived in Williamsburg the 16th, when I waited upon his Honour the Governor, with the letter I had brought from the French commandant, and to give an account of the success of my proceedings. This I beg leave to do by offering the foregoing narrative, as it contains the most remarkable occurrences which happened in my journey.

I hope what has been said will be sufficient to make your Honour satisfied with my conduct, for that was my aim in undertaking the journey, and chief study throughout the prosecution of it.

Part Two

INDEPENDENCE

America 1764–1815

Introduction

With the Treaty of Paris of 1763 in their pocket, the British seemed masters of all they surveyed in America.

It was precisely mastership which proved their undoing. The British wanted to rule the colonies by remote control from London, while the Americans wanted self-government; indeed they had long before created local law-making assemblies. There was another rub between London and America; London tended to treat America as a useful supplier of raw materials and a captive market for its own manufactured goods. The colonists' trade with other countries was either taxed or simply prohibited. Until 1763 the British enforced their regulations lightly. From 1764 they did it with a heavy hand, intent on raising revenues for the defence of America itself (where the Pontiac Indians were on the warpath and the French at Quebec looking mutinous). The British themselves were almost bankrupted by the last war with France.

So it was that the British passed the Sugar Act of 1764, which put stiff duties on imported molasses. This done, the British then introduced the Stamp Act of 1765, which ordered that revenue stamps be fixed to all printed documents circulated in the American colonies. This was a cardinal mistake, for it garnered the enmity of the most vocal, literate and powerful of the colonists: newspaper publishers, lawyers, merchants and clergy.

It was from the lips of such people that first came the call of "No taxation without representation". If the colonists were not represented in the British Parliament, they could not lawfully be taxed by it. At a meeting of colonial representatives in New York in 1765 it was agreed to reply to the Stamp Act: a boycott of British goods.

To this the British yielded, and repealed the Act. However, Parliament maintained the right to tax the colonies and tried again in 1767, and once more backed down – with the exception of a tax on tea. The crisis came on 16 December 1773 when Boston patriots, half-heartedly disguised as Indians, dumped cargoes of tea into the harbour.

Thereafter the logic of conflict was inescapable. Britain was punitive. America was incensed by London's "tyranny". On 5 September, 1774, a Continental Congress of 55 delegates from 12 of the 13 colonies met in Philadelphia and requested George III to remove the "Intolerable Acts". After some saber-rattling, open fighting broke out near Boston on 19 April 1775 between colonial militiamen and British redcoats.

With the war begun, the colonists steeled themselves to break the umbilical cord. A Declaration of Independence was adopted by the Continental Congress on 4 July 1776. For a long dark while, however, independence seemed a ridiculous hope, as British forces persistently routed the Continental Army of George Washington. The winter of 1777–8, which Washington men's spent starving and shivering at Valley Forge in Pennsylvania, reduced the Continental Army to 8000 troops. Yet they endured and remained on the field, and time (plus a useful alliance with a provident France) was on the American side. A rash mistake by the Redcoat commander Lord Cornwallis cost the British the war: he allowed the Americans to hem him in on land, while a French naval squadron under de Grasse blockaded him by sea. On 17 October 1781 Cornwallis surrendered at Yorktown. As the redcoats marched out, their bands played "The World Turned Upside Down".

By the new Treaty of Paris of 1783, the British recognized American independence, and the United States' northern and western frontiers as the Lakes and the Mississippi.

Yet the States – as the former colonies had become – were United mainly by antipathy to British rule. When that went, so did their cohesion. Their jealous guarding of sovereignty made central government unworkable. Not until 1787 did the States agree a workable Constitution, one which gave Federal government exclusive power of war, commerce and diplomacy. Under the Constitution was also established the executive power of the President, and a Congress consisting of two houses, a Senate and House of Representatives.

With good government founded – and much has happened to US government in the ensuing two centuries, but little has needed to be altered – America resumed its relentless westwards expansion. Spurred on by the Northwest Ordinance of 1787, which both blue-printed political organization for new territories and sold off their lands cheap (a dollar an acre), settlers poured by the thousand into lands between the Appalachians and the Mississippi. By 1803 Ohio was a state of the Union. In the selfsame year, America assured her westwards future in the greatest real estate deal of all time. Tiring of her possession of Louisiana, Spain had sold the entire land to France – who was persuaded to part with it cheap by the guileful President Thomas Jefferson. For 800,000 square miles Jefferson paid $15 million. To put it another way: Jefferson paid 3 cents an acre for most of the West beyond the Mississippi.

The Louisiana purchase – which doubled the size of the USA – had another useful aspect. It removed the possibility of French interference in the new nation. This was necessary since the British were proving perfidiously provocative, even firing on the frigate *Chesapeake* because it was suspected of harbouring British deserters. By 1812 America and Britain were at war again in what, to all extents and purposes, was the Revolutionary War II. As John Quincy Adams noted, the United States had no alternative but war "or the abandonment of our right as an independent nation". The ensuing three years of conflict were bloody but inconclusive, and both sides slinked to the negotiating table at Ghent. Little was given, and little was asked, save for a mutual cease-fire. But the 1814 Peace of Ghent brought an era to an end. Britain at last gave up her imperial ambitions towards America. The War of 1812 was the last Anglo-American conflict.

"TO SETTLE THE WILDERNESS": DANIEL BOON IN KENTUCKY, 1769–1782

Daniel Boon

The legendary Boon (1735–1820) was the pre-eminent white explorer and settler of Kentucky (from the Iroquois *Ken-ta-ke*, "great meadow").

It was on the 1st of May, 1769, that I resigned my domestic happiness, and left my family and peaceful habitation on the Yadkin river, in North Carolina, to wander through the wilderness of America, in quest of the country of Kentucky, in company with

John Finley, John Stuart, Joseph Holden, James Monay and William Cool.

On the 7th June, after travelling in a western direction, we found ourselves on Red river, where John Finley had formerly been trading with the Indians, and from the top of an eminence, saw with pleasure the beautiful level of Kentucky. For some time we had experienced the most uncomfortable weather. We now encamped, made a shelter to defend us from the inclement season, and began to hunt and reconnoitre the country. We found abundance of wild beasts in this vast forest. The buffaloes were more numerous than cattle on their settlements, browsing on the leaves of the cane, or crossing the herbage on these extensive plains. We saw hundreds in a drove, and the numbers about the salt springs were amazing. In this forest, the habitation of beasts of every American kind, we hunted with great success until December.

On the 22nd December, John Stuart and I had a pleasant ramble; but fortune changed the day at the close of it. We passed through a great forest, in which stood myriads of trees, some gay with blossoms, others rich with fruits. Nature was here a series of wonders and a fund of delight. Here she displayed her ingenuity and industry in a variety of flowers and fruits, beautifully coloured, elegantly shaped, and charmingly flavoured, and we were favoured with numberless animals presenting themselves perpetually to our view. In the decline of the day, near Kentucky river, as we ascended the brow of a small hill, a number of Indians rushed out of a cane brake and made us prisoners. The Indians plundered us and kept us in confinement seven days. During this we discovered no uneasiness or desire to escape, which made them less suspicious; but in the dead of night, as we lay by a large fire in a thick cane brake, when sleep had locked up their senses, my situation not disposing me to rest, I gently awoke my companion. We seized this favourable opportunity and departed, directing our course toward our old camp, but found it plundered and our company destroyed and dispersed.

About this time, as my brother with another adventurer who came to explore the country shortly after us, was wandering through the forest, they accidentally found our camp. Notwithstanding our unfortunate circumstances, and our dangerous situation, surrounded with hostile savages, our meeting fortunately in the wilderness gave us the most sensible satisfaction.

Soon after this, my companion in captivity, John Stuart, was killed by the savages, and the man who came with my brother (while on a private excursion) was soon after attacked and killed by the wolves. We were now in a dangerous and helpless situation, exposed daily to perils and death, among savages and wild beasts, not a white man in the country but ourselves.

Although many hundred miles from our families in the howling wilderness, we did not continue in a state of indolence, but hunted every day, and prepared a little cottage to defend us from the winter. On the 1st of May, 1770, my brother returned home for a new recruit of horses and ammunition, leaving me alone, without bread, salt or sugar, or even a horse or a dog. I passed a few days uncomfortably – the idea of a beloved wife and family, and their anxiety on my account, would have disposed me to melancholy if I had further indulged the thought.

One day I undertook a tour through the country, when the diversity of beauties of nature I met with in this charming season expelled every gloomy thought. Just at the close of the day, the gentle gales ceased; profound calm ensued; not a breath shook the tremulous leaf. I had gained the summit of a commanding ridge, and looking around with astonishing delight beheld the ample plains and beauteous tracks below. On one hand I surveyed the famous Ohio rolling in silent dignity, and marking the western boundary of Kentucky with inconceivable grandeur. At a vast distance I beheld the mountains lift their venerable brows and penetrate the clouds. All things were still. I kindled a fire near a fountain of sweet water, and feasted on the line [*sic*] of a buck which I had killed a few hours before. The shades of night soon overspread the hemisphere, and the earth seemed to gasp after the hovering moisture. At a distance I frequently heard the hideous yells of savages. My excursion had fatigued my body and amused my mind. I laid me down to sleep, and awoke not until the sun had chased away the night. I continued this tour, and in a few days explored a considerable part of the country, each day equally pleasing as the first; after which I returned to my old camp, which had not been disturbed in my absence. I did not confine my lodging to it, but often reposed in thick cane brakes to avoid the savages, who I believe frequently visited my camp, but fortunately for me, in my absence. No populous city, with all its varieties of commerce and stately structures, could afford so much pleasure to my mind as the beauties of nature I found in this country.

Until the 27th July I spent my time in an uninterrupted scene of sylvan pleasures, when my brother, to my great felicity, met me, according to appointment, at our old camp. Soon after we left the place and proceeded to Cumberland river, reconnoitring that part of the country, and giving names to the different rivers.

In March 1771 I returned home to my family, being determined to bring them as soon as possible, at the risk of my life and fortune, to reside in Kentucky, which I esteemed a second Paradise.

On my return I found my family in happy circumstances. I sold my farm on the Yadkin and what goods we could not carry with us, and on the 25th September, 1773, we took leave of our friends and proceeded on our journey to Kentucky, in company with five more families, and forty men that joined us in Powell's Valley, which is 150 miles from the new settled parts of Kentucky; but this promising beginning was soon overcast with a cloud of adversity.

On the 10th October the rear of our company was attacked by a party of Indians, who killed six and wounded one man. Of these my oldest son was one that fell in the action. Though we repulsed the enemy, yet this unhappy affair scattered our cattle and brought us into extreme difficulty – we returned forty miles to the settlement on Clench river. We had passed over two mountains, Powel's and Walden's, and were approaching Cumberland mountain, when this adverse fortune overtook us. These mountains are in the wilderness, in passing from the old settlements in Virginia to Kentucky, are ranged in a southwest and northeast direction, are of great length and breadth, and not far distant from each other. Over them nature hath formed passes less difficult than might be expected from the view of such huge piles. The aspect of these cliffs are so wild and horrid, that it is impossible to behold them without horror.

Until the 6th June, 1774, I remained with my family on the Clench, until I and another person were solicited by Governor Dunmore of Virginia, to conduct a number of surveyors to the falls of Ohio. This was a tour of 800 miles, and took us sixty-two days.

On my return Gov. Dunmore gave me the command of three garrisons during the campaign against the Shawanese. In March 1775, at the solicitation of a number of gentlemen of North Carolina, I attended their treaty at Wataga with the Cherokee Indians, to purchase the lands on the south side of Kentucky river. After this, I undertook to mark out a road in the best passage from the settlements through the wilderness to Kentucky.

Having collected a number of enterprising men well armed, I soon began this work – we proceeded until we came within fifteen miles of where Boonsborough now stands, where the Indians attacked us, and killed two and wounded two more of our party. This was on the 22nd March, 1775 – two days after we were again attacked by them, when we had two more killed and three wounded. After this we proceeded on to Kentucky river without opposition.

On the 1st April we began to erect the fort of Boonsborough, at a salt lick, sixty yards from the river on the south side. On the 4th the Indians killed one of our men. On the 14th June, having completed the fort, I returned to my family on the Clench, and whom I soon after removed to the fort – my wife and daughter were supposed to be the first white women that ever stood upon the banks of Kentucky river.

On the 24th December an Indian killed one of our men and wounded another; and on the 15th July, 1776, they took my daughter prisoner – I immediately pursued them with eight men, and on the 16th overtook and engaged them; I killed two of them and recovered my daughter.

The Indians having divided themselves into several parties, attacked in one day all our infant settlement and forts, doing a great deal of damage – the husbandmen were ambushed and unexpectedly attacked while toiling in the fields. They continued this kind of warfare until the 15th April, 1777, when nearly 100 of them attacked the village of Boonsborough, and killed a number of its inhabitants. On the 19th Col. Logan's fort was attacked by 200 Indians – there were only thirteen men in the fort, of whom the enemy killed two and wounded one.

On the 20th August Col. Bowman arrived with 100 men from Virginia, with which additional force we had almost daily skirmishes with the Indians, who began now to learn the superiority of the long knife, as they termed the Virginians; being out-generalled in almost every action. Our affairs began now to wear a better aspect, the Indians no longer daring to face us in open field, but sought private opportunities to destroy us.

On the 7th February, 1778, while on a hunting expedition alone, I met a party of 102 Indians and two Frenchmen, marching to attack Boonsborough – they pursued and took me prisoner, and conveyed me to Old Chelicothe, the principal Indian town on little Miami, where we arrived on the 18th February, after an uncomfortable journey. On the 10th March I was conducted to Detroit, and while there was treated with great humanity by Governor Hamilton, the British commander at that port, and Intendant for Indian affairs.

The Indians had such an affection for me, that they refused £100 sterling offered them by the Governor if they would consent to leave me with him, that he might be enabled to liberate me on my parole. Several English gentlemen then at Detroit, sensible of my adverse fortune, and touched with sympathy, generously offered to supply my wants, which I declined with many thanks, adding that I never expected it would be in my power to recompense such unmerited generosity.

On the 10th April the Indians returned with me to Old Chelicothe, where we arrived on the 25th. This was a long and fatiguing march, although through an exceeding fertile country, remarkable for springs and streams of water. At Chelicothe I spent my time as comfortable as I could expect; was adopted according to their custom, into a family where I became a son, and had a great share in the affection of my new parents, brothers, sisters and friends. I was exceedingly familiar and friendly with them, always appearing as cheerful and contented as possible, and they put great confidence in me. I often went a-hunting with them, and frequently gained their applause for my activity at our shooting matches. I was careful not to exceed many of them in shooting, for no people are more envious than they in this sport. I could observe in their countenances and gestures the greatest expressions of joy when they exceeded me, and when the reverse happened, of envy. The Shawanese king took great notice of me, and treated me with profound respect and entire friendship, often entrusting me to hunt at my liberty. I frequently returned with the spoils of the woods, and as often presented some of what I had taken to him, expressive of duty to my sovereign. My food and lodging was in common with them, not so good indeed as I could desire, but necessity made every thing acceptable.

I now began to mediate an escape, and carefully avoided giving suspicion. I continued at Chelicothe until the first day of June, when I was taken to the salt springs on Sciotha, and there employed ten days in the manufacturing of salt. During this time I hunted with my Indian masters, and found the land for a great extent about this river to exceed the soil of Kentucky.

On my return to Chelicothe 150 of the choicest Indian warriors were ready to march against Boonsborough; they were painted and armed in a frightful manner. This alarmed me, and I determined to escape.

On the 16th June, before sun-rise, I went off secretly, and reached Boonsborough on the 20th, a journey of 160 miles, during which I had only one meal. I found our fortress in a bad state, but we immediately repaired our flanks, gates, posterns, and formed double bastions, which we completed in ten days. One of my fellow prisoners escaped after me, brought advice that on account of my flight, the Indians had put off their expedition for three weeks.

About 1st August, I set out with 19 men to surprise Point Creek Town on Sciotha, within four miles of which we fell in with 40 Indians, going against Boonsborough: – we attacked them and they soon gave way without any loss on our part – the enemy had one killed and two wounded – we took three horses and all their baggage.

About this time I returned to Kentucky with my family; for during my captivity my wife, thinking me killed by the Indians, had transported my family and goods on horses through the wilderness, amidst many dangers, to her father's house in North Carolina.

On the 6th of October, 1780, soon after my settling again at Boonsborough, I went with my brother to the Blue Licks, and on our return, he was shot by a party of Indians. They followed me by the scent of a dog, which I shot and escaped. The severity of the winter caused great distress in Kentucky, the enemy during the summer having destroyed most of the corn. The inhabitants lived chiefly on Buffaloe's flesh.

In spring, 1782, the Indians harassed us. In May they ravished, killed, and scalped a woman and her two daughters near Ashton's station, and took a negro prisoner. 8th August two boys were carried off from Major Hoy's station. Our affairs became more and more alarming. The savages infested the country and destroyed the woods as opportunity presented.

18th August Colonels Todd and Trigg, Major Harland and myself, speedily collected 176 men well armed, and pursued the savages. They had marched beyond the Blue Licks, to a remarkable bend of the main fork of Licking River, about 43 miles from Lexington, where we overtook them on the 19th. The savages, observing us, gave way, and we, ignorant of their numbers, passed the river. When they saw our proceedings (having accordingly the advantage in situation) they formed their line of battle from one end of the Licking to the other, about a mile from the Blue Licks. The engagement was close and warm for about fifteen minutes, when we, being overpowered by numbers, were obliged to retreat, with the loss of 67 men, 7 of whom were taken prisoners. The brave and much lamented Colonels Todd and Trigg, Major Harland, and my second son were among the dead.

When General Clark, at the falls of Ohio, heard of our disaster he ordered an expedition to pursue the savages. We overtook them within two miles of their towns, and we should have obtained a great victory had not some of them met us when about two hundred poles from their camp. The savages fled in the utmost disorder, and evacuated all their towns. We burned to ashes Old Chelicothe, Peccaway, New Chelicothe, and Wills Town; entirely destroyed their corn and other fruits; and spread desolation through their country.

In October a party attacked Crab Orchard, and one of them being a good way before the others, boldly entered a house, in which were only a woman and her children and a negro man. The savage used no violence, but attempted to carry off the negro, who happily proved too strong for him, and threw him on the ground, and in the struggle the woman cut off his head with an axe, whilst her little daughter shut the door. The savages instantly came up and applied their tomahawks to the door, when the mother putting an old rusty gun barrel through the crevices, the savages immediately went off.

From that time till the happy return of peace between the United States and Great Britain, the Indians did us no mischief. Soon after this the Indians desired peace.

Two darling sons and a brother I have lost by savage hands, which have also taken from me 40 valuable horses and abundance of cattle. Many dark and sleepless nights have I spent, separated from the cheerful society of men, scorched by the summer's sun, and pinched by the winter's cold, an instrument ordained to settle the wilderness.

A PORTRAIT OF GEORGE WASHINGTON, 1769–99

Thomas Jefferson

George Washington (1732–99), first president of the United States of America; Thomas Jefferson (1743–1826), third president of the USA. The letter below was written by Jefferson in January 1814; the addressed was Walter Jones.

You say that in taking General Washington on your shoulders, to bear him harmless through the federal coalition, you encounter a perilous topic. I do not think so. You have given the genuine history of the course of his mind through the trying scenes in which it was engaged, and of the seductions by which it was deceived, but not depraved. I think I knew General Washington intimately and thoroughly; and were I called on to delineate his character, it would be in terms like these.

His mind was great and powerful, without being of the very first order; his penetration strong, though not so acute as that of a Newton, Bacon, or Locke; and as far as he saw, no judgment was ever sounder. It was slow in operation, being little aided by invention or imagination, but sure in conclusion. Hence the common remark of his officers, of the advantage he derived from councils of war, where hearing all suggestions, he selected whatever was best; and certainly no General ever planned his battles more judiciously. But if deranged during the course of the action, if any member of his plan was dislocated by sudden circumstances, he was slow in readjustment. The consequence was, that he often failed in the field, and rarely against an enemy in station, as at Boston and York. He was incapable of fear, meeting personal dangers with the calmest unconcern. Perhaps the strongest feature in his character was prudence, never acting until every circumstance, every consideration, was maturely weighed; refraining if he saw a doubt, but, when once decided, going through with his purpose, whatever obstacles opposed. His integrity was most pure, his justice the most inflexible I have ever known, no motives of interest or consanguinity, of friendship or hatred, being able to bias his decision. He was, indeed, in every sense of the words, a wise, a good, and a great man. His temper was naturally high toned; but reflection and resolution had obtained a firm and habitual ascendency over it. If ever, however, it broke its bonds, he was most tremendous in his wrath. In his expenses he was honorable, but exact; liberal in contributions to whatever promised utility; but frowning and unyielding on all visionary projects and all unworthy calls on his charity. His heart was not warm in its affections; but he exactly calculated every man's value, and gave him a solid esteem proportioned to it. His person, you know, was fine, his stature exactly what one would wish, his deportment easy, erect and noble; the best horseman of his age, and the most graceful figure that could be seen on horseback. Although in the circle of his friends, where he might be unreserved with safety, he took a free share in conversation, his colloquial talents were not above mediocrity, possessing neither copiousness of ideas, nor fluency of words. In public, when called on for a sudden opinion, he was unready, short and embarrassed. Yet he wrote readily, rather diffusely, in an easy and correct style. This he had acquired by conversation with the world, for his education was merely reading, writing and common arithmetic, to which he added surveying at a later day. His time was employed in action chiefly, reading little, and that only in agriculture and English history. His correspondence became necessarily extensive, and, with journalizing his agricultural proceedings, occupied most of his leisure hours within doors. On the whole, his character was, in its mass, perfect, in nothing bad, in few points indifferent; and it may truly be said, that never did nature and fortune combine more perfectly to make a man great, and to place him in the same constellation with whatever worthies have merited from man an everlasting remembrance. For his was the singular destiny and merit, of leading the armies of his country successfully through an arduous war, for the establishment of its independence; of conducting its councils through the birth of a government, new in its forms and principles, until it had settled down into a quiet and orderly train; and of scrupulously obeying the laws through the whole of his career, civil and military, of which the history of the world furnishes no other example.

How, then, can it be perilous for you to take such a man on your shoulders? I am satisfied the great body of republicans think of him as I do. We were, indeed, dissatisfied with him on his ratification of the British treaty. But this was short lived. We knew his honesty, the wiles with which he was encompassed, and that age had already begun to relax the firmness of his purposes; and I am convinced he is more deeply seated in the love and gratitude of the republicans, than in the Pharisaical homage of the federal monarchists. For he was no monarchist from preference of his judgment. The soundness of that gave him correct views of the rights of man, and his severe justice devoted him to them. He has often declared to me that he considered our new constitution as an experiment on the practicability of republican government, and with what dose of liberty man could be trusted for his own good; that he was determined the experiment should have a fair trial, and would lose the last drop of his blood in support of it. And these declarations he repeated to me the oftener and more pointedly, because he knew my suspicions of Colonel Hamilton's views, and probably had heard from him the same declarations which I had, to wit, "that the British constitution, with its unequal representation, corruption and other existing abuses, was the most perfect government which had ever been established on earth, and that a reformation of those abuses would make it an impracticable government." I do believe that General Washington had not a firm confidence in the durability of our government. He was naturally distrustful of men, and inclined to gloomy apprehensions; and I was ever persuaded that a belief that we must at length end in something like a British constitution, had some weight in his adoption of the ceremonies of levees, birthdays, pompous meetings with Congress, and other forms of the same character, calculated to prepare us gradually for a change which he believed possible, and to let it come on with as little shock as might be to the public mind.

These are my opinions of General Washington, which I would vouch at the judgment seat of God, having been formed on an acquaintance of thirty years. I served with him in the Virginia legislature from 1769 to the Revolutionary War, and again, a short time in Congress, until he left us to take command of the army. During the war and after it we corresponded occasionally, and in the four years of my continuance in the office of Secretary of State, our intercourse was daily, confidential and cordial. After I retired from that office, great and malignant pains were taken by our federal monarchists, and not entirely without effect, to make him view me as a theorist, holding French principles of government, which would lead infallibly to licentiousness and anarchy. And to this he listened the more easily, from my known disapprobation of the British treaty. I never saw him afterwards, or these malignant insinuations should have been dissipated before his just judgment, as mists before the sun. I felt on his death, with my countrymen, that "verily a great man hath fallen this day in Israel."

THE BOSTON MASSACRE, 5 March 1770

Captain Thomas Preston

Preston was among the soldiers dispatched by the British Government to enforce of the Acts of Trade in Boston.

On Monday night about 8 o'clock two soldiers were attacked and beat. But the party of the townspeople in order to carry matters to the utmost length, broke into two meeting houses and rang the alarm bells, which I supposed was for fire as usual, but was soon undeceived. About 9 some of the guard came to and informed me the town inhabitants were assembling to attack the troops, and that the bells were ringing as the signal for that purpose and not for fire, and the beacon intended to be fired to bring in the distant people of the country. This, as I was captain of the day, occasioned my repairing immediately to the main guard. In my way there I saw the people in great commotion, and heard them use the most cruel and horrid threats against the troops. In a few minutes after I reached the guard, about 100 people passed it, and went towards the custom house where the King's money is lodged. They immediately surrounded the sentry posted there, and with clubs and other weapons threatened to execute their vengeance on him. I was soon informed by a townsman their intention was to carry off the soldier from his post and probably murder him: on which I desired him to return for further intelligence, and he soon came back and assured me he heard the mob declare they would murder him. This I feared might be a prelude to their plundering the King's chest. I immediately sent a non-commissioned officer and 12 men to protect both the sentry and the King's money, and very soon followed myself to prevent, if possible, all disorder, fearing lest the officer and soldiers, by the insults and provocations of the rioters, should be thrown off their guard and commit some rash act. They soon rushed through the people, and by charging their bayonets in half-circles, kept them at a little distance. Nay, so far was I from intending the death of any person that I suffered the troops to go to the spot where the unhappy affair took place without any loading in their pieces; nor did I ever give orders for loading them. This remiss conduct in me perhaps merits censure; yet it is evidence, resulting from the nature of things, which is the best and surest that can be offered, that my intention was not to act offensively, but the contrary part, and that not without compulsion. The mob still increased and were more outrageous, striking their clubs or bludgeons one against another, and calling out, "Come on you rascals, you bloody backs, you lobster scoundrels, fire if you dare, G – d damn you, fire and be damned, we know you dare not," and much more such language was used. At this time I was between the soldiers and the mob, parleying with, and endeavouring all in my power to persuade them to retire peaceably, but to no purpose. They advanced to the points of the bayonets, struck some of them and even the muzzles of the pieces, and seemed to be endeavouring to close with the soldiers. On which some well behaved persons asked me if the guns were charged. I replied yes. They then asked me if I intended to order the men to fire. I answered no, by no means, observing to them that I was advanced before the muzzles of the men's pieces, and must fall a sacrifice if they fired; that the soldiers were upon the half cock and charged bayonets, and my giving the word fire under those circumstances would prove me to be no officer. While I was thus speaking, one of the soldiers having received a severe blow with a stick, stepped a little on one side and instantly fired, on which turning to and asking him why he fired without orders, I was struck with a club on my arm, which for some time deprived me of the use of it, which blow had it been placed on my head most probably would have destroyed me. On this a general attack was made on the men by a great number of heavy clubs and snowballs being thrown at them, by which all our lives were in imminent danger, some persons at the same time from behind calling out, "damn your bloods – why don't you fire." Instantly three or four of the soldiers fired, one after another, and directly after three more in the same confusion and hurry. The mob then ran away, except three unhappy men who instantly expired, . . . one more is since dead, three others are dangerously, and four slightly wounded. The whole of this melancholy affair was transacted in almost 20 minutes. On my asking the soldiers why they fired without orders, they said they heard the word fire and supposed it came from me. This might be the case as many of the mob called out fire, fire, but I assured the men that I gave no such order; that my words were, don't fire, stop your firing. In short, it was scarcely possible for the soldiers to know who said fire, or don't fire, or stop your firing. On the people's assembling again to take away the dead bodies, the soldiers supposing them coming to attack them, were making ready to fire again, which I prevented by striking up their firelocks with my hand. Immediately after a townsman came and told me that 4 or 5000 people were assembled in the next street, and had sworn to take my life with every man's with me. On which I judged it unsafe to remain there any longer, and therefore sent the party and sentry to the main guard, where the street is narrow and short, there telling them off into street firings, divided and planted them at each end of the street to secure their rear, momently expecting an attack, as there was a constant cry of the inhabitants "to arms, to arms, turn out with your guns;" and the town drums beating to arms, I ordered my drums to beat to arms, and being soon after joined by the different companies of the 29th regiment, I formed them as the guard into street firings. The 14th regiment also got under arms but remained at their barracks. I immediately sent a sergeant with a party to Colonel Dalrymple, the commanding officer, to acquaint him with every particular. Several officers going to join their regiment were knocked down by the mob, one very much wounded and his sword taken from him. The Lieutenant-Governor and Colonel Carr soon after met at the head of the 29th regiment and agreed that the regiment should retire to their barracks, and the people to their houses, but I kept the picket to strengthen the guard. It was with great difficulty that the Lieutenant-Governor prevailed on the people to be quiet and retire. At last they all went off, excepting about a hundred. . . .

SOME SCOTTISH IMMIGRANTS TO THE AMERICAN COLONIES, 1772

Report of British Customs

Reasons for emigrating to America:

John McBeath, aged 37, by trade a farmer and shoemaker, married; hath 5 children from 13 years to 9 months old. Resided last in Mault in the parish of Kildorman in the county of Sutherland, upon the estate of Sutherland. Intends to go to Wilmington in North Carolina; left his own country because crops failed, he lost his cattle, the rent of his possession was raised, and bread had been long dear; he could get no employment at home whereby he could support himself and family, being unable to buy bread at the prices the factors on the estate of Sutherland and neighbouring estates exacted from him. That he was encouraged to emigrate by the accounts received from his own and his wife's friends already in America, assuring him that he would procure comfortable subsistence in that country for his wife and children, and that the price of labour was very high. He also assigns for the cause of bread being dear in his country that it is owing to the great quantities of corn consumed in brewing risquebah [scotch].

Elizabeth McDonald, aged 29, unmarried, servant to James Duncan in Mointle in the parish of Farr in the county of Sutherland; intends to go to Wilmington in North Carolina, left her own country because several of her friends having gone to Carolina before her, had assured her that she would get much better service and greater encouragement in Carolina than in her own country.

"BOSTON TEA PARTY", 16 December 1773

John Andrews

In which colonial patriots, disguised as American Indians, boarded British merchantmen in Boston Harbor and dumped into the sea their cargoes of tea in protest at the duty laid by the British upon its importation.

18th December 1773.
However precarious our situation may be, yet such is the present calm composure of the people that a stranger would hardly think that ten thousand pounds sterling of the East India Company's tea was destroyed the night, or rather evening, before last, yet it's a serious truth; and if yours, together with the other Southern provinces, should rest satisfied with their quota being stored, poor Boston will feel the whole weight of ministerial vengeance. However, it's the opinion of most people that we stand an equal chance now, whether troops are sent in consequence of it or not; whereas, had it been stored, we should inevitably have had them, to enforce the sale of it.

The affair was transacted with the greatest regularity and despatch. . . . A general muster was assembled, from this and all the neighbouring towns, to the number of five or six thousand, at 10 o'clock Thursday morning in the Old South Meeting House, where they passed a unanimous vote that the Tea should go out of the harbour that afternoon, and sent a committee with Mr Rotch* to the Customhouse to demand a clearance, which the Collector told them it was not in his power to give, without the duties being first paid. They then sent Mr Rotch to Milton, to ask a pass from the Governor, who sent for answer, that "consistent with the rules of government and his duty to the King he could not grant one without they produced a previous clearance from the office". By the time he returned with this message the candles were light in the house, and upon reading it, such prodigious shouts were made, that induced me, while drinking tea at home, to go out and know the cause of it. The house was so crowded I could get no

* Owner of one of the tea ships.

farther than the porch, when I found the moderator was just declaring the meeting to be dissolved, which caused another general shout, outdoors and in, and three cheers. What with that, and the consequent noise of breaking up the meeting, you'd thought that the inhabitants of the infernal regions had broke loose.

For my part, I went contentedly home and finished my tea, but was soon informed what was going forward; but still not crediting it without ocular demonstration, I went and was satisfied. They mustered, I'm told, upon Fort Hill to the number of about two hundred, and proceeded, two by two, to Griffin's wharf, where *Hall, Bruce*, and *Coffin* lay, each with 114 chests of the ill-fated article on board; the two former with only that article, but the latter, arrived at the wharf only the day before, was freighted with a large quantity of other goods, which they took the greatest care not to injure in the least, and before nine o'clock in the evening every chest from on board the three vessels was knocked to pieces and flung over the sides.

They say the actors were Indians from Narragansett. Whether they were or not, to a transient observer they appeared as such, being clothed in blankets with the heads muffled, and copper-coloured countenances, being each armed with a hatchet or axe, and pair pistols, nor was their dialect different from what I conceive these geniuses to speak, as their jargon was unintelligible to all but themselves. Not the least insult was offered to any person, save one Captain Connor, a letter of horses in this place, not many years since removed from dear Ireland, who had ripped up the lining of his coat and waistcoat under the arms, and watching his opportunity had nearly filled them with tea, but being detected, was handled pretty roughly. They not only stripped him of his clothes, but gave him a coat of mud, with a severe bruising into the bargain; and nothing but their utter aversion to make any disturbance prevented his being tarred and feathered.

Should not have troubled you with this, by this post, hadn't I thought you would be glad of a more particular account of so important a transaction than you could have obtained by common report; and if it affords my brother but a temporary amusement, I shall be more than repaid for the trouble of writing it.

THE REVOLUTIONARY WAR: SKIRMISH AT LEXINGTON, 19 April 1775

Lieutenant-Colonel F. Smith, 10th Foot

The opening shots of the Revolutionary War (the War of Independence). On the orders of General Gage, British troops set out in great secrecy from Boston on 18 April to destroy the military stores of the Massachusets militia at Concord, but the plot was uncovered and Paul Revere made his famous night-ride to raise the alarm. The advance British detachment was intercepted by the colonialists at Lexington.

Lieut.-Col. Smith to Governor Gage

Boston, 22 April, 1775.

Sir,

In obedience to your Excellency's commands, I marched on the evening of the 18th inst. with the corps of grenadiers and light infantry for Concord, to execute your Excellency's orders with respect to destroying all ammunition, artillery, tents, &c., collected there, which was effected, having knocked off the trunnions of three pieces of iron ordnance, some new gun carriages, a great number of carriage wheels burnt, a considerable quantity of flour, some gunpowder and musket balls, with other small articles thrown into the river. Notwithstanding we marched with the utmost expedition and secrecy, we found the country had intelligence or strong suspicion of our coming, and fired many signal guns, and rung the alarm bells repeatedly; and were informed, when at Concord, that some cannon had been taken out of the town that day, that others, with some stores, had been carried three days before. . . .

I think it proper to observe, that when I had got some miles on the march from Boston, I detached six light infantry companies to march with all expedition to seize the two bridges on different roads beyond Concord. On these companies' arrival at Lexington, I understand, from the report of Major Pitcairn, who was with them, and from many officers, that they found on a green close to the road a body of the country people drawn up in military order, with arms and accoutrements, and, as appeared after, loaded; and that they had posted some men in a dwelling and Meeting-house. Our troops advanced towards them, without any intention of injuring them, further than to inquire the reason of their being thus assembled, and, if not satisfactory, to have secured their arms; but they in confusion went off, principally to the left, only one of them fired before he went off, and three or four more jumped over a wall and fired from behind it among the soldiers; on which the troops returned it, and killed several of them. They likewise fired on the soldiers from the Meeting and dwelling-house. We had one man wounded, and Major Pitcairn's horse shot in two places. Rather earlier than this, on the road, a country man from behind a wall had snapped his piece at Lieutenants Adair and Sutherland, but it flashed and did not go off. After this we saw some in the woods, but marched on to Concord without anything further happening. While at Concord we saw vast numbers assembling in many parts; at one of the bridges they marched down, with a very considerable body, on the light infantry posted there. On their coming pretty near, one of our men fired on them, which they returned; on which an action ensued, and some few were killed and wounded. In this affair, it appears that after the bridge was quitted, they scalped and other-wise ill-treated one or two of the men who were either killed or severely wounded, being seen by a party that marched by soon after. At Concord we found very few inhabitants in the town; those we met with both Major Pitcairn and myself took all possible pains to convince that we meant them no injury, and that if they opened their doors when required to search for military stores, not the slightest mischief would be done. We had opportunities of convin-cing them of our good intentions, but they were sulky; and one of them even struck Major Pitcairn. On our leaving Concord to return to Boston, they began to fire on us from behind the walls, ditches, trees, etc., which, as we marched, increased to a very great degree, and continued without the intermission of five minutes altogether, for, I believe, upwards of eighteen miles; so that I can't think but it must have been a preconcerted scheme in them, to attack the King's troops the first favourable opportunity that offered, otherwise, I think they could not, in so short a time as from our marching out, have raised such a numerous body, and for so great a space of ground. Notwithstanding the enemy's numbers, they did not make one gallant effort during so long an action, though our men were so very much fatigued, but kept under cover.

I have the honour, etc.
F. Smith, Lt-Col. 10th Foot.

THE REVOLUTIONARY WAR: IN ACTION AGAINST THE BRITISH AT BUNKER HILL, 16–17 June 1775

Israel R. Potter

By the break of day Monday morning I swung my knapsack, shouldered my musket, and with the company commenced my march with a quick step for Charleston, where we arrived about sunset and remained encamped in the vicinity until about noon on the 16th June; when, having been previously joined by the remainder of the regiment from Rhode Island, to which our company was attached, we received orders to proceed and join a detachment of about 1000 American troops, which had that morning taken possession of Bunker Hill and which we had orders immediately to fortify, in the best manner that circumstances would admit of. We laboured all night without cessation and with very little refreshment, and by the dawn of day succeeded in throwing up a redoubt of eight or nine rods square. As soon as our works were discovered by the British in the morning, they commenced a heavy fire upon us, which was supported by a fort on Copp's hill; we however (under the command of the intrepid Putnam) continued to labour like beavers until our breast-work was completed.

About noon, a number of the enemy's boats and barges, filled with troops, landed at Charlestown, and commenced a deliberate march to attack us – we were now harangued by Gen. Putnam, who reminded us, that exhausted as we were, by our incessant labour through the preceding night, the most important part of our duty was yet to be performed, and that much would be expected from so great a number of excellent marksmen – he charged us to be cool, and to reserve our fire until the enemy approached so near as to enable us to see the white of their eyes – when within about ten rods of our works we gave them the contents of our muskets, and which were aimed with so good effect, as soon to cause them to turn their backs and to retreat with a much quicker step than with what they approached us. We were now again harangued by "old General Put," as he was termed, and requested by him to aim at the officers, should the enemy renew the attack – which they did in a few moments, with a reinforcement – their approach was with a slow step, which gave us an excellent opportunity to obey the commands of our General in bringing down their officers. I feel but little disposed to boast of my own performances on this occasion and will only say, that after devoting so many months in hunting the wild animals of the wilderness, while an inhabitant of New Hampshire, the reader will not suppose me a bad or inexperienced marksman, and that such were the fare shots which the epauletted red coats presented in the two attacks, that every shot which they received from me, I am confident on another occasion would have produced me a deer skin.

So warm was the reception that the enemy met with in their second attack, that they again found it necessary to retreat, but soon after receiving a fresh reinforcement, a third assault was made, in which, in consequence of our ammunition failing, they too well succeeded – a close and bloody engagement now ensued – to fight our way through a very considerable body of the enemy, with clubbed muskets (for there were not one in twenty of us provided with bayonets) were now the only means left us to escape the conflict, which was a sharp and severe one, is still fresh in my memory, and cannot be forgotten by me while the scars of the wounds which I then received, remain to remind me of it! Fortunately for me, at this critical moment, I was armed with a cutlass, which although without an edge, and much rust-eaten, I found of infinite more service to me than my musket – in one instance I am certain it was the means of saving my life – a blow with a cutlass was aimed at my head by a British officer, which I parried and received only a slight cut with the point on my right arm near the elbow, which I was then unconscious of, but this slight wound cost my antagonist at the moment a much more serious one, which effectually *dis-armed* him, for with one well-directed stroke I deprived him of the power of very soon again measuring swords with a "yankee rebel!" We finally however should have been mostly cut off, and compelled to yield to a superior and better equipped force, had not a body of three or four hundred Connecticut men formed a temporary breast work, with rails &c. and by which means held the enemy at bay until our main body had time to ascend the heights, and retreat across the neck; – in this retreat I was less fortunate than many of my comrades – I received two musket ball wounds, one in my hip and the other near the ankle of my left leg. I succeeded however without any assistance in reaching Prospect Hill, where the main body of the Americans had made a stand and commenced fortifying – from thence I was soon after conveyed to the Hospital in Cambridge, where my wounds were dressed and the bullet extracted from my hip by one of the Surgeons; the house was nearly filled with the poor fellows who like myself had received wounds in the late engagement, and presented a melancholy spectacle.

Bunker Hill fight proved a sore thing for the British, and will I doubt not be long remembered by them; while in London I heard it frequently spoken of by many who had taken an active part therein, some of whom were pensioners, and bore indelible proofs of American bravery – by them the Yankees, by whom they were opposed, were not infrequently represented as a set of infuriated beings, whom nothing could daunt or intimidate: and who, after their ammunition failed, disputed the ground, inch by inch, for a full hour with clubbed muskets, rusty swords, pitchforks and billets of wood, against the British bayonets.

THE WRITING OF THE DECLARATION OF INDEPENDENCE, June–July 1776

John Adams

In the summer of 1776 Thomas Jefferson was selected by a committee of the Continental Congress to draft a declaration of independence from Britain. This was revised by the committee – which numbered Jefferson himself, John Adams, Benjamin Franklin, Robert R. Livingston and Roger Sherman – before submission to the Continental Congress on 28 June. On 2nd July the Congress voted for independence. The Declaration of Independence was released to the American public on 4th July. Below Adams, writing to a correspondent in 1822, recalls the writing of the Declaration.

You inquire why so young a man as Mr Jefferson was placed at the head of the committee for preparing a Declaration of Independence? I answer: It was the Frankfort advice, to place Virginia at the head of everything. Mr Richard Henry Lee might be gone to Virginia, to his sick family, for aught I know, but that was not the reason of Mr Jefferson's appointment. There were three committees appointed at the same time, one for the Declaration of Independence, another for preparing articles of confederation, and another for preparing a treaty to be proposed to France. Mr Lee was chosen for the Committee of Confederation, and it was not thought convenient that the same person should be upon both. Mr Jefferson came into Congress in June, 1775, and brought with him a reputation for literature, science, and a happy talent of composition. Writings of his were handed about, remarkable for the peculiar felicity of expression. Though a silent member in Congress, he was so prompt, frank, explicit, and decisive upon committees and in conversation – not even Samuel Adams was more so – that he soon seized upon my heart; and upon this occasion I gave him my vote, and did all in my power to procure the votes of others. I think he had one more vote than any other, and that placed him at the head of the committee. I had the next highest number, and that placed me the second. The committee met, discussed the subject, and then appointed Mr Jefferson and me to make the draft, I suppose because we were the two first on the list.

The subcommittee met. Jefferson proposed to me to make the draft. I said, "I will not," "You should do it." "Oh! no." "Why will you not? You ought to do it." "I will not." "Why?" "Reasons enough." "What can be your reasons?" "Reason first, you are a Virginian, and a Virginian ought to appear at the head of this business. Reason second, I am obnoxious, suspected, and unpopular. You are very much otherwise. Reason third, you can write ten times better than I can." "Well," said Jefferson, "if you are decided, I will do as well as I can." "Very well. When you have drawn it up, we will have a meeting."

A meeting we accordingly had, and conned the paper over. I was delighted with its high tone and the flights of oratory with which it abounded, especially that concerning Negro slavery, which, though I knew his Southern brethren would never suffer to pass in Congress, I certainly never would oppose. There were other expressions which I would not have inserted if I had drawn it up, particularly that which called the King tyrant. I thought this too personal, for I never believed George to be a tyrant in disposition and in nature; I always believed him to be deceived by his courtiers on both sides of the Atlantic, and in his official capacity, only, cruel. I thought the expression too passionate, and too much like scolding, for so grave and solemn a document; but as Franklin and Sherman were to inspect it afterwards, I thought it would not become me to strike it out. I consented to report it, and do not now remember that I made or suggested a single alteration.

We reported it to the committee of five. It was read, and I do not remember that Franklin or Sherman criticized anything. We were all in haste. Congress was impatient, and the instrument was reported, as I believe, in Jefferson's handwriting, as he first drew it. Congress cut off about a quarter of it, as I expected they would; but they obliterated some of the best of it, and left all that was exceptionable, if anything in it was. I have long wondered that the original draft had not been published. I suppose the reason is the vehement philippic against Negro slavery.

As you justly observe, there is not an idea in it but what had been hackneyed in Congress for two years before. The substance of it is contained in the declaration of rights and the violation of those rights in the Journals of Congress in 1774. Indeed, the essence of it is contained in a pamphlet, voted and printed by the town of Boston, before the first Congress met, composed by James Otis, as I suppose, in one of his lucid intervals, and pruned and polished by Samuel Adams.

VALLEY FORGE, 14–29 December 1777

Albigence Waldo

Valley Forge, in eastern Pennsylvania, was the winter camp of the army of the Continental Congress during 1777–8. As Waldo, a surgeon with the Connecticut Infantry Regiment, records in his journal, the privations suffered by the colonial army were immense. Even so, Washington's force re-emerged in the new year as a more effective military force.

Journal: December 14, 1777 – Prisoners & Deserters are continually coming in. The Army which has been surprisingly healthy hitherto, now begins to grow sickly from the continued fatigues they have suffered this Campaign. Yet they still show a spirit of Alacrity and Contentment not to be expected from so young Troops. I am Sick-discontented and out of humor. Poor food hard lodging – cold weather – fatigue – Nasty Cloaths – Nasty Cookery – Vomit half my time – smoak'd out of my senses – the Devil's in't – I can't Endure it – Why are we sent here to starve and freeze – What sweet Felicities have I left at home; A charming Wife – pretty Children – Good Beds – good food – good Cookery – all agreeable – all harmonious. Here all Confusion – smoke and Cold – hunger and filthyness – A pox on my bad luck. There comes a bowl of beef soup – full of burnt leaves and dirt, sickish enough to make a Hector spue – away with it boys – I'll live like the Chameleon upon air.

Poh! Poh! crys Patience within me – you talk like a fool. Your being sick Covers your mind with a Melanchollie Gloom, which makes everything about you appear gloomy. See the poor soldier, when in health – with what cheerfulness he meets his foes and encounters every hardship – if barefoot he labors thro' the Mud & every hardship – if barefoot he labors thro' the Mud & Cold with a song in his mouth extolling War & Washington – if his food be bad, he eats it notwithstanding with seeming content – blesses God for a good stomach and Whistles it into digestion. But harkee Patience, a moment – There comes a Soldier, his bare feet are seen thro' his worn out Shoes, his legs nearly naked from the tatter'd remains of an only pair of stockings, his Breeches not sufficient to cover his nakedness, his Shirt hanging in Strings, his hair disheveled, his face meager; his whole appearance pictures a person forsaken and discouraged. He comes, and crys with an air of wretchedness and despair, I am Sick, my feet lame, my legs are sore, my body cover'd with this tormenting Itch – my Cloaths are worn out, my Constitution is broken, my formed Activity is exhausted by fatigue, hunger and Cold, I fail fast. I shall soon be no more! and all the reward I shall get will be – "Poor Will is dead." People who live at home in Luxury and Ease, quietly possessing their habitation. Enjoying their Wives and Families in peace, have but a very faint idea of the unpleasing sensations, and continual Anxiety the man endures who is in a Camp, and is the husband and parent of an agreeable family. These same People are willing we should suffer everything for their Benefit and advantage, and yet are the first to Condemn us for not doing more!!

December 15 – Quit. Eat Pessimmens [persimmons], found myself better for their Lenient Operation. Went to a house, poor & small, but good food within – eat too much from being so long Abstemious, thro' want of palatables. Mankind are never truly thankfull for the Benefits of life, until they have experienced the want of them. The Man who has seen misery knows best how to enjoy good. He who is always at ease & has enough of the Blessings of common life is an Impotent Judge of the feelings of the unfortunate . . .

December 16 – Cold Rainy Day, Baggage ordered over the Gulph of our Division, which were to march at Ten, but the baggage was order'd back and for the first time since we have been here the Tents were pitch'd, to keep the men more comfortable. Good morning Brother Soldier (says one to another) how are you? All wet I thank'e, hope you are so (says the other). The Enemy have been at Chestnut Hill Opposite to us near our last encampment the other side of Schuylkill, made some Ravages, kill'd two of our Horsemen, taken some prisoners. We have done the like by them. . . .

December 18 – Universal Thanksgiving – a roasted Pig at Night. God be thanked for my health which I have pretty well recovered. How much better should I feel, were I assured my family were in health. But the same good Being who graciously preserves me, is able to preserve them & bring me to the ardently wish'd for enjoyment of them again.

Our brethren who are unfortunately Prisoners in Philadelphia meet with the most savage and inhumane treatments that Barbarians are capable of inflicting. Our Enemies do not knock them in the head or burn them with torches to death, or flay them alive, or gradually dismember them till they die, which is customary among Savages and Barbarians. No, they are worse by far. They suffer them to starve, to linger out their lives in extreem hunger. One of these poor unhappy men, drove to the last extreem by the rage of hunger, eat his own fingers up to the first joint from the hand, before he died. Others eat the Clay, the Lime, the Stones of the Prison Walls. Several who died in the Yard had pieces of Bark, Wood, Clay and Stones in their mouths, which the ravings of hunger had caused them to take in for food the last Agonies of Life! "These are thy mercies, O Britain!"

December 21 – [Valley Forge] Preparations made for huts. Provisions Scarce. Mr Ellis went homeward – sent a Letter to my Wife. Heartily wish myself at home, my Skin & eyes are almost spoil'd with continual smoke. A general cry thro' the Camp this Evening among the Soldiers, "No Meat! No Meat!" – the Distant vales Echoed back the melancholy sound – "No Meat! No Meat!" Imitating the noise of Crows and Owls, also, made a part of the confused Musick. What have you for your Dinner Boys? "Nothing but Fire Cake and Water, Sir." At night, "Gentlemen the Supper is ready." What is your Supper Lads? "Fire Cake and Water, Sir." Very poor beef has been drawn in our Camp the greater part of this season. A Butcher bringing a Quarter of this kind of Beef into Camp one day who had white Buttons on the knees of his breeches, a soldier cries out – "There, there Tom is some sort of your fat Beef, by my soul I can see the Butcher's breeches buttons through it."

December 22 – Lay excessive Cold and uncomfortable last Night –

my eyes are started out from their Orbits like a Rabbit's eyes, occasion'd by a great Cold and Smoke. "What have you got for Breakfast, Lads? Fire Cake and Water, Sir." The Lord send our Commissary of Purchases may live [on] Fire Cake and water, 'till their glutted Gutts are turned to Pasteboard.

Our Division are under Marching Orders this morning. I am ashamed to say it, but I am tempted to steal Fowls if I could find them, or even a whole Hog, for I feel as if I could eat one, But the Impoverish'd Country about us, affords but little matter to employ a Thief, or keep a Clever Fellow in good humor. But why do I talk of hunger & hard usage, when so many in the World have not even Fire Cake & Water to eat.

The human mind is always poreing upon the gloomy side of Fortune, and while it inhabits this lump of Clay, will always be in any uneasy and fluctuating State produced by a thousand Incidents in common Life, which are deemed misfortunes, while the mind is taken off from the nobler pursuit of matters in Futurity. The sufferings of the Mind, and this Attention is more or less strong, in greater or lesser souls, althou' I believe that Ambition & a high Opinion of Fame, makes many People endure hardships and pains with that fortitude we after times Observe them to do. On the other hand, a despicable opinion of the enjoyments of this Life, by a continued series of Misfortunes, and a long acquaintance with Grief, induces others to bear afflictions with becoming serenity and Calmness.

It is not in the power of Philosophy however, to convince a man he may be happy and Contented if he will, with a Hungry Belly. Give me Food, Cloaths, Wife & Children, kind Heaven! and I'll be as contented as my Nature will permit me to be.

This Evening a Party with two field pieces were order'd out. At 12 of the Clock at Night, Providence sent us a little mutton, with which we immediately had some Broth made, and a fine Stomach for same. Ye who Eat Pumpkin Pie and Roast Turkies, and yet Curse fortune for using you ill, Curse her no more, least she reduce your Allowance of her favors to a bit of Fire Cake, & a draught of Cold Water, & in Cold Weather too.

December 25 – Christmas – We are still in Tents – when we ought to be in huts – the poor sick, suffer much in Tents this cold weather. But now we treat them differently from what they used to be at home, under the inspection of Old Women and Doct. Bolus Linctus [Pill and Syrup]. We give them Mutton and Grogg

and a Capital Medicine once in a while, to start the Disease from
its foundation at once. We avoid Piddling Pills, Powders, Bolus's
Linctus Cordials and all such insignificant matters whose powers
are Only render'd important by causing the Patient to vomit up
his money instead of his disease. But very few of the sick Men die.

December 26 – The Enemy have been some Days the west
Schuykill from Opposite the City to Derby. Their intentions
not yet known. The City is at present pretty Clear of them.
Why don't his Excellency [George Washington] rush in and retake
the City, in which he will doubtless find much Plunder? Because he
knows better than to leave his Post and be catch'd like a d—d fool
cooped up in the City. He has always acted wisely hitherto. His
conduct when closely scrutinised is uncensurable. Were his Inferior
Generals as skillful as himself, we should have the Grandest Choir
of Officers ever God made. Many Country Gentlemen in the
interior parts of the States who get wrong information of the
Affairs and State of our Camp, are very much Surprised at G
Washington's delay to drive off the Enemy, being falsely inform'd
that his Army, consists of double the Number of the Enemyies such
wrong information serves not to keep up the spirit of the People, as
they must be by and by undeceiv'd to their no small disappointment – it brings blame on his Excellency, who is deserving of the
greatest encomiums; it brings disgrace on the Continental Troops,
who have never evidenced the least backwardness in doing their
duty, but on the contrary, have cheerfully endur'd a long and very
fatiguing Campaign.

December 28 – Yesterday upwards of fifty officers in Gen Greene's
Division resigned their Commissions – Six or Seven of our Regiment are doing the hike to-day. All this is occasion'd by Officers
Families being so much neglected at home on account of Provisions. Their Wages will not buy considerable, purchase a few
trifling Comfortables here in camp, and maintain their families at
home, while such extravagant prices are demanded for the common necessaries of Life – What then have they to purchase Cloaths
and other necessaries with? It is a Melancholy reflection that what
is of the most universal importance, is most universally neglected –
I mean keeping up the Credit or Money. The present Circumstances of the Soldier is better by far than the Officers – for the
family of the Soldier is provided for at the public expense if the
Articles they want are above the common price – but the Officer's
family, are obliged not only to beg in the most humble manner for

the necessaries of Life – but also to pay for them afterwards at the most exorbitant rates – and even in this manner, many of them who depend entirely on their Money, cannot procure half the material comforts that are wanted in a family – this produces continual letters of complaint from home.

When the Officer has been fatiguing thro wet and cold and returns to his tent where he finds a letter directed to him from his Wife, fill'd with the most heart aching tender Complaints, a Woman is capable of writing . . . What man is there – who has the least regard for his family – whose soul would not shrink within him? Who would not be disheartened?

December 29 – Snow'd all day pretty briskly . . . So much talk about discharges among the officers – and so many are discharged – his Excellency lately expressed his fears of being left Alone with the Soldiers only. Strange that our Country will not exert themselves for his support, and save so good – so great a Man from entertaining the least anxious doubt of their Virtue and perseverance in supporting a Cause of such unparallel'd importance!

CAPTURED BY OTTAWA INDIANS, c. 1795

John Tanner

Tanner was a white boy seized by Ottawa Indians. The lure of Native life proved strong, and Tanner later chose, of his own volition, to live with the tribes of the Northwest territory. When, after thirty years, he emerged from the woods he was more Indian than white and was treated as a pariah. Eventually, he disappeared back into the wilderness.

It was early in the spring when we arrived at the mouth of the Big Miami, and we were soon engaged in preparing a field to plant corn. I think it was not more than ten days after our arrival, when my father told us in the morning, that from the actions of the horses, he perceived there were Indians lurking about in the woods, and he said to me, "John, you must not go out of the house today." After giving strict charge to my stepmother to let none of the little children go out, he went to the field with the Negroes, and my elder brother, to drop corn.

Three little children, beside myself, were left in the house with my stepmother. To prevent me from going out, my stepmother required me to take care of the little child, then not more than a few months old; but as I soon became impatient of confinement, I began to pinch my little brother, to make him cry. My mother perceiving his uneasiness, told me to take him in my arms and walk about the house; I did so, but continued to pinch him. My mother at length took him from me to give him suck. I watched my opportunity, and escaped into the yard; thence through a small door in the large gate of the wall into the open field. There was a walnut tree at some distance from the house, and near the side of the field, where I had been in the habit of finding some of the last year's nuts. To gain this tree without being seen by my father, and those in the field, I had to use some precaution. I remember perfectly well having seen my father, as I skulked toward the tree; he stood in the middle of the field, with his gun in his hand, to watch for Indians, while the others were dropping corn. As I came near the tree, I thought to myself, "I wish I could see these Indians." I had partly filled with nuts a straw hat which I wore, when I heard a crackling noise behind me; I looked round, and saw the Indians; almost at the same instant, I was seized by both hands, and dragged off betwixt two. One of them took my straw hat, emptied the nuts on the ground, and put it on my head. The Indians who seized me were an old man and a young one; these were, as I learned subsequently, Manito-o-geezhik, and his son Kish-kau-ko. Since I returned from Red River, I have been at Detroit while Kish-kau-ko was in prison there; I have also been in Kentucky, and have learned several particulars relative to my capture, which were unknown to me at the time. It appears that the wife of Manito-o-geezhik had recently lost by death her youngest son – that she had complained to her husband, that unless he should bring back her son, she could not live. This was an intimation to bring her a captive whom she might adopt in the place of the son she had lost. Manito-o-geezhik, associating with him his son, and two other men of his band, living at Lake Huron, had proceeded eastward with this sole design. On the upper part of Lake Erie, they had been joined by three other young men, the relations of Manito-o-geezhik, and had proceeded on, now seven in number, to the settlements on the Ohio. They had arrived the night previous to my capture at the mouth of the Big Miami, had crossed the Ohio, and concealed themselves within sight of my father's house. Several times in the course of the morning, old Manito-o-geezhik had been compelled to repress the ardor of his young men, who becoming impatient at seeing no opportunity to steal a boy, were anxious to fire upon the people dropping corn in the field. It must have been about noon when they saw me coming from the house to the walnut tree, which was probably very near the place where one or more of them were concealed.

It was but a few minutes after I left the house, when my father, coming from the field, perceived my absence. My stepmother had not yet noticed that I had gone out. My elder brother ran immediately to the walnut tree, which he knew I was fond of visiting, and seeing the nuts which the Indian had emptied out of my hat, he immediately understood that I had been made captive. Search was instantly made for me, but to no purpose. My father's distress, when he found I was indeed taken away by the Indians, was, I am told, very great.

After I saw myself firmly seized by both wrists by the two Indians, I was not conscious of anything that passed for a considerable time. I must have fainted, as I did not cry out, and I can remember nothing that happened to me, until they threw me over a large log, which must have been at a considerable distance from the house. The old man I did not now see; I was dragged along between Kish-kau-ko and a very short thick man. I had probably made some resistance, or done something to irritate this last, for he took me a little to one side, and drawing his tomahawk, motioned to me to look up. This I plainly understood, from the expression of his face, and his manner, to be a direction for me to look up for the last time, as he was about to kill me. I did as he directed, but Kish-kau-ko caught his hand as the tomahawk was descending and prevented him from burying it in my brains. Loud talking ensued between the two, Kish-kau-ko presently raised a yell; the old man and the four others answered it by a similar yell; and came running up. I have since understood that Kish-kau-ko complained to his father, that the short man had made an attempt to kill his little brother, as he called me. The old chief, after reproving him, took me by one hand, and Kish-kau-ko by the other, and dragged me betwixt them; the man who had threatened to kill me, and who was now an object of terror, being kept at some distance. I could perceive, as I retarded them somewhat in their retreat, that they were apprehensive of being overtaken; some of them were always at some distance from us.

It was about one mile from my father's house to the place where they threw me into a hickory bark canoe, which was concealed under the bushes, on the bank of the river. Into this they all seven jumped, and immediately crossed the Ohio, landing at the mouth of the Big Miami, and on the south side of that river. Here they abandoned their canoe, and stuck their paddles in the ground, so that they could be seen from the river. At a little distance in the woods, they had some blankets and provisions concealed; they offered me some dry venison and bear's grease, but I could not eat. My father's house was plainly to be seen from the place where we stood; they pointed at it, looked at me, and laughed, but I have never known what they said.

After they had eaten a little, they began to ascend the Miami, dragging me along as before. The shoes I had on when at home, they took off, as they seemed to think I could run better without them. Although I perceived I was closely watched, all hope of escape did not immediately forsake me. As they hurried me along, I endeavored, without their knowledge, to take notice of such objects as would serve as landmarks on my way back. I tried also, where I passed long grass, or soft ground, to leave my tracks. I hoped to be able to escape after they should have fallen asleep at night. When night came, they lay down, placing me between the old man and Kish-kau-ko, so close together, that the same blanket covered all three. I was so fatigued that I fell asleep immediately, and did not wake until sunrise next morning, when the Indians were up and ready to proceed on their journey. Thus we journeyed for about four days, the Indians hurrying me on, and I continuing to hope that I might escape, but still every night completely overpowered by sleep. As my feet were bare, they were often wounded, and at length much swollen. The old man perceiving my situation, examined my feet one day, and after removing a great many thorns and splinters from them, gave me a pair of moccasins, which afforded me some relief. Most commonly I traveled between the old man and Kish-kau-ko, and they often made me run until my strength was quite exhausted. For several days I could eat little or nothing. It was, I think, four days after we left the Ohio, that we came to a considerable river, running, as I suppose, into the Miami. This river was wide, and so deep, that I could not wade across it; the old man took me on his shoulders and carried me over; the water was nearly up to his armpits. As he carried me across, I though I should never be able to pass this river alone, and gave over all hope of immediate escape. When he put me down on the other side, I immediately ran up the bank, and a short distance into the woods, when a turkey flew up a few steps before me. The nest she had left contained a number of eggs; these I put in the bosom of my shirt, and returned towards the river. When the

Indians saw me they laughed, and immediately took the eggs from me, and kindling a fire, put them in a small kettle to boil. I was then very hungry, and as I sat watching the kettle, I saw the old man come running from the direction of the ford where we had crossed; he immediately caught up the kettle, threw the eggs and the water on the fire, at the same time saying something in a hurried and low tone to the young men. I inferred we were pursued, and have since understood that such was the case; it is probable some of my friends were at that time on the opposite side of the river searching for me. The Indians hastily gathered up the eggs and dispersed themselves in the woods, two of them still urging me forward to the utmost of my strength.

It was a day or two after this that we met a party of twenty or thirty Indians, on their way toward the settlements. Old Manito-o-geezhik had much to say to them; subsequently I learned that they were a war party of Shawneese; that they received information from our party, of the whites who were in pursuit of us about the forks of the Miami; that they went in pursuit of them, and that a severe skirmish happened between them, in which numbers were killed on both sides.

Our journey through the woods was tedious and painful: it might have been ten days after we met the war party, when we arrived at the Maumee river. As soon as we came near the river, the Indians were suddenly scattered about the woods examining the trees, yelling and answering each other. They soon selected a hickory tree, which was cut down, and the bark stripped off, to make a canoe. In this canoe we all embarked, and descended till we came to a large Shawnee village, at the mouth of a river which enters the Maumee. As we were landing in this village, great numbers of the Indians came about us, and one young woman came crying directly toward me, and struck me on the head. Some of her friends had been killed by the whites. Many of these Shawneese showed a disposition to kill me, but Kish-kau-ko and the old man interposed, and prevented them. I could perceive that I was often the subject of conversation, but could not as yet understand what was said. Old Manito-o-geezhik could speak a few words of English, which he used occasionally, to direct me to bring water, make a fire, or perform other tasks, which he now began to require of me. We remained two days at the Shawnee village, and then proceeded on our journey in the canoe. It was not very far from the village that we came to a trading house, where were three or four men who could speak English; they talked much with me, and said they wished to have purchased me from the Indians, that I might return to my friends; but as the old man would not consent to part with me, the traders told me I must be content to go with the Indians, and to become the old man's son, in place of one he had lost, promising at the same time that after ten days they would come to the village and release me. They treated me kindly while we stayed, and gave me plenty to eat, which the Indians had neglected to do. When I found I was compelled to leave this house with the Indians, I began to cry, for the first time since I had been taken. I consoled myself, however, with their promise that in ten days they would come for me. Soon after leaving this trading house, we came to the lake; we did not stop at night to encamp, but soon after dark the Indians raised a yell, which was answered from some lights on shore, and presently a canoe came off to us, in which three of our party left us. I have little recollection of any thing that passed from this time until we arrived at Detroit. At first we paddled up in the middle of the river until we came opposite the center of the town; then we ran in near the shore, where I saw a white woman, with whom the Indians held a little conversation, but I could not understand what was said. I also saw several white men standing and walking on shore, and heard them talk, but could not understand them; it is likely they spoke French. After talking a few minutes with the woman, the Indians pushed off, and ran up a good distance above the town.

It was about the middle of the day when we landed in the woods, and drew up the canoe. They presently found a large hollow log, open at one end, into which they put their blankets, their little kettle, and some other articles; they then made me crawl into it, after which they closed up the end at which I had entered. I heard them for a few minutes on the outside, then all was still, and remained so for a long time. If I had not long since relinquished all hope of making my escape, I soon found it would be in vain for me to attempt to release myself from my confinement. After remaining many hours in this situation, I heard them removing the logs with which they had fastened me in, and on coming out, although it was very late in the night, or probably near morning, I could perceive that they had brought three horses. One of these was a large iron-gray mare, the others were two small bay horses. On one of these they placed me, on the others their baggage, and sometimes one, sometimes another of the Indians riding, we traveled rapidly, and in about three days reached Sau-ge-nong, the village to which old Manito-o-geezhik belonged. This village or settlement consisted of several scattered houses. Two of the Indians left us soon after we entered it; Kish-kau-ko and his father only remained, and instead of proceeding immediately home, they left their horses and borrowed a canoe, in which we at last arrived at the old man's house. This was a hut or cabin built of logs, like some of those in Kentucky. As soon as we landed, the old woman came down to us to the shore, and after Manito-o-geezhik had said a few words to her, she commenced crying, at the same time hugging and kissing me, and thus she led me to the house. Next day they took me to the place where the old woman's son had been buried. The grave was enclosed with pickets, in the manner of the Indians, and on each side of it was a smooth open place. Here they all took their seats; the family and friends of Manito-o-geezhik on the one side, and strangers on the other. The friends of the family had come provided with presents; mukkuks of sugar, sacks of corn, beads, strouding, tobacco, and the like. They had not been long assembled when my party began to dance, dragging me with them about the grave. Their dance was lively and cheerful, after the manner of the scalp dance. From time to time as they danced, they presented me something of the articles they had brought, but as I came round in the dancing to the party on the opposite side of the grave, whatever they had given me was snatched from me: thus they continued a great part of the day, until the presents were exhausted, when they returned home.

It must have been early in the spring when we arrived at Sau-ge-nong, for I can remember that at this time the leaves were small, and the Indians were about planting their corn. They managed to make me assist at their labors, partly by signs, and partly by the few words of English old Manito-o-geezhik could speak. After planting, they all left the village, and went out to hunt and dry meat. When they came to their hunting grounds, they chose a place where many deer resorted, and here they began to build a long screen like a fence; this they made of green boughs and small trees. When they had built a part of it, they showed me how to remove the leaves and dry brush from that side of it to which the Indians were to come to shoot the deer. In this labor I was sometimes assisted by the squaws and children, but at other times I was left alone. It now began to be warm weather, and it happened one day that having been left alone, as I was tired and thirsty, I fell asleep. I cannot tell how long I slept, but when I began to awake, I thought I heard some one crying a great way off. Then I tried to raise up my head, but could not. Being now more awake, I saw my Indian mother and sister standing by me, and perceived that my face and head were wet. The old woman and her daughter were crying bitterly, but it was some time before I perceived that my head was badly cut and bruised. It appears that after I had fallen asleep, Manito-o-geezhik, passing that way, had perceived me, had tomahawked me, and thrown me in the bushes; and that when he came to his camp he had said to his wife, "Old woman, the boy I brought you is good for nothing; I have killed him, and you will find him in such a place." The old woman and her daughter having found me, discovered still some signs of life, and had stood over me a long time, crying, and pouring cold water on my head, when I waked. In a few days I recovered in some measure from this hurt, and was again set to work at the screen, but I was more careful not to fall asleep; I endeavored to assist them at their labors, and to comply in all instances with their directions, but I was notwithstanding treated with great harshness, particularly by the old man, and his two sons She-mung and Kwo-tash-e. While we remained at the hunting camp, one of them put a bridle in my hand, and pointing in a certain direction, motioned me to go. I went accordingly, supposing he wished me to bring a horse; I went and caught the first I could find, and in this way I learned to discharge such services as they required of me.

When we returned from hunting, I carried on my back a large pack of dried meat all the way to the village; but though I was almost starved, I dared not touch a morsel of it. My Indian mother, who seemed to have some compassion for me, would sometimes steal a little food, and hide it for me until the old man was gone away, and then give it me. After we returned to the village, the young men, whenever the weather was pleasant, were engaged in spearing fish, and they used to take me to steer the canoe. As I did not know how to do this very well, they commonly turned upon me, beat me, and often knocked me down with the pole of the spear. By one or the other of them I was beaten almost every day. Other Indians, not of our family, would sometimes seem to pity me, and when they could without being observed by the old man, they would sometimes give me food, and take notice of me.

After the corn was gathered in the fall, and disposed of in the Sun-je-gwun-nun, or Ca-ches, where they hide it for the winter, they went to hunt on the Sau-ge-nong River. I was here, as I had always been, when among them, much distressed with hunger. As I was often with them in the woods, I saw them eating something, and I endeavored to discover what it was, but they carefully concealed it from me. It was some time before I accidentally found some beechnuts, and though I knew not what they were, I was tempted to taste them, and finding them very good, I showed them to the Indians, when they laughed, and let me know these were what they had all along been eating. After the snow had fallen, I was compelled to follow the hunters, and oftentimes to drag home to the lodge a whole deer, though it was with the greatest difficulty I could do so.

At night I had always to lie between the fire and the door of the lodge, and when any one passed out or came in, they commonly gave me a kick; and whenever they went to drink, they made a practice to throw some water on me. The old man constantly treated me with much cruelty, but his ill humor showed itself more on some occasions than others. One morning, he got up, put on his moccasins, and went out; but presently returning, he caught me by the hair of my head, dragged me out, rubbed my face for a long time in a mass of recent excrement, as one would do the nose of a cat, then tossed me by the hair into a snow bank. After this I was afraid to go into the lodge; but at length my mother came out and gave me some water to wash. We were now about to move our camp, and I was as usual made to carry a large pack; but as I had not been able to wash my face clean, when I came among other Indians they perceived the smell, and asked me the cause. By the aid of signs, and some few words I could now speak, I made them comprehend how I had been treated. Some of them appeared to pity me, assisted me to wash myself, and gave me something to eat.

HAMILTON v BURR: THE DUEL, New Jersey, 7.00 11 July 1804

Nathaniel Pendleton and W. P. Van Ness

Hamilton was first Secretary of the Treasury and principal author of *The Federalist Papers*. Burr was a stalwart of the old Republican Party. The long animosity between the two men came to a head in 1804 when Hamilton blocked Burr's renomination for the Vice Presidency and his bid for the governorship of New York. Burr's response was to challenge Hamilton to a duel. Pendleton and Van Ness were the duellists' seconds.

Colonel Burr arrived first on the ground, as had been previously agreed. When General Hamilton arrived, the parties exchanged salutations, and the seconds proceeded to make their arrangements. They measured the distance, ten full paces, and cast lots for the choice of position, as also to determine by whom the word should be given, both of which fell to the second of General Hamilton. They then proceeded to load the pistols in each other's presence, after which the parties took their stations. The gentleman who was to give the word then explained to the parties the roles which were to govern them in firing, which were as follows:

The parties being placed at their stations, the second who gives the word shall ask them whether they are ready; being answered in the affirmative, he shall say *present*! After this the parties shall present and fire *when they please*. If one fires before the other, the opposite second shall say *one, two, three, fire*, and he shall then fire or lose his fire.

He then asked if they were prepared; being answered in the affirmative, he gave the word *present*, as had been agreed on, and both parties presented and fired in succession. The intervening time is not expressed, as the seconds do not precisely agree on that point. The fire of Colonel Burr took effect, and General Hamilton almost instantly fell. Colonel Burr advanced toward General Hamilton with a manner and gesture that appeared to General Hamilton's friend to be expressive of regret; but, without speaking, turned about and withdrew, being urged from the field by his friend, as has been subsequently stated, with a view to prevent his being recognized by the surgeon and bargemen who were then approaching. No further communication took place between the principals, and the barge that carried Colonel Burr immediately returned to the city. We conceive it proper to add, that the conduct of the parties in this interview was perfectly proper, as suited the occasion.

THE HAMILTON v BURR DUEL: A PHYSICIAN TENDS THE MORTALLY WOUNDED HAMILTON, New Jersey, 11 July 1804

Dr Hosack

When called to him upon his receiving the fatal wound, I found him half sitting on the ground, supported in the arms of Mr Pendleton. His countenance of death I shall never forget. He had at that instant just strength to say, "This is a mortal wound, doctor;" when he sunk away, and became to all appearance lifeless. I immediately stripped up his clothes, and soon, alas I ascertained that the direction of the ball must have been through some vital part. His pulses were not to be felt, his respiration was entirely suspended, and, upon laying my hand on his heart and perceiving no motion there, I considered him as irrecoverably gone. I, however, observed to Mr Pendleton, that the only chance for his reviving was immediately to get him upon the water. We therefore lifted him up, and carried him out of the wood to the margin of the bank, where the bargemen aided us in conveying him into the boat, which immediately put off. During all this time I could not discover the least symptom of returning life. I now rubbed his face, lips, and temples with spirits of hartshorn, applied it to his neck and breast, and to the wrists and palms of his hands, and endeavoured to pour some into his mouth.

When we had got, as I should judge, about fifty yards from the shore, some imperfect efforts to breathe were for the first time manifest; in a few minutes he sighed, and became sensible to the impression of the hartshorn or the fresh air of the water. He breathed; his eyes, hardly opened, wandered, without fixing upon any object; to our great joy, he at length spoke. "My vision is indistinct," were his first words. His pulse became more percept-ible, his respiration more regular, his sight returned. I then examined the wound to know if there was any dangerous discharge of blood; upon slightly pressing his side it gave him pain, on which I desisted.

Soon after recovering his sight, he happened to cast his eye upon the case of pistols, and observing the one that he had had in his hand lying on the outside, he said, "Take care of that pistol; it is undischarged, and still cocked; it may go off and do harm. Pendleton knows" (attempting to turn his head towards him) "that I did not intend to fire at him." "Yes," said Mr Pendleton, understanding his wish, "I have already made Dr Hosack ac-quainted with your determination as to that." He then closed his eyes and remained calm, without any disposition to speak; nor did he say much afterward, except in reply to my questions. He asked me once or twice how I found his pulse; and he informed me that his lower extremities had lost all feeling, manifesting to me that he entertained no hopes that he should long survive.

* Hamilton, with the pistol ball lodged next to his spine, died in agony the following day.

THE VOYAGE OF DISCOVERY: MEETING THE LAKOTA, Bad River, 24–25 September 1804

Captain Meriwether Lewis and Captain William Clark

Lewis and Clark were charged by President Thomas Jefferson with the exploration of the continent from the Missouri River to the Pacific Ocean. On 14 May 1804, accompanied by 27 members of their "Corps of Discovery", Lewis and Clark began ascent of the Missouri in a keelboat. Most Indians they encountered were "peaceable"; the Lakota were less tractable.

Monday 24th September 1804

[Clark]
we prepared Some Clothes and a fiew Meadels for the Chiefs of the Teton's bands of Seoux which we expect to See to day at the next river, observe a great Deel of Stone on the Sides of the hills on the S. S. we Saw one Hare, to day, prepared all things for Action in Case of necessity, our Perogus went to the Island for the Meet, Soon after the man on Shore run up the bank and reported that the Indians had Stolen the horse We Soon after Met 5 Inds. and ankered out Som distance & Spoke to them informed them we were friends, & Wished to Continue So but were not afraid of any Indians, Some of their young men had taken the horse Sent by their Great father for their Cheif and we would not Speek to them untill the horse was returned to us again.

25th Sept.
A fair Morning the Wind from the S. E. all well, raised a Flag Staff & made a orning or Shade on a Sand bar in the mouth of Teton River, for the purpose of Speeking with the Indians under, the Boat Crew on board at 70 yards Distance from the bar The 5 Indians which we met last night Continued, about 11 oClock the 1t. & 2d. Chief Came we gave them Some of our Provisions to eat, they gave us great Quantitis of Meet Some of which was Spoiled we feel much at a loss for the want of an interpeter the one we have can Speek but little.
    Met in Council at 12 oClock and after Smokeing, agreeable to the useal Custom, Cap. Lewis proceeded to Deliver a Speech which we [were] oblige[d] to Curtail for want of a good interpreter. all our party paraded. gave a Medal to the Grand Chief

Calld. in Indian *Un ton gar Sar bar* in French *Beeffe nure* [Beuffle noir] Black Buffalow. Said to be a good Man, 2nd Chief *Torto hon gar* or the *Parti sin* or Partizan *bad* the 3rd. is the Beffe De Medison [Beuffe de Medecine] his name is *Tar ton gar Wa ker* 1st. Considerable Man, *War zing go.* 2nd. Considerable Man *Second Bear − Mato co que par*.

Envited those Chiefs on board to Show them our boat and such Curiossities as was Strange to them, we gave them ¼ a glass of whiskey which they appeared to be verry fond of, Sucked the bottle after it was out & Soon began to be troublesom, one the 2d. Chief assuming Drunkness, as a Cloake for his rascally intentions I went with those Chiefs (which left the boat with great reluctiance) to Shore with a view of reconsileing those men to us, as Soon as I landed the Perogue three of their young Men Seased the Cable of the Perogue, the Chiefs Soldr. Huged the mast, and the 2d. Chief was verry insolent both in words & justures (*pretended Drunkenness & staggered up against me*) declareing I should not go on, Stateing he had not receved presents sufficent from us, his justures were of Such a personal nature I felt My self Compeled to Draw my Sword (*and Made a Signal to the boat to prepare for action*) at this Motion Capt. Lewis ordered all under arms in the boat, those with me also Showed a Disposition to Defend themselves and me, the grand Chief then took hold of the roap & ordered the young Warrers away, I felt My Self warm & Spoke in verry positive terms.

Most of the Warriers appeared to have ther Bows strung and took out their arrows from the quiver. as I (*being surrounded*) was not permited to return, I Sent all the men except 2 Inps. [Interpreters] to the boat, the perogue Soon returned with about 12 of our determined men ready for any event. this movement caused a no: of the Indians to withdraw at a distance. Their treatment to me was very rough & I think justified roughness on my part, they all lift my Perogue, and Councild. with themselves the result I could not lern and nearly all went off after remaining in this Situation Some time I offered my hand to the 1. & 2. Chiefs who refusd. to receve it. I turned off & went with my men on board the perogue, I had not prosd. more the [than] 10 paces before the 1st. Chief 3rd. & 2 Brave Men Waded in after me. I took them in & went on board

We proceeded on about 1 Mile & anchored out off a Willow Island placed a guard on Shore to protect the Cooks &a guard in the boat, fastened the Perogues to the boat, I call this Island bad humered Island as we were in a bad humer.

THE VOYAGE OF DISCOVERY: SACAGAWEA'S BABY IS BORN, North Dakota, 11 February 1805

Lewis and Clark

Sacagewea was a Shoshone who guided Lewis and Clark's expedition.

11th February Monday 1805

[Lewis]
about five Ocock this evening one of the wives of Charbono was delivered of a fine boy. it is worthy of remark that this was the first child which this woman had boarn, and as is common in such cases her labour was tedious and the pain violent; Mr. Jessome informed me that he had frequently administered a small portion of the rattle of the rattle-snake, which he assured me had never failed to produce the desired effect, that of hastening the birth of the child; having the rattle of a snake by me I gave it to him and he administered two rings of it to the woman broken in small pieces with the fingers and added to a small quantity of water. Whether this medicine was truly the cause or not I shall not undertake to determine, but I was informed that she had not taken it more than ten minutes before she brought forth perhaps this remedy may be worthy of future experiments, but I must confess that I want faith as to it's efficacy.

THE VOYAGE OF DISCOVERY: SACAGAWEA MEETS HER RELATIVES, Rocky Mountains, 17 August 1805

Lewis and Clark

[Lewis; with a small advance party he had already entered the Shoshone camp.]

Saturday 17th August 1805.—
an Indian who had straggled some little distance down the river returned and reported that the whitemen were coming, that he had seen them just below. they all appeared transported with joy, & the ch[i]ef repeated his fraturnal hug. I felt quite as much

gratifyed at this information as the Indians appeared to be. Shortly after Capt. Clark arrived with the Interpreter Charbono, and the Indian woman, who proved to be a sister of the Chief Cameahwait. the meeting of those people was really affecting, particularly between Sah-cah-gar-we-ah and an Indian woman, who had been taken prisoner at the same time with her and who, had afterwards escaped from the Minnetares and rejoined her nation. At noon the Canoes arrived, and we had the satisfaction once more to find ourselves all together, with a flattering prospect of being able to obtain as many horses shortly as would enable us to prosicute our voyage by land should that by water be deemed unadvisable.

Saturday 17th August 1805

[Clark]

I had not proceeded on one mile before I saw at a distance Several Indians on horsback comeing towards me, The Interpreter & Squar who were before me at Some distance danced for the joyful sight, and She made signs to me that they were her nation, as I aproached nearer them descovered one of Capt Lewis party With them dressed in their Dress; the[y] met me with great Signs of joy, as the Canoes were proceeding on nearly opposit me, I turned those people & Joined Capt Lewis who had Camped with 16 of those Snake Indians at the forks 2 miles in advance, those Indians Sung all the way to their Camp where the others had provd a cind [kind] of Shade of Willows Stuck up in a Circle the Three Chiefs with Capt. Lewis met me with great cordiallity embraced and took a Seat on a white robe, the Main Chief imediately tied to my hair Six Small pieces of Shells resembling *perl* which is highly Valued by those people and is pr[o]cured from the nations resideing near the *Sea* Coast. we then Smoked in their fassion without Shoes and without much ceremoney and form.

Capt. Lewis informed me he found those people on the *Columbia* River about 40 miles from the forks at that place there was a large camp of them, he had purswaded those with him to Come and see that what he said was the truth, they had been under great apprehension all the way, for fear of their being deceived. The Great Chief of this nation proved to be the brother of the *woman* with us and is a man of Influence Sence & easey & reserved manners, appears to possess a great deel of Cincerity. The Canoes arrived & unloaded. every thing appeared to astonish those people. the appearance of the men, their arms, the Canoes, the Clothing my black Servent & the Segassity of Capt Lewis's Dog.

we spoke a fiew words to them in the evening respecting our rout intentions our want of horses &c. & gave them a fiew presents & medals. we made a number of enquires of those people about the Columbia River the Countrey game &c. The account they gave us was verry unfavourable, that the River abounded in emence falls, one perticularly much higher than the falls of the Missouri & at the place the mountains Closed so Close that it was impracticable to pass, & that the ridge Continued on each Side of perpendicular Clifts inpenetratable, and that no Deer Elk or any game was to be found in that Countrey, aded to that they informed us that there was no timber on the river Sufficiently large to make Small Canoes

This information (if true is alarming) I deturmined to go in advance and examine the Countrey, See if those dificueltes presented themselves in the gloomey picture in which they painted them, and if the river was practi[c]able and I could find timber to build Canoes, those Ideas & plan appear[e]d to be agreeable to Capt Lewis's ideas on this point, and I selected 11 men, directed them to pack up their baggage Complete themselves with amunition, take each an ax and Such tools as will be Soutable to build Canoes, and be ready to Set out at 10 oClock tomorrow morning.

Those people greatly pleased. our hunters killed three Deer & an antilope which was eaten in a Short time the Indians being so harrassed & compelled to move about in those rugid mountains that they are half Starved liveing at this time on berries & roots which they geather in the plains. Those people are not begerley but generous, only one has asked me for anything and he for powder.

"I HAVE BEEN WET AND AS COLD IN EVERY PART AS I EVER WAS IN MY LIFE": CROSSING THE ROCKY MOUNTAINS, 29 August–7 October 1805

Lewis and Clark

August 29th. Thursday 1805

[Clark]
I left our baggage in possession of 2 men and proceeded on up to

join Capt. Lewis at the upper Village of Snake Indians where I arrived at 1 oClock found him much engaged in Councelling and attempting to purchase a fiew more horses. I spoke to the Indians on various Subjects endeavoring to impress on theire minds the advantage it would be to them for to sell us horses and expedite the [our] journey the nearest and best way possibly that we might return as soon as possible and winter with them at Some place where there was plenty of buffalow, our wish is to get a horse for each man to carry our baggage and for Some of the men to ride occasionally, The horses are handsom and much acustomed to be changed as to their Parsture, we cannot calculate on their carrying large loads & feed on the Grass which we may calculate on finding in the Mountain thro' which we may expect to pass on our rout

August 30th. Friday 1805 finding that we Could purchase no more horse[s] than we had for our goods &c. (and those not a Sufficint number for each of our Party to have one which is our wish) I Gave my Fuzee to one of the men & Sold his musket for a horse which Completed us to 29 total horses, we Purchased pack cords Made Saddles & Set out on our rout down the [Lemhi] river by land guided by my old guide [and] one other who joined him, the old gu[i]de's 3 Sons followed him, before we Set out our hunters killed three Deer proceeded on 12 Miles and encamped on the river South Side.

at the time we Set out from the Indian Camps the greater Part of the Band Set out over to the waters of the Missouri. we had great attention paid to the horses, as they were nearly all Sore Backs, and Several pore, & young Those horses are indifferent, maney Sore backs and others not acustomed to pack, and as we cannot put large loads on them are Compelled to purchase as maney as we can to take our Small proportion of baggage of the Parties, (& Eate if necessary) Proceeded on *12* Miles to day.

September 2nd. Monday 1805 proceded on up the Creek, proceded on thro' thickets in which we were obliged to Cut a road, over rockey hill Sides where our horses were in [per]peteal danger of Slipping to their certain distruction & up & Down Steep hills, where Several horses fell, Some turned over, and others Sliped down Steep hill Sides, one horse Crippeled & 2 gave out.

September 3rd. Tuesday 1805
hills high & rockey on each Side, in the after part of the day the
high mountains closed the Creek on each Side and obliged us to
take on the Steep Sides of those Mountains, So Steep that the
horses Could Scur[ce]ly keep from Slipping down, Several sliped
& Injured themselves verry much, with great dificuelty we made
[blank space in MS.] miles & Encamped on a branch of the Creek
we assended after crossing Several Steep points & one mountain,
but little to eate

The mouintains to the East Covered with Snow. we met with a
great misfortune, in haveing our last Th[er]mometer broken, by
accident This day we passed over emence hils and Some of the
worst roads that ever horses passed, our horses frequently fell Snow
about 2 inches deep when it began to rain which termonated in a
Sleet [storm]

Septr. 3rd. Tuesday 1805

N. 25.° W. 2½   Miles to a Small fork on the left Hilley and
thick assending

N. 15.° W. 2   miles to a fork on the right assending

N. 22.° W. 2½   miles to a fork on the left passing one on the
left Several Spring runs on the right Stoney
hills & much falling timber

N. 18.° E. 2   miles passing over Steep points & winding
ridges to a high Point passed a run on the
right

N. 32.° W. 2   miles to the top of a high hill passed 2 runs
from the left, passing on the Side of a Steep
ridge, no road

N. 40.° W. 3¼   miles leaveing the waters of the Creek to the
right & passing over a high pine Mountn.
o the head of a Drean running to the left

September 4th. Wednesday 1805
a verry cold morning every thing wet and frosed, Groun[d]
covered with Snow, we assended a mountain & took a Divideing
ridge* which we kept for Several Miles & fell on the head of a
Creek which appeared to run the Course we wished to go

prosued our Course down the Creek to the forks about 5 miles

* Lost Trail Pass into Montana on the west slope of the Continental Divide.

where we met a part[y] of the Tushepau* nation, of 33 Lodges about 80 men 400 Total and at least 500 horses, those people rec[e]ved us friendly, threw white robes over our Sholders & Smoked in the pipes of peace, we Encamped with them & found them friendly but nothing but berries to eate a part of which they gave us, those Indians are well dressed with Skin shirts & robes, they [are] Stout & light complected more So than Common for Indians, The Chief harangued untill late at night, Smoked in our pipe and appeared Satisfied. I was the first white man who ever wer on the waters of this river.

September 5th. Thursday 1805 we assembled the Chiefs & warriers and Spoke to them (with much dificuel[t]y as what we Said had to pass through Several languages before it got into theirs, which is a gugling kind of language Spoken much thro the throught [throat]) we informed them who we were, where we came from, where bound and for what purpose &c. &c. and requested to purchase & exchange a fiew horses with them, in the Course of the day I purchased 11 horses & exchanged 7 for which we gave a fiew articles of merchendize, those people possess ellegant horses.

September 6th. Friday 1805 took a Vocabelary of the language litened our loads & packed up, rained contd. untill 12 oClock

all our horses purchased of the flat heads (*oote-lash-shutes*) we Secured well for fear of their leveing of us, and Watched them all night for fear of their leaving us or the Indians prosuing & Steeling them.

Monday September 9th. 1805
[Lewis]
two of our hunters have arrived, one of them brought with him a redheaded woodpecker of the large kind common to the U States. this is the first of the kind I have seen since I left the Illinois. just as we were seting out Drewyer arrived with two deer. we continued our rout down the valley about 4 miles and crossed the river; it is hear a handsome stream about 100 yards wide and affords a considerable quantity of very clear water, the banks are low and it's bed entirely gravel. the stream appears navigable, but from the circumstance of their being no sammon in it I believe that there must be a considerable fall in it below.

---

* Flathead.

our guide could not inform us where this river* discharged itself
into the columbia river, he informed us that it continues it's course
along the mountains to the N. as far as he knew it and that not very
distant from where we then were it formed a junction with a stream
nearly as large as itself which took it's rise in the mountains near
the Missouri to the East of us and passed through an extensive
valley generally open prarie which forms an excellent pass to the
Missouri, the point of the Missouri where this Indian pass inter-
sects it, is about 30 miles above the *gates of the rocky Mountain*, or the
place where the valley of the Missouri first widens into an extensive
plain after entering the rockey Mountains, the guide informed us
that a man might pass to the missouri from hence by that rout in
four days.

we continued our rout down the W. side of the river about 5
miles further and encamped on a large creek which falls in on the
West. as our guide inform[ed] me that we should leave the river at
this place and the weather appearing settled and fair I determined
to halt the next day rest our horses and take some scelestial
Observations. we called this Creek *Travellers rest*.

September 11th Wednesday 1805

[Clark]
proceeded on up the *Travelers rest Creek* accompanied by the Flat
head Indian about 7 miles our guide tels us a fine large roade
passes up this river to the Missouri. The loss of 2 of our horses
detained us unl. 3 oClock P.M. our *Flat head* Indian being restless
thought proper to leave us and proceed on alone, Sent out the
hunters to hunt in advance as usial. (we have Selected 4 of the best
hunters to go in advance to hunt for the party. This arrangement
has been made long since)

Encamped at Some old Indian Lodges, nothing killed this
evening hills on the right high & ruged, the mountains on the
left high & Covered with Snow. The day Verry worm

September 12th Thursday 1805.
The road through this hilley Countrey is verry bad passing over
hills & thro' Steep hollows, over falling timber &c. &c. continued on & passed Some most intolerable road on the Sides of
the Steep Stoney mountains, which might be avoided by keeping up the Creek which is thickly covered with under groth &
falling timber, Crossed a Mountain 8 miles with out water

* Bitterroot River, originally named Clark's River by the explorers.

& encamped on a hill Side on the Creek after Decending a long
Steep mountain, Some of our Party did not get up until 10 oClock
P M.

September 14th Thursday (*Saturday*) 1805
a verry high Steep mountain for 9 miles to a large fork from the
left which appears to head in the Snow toped mountains we
Encamped opposit a Small Island at the mouth of a branch on
the right side of the river which is at this place 80 yards wide,
Swift and Stoney, here we were compelled to kill a Colt for our
men & Selves to eat for the want of meat & we named the South
fork Colt killed Creek, and this river we Call *Flat head* River the
flat head name is Koos koos ke* The Mountains which we passed
to day much worst than yesterday the last excessively bad &
thickly Strowed with falling timber & Pine Spruce fur Hackma-
tak & Tamerack, Steep & Stoney our men and horses much
fatigued

Wednesday (*Sunday*) Septr. 15th. 1805
Several horses Sliped and roled down Steep hills which hurt them
verry much the one which Carried my desk & Small trunk Turned
over & roled down a mountain for 40 yards & lodged against a
tree, broke the Desk the horse escaped and appeared but little hurt
Some others verry much hurt, from this point I observed a range of
high mountains Covered with Snow from S E. to S W with their
tops bald or void of timber,

after two hours delay we proceeded on up the mountain Steep &
ruged as usial, more timber near the top, when we arrived at the
top As we Conceved, we could find no water and Concluded to
Camp and make use of the Snow we found on the top to cook the
remns. of our Colt & make our Supe, evening verry cold and
cloudy. Two of our horses gave out, pore and too much hurt to
proceed on and left in the rear. nothing killed to day except 2
Phests.

From this mountain I could observe high ruged mountains in
every direction as far as I could see. with the greatest exertion we
could only make 12 miles up this mountain

Saturday (*Monday*) Septr. 16th. 1805
began to Snow about 3 hours before Day and continued all day the
Snow in the morning 4 inches deep on the old Snow, and by night
we found it from 6 to 8 inches deep, I walked in front to

* Clearwater River.

keep the road and found great dificuelty in keeping it as in maney places the Snow had entirely filled up the track, and obliged me to hunt Several-minits for the track, at 12 oClock we halted on the top of the mountain to worm & dry our Selves a little as well as to let our horses rest and graze a little on Some long grass which I observed, (on) The (South) Knobs Steep hill Sides & falling timber Continue to day, and a thickly timbered Countrey of 8 different kinds of pine, which are so covered with Snow, that in passing thro' them we are continually covered with Snow,

I have been wet and as cold in every part as I ever was in my life, indeed I was at one time fearfull my feet would freeze in the thin Mockirsons which I wore, after a Short Delay in the middle of the Day, I took one man and proceeded on as fast as I could about 6 miles to a Small branch passing to the right, halted and built fires for the party agains[t] their arrival which was at Dusk, verry cold and much fatigued, we Encamped at this Branch in a thickly timbered bottom which was scurcely large enough for us to lie leavil, men all wet cold and hungary. Killed a Second Colt which we all Suped hartily on and thought it fine meat.

Wednesday September 18th. 1805

[Lewis]

Cap Clark set out this morning to go a head with six hunters. there being no game in these mountains we concluded it would be better for one of us to take the hunters and hurry on to the leavel country a head and there hunt and provide some provisions while the other remained with and brought on the party. the latter of these was my part; accordingly I directed the horses to be gotten up early being determined to force my march as much as the abilities of our horses would permit.

this morning we finished the remainder of our last coult. we dined & suped on a skant proportion of portable soupe, a few canesters of which, a little bears oil and about 20 lbs. of candles form our stock of provision, the only resources being our guns & packhorses. the first is but a poor dependance in our present situation where there is nothing upon earth ex[c]ept ourselves and a few small pheasants, small grey Squirrels, and a blue bird of the vulter kind about the size of a turtle dove or jay bird.

Monday (*Wednesday*) 18th Septr. 1805

[Clark]

I proceeded on in advance with Six hunters to try and find deer or Something to kill

Thursday September 19th 1805.

[Lewis]

Fraziers horse fell from this road in the evening, and roled with his load near a hundred yards into the Creek. we all expected that the horse was killed but to our astonishment when the load was taken off him he arose to his feet & appeared to be but little injured, in 20 minutes he proceeded with his load. this was the most wonderful escape I ever witnessed, the hill down which he roled was almost perpendicular and broken by large irregular and broken rocks.

we took a small quantity of portable soup, and retired to rest much fatiegued. several of the men are unwell of the disentary. brakings out, or irruptions of the Skin, have also been common with us for some time.

Tuesday (*Thursday*) 19th Septr. 1805

[Clark]

Set out early proceeded on up the [Hungry] Creek passing through a Small glade at 6 miles at which place we found a horse. I derected him killed and hung up for the party after takeing a brackfast off for our Selves which we thought fine

Friday September 20th. 1805.

[Lewis]

This morning my attention was called to a species of bird which I had never seen before.* It was reather larger than a robbin, tho' much it's form and action. the colours were a blueish brown on the back the wings and tale black, as wass a stripe above the croop $\frac{3}{4}$ of an inch wide in front of the neck, and two others of the same colour passed from it's eyes back along the sides of the head. the top of the head, neck brest and belley and butts of the wing were of a fine yellowish brick reed [red]. it was feeding on the buries of a species of shoemake or ash which grows common in [this] country & which I first observed on 2d. of this month. I have also observed two birds of a blue colour both of which I believe to be of the haulk or vulter kind. the one of a blue shining colour with a very high tuft of feathers on the head a long tale, it

* Steller's jay (*Cyanocritta stelleri*).

feeds on flesh the beak and feet black. it's note is chă-ăh, chă-ăh. it is about the size of a pigeon, and in shape and action resembles the jay bird.

Three species of Phesants, a large black species, with some white feathers irregularly scattered on the brest neck and belley – a smaller kind of a dark uniform colour with a red stripe above the eye, and a brown and yellow species that a gooddeel resembles the phesant common to the Atlantic States.

We were detained this morning until ten oclock in consequence of not being enabled to collect our horses. we had proceeded about 2 Miles when we found the greater part of a horse which Capt. Clark had met with and killed for us. he informed me by note that he should proceed as fast as possible to the leavel country which lay to the S. W. of us, which we discovered from the hights of the mountains on the 19th. there he intended to hunt until our arrival. at one oclock we halted on a small branch runing to the left and made a hearty meal on our horse beef much to the comfort of our hungry stomachs. here I larnt that one of the Packhorses with his load was missing and immediately dispatched Baptiest Lapage who had charge of him, to surch for him. he returned at 3 OC. without the horse. The load of the horse was of considerable value consisting of merchandize and all my stock of winter cloathing. I therefore dispatched two of my best woodsmen in surch of him, and proceeded with the party.

Our road was much obstructed by fallen timber particularly in the evening. we encamped on a ridge where ther was but little grass for our horses, and at a distance from water. however we obtained as much as served our culinary purposes and suped on our beef. the soil as you leave the hights of the mountains becomes gradually more fertile. the land through which we passed this evening is of an excellent quality tho' very broken, it is a dark grey soil. a grey free stone appearing in large masses above the earth in many places. saw the hucklebury, honeysuckle, and alder common to the Atlantic states, also a kind of honeysuckle which bears a white bury and rises about 4 feet high not common but to the western side of the rockey mountains. a growth which resembles the choke cherry bears a black bury with a single stone of a sweetish taste, it rises to the hight of 8 or 10 feet and grows in thick clumps. the Arborvita is also common and grows to an immence size, being from 2 to 6 feet in diameter.

Wednesday (*Friday*) 20th September 1805
[Clark]

I set out early and proceeded on through a Countrey as ruged as usial at 12 miles decended the mountain to a leavel pine Countrey proceeded on through a butifull Countrey for three miles to a Small Plain in which I found maney Indian lodges, a man Came out to meet me, & Conducted me to a large Spacious Lodge which he told me (by Signs) was the Lodge of his great Chief who had Set out 3 days previous with all the Warriers of the nation to war on a South West derection & would return in 15 or 18 days. the fiew men that were left in the Village and great numbers of women geathered around me with much apparent signs of fear, and apr. pleased they those people gave us a Small piece of Buffalow meat, Some dried Salmon beries & roots in different States, Some round and much like an onion which they call Pas she co [*quamash. the Bread or Cake is called Pas-shi-co*] Sweet, of this they make bread & Supe they also gave us, the bread made of this root all of which we eate hartily, I gave them a fiew Small articles as preasents, and proceeded on with a Chief to his Village 2 miles in the Same Plain, where we were treated kindly in their way and continued with them all night Those two Villages consist of about 30 double lodges, but fiew men a number of women & children, they call themselves *Cho pun-nish or Pierced noses* Their diolect appears verry different from the flat heads, [*Tushapaws*], altho origineally the Same people

Emence quantity of the [*quawmash or*] *Pas-shi-co* root gathered & in piles about the plain, those roots grow much like an onion in marshey places the seed are in triangular Shells, on the Stalk. they sweat them in the following manner i.e. dig a large hole 3 feet deep, cover the bottom with Split wood on the top of which they lay Small Stones of about 3 or 4 Inches thick, a Second layer of Splited wood & Set the whole on fire which heats the Stones, after the fire is extinguished they lay grass & mud mixed on the Stones, on that dry grass which Supports the Pâsh-shi-co root a thin Coat of the Same grass is laid on the top, a Small fire is kept when necessary in the Center of the kill &c.

I find myself verry unwell all the evening from eateing the fish & roots too freely Sent out hunters they killed nothing

Saturday September 21st. 1805
[Lewis]
we killed a few Pheasants, and I killed a prarie woolf which
together with the ballance of our horse beef and some crawfish
which we obtained in the creek enabled us to make one more
hearty meal, not knowing where the next was to be found.

the Arborvita increases in quantity and size. I saw several sticks
today large enough to form eligant perogues of at least 45 feet in
length. I find myself growing weak for the want of food and most of
the men complain of a similar deficiency, and have fallen off very
much.

Thursday (*Saturday*) 21st. Septr. 1805
[Clark]
A fine Morning Sent out all the hunters in different directions to
hunt deer, I my self delayed with the Chief to prevent Suspission
and to Collect by Signs as much information as possible about the
river and Countrey in advance. The Chief drew me a kind of
chart of the river, and informed me that a greater Chief than
himself was fishing at the river half a days march from his Village
called the twisted hare [hair], and that the river forked a little
below his Camp and at a long distance below & below 2 large
forks one from the left & the other from the right the river passed
thro' the mountains at which place was a great fall of the Water
passing through the rocks, at those falls white people lived from
whome they precured the white Beeds & Brass &c. which the
womin wore

I am verry sick to day and puke which relive me

Sunday September 22nd. 1805.
[Lewis]
Notwithstanding my positive directions to hubble the horses last
evening one of the men neglected to comply. he plead[ed] ignorance of the order. this neglect however detained us until ½ after
eleven OCk. at which time we renewed our march, our course
being about west. we had proceeded about two and a half miles
when we met Reubin Fields one of our hunters, whom Capt. Clark
had dispatched to meet us with some dryed fish and roots that he
had procured from a band of Indians, whose lodges were about
eight miles in advance. I ordered the party to halt for the purpose
of taking some refreshment. I divided the fish roots and buries, and
was happy to find a sufficiency to satisfy compleatly all our
appetites.

The pleasure I now felt in having tryumphed over the rockey Mountains and decending once more to a level and fertile country where there was every rational hope of finding a comfortable subsistence for myself and party can be more readily conceived than expressed, nor was the flattering prospect of the final success of the expedition less pleasing. on our approach to the village which consisted of eighteen lodges most of the women fled to the neighbouring woods on horseback with their children, a circumstance I did not expect as Capt. Clark had previously been with them and informed them of our pacific intentions towards them and also the time at which we should most probably arrive. the men seemed but little concerned, and several of them came to meet us at a short distance from their lodges unarmed.

Friday (*Sunday*) 22nd. Septr. 1805

[Clark]
Set out with the Chief & his Son on a young horse for the Village at which place I expected to meet Capt Lewis this young horse in fright threw himself & me 3 times on the Side of a Steep hill & hurt my hip much, Cought a Coalt which we found on the roade & I rode it for Several miles untill we saw the Chiefs horses, he Cought one & we arrived at his Village at Sunset, & himself and mys[el]f walked upto the 2d Village where I found Capt Lewis & the party Encamped, much fatigued, & hungery, much rejoiced to find something to eate of which they appeared to partake plentifully I cautioned them of the Consequences of eateing too much &c.

The planes appeared covered with Spectators viewing the white men and the articles which we had, our party weakened and much reduced in flesh as well as Strength

I got the Twisted hare to draw the river from his Camp down which he did with great Cherfullness on a white Elk skin, from the 1st. fork which is few miles below, to the large fork on which the *So So ne* or Snake Indians fish, is South 2 Sleeps; to a large river which falls in on the N W. Side and into which The *Clarks river* empties itself is 5 Sleeps from the mouth of that river to the *falls* is 5 Sleeps at the falls he places Establishments of white people &c. and informs that the great numbers of Indians reside on all those fo[r]ks as well as the main river; one other Indian gave me a like account of the Countrey. Some few drops of rain this evening. I precured maps of the Countrey & river with the Situation of

Indians, Towns from Several men of note Seperately which varied verry little.

Saturday (*Monday*) 23rd. Septr. 1805 gave a Shirt to the *Twisted hare* & a knife & Handkerchief with a Small pece of Tobacco to each. Finding that those people gave no provisions to day we deturmined to purchase with our Small articles of Merchindize, accord[ingly] we purchased all we could, Such as roots dried, in bread, & in their raw State, Berries of red Haws & *Fish*

Capt. Lewis & 2 men Verry Sick this evening, my hip Verry Painfull, the men trade a few old tin Canisters for dressed Elk Skin to make themselves Shirts. at dark a hard wind from the S W accompanied with rain which lasted half an hour. The *twisted hare* envited Capt. Lewis & myself to his lodge which was nothin[g] more than Pine bushes & bark, and gave us Some broiled dried *Salmon* to eate, great numbers about us all night. at this village the women were busily employed in gathering and drying the *Pas-she-co* root of which they had great quantities dug in piles

Sunday (*Tuesday*) 24th. Septr. 1805 despatched J. Colter back to hunt the horses lost in the mountains & bring up Some Shot left behind, and at 10 oClock we all Set out for the river and proceeded on by the Same rout I had previously traveled, and at Sunset we arrived at the Island on which I found the *Twisted hare*, and formed a Camp on a large Island a little below, Capt. Lewis sccrcely able to ride on a jentle horse which was furnished by the Chief, Several men So unwell that they were Compelled to lie on the Side of the road for Some time others obliged to be put on horses. I gave rushes Pills to the Sick this evening. Several Indians follow us.

Monday (*Wednesy.*) 25th. of September 1805 I Set out early with the Chief and 2 young men to hunt Some trees Calculated to build Canoes, as we had previously deturmined to proceed on by water, I was furnished with a horse and we proceeded on down the river Passed down on the N side of the river to a fork from the North we halted about an hour, one of the young men took his guig and killed 6 fine Salmon two of them were roasted and we eate, I Saw fine timber for Canoes.

Tuesday (*Thursday*) 26th. Septr. 1805 I had the axes distributed and handled and men apotned. [apportioned] ready to commence building canoes on tomorrow, our axes are Small & badly calculated to build Canoes of the large Pine, Capt Lewis Still very unwell, Several men taken Sick on the way down, I administered *Salts* Pils Galip, [jalap] Tarter emetic &c. I feel unwell this evening, two Chiefs & their families follow us and encamp near us, they have great numbers of horses. This day proved verry hot, we purchase fresh Salmon of the Indians.

Thursday (*Saturday*) 28th. Septr. 1805
Our men nearly all Complaining of their bowels, a heaviness at the Stomach & Lax, Some of those taken first getting better, a number of Indians about us gazeing This day proved verry worm and Sultery, nothing killed men complaining of their diat of fish & roots. all that is able working at the Canoes.

October 5th Friday (*Saty*) 1805
had all our horses 38 in number Collected and branded Cut off their fore top and delivered them to the 2 brothers and one son of one of the Chiefs who intends to accompany us down the river to each of those men I gave a Knife & Some Small articles &c. they promised to be attentive to our horses untill we Should return.

Nothing to eate except dried fish & roots. Capt Lewis & myself eate a Supper of roots boiled, which Swelled us in Such a manner that we were Scercely able to breath for Several hours. finished and lanced (*launched*) 2 of our canoes this evening which proved to be verry good our hunters with every diligence Could kill nothing. The hills high and ruged and woods too dry to hunt the deer which is the only game in our neighbourhood. Several Squars Came with fish and roots which we purchased of them for Beeds, which they were fond of. *Capt Lewis not So well to day as yesterday.*

October 7th. Monday 1805
I continue verry unwell but obliged to attend every thing all the Canoes put into the water and loaded, fixed our Canoes as well as possible and Set out as we were about to Set out we missd. both of the Chiefs who promised to accompany us, I also missed my Pipe Tomahawk which could not be found.

The after part of the day cloudy proceded on passed 10 rapids which wer dangerous the Canoe in which I was Struck a rock and Sprung a leak in the 3rd. rapid, we proceeded on.

After taking to the water, the Corps of Discovery descended the Snake and the Columbia, reaching the Pacific Ocean on 15 November. They wintered at Fort Clatsop, starting for home on 23 March 1806.

VOYAGE OF DISCOVERY: MELEE WITH PIEGANS, Montana, 27 July 1806

Captain Meriwether Lewis

On 23 March 1806 the Corps of Discovery split, with Clark exploring the Yellowstone and Lewis the Marias into northern Montana. At Cut Bank Creek a meeting with Piegan (Alongonquian-speaking Blackfeet) turned sour:

July 27th. 1806. Sunday.

[Lewis]

This morning at daylight the indians got up and crouded around the fire, J. Fields who was on post had carelessly laid his gun down behi[n]d him near where his brother was sleeping, one of the indians the fellow to whom I had given the medal last evening sliped behind him and took his gun and that of his brother unperceived by him, at the same instant two others advanced and seized the guns of Drewyer and myself, J. Fields seeing this turned about to look for his gun and saw the fellow just runing off with her and his brother's he called to his brother who instantly jumped up and pursued the indian with him whom they overtook at the distance of 50 or 60 paces from the camp s[e]ized their guns and rested them from him and R. Fields as he seized his gun stabed the indian to the heart with his knife the fellow ran about 15 steps and fell dead; of this I did not know untill afterwards, having recovered their guns they ran back instantly to the camp;

Drewyer who was awake saw the indian take hold of his gun and instantly jumped up and s[e]ized her and rested her from him but the indian still retained his pouch, his jumping up and crying damn you let go my gun awakened me I jumped up and asked what was the matter which I quickly learned when I saw drewyer in a scuffle with the indian for his gun. I reached to seize my gun but found her gone, I then drew a pistol from my holster and terning myself about saw the indian making off with my gun I ran at him with my pistol and bid him lay down my gun which he was in the act of doing when the Fieldses returned and drew up their guns to shoot him which I forbid as he did not appear to be about to make any resistance or commit any offensive act, he droped the gun and walked slowly off, I picked her up instantly, Drewyer having about this time recovered his gun and pouch asked me if he might not kill the fellow which I also forbid as the indian did not appear to wish to kill us, as soon as they found us all in possession of our arms they ran and indeavored to drive off all the horses I now hollowed to the men and told them to fire on them if they attempted to drive off our horses, they accordingly pursued the main party who were dr[i]ving the horses up the river and I pursued the man who had taken my gun who with another was driving off a part of the horses which were to the left of the camp.

I pursued them so closely that they could not take twelve of their own horses but continued to drive one of mine with some others: at the distance of three hundred paces they entered one of those steep nitches in the bluff with the horses before them being nearly out of breath I could pursue no further, I called to them as I had done several times before that I would shoot them if they did not give me my horse and raised my gun, one of them jumped behind a rock and spoke to the other who turned arround and stoped at the distance of 30 steps from me and I shot him through the belly, he fell to his knees and on his wright elbow from which position he partly raised himself up and fired at me, and turning himself about crawled in behind a rock which was a few feet from him, he overshot me, being bearheaded I felt the wind of his bullet very distinctly. not having my shotpouch I could not reload my peice and as there were two of them behind good shelters from me I did not think it prudent to rush on them with my pistol which had I discharged I had not the means of reloading untill I reached camp; I therefore returned leasurely towards camp.

On my way I met with Drewyer who having heared the report of the guns had returned in surch of me and left the Fieldes to pursue the indians, I desired him to haisten to the camp with me and assist in catching as many of the indian horses as were necessary and to call to the Fieldes if he could make them hear to come back that we still had a sufficient number of horses, this he did but they were too far to hear him. we reached the camp and began to catch the horses and saddle them and put on the packs. the reason I had not my pouch with me was that I had not time to return about 50 yards to camp after geting my gun before I was obliged to pursue the indians or suffer them to collect and drive off all the horses. we had caught and saddled the horses and began to arrange the packs when the Fieldses returned with four of our horses; we left one of our horses and took four of the best of those of the indian's; while the men were preparing the horses I put four sheilds and two bows and quivers of arrows which had been left on the fire, with sundry other articles; they left all their baggage at our mercy. they had but 2 guns and one of them they left the others were armed with bows and arrows and eyedaggs. the gun we took with us. I also retook the flagg but left the medal about the neck of the dead man that they might be informed who we were.

We took some of their buffaloe meat and set out ascending the bluffs by the same rout we had decended last evening leaving the ballance of nine of their horses which we did not want. the Fieldses told me that three of the indians whom they pursued swam the river one of them on my horse. and that two others ascended the hill and escaped from them with a part of their horses, two I had pursued into the nitch one lay dead near the camp and the eighth we could not account for but suppose that he ran off early in the contest. having ascended the hill we took our course through a beatifull level plain a little to the S. of East. My design was to hasten to the entrance of Maria's river as quick as possible in the hope of meeting with the canoes and party at that place having no doubt but that they [the Indians] would pursue us with a large party and as there was a band near the broken mountains or probably between them and the mouth of that river we might expect them to receive inteligence from us and arrive at that place nearly as soon as we could, no time was therefore to be lost and we pushed our horses as hard as they would bear.

At 8 miles we passed a large branch 40 yds. wide which I called battle river. At 3 P. M. we arrived at rose river about 5 miles above where we had passed it as we went out, having traveled by my estimate compared with our former distances and cou[r]ses about 63 ms. here we halted an hour and a half took some refreshment and suffered our horses to graize; the day proved warm but the late rains had supplyed the little reservors in the plains with water and had put them in fine order for traveling, our whole rout so far was as level as a bowling green with but little stone and few prickly pears. after dinner we pursued the bottoms of rose river but finding [it] inconvenient to pass the river so often we again ascended the hills on the S. W. side and took the open plains; by dark we had traveled about 17 miles further, we now halted to rest ourselves and horses about 2 hours, we killed a buffaloe cow and took a small quantity of the meat.

After refreshing ourselves we again set out by moonlight and traveled leasurely, heavy thunderclouds lowered arround us on every quarter but that from which the moon gave us light. we continued to pass immence herds of buffaloe all night as we had done in the latter part of the day. we traveled untill 2 OCk in the morning having come by my estimate after dark about 20 ms. we now turned out our horses and laid ourselves down to rest in the plain very much fatiegued as may be readily conceived. my indian horse carried me very well in short much better than my own would have done and leaves me with but little reason to complain of the robery.

Lewis reunited with Clark near the junction of the Yellowstone and Missouri, and the explorers made haste to St Louis, which they reached on 23 September 1806. They had been gone two years, four months and ten days. They had travelled 8000 miles, and been the first people to cross the continent within the borders of the present-day USA.

THE WAR OF 1812: THE DEFEAT OF HMS *GUERRIERE*, 19 August 1812

Isaac Hull

The War of 1812, between Britain and the USA, was an encore to the War of Independence. The reasons for the conflict – outside of a mutual sense of unfinished business – were to be found in obscure violations of maritime law.

Although the US Navy was minuscule (8 frigates, 12 sloops and some runarounds for the Great Lakes), its crews were highly trained and its 44-gun frigates the meanest frigates at sea – as US Navy Captain Isaac Hull found to his pleasure in August 1812.

United State's frigate *Constitution*, off Boston Light, 30 August 1812 I have the honour to inform you, that on the 19th instant, at 2 p.m. being in latitude 41, 42, longitude 55, 48, with the *CONSTITUTION* under my command, a sail was discovered from the mast-head bearing E. by S. or E.S.E. but at such a distance we could not tell what she was. All sail was instantly made in chase, and soon found we came up with her. At 3 p.m. could plainly see that she was a ship on the starboard tack, under easy sail, close on a wind; at half past 3 p.m. made her out to be a frigate; continued the chase until we were within about three miles, when I ordered the light sails taken in, the courses hauled up, and the ship cleared for action. At this time the chase had backed his main top-sail, waiting for us to come down. As soon as the *CONSTITUTION* was ready for action, I bore down with an intention to bring him to close action immediately; but on our coming within gun-shot she gave us a broadside and filled away, and then were giving us a broadside on the other tack, but without effect; her shot falling short. She continued wearing and manoeuvreing for about three quarters of an hour, to get a raking position, but finding she could not, she bore up, and run under top-sails and gib, with the wind on the quarter. Immediately made sail to bring the ship up with her, and 5 minutes before 6 p.m. being along side within half pistol shot, we commenced a heavy fire from all our guns, double shotted with round and grape, and so well directed were they, and so warmly kept up, that in 15 minutes his mizen-mast went by the board, and his main-yard in the slings, and the hull, rigging and sails very much torn to pieces. The fire was kept up with equal warmth for 15 minutes longer, when his main-mast and fore-mast went, taking with them every spar, excepting the bowsprit; on seeing this we ceased firing, so that in 30 minutes after we got fairly along side the enemy she surrendered, and had not a spar standing, and her hull below and above water so shattered, that a few more broadsides must have carried her down.

After informing you that so fine a ship as the *GUERRIERE*, commanded by an able and experienced officer, had been totally dismasted, and otherwise cut to pieces, so as to make her not worth towing into port, in the short space of 30 minutes, you can have no doubt of the gallantry and good conduct of the officers and ship's company I have the honour to command. It only remains, therefore, for me to assure you, that they all fought with great bravery; and it gives me great pleasure to say, that from the smallest boy in the ship to the oldest seaman, not a look of fear was seen. They all went into action, giving three cheers, and requesting to be laid close along side the enemy.

Enclosed I have the honour to send you a list of killed and

wounded on board the *CONSTITUTION*, and a report of the damages she has sustained; also, a list of the killed and wounded on board the enemy, with his quarter bill, &c.

Killed and wounded on board the United States' frigate *CON-STITUTION*, Isaac Hull, Esqr. Captain, in the action with his Britannic majesty's frigate *GUERRIERE*, James A. Dacres, Esqr. Captain, on the 20th of August, 1812:

Killed	W. S. Bush, lieutenant of Marines, and six seamen,	7
Wounded	lieutenant C. Morris J. C. Aylwin, four seamen, one marine,	7
Total	killed and wounded,	14

Killed and wounded on board the *GUERRIERE*.

Killed	3 officers, 12 seamen and marines,	15
Wounded	J. A. Dacres, captain, 4 officers, 57 seamen and marines,	62
Missing	lieutenants Pullman and Roberts, and 22 seamen and marines	24
Total	killed, wounded and missing,	101

THE WAR OF 1812: CORPORAL STUBBS FIGHTS THE REDCOATS, 1812–1815

Corporal Samuel Stubbs

Stubbs served with the Kentucky Militia. He was aged 63 in 1812.

Brother Ephram,
I just write you to enform you that I'm still alive and in tolerable helth and choice spirits – altho as well as my brother *officers*, I have had some hair bredth escapes. Sposing that you would like to know something about my military life since I quit home, I'll give you the whole story.

When the express first came into our neighborhood, calling upon us all to turn out and march against the Canadians, I was like another [Israel] Putnam, ploughing in my field – but I immediately unharnest the old daples, swung my napsack, shoul-dered my old gun that had killed me forty-five deer the three months past, and marched away for head quarters.

In four days time I joined the army with a dozen more of my

neighbors, near Queenstown. The brave Col. Van Rensselare was our commander in chief, under whose command we the next day (which being the 13th day of October 1812) in boats crossed over to Canada – But, ah, in the end it liked to have proved rather a bad job for us, for the opposite shore was lined with redcoats as thick as bees upon a sugar maple – but after exchanging a few shots our brave Colonel buzzed in among them, while I and the rest followed close to his heels, and drove them all up a steep bank. We now got a fair footing and stuck up the American colours in Canada! We did not obtain this much however without some loss on our part, and what was unfortunate for us all, our Colonel was severely wounded – but he was still able to keep upon his legs and with great courage ordered us to push forward and storm their fort, and that we did, and made them one and all scamper off into the woods.

But we were now in our turn unfortunate, for one half of our army was yet on the other side of the river, nor would the cowardly dogs come over to assist us when they saw the d–d redcoats cutting us up like slain venison!* The enemy now doubled their numbers while every shot diminished ours; in truth they got the better of us, and again got possession of their batteries, altho we let fly showers of ball and buck shot into their very teeth and eyes! Ah! the poor Yankee lads, this was a sorry moment for ye! They dropped my brave companions like wild pigeons, while their balls whistled like a northwest wind through a dry cane break! Our Commander ordered a retrete, but nature never formed any of our family you know for runners, so I wadled along as well as I could behind; but the redcoat villains overhaul'd me, and took me prisoner! But not until I had a fare shot at their head commander General Brock, who galloping his horse after my retreting comrads, bellowed out to 'um like a wounded buffalo to surrender; but I leveled my old fatheful Bess, which never disappointed me in so fare a mark, and I heard no more of his croaking afterwards.

Oh one thousand which crossed over, but a few escaped biting the dust! As for poor me, I expected they'd kill and scalp me, but

* Colonel Van Resnnelare (aka van Renselaer) crossed the Niagara River at Queenston with 900 regulars and some militia; most of his 2,270 militiamen refused to cross on the ground that they were only raised to fight within the US. At the ensuing battle of Queenston Heights, the British General Brock, heading 600 British regulars and 400 Canadian militia, inflicted 250 casualties and took over 700 prisoners.

after stareing at me as if I had been born with two heads, and enquiring of what nation I was, and from what part of the world I came, their Colonel ordered me liberated, who said to me, "Old daddy, your age and odd appearance induces me now to set you at liberty; return home to your family and think no more of invading us!" This I promised him I would do, but I didn't mean so, for I was determined I wouldn't give up the chase so, but at 'um again.

So I hastened off and joined General Deerbon's army; and on the 27th day of April [1813] we took Little York, which is the chief town of the Upper Province. We went in boats, and the redcoats peppered a good many of us before we reeched the shore. But when we got footing, they fled before us like an affrighted flock of redwinged boblinkons. We drove 'um, from their battery, and then in a powerful body of pursuing 'um, when on a sudden, as if the whole earth was paring asunder and discharging from its bowels huge rocks and stones, a dreadful exploshon took place from the maggazeen, which the arch dogs had fixed for the purpose! And a serious exploshon it proved for us, I tell ye, for it killed one hundred of our men, including our brave commander General Pike. For my own part, I scaped with just my life as you may say, for a stone as big as your fist struck me on the head, and nocked off a piece of my scalp as broad as your hand! But, faith, this I didn't mind much, but waddled on with the rest, over dead bodies as thick as cowslops, and soon got posesshon of the town. The cowerdly British chief, General Sheaff, had thought it best to scamper off with his soldiers and Indians before we entered the town, so that I got but one fare shot at one of their copper-colour'd sanups, whose heels I soon made too light for his head, and would have scalped the dog, but my captin would'nt allow it.

As all the work appeared now to be done in this quarter, I marched off. And on the 20th June [1814] joined General Browne's army, which amounting to about three thousand brave boys of us, on the 3d day of July, crossed the Niagara. General Scott commanded the first brigade, Gen. Ripley the second, Gen. Porter the militia, and Farmers' Brother the Indians, who were painted as red as maple blosums. Fort Eree* surrendered to us that very day, and on the next we marched to

* i.e. Fort Erie.

Chippewa, driving the enemy before us like so many fire-frigh-
tened antelopes!

On the 5th, the enemy's commander, General Riall, came out
upon Chippewa plain, with two thousand two hundred regelers,
while my militia boys and the Indians on both sides were engaged
in the woods. For my own part, I climed a sturdy oak, where I
assure you I did not suffer my old Bess to grow cold, for whenever I
saw an Indian creeping like an allegator upon his belly, I gave him
the contents in full, and made him hug the ground to sum purpose.
I'm sure I killed fifteen of 'um in fifteen minnits, and shood have
been glad to have fleeced them; but the New England men don't
approve of scalping. At this time our brave troops under Gen.
Scott* was hotly engaged with Gen. Riall's redcoats, who after an
hour's hard fighting, they turn'd tail to and run in all directions,
and saved their pork by gaining their works at Chippewa. We
killed about five hundred of them, while our loss was three
hundred twenty-nine killed wounded and prisoners. And thus
ended this engagement.

On the 25th, I agin marched with Gen. Scott, who advanced
with his brigade, betwixt eight and nine hundred, about a mile in
the Queenstown road, where we found the enemies, and engaged
'um about sunset.† The enemies were guessed to be four thousand‡
stout, and were cummanded by Gen. Drummond. The tussel
lasted til about leven a'clock, when, gad! I believe both parties
were willing to quit the field. We took twenty pieces of artilary
from 'um; one of 'um I took, faith, myself alone with charg'd
bagnut [bayonet]! The loss on both sides was about nine hundred;
the redcoats commander, Gen. Riall, and about twenty officers
were taken prisoners. Our Gen. Brown and Gen. Scott were
wounded. The next day, we return'd to Fort Eree, under command of Gen. Ripley.

August 15th, Gen. Drummond ordered an assalt upon our fort
in three columns, consisting of the bestest men of his army, to the
amount of three thousand. There was about one thousand five
hundred of us, under Gen. Gaines, who took cummand of us
about the first of August. We repulsed the redcoats with great
loss. We killed, mangled and made prisoners of about one

* General Winfield Scott; the grey coats of his regular brigade became the model for
the dress uniform at West Point.
† This was the battle of Lundy's Lane, perhaps the most vicious firefight of the War.
‡ British forces were closer to 3,000.

thousand five hundred of 'um. They lay as thick as slartered mutton around. Ha, brother Ephe, a fine picking for skelpers! Our loss was sixty killed and wounded.

I continued with the American troops until they were about to go into winter quarters, when with the thanks of my General, like another Cincinnaty, I started home, to exchange my rifle and bagnut for the ploughshare and pruning hook. But I did not get half way when I was summoned to repair to New Orlenes, where the redcoats had landed and were thretening to over run the whole country! Accordingly, I right-about-face, and with quick step steered my course for New Orlenes, where by land and water tacks I arrived in seven days.

I found the whole place in alarm. They had had some skermishing with the redcoats, but the desisive battle was yet to be fought, as you shall here. I joined capt. Copp's company, a nice man, who gladly receiv'd me, and in three days promoted me to the office of a CORPORAL! As I never held any office before, you know, it made me feel kinder queer at first; but I soon learnt my duty, and the grate responsibility attached to my office.

On the morning of the 8th [January 1815] before day-light, the enemy silently drew out a large force to storm our lines, where we were entrenched up to our chins. There was a great fog, and their columns advanced unperceived to within about half a mile of our camp, and drove in our piquet [picket] guard. About the break of day, they as bold as hunger wolves advanced to our entrenchments, led on by their foolish officers up to the very muzels of our guns. I could have dropped them as easy as a flock of benumb'd wild turkeys in a frosty morning. But I picked for those who had frog paws upon their shoulders, and the most lace upon their frocks. Aye, the Corporal did his duty that day I'll warrant ye. Some of the foolish redcoats penetrated into our lines, where they were soon baganuted or taken prisoners; many fell mounting the brest works; others upon the works themselves. The roar of artillery from our lines was insessant, while an unremitted rolling fire was kept up from our muskets. Ah, *my men* performed wonders. For an hour and a quarter the enemy obstinately continued the assault; nor did they faulter until almost all their officers had fallen. They then retreted, leaving from one thousand five hundred to two thousand in killed mangled and prisoners. On our side the loss

was confined to about twenty men – but I lost but one out of
my company!

So I remain, yours, &c.
Corporal Samuel Stubbs

DOLLEY MADISON RESCUES THE NATIONAL TREASURE, Washington D.C., 24 August 1814

Dolley Madison

In the twilight of the War of 1812, the British marched on Washington
D.C., at which government officials hastily removed national treasures.
Unfortunately the portrait of George Washington in the dining room of
the White House refused to leave the wall. Dolley Madison, the wife of the
fourth president, saved the day.

Tuesday, August 23, 1814

Dear Sister:
My husband left me yesterday morning to join General Winder. He
inquired anxiously whether I had courage or firmness to remain in
the President's house until his return on the morrow, or succeeding
day, and on my assurance that I had no fear but for him, and the
success of our army, he left, beseeching me to take care of myself,
and of the Cabinet papers, public and private. I have since received
two dispatches from him, written with a pencil. the last is alarming,
because he desires I should be ready at a moment's warning to enter
my carriage, and leave the city; that the enemy seemed stronger
than had at first been reported, and it might happen that they
would reach the city with the intention of destroying it. I am
accordingly ready; I have pressed as many Cabinet papers into
trunks as to fill one carriage; our private property must be sacrificed,
as it is impossible to procure wagons for its transportation.

I am determined not to go myself until I see Mr Madison safe, so
that he can accompany me, as I hear of much hostility toward him.
Disaffection stalks around us. My friends and acquaintances are all
gone, even Colonel C. with his hundred, who were stationed as a
guard in this enclosure. French John [a faithful servant], with his
usual activity and resolution, offers to spike the cannon at the gate,
and lay a train of powder, which would blow up the British, should
they enter the house. To this last proposition I positively object,
without being able to make him understand why all advantages in
war may not be taken.

Wednesday morning, twelve o'clock. Since sunrise I have been turning my spy-glass in every direction, and watching with unwearied anxiety, hoping to discover the approach of my dear husband and his friends; but, alas! I can descry only groups of military, wandering in all directions, as if there was a lack of arms, or of spirit to fight for their own fireside.

Three o'clock. Will you believe it, my sister? we have had a battle, or skirmish, near Bladensburg, and here I am still, within sound of the cannon! Mr Madison comes not. May God protect us! Two messengers, covered with dust, come to bid me fly; but here I mean to wait for him . . . At this late hour a wagon has been procured, and I have had it filled with plate and the most valuable portable articles, belonging to the house. Whether it will reach its destination, the "Bank of Maryland," or fall into the hands of British soldiery, events must determine. Our kind friend, Mr Carroll, has come to hasten my departure, and in a very bad humor with me, because I insist on waiting until the large picture of General Washington is secured, and it requires to be unscrewed from the wall. This process was found too tedious for these perilous moments; I have ordered the frame to be broken, and the canvas taken out. It is done! and the precious portrait placed in the hands of two gentlemen of New York, for safekeeping. And now, dear sister, I must leave this house, or the retreating army will make me a prisoner of it by filling up the road I am directed to take. When I shall again write to you, or where I shall be tomorrow, I cannot tell!

Dolley

Part Three

DESTINY
America 1816–1900

Introduction

The 1812 War finally shrugged America free of the colonial interference of Britain. Henceforth she would be mistress of her own block. In case anyone was in any doubt, the fifth president, James Monroe, fashioned a Doctrine in 1823 by which the USA disbarred European powers from colonization in the Western hemisphere. The Monroe Doctrine became the guiding light for US foreign policy thereafter; all the "international" wars the USA would fight for the next century would be wars – Mexico in 1846, and Spain in 1898 – to stem or reverse Old World imperialism.

America's splendid isolationism in world affairs allowed her to direct attention to some colonization of her own: the settlement of the American West. From 1843 there were major overland migrations to Oregon, and in 1845 Texas became the 28th state of the Union. It seemed, in the phrase of the year, the "Manifest Destiny" of America to rule the northern Continent. Proof, if it were needed, came in the discovery of gold at Sutter's Mill, California, in 1848, which began the great gold rush, and so brought California into the US. Yet for all the glittering allure of gold, the big bait out West was land for farming. It mattered little that the West was already occupied by the Native Americans; in the name of Manifest Destiny they were killed, removed and simply swamped. In only a handful of years after 1843, the number of whites living in trans-Mississppi America vastly outnumbered the 350,000 Native Americans there.

Ironically it was America's very success in the conquest of the West which provided the pretext for a national suicide attempt.

While some Western states were admitted under the Northwest ordinance of 1787, which forbade slavery, others were admitted under cobbled-together comprises such as the 1854 Kansas–Nebraska Act were allowed to maintain slavery. Faced with the Act, and the Dred Scott decision in the Supreme Court in 1857, abolitionists in the Democratic and Whig parties split to found the Republican Party. In 1860 the Republican candidate, Abraham Lincoln, was elected president. With the possibility of slavery being constitutionally abolished, South Carolina seceded, to be joined by six other states in the Confederate States of America in February 1861. (Four more states joined later). On 12 April Confederate forces began the bombardment of the Federal arsenal at Fort Sumter, South Carolina. The Civil War had begun. Four years later, at the village of Appomattox Courthouse, the Confederate army of General Robert E. Lee surrendered. Between Fort Sumter and Appomattox Courthouse 600,000 American soldiers had died of wounds and disease, and much of America, from Virginia to Arkansas, had been reduced to a battlefield.

The American Civil War was a peculiarly bloody affray. In Pickett's charge at Gettysburg, 8000 (60%) of the participants died in a single attack. In part the bloodiness was caused by the passions involved; in part it was because of the advanced technologies available – mass-produced rifles, artillery, battleships, even machine guns. The American Civil War was the world's first industrialized slaughter. Consequently, the North was always going to win – not least because the North did not rely on such an outmoded economic system as slavery. The North had more factories, more rail network, more (white) people. From 1862 the North also began the enlistment of black soldiers. At its peak, the Union army was one million strong; the most the South could put into grey was 500,000 men.

The price of victory was high: Lincoln himself was assassinated, while the South, to ensure it obeyed the abolition of slavery, was placed under military occupation and coerced into democracy. (This failed singularly: when the last troops were withdrawn from the South in 1877, Southerners imposed "Jim Crow" laws which imposed segregation of the races. Not until 1954 would segregation be banned by the Supreme Court). Even so, only victory allowed the reunion of the States and the continued westwards march of the American Empire. The thirty years after the Civil War were the great decades of the "taming" of the West, the spanning of

America from sea to shining sea with ribbons of rail, and transformation of the Great Plains into the world's most lavish beef butchery and bread basket. More American soil – 430 million acres – was occupied and placed under cultivation between 1870 and 1890 than in the entire two and half centuries since the landing at Jamestown. Effectively, by 1890, America had colonized its own West. The last gasp of the free Plains Indians had come at Wounded Knee, and the Census of that year could find no meaningful "frontier" between the wilderness and the zone of settlement.

Freely able to exploit the agricultural land of the West, along with its vast reserves of raw materials (oil, coal, iron ore and timber principal among them), American industry was able to grow at a stunning pace. One measure will serve: in 1865 production of steel ingots and castings was less than 20,000 long tons; in 1898 it had reached 9,000,000 tons. By 1900 the USA was producing 23.6% of the world's manufactured goods – more even than the United Kingdom. To labor in America's factories, millions of immigrants were siren-called across the Atlantic. Between 1860 and 1890 the population of America doubled from 31,443, 321 to 62,947,714.

Such a population was good for laboring and good for the business of buying, but not quite good enough for the hyper-efficiency of US industry. Goods needed to be sold abroad, and pushes to "open doors" in foreign lands were urged on the government. Under such pressure, inevitably enough, American foreign policy changed from isolationism to imperialism: the new compass direction for Manifest Destiny was Abroad. The war with Spain of 1898 was begun in Cuba but concluded with the USA seizing Spain's Philippines, Guam and Puerto Rico. By 1900 the signs were there for all the world to see. America had the money, the people, the guns, the self-belief to be a superpower. The overseas possessions were just the baubles of confirmation. Most Old World nations had already recognized America's new status; in 1892 they had upgraded their representatives in Washington D.C. from mere ministers to full-blown diplomats.

EXPLORATIONS IN THE AMERICAN DESERT, 1826–7

Jedediah Strong Smith

Seeking fresh beaver grounds trapper, Jed Smith (1799–1831) became the first white man to cross the Sierra Nevada mountains and the Great Salt Lake Desert. Smith was killed by Comanches in 1831.

Little Lake of Bear River, July 17th 1827.

Genl. Wm. Clark, Supt. of Indian Affairs

Sir, My situation in this country has enabled me to collect information respecting a section of the country which has hitherto been measurably veiled in obscurity to the citizens of the United States. I allude to the country S.W. of the *Great Salt Lake* west of the Rocky mountains.

I started about the 22d of August 1826, from the Great Salt Lake, with a party of fifteen men, for the purpose of exploring the country S.W. which was entirely unknown to me, and of which I could collect no satisfactory information from the Indians who inhabit this country on its N.E. borders.

My general course on leaving the Salt Lake was S.W. and W. Passing the Little Uta Lake and ascending Ashley's river, which empties into the Little Uta Lake. From this lake I found no more signs of buffalo; there are a few antelope and mountain sheep, and an abundance of *black tailed hares*. On Ashley's river, I found a nation of Indians who call themselves *Sampatch*; they were friendly disposed towards us. I passed over a range of mountains running S.E. and N.W. and struck a river running S.W. which I called *Adams River*, in compliment to our President. The water is of a muddy cast, and is a little brackish. The country is mountainous to East; towards the West there are sandy plains and detached rocky hills.

Passing down this river some distance, I fell in with a nation of Indians who call themselves *Pa-Ulches* (those Indians as well as those last mentioned, wear rabbit skin robes) who raise some little corn and pumpkins. The country is nearly destitute of game of any description, except a few hares. Here (about ten days march down it) the river turns to the South East. On the S.W. side of the river there is a *cave*, the entrance of which is about 10 or 15 feet high, and 5 or 6 feet in width; after descending about 15 feet, a room opens out from 25 to 30 in length and 15 to 20 feet in width; the roof, sides and floor are solid rock salt, a sample of which I send you, with some other articles which will be hereafter described. I here found a kind of plant of the prickly pear kind, which I called the cabbage pear, the largest of which grows about two feet and a half high and 1½ feet in diameter; upon examination I found it to be nearly of the substance of a turnip, altho' by no means palatable; its form was similar to that of an egg, being smaller at the ground and top than in the middle; it is covered with pricks similar to the prickly pear with which you are acquainted.

There are here also a number of shrubs and small trees with which I was not acquainted previous to my route there, and which I cannot at present describe satisfactorily, as it would take more space than I can here allot.

The *Pu Ulches* have a number of marble pipes, one of which I obtained and send you, altho it has been broken since I have had it in my possession; they told me there was a quantity of the same material in their country. I also obtained of them a knife of *flint*, which I send you, but it has likewise been broken by accident.

I followed Adams river two days further to where it empties into the Seedekeeden a South East course. I crossed the Seedskeeder, and went down it four days a south east course; I here found the country remarkably barren, rocky, and mountainous; there are a good many rapids in the river, but at this place a valley opens out about 5 to 15 miles in width, which on the river banks is timbered and fertile. I here found a nation of Indians who call themselves *Ammuchabas*; they cultivate the soil, and raise corn, beans, pumpkins, watermelons and muskmelons in abundance, and also a little wheat and cotton. I was now nearly destitute of horses, and had learned what it was to do without food; I therefore remained fifteen days and recruited my men, and I was enabled also to exchange my horses and purchase a few more of a few runaway Indians who stole some horses of the Spaniards. I here got information of the Spanish country (the Californias) and obtained two guides, recrossed the Seedskadeer, which I afterwards found emptied into the Gulf of California about 80 miles from this place by the name of the Collarado; many render the river *Gild* from the East.

I travelled a west course fifteen days over a country of complete barrens, generally travelling from morning until night without water. I crossed a Salt plain about 20 miles long and 8 wide; on the surface was a crust of beautiful white salt, quite thin. Under this surface there is a layer of salt from a half to one and a half inches in depth; between this and the upper layer there is about four inches of yellowish sand.

On my arrival in the province of Upper California, I was looked upon with suspicion, and was compelled to appear in presence of the Governor of the Californias residing at San Diego, where, by the assistance of some American gentlemen (especially Capt. W. H. Cunningham of the ship Courier from Boston) I was enabled to obtain permission to return with my men the route I came, and purchased such supplies as I stood in want of. The Governor would not allow me to trade up the Sea coast towards Bodaga. I returned to my party and purchased such articles as were necessary, and went Eastward of the Spanish settlements on the route I had come in. I then steered my course N.W. keeping from 150 miles to 200 miles from the sea coast. A very high range of mountains lay on the East. After travelling three hundred miles in that direction through a country somewhat fertile, in which there was a great many Indians, mostly naked and destitute of arms, with the exception of a few Bows and Arrows and what is very singular amongst Indians, they cut their hair to the length of three inches; they proved to be friendly; their manner of living is on fish, roots, acorns and grass.

On my arrival at the river which I named the *Wim-mul-che* (named after a tribe of Indians which resides on it, of that name) I found a few beaver, and elk, deer, and antelope in abundance. I here made a small hunt, and attempted to take my party across the [mountain] which I before mentioned, and which I called *Mount Joseph*, to come on and join my partners at the Great Salt Lake. I found the snow so deep on Mount Joseph that I could not cross my horses, five of which starved to death; I was compelled therefore to return to the valley which I had left, and there, leaving my party, I started with two men, seven horses and two mules, which I loaded with hay for the horses and provisions for ourselves, and started on the 20th of May, and succeeded in crossing it in eight days, having lost only two horses and one mule. I found the snow on the top of this mountain from 4 to 8 feet deep, but it was so consolidated by the heat of the sun that my horses only sunk from half a foot to one foot deep.

After travelling twenty days from the east side of Mount Joseph, I struck the S.W. corner of the Great Salt Lake, travelling over a country completely barren and destitute of game. We frequently travelled without water sometimes for two days over sandy deserts, where there was no sign of vegetation and when we found water in some of the rocky hills, we most generally found some Indians who appeared the most miserable of the human race having nothing to subsist on (nor any clothing) except grass seed, grasshoppers, etc. When we arrived at the Salt Lake, we had but one horse and one mule remaining, which were so feeble and poor that they could scarce carry the little camp equipage which I had along; the balance of my horses I was compelled to eat as they gave out.

The company are now starting, and therefore must close my communication. Yours respectfully,

(signed) Jedediah S. Smith, of the firm of
Smith, Jackson and Sublette.

AN ENGLISH IMMIGRANT IN NEW YORK, August 1830

John Downe

Downe had emigrated to America to work as a weaver. Here he writes to his wife – who remained behind in England until he could afford her passage – recording his impressions of New York.

New York, United States
August 12, 1830

My dear wife,
I have got a situation in a Factory, in a very pleasant vale about 7 miles from Hudson, and I am to have the whole management of the factory and the master is going to board me till you come in his house. A Farmer took me one day in his waggon into the country, from Hudson, to see a factory, and I dined with him, and he would not have a farthing, and told me I was welcome to come to his house at any time; they had on the table pudding, pyes, and fruit of all kind that was in season, and preserves, pickles, vegetables, meat, and everything that a person could wish, and the servants set down at the same table with their masters. They do not think of locking the doors in the country, and you can gather peaches, apples, and all kinds of fruit by the

side of the roads. And I can have a barrel of cider holding 32 gallons, for 4s., and they will lend me the barrel till I have emptied it. And I can have 100 lbs. of Beef for 10s. English money. Lamb is about five farthings the pound, and the butcher brings it to your door. And as for the bullocks' heads, sheep and lambs', they are thrown away, no one will eat them. I went into the market yesterday at New York, and on the outside of the market there was bullocks' and sheep and lambs' heads laying underfoot like dogs' meat. They cut the tongue, and throw the rest away. And I can go into a store, and have as much brandy as I like to drink for three half-pence and all other spirits in proportion. If a man like work he need not want victuals. It is a foolish idea that some people have, that there is too many people come here, it is quite the reverse; there was more than 1000 emigrants came in the day after I landed, and there is four ships have arrived since with emigrants. But there is plenty of room yet, and will for a thousand years to come.

My dear Sukey, all that I want now is to see you, and the dear children here, and then I shall be happy, and not before. You know very well that I should not have left you behind me, if I had money to have took you with me. It was sore against me to do it. But I do not repent of coming, for you know that there was nothing but poverty before me, and to see you and the dear children want was what I could not bear. *I would rather cross the Atlantic ten times than hear my children cry for victuals once.* Now, my dear, if you can get the Parish to pay for your passage, come directly; for I have not a doubt in my mind I shall be able to keep you in credit. You will find a few inconveniences in crossing the Atlantic, but it will not be long, and when that is over, all is over, for I know that you will like America.

America is not like England, for here no man thinks himself your superior. There is no improper or disgusting equality, for Character has its weight and influence, and the man which is really your superior does not plume himself on being so. An American, however low his station, never feels himself abashed when entering the presence of the highest. This is a country where a man can stand as a man, and where he can enjoy the fruits of his own exertions, with rational liberty to its fullest extent.

There is much attention paid to dress as at any of the watering places in England. Out in the country where I have been you see the young women with their veils and parasols, at the lowest that I saw. Poverty is unknown here. You see no beggars.

Give all the little ones a kiss for me, etc.

A SLAVE-MART, Natchez, America, c. 1834

Joseph Ingraham

"Will you ride with me into the country?" said a young planter. "I am about purchasing a few negroes and a peep into a slave-mart may not be uninteresting to you." I readily embraced the opportunity and in a few minutes our horses were at the door.

A mile from Natchez we came to a cluster of rough wooden buildings, in the angle of two roads, in front of which several saddle-horses, either tied or held by servants, indicated a place of popular resort.

"This is the slave market," said my companion, pointing to a building in the rear; and alighting, we left our horses in charge of a neatly dressed yellow boy belonging to the establishment. Entering through a wide gate into a narrow court-yard, partially enclosed by low buildings, a scene of a novel character was at once presented. A line of negroes, commencing at the entrance with the tallest, who was not more than five feet eight or nine inches in height – for negroes are a low rather than a tall race of men – down to a little fellow about ten years of age, extended in a semicircle around the right side of the yard. There were in all about forty. Each was dressed in the usual uniform of slaves, when in market, consisting of a fashionably shaped, black fur hat, roundabout and trowsers of coarse corduroy velvet, precisely such as are worn by Irish labourers, when they first "come over the water"; good vests, strong shoes, and white cotton shirts, completed their equipment. This dress they lay aside after they are sold, or wear out as soon as may be; for the negro dislikes to retain the indication of his having recently been in the market. With their hats in their hands, which hung down by their sides, they stood perfectly still, and in close order, while some gentlemen were passing from one to another examining for the purpose of buying. With the exception of displaying their teeth when addressed, and rolling their great white eyes about the court – they were so many statues of the most glossy ebony.

As we entered the mart, one of the slave merchants – for a "lot" of slaves is usually accompanied, if not owned, by two or three individuals – approached us, saying "Good morning, gentlemen! Would you like to examine my lot of boys? I have as fine a lot as ever came into market." – We approached them, one of us as a curious spectator, the other as a purchaser; and as my friend passed along the line, with a scrutinizing eye – giving that singular look, peculiar to the buyer of slaves as he glances from head to foot over each individual – the passive subjects of his observations betrayed no other signs of curiosity than that evinced by an occasional glance. The entrance of a stranger into a mart is by no means an unimportant event to the slave, for every stranger may soon become his master and command his future destinies.

"For what service in particular did you want to buy?" inquired the trader of my friend, "A coachman." 'There is one I think may suit you, sir," said he; "George, step out here." Forthwith a light-coloured negro, with a fine figure and good face, bating an enormous pair of lips, advanced a step from the line, and looked with some degree of intelligence, though with an air of indifference, upon his intended purchaser.

"How old are you, George?" he inquired. "I don't recollect, sir 'zactly – b'lieve I'm somewhere 'bout twenty-dree." "Where were you raised?" "On master R – 's farm in Wirginny." "Then you are a Virginia negro." "Yes, master, me full blood Wirginny." "Did you drive your master's carriage?" "Yes, master, I drove ole missus' carage, more dan four year." "Have you a wife?" "Yes, master, I lef' young wife in Richmond, but I got new wife here in de lot. I wishy you buy her, master, if you gwine to buy me."

Then came a series of the usual questions from the intended purchaser. "Let me see your teeth – your tongue – open your hands – roll up your sleeves – have you a good appetite? are you good tempered?" "Me get mad sometime," replied George to the last query, "but neber wid my horses." "What do you ask for this boy, sir?" inquired the planter, after putting a few more questions to the unusually loquacious slave. "I have held him at one thousand dollars, but I will take nine hundred and seventy-five cash." The bargain was in a few minutes concluded, and my companion took the negro at nine hundred and fifty, giving negotiable paper – the customary way of paying for slaves – at

four months. It is, however, generally understood, that if servants
prove unqualified for the particular service for which they are
bought, the sale is dissolved. So there is general perfect safety in
purchasing servants untried, and merely on the warrant of the
seller.

George, in the meanwhile, stood by, with his hat in his hand,
apparently unconcerned in the negotiations going on, and when
the trader said to him, "George, the gentleman has bought you;
get ready to go with him," he appeared gratified at the tidings, and
smiled upon his companions apparently quite pleased, and then
bounded off to the buildings for his little bundle. In a few minutes
he returned and took leave of several of his companions, who,
having been drawn up into line only to be shown to purchasers,
were now once more at liberty, and moving about the court, all the
visitors having left except my friend and myself. "You mighty
lucky, George," said one, congratulating him, "to get sol so
quick," "Oh, you neber min', Charly," replied the delighted
George; "your turn come soon too."

"VICTORY OR DEATH": THE STAND AT THE ALAMO, Texas, 24 February 1836

Lieutenant-Colonel William Barrett Travis

A former Franciscan mission, the Alamo was the site chosen by a garrison
of American settlers to make a stand against Mexican rule.

Commandancy of the Almo
Bexar, Feby 24th 1836

Fellow citizens and compatriots,
I am besieged by a thousand or more of the Mexicans under Santa
Anna – I have sustained a continual bombardment and cannonade for 24 hours and have not lost a man. The enemy has
demanded a surrender at discretion, otherwise the garrison are
to be put to the sword, if the fort is taken. I have answered the
demand with a cannon shot, and our flag still waves proudly from
the walls. I shall never surrender or retreat.

Then, I call on you in the name of liberty, of patriotism and
everything dear to the American character to come to our aid,
with all dispatch. The enemy is receiving reinforcements daily and
will no doubt increase to three or four thousand in four or five days.

If this call is neglected, I am determined to sustain myself as long

as possible and die like a soldier who never forgets what is due to
his own honour or that of his country.

Victory or death.

WILLIAM BARRETT TRAVIS
Lt. Col. Comd.

P.S. The Lord is on our side. When the enemy appeared in
sight we had not three bushels of corn. We have since found in
deserted houses 80 or 90 bushels and got into the wall 20 or 30
head beeves.

TRAVIS

The Alamo fell on 6 March. Aside from Travis, those who died in the
defence included such frontier legends as Jim Bowie and Davy Crockett.
To overcome the 200 Texans who held the Alamo cost the Mexican army
over 1000 men.

DINNER WITH A MANDAN CHIEF, c. 1838

George Catlin

George Catlin (1796–1872), artist and traveller. Within 20 years of
Catlin's meal with Mah-to-toh-pa (Four Bears), the Mandan would be
wiped out by smallpox contracted from Caucasian pioneers.

I spoke in a former Letter of Mah-to-toh-pa (the four bears), the
second chief of the nation, and the most popular man of the
Mandans – a high-minded and gallant warrior.

About a week since, this noble fellow stepped into my painting-
room about twelve o'clock in the day, in full and splendid dress,
and passing his arm through mine, pointed the way, and led me in
the most gentlemanly manner, through the village and into his
own lodge, where a feast was prepared in a careful manner and
waiting our arrival. The lodge in which he dwelt was a room of
immense size, some forty or fifty feet in diameter, in a circular
form, and about twenty feet high – with a sunken curb of stone in
the centre, of five or six feet in diameter and one foot deep, which
contained the fire over which the pot was boiling. I was led near
the edge of this curb, and seated on a very handsome robe, most
ingeniously garnished and painted with hieroglyphics; and he
seated himself gracefully on another one at a little distance from
me; with the feast prepared in several dishes, resting on a beautiful
rush mat, which was placed between us.

The simple feast which was spread before us consisted of three dishes only, two of which were served in wooden bowls, and the third in an earthen vessel of their own manufacture, somewhat in shape of a bread-tray in our own country. This last contained a quantity of *pem-i-can* and *marrow-fat*; and one of the former held a fine brace of buffalo ribs, delightfully roasted; and the others was filled with a kind of paste or pudding, made of the flour of the *"pomme blanche"*, as the French call it, a delicious turnip of the prairie, finely flavoured with the buffalo berries, which are collected in great quantities in this country, and used with divers dishes in cooking, as we in civilized countries use dried currants, which they very much resemble.

A handsome pipe and a tobacco-pouch made of the otter skin, filled with k'nick-k'neck (Indian tobacco), laid by the side of the feast; and when we were seated, mine host took up his pipe, and deliberately filled it; and instead of lighting it by the fire, which he could easily have done, he drew from his pouch his flint and steel, and raised a spark with which he kindled it. He drew a few strong whiffs through it, and presented the stem of it to my mouth, through which I drew a whiff or two while he held the stem in his hands. This done, he laid down the pipe, and drawing his knife from his belt, cut off a very small piece of the meat from the ribs, and pronouncing the word "Ho-pe-ne-chee-wa-pa-shee" (meaning a *medicine* sacrifice), threw it into the fire.

He then (by signals) requested me to eat, and I commenced, after drawing out from my belt my knife (which it is supposed that every man in this country carries about him, for at an Indian feast a knife is never offered to a guest). Reader, be not astonished that I sat and ate my dinner *alone*, for such is the custom of this strange land. In all tribes in these western regions it is an invariable rule that a chief never eats with his guests invited to a feast; but while they eat, he sits by, at their service, and ready to wait upon them; deliberately charging and lighting the pipe which is to be passed around after the feast is over. Such was the case in the present instance, and while I was eating, Mah-to-toh-pa sat cross-legged before me, cleaning his pipe and preparing it for a cheerful smoke when I had finished my meal. For this ceremony I observed he was making unusual preparation, and I observed as I ate, that after he had taken enough of the k'nick-k'neck or bark of the red willow, from his pouch, he rolled out of it also a piece of the *"castor"*, which it is customary amongst these folks to carry in their tobacco-sack to give it a flavour; and, shaving off a small quantity of it, mixed it with the bark, with which he charged his pipe. This done, he drew also from his sack a small parcel containing a fine powder, which was made of dried buffalo dung, a little of which he spread over the top, (according also to custom), which was like tinder, having no other effect than that of lighting the pipe with ease and satisfaction. My appetite satiated, I straightened up, and with a whiff the pipe was lit, and we enjoyed together for a quarter of an hour the most delightful exchange of good feeling, amid clouds of smoke and pantomimic signs and gesticulations.

The dish of "pemican and marrow-fat", of which I spoke, was thus: – The first, an article of food used throughout this country, as familiarly as we use bread in the civilized world. It is made of buffalo meat dried very hard, and afterwards pounded in a large wooden mortar until it is made nearly as fine as sawdust, then packed in this dry state in bladders or sacks of skin, and is easily carried to any part of the world in good order. "Marrow-fat" is collected by the Indians from the buffalo bones which they break to pieces, yielding a prodigious quantity of marrow, which is boiled out and put into buffalo bladders which have been distended; and after it cools, becomes quite hard like tallow, and has the appearance, and very nearly the flavour, of the richest yellow butter. At a feast, chunks of this marrow-fat are cut off and placed in a tray or bowl, with the pemican, and eaten together.

In this dish laid a spoon made of the buffalo's horn, which was black as jet, and beautifully polished; in one of the other there was another of still more ingenious and beautiful workmanship, made of the horn of the mountain-sheep, or "Gros corn", as the French trappers call them; it was large enough to hold of itself two or three pints, and was almost entirely transparent.

I spoke also of the earthen dishes or bowls in which these viands were served out; they are a familiar part of the culinary furniture of every Mandan lodge, and are manufactured by the women of this tribe in great quantities, and modelled into a thousand forms and tastes. They are made by the hands of the women, from a tough black clay, and baked in kilns which are made for the purpose, and are nearly equal in hardness to our own manufacture of pottery; though they have not yet got the art of glazing, which would be to them a most valuable secret. They make them so strong and serviceable, however, that they hang them over the fire as we do our iron pots, and boil their meat in them with perfect success. I have seen some few specimens of such manufacture, which have been dug up in Indian mounds and tombs in the southern and middle states, placed in our Eastern Museums and looked upon as a great wonder, when here this novelty is at once done away with, and the whole mystery; where women can be seen handling and using them by hundreds, and they can be seen every day in the summer also, moulding them into many fanciful forms, and passing them through the kiln where they are hardened.

Whilst sitting at this feast the wigwam was as silent as death, although we were not alone in it. This chief, like most others, had a plurality of wives, and all of them (some six or seven) were seated around the sides of the lodge, upon robes or mats placed upon the ground, and not allowed to speak, though they were in readiness to obey his orders or commands, which were uniformly given by signs-manual, and executed in the neatest and most silent manner.

When I arose to return, the pipe through which we had smoked was presented to me; and the robe on which I had sat, he gracefully raised by the corners and tendered it to me, explaining by signs that the paintings which were on it were the representations of the battles of his life, where he had fought and killed with his own hand fourteen of his enemies; that he had been two weeks engaged in painting it for me, and that he had invited me here on this occasion to present it to me.

ESCAPE FROM SLAVERY, Baltimore, 1838

Frederick Douglass

Douglass was born a slave in Tuckahoe, Maryland, in 1817. After his escape from slavery in a Baltimore shipyard he changed his name, settled in New Bedford, Massachussetts, and became a leading abolitionist. His autobiography was published as *Life and Times of Frederick Douglass: Written by Himself.*

My condition during the year of my escape, 1838, was comparatively a free and easy one, so far, at least, as the wants of the physical man were concerned; but the reader will bear in mind that my troubles from the beginning had been less physical than mental, and he will thus be prepared to find slave life was adding nothing to its charms for me as I grew older, and became more and more acquainted with it. The practice from week to week of openly robbing me of all my earnings, kept the nature and character of slavery constantly before me. I could be robbed by indirection, but this was too open and barefaced to be endured. I could see no reason why I should, at the end of each week, pour the reward of my honest toil into the purse of my master. My obligation to do this vexed me, and the manner in which Master Hugh received my wages vexed me yet more. Carefully counting the money, and rolling it out dollar by dollar, he would look me in the face as if he would search my heart as well as my pocket, and reproachfully ask me, "Is that all?" – implying that I had perhaps kept back part of my wages; or, if not so, the demand was made possibly to make me feel that, after all, I was an "unprofitable servant". Draining me of the last cent of my hard earnings, he would, however, occasionally, when I brought home an extra large sum, dole out to me a sixpence or shilling, with a view, perhaps, of enkindling my gratitude. But it had the opposite effect; it was an admission of my right to the whole sum. The fact that he gave me any part of my wages, was proof that he suspected I had a right to the whole of them; and I always felt uncomfortable after having received anything in this way, lest his giving me a few cents might possibly ease his conscience, and make him feel himself to be a pretty honourable robber, after all.

Held to a strict account, and kept under a close watch – the old suspicion of my running away not having been entirely removed – to accomplish my escape seemed a very difficult thing. The railroad from Baltimore to Philadelphia was under regulations so stringent, that even *free* coloured travellers were almost excluded. They must have free papers; they must be measured, and carefully examined, before they could enter the cars, and could go only in the daytime, even when so examined. The steamboats were under regulations equally stringent. And still more, and worse than all, all the great turnpikes leading Northward, were beset with kidnappers; a class of men who watched the newspapers for advertisements for runaway slaves, thus making their living by the accursed reward of slave-hunting.

My discontent grew upon me, and I was on the constant lookout for means to get away. With money I could easily have managed the matter, and from this consideration I hit upon the plan of soliciting the privilege of hiring my time. It was quite common in Baltimore to allow slaves this privilege, and was the practice also in New Orleans. A slave who was considered trustworthy could, by paying his master a definite sum regularly, at the end of each week, dispose of his time as he liked. It so happened that I was not in very good odour, and I was far from being a trustworthy slave. Nevertheless, I watched my opportunity when Master Thomas came to Baltimore – for I was still his property, Hugh only acting as his agent – in the spring of 1838, to purchase his spring supply of goods, and applied to him directly for the much-coveted privilege of hiring my time. This request Master Thomas unhesitatingly refused to grant; and he charged me, with some sternness, with inventing this stratagem to make my escape. He told me I could go *nowhere* but he would catch me; and, in the event of my running away, I might be assured he should spare no pains in his efforts to recapture me. He recounted, with a good deal of eloquence, the many kind offices he had done me, and exhorted me to be contented and obedient. "Lay out no plans for the future," said he; "if you behave yourself properly, I will take care of you." Now, kind and considerate as this offer was, it failed to soothe me into repose. In spite of all Master Thomas had said, and in spite of my own efforts to the contrary, the injustice and wickedness of slavery was always uppermost in my thoughts, strengthening my purpose to make my escape at the earliest moment possible.

About two months after applying to Master Thomas for the privilege of hiring my time, I applied to Master Hugh for the same liberty, supposing him to be unacquainted with the fact, that I had made a similar application to Master Thomas, and had been refused. My boldness in making this request fairly astounded him at first. He gazed at me in amazement. But I had many good reasons for pressing the matter, and, after listening to them awhile he did not absolutely refuse, but told me he would think of it. There was hope for me in this. Once master of my own time, I felt sure that I could make over and above my obligation to him – a dollar or two every week. Some slaves had made enough in this way to purchase their freedom. It was a sharp spur to their industry; and some of the most enterprising coloured men in Baltimore hired themselves in that way.

After mature reflection, as I suppose it was, Master Hugh granted me the privilege in question, on the following terms: I was to be allowed all my time; to make all bargains for work, and to collect my own wages; and in return for this liberty, I was required or obliged to pay him three dollars at the end of week, and to board and clothe myself, and buy my own caulking tools. A failure in any of these particulars would put an end to the privilege. This was a hard bargain. The wear and tear of clothing, the losing and breaking of tools, and the expense of board made it necessary for me to earn at least six dollars per week to keep even with the world. All who are acquainted with caulking know how uncertain and irregular that employment is. It can be done to advantage only in dry weather, for it is useless to put wet oakum into a ship's seam. Rain or shine, however, work or no work, at the end of each week the money must be forthcoming.

Master Hugh seemed much pleased with this arrangement for a time; and well he might be, for it was decidedly in his favour. It relieved him of all anxiety concerning me. His money was sure. He had armed my love of liberty with a lash and a driver far more efficient than any I had before known; and while he derived all the benefits of slave-holding by the arrangement, without its evils, I endured all the evils of being a slave, and yet suffered all the care and anxiety of a responsible freeman. "Nevertheless," thought I, "it is a valuable privilege – another step in my career toward freedom." It was something, even to be permitted to stagger under the disadvantages of liberty, and I was determined to hold on to the newly-gained footing by all proper industry. I was ready to work by night as by day, and being in the possession of excellent health, I was not only able to meet my current expenses, but also to lay by a small sum at the end of each week. All went on thus from the months of May till August; then, for reasons which will become apparent as I proceed, my much-valued liberty was wrested from me.

During the week previous to this calamitous event, I had made arrangements with a few young friends to accompany them on Saturday night to a camp-meeting, to be held about twelve miles from Baltimore. On the evening of our intended start for the camp-ground, something occurred in the shipyard where I was at work, which detained me unusually late, and compelled me either to disappoint my friends, or to neglect carrying my weekly dues to Master Hugh. Knowing that I had the money and could hand it to him on another day, I decided to go on the camp-meeting, and to pay him the three dollars for the past week on my return. Once on the camp-ground, I was induced to remain one day longer then I intended when I left home. But as soon as I returned I went directly to his home in Fell Street, to hand him his (my) money. Unhappily the fatal mistake had been made. I found him exceedingly angry. He exhibited all the signs of apprehension and wrath which a slave-holder might be surmised to exhibit on the supposed escape of a favourite slave. "You rascal! I have a great mind to give you a sound whipping. How dare you go out of the city without first asking and obtaining my permission?" "Sir," I said, "I hired my time and paid you the price you asked for it. I did not know that it was any part of the bargain that I should ask you when or where I should go." "You did not know, you rascal! You are bound to show yourself here every Saturday night." After reflecting a few moments, he became somewhat cooled down; but evidently greatly troubled, and said; "Now, you scoundrel, you have done for yourself; you shall hire your time no longer. The next thing I shall hear of, will be your running way. Bring home your tools at once. I'll teach you how to go off in this way."

Thus ended my partial freedom. I could hire my time no longer; and I obeyed my master's orders at once. The little taste of liberty which I had had – although as it will be seen, that taste was far from being unalloyed – by no means enhanced my contentment with slavery. Punished by Master Hugh, it was now my turn to punish him. "Since," thought I, "you *will* make a slave of me, I will await your order in all things." So, instead of going to look for work on Monday morning, as I had formerly done, I remained at home during the entire week, without the performance of a single stroke of work. Saturday night came, and he called upon me as usual for my wages. I, of course, told him I had done no work, and had no wages. Here we were at the point of coming to blows. His wrath had been accumulating during the whole week; for he evidently saw that I was making no effort to get work, but was most aggravatingly awaiting his orders in all things. As I look back to this behaviour of mine, I scarcely know what possessed me, thus to trifle with one who had such unlimited power to bless or blast me. Master Hugh raved, and swore he would "get hold of me", but wisely for *him*, and happily for *me*, his wrath employed only those harmless, impalpable missiles which roll from a limber tongue. In my desperation I had fully made up my mind to measure strength with him, in case he should attempt to execute his threats. I am glad there was no occasion for this, for resistance to him could not

have ended so happily for me, as it did in the case of Covey. Master
Hugh was not a man to be safely resisted by a slave; and I freely
own that in my conduct toward him, in this instance, there was
more folly than wisdom. He closed his reproof, by telling me that
hereafter I need give myself no uneasiness about getting work; he
"would himself see to getting work for me, and enough of it at
that". This threat, I confess, had some terror in it, and on thinking
the matter over during the Sunday, I resolved not only to save him
the trouble of getting me work, but that on the third day of
September I would attempt to make my escape. His refusal to
allow me to hire my time therefore hastened the period of my
flight. I had three weeks in which to prepare for my journey.

Once resolved, I felt a certain degree of repose, and on Monday
morning, instead of waiting for Master Hugh to seek employment
for me, I was up by break of day, and off to the shipyard of Mr
Butler, on the City Block, near the drawbridge. I was a favourite
with Mr Butler, and, young as I was, I had served as his foreman,
on the float-stage, at caulking. Of course I easily obtained work,
and at the end of the week, which, by-the-way, was exceedingly
fine, I brought Master Hugh nine dollars. The effect of this mark of
returning good sense on my part, was excellent. He was very much
pleased; he took the money, commended me, and told me I might
have done the same thing the week before. It is a blessed thing that
the tyrant may not always know the thoughts and purposes of his
victim. Master Hugh little knew my plans. The going to camp-
meeting without asking his permission, the insolent answers to his
reproaches, the sulky deportment of the week, after being deprived
of the privilege of hiring my time, had awakened the suspicion that
I might be cherishing disloyal purposes. My object, therefore, in
working steadily, was to remove suspicion; and in this I succeeded
admirably. He probably thought I was never better satisfied with
my condition than at the very time I was planning my escape. The
second week passed, and I again carried him my full week's wages
– *nine dollars*; and so well pleased was he that he gave me *twenty-five
cents!* and bade me "make good use of it". I told him I would do so;
for one of the uses to which I intended to put it was to pay my fare
on the "underground railroad".

Things without went on as usual; but I was passing through the
same internal excitement and anxiety which I had experienced
two years and a half before. The failure in that instance was not
calculated to increase my confidence in the success of this, my

second attempt; and I knew that a second failure could not leave
me where my first did. I must either get to the *far North* or *be sent* to
the *far South*. Besides the exercise of mind from this state of facts, I
had the painful sensation of being about to separate from a circle of
honest and warm-hearted friends. The thought of such a separa-
tion, where the hope of ever meeting again was excluded, and
where there could be no correspondence was very painful. It is my
opinion that thousands more would have escaped from slavery but
for the strong affection which bound them to their families,
relatives, and friends. The daughter was hindered by the love
she bore her mother, and the father by the love he bore his wife and
children, and so on to the end of the chapter. I had no relations in
Baltimore, and I saw no probability of ever living in the neighbourhood of sisters and brothers; but the thought of leaving my
friends was the strongest obstacle to my running away. The last
two days of the week, Friday and Saturday, were spent mostly in
collecting my things together for my journey. Having worked four
days that week for my master, I handed him six dollars on
Saturday night. I seldom spent my Sundays at home, and for
fear that something might be discovered in my conduct, I kept up
my custom and absented myself all day. On Monday, the third day
of September 1838, in accordance with my resolution, I bade
farewell to the city of Baltimore, and to that slavery which had
been my abhorrence from childhood.

In the first narrative of my experience in slavery, written nearly
forty years ago, and in various writings since, I have given the
public what I considered very good reasons for withholding the
manner of my escape. In substance these reasons were, first, that
such publication at any time during the existence of slavery might
be used by the master against the slave, and prevent the future
escape of any who might adopt the same means that I did. The
second reason was, if possible, still more binding to silence – for
publication of details would certainly have put in peril the persons
and property of those who assisted. Murder itself was not more
sternly and certainly punished in the State of Maryland, than that
of aiding and abetting the escape of a slave. Many coloured men,
for no other crime than that of giving aid to a fugitive slave, have,
like Charles T. Torrey, perished in prison. The abolition of slavery
in my native state and throughout the country, and the lapse of
time, render the caution hitherto observed no longer necessary.

But even since the abolition of slavery, I have sometimes thought it well enough to baffle curiosity, by saying that while slavery existed there were good reasons for not telling the manner of my escape, and since slavery had ceased to exist, there was no reason for telling it. I shall now, however, cease to avail myself of this formula, and as far as I can, endeavour to satisfy this very natural curiosity. I should perhaps have yielded to that feeling sooner, had there been anything very heroic or thrilling in the incidents connected with my escape, but I am sorry to say I have nothing of that sort to tell; and yet, the courage that could risk betrayal, and the bravery which was ready to encounter death, if need be, in pursuit of freedom, were essential features in the undertaking. My success was due to address rather than courage; to good luck rather than bravery. My means of escape were provided for me by the very men who were making laws to hold and bind me more securely in slavery. It was the custom in the State of Maryland to require the free coloured people to have what were called free papers. This instrument they were required to renew very often, and by charging a fee for this writing, considerable sums, from time to time, were collected by the State. In these papers the name, age, colour, height, and form of the free man were described, together with any scars or other marks upon his person, which could assist in his identification. This device of slave-holding ingenuity, like other devices of wickedness, in some measure defeated itself – since more than one man could be found to answer the same general description. Hence many slaves could escape by personating the owner of one set of papers; and this was often done as follows: A slave nearly or sufficiently answering the description set forth in papers, would borrow or hire them till he could by their means escape to a free State, and then, by mail or otherwise, return them to the owner. The operation was a hazardous one for the lender as well as the borrower. A failure on the part of the fugitive to send back the papers would imperil his benefactor, and the discovery of the papers in possession of the wrong man, would imperil both the fugitive and his friend. It was, therefore, an act of supreme trust on the part of a freeman of colour thus to put in jeopardy his own liberty, that another might be free. It was, however, not unfrequently bravely done, and was seldom discovered. I was not so fortunate to sufficiently resemble any of my free acquaintances as to answer the description of their papers. But I had one friend – a sailor – who owned a sailor's protection, which answered somewhat the purpose of free papers – describing his person, and certifying to the fact that he was a free American sailor. The instrument had at its head the American eagle, which gave it the appearance at once of an authorised document. This protection did not, when in my hands, describe its bearer very accurately. Indeed, it culled for a man much darker than myself, and close examination of it would have caused my arrest at the start. In order to avoid this fatal scrutiny on the part of the railroad official, I had arranged with Isaac Rolls, a hackman, to bring my baggage to the train just on the moment of its starting, and I jumped upon the car myself when the train was already in motion. Had I gone into the station and offered to purchase a ticket, I should have been instantly and carefully examined, and undoubtedly arrested. In choosing this plan upon which to act, I considered the jostle of the train, and the natural haste of the conductor, in a train crowded with passengers, and relied upon my skill and address in playing the sailor as described in my protection, to do the rest. One element in my favour, was the kind feeling which prevailed in Baltimore and other seaports at the time, towards "those who go down to the sea in ships". "Free trade and sailors' rights" expressed the sentiment of the country just then. In my clothing, I was rigged out in sailor style. I had on a red shirt and a tarpaulin hat and black cravat, tied in sailor fashion, carelessly and loosely about my neck. My knowledge of ships and sailor's talk came much to my assistance, for I knew a ship from stem to stern, and from keelson to cross-trees, and could talk sailor like an "old salt". On sped the train, and I was well on the way to Havre de Grace before the conductor came into the negro car to collect tickets and examine the papers of his black passengers. This was a critical moment in the drama. My whole future depended upon the decision of this conductor. Agitated I was while this ceremony was proceeding, but still externally, at least, I was apparently calm and self-possessed. He went on with his duty – examining several coloured passengers before reaching me. He was somewhat harsh in tone, and peremptory in manner until he reached me, when, strangely enough, and to my surprise and relief, his whole manner changed. Seeing that I did not readily produce my free papers, as the other coloured persons in the car had done, he said to me, in a friendly contrast with that observed towards the others: "I suppose you have your free papers?" To which I answered: "No, sir; I never carry my free papers to sea with me." 'But you have something to show that you are a free man, have you not?" "Yes, sir," I answered; "I have a paper with the American eagle on it, and that will carry me round the world." With this I drew from my deep sailor's pocket my seaman's protection, as before described. The merest glance at the paper satisfied him, and he took my fare and went on about his business. This moment of time was one of the most anxious I ever experienced. Had the conductor looked closely at the paper, he could not have failed to discover that it called for a very different looking person from myself, and in that case, it would have been his duty to arrest me on that instant, and send me back to Baltimore from the first station. When he left me with the assurance that I was all right, though much relieved, I realised that I was still in great danger. I was still in Maryland, and subject to arrest at any moment. I saw on the train several persons who would have known me in any other clothes, and I feared they might recognise me, even in my sailor "rig", and report me to the conductor, who would then subject me to a closer examination, which I knew well would be fatal to me.

Though I was not a murderer fleeing from justice, I felt perhaps quite as miserable as such a criminal. The train was moving at a very high rate of speed for that time of railroad travel, but to my anxious mind, it was moving far too slowly. Minutes were hours, and hours were days, during this part of my flight. After Maryland, I was to pass through Delaware – another slave State, where slave-catchers generally awaited their prey, for it was not in the interior of the State, but on its borders, that these human hounds were most vigilant and active. The border lines between slavery and freedom were the dangerous ones, for the fugitives. The heart of no fox or deer, with hungry hounds on his trail in full chase, could have beaten more anxiously or noisily than did mine, from the time I left Baltimore till I reached Philadelphia. The passage of the Susquehanna river at Havre de Grace was made by ferry boat at that time, on board of which I met a young coloured man by the name of Nichols, who came very near betraying me. He was a "hand" on the boat, but instead of minding his business, he insisted upon knowing me, and asking me dangerous questions as to where I was going, and when I was coming back, etc. I got away from my old and inconvenient acquaintance as soon as I could decently do so, and went to another part of the boat. Once across the river I encountered a new danger. Only a few days before, I had been at work on a revenue-cutter, in Mr Price's shipyard, under the care of

Captain McGowan. On the meeting at this point of the two trains, the one going South stopped on the track just opposite to the one going North, and it so happened that this Captain McGowan sat at a window where he could see me very distinctly, and would certainly have recognised me had he looked at me but for a second. Fortunately, in the hurry of the moment, he did not see me; and the trains soon passed each other on their respective ways. But this was not my only hair's breadth escape. A German blacksmith whom I knew well, was on the train with me, and looked at me very intently, as if he thought he had seen me somewhere before in his travels. I really believe he knew me, but had no heart to betray me. At any rate he saw me escaping and held his peace.

The last point of imminent danger, and the one I dreaded most, was Wilmington. Here we left the train, and took the steamboat for Philadelphia. In making the change here I again apprehended arrest, but no one disturbed me, and I was soon on the broad and beautiful Delaware, speeding away to the Quaker City. On reaching Philadelphia in the afternoon, I enquired of a coloured man how I could get on to New York. He directed me to the William Street depot, and thither I went, taking the train that night. I reached New York on Tuesday morning, having completed the journey in less than twenty-four hours. Such is briefly the manner of my escape from slavery – and the end of my experience as a slave. Other chapters will tell the story of my life as a freeman.

"WHERE FLAG NEVER WAVED BEFORE": FREMONT SUMMITS THE ROCKY MOUNTAINS, 12–15 August 1842

John Charles Fremont

Fremont (1813–90) led two major expeditions into the interior of North America, his 1842 exploration of the Rocky Mountains opening the way for overland crossings of the continent. In 1856 Fremont stood for the presidency as a Republican.

Early in the morning [12 August] we left the camp, fifteen in number, well armed, of course, and mounted on our best mules. A pack-animal carried our provisions, with a coffee-pot and kettle, and three or four tin cups. Every man had a blanket strapped over his saddle, to serve for his bed, and the instruments were carried by turns on their backs. We entered directly on rough and rocky ground; and, just after crossing the ridge, had the good fortune to shoot an antelope. We heard the roar, and had a glimpse of a waterfall as we rode along, and, crossing in our way two fine streams, tributary to the Colorado, in about two hours ride we reached the top of the first row or range of the mountains. Here, again, a view of the most romantic beauty met our eyes. It seemed as if, from the vast expanse of uninteresting prairie we had passed over, Nature had collected all her beauties together in one chosen place. We were overlooking a deep valley, which was entirely occupied by three lakes, and from the brink to the surrounding ridges rose precipitously five hundred and a thousand feet, covered with the dark green of the balsam pine, relieved on the border of the lake with the light foliage of the aspen. They all communicated with each other, and the green of the waters, common to mountain lakes of great depth, showed that it would be impossible to cross them. The surprise manifested by our guides when these impassable obstacles suddenly barred our progress proved that they were among the hidden treasures of the place, unknown even to the wandering trappers of the region. Descending the hill, we proceeded to make our way along the margin to the southern extremity. A narrow strip of angular fragments of rock sometimes afforded a rough pathway for our mules, but generally we rode along the shelving side, occasionally scrambling up, at a considerable risk of tumbling back into the lake. . . .

The hills on this southern end were low, and the lake looked like a mimic sea, as the waves broke on the sandy beach in the force of a strong breeze. There was a pretty open spot, with fine grass for our mules; and we made our noon halt on the beach, under the shade of some large hemlocks. We resumed our journey after a halt of about an hour, making our way up the ridge on the western side of the lake. In search of smoother ground, we rode a little inland; and, passing through groves of aspen, soon found ourselves again among the pines. Emerging from these, we struck the summit of the ridge above the upper end of the lake.

We had reached a very elevated point, and in the valley below, and among the hills, were a number of lakes of different levels; some two or three hundred feet above others, with which they communicated by foaming torrents. Even to our great height the roar of the cataracts came up, and we could see them leaping down in lines of snowy foam. From this scene of busy waters, we turned abruptly into the stillness of a forest . . . Towards evening we reached a defile, or rather a hole in the mountains, entirely shut in by dark, pine-covered rocks.

A small stream, with scarcely perceptible current, flowed through a level bottom of perhaps eighty yards width, where the grass was saturated with water. Into this the mules were turned, and were neither hobbled nor picketed during the night, as the fine pasturage took away all temptation to stray; and we made our bivouac in the pines. The surrounding masses were all of granite. While supper was being prepared, I set out on an excursion in the neighbourhood, accompanied by one of my men. We wandered about among the crags and ravines until dark, richly repaid for our walk by a fine collection of plants, many of them in full bloom. Ascending a peak to find the place of our camp, we saw that the little defile in which we lay, communicated with the long green valley of some stream, which, here locked up in the mountains, far away to the south, found its way in a dense forest to the plains.

Looking along its upward course, it seemed to conduct, by a smooth gradual slope, directly towards the peak, which, from long consultation as we approached the mountain, we had decided to be the highest of the range. Pleased with the discovery of so fine a road for the next day, we hastened down to the camp, where we arrived just in time for supper. Our table-service was rather scant; and we held the meat in our hands, and clean rocks made good plates, on which we spread our macaroni. Among all the strange places on which we had occasion to encamp during our long journey, none have left so vivid an impression on my mind as the camp of this evening. The disorder of the masses which surrounded us – the little hole through which we saw the stars overhead – the dark pines where we slept – and the rocks lit up with the glow of our fires, made a night-picture of very wild beauty.

13th. The morning was bright and pleasant, just cool enough to make exercise agreeable, and we soon entered the defile I had seen the preceding day. . . . This road continued for about three miles, when we suddenly reached its termination in one of the grand views which, at every turn, meet the traveller in this magnificent region. Here the defile up which we had travelled opened out into a small lawn, where, in a little lake, the stream had its source. . . . I determined to leave our animals here, and make the rest of our way on foot. The peak appeared so near that there was no doubt of our returning before night; and a few men were left in charge of the mules, with our provisions and blankets. We took with us nothing but our arms and instruments, and, as the day had become warm, the greater part left our coats.

Having made an early dinner, we started again. We were soon involved in the most ragged precipices, nearing the central chain very slowly, and rising but little. The first ridge hid a succession of others; and when, with great fatigue and difficulty, we had climbed up five hundred feet, it was but to make an equal descent on the other side; all these intervening places were filled with small deep lakes, which met the eye in every direction, descending from one level to another, sometimes under bridges formed by huge fragments of granite, beneath which was heard the roar of the water. These constantly obstructed our path, forcing us to make long detours, frequently obliged to retrace our steps, and frequently falling among the rocks. Maxwell was precipitated towards the face of a precipice, and saved himself from going over by throwing himself flat on the ground. We clambered on, always expecting, with every ridge that we crossed, to reach the foot of the peaks, and always disappointed, until about four o'clock, when, pretty well worn out, we reached the shore of a little lake, in which was a rocky island. We remained here a short time to rest, and continued on around the lake, which had in some places a beach of white sand, and in others was bound with rocks, over which the way was difficult and dangerous, as the water from innumerable springs made them very slippery.

By the time we had reached the further side of the lake, we found ourselves all exceedingly fatigued, and, much to the satisfaction of the whole party, we encamped. . . . We had nothing to eat tonight. Lajeunesse, with several others, took their guns and sallied out in search of a goat, but returned unsuccessful. At sunset, the barometer stood at 20.522; the attached thermometer 50°. Here we had the misfortune to break our thermometer, having now only that attached to the barometer. I was taken ill shortly after we had encamped, and continued so until late in the night, with violent headache and vomiting. This was probably caused by the excessive fatigue I had undergone, and want of food, and perhaps also, in some measure, by the rarity of the air. The night was cold, as a violent gale from the north had sprung up at sunset, which entirely blew away the heat of the fires. The cold, and our granite beds, had not been favorable to sleep, and we were glad to see the face of the sun in the morning. Not being delayed by any preparation for breakfast, we set out immediately.

On every side, as we advanced, was heard the roar of waters, and of a torrent, which we followed up a short distance, until it expanded into a lake about one mile in length. On the northern side of the lake was a bank of ice, or rather of snow covered with a crust of ice. Carson had been our guide into the mountains, and, agreeably to his advice, we left this little valley, and took to the ridges again, which we found extremely broken, and where we were again involved among precipices. Here were ice-fields; among which we were all dispersed, seeking each the best path to ascend the peak. Mr Preuss attempted to walk along the upper edge of one of these fields, which sloped away at an angle of about twenty degrees; but his feet slipped from under him, and he went plunging down the plain. A few hundred feet below, at the bottom, were some fragments of sharp rock, on which he landed and, though he turned a couple of somersets, fortunately received no injury beyond a few bruises. Two of the men, Clement Lambert and Descoteaux, had been taken ill, and lay down on the rocks, a short distance below; and at this point I was attacked with headache and giddiness, accompanied by vomiting, as on the day before. Finding myself unable to proceed, I sent the barometer over to Mr Preuss, who was in a gap two or three hundred yards distant, desiring him to reach the peak if possible, and take an observation there. He found himself unable to proceed further in that direction . . . Carson, who had gone over to him, succeeded in reaching one of the snowy summits of the main ridge, whence he saw the peak towards which all our efforts had been directed, towering eight or ten hundred feet into the air above him. In the mean time, finding myself grow rather worse than better, and doubtful how far my strength would carry me, I sent Basil Lajeunesse, with four men, back to the place where the mules had been left.

We were now better acquainted with the topography of the country, and I directed him to bring back with him, if it were in any way possible, four or five mules, with provisions and blankets. With me were Maxwell and Ayer; and after we had remained nearly an hour on the rock, it became so unpleasantly cold, though the day was bright, that we set out on our return to the camp, at which we all arrived safely, straggling in one after the other. I continued ill during the afternoon, but became better towards sundown, when my recovery was completed by the appearance of Basil and four men, all mounted. The men who had gone with him had been too much fatigued to return, and were relieved by those in charge of the horses; but in his powers of endurance Basil resembled more a mountain-goat than a man. They brought blankets and provisions, and we enjoyed well our dried meat and a cup of good coffee. We rolled ourselves up in our blankets, and with our feet turned to a blazing fire, slept soundly until morning.

15th. . . . When we had secured strength for the day by a hearty breakfast, we covered what remained, which was enough for one meal, with rocks, in order that it might be safe from any marauding bird, and, saddling our mules, turned our faces once more towards the peaks. This time we determined to proceed quietly and cautiously, deliberately resolved to accomplish our object if it were within the compass of human means. We were of opinion that a long defile which lay to the left of yesterday's route would lead us to the foot of the main peak. Our mules had been refreshed by the fine grass in the little ravine at the Island camp, and we intended to ride up the defile as far as possible, in order to husband our strength for the main ascent. . . .

We managed to get our mules up to a little bench about a hundred feet above the lakes, where there was a patch of good grass, and turned them loose to graze. During our rough ride to this place, they had exhibited a wonderful surefootedness. Parts of the defile were filled with angular, sharp fragments of rock, three or four and eight or ten feet cube; and among these they had worked their way, leaping from one narrow point to another, rarely making a false step, and giving us no occasion to dismount. Having divested ourselves of every unnecessary encumbrance, we commenced the ascent. This time, like experienced travellers, we did not press ourselves, but climbed leisurely, sitting down as soon as we found breath beginning to fail. At intervals we reached places where a number of springs gushed from the rocks, and about 1,800 feet above the lakes came to the snow line. From this point our progress was uninterrupted climbing. Hitherto I had worn a pair of thick moccasins, with soles of *parflèche*, but here I put on a light, thin pair, which I had brought for the purpose, as now the use of our toes became necessary to a further advance. I availed myself of a sort of comb of the mountain, which stood against the wall like a buttress, and which the wind and the solar radiation, joined to the steepness of the smooth rock, had kept almost entirely free from snow. Up this I made my way rapidly. Our cautious method of advancing at the outset had spared my strength; and, with the exception of a slight disposition to headache, I felt no remains of yesterday's illness. In a few minutes we reached a point where the buttress was overhanging, and there was no other way of surmounting the difficulty than by passing around one side of it, which was the face of a vertical precipice of several hundred feet.

Putting hands and feet in the crevices between the blocks, I succeeded in getting over it, and, when I reached the top, found my companions in a small valley below. Descending to them, we continued climbing, and in a short time reached to the crest. I sprang upon the summit, and another step would have precipitated me into an immense snow-field five hundred feet below. To the edge of this field was a sheer icy precipice; and then, with a gradual fall, the field sloped off for about a mile, until it struck the foot of another lower ridge. I stood on a narrow crest, about three feet in width . . . As soon as I had gratified the first feelings of curiosity, I descended, and each man ascended in his turn; for I would only allow one at a time to mount the unstable and precarious slab, which it seemed a breath would hurl into the abyss below. We mounted the barometer in the snow of the summit, and fixing a ramrod in a crevice, unfurled the national flag to wave in the breeze where never flag waved before. During our morning's ascent, we had met no sign of animal life, except the small sparrow-like bird . . . A stillness the most profound and a terrible solitude-forced themselves constantly on the mind as the great features of the place. Here, on the summit, where the stillness was absolute, unbroken by any sound, and solitude complete, we thought ourselves beyond the region of animated life; but while we were sitting on the rock, a solitary bee came winging his flight from the eastern valley, and lit on the knee of one of the men.

It was a strange place, the icy rock and the highest peak of the Rocky mountains, for a lover of warm sunshine and flowers; and we pleased ourselves with the idea that he was the first of his species to cross the mountain barrier – a solitary pioneer to foretell the advance of civilization. I believe that a moment's thought would have made us let him continue his way unharmed; but we carried out the law of this country, where all animated nature seems at war; and, seizing him immediately, put him in at least a fit place – in the leaves of a large book, among the flowers we had collected on

our way. The barometer stood at 18.293, the attached thermometer at 44°; giving for the elevation of this summit 13,570 feet
above the Gulf of Mexico, which may be called the highest flight of
the bee. It is certainly the highest known flight of that insect. From
the description given by Mackenzie of the mountains where he
crossed them, with that of a French officer still further to the north,
and Colonel Long's measurements to the south, joined to the
opinion of the oldest traders of the country, it is presumed that
this is the highest peak of the Rocky mountains.

ENCOUNTER WITH A GRIZZLY BEAR, Rocky Mountains, 20 August 1843

Osborne Russell

Russell was a trapper. The 1840s was the death decade of the fur trade,
and shortly after his 1843 expedition Russell gave up trapping. He settled
in Oregon, before becoming a judge in a California mining camp.

On the 20th of August we started again to hunt meat: we left the
Fort and travelled abot 6 miles when we discovered a Grizzly Bear
digging and eating roots in a piece of marshy ground near a large
bunch of willows. The Mullattoe approached within 100 yards and
shot him thro the left shoulder he gave a hideous growl and sprang
into the thicket. The Mullattoe then said "let him go he is a
dangerous varmint" but not being acquainted with the nature of
these animals I determined on making another trial, and persuaded the Mullattoe to assist me we walked round the bunch of
willows where the Bear lay keeping close together, with our rifles
ready cocked and presented towards the bushes until near the
place where he had entered, when we heard a sullen growl about
10 ft from us, which was instantly followed by a spring of the Bear
toward us; his enormous jaws extended and eyes flashing fire. Oh
Heavens! was ever anything so hideous? We could not retain
sufficient presence of mind to shoot at him but took to our heels
separating as we ran the Bear taking after me, finding I could
outrun him he left and turned to the other who wheeled about and
discharged his rifle covering the Bear with smoke and fire the ball
however missing him he turned and bounding toward me – I could
go no further without jumping into a large quagmire which
hemmed me on three sides, I was obliged to turn about and face
him he came within about 10 paces of me then suddenly stopped

and raised his ponderous body erect, his mouth wide open, gazing at me with a beastly laugh at this moment I pulled trigger and I knew not what else to do and hardly knew that I did this but it accidentally happened that my rifle was pointed towards the Bear when I pulled and the ball piercing his heart, he gave one bound from me uttered a deathly howl and fell dead: but I trembled as if I had an ague fit for half an hour after, we butchered him as he was very fat packed the meat and skin on our horses and returned to the Fort with the trophies of our bravery, but I secretly determined in my own mind never to molest another wounded Grizzly Bear in a marsh or thicket.

SUN DANCE OF THE SIOUX, Great Plains, c. 1843

George Catlin

At its most complex, the Sun Dance required young warriors to indulge in the self-torture Catlin describes below. Although the Sun Dance was Teton in origin, it was borrowed by many other Plains tribes.

An inch or more of the flesh on each shoulder, or each breast was taken up between the thumb and finger by the man who held the knife in his right hand; and the knife, which had been ground sharp on both edges, and then hacked and notched with the blade of another, to make it produce as much pain as possible, was forced through the flesh below the fingers, and being withdrawn, was followed with a splint or skewer, from the other, who held a bunch of such in his left hand, and was ready to force them through the wound. There were then two cords lowered down from the top of the lodge, which were fastened to these splints or skewers, and they instantly began to haul him up; he was thus raised until his body was suspended from the ground where he rested, until the knife and a splint were passed through the flesh or integuments in a similar manner on each arm below the shoulder, below the elbow, on the thighs, and below the knees.

In some instances they remained in a reclining position on the ground until this painful operation was finished, which was performed, in all instances, exactly on the same parts of the body and limbs; and which, in its progress, occupied some five or six minutes.

Each one was then instantly raised with the cords, until the weight of his body was suspended by them, and then, while the

blood was streaming down their limbs, the bystanders hung upon
the splints each man's appropriate shield, bow and quiver, and in
many instances, the skull of a buffalo with the horns on it. was
attached to each lower arm and each lower leg, for the purpose,
probably, of preventing by their great weight, the struggling,
which might otherwise have taken place to their disadvantage
whilst they were hung up.

OVERLAND TO CALIFORNIA: THE PIONEER'S VIEW, 1846

William E. Taylor

In 1843 1000 pioneers drove off in their wagons into the Wilderness at
Independence, Missouri, determined to go the "plains across" to the
Pacific Coast. Their success prompted thousands of other pioneers to surge
to the promised lands of California and Oregon. William E. Taylor was
among them. His personal diary is a laconic record of all the dangers,
boredoms and triumphs which faced the pioneers in their "prarie schoon-
ers" on the 2000-mile journey West.

Monday April the 20th 1846. We this day lef home for Oregon and
proceeded 5 [15?] miles to Elk horn whare we got some work done
on our waggon Our company consisting of Craig Shreve and myself

Tuesday, the 21. We Left at 10 O'clock and Standlly's wagon
Broak 2 miles from Elk horn whare we continued all night

Wed. 22. Left at 12 O'clock after having finished all the repares
our waggon proceeded about 3 miles This day one of our Crowd
(Shreve) took his *[illegible]* Mr Lad Joined us

Th. 23. went 12 miles

Friday 24. passed plattsburg travailed 12 miles

Sat. 25. traveled 20 miles

Sund. 26. got to St. Josephs, traveled 3 miles

Monday 27 Tuesday 28 we remained at St. Josephs

Wen. 29 we Left St. Josephs went to parrots ferry 5 miles above
town. Weather fair wind high

Th 30 Remained In Camp Wind prevents us from Crossing

May 1 Crossed over the river which was very hig for the season
we find an abundance of grass for the oxen

2 Remained in camp

3. Struck our tents and proceeded to wolf River whare we had
some difficulty in getting over went 14 mils

4. Started Early passed the Iowa Agency, distance 25 [miles]

5. Left camp Early travled 15 miles

6. We overtook 18 waggons at the Nemihaw River crossed over found 6 wagons encamped making 27 waggons and 50 men. A view from the prairie hills of this Little River is very sublime and beautiful it Surpasses any thing I have yet seen

7 we traveled about 20 miles the road verry undulating and the Land of the Richest kind Scarcely any timber or Water Some symptoms of discord in camp owing to all not being present at the Election of officers

8 we travel^d over Level wet prairie 18 ms

9 we traveld 2½ miles Crossed one fork of the Blue. Staid all day found we were wrong

10 Changed our course Crossed over the other fork of Blue came to Independence trail we are ahead of all distance 16 miles

11 traveled 14 miles Camped in a small grove on a tributary of Blue

12 Camped on Horse Creek 7 miles

13 Travailed 7 miles Camped on Blue

14 Camped on Sandy a tributary of the Blue after travling 20 miles

15 Camped on the blue 16 miles verry warm The Mercury stands 76 at noon in the shade

16 traveld up Blue 16 miles Stanley killed a deer Mercury Stood at 86 at noon in the shade

17 traveled 4 miles

18 we went But 2 miles owing to the indisposition of Mrs Munkerass who brough an increase in to the emigration

19 travailed 8 miles

20 traveled 16 up Blue

21 Arrived at the Nebraska, travailed 17 miles

22 to day we saw a party of pawnees some hunters quite friendly distance 18 miles

23 traveld 8 miles

24 traveld 20 miles Saw and killed some Buffalo

25 traveled 18 miles thousands of Buffalo

26 traveled 18 A sevier h[a]il storm in the Evning.

27   "   16 miles quite Cool Mercury at 57

28   "   23 another hail Storm Reached the South fork of platt

the 29 travaled 16 miles first used the excrement of the Buffalo for fuel

30 Crossed the South fork which is one mill wide with an average depth of 18 inches dis. 12 miles this evening we had the most sevier storm I ever saw

31 Lay by all day owing to incessant Rain and intense Cold with Some Snow Tem. 48 Fah[renheit]

June the first today there was quit a snow storm passed over to the Ash hollow distance 25 miles Tem. 38 deg. Fah.

2 Staid here all day

3 went 10 miles Camped out of the Rain Tem. 57 deg

4 travelled 20 miles Saw wild horses

5 travaled 20 miles. Came in sight of Castle Rock also the Chimney Rock Crossed Sandy

6 passed the Chimney Rock dist. 25 miles

7 passed Scotts Bluff Beautiful Scenry dist 18 miles

8 Company divided distance 19 miles

9 Travelled 15 miles Temp. 90 deg of Fah

10 Went 7 miles came to Laramie. Tem. 100 deg of Fah

11 Lay By. mercury at 100 Fah.

12 travelled 20 miles through the Black hills Camped on the Bitter Cotton Wood a Smal Stream

13 Came 20 miles camped on horse Shoe Creek

14 camped on Butte creek distance 20 miles

15 camped on Black Creek dist 20 miles Red Rock

16 travelled 18 miles camped on deer creek

17 traveled 16 miles Tem 90 deg of Fah.

18 Came to the Crossing of platt not fordable met some Return emigrants Tem. 81 deg. of Fah.

19 Remained trying to cross our Cattle

20 Do Do 16 more waggons Came up

21 got all over Rafted the waggons Swam the Cattle

22 passed the Red Butt[e]s dist 12 miles a good Spring

23 Came to the Willow Spring distance 20 miles

24 20 miles Braught us to the Rock Independence

25 Passed the Kenion on Sweet water saw mountain sheep travelled 16 miles

26 Went 18 miles, passed a party of men

27 traveled 25 miles Thousands of buffalo

28 Lay By all day

29 Traveled 20 miles a plain view of the wind River mountains Covered with snow Bad roads Some Sick

30 Came to the South Pass at 16 miles

July the 1 23 miles Braught us to Little Sandy extremely sterile country in sight of eternal snow on the Bear River mountan

2 Broak a waggon a man sick dist 10 miles Camped on Big Seany [Sandy] Mr L W Hastings visited our camp

3 travelled 18 miles Tem. 29 deg. of Fah.

4 crossed the colorado of the west a stream of 40 Rods wide 2 feet deep dis. 16 miles

5 traveled 15 miles camped on Blacks Fork near half the company confined by sickness

6 traveled 2 miles Lay By on account of the sick Tem 90 Deg. of Fah.

7 Lay By Sick get worse Mr S Sublett & three others staid with us they ware from California Wrote home By them. Tem. 105

8 We Left the main croud with 7 waggons travelled 16 miles some Rain

9 16 miles Braught us to Bridger Shoshone in abundane Mr Joseph Walker et al from California

10 Lay By Indians visited us in great numbers

11 traveled 18 miles Cam[p]ed on muddy a bad camp

12 traveled 18 miles Camped at a good Spring

13 Crossed the Bear River mountain Rain 25 miles

14 16 miles Brought us to Smiths fork

15 traveled 22 verr[y] Bad Roads hard Rain

16 traveled 14 miles more Rain

17 21 Braught us to the Soda Spring

18 Lay By Rain thunder and Lightning

19 Left our company with our 2 waggons alon never shall I forget the deep Regret at a Leaving our friends passed the old Crater traveled 12 miles

20 our oxen sensable of the impropriety of Leaving their as well as our friends Left camp and ware overtaken 3 miles from the Soda Spring so that we only got to portneif River 7 miles

21 traveled 22 miles Crossed divers streams

22 traveled 21 to the Blue Spring 5 miles from fort Hall

23 passed Ft hall traveled 14 miles to portneiffe River.

24 traveled 18 mils passed the American falls of Snake or Saptin River.

25 travelled 18 miles to Casua Bad Road

26 Left the Oregon Road traveled 22 miles up the casua or Raft River good Road

27 traveled up casua 18 miles Rain Lightning and thunder

28 20 miles Braught us to a good Spring Road Bad Crossed over to goose creek [*deleted:* 10 miles]

29 we came 10 miles

30 travelled 15 miles

31 we came 18 miles Tem. 30 deg. Fah morning

August the 1 traveled 17 miles

2 passed a verry hot Spring 20 miles Struck the head of Marys River

3 met Black harriis and applegate who had Been to view a new Road to oregon and designed meeting the emigrants to turn them into it travelled 20 miles Tem 88 of Fah.

4 Traveled 17 miles down Marys Rive. Tem. 90

5 This day we came 20 miles sevral diggers [Indians]

6 passed sevral Remarkabley hot Springs 20 miles

7 Came 14 miles

8   "   17 miles hot Springs

9   "   16 miles

10   "   20 miles quit steril[e]

11   "   23 miles   "   "

12   "   18 miles Natural Soap

13   "   18 miles Salaeratus visited by Large party of Indians

14 Travelled 22 miles (Rain Lightning

15   "   20 miles. divergence of new oregon road

16   "   20   "   Extreme Sterility

17   "   25   "   to day we Suffered for water as the Road Left the River for 14 miles Rain

18 Lay By Joined By Col. Russell of Mo. & 8 others packing Tem. 42 morning 96 noon

19 20 miles Braught us to the Sink of Marys Riv Vegetation entirely disappear water verry bad

20 traveled all day and all night passed some Boiling Springs quite salt distance 40 miles making 60 miles that 8 of us had 12 gallons of Water Extreme suffering Reached Trucky

21 Lay by all day Tem 100 of Fah.

22 Entered the Siera Nevada or Cascade mts up Trucky vally 15 miles Tem 87 deg of Fah.

23 Traveled 18 miles Bad Road

24   "   10 miles came to timber Tem 94 deg Fah

25 Crossed a spur of the mts 12 miles Tem 84.

26 travelled 12 miles good Road Tem 32.

27   "   8 miles Trucky Lake Tem 30

28 travelled 1 mile up the worst mountain that waggons ever crossed sevier frost Tem 28

29 got up the mts. Distance 2 miles

30 travelled 3 miles Lay by the Ballance of day

31   "   15 miles on top of the mt. Bad Road Tem 22 at day Light & 60 at Sun down

Sept 1 travelled 7 miles Bad Bad Road Bear sign Tem. 40 deg morn

2 traveled 7 miles of distressing Road

3rd   "   8 miles ove if possable worse Road

4 Lay by to Rest our oxen

5 travled 16 miles principally upon the top of a high Spur of the mountain our Oxen are worn nearly out we have but three that are able to Render service and we have as steep a hill befor us as we have Left behind us Heaven only knows how we are to get Along Our Oxen are almost perishing for food and nothing grows in this hateful valley that will sustain life.

6 Lay by to day as yestardys Long drive has well nigh done for the oxen. We cut down Oak Bushes and trees, for them to Brows on, or such of them, as are able to Stand on their feet.

7 the indians drove off two of Mr Stanley's ablest Oxen; tho' we succeeded in Recapturing one of them We unloaded our waggons and packed the Load near a mile on our horses We then took four of the best yoaks of Oxen and put to the empty waggons with a man at each wheel and by such exertions as I have seldom saw used we got the wagons up one at a time and proceeded about 5 miles grass verry Scarce and dry Our oxen are as near gone as I ever saw oxen to be driven at all

8 This morning we found that the Indians had taken off another one of Stanley's oxen, it was seen by following the trail that they had taken him up a steep hill and carfully Covered Evry track for the distance of a mile he was taken probably whilst I was on guard. I do not know how he managed to affect this Roguery it must have been very Sly W[e] travelled 11 miles and Stoped at a Small patch of dry grass and no water for the Cattle or horses

9 we traveled 3 miles and Stoped for the day at a Little grass and a hole of water one of Mr Craigs Best oxen has gave out; the hills have got much Smaller and the Rocks are not so much in the way as on any part of the Road Since we Struck the waters of Trucky River

10 Lay by all day our oxen are so near worn out and our provisions are getting scarce

11 Started on slow went about 6 miles today we had to Leave an ox on the Road

12 we traveled 7 miles and Stopt we are in five miles of the first settlement today we left another ox we have but two oxen to our waggon

13 We this morning got into the Valley and stoped at Cap. Wm. Johnsons Whare we ware Recieved in the most Kind and hospitable manner We made several trades Bought a beef swaped our broak down oxen for fresh ons this day our company Lay by and so for several days distance 5 miles

So Ends my Diary

STEAMBOATS ON THE MISSISSIPPI, Hannibal, Missouri, c. 1845

Mark Twain

Twain's recollection was written in 1875.

When I was a boy, there was but one permanent ambition among my comrades in our village [Hannibal, Missouri] on the west bank of the Mississippi River. That was, to be a steamboatman. We had transient ambitions of other sorts, but they were only transient. When a circus came and went, it left us all burning to become clowns; the first negro minstrel show that came to our section left us all suffering to try that kind of life; now and then we had a hope that if we lived and were good, God would permit us to be pirates. These ambitions faded out, each in its turn; but the ambition to be a steamboatman always remained.

Once a day a cheap, gaudy packet arrived upward from St Louis, and another downward from Keokuk. Before these events, the day was glorious with expectancy; after them, the day was a dead and empty thing. Not only the boys, but the whole village, felt this. After all these years I can picture that old time to myself now, just as it was then: the white town drowsing in the sunshine of a summer's morning; the streets empty, or pretty nearly so; one or two clerks sitting in front of the Water Street stores, with their splint-bottomed chairs tilted back against the wall, chins on breasts, hats slouched over their faces, asleep – with shingle-shavings enough around to show what broke them down; a sow and a litter of pigs loafing along the sidewalk, doing a good business in watermelon rinds and seeds; two or three lonely little freight piles scattered about the "levee"; a pile of "skids" on the slope of the stone-paved wharf, and the fragrant town drunkard asleep in the shadow of them; two or three wood flats at the head of the wharf, but nobody to listen to the peaceful lapping of the wavelets against them; the great Mississippi, the majestic, the magnificent Mississippi, rolling its mile-wide tide along, shining in the sun; the dense forest away on the other side; the "point" above the town, and the "point" below, bounding the river-glimpse and turning it into a sort of sea, and withal a very still and brilliant and lonely one. Presently a film of dark smoke appears above one of those remote "points"; instantly a negro drayman, famous for his quick eye and prodigious voice, lifts up the cry, "S-t-e-a-m-boat a-comin'!" and the scene changes! The town drunkard stirs, the clerks wake up, a furious clatter of drays follows, every house and store pours out a human contribution, and all in a twinkling the dead town is alive and moving. Drays, carts, men, boys, all go hurrying from many quarters to a common centre, the wharf. Assembled there, the people fasten their eyes upon the coming boat as upon a wonder they are seeing for the first time. And the boat *is* rather a handsome sight, too. She is long and sharp and trim and pretty; she has two tall, fancy-topped chim-neys, with a gilded device of some kind swung between them; a fanciful pilot-house, all glass and "gingerbread", perched on top of the "texas" deck behind them; the paddle-boxes are gorgeous with a picture or with gilded rays above the boat's name; the boiler deck, the hurricane deck, and the texas deck are fenced and ornamented with clean white railings; there is a flag gallantly flying from the jack-staff; the furnace doors are open and the fires glaring bravely; the upper decks are black with passengers; the captain stands by the big bell, calm, imposing, the envy of all; great volumes of the blackest smoke are rolling and tumbling out of the chimneys – a husbanded grandeur created with a bit of pitch pine just before arriving at a town; the crew are grouped on the forecastle; the broad stage is run far out over the port bow, and an envied deck-hand stands picturesquely on the end of it with a coil of rope in his hand; the pent steam is screaming through the gauge-cocks, the captain lifts his hand, a bell rings, the wheels stop; then they turn back, churning the water to foam, and the steamer is at rest. Then such a scramble as there is to get aboard, and to get ashore, and to take in freight and to discharge freight, all at one and the same time; and such a yelling and cursing as the mates facilitate it all with! Ten minutes later the steamer is under way again, with no flag on the jack-staff and no black smoke issuing from the chimneys. After ten more minutes the town is dead again, and the town drunkard asleep by the skids once more.

Twain achieved his ambition to become a steamboatman; he was a pilot on the Mississippi between 1857–61. Steamboating also gave Samuel Clemens – to give Twain his real name – his *nom de plume*: "mark twain" is the call to sound two fathoms of depth.

BUFFALO HUNT, Great Plains, 1846

Francis Parkman

Within forty years of Parkman's exploit, *bos bison Americanus* was almost exterminated by hunting (Buffalo Bill Cody accounted for 4280 beasts alone in eight months over 1867–8), brucellosis, tuberculosis, white settlement, and the competition for grazing and water given by ranching and Indian horse herds.

At length I was fairly among the buffalo. They were less densely crowded than before, and I could see nothing but bulls, who always run at the rear of a herd to protect their females. As I passed among them they would lower their heads, and turning as they ran, try to gore my horse; but as they were already at full speed there was no force in their onset, and as Pauline ran faster than they, they were always thrown behind her in the effort. I soon began to distinguish cows amid the throng. One just in front of me seemed to my liking, and I pushed close to her side. Dropping the reins I fired, holding the muzzle of the gun within a foot of her shoulder. Quick as lightning she sprang at Pauline; the little mare dodged the attack, and I lost sight of the wounded animal amid the tumult. Immediately after, I selected another, and urging forward Pauline, shot into her both pistols in succession. For a while I kept her in view, but in attempting to load my gun lost sight of her also in the confusion. Believing her to be mortally wounded and unable to keep up with the herd, I checked my horse. The crowd rushed onwards. The dust and tumult passed away, and on the prairie, far behind the rest, I saw a solitary buffalo galloping heavily. In a moment I and my victim were running side by side. My firearms were all empty, and I had in my pouch nothing but rifle bullets, too large for the pistols and too small for the gun. I loaded the gun,

however, but as often as I levelled it to fire, the bullets would roll
out of the muzzle and the gun returned only a report like a squib as
the powder harmlessly exploded. I rode in front of the buffalo and
tried to turn her back; but her eyes glared, her mane bristled, and,
lowering her head, she rushed at me with the utmost fierceness and
activity. Again and again I rode before her, and again and again
she repeated her furious charge. But little Pauline was in her
element. She dodged her enemy at every rush, until at length the
buffalo stood still, exhausted with her own efforts, her tongue
lolling from her jaws.

Riding to a little distance, I dismounted, thinking to gather a
handful of dry grass to serve the purpose of wadding, and load the
gun at my leisure. No sooner were my feet on the ground than the
buffalo came bounding in such a rage towards me that I jumped
back again into the saddle with all possible despatch. After waiting
a few minutes more, I made an attempt to ride up and stab her
with my knife; but Pauline was near being gored in the attempt. At
length, bethinking me of the fringes at the seams of my buckskin
trousers, I jerked off a few of them and, reloading the gun, forced
them down the barrel to keep the bullet in its place; then
approaching, I shot the wounded buffalo through the heart.
Sinking to her knees, she rolled over lifeless on the prairie. To
my astonishment, I found that, instead of cow, I had been
slaughtering a stout young bull. No longer wondering at his
fierceness, I opened his throat, and cutting out his tongue tied
it at the back of my saddle. My mistake was one which a more
experienced eye than mine might easily make in the dust and
confusion of such a chase.

PUNISHMENT OF A FEMALE SLAVE,
New Orleans, 1846

Samuel Gridley Howe

Howe was a leading educationalist of the 19th century.

I have passed ten days in New Orleans, not unprofitably, I trust, in
examining the public institutions – the schools, asylums, hospitals,
prisons, etc. With the exception of the first, there is little hope of
amelioration. I know not how much merit there may be in their
system; but I do know that, in the administration of the penal code,
there are abominations which should bring down the fate of

Sodom upon the city. If Howard or Mrs Fry ever discovered so ill-administered a den of thieves as the New Orleans prison, they never described it. In the negroes' apartment I saw much which made me blush that I was a white man, and which, for a moment, stirred up an evil spirit in my animal nature. Entering a large paved courtyard, around which ran galleries filled with slaves of all ages, sexes, and colours, I heard the snap of a whip, every stroke of which sounded like the sharp crack of a pistol. I turned my head, and beheld a sight which absolutely chilled me to the marrow of my bones, and gave me, for the first time in my life, the sensation of my hair stiffening at the roots. There lay a black girl flat upon her face, on a board, her two thumbs tied, and fastened to one end, her feet tied and drawn tightly to the other end, while a strap passed over the small of her back, and, fastened around the board, compressed her closely to it. Below the strap she was entirely naked. By her side, and six feet off, stood a huge negro, with a long whip, which he applied with dreadful power and wonderful precision. Every stroke brought away a strip of skin, which clung to the lash, or fell quivering on the pavement, while the blood followed after it. The poor creature writhed and shrieked, and, in a voice which showed alike her fear of death and her dreadful agony, screamed to her master, who stood at her head, "O, spare my life! don't cut my soul out!" But still fell the horrid lash; still strip after strip peeled off from the skin; gash after gash was cut in her living flesh, until it became a livid and bloody mass of raw and quivering muscle. It was with the greatest difficulty I refrained from spring-ing upon the torturer, and arresting his lash; but, alas! what could I do, but turn aside to hide my tears for the sufferer, and my blushes for humanity? This was in a public and regularly orga-nized prison; the punishment was one recognized and authorized by the law. But think you the poor wretch had committed a heinous offence, and had been convicted thereof, and sentenced to the lash? Not at all. She was brought by her master to be whipped by the common executioner, without trial, judge or jury, just at his beck or nod, for some real or supposed offence, or to gratify his own whim or malice. And he may bring her day after day, without cause assigned, and inflict any number of lashes he pleases, short of twenty-five, provided only he pays the fee. Or, if he choose, he may have a private whipping-board on his own premises, and brutalize himself there. A shocking part of this horrid punishment was its publicity, as I have said; it was in a courtyard surrounded by galleries, which were filled with coloured persons of all sexes – runaway slaves, committed for some crime, or slaves up for sale. You would naturally suppose they crowded forward, and gazed, horror-stricken, at the brutal spectacle below; but they did not; many of them hardly noticed it, and many were entirely indifferent to it. They went on in their childish pursuits, and some were laughing outright in the distant parts of the galleries; so low can man, created in God's image, be sunk in brutality.

CANNIBALISM AT THE DONNER CAMPS, California, 17 April 1847

Captain Fellun

Trapped by snow in the high sierras, a party of California-bound emigrants led by George Donner resorted to eating human flesh. The author led one of the relief expeditions which eventually struggled through to the Donner camps.

April, 17th. Reached the Cabins between 12 and 1 o'clock. Expected to find some of the sufferers alive, Mrs Donner and Kiesburg in particular. Entered the cabins and a horrible scene presented itself, – human bodies terribly mutilated, legs, arms, and sculls scattered in every direction. One body, supposed to be that of Mrs Eddy, lay near the entrance, the limbs severed off and a frightful gash in the scull. The flesh from the bones was nearly consumed and a painful stillness pervaded the place. The supposition was that all were dead, when a sudden shout revived our hopes, and we flew in the direction of the sound, three Indians [who] were hitherto concealed, started from the ground and fled at our approach, leaving behind their bows and arrows. We delayed two hours in searching the cabins, during which we were obliged to witness sights from which we would have fain turned away, and which are too dreadful to put on record. We next started for "Donner's camp" 8 miles distant over the mountains. After traveling about half way, we came upon a track in the snow, which excited our suspicion, and we determined to pursue it. It brought us to the camp of Jacob Donner, where it had evidently left that morning. There we found property of every discription, books, calicoes, tea, coffee, shoes, purcussion caps, household and kitchen furniture scattered in every direction, and mostly in the water. At the mouth of the tent stood a large iron kettle, filled with

human flesh cut up, it was the body of Geo. Donner, the head had
been split open, and the brains extracted therefrom, and to the
appearance, he had not been long dead, not over three or four days
at the most. Near by the kettle stood a chair, and thereupon three
legs of a bullock that had been shot down in the early part of the
winter, and snowed under before it could be dressed. The meat was
found sound and good, and with the exception of a small piece out
of the shoulder, wholly untouched. We gathered up some property
and camped for the night.

THE HANGING OF JOHN BROWN, Harper's Ferry, Virginia, 1859

David Hunter Strother

The slave-abolitionist John Brown was captured by Virginian forces
during a raid on the Harper's Ferry arsenal, and subsequently sentenced
to death for treason.

At eleven o'clock, escorted by a strong column of soldiers, the
prisoner entered the field. He wore the same seedy and dilapidated
dress he had at Harper's Ferry and during his trial, but his rough
boots had given place to a pair of parti-coloured slippers and he
wore a low crown broad brimmed hat (the first time I had ever
seen him with a hat) . . . He stepped from the waggon with
surprising agility and walked hastily toward the scaffold pausing
a moment as he passed our group to wave his pinioned arm and bid
us good morning. I thought I could observe in this a trace of
bravado – but perhaps I was mistaken, as his natural manner was
short, ungainly and hurried. He mounted the steps of the scaffold
with the same alacrity and there, as if by previous arrangement, he
immediately took off his hat and offered his neck for the halter
which was as promptly adjusted by Mr Avis the jailer. A white
muslin cap or hood was then drawn over his face and the Sheriff
not remembering that his eyes were covered requested him to
advance to the platform. The prisoner replied in his usual tone,
"You will have to guide me there."
    The breeze disturbing the arrangement of the hood, the Sheriff
asked his assistant for a pin. Brown raised his hand and directed
him to the collar of his coat where several old pins were quilted in.
The Sheriff took the pin and completed his work.
    He was accordingly led forward to the drop, the halter hooked

to the beam and the officers supposing that the execution was to follow immediately took leave of him. In doing so, the Sheriff enquired if he did not want a handkerchief to throw as a signal to cut the drop. Brown replied, "No, I don't care; I don't want you to keep me waiting unnecessarily."

These were his last words, spoken with that sharp nasal twang peculiar to him, but spoken quietly and civilly without impatience or the slightest apparent emotion. In this position he stood for five minutes or more, while the troops that composed the escort were wheeling into the positions assigned them. I stood within a few paces of him and watched narrowly during these trying moments to see if there was any indication of his giving way. I detected nothing of the sort . ,

Colonel Smith said to the Sheriff in a low voice, "We are ready."

The civil officers descended from the scaffold. One who stood near me whispered earnestly, "He trembles, his knees are shaking."

"You are mistaken," I replied, "it is the scaffold that shakes under the footsteps of the officers."

A VISIT TO BRIGHAM YOUNG, Salt Lake City, Utah, 1860

Richard F. Burton

Brigham Young (1801–77) succeeded Joseph Smith as president of the Mormons in 1844, and was leader of their 1847 exodus to Utah.

The "President of the Church of Jesus Christ of Latter-Day Saints all over the World" is obliged to use caution in admitting strangers, not only for personal safety, but also to defend his dignity from the rude and unfeeling remarks of visitors, who seem to think themselves entitled, in the case of a Mormon, to transgress every rule of civility.

About noon, after a preliminary visit to Mr Gilbert – and a visit in these lands always entails a certain amount of smiling – I met Governor Cumming in Main Street, and we proceeded together to our visit. After a slight scrutiny we passed the guard – which is dressed in plain clothes and to the eye unarmed – and walking down the verandah, entered the Prophet's private office. Several people who were sitting there rose at Mr Cumming's entrance. At a few words of introduction, Mr Brigham Young advanced, shook hands with complete simplicity of manner, asked me to be seated on a sofa at one side of the room, and presented me to those present.

Under ordinary circumstances it would be unfair in a visitor to draw the portrait of one visited. But this is no common case. I have violated no rites of hospitality. Mr Brigham Young is a "seer, revelator, and prophet, having all the gifts of God which He bestows upon the Head of the Church": his memoirs, lithographs, photographs, and portraits have been published again and again; I add but one more likeness; and, finally, I have nothing to say except in his favour.

The Prophet was born at Whittingham, Vermont, on the 1st of June, 1801; he was consequently, in 1860, fifty-nine years of age: he looks about forty-five. *La célébrité vieillit* – I had expected to see a venerable-looking old man. Scarcely a grey thread appears in his hair, which is parted on the side, light coloured, rather thick, and reaches below the ears with a half curl. He formerly wore it long after the Western style, now it is cut level with the ear lobes. The forehead is somewhat narrow, the eyebrows are thin, the eyes between grey and blue, with a calm, composed, and somewhat reserved expression: a slight droop in the left lid made me think that he had suffered from paralysis, I afterwards heard that the ptosis is the result of a neuralgia which has long tormented him. For this reason he usually covers his head – except in his own house or in the tabernacle. Mrs Ward, who is followed by the "Revue des deux Mondes", therefore errs again in asserting that "his Mormon majesty never removes his hat in public." The nose, which is fine and somewhat sharp pointed, is bent a little to the left. The lips are close like the New Englander's, and the teeth, especially those of the under jaw, are imperfect. The cheeks are rather fleshy, and the line between the bottom of the nose and the mouth is broken; the chin is somewhat peaked, and the face clean shaven, except under the jaws, where the beard is allowed to grow. The hands are well made, and not disfigured by rings. The figure is somewhat large, broad-shouldered, and stooping a little when standing.

The Prophet's dress was neat and plain as a Quaker's, all grey homespun, except the cravat and waistcoat. His coat was of antique cut, and, like the pantaloons, baggy, and the buttons were black. A necktie of dark silk, with a large bow, was loosely passed round a starchless collar, which turned down of its own accord. The waistcoat was of black satin – once an article of almost national dress – single-breasted and buttoned nearly to the neck, and a plain gold chain was passed into the pocket. The boots were Wellingtons, apparently of American make.

Altogether the Prophet's appearance was that of a gentleman farmer in New England – in fact such as he is: his father was an agriculturist and revolutionary soldier, who settled "down East". He is a well-preserved man; a fact which some attribute to his habit of sleeping, as the Citizen Proudhon so strongly advises, in solitude. His manner is at once affable and impressive, simple and courteous: his want of pretension contrasts favourably with certain pseudo-prophets that I have seen, each and every one of whom holds himself to be a "Logos" without other claim save a semi-maniacal self-esteem. He shows no signs of dogmatism, bigotry, or fanaticism, and never once entered – with me at least – upon the subject of religion. He impresses a stranger with a certain sense of power: his followers are, of course, wholly fascinated by his superior strength of brain. It is commonly said there is only one chief in G[reat] S[alt] L[ake] City, and that is "Brigham". His temper is even and placid, his manner is cold, in fact, like his face, somewhat bloodless, but he is neither morose nor methodistic, and where occasion requires he can use all the weapons of ridicule to direful effect, and "speak a bit of his mind" in a style which no one forgets. He often reproves his erring followers in purposely violent language, making the terrors of a scolding the punishment in lieu of hanging for a stolen horse or cow. His powers of observation are intuitively strong, and his friends declare him to be gifted with an excellent memory and a perfect judgment of character. If he dislikes a stranger at the first interview, he never sees him again. Of his temperance and sobriety there is but one opinion. His life is ascetic: his favourite food is baked potatoes with a little buttermilk, and his drink water: he disapproves, as do all strict Mormons, of spirituous liquors, and never touches anything stronger than a glass of thin Lager-bier; moreover, he abstains from tobacco. Mr Hyde has accused him of habitual intemperance: he is, as his appearance shows, rather disposed to abstinence than to the reverse. Of his education I cannot speak: "men not books, deeds not words", has ever been his motto: he probably has, as Mr Randolph said of Mr Johnston, "a mind uncorrupted by books". In the only discourse which I heard him deliver, he pronounced impĕtus, impētus. Yet he converses with ease and correctness, has neither snuffle nor pompousness, and speaks as an authority upon certain subjects, such as agriculture and stock-breeding. He assumes no airs of extra sanctimoniousness, and has the plain, simple manners of honesty. His followers deem him an angel of light, his foes, a goblin damned: he is, I presume, neither one nor the other. I cannot pronounce about his scrupulousness: all the world over, the sincerest religious belief, and the practice of devotion, are sometimes compatible not only with the most disorderly life but also with the most terrible crimes; for mankind mostly believes that –

> *"Il est avec le ciel des accommodements."*

He has been called hypocrite, swindler, forger, murderer. – No one looks it less. The best authorities – from those who accuse Mr Joseph Smith of the most heartless deception, to those who believe that he began as an impostor and ended as a prophet – find in Mr Brigham Young "an earnest, obstinate egotistic enthusiasm, fanned by persecution and inflamed by bloodshed". He is the St Paul of the New Dispensation: true and sincere, he gave point, and energy, and consistency to the somewhat disjointed, turbulent, and unforeseeing fanaticism of Mr Joseph Smith; and if he has not been able to create, he has shown himself great in controlling, circumstances. Finally, there is a total absence of pretension in his manner, and he has been so long used to power that he cares nothing for its display. The arts by which he rules the heterogeneous mass of conflicting elements are indomitable will, profound secrecy, and uncommon astuteness.

Such is His Excellency President Brigham Young, "painter and glazier", – his earliest craft – prophet, revelator, translator and seer; the man who is revered as king or kaiser, pope or pontiff never was; who, like the Old Man of the Mountain, by holding up his hand could cause the death of any one within his reach; who, governing as well as reigning, long stood up to fight with the sword of the Lord, and with his few hundred guerillas, against the then mighty power of the United States; who has outwitted all diplomacy opposed to him; and finally, who made a treaty of peace with the President of the Great Republic as though he had wielded the combined power of France, Russia, and England.

It is observable that, although every Gentile writer has represented Mr Joseph Smith as an heartless impostor, few have ventured to apply the term to Mr Brigham Young. I also remarked an instance of the veneration shown by his followers, whose affection for him is equalled only by the confidence with which they entrust to him their dearest interests in this world and in the next. After my visit many congratulated me, as would the followers of the Tien Wong or Heavenly King, upon having at last seen what they consider "a per se" the most remarkable man in the world.

ROUGHING IT: RIDING THE OVERLAND STAGE, 1861

Mark Twain

Twain's brother had secured an appointment as secretary to the Governor of Nevada. Twain went along for the ride – from St. Joseph, Missouri, to Carson City, Nevada, by stagecoach. Twain's ticket cost $150 dollars, some $2500 in contemporary money.

Leaving St. Jo:

It was a superb summer morning, and all the landscape was brilliant with sunshine. There was a freshness and breeziness, too, and an exhilarating sense of emancipation from all sorts of cares and responsibilities, that almost made us feel that the years we had spent in the close, hot city, toiling and slaving, had been wasted and thrown away. We were spinning along through Kansas, and in the course of an hour and a half we were fairly abroad on the great Plains. Just here the land was rolling – a grand sweep of regular elevations and depressions as far as the eye could reach – like the stately heave and swell of the ocean's bosom after a storm. And everywhere were cornfields, accenting with squares of deeper green this limitless expanse of grassy land. But presently this sea upon dry ground was to lose its "rolling" character and stretch away for seven hundred miles as level as a floor!

Our coach was a great swinging and swaying stage, of the most sumptuous description – an imposing cradle on wheels. It was drawn by six handsome horses, and by the side of the driver sat the "conductor," the legitimate captain of the craft; for it was his business to take charge and care of the mails, baggage, express matter, and passengers. We three were the only passengers, this trip. We sat on the back seat, inside. About all the rest of the coach was full of mailbags – for we had three days' delayed mails with us. Almost touching our knees, a perpendicular wall of mail matter rose up to the roof. There was a great pile of it strapped on top of the stage, and both the fore and hind boots were full. We had twenty-seven hundred pounds of it aboard, the driver said – "a little for Brigham, and Carson, and 'Frisco, but the heft of it for the Injuns, which is powerful troublesome 'thout they get plenty of truck to read." But as he just then got up a fearful convulsion of his countenance which was suggestive of a wink being swallowed by an earthquake, we guessed that his remark was intended to be facetious, and to mean that we would unload the most of our mail matter somewhere on the Plains and leave it to the Indians, or whosoever wanted it.

We changed horses every ten miles, all day long, and fairly flew over the hard, level road. We jumped out and stretched our legs every time the coach stopped, and so the night found us still vivacious and unfatigued.

After supper a woman got in, who lived about fifty miles further on, and we three had to take turns at sitting outside with the driver and conductor. Apparently she was not a talkative woman. She would sit there in the gathering twilight and fasten her steadfast eyes on a mosquito rooting into her arm, and slowly she would raise her other hand till she had got his range, and then she would launch a slap at him that would have jolted a cow; and after that she would sit and contemplate the corpse with tranquil satisfaction – for she never missed her mosquito; she was a dead shot at short range. She never removed a carcass, but left them there for bait. I sat by this grim Sphinx and watched her kill thirty or forty mosquitoes – watched her, and waited for her to say something, but she never did. So I finally opened the conversation myself. I said:

"The mosquitoes are pretty bad, about here, madam."

"You bet!"

"What did I understand you to say, madam?"

"YOU BET!"

Then she cheered up, and faced around and said:

"Danged if I didn't begin to think you fellers was deef and dumb. I did, b' gosh. Here I've sot, and sot, and sot, a-bust'n' muskeeters and wonderin' what was ailin' ye. Fust I thot you was deef and dumb, then I thot you was sick or crazy, or suthin', and then by and by I begin to reckon you was a passel of sickly fools that couldn't think of nothing to say. Where'd ye come from?"

The Sphinx was a Sphinx no more! The fountains of her great deep were broken up, and she rained the nine parts of speech forty days and forty nights, metaphorically speaking, and buried us under a desolating deluge of trivial gossip that left not a crag or pinnacle of rejoinder projecting above the tossing waste of dislocated grammar and decomposed pronunciation!

How we suffered, suffered, suffered! She went on, hour after hour, till I was sorry I ever opened the mosquito question and gave her a start. She never did stop again until she got to her journey's end toward daylight; and then she stirred us up as she was leaving the stage (for we were nodding, by that time), and said:

"Now you git out at Cottonwood, you fellers, and lay over a couple o' days, and I'll be along some time to-night, and if I can do ye any good by edgin' in a word now and then, I'm right thar. Folks 'll tell you 't I've always ben kind o' offish and partic'lar for a gal that's raised in the woods, and I *am*, with the ragtag and bobtail, and a gal *has* to be, if she wants to *be* anything, but when people comes along which is my equals, I reckon I'm a pretty sociable heifer after all."

We resolved not to "lay by at Cottonwood."

As the sun went down and the evening chill came on, we made preparation for bed. We stirred up the hard leather letter-sacks, and the knotty canvas bags of printed matter (knotty and uneven because of projecting ends and corners of magazines, boxes and books). We stirred them up and redisposed them in such a way as to make our bed as level as possible. And we *did* improve it, too, though after all our work it had an upheaved and billowy look about it, like a little piece of a stormy sea. Next we hunted up our boots from odd nooks among the mail-bags where they had settled, and put them on. Then we got down our coats, vests, pantaloons and heavy woolen shirts, from the armloops where they had been swinging all day, and clothed ourselves in them – for, there being no ladies either at the stations or in the coach, and the weather being hot, we had looked to our comfort by stripping to our underclothing, at nine o'clock in the morning. All things being now ready, we stowed the uneasy Dictionary where it would lie as quiet as possible, and placed the water-canteen and pistols where we could find them in the dark. Then we smoked a final pipe, and swapped a final yarn; after which, we put the pipes, tobacco, and bag of coin in snug holes and caves among the mail-bags, and then fastened down the coach curtains all around and made the place as "dark as the inside of a cow," as the conductor phrased it in his picturesque way. It was certainly as dark as any place could be – nothing was even dimly visible in it. And finally, we rolled ourselves up like silkworms, each person in his own blanket, and sank peacefully to sleep.

Whenever the stage stopped to change horses, we would wake up, and try to recollect where we were – and succeed – and in a minute or two the stage would be off again, and we likewise. We began to get into country, now, threaded here and there with little streams. These had high, steep banks on each side, and every time we flew down one bank and scrambled up the other, our party inside got mixed somewhat. First we would all be down in a pile at the forward end of the stage, nearly in a sitting posture, and in a second we would shoot to the other end, and stand on our heads. And we would sprawl and kick, too, and ward off ends and corners of mail-bags that came lumbering over us and about us; and as the dust rose from the tumult, we would all sneeze in chorus, and the majority of us would grumble, and probably say some hasty thing, like: "Take your elbow out of my ribs! – can't you quit crowding?"

Every time we avalanched from one end of the stage to the other, the Unabridged Dictionary would come too; and every time it came it damaged somebody. One trip it "barked" the Secretary's elbow; the next trip it hurt me in the stomach, and the third it tilted Bemis's nose up till he could look down his nostrils – he said. The pistols and coin soon settled to the bottom, but the pipes, pipe-stems, tobacco, and canteens clattered and floundered after the Dictionary every time it made an assault on us, and aided and abetted the book by spilling tobacco in our eyes, and water down our backs.

The Way Station:

The station buildings were long, low huts, made of sun-dried, mud-colored bricks, laid up without mortar (*adobes*, the Spaniards call these bricks, and Americans shorten it to '*dobies*). The roofs, which had no slant to them worth speaking of, were thatched and then sodded or covered with a thick layer of earth, and from this sprung a pretty rank growth of weeds and grass. It was the first time we had ever seen a man's front yard on top of his house. The buildings consisted of barns, stable-room for twelve or fifteen horses, and a hut for an eating-room for passengers. This latter had bunks in it for the station-keeper and a hostler or two. You could rest your elbow on its eaves, and you had to bend in order to get in at the door. In place of a window there was a square hole about large enough for a man to crawl through, but this had no glass in it. There was no flooring, but the ground was packed hard. There was no stove, but the fireplace served all needful purposes. There were no shelves, no cupboards, no closets. In a corner stood an open sack of flour, and nestling against its base were a couple of black and venerable tin coffee-pots, a tin teapot, a little bag of salt, and a side of bacon.

By the door of the station-keeper's den, outside, was a tin wash-basin, on the ground. Near it was a pail of water and a piece of yellow bar-soap, and from the eaves hung a hoary blue woolen shirt, significantly – but this latter was the station-keeper's private towel, and only two persons in all the party might venture to use it – the stage-driver and the conductor. The latter would not, from a sense of decency; the former would not, because he did not choose to encourage the advances of a station-keeper. We had towels – in the valise; they might as well have been in Sodom and Gomorrah. We (and the conductor) used our handkerchiefs, and the driver his pantaloons and sleeves. By the door, inside, was fastened a small old-fashioned looking-glass frame, with two little fragments of the original mirror lodged down in one corner of it. This arrangement afforded a pleasant double-barreled portrait of you when you looked into it, with one half of your head set up a couple of inches above the other half. From the glass frame hung the half of a comb by a string – but if I had to describe that patriarch or die, I believe I would order some sample coffins. It had come down from Esau and Samson, and had been accumulating hair ever since – along with certain impurities. In one corner of the room stood three or four rifles and muskets, together with horns and pouches of ammunition. The station-men wore pantaloons of coarse, country-woven stuff, and into the seat and the inside of the legs were sewed ample additions of buckskin, to do duty in place of leggings, when the man rode horseback – so the pants were half dull blue and half yellow, and unspeakably picturesque. The pants were stuffed into the tops of high boots, the heels whereof were armed with great Spanish spurs, whose little iron clogs and chains jingled with every step. The man wore a huge beard and mustachios, an old slouch hat, a blue woolen shirt, no suspenders, no vest, no coat – in a leathern sheath in his belt, a great long "navy" revolver (slung on right side, hammer to the front), and projecting from his boot a horn-handled bowie-knife. The furniture of the hut was neither gorgeous nor much in the way. The rocking-chairs and

sofas were not present, and never had been, but they were
represented by two three-legged stools, a pine-board bench four
feet long, and two empty candle-boxes. The table was a greasy
board on stilts, and the table-cloth and napkins had not come –
and they were not looking for them, either. A battered tin platter, a
knife and fork, and a tin pint cup, were at each man's place, and
the driver had a queens-ware saucer that had seen better days. Of
course, this duke sat at the head of the table. There was one
isolated piece of table furniture that bore about it a touching air of
grandeur in misfortune. This was the caster. It was German silver,
and crippled and rusty, but it was so preposterously out of place
there that it was suggestive of a tattered exiled king among
barbarians, and the majesty of its native position compelled respect
even in its degradation. There was only one cruet left, and that was
a stopperless, fly-specked, broken-necked thing, with two inches of
vinegar in it, and a dozen preserved flies with their heels up and
looking sorry they had invested there.

The station-keeper up-ended a disk of last week's bread, of the
shape and size of an old-time cheese, and carved some slabs from it
which were as good as Nicholson pavement, and tenderer.

He sliced off a piece of bacon for each man, but only the experienced old hands made out to eat it, for it was condemned army bacon
which the United States would not feed to its soldiers in the forts, and
the stage company had bought it cheap for the sustenance of their
passengers and employees. We may have found this condemned
army bacon further out on the Plains than the section I am locating it
in, but we *found* it – there is no gainsaying that.

Then he poured for us a beverage which he called "*Slumgullion*,"
and it is hard to think he was not inspired when he named it. It
really pretended to be tea, but there was too much dish-rag, and
sand, and old bacon-rind in it to deceive the intelligent traveler.
He had no sugar and no milk – not even a spoon to stir the
ingredients with.

We could not eat the bread or the meat, nor drink the "Slumgullion." And when I looked at that melancholy vinegar-cruet, I
thought of the anecdote (a very, very old one, even at that day) of
the traveler who sat down to a table which had nothing on it but a
mackerel and a pot of mustard. He asked the landlord if this was
all. The landlord said:

"*All!* Why, thunder and lightning, I should think there was
mackerel enough there for six."

"But I don't like mackerel."

"Oh – then help yourself to the mustard."

In other days I had considered it a good, a very good, anecdote, but there was a dismal plausibility about it, here, that took all the humor out of it.

Our breakfast was before us, but our teeth were idle.

I tasted and smelt, and said I would take coffee, I believed. The station-boss stopped dead still, and glared at me speechless. At last, when he came to, he turned away and said, as one who communes with himself upon a matter too vast to grasp:

"*Coffee!* Well, if that don't go clean ahead of me, I'm d–d!"

THE PONY EXPRESS RIDER

The Pony Express had been founded the year before. A relay of fast riders carried mail the 2000 miles between St. Joseph and San Francisco in as little as 7 days and 17 hours. Yet the service was soon made obsolete by the transcontinental telegraph.

Presently the driver exclaims:
"HERE HE COMES!"
Every neck is stretched further, and every eye strained wider. Away across the endless dead level of the prairie a black speck appears against the sky, and it is plain that it moves. Well, I should think so! In a second or two it becomes a horse and rider rising and falling, rising and falling – sweeping toward us nearer and nearer and still nearer   growing more and more distinct, more and more sharply defined – nearer and still nearer, and the flutter of the hoofs comes faintly to the ear – another instant a whoop and a hurrah from our upper deck, a wave of the rider's hand, but no reply, and a man and horse burst past our excited faces, and go winging away like a belated fragment of a storm!

CIVIL WAR: CONFEDERATE FORCES ATTACK FORT SUMTER, South Carolina, 12 April 1861

B.S. Osbon

B.S. Osbon was a journalist for the New York *World*.

On April 12, 1861, Confederate forces began the bombardment of the Federal arsenal at Fort Sumter, South Carolina. Four years later, almost to the day, on April 9 1865, in the silence of Appomattox Courthouse, the

Confederate army of General Lee surrendered. In between times, over 600,000 soldiers had died of wounds and disease, and much of America, from Virginia to Arkansas, had been reduced to a battlefield.

Charleston, April 12

The batteries of Sullivan's Island, Morris Island, and other points were opened on Fort Sumter at four o'clock this morning. Fort Sumter has returned the fire, and a brisk cannonading has been kept up.

The military are under arms, and the whole of our population are on the streets. Every available space facing the harbor is filled with anxious spectators.

The firing has continued all day without intermission.

Two of Fort Sumter's guns have been silenced, and it is reported that a breach has been made in the southeast wall.

The answer to General Beauregard's demand by Major Anderson was that he would surrender when his supplies were exhausted; that is, if he was not reinforced.

CIVIL WAR HAS AT LAST BEGUN. A terrible fight is at this moment going on between Fort Sumter and the fortifications by which it is surrounded. The issue was submitted to Major Anderson of surrendering as soon as his supplies were exhausted, or of having fire opened on him within a certain time. He refused to surrender, and accordingly at twenty-seven minutes past four o'clock this morning Fort Moultrie began the bombardment by firing two guns.

Major Anderson has the greater part of the day been directing his fire principally against Fort Moultrie, the Stevens and floating battery, these and Fort Johnson being the only ones operating against him. The remainder of the batteries are held in reserve.

The Stevens battery is eminently successful and does terrible execution on Fort Sumter. Breaches, to all appearances, are being made in the several sides exposed to fire. Portions of the parapet have been destroyed, and several of the guns there mounted have been shot away.

The excitement in the community is indescribable. With the first boom of the gun, thousands rushed from their beds to the harbor front, and all day every available place has been thronged by ladies and gentlemen, viewing the solemn spectacle through their glasses. Most of these have relatives in the several fortifications, and many a tearful eye attested the anxious affection of the mother, wife, and sister, but not a murmur came from a single individual.

Business is entirely suspended. Only those stores are open necessary to supply articles required by the army.

Troops are pouring into the town by hundreds, but are held in reserve for the present, the force already on the islands being ample. The thunder of the artillery can be heard for fifty miles around, and the scene is magnificently terrible.

CIVIL WAR: A DIARY FROM DIXIE, 1861

Mary Boykin Chesnut

Chesnut was the wife of a South Carolina slaveholder and senator.

May 19 [1861] Back in Montgomery. Mrs Fitzpatrick said Mr [Jefferson] Davis is too gloomy for her. He says we must prepare for a long war and unmerciful reverses at first, because they are readier for war, and so much stronger numerically. Men and money count so in war. "As they do everywhere else," said I, doubting her accurate account of Mr Davis's spoken words, though she tried to give it faithfully. We need patience and persistence. There is enough and to spare of pluck and dash among us; the do-and-dare style.

[May 27, 1861] Johnny [Mary Chesnut's nephew] has gone as a private in Gregg's regiment. He could not stand it at home any longer. Mr Chesnut was willing for him to go, because those sandhill men said: "This is a rich man's war," and that the rich men could be officers and have an easy time, and the poor ones be privates. So he said: "Let the gentlemen set the example; let them go in the ranks." So John Chesnut is a gentleman private. He took his servant with him, all the same.

[June 10, 1861] The war is making us all tenderly sentimental. No casualties yet, no real mourning, nobody hurt; so it is all parade, fuss and fine feathers. There is no imagination here to forestall woe, and only the excitement and wild awakening from everyday stagnant life is felt; that is, when one gets away from the two or three sensible men who are still left in the world.

In Charleston, a butcher has been clandestinely supplying the Yankee fleet outside of the Bar with beef. They say he gave the information which led to the capture of the *Savannah*. They will hang him. Mr Petigru alone, in South Carolina, has not seceded.

When they pray for our President, he gets up from his knees. He might risk a prayer for Mr Davis, though I doubt if it would do Mr Davis any good. Mr Petigru is too clever to think himself one of the righteous, whose prayers avail so overly much. Mr Petigru's disciple, Mr Bryan, followed his example. Mr Petigru has such a keen sense of the ridiculous, he must be laughing in his sleeve at the hubbub this untimely trait of independence has raised.

Harper's Ferry has been evacuated, and we are looking out for a battle at Manassas Station. I am always ill. The name of my disease is a longing to get away from here, and go to Richmond. Good Lord, forgive me! Your commandment I cannot keep. How can I honor what is so dishonorable, or respect what is so little respectable, or love what is so utterly unlovely. Then I must go, indeed; go away from here.

[June 28, 1861] In Mrs Davis's drawing-room last night, the President took a seat by me on the sofa where I sat. He talked for nearly an hour. He laughed at our faith in our own prowess. We are like the British; we think every Southerner equal to three Yankees at least, but we will have to be equivalent to a dozen now. After his experience of the fighting qualities of Southerners in Mexico, Mr Davis believes that we will do all that can be done by pluck and muscle, endurance and dogged courage, dash and red-hot patriotism, and yet his tone was not sanguine. There was a sad refrain running through it all. For one thing, either way, he thinks it will be a long war. That floored me at once. It has been too long for me already. Then he said that before the end came we would have many a bitter experience. He said only fools doubted the courage of the Yankees, or their willingness to fight when they saw fit. And now we have stung their pride, we have roused them till they will fight like devils. He said Mr Chesnut's going as aide-de-camp to Beauregard was a mistake, and that he ought to raise a regiment of his own.

[July 11, 1861] The spy, so called, gave us a parting shot. She said Beauregard arrested her brother so that he might take a fine horse aforesaid brother was riding. Why? Beauregard could have at a moment's notice any horse in South Carolina – or Louisiana, for that matter – at a word. The brother was arrested and sent to Richmond, and "will be acquitted as they always are," said Brewster. They send them first to Richmond to see and hear everything there; then they acquit them, and send them out of the country by way of Norfolk to see everything there. But after all, what does it matter? The Yankees have no need of spies. Our newspapers keep no secrets hid. The thoughts of our hearts are all revealed. Everything with us is open and above board. At Bethel, the Yankees fired too high, and every daily is jeering them about it even now. They'll fire low enough next time, but no newspaper man will be there to get the benefit of their improved practice! Alas!

[September 19, 1861] Mr Chesnut and Uncle John, both *ci-devant* [heretofore] Union men, are now utterly for State's Rights.

. . . An iron steamer has run the blockade at Savannah. We raise our wilted heads like flowers after a shower. This drop of good news revives us.

September 24 [1861] The men who went to Society Hill (the Witherspoon home) have come home again with nothing very definite. William and Cousin Betsey's old maid, Rhody, are in jail; strong suspicion but as yet no proof of their guilt. The neighborhood is in a ferment. Evans and Wallace say these Negroes ought to be burnt. Lynching proposed! But it is all idle talk. They will be tried as the law directs, and not otherwise. John Witherspoon will not allow anything wrong or violent to be done. He has a detective there from Charleston.

Hitherto I have never thought of being afraid of Negroes. I had never injured any of them; why should they want to hurt me? Two thirds of my religion consists in trying to be good to Negroes, because they are so in our power, and it would be so easy to be the other thing. Somehow today I feel that the ground is cut away from under my feet. Why should they treat me any better than they have done Cousin Betsey Witherspoon?

Kate and I sat up late and talked it all over. Mrs Witherspoon was a saint on this earth, and this is her reward. Kate's maid Betsey came in – a strong-built, mulatto woman – dragging in a mattress. "Missis, I have brought my bed to sleep in your room while Mars' David is at Society Hill. You ought not to stay in a room by yourself these times." She went off for more bed gear. "For the life of me," said Kate gravely. "I cannot make up my mind. Does she mean to take care of me, or to murder me?" I do not think Betsey heard, but when she came back she said: "Missis, as I have a soul to be saved, I will keep you safe. I will guard you." We know Betsey well, but has she soul enough to swear by? She is a great stout, jolly, irresponsible, unreliable, pleasant-tempered, bad-behaved woman, with ever so many good points. Among others, she is so

clever she can do anything, and she never loses her temper; but she
has no moral sense whatever.

That night, Kate came into my room. She could not sleep. The
thought of those black hands strangling and smothering Mrs
Witherspoon's grey head under the counterpane haunted her;
we sat up and talked the long night through.

[October 7, 1861] An appalling list of foreigners in the Yankee
army, just as I feared; a rush of all Europe to them, as soon as they
raised the cry that this war is for the extirpation of slavery. If our
people had read less of Mr Calhoun's works, and only read the
signs of the times a little more; if they had known more of what was
going on around them in the world.

[October 13, 1861] I was shocked to hear that dear friends of
mine refused to take work for the soldiers because their seamstresses
had their winter clothes to make. I told them true patriotesses would
be willing to wear the same clothes until our siege was raised. They
did not seem to care. They have seen no ragged, dirty, sick and
miserable soldiers lying in the hospital, no lack of woman's nursing,
no lack of woman's tears, but an awful lack of a proper change in
clean clothes. They know nothing of the horrors of war. One has to
see to believe. They take it easy, and are not yet willing to make
personal sacrifices. The time is coming when they will not be given a
choice in the matter. The very few stay-at-home men we have are
absorbed as before in plantation affairs; cotton-picking, Negro
squabbles, hay stealing, saving the corn from the freshet. They
are like the old Jews while Noah was building the Ark.

Woe to those who began this war, if they were not in bitter
earnest. Lamar (L. Q. C., and the cleverest man I know) said in
Richmond in one of those long talks of ours: "Slavery is too heavy a
load for us to carry."

[October 25, 1861] The Yankees' principal spite is against
South Carolina. Fifteen war steamers have sailed – or steamed
– out against us. Hot work will be cut out for us whenever they
elect to land. They hate us, but they fear us too. They do not move
now until their force is immense; overwhelming is their word.
Enormous preparations and a cautious approach are the lessons we
taught them at Manassas.

November 6 [1861] Mr Chesnut has gone to Charleston, and
Kate to Columbia, on her way to Flat Rock. Partings are sorrowful
things now.

As for the dunderheads here, I can account for their stolidity only in one way. They have no imagination. They cannot conceive what lies before them. They can only see what actually lies under their noses. To me it is evident that Russell, the Times [of London] correspondent, tries to tell the truth, unpalatable as it is to us. Why should we expect a man who recorded so unflinchingly the wrongdoing in India, to soften matters for our benefit, sensitive as we are to blame. He described slavery in Maryland, but says that it has worse features further South; yet his account of slavery in Maryland might stand as a perfectly accurate picture of it here. God knows I am not inclined to condone it, come what may. His work is very well done for a stranger who comes and in his haste unpacks his three P's – pen, paper, and prejudices – and hurries through his work.

STEAMBOAT TRIP ON THE MISSISSIPPI, 1861

Anthony Trollope

The English novelist sojourned in the USA between August 1861 and 1862. His subsequent travelogue, *North America*, was restitution for his mother's infamous attack on the crudity of the *Domestic Manners of the Americans* from 1832.

From La Crosse to St Paul, the distance up the river is something over 200 miles, and from St Paul down to Dubuque, in Iowa, to which we went on our return, the distance is 450 miles. On the whole we slept on board four nights, and lived on board as many days. I cannot say that the life was comfortable, though I do not know that it could be made more so by any care on the part of the boat-owners. My first complaint would be against the great heat of the cabins. The Americans as a rule live in an atmosphere which is almost unbearable to an Englishman. To this cause, I am convinced, is to be attributed their thin faces, the pale skins, the unenergetic temperament, unenergetic as regards physical motion, and their early old age. The winters are long and cold in America, and mechanical ingenuity is far extended. The two facts together have created a system of stoves, hot-air pipes, steam chambers, and heating apparatus, so extensive that from autumn till the end of spring all inhabited rooms are filled with the atmosphere of a hot oven. An Englishman fancies that he is to be baked, and for a while finds it almost impossible to exist in the air prepared for him. How the heat is engendered on board the river steamers I do not know, but it is engendered to so great a degree that the sitting-cabins are unendurable.

That is my first complaint. My second complaint is equally unreasonable, and is quite as incapable of a remedy as the first. Nine-tenths of the travellers carry children with them. They are not tourists engaged on pleasure excursions, but men and women intent on the business of life. They are moving up and down, looking for fortune, and in search of new homes. Of course they carry with them all their household gods. Do not let any critics say that I grudge these young travellers their right to locomotion. Neither their right to locomotion is grudged by me, nor any of those privileges which are accorded in America to the rising generation. The habits of their country and the choice of the parents give to them full dominion over all hours and over all places, and it would ill become a foreigner to make such habits and such choice a ground of serious complaint.

But nevertheless the uncontrolled energies of twenty children round one's legs do not convey comfort or happiness, when the passing events are producing noise and storm rather than peace and sunshine. I must protest that American babies are an unhappy race. They eat and drink just as they please; they are never punished; they are never banished, snubbed, and kept in the background as children are kept with us; and yet they are wretched and uncomfortable. My heart has bled for them as I have heard them squalling by the hour together in agonies of discontent and dyspepsia. Can it be, I wonder, that children are happier when they are made to obey orders and are sent to bed at six o'clock, than when allowed to regulate their own conduct; that bread and milk is more favourable to laughter and soft childish ways than beefsteaks and pickles three times a day; that an occasional whipping, even, will conduce to rosy cheeks?

But there was a third reason why travelling on these boats was not as pleasant as I had expected. I could not get my fellow-travellers to talk to me. It must be understood that our fellow-travellers were not generally of that class which we Englishmen, in our pride, designate as gentlemen and ladies. They were people, as I have said, in search of new homes and new fortunes. But I protest that as such they would have been in those parts much more agreeable as companions to me than any gentlemen or any ladies, if only they would have talked to me.

A western American man is not a talking man. He will sit for hours over a stove with his cigar in his mouth, and his hat over his eyes, chewing the cud of reflection. A dozen will sit together in the same way, and there shall not be a dozen words spoken between them in an hour. With the women one's chance of conversation is still worse. It seemed as though the cares of the world had been too much for them, and that all talking excepting as to business – demands for instance on the servants for pickles for their children – had gone by the board. They were generally hard, dry, and melancholy. I am speaking of course of aged females – from five and twenty perhaps to thirty, who had long since given up the amusements and levities of life. I very soon abandoned any attempt at drawing a word from these ancient mothers of families; but not the less did I ponder in my mind over the circumstances of their lives. Had things gone with them so sadly, was the struggle for independence so hard, that all the softness of existence had been trodden out of them? In the cities too it was much the same. It seemed to me that a future mother of a family in those parts had left all laughter behind her when she put out her finger for the wedding ring.

For these reasons I must say that life on board these steamboats was not as pleasant as I had hoped to find it, but for our discomfort in this respect we found great atonement in the scenery through which we passed. I protest that of all the river scenery that I know, that of the Upper Mississippi is by far the finest and the most continued. One thinks of course of the Rhine; but, according to my idea of beauty, the Rhine is nothing to the Upper Mississippi.

For miles upon miles, for hundreds of miles, the course of the river runs through low hills, which are there called bluffs. These bluffs rise in every imaginable form, looking sometimes like large straggling unwieldy castles, and then throwing themselves into sloping lawns which stretch back away from the river till the eye is lost in their twists and turnings. Landscape beauty, as I take it, consists mainly in four attributes: in water, in broken land, in scattered timber – timber scattered as opposed to continuous forest timber – and in the accident of colour. In all these particulars the banks of the Upper Mississippi can hardly be beaten. There are no high mountains, but there is a succession of hills which group themselves for ever without monotony. It is perhaps the ever-variegated forms of these bluffs which chiefly constitute the wonderful loveliness of this river.

To my taste the finest stretch of the river was that immediately above Lake Pepin; but then, at this point, we had all the glory of

the setting sun. It was like fairy land, so bright were the golden
lines, so fantastic were the shapes of the hills, so broken and twisted
the course of the waters! But the noisy steamer went groaning up
the narrow passages with almost unabated speed, and left the fairy
land behind all too quickly. Then the bell would ring for tea, and
the children with the beefsteaks, the pickled onions, and the light
fixings would all come over again. The care-laden mothers would
tuck the bibs under the chins of their tyrant children, and some
embryo senator of four years old would listen with concentrated
attention, while the Negro servant recapitulated to him the
delicacies of the supper-table, in order that he might make his
choice with due consideration.

"Beefsteak," the embryo four-year-old senator would lisp, "and
stewed potato, and buttered toast, and corn cake, and coffee – and
– and – and – mother, mind you get me the pickles."

CIVIL WAR: LAST LETTER HOME, 14 July 1861
Major Sullivan Ballou

Ballou was an officer in the 2nd Rhode Island Volunteers. He writes to his
wife in Smithfield.

July 14, 1861
Camp Clark

My very dear Sarah:
The indications are very strong that we shall move in a few days –
perhaps tomorrow. Lest I should not be able to write you again, I
feel impelled to write lines that may fall under your eye when I
shall be no more.

Our movement may be one of a few days duration and full of
pleasure – and it may be one of severe conflict and death to me.
Not my will, but thine O God, be done. If it is necessary that I
should fall on the battlefield for my country, I am ready. I have no
misgivings about, or lack of confidence in, the cause in which I am
engaged, and my courage does not halt or falter. I know how
strongly American Civilization now leans upon the triumph of the
Government, and how great a debt we owe to those who went
before us through the blood and suffering of the Revolution. And I
am willing – perfectly willing – to lay down all my joys in this life,
to help maintain this Government, and to pay that debt.

But, my dear wife, when I know that with my own joys I lay

down nearly all of yours, and replace them in this life with cares and sorrows – when, after having eaten for long years the bitter fruit of orphanage myself, I must offer it as their only sustenance to my dear little children – is it weak or dishonorable, while the banner of my purpose floats calmly and proudly in the breeze, that my unbounded love for you, my darling wife and children, should struggle in fierce, though useless, contest with my love of country?

I cannot describe to you my feelings on this calm summer night, when two thousand men are sleeping around me, many of them enjoying the last, perhaps, before that of death – and I, suspicious that Death is creeping behind me with his fatal dart, am communing with God, my country, and thee.

I have sought most closely and diligently, and often in my breast, for a wrong motive in thus hazarding the happiness of those I loved and I could not find one. A pure love of my country and of the principles have often advocated before the people and "the name of honor that I love more than I fear death" have called upon me, and I have obeyed.

Sarah, my love for you is deathless, it seems to bind me to you with mighty cables that nothing but Omnipotence could break; and yet my love of Country comes over me like a strong wind and bears me irresistibly on with all these chains to the battlefield.

The memories of the blissful moments I have spent with you come creeping over me, and I feel most gratified to God and to you that I have enjoyed them so long. And hard it is for me to give them up and burn to ashes the hopes of future years, when God willing, we might still have lived and loved together and seen our sons grow up to honorable manhood around us. I have, I know, but few and small claims upon Divine Providence, but something whispers to me – perhaps it is the wafted prayer of my little Edgar – that I shall return to my loved ones unharmed. If I do not, my dear Sarah, never forget how much I love you, and when my last breath escapes me on the battlefield, it will whisper your name.

Forgive my many faults, and the many pains I have caused you. How thoughtless and foolish I have oftentimes been! How gladly would I wash out with my tears every little spot upon your happiness, and struggle with all the misfortune of this world, to shield you and my children from harm. But I cannot. I must watch you from the spirit land and hover near you, while you buffet the storms with your precious little freight, and wait with sad patience till we meet to part no more.

But, O Sarah! If the dead can come back to this earth and flit unseen around those they loved, I shall always be near you; in the garish day and in the darkest night – amidst your happiest scenes and gloomiest hours – always, always; and if there be a soft breeze upon your cheek, it shall be my breath; or the cool air fans your throbbing temple, it shall be my spirit passing by.

Sarah, do not mourn me dead; think I am gone and wait for thee, for we shall meet again.

As for my little boys, they will grow as I have done, and never know a father's love and care. Little Willie is too young to remember me long, and my blue-eyed Edgar will keep my frolics with him among the dimmest memories of his childhood. Sarah, I have unlimited confidence in your maternal care and your development of their characters. Tell my two mothers his and hers I call God's blessing upon them. O Sarah, I wait for you there! Come to me, and lead thither my children.

Sullivan

Sullivan Ballou was killed a week later at the first battle of Bull Run.

CLASH OF THE IRONCLADS: THE *MONITOR* v. THE *MERRIMAC*, 8–9 March 1862

Lieutenant Dana Green

The naval battle between Union and Confederate forces at Hampton Roads on 8–9 March was the first engagement in history between "ironclad" warships. Federal Lieutenant Green was an officer aboard the USS *Monitor*.

At daylight we discovered the Merrimac at anchor with several vessels under Sewell's Point. We immediately made every preparation for battle. At 8 a.m. on Sunday the Merrimac got underweigh accompanied by several steamers and steered direct for the Minnesota (a wooden battleship). When a mile distant she fired two guns at the Minnesota. By this time our anchor was up, the men at quarters, the guns loaded, and everything ready for action. As the Merrimac came close the Captain passed the word to commence firing. I triced up the port, ran the gun out and fired the first gun and thus commenced the great battle between the Monitor and the Merrimac.

Now mark the condition our men were in. Since Friday morning, 40 hours, they had had no rest and very little food, as we could not conveniently cook. They had been hard at work all night, had nothing to eat for breakfast except hard bread, and were thoroughly worn out. As for myself, I had not slept a wink for 51 hours, and had been on my feet almost constantly. But, after the first gun was fired we forgot all fatigue, hard work and everything else, and went to work fighting as hard as men ever fought.

We loaded and fired as fast as we could . . . Our tower was struck several times, and though the noise was pretty loud it did not affect us any. At about 11:30 the Captain sent for me.

I went forward, and there stood as noble a man as lives at the foot of the ladder of the Pilot House. His face was perfectly black with powder and iron and he was apparently perfectly blind. He said a shot had struck the Pilot House and blinded him. He told me to take charge of the ship and use my own discretion. I led him to his room and laid him on the sofa and then took his position. We still continued firing, the tower being under the direction of Stimers. We were now between two fires, the Minnesota on one side, and the Merrimac on the other. The latter was retreating to Sewell's Point.

The fight was over now and we were victorious. My men and myself were perfectly black, and my person in the same condition . . . Batsy, my old roommate was on board the Merrimac. Little did we ever think at the Academy we should be firing 150 lb. balls at each other. But, so goes the world.

SHILOH, 6–7 April 1862

Anon

The author – possibly W.W. Worthington – was a private soldier in the Union army.

Field of Shiloh, Tennessee, April 14th, 1862
Dear King: – I commence writing you a letter, which, I know, you will be glad to get; for I mean to tell you what our battalion did on the 6th and 7th inst., whilst the great battle at this place was progressing. . . . Leaving Columbia, we took up the line of march for Savannah, a distance of eighty-two miles through a country almost uninhabited and barren to the last degree. On Saturday night we encamped at a place seventeen miles from the latter town. Starting again the next morning, we had proceeded but a little

way when the noise of the battle of that disastrous day broke upon
our ears. As we advanced the cannonading became each moment
more distinct. It was plain that a desperate fight was going on
somewhere: but not one of our number dreamed that Grant had
been attacked and was at that instant slowly losing ground before
the enemy. Indeed the general belief was created by reports
brought from the front that our gunboats were attacking some
batteries at a place called Hamburg. About noon, however, we
began to think it possible that in some way or other our aid might
be needed; for we were halted in an old cotton field, our arms were
inspected, and rations and ammunition were issued. Still we were
ignorant of the terrible conflict then going on, though by this time
the ground fairly trembled under our feet with the rapid discharge
of artillery. Again pushing on, sweltering in the hot southern sun,
travelling over roads almost impassable and fording several
streams, about dark we halted for a few hours at a creek three
miles inland from Savannah. There we learned for the first time,
that instead of a gunboat bombardment, that day had been fought
at Pittsburg.

 Landing, the bloodiest battle in which American troops were ever
engaged. The accounts of the conflict were most cheering. They
represented that Grant had that morning attacked the immense
army under Albert Sidney Johnston and Beauregard, completely
defeating and routing it after a desperate fight of fifteen hours
duration. The cannon we continued to hear at intervals were said
to be those hurried forward in pursuit of the flying enemy. You
may be sure we were jubilant at this news; although we declaimed
somewhat against the selfishness that precipitated the engagement
and won the victory before Buell's column had an opportunity to
take a part. Little did we dream that so far from having gained a
triumph, Grant's force was then defeated and panic-stricken, with
an insolent foe occupying most of his camps, and that the morrow
would introduce us to scenes of carnage the mere imagination of
which sickens the heart.

    It was quite dark, though still early in the night, when we moved
on again. The men were in the best of spirits, rude witticisms,
laughter and snatches of song ran along the whole line. Here and
there some fellow boasted of the gallant deeds he would have
performed had he been in the day's engagement. The officers, on
the other hand, were more quiet than usual. They marched in
silence or gathered in little knots and conversed in whispers. At

length, the town of Savannah was entered. Every house in the place seemed to be illuminated; for each had been converted into an hospital and was packed from attic to basement with the dying and wounded who had been conveyed thither by the steamer.

Groans and cries of pain saluted our ears from all the buildings we passed. Through the windows, the sash of which were removed to give air to the injured, we could see the surgeons plying their horrid profession. The atmosphere was that of a vast dissecting room. The streets were crowded with ambulances, baggage trains, parties bearing the victims of the fight on stretchers, on rails, on rude litters of muskets and on their shoulders, and with batteries of artillery and long lines of infantry waiting to be taken to the scene of the struggle. The confusion everywhere visible, the shouting, cursing, quarrelling, beggars descriptions. Teams of mules, abandoned by their drivers, ran away trampling down every thing in their course. Quartermasters rode about at furious pace trying to extricate their transportation from the general mass. Doctors, one hand full of instruments, the other of bandages, and covered with blood, wildly rushed through the immense crowd in search of additional subjects of their art. Still, from all that could be gathered, the idea appeared to be that we had achieved a great victory. No one could exactly tell the events of the day; but the fact of our decisive triumph was unquestioned. The falsity of this common opinion every reader of the newspapers already knows.

Getting on board the "Hiawatha," by midnight we were ploughing the turbid Tennessee river *en route* for Pittsburg Landing, by water a distance of fourteen miles. From the officers of the steamer we got other accounts of the battle, which we afterwards ascertained to be correct. Their statements were, that Johnston and Beauregard, hoping to destroy Grant before he was joined by Buell, then close at hand, made a furious attack upon him, in great strength, that Sunday morning immediately after daylight. There is some dispute whether or not we had outposts; those who maintain we had, admit that they were playing cards at the time of the assault. At all events our troops were completely and criminally surprised. Unable to form to resist the onslaught, hundreds of them were mercilessly shot down in their tents and company streets. Those who escaped fled in the greatest terror through the camps in their rear, spreading the panic and closely followed by the successful foe. At least two miles of the ground occupied by our forces was thus abandoned before the regiments near the river could be brought to present a front to the rebels. A temporary check was then given to the enemy's impetuous advance, but being strongly reinforced they pushed our army slowly and surely towards the landing. During the whole day the battle raged with violence. Several corps of our volunteers behaved with great gallantry; but others ran at the first fire, and with those surprised in the morning (at least 10,000 men) could not again be brought into action. But the Secessionists steadily gained upon us. Seven batteries of our light artillery and a large number of our soldiers fell into their hands, as well as thousands of tents, and immense quantities of Commissary and Quartermaster's stores. When night closed upon the struggle we were driven within three hundred yards of the river, and would have been pushed into it had not the spiteful little gunboats then been enabled to come to our relief. Our loss in the engagement was terrible; but it was not all we suffered. At times when the fortune of war was most decidedly against us, the skulkers under the bluff, would rush in crowds to reach the steamers moored in the Tennessee, and by jostling and pushing each other into and struggling together in the water, hundreds of them were drowned. Little pity is felt for their fate, of course; but still these help to swell the casualties of that disastrous day.

Regaled, as we were, during the entire passage from Savannah to Pittsburg Landing, with stories of defeat and forebodings of what would occur the next day, you may be certain that we were not as comfortable as if we were in the old barracks. It was plain to the dullest comprehension that McCook's, Nelson's and Crittenden's divisions of Buell's army, then arrived at the scene of action, would have work enough to do early in the morning, and that too against an enemy flushed with recent victory. It seemed like folly to hope for success; for our strength did not exceed thirty thousand. From Grant's badly beaten and demoralized force we expected nothing, unless it was a mere show of numbers. On the other hand, the rebels were estimated at from 60,000 to 80,000. These considerations did not do much to inspirit, whilst throughout the night our anxiety was kept alive and our consciousness of the immediate presence of the foe not permitted to slumber by the regular firing from the gunboats upon the camps of the enemy close beside those of our own.

At daybreak on Monday the 7th inst. our battalion was disembarked. Forcing its way with difficulty through the vast crowd of fugitives from the previous day's fight gathered on the river bank, we scrambled up the bluff in the best way we could and formed in the camp of the Missouri Artillery. Here there were more refugees, their officers riding among them and urging them to rally, but without the least success. I never witnessed such abject fear as these fellows exhibited. Without a single avenue of escape in the event of defeat, they were unable, even, to muster up the desperation of cornered cowards. It is said that several in high command set them the example of pusillanimity. As we moved among them they inquired "what regiment is that?" "15th Regulars," replied some of our men. "Well, you'll catch regular hell today," was their rejoinder. Others said "Boys, it's of no use; we were beaten yesterday and you'll be beaten now." But still our men got into line well, and were marched by the right flank a few hundred yards to the place where the action of the previous day had ended. Here Capt. Swaine and Major King joined us, knapsacks were unslung, and we made the final preparations for the conflict we knew to be imminent. Being informed that we were the reserve of Rousseau's Brigade, we were slowly moved forward in column at half distance, through camps our troops had abandoned in the fight of the 6th inst. Other corps, all the while, were passing us on either side, and disappearing from view in a dip of ground in front, but as yet the engagement had not begun.

Let me try, at this point, to give you as good an idea of the field of battle as I am able. The Tennessee river at Pittsburg Landing describes a considerable curve; in the neck formed by this bend and some distance outside of it were the camps of Gen. Grant's command. On the morning of the 7th, the rebels were posted some distance inside of the ground formerly occupied by us, so that the line of conflict was pretty nearly straight between the two points of the semi-circle. Nelson's division was on our extreme left, resting on the river; Crittenden was next to him on his right, then came McCook in the centre, and joined to him was McClernand, who had other of Grant's generals beyond him. This order continued unbroken until the struggle was over.

Nelson and Crittenden's commands having passed the left flank of our battalion speedily became engaged. A few scattering shots were heard from their direction, which were soon followed by such a heavy firing of small arms that it was plain our men had found the enemy. The field artillery also broke in with its thunder, increasing the din already so great that it was difficult to hear one's self speak. As further evidence that the battle had begun in earnest, a mounted officer dashed by, crying, "bring on the ambulances," and those vehicles were at once taken to the front, to return in a few minutes laden with mangled freight. Other wounded men, some on foot, others carried by their comrades, likewise now came to the rear. From these we learned that Nelson and Crittenden, although suffering severely, were steadily pushing the rebels back, a story attested by the frequent cheers that arose from their gallant fellows.

A sharp firing that now took place almost immediately in our front, showed that the left and centre of our (McCook's) division had got into action, and that the battle was rapidly becoming general. Our battalion was instantly deployed into line to receive the foe should the troops in advance give way. While in this position, Generals Buell and Rousseau rode up, ordered us to proceed to the right of the brigade, which was the right of the division, and be ready for any emergency, and to send out at the same time a company of skirmishers to provoke an attack. This converted us from a reserve into an assaulting party.

Forming in column by division on the first, we marched by the right flank to the position we were to occupy, Captain Haughey with his command, being thrown forward to feel the enemy. (I will state here that battalions of the 16th and 19th regiments US Infantry, the whole under Major John H. King, were with us and shared in all our operations.) At this place we again deployed, then moved by the right of companies to the front, until a little hill between us and the rebels was surmounted, when we were again brought into line. Rapid discharges of small arms forward of our left flank, now showed that our skirmishers were successful in their search. Again we were advanced, until having gained some distance, we were ordered to lie close to the ground. Immediately we were exposed to a cannonade and fire of musketry, whose severity defies description. From three batteries and their strong support of infantry just before us, masked by the underbrush, came a shower of grape, canister, spherical case, rifle balls, &c., that would have swept every one of us away had we been standing on our feet. An examination I have since made of the ground exhibits the fact that every tree and sapling bears the marks of shot. Protecting ourselves as we did, our loss was still severe. Among the injured were Capt. Acker of the 16th, killed, and Capt. Peterson of the 15th, wounded in the head. As yet, as I have said before, the foe was concealed in

the thick woods so that we could not see them; but now emboldened, perhaps, by what they supposed their irresistible attack,
they emerged from their cover. Never did they commit a more fatal
mistake. Our men, restrained by their officers, had not discharged
a piece up to this time. But now each coolly marked his man; and
when Capt. Swaine, in a voice that could be heard along the whole
line, gave the command to fire, our Springfield rifles dealt a
destruction that was awful. After pelting the rebels a little while
longer, we again moved forward to the sound of the bugle, taking
to the earth once more when the enemy opened upon us. Here
Lieut. Mitchell of the 16th was killed, and Lieut. Lyster of the
19th, and 1st Sergeants Williams and Kiggins of the 15th dangerously wounded. Halting a few moments to reply, we moved down
upon the traitors a third time, subjected the while to a fearful storm
of missiles, by which Capt. Curtiss and Lieut. Wykoff of the 15th
were very severely hurt, and 1st Sergeant Killink of the same corps
instantly killed. But at length the artillery of the enemy, that had
been playing upon us so long, came in sight. Hastily fixing
bayonets, we charged upon it at a double-quick. Capt. Keteltas
of the 15th being then shot through the body. Unable to withstand
our desperate assault, the rebel cannoneers abandoned their guns,
and with the infantry supports fled across an open space into the
woods beyond. An opportunity offered at this point to ascertain
the havoc we had done. Every horse in each piece and caisson lay
dead in his harness, and the ground was covered with the killed
and dying. Among the latter was the Chief of the Artillery. As we
came up he said, "You have slain all my men and cattle, and you
may take the battery and be damned." But we had not leisure to
stop and talk with him or any other person; for we were already
being fired upon from the new covert of the foe. Pushing forward
amid great danger across the field, we gained the edge of the
timber and continued the fight in which we had then been engaged
for more than five hours.

The foregoing was the state of affairs at high noon. Let us pause
a moment to see what was the condition of the battle field at that
hour. There was no fighting on the right of the centre; indeed it
had not been severe in that quarter during the day. On the left,
Nelson and Crittenden having repulsed the enemy, were resting on
their arms; for the foe in their front had mysteriously disappeared.
Our three battalions were our only troops then hotly engaged. You
inquire, "where were the rest of the rebels?" That is just what I

propose telling you. Leaving only enough of men before the other divisions to mask their purpose, they were engaged massing their troops, those that had been engaged as well as their reserves, for an overwhelming onslaught upon the right of our centre, where we had contested all morning without support. I think it possible that Gen. Rousseau suspected their scheme; for whilst we strove in the edge of the timber, two regiments of volunteers took position on our right, and a section of a battery quietly unlimbered on our left. Scarcely were these dispositions completed, when down upon us came the enemy, pouring in a withering, staggering fire, that compelled the regiments just mentioned to break and fly, in such confusion that they could not be rallied again. This panic not only left us alone to sustain the dreaded onset, but in addition, put us in extraordinary peril by the total exposure of our left flank. The occasion was indeed critical. But before the enemy could take any advantage of the condition of things, Capt. Swaine averted the danger by causing our battalion to charge front, thus giving the 15th, 16th and 19th the form of two sides of a triangle. Here we fought for a time that seemed interminable, holding the rebel force in check, until Col. Gibson's brigade, hastily brought up to our relief, assisted by a flanking attack from Nelson and Crittenden's divisions started the foe in the retreat, that shortly became a rout. Falling back, then, only long enough to replenish our ammunition, we joined in the pursuit, keeping it up, notwithstanding our exhausted condition, until we got beyond the line of the camps captured from our troops the day before.

I do not undertake to say what body of troops engaged in the battle of Shiloh, is entitled to the most honor. But I unhesitatingly assert that the 1st Battalion of the 15th US Infantry did its whole duty. For seven hours it fought without ceasing, that, too, after it had marched seventeen miles the day before, and been deprived of sleep the night previous. And when the dreadful attack upon our centre was made, which caused Willich's German veterans to scatter like cattle upon a thousand hills, it still stood up to its work as though there was no such word as defeat in its lexicon. Throughout the struggle, Major King, Capt. Swaine and the company officers conducted themselves with great gallantry. In our company, nine men are killed and wounded. The loss of the command is sixty-three. Curtenius escaped without a scratch.

Dr Parry informs me that our loss in killed and wounded, will not fall short of nine thousand men, and may exceed that number.

From what I have seen myself, I give the fullest credence to his statement. On the evening of the engagement, the dead were everywhere. There never has been such carnage on this continent. I trust I may never again see anything of the kind.

The battle was fought in the woods, which were as serviceable to the enemy as fortifications. You may travel for a day around here and you will scarcely find a tree, sapling or twig, that has not been struck by a bullet. How any of us escaped is more than I can imagine.

CIVIL WAR: ONE MAN'S WAR, August–September 1862

Dennis Ford, 28th Massachusetts Volunteers

Washington, September 6th, 1862

Dear wife and neighbors. I am living still, thank God. I been in four battles since I left Newport News. We had two severe ones. We lost half our regiment. The last fight, my clothes were riddled with balls. I was grazed in the right arm. It knocked my arm dead, though thank God I have not seen one drop of blood as yet. The rubber blanket I had on my back was riddled. A ball struck me on the shoe. They fell around me like hail. James Phillips is shot dead. The rest of the boys are safe. John Maher was wounded. Peter King got something like a wound, it is nothing. John Fenning was wounded. Con Roach came out safe. Maurice and the Donnellys are safe. We lost in the last fight 130 men out of our regiment.

It would be too tedious for me to tell what I went through – the long marching for the last 26 days. Half hungry, some would kill cows and skin a part of them, cut off a piece and waste it, and never open them. Some would shoot pigs and sheep, and would never open them, only cut a piece and roast it and leave the rest behind. Some would carry their coffee in their hand and march in the ranks and drink it, some would spill it. Sometimes, the dinner and breakfast would be cooking, they would get word to march, they would have to spill it and throw it away and march. The rebels fare worse than we do.

Let me know how are the children. Let me know about the note. I did not receive an answer to the last letter I wrote you from Newport News. Write as soon as you receive this, as we don't know the hour we will be on the march.

The war is raging in every direction the rebels fight in the woods. So I must conclude. Give my best love and respects to all the friends and neighbors. Let me know how times are in Haverhill. We received no pay for the last two months. When you write, let me know all the particulars. Our priest can't stand the hardship, we fear he will leave though he is a smart young man. They treat him very bad.

So I must conclude. Do pray for us, we look shabby and thin, though we were called a clean regiment. I saw a great deal shot and wounded. Balls drove through their [lines]. The 28th Mass. suffered [along with] the 79th New York. Our regiment stood the severest fire that was witnessed. During the war, when we got into the woods, we ran through what we did not shoot. We bayoneted them. One man begged and got no mercy, a yankee ran him through. Thank God it was not an Irishman did it.

So I must conclude. I remain your humble husband Dennis Ford until death. I am in hopes I will see Haverhill once more before I die with the help of God. Direct to Washington, to me, Company H, 28 Regiment Mass. Vol. Tell Mrs. McCormick her friend Thomas Cline is well. There was one James Short from Lawrence [who] fell in the last battle.

GRANT BESIEGES VICKSBURG, May 1863
Special Correspondent, Cleveland Herald

General Ulysses S. Grant besieged Confederate forces at Vicksburg from May to 4 July 1863. His victory there brought the Mississippi under Union control.

. . . Let us climb the parapet and see the siege by moonlight. In front of us, beyond the enemy's works, but hidden from us, lies the city of Vicksburg. Look carefully, and you can distinguish the spires of the courthouse and two or three churches. The rebels had a signal station on the former when we came, but our shells made it too warm for them, and they withdrew. The mortars are playing tonight, and they are well worth seeing. We watch a moment, and in the direction of Young's Point, beyond the city, suddenly up shoots a flash of light, and in a moment the ponderous shell, with its fuse glowing and sparkling, rises slowly from behind the bluffs; up, up, it goes, as though mounting to the zenith, over it comes towards us, down through its flight trajectory into the city, and explodes with a shock that jars the ground for miles. There are women and tender children where those shells fall, but war is war.

Sherman's eight-inch monsters are grumbling far way on the right. Nearer, McPherson's, too, are playing – we can even see the cannoneers beside them at each flash. Ours will open at midnight; then there will be music to your heart's content. Meanwhile, let us go to the front. A hundred yards to the right of where we now are we enter a deep trench. Following this, as it winds down around the hill, we reach the opening of a cave or mine. The air within is damp and close, like that of a vault. Candles are burning dimly at intervals, and we hear a hum of voices far within and out of sight. We proceed, and presently meet two men carrying a barrow of earth, for our boys are at work night and day. Finally, we reach the moonlight again, and emerge into a wide, deep trench, cut across the line of the covered way. This is open, and filled with troops, who protect the working party. A heavy parapet of cotton bales and earth is built on the side towards the enemy, and we must mount them to look over.

We are now within sociable distance of the chivalry. Those men lying on the ground, ten to thirty yards from us, are our boys, our advance pickets; but that grey fellow, with the bright musket, which glistens so, a few steps beyond, is a "reb.", long-haired and hot-blooded, one of Wall's famous Texas legion – a bulldog to fight, you may be sure.

Now jump down and enter the mouth of the other mine, which leads toward the salient of the enemy's work. Stumbling along, we reach the end where the men are digging. The candle burns very dimly – the air is almost stifling. Never mind, let us watch them. See that slender, bright-looking fellow swinging that pick. Great beaded drops of perspiration trickle down his face; there is not a dry thread in his coarse, grey shirt; but no matter, the pick swings, and each stroke slices down six inches of the tough subsoil of Mississippi. That fellow was "Jim", once a tender-handed, smooth-faced, nice young man, whose livery-stable, billiard and cigar bills were a sore trial to his worthy governor. Jim says that he used to wear gloves and "store-clothes", and that girls called him good-looking, but that's played out now; he is going for Uncle Sam.

But we return to the fresh air. Look over the parapet again towards the turret, where we saw the rebel picket. Do you see the little grey mounds which cover the hillside so thickly? – ten, twenty, thirty, you can count on a few square rods. Ah, my friend, this is sacred ground you are looking upon. There our boys charged; there they were slain in heaps; but they pressed on, and leaped into the ditch. They climbed the parapet, and rolled back into eternity. Others followed them; their flag was planted, and they sprang over, to meet their certain death. An hour passed, and *one* returned; the rest were dead.

THE AMERICAN ASSAULT ON THE PYRAMIDS, Egypt, 1864

Mark Twain

In 1864 Twain was hired by the *Daily Alta California* newspaper to accompany one of the first organized tours of the Old World. Twain's dispatches were subsequently expanded into *Innocents Abroad*.

At the distance of a few miles the Pyramids, rising above the palms, looked very clean-cut, very grand and imposing, and very soft and filmy as well. They swam in a rich haze that took from them all suggestions of unfeeling stone, and made them seem only the airy nothings of a dream – structures which might blossom into tiers of vague arches, or ornate colonnades, may be, and change and change again into all graceful forms of architecture, while we looked, and then melt deliciously away and blend with the tremulous atmosphere.

At the end of the levee we left the mules and went in a sail-boat across an arm of the Nile, or an overflow, and landed where the sands of the Great Sahara left their embankment, as straight as a wall, along the verge of the alluvial plain of the river. A laborious walk in the flaming sun brought us to the foot of the great Pyramid of Cheops. It was a fairy vision no longer. It was a corrugated, unsightly mountain of stone. Each of its monstrous sides was a wide stairway which rose upward, step above step, narrowing as it went, till it tapered to a point far aloft in the air. Insect men and women – pilgrims from the *Quaker City* – were creeping about its dizzy perches, and one little black swarm were waving postage stamps from the airy summit – handkerchiefs will be understood.

Of course we were besieged by a rabble of muscular Egyptians and Arabs who wanted the contract of dragging us to the top – all tourists are. Of course you could not hear your own voice for the din that was around you. Of course the Sheiks said *they* were the only responsible parties; that all contracts must be made with them, all moneys paid over to them, and none exacted from us by any but themselves alone. Of course they contracted that the varlets who dragged us up should not mention backsheesh once. For such is the usual routine. Of course we contracted with them, paid them, were delivered into the hands of the draggers, dragged up the Pyramids, and harried and be-devilled for backsheesh from the foundation clear to the summit. We paid it, too, for we were purposely spread very far apart over the vast side of the Pyramid. There was no help near if we called, and the Herculeses who dragged us had a way of asking sweetly and flatteringly for backsheesh, which was seductive, and of looking fierce and threatening to throw us down the precipice, which was persuasive and convincing.

Each step being full as high as a dinner-table; there being very, very many of the steps; an Arab having hold of each of our arms and springing upward from step to step and snatching us with them, forcing us to lift our feet as high as our breasts every time, and do it rapidly and keep it up till we were ready to faint – who shall say it is not lively, exhilarating, lacerating, muscle-straining, bone-wrenching and perfectly excruciating and exhausting pastime, climbing the Pyramids? I beseeched the varlets not to twist *all* my joints asunder; I iterated, reiterated, even *swore* to them that I did not wish to beat anybody to the top; did all I could to convince them that if I got there the last of all I would feel blessed above men and grateful to them for ever; I begged them, prayed them, pleaded with them to let me stop and rest a moment – only one little moment: and they only answered with some more frightful springs, and an unenlisted volunteer behind opened a bombardment of determined boosts with his head which threatened to batter my whole political economy to wreck and ruin.

Twice, for one minute, they let me rest while they extorted backsheesh, and then continued their maniac flight up the pyramid. They wished to beat the other parties. It was nothing to them that I, a stranger, must be sacrificed upon the altar of their unholy ambition. But in the midst of sorrow, joy blooms. Even in this dark hour I had a sweet consolation. For I knew that except these Mohammedans repented they would go straight to perdition some day. And *they* never repent – they never forsake their paganism. This thought calmed me, cheered me, and I sank down, limp and exhausted, upon the summit, but happy, *so* happy and serene within.

On the one hand, a mighty sea of yellow sand stretched away toward the ends of the earth, solemn, silent, shorn of vegetation, its solitude uncheered by any forms of creature life; on the other, the Eden of Egypt was spread below us – a broad green floor, cloven by the sinuous river, dotted with villages, its vast distances measured and marked by the diminishing stature of receding clusters of palms. It lay asleep in an enchanted atmosphere. There was no sound, no motion. Above the date-plumes in the middle distance swelled a domed and pinnacled mass, glimmering through a tinted, exquisite mist; away toward the horizon a dozen shapely pyramids watched over ruined Memphis; and at our feet the bland impassible Sphynx looked out upon the picture from her throne in the sands as placidly and pensively as she had looked upon its like full fifty lagging centuries ago.

We suffered torture no pen can describe from the hungry appeals for backsheesh that gleamed from Arab eyes and poured incessantly from Arab lips. Why try to call up the traditions of vanished Egyptian grandeur; why try to fancy Egypt following dead Rameses to his tomb in the Pyramid, or the long multitude of Israel departing over the desert yonder? Why try to think at all? The thing was impossible. One must bring his meditations cut and dried, or else cut and dry them afterward.

The traditional Arab proposed, in the traditional way, to run down Cheops, cross the eighth of a mile of sand intervening between it and the tall Pyramid of Cephron, ascend to Cephron's summit and return to us on the top of Cheops – all in nine minutes by the watch, and the whole service to be rendered for a single dollar. In the first flush of irritation, I said let the Arab and his exploits go to the mischief. But stay. The upper third of Cephron was coated with dressed marble, smooth as glass. A blessed thought entered my brain. He must infallibly break his neck. Close the contract with dispatch, I said, and let him go. He started. We watched. He went bounding down the vast broadside, spring after spring, like an ibex. He grew smaller and smaller till he became a bobbing pigmy, away down toward the bottom – then disappeared. We turned and peered over the other side – forty seconds – eighty seconds – a hundred – happiness, he is dead already; – two minutes – and a quarter – "There he goes!" Too true – it was too true. He was very small now. Gradually, but surely, he overcame

the level ground. He began to spring and climb again. Up, up, up
– at last he reached the smooth coating – now for it. But he clung to
it with toes and fingers, like a fly. He crawled this way and that –
away to the right, slanting upward – away to the left, still slanting
upward – and stood at last, a black peg on the summit, and waved
his pigmy scarf! Then he crept downward to the raw steps again,
then picked up his agile heels and flew. We lost him presently. But
presently again we saw him under us, mounting with undiminished energy. Shortly he bounded into our midst with a gallant
war-whoop. Time, eight minutes, forty-one seconds. He had won.
His bones were intact. I was a failure. I reflected. I said to myself,
he is tired and must grow dizzy. I will risk another dollar on him.

He started again. Made the trip again. Slipped on the smooth
coating – I almost had him. But an infamous crevice saved him. He
was with us once more perfectly sound. Time, eight minutes, forty-
six seconds.

I said to Dan, "Lend me a dollar – I can beat this game yet."

Worse and worse. He won again. Time, eight minutes, forty-
eight seconds. I was out of all patience, now. I was desperate. –
Money was no longer of any consequence. I said, "Sirrah, I will
give you a hundred dollars to jump off this pyramid head first. If
you do not like the terms, name your bet. I scorn to stand on
expenses now. I will stay right here and risk money on you as long
as Dan has got a cent."

I was in a fair way to win, now, for it was a dazzling opportunity
for an Arab. He pondered a moment, and would have done it, I
think, but his mother arrived, then, and interfered. Her tears
moved me – I never can look upon the tears of woman with
indifference – and I said I would give her a hundred to jump off,
too.

But it was a failure. The Arabs are too high-priced in Egypt.
They put on airs unbecoming to such savages.

We descended, hot and out of humour. The dragoman lit
candles, and we all entered a hole near the base of the pyramid,
attended by a crazy rabble of Arabs who thrust their services upon
us uninvited. They dragged us up a long inclined chute, and
dripped candle-grease all over us. This chute was not more than
twice as wide and high as a Saratoga trunk, and was walled,
roofed, and floored with solid blocks of Egyptian granite as wide as
a wardrobe, twice as thick and three times as long. We kept on
climbing, through the oppressive gloom, till I thought we ought to

be nearing the top of the pyramid again, and then came to the
"Queen's Chamber," and shortly to the Chamber of the King.
These large apartments were tombs. The walls were built of
monstrous masses of smoothed granite, neatly joined together.
Some of them were nearly as large square as an ordinary parlour.
A great stone sarcophagus like a bath-tub stood in the centre of the
King's Chamber. Around it were gathered a picturesque group of
Arab savages and soiled and tattered pilgrims, who held their
candles aloft in the gloom while they chattered, and the winking
blurs of light shed a dim glory down upon one of the irrepressible
memento-seekers who was pecking at the venerable sarcophagus
with his sacrilegious hammer.

We struggled out to the open air and the bright sunshine, and
for the space of thirty minutes received ragged Arabs by couples,
dozens and platoons, and paid them backsheesh for services they
swore and proved by each other that they had rendered, but which
we had not been aware of before – and as each party was paid, they
dropped into the rear of the procession and in due time arrived
again with a newly invented delinquent list for liquidation.

We lunched in the shade of the pyramid, and in the midst of this
encroaching and unwelcome company, and then Dan and Jack
and I started away for a walk. A howling swarm of beggars
followed us – surrounded us – almost headed us off. A Sheik, in
flowing white bournous and gaudy head-gear, was with them. He
wanted more backsheesh. But we had adopted a new code – it was
millions for defence, but not a cent for backsheesh. I asked him if he
could persuade the others to depart if we paid him. He said yes –
for ten francs. We accepted the contract, and said –

"Now persuade your vassals to fall back."

He swung his long staff round his head and three Arabs bit the
dust. He capered among the mob like a very maniac. His blows fell
like hail, and wherever one fell a subject went down. We had to
hurry to the rescue and tell him it was only necessary to damage
them a little, he need not kill them. – In two minutes we were alone
with the Sheik, and remained so. The persuasive powers of this
illiterate savage were remarkable.

Each side of the Pyramid of Cheops is about as long as the
Capitol at Washington, or the Sultan's new palace on the Bos-
porus, and is longer than the greatest depth of St. Peter's at Rome
– which is to say that each side of Cheops extends seven hundred
and some odd feet. It is about seventy-five feet higher than the

cross on St. Peter's. The first time I ever went down the Mississippi, I thought the highest bluff on the river between St. Louis and New Orleans – it was near Selma, Missouri – was probably the highest mountain in the world. It is four hundred and thirteen feet high. It still looms in my memory with undiminished grandeur. I can still see the trees and bushes growing smaller and smaller as I followed them up its huge slant with my eye, till they became a feathery fringe on the distant summit. This symmetrical Pyramid of Cheops – this solid mountain of stone reared by the patient hands of men – this mighty tomb of a forgotten monarch – dwarfs my cherished mountain. For it is four hundred and eighty feet high. In still earlier years than those I have been recalling, Holliday's Hill, in our town, was to me the noblest work of God. It appeared to pierce the skies. It was nearly three hundred feet high. In those days I pondered the subject much, but I never could understand why it did not swathe its summit with never-failing clouds, and crown its majestic brow with everlasting snows. I had heard that such was the custom of great mountains in other parts of the world. I remembered how I worked with another boy, at odd afternoons stolen from study and paid for with stripes, to undermine and start from its bed an immense boulder that rested upon the edge of that hill-top; I remembered how, one Saturday afternoon, we gave three hours of honest effort to the task, and saw at last that our reward was at hand; I remembered how we sat down, then, and wiped the perspiration away, and waited to let a picnic party get out of the way in the road below – and then we started the boulder. It was splendid. It went crashing down the hill-side, tearing up saplings, mowing bushes down like grass, ripping and crushing and smashing everything in its path – eternally splintered and scattered a wood pile at the foot of the hill and then sprang from the high bank clear over a dray in the road – the negro glanced up once and dodged – and the next second it made infinitesimal mincemeat of a frame cooper shop, and the coopers swarmed out like bees. Then we said it was perfectly magnificent, and left. Because the coopers were starting up the hill to inquire.

Still, that mountain, prodigious as it was, was nothing to the Pyramid of Cheops. I could conjure up no comparison that would convey to my mind a satisfactory comprehension of the magnitude of a pile of monstrous stones that covered thirteen acres of ground and stretched upward four hundred and eighty tiresome feet, and so I gave it up and walked down to the Sphynx.

THE MARCH ON GEORGIA, 1864

Frederick C. Buerstatte

Private Buerstatte served with the 26th Regiment Wisconsin Volunteers in Sherman's historic march on Georgia.

Diary: 12th February 1864 Tonight I volunteered for duty with the 26th Regiment Wis. Infantry Volunteers for 3 years or duration of the war.

6th March – I received a physical examination by the doctor at Camp Randall and was declared fit.

15th March – We were mustered into the service of the U.S.

18th April – We left Camp Randall and were sent to the regiment.

23rd April – We arrived at the regiment at Lookout Valley, Tennessee.

27th April – We finally received *rifles*.

2nd May – We left on march from Lookout Valley this morning. We are now 15 miles from Georgia. We came to Missionary Ridge battlefield on the way. The roadside was full of graves and the cannonballs and rifle balls were buried in the trees.

5th May – Today in Georgia it is [?] day. We marched here yesterday. The Rebs are not far from here. Weather is beautiful and the air warm.

7th May – The entire army is on the move. We marched farther south yesterday and today. The area is hilly. We see few men but often women and children.

8th May – We marched to Tunnel Hill where the Rebs were. In the afternoon we had an encounter with the Rebs in which they were driven from their first position. We lost 2 dead and some wounded.

11th May – We marched in the direction of Rome. We drove the enemy before us and we heard General Grant had beaten the Rebs in Virginia. The soldiers hope to see the war come to an end this year. So do the enemy prisoners, some of whom look quite bewildered.

14th May – Since yesterday and today a lively skirmish has been occurring in front of us. We are lying here in a battle line. The enemy is resisting heavily and we will soon get into the fire because our advance troops are already in it. The Adjutant had acquired a detachment from the Army of the Potomac with which General Grant had beaten the Rebs after a 4 day battle. He captured 30 cannons and an entire division. We hear loud gunfire to the left and in front of us and it seems the enemy is being driven back.

15th May – Today is Pentecost day. The battle lasted yesterday into the night and this morning it continues again. We were relieved last night. Our entire division is on the march to try to surround the enemy. We marched until noon and set up a battle line and moved out. Our brigade attacked the enemy defenses but we were thrown back. We regrouped and attacked again. Our regiment moved ahead in good formation, but the other regiments broke up and we had to retreat again. We attacked again but did not succeed. We received reinforcements and took the defenses. This was a horrible fight. Dead and wounded lay everywhere. We were taken to the rear and spent a quiet night we are considerably disappointed since our regiment lost 70 men of 370 total.

16th May – The enemy was beaten this morning. We have the last stragglers of the Rebs behind us. We captured more material and ammunition. The guns they left behind are all destroyed. The road is scattered full of dead, horses, pieces of clothing, weapons. cartridge containers, etc. These are the tracks of an army in flight.

17th May – Last night we marched until 1:00 o'clock. Our cavalry is following the enemy. We are finding while marching many dead and wounded left behind by the enemy.

18th May – In the evening we got to the enemy area and built breastworks overnight. Enemy cavalry is in front of us. We are extremely exhausted from the long march.

19th May – At noon we engaged the enemy and the battle started. In spite of this, our regiment did not get into it. Good news from Virginia.

21st May – Rest day.

22nd May – One does not realize it, but today is Sunday. Tomorrow we march again. The heat is terrible and we are all almost "finished".

23rd May – Our company was assigned to train guard duty.

27th May – We were relieved of train guard duty and at midnight returned to our regiment encamped at Burnt Hickory.

28th May – The Rebs greeted us with cannon fire this morning. We relieved the 1st Brigade which was positioned behind breastworks. The entire area is thickly wooded.

30th May – The Rebs attacked last night but were driven off.

31st May – We were relieved last night and lay in reserve today.

2nd June – We marched on the right flank today. It rained a great deal. We are all wet through and through and there is an awful lot of mud! mud!

5th June – Today is Sunday, a beautiful day at home, but here we must keep our thoughts together, otherwise one does not know it is Sunday. The weather is finally clearing up after a long period of rain. Rations are becoming scarce.

7th June – Today we are encamped on a hill. We had to build breastworks deep into last night and are learning what the word hunger means.

8th June – Rest day.

16th June – We marched out at 2:00 o clock and met the Rebs at 6:00 o clock at Big Shanty. We laid for 2 hours through cannon and rifle fire on the ground and dared not get up. Two men were wounded from our regiment.

17th June – Last night we had to lay at night with rifles in our arms and then we built breastworks.

19th June – We advanced 2 miles. The Rebs left their defenses, strong defenses, which were built a long time ago.

20th June – We got into a skirmish yesterday in which we lost a lot of men.

22nd June – Today was again another bloody day near Marietta. We had to attack the well-entrenched enemy at noon. We ran across a wide open field with shouts and into the next woods where we came upon the enemy outpost defenses and got to within 300 yards of their main defenses. Our regiment lost 45 dead and wounded.

23rd June – We were relieved last night and marched farther to the right where today we built breastworks in view of the enemy who provided us with cannonball music.

3rd July – While we were on the march, the Rebs gave up their forward defenses and retreated with us at their heels.

4th July – Today we stood watch and returned at noon. All day long a terrible cannonade has been going on in front and to the left of us. Toward evening we marched about 3 miles and built breastworks.

6th July – Today we are positioned on a hill about 2 miles from the Chattahoochie River. The Rebs are in retreat. We marched here yesterday in the greatest heat in which many of our men collapsed from exhaustion.

9th July – We established our camp here. Weather is beautiful.

16th July – We stood general inspection today.

17th July – Today is Sunday. We had to clean up the camp after which we received orders to march.

18th July – Yesterday evening we crossed the river on pontoons and marched back and forth in the woods.

19th July – We rested today.

20th July – Today we are engaged in a terrible battle with the Rebs at Peach Tree Creek. At 2:00 o'clock PM. our brigade which was at the left Rank of the corps, joined the 4th Corps in battle line. The enemy attacked at which time we advanced. Our regiment was as always in the forward battle line. We advanced over a small hill and into a valley in which a small creek flowed. Then the Rebs came toward us down the hill in front of us. Now the firing really began. The gunfire exceeded anything I had ever heard before. We loaded and fired as fast as possible. The Rebs came to within 10 paces of us, at which time our musket balls became too thick for them. They turned to the right and retreated up the hill with us behind them. This was a sight which I had never seen before and hope never to see again. The entire field was scattered with dead, wounded and dying. The wounded moaned so much that I could hardly watch. However, we had no time and had to advance up the hill. There stood a fence behind which we petitioned ourselves. The Rebs tried to advance again but did not succeed, because a battery was placed on the hill behind us which greeted the enemy terribly with cannonballs. After 4 hours of firing, we were finally relieved and went to the second battle line. The firing lasted into the night. At night I helped carry more wounded from the field. We also captured a flag from the 33rd Mississippi Regiment.

21st July – This morning our regiment, after a sleepless night, had to bury the dead Rebs which laid before our regiment. They were all from the 33rd Mississippi Regiment. Our regiment lost 9 dead and 36 wounded. We buried over 50 Rebs, among them Colonel Drake and most of the officers of the 33rd Miss. Regiment. Now we had to clean our guns.

22nd July – Today we marched toward Atlanta and built breastworks. Toward evening the Rebs greeted us with cannon fire. Four cannons are positioned between our regiment. One can see the towers of Atlanta.

23rd July – We changed our position again. We marched further to the right near the First Division and lay behind "Dulgars Battery". Now the bombardment of Atlanta has begun. Heavy defenses rise before us.

29th July – A bloody battle occurred yesterday to our right and in front of us at the 15th Corps.

21st August – Today is Sunday. One almost doesn't realize it because the bombardment continues without letup. We received a little whiskey today. The Rebs bothered us very much. They lobbed 64-pounders at us.

27th August – Last night we quietly left our breastworks and retreated to the Chattahoochie River where we burnt breastworks today.

28th August – Today is Sunday. Yesterday the Rebel cavalry attacked our outposts and took several prisoners. Our Corps is stationed at the river as bridge guard.

2nd Sept. – This morning we left our quarters at the river at 5:00 o'clock and filed through wood and field over hill and dale toward Atlanta. We came to the city at 10:00 o'clock. The city immediately surrendered. We drove 30 Reb cavalry before us through the city. Several stores were broken into and tobacco was taken from them. Many Germans live here.

6th Sept. – We have established summer encampment on the south side of Atlanta.

8th Sept. – The Army finally returned with 6000 prisoners.

11th Sept. – Today is Sunday. The bells in the city are ringing but one cannot go to church no matter how hard one tries because one must "stay home" and clean rifles.

19th Sept. – We signed our pay lists.

26th Sept. – Today our division stood review before Major General Slocum. Our regiment was highly praised.

1st Oct. – Our tie with the North was again cut by the Reb General Wheeler with his cavalry.

5th Oct. – Hood's Army is to our rear and our whole army including our Corps chased him. We were paid today.

8th Oct. – Our regiment marched away from Atlanta to the river to a position at the railroad bridge.

19th Oct. – This morning we took 3 days ration and patrolled and foraged toward Roswell.

21st Oct. – We returned today at noon. Yesterday we camped 1 mile on this side of Roswell overnight. Yesterday the wagons were loaded with corn. At noon we marched toward Marietta and today we marched 16 miles in 6 hours.

9th Nov. – Today we heard loud cannon and musket fire near Atlanta.

10th Nov. – We heard that yesterday 2 Reb infantry regiments and 1 Reb cavalry regiment were seen near the city but retreated quickly.

14th Nov. – This morning we burned our camp and marched to Atlanta to our brigade. We received more whiskey last night.

15th Nov. – This morning the entire Army of the HAC. 15 A.C. 19 A.C. and the 20th Army Corps [A.C.] was on the move toward Atlanta.

19th Nov. – Tonight we are about 45 miles from Atlanta. We began to live from that which we found on the plantations such as potatoes, pigs, chickens, sheep and cornmeal.

20th Nov. – Today is Sunday but just the same we are marching in rainy weather and mud. We came through the little town of Madison.

21st–22nd Nov. – Rain and mud.

23rd Nov. – It cleared up today. We had strong winds. During last 3 days of marching through rain and mud, we crowded ourselves quite close together. We passed through Milledgeville which was the governor's residence. He fled 3 days ago; it is the capital city of Georgia.

26th Nov.   Tonight we came upon Andersonville.

27th Nov. – This morning we had inspection of rifles cartridges and cartridge cases. We moved on at 10:00 o clock.

29th Nov. – Today we marched through the considerably larger town of Louisville.

30th Nov. – We had a well-deserved rest day today.

4th Dec. – Today is Sunday but we had to march anyhow. The entire area around Andersonville is swampy and roads are bad.

7th Dec. – We marched among ruins and mud. It is still 25 miles to Savannah.

9th Dec. – We hear cannon fire to our left in front of us near the 14th Army Corps.

10th Dec. – Before us and near us we hear cannon fire near the 14th Corps and 17 A.C. The 14th is to our left and 17 A.C. is to our right and in front of us. We were formed into a battle line at noon.

11th Dec. – The bombing continues without stopping near us. Our rations are now short and one discovers what hunger feels like.

12th Dec. – All the trains which we encountered from Atlanta to Savannah were destroyed.

14th Dec. – The bombing still continues vigorously. This morning the 2nd Div. of the 15th Army Corps attacked Fort McEllister and captured it on the first advance. They captured 26 cannons and 1500 men which was the entire complement of the fort. Our food line should now be open again. We now have too little to live on and too many dying. We have only a small amount of rice and an ounce of meat per day.

16th Dec. – One hears that a 15 ton food supply for this army is on the way which should arrive in about 2 days.

17th Dec. – Another food supply arrived which made us very happy.

19th Dec. – We received ½ rations again.

21st Dec. – This morning the order came to advance. The Rebs have left and we had to pack in 5 minutes and march toward Savannah, where we set up quarters 1 mile west of the city. We now have as much rice as we want. The Rebs have fled to South Carolina. We captured much rice, cannons and munitions which the enemy left behind. We also captured many prisoners.

24th Dec. – We cleaned our quarters. Each person planted a Christmas tree in front of his tent.

25th Dec. – Christmas morning inspection. We received a ½ unit crackers, rice and meat.

26th Dec. – We received orders to march tomorrow across the Savannah River.

27th Dec. – The march orders were rescinded. Good news from Tennessee. General Hood's army is completely demoralized.

30th Dec. – Today the entire 20th Army Corps was reviewed by General Sherman in Savannah in beautiful weather. We received orders to march tonight.

31st Dec. – We marched in the rain 2 miles east of the city. It was cold and returned to our old quarters for the first time since November 14th. We received sugar and full cracker rations. Cold wind.

End of 1864.

CIVIL WAR: LEE SURRENDERS AT
APPOMATTOX COURTHOUSE, 9 April 1865
General Horace Porter

With the fall of Richmond on 3 April, Robert E. Lee realized that he had
little choice but to surrender his Army of Northern Virginia to Ulysses S.
Grant. The two men met at the house of Wilmer McClean in the village of
Appomattox Courthouse. Horace Porter served on the staff of Grant.

We entered, and found General Grant sitting at a marble-topped
table in the center of the room, and Lee sitting beside a small oval
table near the front window, in the corner opposite to the door by
which we entered, and facing General Grant. We walked in softly
and ranged ourselves quietly about the sides of the room, very
much as people enter a sick-chamber when they expect to find the
patient dangerously ill.

The contrast between the two commanders was striking, and
could not fail to attract marked attention; they sat ten feet apart
facing each other. General Grant, then nearly forty-three years of
age, was five feet eight inches in height, with shoulders slightly
stooped. His hair and full beard were a nut-brown, without a
trace of gray in them. He had on a single-breasted blouse, made
of dark-blue flannel, unbuttoned in front, and showing a waistcoat underneath. He wore an ordinary pair of top-boots, with his
trousers inside, and was without spurs. The boots and portions of
his clothes were spattered with mud. He had no sword, and a pair
of shoulder-straps was all there was about him to designate his
rank. In fact, aside from these, his uniform was that of a private
soldier.

Lee, on the other hand, was fully six feet in height, and quite
erect for one of his age, for he was Grant's senior by sixteen years.
His hair and full beard were silver-gray, and quite thick, except
that the hair had become a little thin in the front. He wore a new
uniform of Confederate gray, buttoned up to the throat, and at his
side he carried a long sword of exceedingly fine workmanship, the
hilt studded with jewels. His top-boots were comparatively new,
and seemed to have on them some ornamental stitching of red silk.
Like his uniform, they were singularly clean, and but little travel-
stained. On the boots were handsome spurs, with large rowels. A
felt hat, which in color matched pretty closely that of his uniform,
and a pair of long buckskin gauntlets lay beside him on the table.

General Grant began the conversation by saying "I met you once before, General Lee, while we were serving in Mexico, when you came over from General Scott's headquarters to visit Garland's brigade, to which I then belonged. I have always remembered your appearance, and I think I should have recognized you anywhere."

"Yes," replied General Lee, "I know I met you on that occasion, and I have often thought of it and tried to recollect how you looked, but I have never been able to recall a single feature.'"

[There ensued more discussion about Mexico before Lee asked Grant to write down the surrender terms]

"Very well," replied General Grant, "I will write them out." And calling for his manifold order-book, he opened it on the table before him and proceeded to write the terms. The leaves had been so prepared that three impressions of the writing were made. He wrote very rapidly, and did not pause until he had finished the sentence ending with "officers appointed by me to receive them." Then he looked toward Lee, and his eyes seemed to be resting on the handsome sword that hung at that officer's side. He said afterward that this set him to thinking that it would be an unnecessary humiliation to require officers to surrender their swords, and a great hardship to deprive them of their personal baggage and horses, and after a short pause he wrote the sentence: "This will not embrace the side-arms of the officers, nor their private horses or baggage."

[After perusing the document, Lee pointed out that his cavalrymen and artillerymen owned their own horses and asked that they might keep them. Grant acceded, and Lee then formally accepted the surrender before exiting the house]

At a little before 4 o'clock General Lee shook hands with General Grant, bowed to the other officers, and with Colonel Marshall left the room. One after another we followed, and passed out to the porch. Lee signaled to his orderly to bring up his horse, and while the animal was being bridled the general stood on the lowest step and gazed sadly in the direction of the valley beyond where his army lay – now an army of prisoners. He smote his hands together a number of times in an absent sort of way; seemed not to see the group of Union officers in the yard who rose respectfully at his approach, and appeared unconscious of everything about him. All appreciated the sadness that overwhelmed him, and he had the personal sympathy of every one who beheld him at this supreme moment of trial. The approach of his horse seemed to recall him from his reverie, and he at once mounted. General Grant now stepped down from the porch, and, moving toward him, saluted him by raising his hat. He was followed in this act of courtesy by all our officers present; Lee raised his hat respectfully, and rode off to break the sad news to the brave fellows whom he had so long commanded.

ASSASSINATION OF PRESIDENT LINCOLN, 14 April 1865

Daniel Dean Beekman

Abraham Lincoln (1809–65), 19th President of the USA, was killed by John Wilkes Booth, a pro-slavery fanatic.

I was in my seat at 7:30 facing the President's box when he came at 8:30 with his wife, Miss Harris (Senator Harris' daughter), and Major Henry R. Rathbone – Grant and his wife leaving the city at six o'clock that night. As the President walked along the gallery to his box, the orchestra played "Hail to the Chief" and the audience arose and cheered him. I remarked to my friend, "He is the homeliest man I have ever seen," but when he acknowledged the applause by bowing and smiling, it so changed his countenance, that I said, it was the most heavenly smile I ever saw on a man's face. He sat in the right-hand corner of the box, in a rocking chair, his head resting on his hand, elbow leaning on the arm of his chair, looking utterly worn out and apparently in deep thought.

Upon the closing of the second scene in the third act of the play, about twenty minutes past ten, I heard the report of a pistol, and I said to my friend, "that is strange, there is no shooting in this play," and just as I said that, Wilkes Booth, whom I took to be Edwin Booth, (the actor), threw one leg over the President's box, brandishing his dagger, crying out in a loud voice, "Sic Semper Tyrannis," Virginia's motto, which means, "Thus always with Tyrants." Booth's spur caught in the flag which decorated the President's box, and he fell on his knee, a distance of nine feet, causing him to limp as he ran across the stage, still theatrically brandishing his dagger, then disappeared behind the curtain before anyone in the audience realised what had happened.

Then I heard a woman scream, and some one called out, "The President is shot" – and then, there was an uproar. The man sitting

ahead of me was on the stage second, and I was the third one. I
noticed a surgeon of the army, standing beside me, whom I knew
by his straps, (having two brothers in the war, both Lieutenants,
serving under Sherman, in the 135th N.J. Regiment) looking
anxiously up to the President's box, and I said to him, "Do
you want to get up there?" and he said, "Yes." I told him to
put his foot on my hand, the other foot on my shoulder, and I
boosted him up into the President's box, which was about nine feet
from the stage. No one could get in the box from the back, as Booth
had barricaded the door after he got in by putting a piece of plank
across, one end of which was secured in the wall, the other against
the door.

The President was shot in the head, back of the left ear, so the
surgeon told me after.

Everyone rushed out of the theatre as the report was circulated
around that there were conspirators in Washington, and that all
the Cabinet were killed. I told my friend, I was going to stay to see
the President carried out which I did, taking hold of his elbow,
lifting up his arm and putting my other hand on his wrist. I knew
by his pulse, which was very irregular and weak, that he was
fatally shot, which remark I made to my friend. They carried him
across the street, where he died twenty minutes past seven the next
morning just nine hours after he was shot.

THE DEATH OF JOHN WILKES BOOTH, Garrett Farm, Virginia, 2.00 26 April 1865

Lieutenant Edward Doherty, 16th New York Cavalry

After assassinating President Lincoln, Wilkes jumped to the floor of the
Ford Theater (breaking his leg on landing) and fled on horseback. He was
eventually tracked down, together with his accomplice David Herold, to
Garrett Farm in Virginia by a detachment of 16th New York Cavalry.

I dismounted, and knocked loudly at the front door. Old Mr
Garrett came out. I seized him, and asked him where the men were
who had gone to the woods when the cavalry passed the previous
afternoon. While I was speaking with him some of the men had
entered the house to search it. Soon one of the soldiers sang out, "O
Lieutenant! I have a man here I found in the corn-crib." It was
young Garrett, and I demanded the whereabouts of the fugitives.
He replied, "In the barn." Leaving a few men around the house,

we proceeded in the direction of the barn, which we surrounded. I kicked on the door of the barn several times without receiving a reply. Meantime another son of the Garrett's had been captured. The barn was secured with a padlock, and young Garrett carried the key. I unlocked the door, and again summoned the inmates of the building to surrender.

After some delay Booth said, "For whom do you take me?"

I replied, "It doesn't make any difference. Come out."

He said, "I am a cripple and alone."

I said, "I know who is with you, and you had better surrender."

He replied, "I may be taken by my friends, but not by my foes."

I said, "If you don't come out, I'll burn the building." I directed a corporal to pile up some hay in a crack in the wall of the barn and set the building on fire.

As the corporal was picking up the hay and brush Booth said, "If you come back here I will put a bullet through you."

I then motioned to the corporal to desist, and decided to wait for daylight and then to enter the barn by both doors and overpower the assassins.

Booth then said in a drawling voice. "Oh Captain! There is a man here who wants to surrender awful bad."

I replied, "You had better follow his example and come out."

His answer was, "No, I have not made up my mind; but draw your men up fifty paces off and give me a chance for my life."

I told him I had not come to fight; that I had fifty men, and could take him.

Then he said, "Well, my brave boys, prepare me a stretcher, and place another stain on our glorious banner."

At this moment Herold reached the door. I asked him to hand out his arms; he replied that he had none. I told him I knew exactly what weapons he had. Booth replied, "I own all the arms, and may have to use them on you, gentlemen." I then said to Herold, "Let me see your hands." He put them through the partly opened door and I seized him by the wrists. I handed him over to a non-commissioned officer. Just at this moment I heard a shot, and thought Booth had shot himself. Throwing open the door, I saw that the straw and hay behind Booth were on fire. He was half-turning towards it.

He had a crutch, and he held a carbine in his hand. I rushed into the burning barn, followed by my men, and as he was falling caught him under the arms and pulled him out of the barn. The

burning building becoming too hot, I had him carried to the
veranda of Garrett's house.

Booth received his death-shot in this manner. While I was taking
Herold out of the barn one of the detectives went to the rear, and
pulling out some protruding straw set fire to it. I had placed
Sergeant Boston Corbett at a large crack in the side of the barn,
and he, seeing by the igniting hay that Booth was leveling his
carbine at either Herold or myself, fired, to disable him in the arm;
but Booth making a sudden move, the aim erred, and the bullet
struck Booth in the back of the head, about an inch below the spot
where his shot had entered the head of Mr Lincoln. Booth asked
me by signs to raise his hands. I lifted them up and he gasped,
"Useless, useless!" We gave him brandy and water, but he could
not swallow it. I sent to Port Royal for a physician, who could do
nothing when he came, and at seven o'clock Booth breathed his
last. He had on his person a diary, a large bowie knife, two pistols,
a compass and a draft on Canada for 60 pounds.

GOLD-RUSH DAYS: VIRGINIA CITY, Nevada 1865

J. Ross Browne

Discovery of the "Comstock Lode" in 1859 set off a stampede of pro-
spectors to an isolated corner of Nevada which boomed into Virginia City.
The gold and silver of Virginia City mines did much to finance the Union
in the Civil War.

I was prepared to find great changes on the route from Carson to
Virginia City. At Empire City – which was nothing but a sage-
desert inhabited by Dutch Nick on the occasion of my early
exploration – I was quite bewildered with the busy scenes of life
and industry. Quartz-mills and saw-mills had completely usurped
the valley along the head of the Carson River; and now the
hammering of stamps, the hissing of steam, the whirling clouds
of smoke from tall chimneys, and the confused clamor of voices
from a busy multitude, reminded one of a manufacturing city.
Here, indeed, was progress of a substantial kind.

Further beyond, at Silver City, there were similar evidences of
prosperity. From the descent into the cañon through the Devil's
Gate, and up the grade to Gold Hill, it is almost a continuous line
of quartz-mills, tunnels, dumps, sluices, water-wheels, frame shanties, and grog-shops.

Gold Hill itself has swelled into the proportions of a city. It is now practically a continuation of Virginia. Here the evidences of busy enterprise are peculiarly striking. The whole hill is riddled and honey-combed with shafts and tunnels. Engine-houses for hoisting are perched on points apparently inaccessible; quartz-mills of various capacities line the sides of the cañon; the main street is well flanked by brick stores, hotels, express-offices, saloons, restaurants, groggeries, and all those attractive places of resort which go to make up a flourishing mining town. Even a newspaper is printed here, which I know to be a spirited and popular institution, having been viciously assailed by the same. A runaway team of horses, charging full tilt down the street, greeted our arrival in a lively and characteristic manner, and came very near capsizing our stage. One man was run over some distance below, and partially crushed; but as somebody was killed nearly every day, such a meagre result afforded no general satisfaction.

Descending the slope of the ridge that divides Gold Hill from Virginia City a strange scene attracts the eye. He who gazes upon it for the first time is apt to doubt if it be real. Perhaps there is not another spot upon the face of the globe that presents a scene so weird and desolate in its natural aspect, yet so replete with busy life, so animate with human interest. It is as if a wondrous battle raged, in which the combatants were man and earth. Myriads of swarthy, bearded, dust-covered men are piercing into the grim old mountains, ripping them open, thrusting murderous holes through their naked bodies; piling up engines to cut out their vital arteries; stamping and crushing up with infernal machines their disemboweled fragments, and holding fiendish revels amidst the chaos of destruction; while the mighty earth, blasted, barren, and scarred by the tempests of ages, fiercely affronts the foe – smiting him with disease and death; scoffing at his puny assaults with a grim scorn; ever grand in his desolation, ever dominant in the infinity of his endurance. "Come!" he seems to mutter, "dig, delve, pierce, and bore, with your picks, your shovels, and your infernal machines; wring out of my veins a few globules of the precious blood; hoard it, spend it, gamble for it, bring perdition to your souls with it – do what you will, puny insects! Sooner or later the death-blow-smites you, and Earth swallows you! From earth you came – to earth you go again!"

The city lies on a rugged slope, and is singularly diversified in its uprisings and downfallings. It is difficult to determine, by any system of observation or measurement, upon what principle it was laid out. My impression is that it was never laid out at all, but followed the dips, spurs, and angles of the immortal Comstock. Some of the streets run straight enough; others seem to dodge about at acute angles in search of an open space, as miners explore the subterranean regions in search of a lead. The cross streets must have been forgotten in the original plan – if ever there was a plan about this eccentric city. Sometimes they happen accidentally at the most unexpected points; and sometimes they don't happen at all where you are sure to require them. A man in a hurry to get from the upper slope of the town to any opposite point below must try it under-ground or over the roofs of the houses, or take the customary circuit of half a mile. Every body seems to have built wherever he could secure a lot. The two main streets, it must be admitted, are so far regular as to follow pretty nearly the direction of the Comstock lead. On the lower slope, or plateau, the town, as viewed from any neighboring eminence, presents much the appearance of a vast number of shingle-roofs shaken down at random, like a jumbled pack of cards. All the streets are narrow, except where there are but few houses, and there they are wide enough at present. The business part of the town has been built up with astonishing rapidity. In the spring of 1860 there was nothing of it save a few frame shanties and canvas tents, and one or two rough stone cabins. It now presents some of the distinguishing features of a metropolitan city. Large and substantial brick houses, three or four stories high, with ornamental fronts, have filled up most of the gaps, and many more are still in progress of erection. The oddity of the plan, and variety of its architecture – combining most of the styles known to the ancients, and some but little known to the moderns – give this famous city a grotesque, if not picturesque, appearance, which is rather increased upon a close inspection. . . .

Entering the main street you pass on the upper side huge piles of earth and ore, hoisted out of the shafts or run out of the tunnels, and cast over the "dumps." The hill-sides, for a distance of more than a mile, are perfectly honeycombed. Steam-engines are puffing off their steam; smoke-stacks are blackening the air with their thick volumes of smoke; quartz-batteries are battering; hammers are hammering; subterranean blasts are bursting up the earth; picks and crow-bars are picking and crashing into the precious rocks; shanties are springing up, and carpenters are sawing and ripping and nailing; store-keepers are rolling their merchandise in and out along the way-side; fruit vendors are peddling their fruits; wagoners are tumbling out and piling in their freights of dry goods and ore; saloons are glittering with their gaudy bars and fancy glasses, and many-colored liquors, and thirsty men are swilling the burning poison; auctioneers, surrounded by eager and gaping crowds of speculators, are shouting off the stocks of delinquent stock-holders; organ-grinders are grinding their organs and torturing consumptive monkeys; hurdy-gurdy girls are singing bacchanalian songs in bacchanalian dens; Jew clothiers are selling off prodigious assortments of worthless garments at ruinous prices; billstickers are sticking up bills of auctions, theatres, and new saloons; newsboys are crying the city papers with the latest telegraphic news; stages are dashing off with passengers for "Reese;" and stages are dashing in with passengers from "Frisco;" and the inevitable Wells, Fargo, and Co. are distributing letters, packages, and papers to the hungry multitude, amidst tempting piles of silver bricks and wonderful complications of scales, letter-boxes, clerks, account-books, and twenty-dollar pieces. All is life, excitement, avarice, lust, deviltry, and enterprise. A strange city truly, abounding in strange exhibitions and startling combinations of the human passions. Where upon earth is there such another place? . . .

Making due allowance for the atmosphere of exaggeration through which a visitor sees every thing in this wonderful mining metropolis, its progress has been sufficiently remarkable to palliate in some measure the extraordinary flights of fancy in which its inhabitants are prone to indulge. I was not prepared to see so great a change within the brief period of three years; for when people assure me "the world never saw any thing like it," "California is left in the shade," "San Francisco is eclipsed" "Montgomery Street is nowhere now," my incredulity is excited, and it takes some little time to judge of the true state of the case without prejudice. Speaking then strictly within bounds, the growth of this city is remarkable. When it is considered that the surrounding country affords but few facilities for the construction of houses; that lumber has to be hauled a considerable distance at great expense; that lime, bricks, iron-works, sashes, doors, etc., cost three or four times what similar articles do in San Francisco; that much indispensable material can only be had by transporting it over the mountains a distance of more than a hundred and fifty miles; and that the average of mechanical labor, living, and other expenses is correspondingly higher than in California, it is really wonderful how much has been done in so short a space of time.

Yet, allowing all this, what would be the impressions of a Fejee Islander sent upon a mission of inquiry to this strange place? His earliest glimpse of the main street would reveal the curious fact that it is paved with a conglomerate of dust, mud, splintered planks, old boots, clippings of tinware, and playing-cards. It is especially prolific in the matter of cards. Mules are said to fatten on them during seasons of scarcity when the straw gives out. The next marvelous fact that would strike the observation of this wild native is that so many people live in so many saloons, and do nothing from morning till night, and from night till morning again, but drink fiery liquids and indulge in profane language. How can all these ablebodied men afford to be idle? Who pays their expenses? And why do they carry pistols, knives, and other deadly weapons, when no harm could possibly befall them if they went unarmed and devoted themselves to some useful occupation? Has the God of the white men done them such an injury in furnishing all this silver for their use that they should treat His name with contempt and disrespect? Why do they send missionaries to the Fejee Islands and leave their own country in such a dreadful state of neglect? The Fejeeans devour their enemies occasionally as a war measure; the white man swallows his enemy all the time without regard to measure. Truly the white man is a very uncertain native! Fejeeans can't rely upon him.

When I was about to start on my trip to Washoe, friends from Virginia assured me I would find hotels there almost, if not quite, equal to the best in San Francisco. There was but little difference, they said, except in the matter of extent. The Virginia hotels were quite as good, though not quite so large. Of course I believed all they told me. Now I really don't consider myself fastidious on the subject of hotels. Having traveled in many different countries I have enjoyed an extensive experience in the way of accommodations, from my mother-earth to the foretop of a whale-ship, from an Indian wigwam to a Parisian hotel, from an African palm-tree to an Arctic snowbank. I have slept in the same bed with two donkeys, a camel, half a dozen Arabs, several goats, and a horse. I have slept on beds alive with snakes, lizards, scorpions, centipeds, bugs, and fleas – beds in which men stricken with the plague had died horrible deaths – beds that might reasonably be suspected of small-pox, measles, and Asiatic cholera. I have slept in beds of rivers and beds of sand, and on the bare bed rock. Standing, sitting, lying down, doubled up, and hanging over; twisted, punched, jammed and elbowed by drunken men; snored at in the ears; sat upon and smothered by the nightmare; burnt by fires, rained upon, snowed upon, and bitten by frost – in all these positions, and subject to all these discomforts. I have slept with comparative satisfaction. There are pleasanter ways of sleeping, to be sure, but there are times when any way is a blessing. In respect to the matter of eating I am even less particular. Frogs, horse-leeches, snails, and grasshoppers are luxuries to what I have eaten. It has pleased Providence to favor me with appetites and tastes appropriate to a great variety of circumstances and many conditions of life. These facts serve to show that I am not fastidious on the subject of personal accommodations.

Perhaps my experience in Virginia was exceptional; perhaps misfortune was determined to try me to the utmost extremity. I endeavored to find accommodations at a hotel recommended as the best in the place and was shown a room over the kitchen stove, in which the thermometer ranged at about 130 to 150 degrees of Fahrenheit. To be lodged and baked at the rate of $2 per night, cash in advance, was more than I could stand, so I asked for another room. There was but one more, and that was preempted by a lodger who might or might not come back and claim possession in the middle of the night. It had no windows except one that opened into the passage, and the bed was so arranged that every other lodger in the house could take a passing observation of the sleeper and enjoy his style of sleeping. Nay, it was not beyond the resources of the photographic art to secure his negative and print his likeness for general distribution. It was bad enough to be smothered for want of light and air; but I had no idea of paying $2 a night for the poor privilege of showing people how I looked with my eyes shut, and possibly my mouth open. A man may have an attack of nightmare, his countenance may be distorted by horrible dreams; he may laugh immoderately at a very bad pun made in his sleep – in all which conditions of body and mind he doubtless presents an interesting spectacle to the critical eyes of a stranger, but he doesn't like to wake up suddenly and be caught in the act.

The next hotel to which I was recommended was eligibly located on a street composed principally of grog-shops and gambling-houses. I was favored with a frontroom about eight feet square. The walls were constructed of boards fancifully decorated with paper, and afforded this facility to a lodger – that he could hear all that was going on in the adjacent rooms. The partitions might deceive the eye, but the ear received the full benefit of the various oaths, ejaculations, conversations, and perambulations in which his neighbors indulged. As for the bed, I don't know how long it had been in use, or what race of people had hitherto slept in it, but the sheets and blankets seemed to be sadly discolored by age – or lack of soap and water. It would be safe to say washing was not considered a paying investment by the managers of this establishment. Having been over twenty-four hours without sleep or rest I made an attempt to procure a small supply, but miserably failed in consequence of an interesting conversation carried on in the passage between the chamber-maids, waiters, and other ladies and gentlemen respecting the last free fight. From what I could gather this was considered the best neighborhood in the city for free fights. Within the past two weeks three or four men had been shot, stabbed, or maimed close by the door. "Oh, it's a lively place, you bet!" said one of the ladies (the chamber-maid, I think), "an oncommon lively place – reely hexcitin'. I look out of the winder every mornin' jist to see how many dead men are layin' around. I declare to gracious the bullets flies around here sometimes like hailstones!" "An' shur," said a voice in that rich brogue which can never be mistaken, "it's no wondher the boys shud be killin' an' murtherin' themselves forninst the door, whin they're all just like me, dyin' in love wid yer beauteeful self!" A smart slap and a general laugh followed this suggestion. "Git away wid ye, Dinnis; yer always up to yer mischief! As I was sayin', no later than this mornin', I see two men a poppin' away at each other wid six-shooters – a big man an' a little man. The big man he staggered an' fell right under the winder, wid his head on the curb-stone, an' his legs a stickin' right up in the air. He was all over-blood, and when the boys picked him up he was dead as a brickbat. 'Tother chap he run into a saloon. You better b'leeve this is a lively neighborhood. I tell you hailstones is nothink to the way the bullets flies around." "That's so," chimes in another female voice; "I see myself, with my own eyes, Jack's corpse an' two more carried away in the last month. If I'd a had a six-shooter then you bet they'd a carried away the fellow that nipped Jack!"

Now taking into view the picturesque spectacle that a few dead men dabbled in blood must present to the eye on a fine morning, and the chances of a miscellaneous ball carrying away the top of one's cranium, or penetrating the thin board wall and ranging upward through his body as he lies in bed, I considered it best to seek a more secluded neighborhood, where the scenery was of a less stimulating character and the hail-storms not quite so heavy. By the kind aid of a friend I secured comparatively agreeable quarters in a private lodging-house kept by a widow lady. The rooms were good and the beds clean, and the price not extravagant for this locality – $12 a week without board.

So much for the famous hotels of Virginia. If there are any better, neither myself, nor some fellow-travelers who told me their experiences, succeeded in finding them. The concurrent testimony was that they are dirty, ill-kept, badly attended by rough, ill-mannered waiters – noisy to such a degree that a sober man can get but little rest, day or night, and extravagantly high in proportion to the small comfort they afford. One of the newspapers published a statement which the author probably intended for a joke, but which is doubtless founded upon fact – namely, that a certain hotel advertised for 300 chickens to serve the same number of guests. Only one chicken could be had for love or money – a very ancient rooster, which was made into soup and afterward served up in the form of a fricassee for the 300 guests. The flavor was considered extremely delicate – what there was of it; and there was plenty of it such as it was.

Still if we are to credit what the Virginia newspapers say – and it would be dangerous to intimate that they ever deal in any thing save the truth – there are other cities on the eastern slope of the Sierras which afford equally attractive accommodations. On the occasion of the recent Senatorial contest at Carson City, the prevailing rates charged for lodgings, according to the Virginia *Enterprise*, were as follows: "For a bed in a house, barn, black-smithshop, or hay-yard (none to be had – all having been engaged shortly before election); horse-blanket in an old sugar hogshead per night, $10; crockery-crate, with straw, $7.50; without straw, $5.75; for cellar-door, $4; for roosting on a smooth pole, $3.50; pole, common, rough, $3; plaza fence, $2.50; walking up and down the Warm Springs road – if cloudy, $1.50; if clear, $1.25. (In case the clouds are very thick and low $1.75 is generally asked.) Very good roosting in a pine-tree, back of Camp Nye, may still be had free, but we understand that a company is being formed to monopolize all the more accessible trees. We believe they propose to improve by putting two pins in the bottom of each tree, or keep a man to boost regular customers. They talk of charging six bits."

I could scarcely credit this, if it were not that a friend of mine, who visited Reese River last summer, related some experiences of a corroborative character. Unable to secure lodgings elsewhere, he undertook to find accommodations in a vacant sheep corral. The proprietor happening to come home about midnight found him spread out under the lee of the fence. "Look-a-here, stranger!" said he, gruffly, "that's all well enough, but I gen'rally collect in advance. Just fork over four bits or mizzle!" My friend indignantly mizzled. Cursing the progressive spirit of the age, he walked some distance out of town, and was about to finish the night under the lee of a big quartz boulder, when a fierce-looking speculator, with a six-shooter in his hand, suddenly appeared from a cavity in the rock, saying, "No yer don't! Take a fool's advice now, and git! When you go a prospectin' around ov nights again, jest steer ov this boulder ef you please!" In vain my friend attempted to explain. The rising wrath of the squatter was not to be appeased by soft words, and the click of the trigger, as he raised his pistol and drew a bead, warned the trespasser that it was time to be off. He found lodgings that night on the public highway to Virginia City and San Francisco.

WASHITA: THE VIEW FROM THE SEVENTH CAVALRY, 26–27 November 1867

Edward S. Godfrey

The Seventh Cavalry's attack on the Cheyenne camp at Washita was only one of the many controversies to trail the career of George Armstrong Custer. The camp flew a white flag and of the 103 Indians killed, a mere eleven were warriors; the rest were women and children. Yet, as the Seventh Cavalry claimed, Black Kettle's camp did indisputably harbour "hostiles". Washita was a tragedy but it was not a genocidal massacre like Sand Creek. Godfrey was a lieutenant in Custer's Seventh Cavalry.

Soon the regiment was ready to move and we struck in a direction to intercept the trail of Elliott's advance. We pushed along almost without rest till about 9 p. m. before we came to Elliott's halting place. There we had coffee made, care being taken to conceal the fires as much as possible. Horses were unsaddled and fed. At 10 p.m. we were again in the saddle with instructions to make as little noise as possible, – no loud talking, no matches were to be lighted. Tobacco users were obliged to console themselves with the quid. Little Beaver, Osage Chief, with one of his warriors, had the lead dismounted as trailers; then followed the other Indian and white scouts with whom General Custer rode to be near the advance. The cavalry followed at a distance of about a half mile. The snow had melted during the day but at night the weather had turned cold and the crunching noise could be heard for a considerable distance.

After a couple of hours' march, the trailers hurried back for the command to halt. General Custer rode up to investigate when Little Beaver informed him that he "smelled smoke." Cautious investigation disclosed the embers of a fire which the guides decided from conditions had been made by the boy herders while grazing the pony herds and from this deduced that the village could not be far distant. The moon had risen and there was little difficulty in following the trail and General Custer rode behind the trailers to watch the developments. On nearing the crest of any rise, the trailer would crawl to the crest to reconnoiter, but seeing Little Beaver exercise greater caution than usual and then shading his eyes from the moon, the General felt there was something unusual. On his return the General asked, "What is it?" and Little Beaver replied, "Heap Injuns down there." Dismounting and advancing with the same caution as the guide, he made his personal investigation, but could only see what appeared to be a herd of animals. Asking why he thought there were Indians down there, Little Beaver replied, "Me heard dog bark." Listening intently they not only heard the bark of a dog, but the tinkling of a bell, indicating a pony herd, and then the cry of an infant.

Satisfied that a village had been located, the General returned to the command, assembled the officers, and, after removing sabres, took us all to the crest where the situation was explained or rather conjectured. The barking of the dogs and the occasional cry of infants located the direction of the village and the tinkling of the bells gave the direction of the herds. Returning and resuming our sabres, the General explained his plans and assigned squadron commanders their duties and places. Major Elliott, with Troops G, H, and M was to march well to our left and approach the village from the northeast or easterly direction as determined by the ground, etc. Captain Thompson, with B and F, was to march well to our right so as to approach from the southeast, connecting with Elliott. Captain Myers, with E and I, was to move by the right so as to approach from a southerly direction. The wagons under Lieutenant Bell and Captain Benteen's squadron – H and M – had been halted about two or three miles on the trail to await the outcome of the investigations.

Just after dismissing the officers and as we were separating, General Custer called my name. On reporting, he directed me to take a detail, go back on the trail to where Captain Benteen and the wagons were, give his compliments to Captain Benteen and instruct him to rejoin the command, and Lieutenant Bell to hold the wagons where they were till he heard the attack which would be about daybreak. "Tell the Adjutant the number of men you want and he will make the detail. How many do you want?" I replied, "One orderly." He then said, "Why do you say that? You can have all you want." I replied that one was all I wanted – "to take more would increase the chances of accident and delay."

I delivered my messages and returned with Captain Benteen's squadron. The camp guard remained with the wagons.

Upon the arrival of Captain Benteen's squadron, Major Elliott proceeded to take position, also Captain Thompson and later Captain Myers.

Before the first streak of dawn, General Custer's immediate command as quietly as possible moved into place facing nearly east, Lieutenant Cooke's sharpshooters in advance of the left dismounted. General Custer and staff were followed by the band mounted. Captain West's squadron was on the right and Captain Hamilton's on the left, the standard and guard in the center. Troop K (West's) was on the right flank and I had command of the first platoon.

With the dawn we were ordered to remove overcoats and haversacks, leaving one man of each organization in charge with orders to load them in the wagons when Lieutenant Bell came up. Following the General, the command marched over the crest of the ridge and advanced some distance to another lower ridge. Waiting till sunrise we began to feel that the village had been abandoned although the dogs continued their furious barkings. Then "little by little" we advanced. Captain West came to me with orders to charge through the village but not to stop, to continue through and round up the pony herds.

With all quiet in the early dawn, Major Elliott's command had reached a concealed position close to the village, but was waiting for the signal from headquarters. The furious barking of the dogs aroused an Indian who came from his lodge, ran to the bank of the Washita, looked about and fired his rifle. I was told that a trooper had raised his head to take aim and was seen by this Indian. With the alarm thus given, the command opened fire. The trumpeters sounded the charge and the band began to play "Garry Owen," but by the time they had played one strain their instruments froze up.

My platoon advanced as rapidly as the brush and fallen timbers would permit until we reached the Washita which I found with steep, high banks. I marched the platoon by the right flank a short distance, found a "pony crossing," reformed on the right bank, galloped through the right of the village without contact with a warrior, and then proceeded to round up the pony herds.

As I passed out of the village, Captain Thompson's and Captain Myers' squadrons came over the high ridge on my right. Both had lost their bearings during their night marching and failed to make contacts for the opening attack.

At the opening of the attack, the warriors rushed to the banks of the stream. Those in front of Custer's command were soon forced to retire in among the tepees, and most of them being closely followed retreated to ravines and behind trees and logs, and in depressions where they maintained their positions till the last one was killed. A few escaped down the valley. This desperate fighting was carried on mostly by sharpshooters, waiting for a head to show. Seventeen Indians were killed in one depression.

Lieutenant Bell, when he heard the firing, rushed his teams to join the command and while loading the overcoats and haversacks was attacked by a superior force and the greater part of them had to be abandoned. His arrival with the reserve ammunition was a welcome reinforcement.

While the fighting was going on, Major Elliott seeing a group of dismounted Indians escaping down the valley called for volunteers to make pursuit. Nineteen men, including Regimental Sergeant Major Kennedy responded. As his detachment moved away, he turned to Lieutenant Hale waved his hand and said: "Here goes for a brevet or a coffin."

After passing through the village, I went in pursuit of pony herds and found them scattered in groups about a mile below the village.

I deployed my platoon to make the roundup and took a position for observation. While the roundup was progressing, I observed a group of dismounted Indians escaping down the opposite side of the valley. Completing the roundup, and starting them toward the village, I turned the herd over to Lieutenant Law who had come with the second platoon of the troop and told him to take them to the village, saying that I would take my platoon and go in pursuit of the group I had seen escaping down the valley.

Crossing the stream and striking the trail, I followed it till it came to a wooded draw where there was a large pony herd. Here I found the group had mounted. Taking the trail which was well up on the hillside of the valley, and following it about a couple of miles, I discovered a lone tepee, and soon after two Indians circling their ponies. A high promontory and ridge projected into the valley and shut off the view of the valley below the lone tepee. I knew the circling of the warriors meant an alarm and rally, but I wanted to see what was in the valley beyond them. Just then Sergeant Conrad, who had been a captain of Ohio volunteers, and Sergeant Hughes, who had served in the 4th U.S. Cavalry in that country before the Civil War, came to me and warned me of the danger of going ahead. I ordered them to halt the platoon and wait till I could go to the ridge to see what was beyond. Arriving at and peering over the ridge, I was amazed to find that as far as I could see down the well wooded, tortuous valley there were tepees – tepees. Not only could I see tepees, but mounted warriors scurrying in our direction. I hurried back to the platoon and returned at the trot till attacked by the hostiles, when I halted, opened fire, drove the hostiles to cover, and then deployed the platoon as skirmishers.

The hillsides were cut by rather deep ravines and I planned to retreat from ridge to ridge. Under the cavalry tactics of 1841, the retreat of skirmishers was by the odd and even numbers, alternating in lines to the rear. I instructed the line in retreat to halt on the next ridge and cover the retreat of the advance line. This was successful for the first and second ridges, but at the third I found men had apparently forgotten their numbers and there was some confusion, so I divided the skirmishers into two groups, each under a sergeant, and thereafter had no trouble.

Finally the hostiles left us and we soon came to the pony herd where the group we had started to pursue had mounted. I had not had a single casualty. During this retreat we heard heavy firing on the opposite side of the valley, but being well up on the side hills we could not see through the trees what was going on. There was a short lull when the firing again became heavy and continued till long after we reached the village, in fact, nearly all day.

In rounding up the pony herd, I found Captain Barnitz' horse, *General*, saddled but no bridle. On reaching the village I turned over the pony herd and at once reported to General Custer what I had done and seen. When I mentioned the "big village," he exclaimed, "What's that?" and put me through a lot of rapid fire questions. At the conclusion I told him about finding Captain Barnitz' horse and asked what had happened. He told me that Captain Barnitz had been severely and probably mortally wounded.

Leaving the General in a "brown study" I went to see my friend and former Captain, Barnitz. I found him under a pile of blankets and buffalo robes, suffering and very quiet. I hunted up Captain Lippincott, Assistant Surgeon, and found him with his hands over his eyes suffering intense pain from snowblindness. He was very pessimistic as to Barnitz' recovery and insisted that I tell him that there was no hope unless he could be kept perfectly quiet for several days as he feared the bullet had passed through the bowels. I went back to Captain Barnitz and approached the momentous opinion of the surgeon as bravely as I could and then blurted it out, when he exclaimed, "Oh hell! they think because my extremities are cold I am going to die, but if I could get warm I'm sure I'll be all right. These blankets and robes are so heavy I can hardly breathe." I informed the first sergeant and the men were soon busy gathering fuel and building fires.

In the midst of this, the general sent for me and again questioned me about the big village. At that time many warriors were assembling on the high hills north of the valley overlooking the village and the General kept looking in that direction. At the conclusion of his inquiry, I told him that I had heard that Major Elliott had not returned and suggested that possibly the heavy firing I had heard on the opposite side of the valley might have been an attack on Elliott's party. He pondered this a bit and said slowly, "I hardly think so, as Captain Myers has been fighting down there all morning and probably would have reported it."

I left him and a while later he sent for me again, and, on reporting, told me that he had Romeo, the interpreter, make inquiries of the squaw prisoners and they confirmed my report of the lower village. He then ordered me to take Troop K and destroy all property and not allow any looting – but destroy everything.

I allowed the prisoners to get what they wanted. As I watched them, they only went to their own tepees. I began the destruction at the upper end of the village, tearing down tepees and piling several together on the tepee poles, set fire to them. (All tepees were made of tanned buffalo hides.) As the fires made headway, all articles of personal property – buffalo robes, blankets, food, rifles, pistols, bows and arrows, lead and caps, bullet molds, etc. – were thrown in the fires and destroyed. I doubt but that many small curios went into the pockets of men engaged in this work. One man brought to me that which I learned was a bridal gown, a "one piece dress," adorned all over with bead work and elks' teeth on antelope skins as soft as the finest broadcloth. I started to show it to the General and ask to keep it, but as I passed a big fire, I thought, "What's the use, 'orders is orders' " and threw it in the blaze. I have never ceased to regret that destruction. All of the powder found I spilled on the ground and "flashed".

I was present in August 1868, at Fort Larned, Kansas, when the annuities were issued, promised by the Medicine Lodge Peace Treaties of 1867, and saw the issue of rifles, pistols, powder, caps, lead and bullet molds to these same Cheyennes.

While this destruction was going on, warriors began to assemble on the hill slopes on the left side of the valley facing the village, as if to make an attack. Two squadrons formed near the left bank of the stream and started on the "Charge" when the warriors scattered and fled. Later, a few groups were seen on the hill tops but they made no hostile demonstrations.

As the last of the tepees and property was on fire, the General ordered me to kill all the ponies except those authorised to be used by the prisoners and given to scouts. We tried to rope them and cut their throats, but the ponies were frantic at the approach of a white man and fought viciously. My men were getting very tired so I called for reinforcements and details from other organizations were sent to complete the destruction of about eight hundred ponies. As the last of the ponies were being shot nearly all the hostiles left. This was probably because they could see our prisoners and realized that any shooting they did might endanger them.

Searching parties were sent to look for dead and wounded of both our own and hostiles. A scout having reported that he had seen Major Elliott and party in pursuit of some escapes down the right side of the valley, Captain Myers went down the valley about two miles but found no trace.

A while before sunset, as the command was forming to march down the valley, the General sent for me to ride with him to show him the place from which we could see the village below. There was no attempt to conceal our formation or the direction of our march. The command in column of fours, covered by skirmishers, the prisoners in the rear of the advance troops, standard and guidons "to the breeze," the chief trumpeter sounded the advance and we were "on our way," the band playing, "Ain't I Glad to Get Out of the Wilderness." The observing warriors followed our movement till twilight, but made no hostile demonstration. Then as if they had divined our purpose there was a commotion and they departed down the valley.

When we came in sight of the promontory and ridge from which I had discovered the lower villages, I pointed them out to the General. With the departure of the hostiles our march was slowed down till after dark, when the command was halted, the skirmishers were quietly withdrawn to rejoin their troops, the advance counter-marched, joined successively by the organizations in the rear, and we were on our way on our back trail. We marched briskly till long after midnight when we bivouacked till daylight with the exception of one squadron which was detached to hurry on to our supply train, the safety of which caused great anxiety. I was detailed to command the prisoners and special guard.

At daylight the next morning, we were on the march to meet our supply train and encountered it some time that forenoon. We were glad that it was safe, but disappointed that Major Elliott and party had not come in. After supper in the evening, the officers were called together and each one questioned as to the casualties of enemy warriors, locations, etc. Every effort was made to avoid duplications. The total was found to be one hundred and three.

GUNFIGHT IN DODGE CITY, Kansas c. 1868

Andy Adams

Adams (1859) spent ten years on "the hurricane deck of a Texas horse" driving cattle to the Powder River country.

Quince Forrest was spending his winnings as well as drinking freely, and at the end of a quadrille gave vent to his hilarity in an

old-fashioned Comanche yell. The bouncer of the dance hall of
course had his eye on our crowd, and at the end of a change, took
Quince to task. He was a surly brute, and instead of couching his
request in appropriate language, threatened to throw him out of
the house. Forrest stood like one absentminded and took the abuse,
for physically he was no match for the bouncer, who was armed,
moreover, and wore an officer's star. I was dancing in the same set
with a redheaded, freckle-faced girl, who clutched my arm and
wished to know if my friend was armed. I assured her that he was
not, or we would have had notice of it before the bouncer's
invective was ended. At the conclusion of the dance, Quince
and The Rebel passed out, giving the rest of us the word to remain
as though nothing was wrong. In the course of half an hour, Priest
returned and asked us to take our leave one at a time without
attracting any attention, and meet at the stable. I remained until
the last, and noticed The Rebel and the bouncer taking a drink
together at the bar – the former apparently in a most amiable
mood. We passed out together shortly afterward, and found the
other boys mounted and awaiting our return, it being now about
midnight. It took but a moment to secure our guns, and once in the
saddle, we rode through the town in the direction of the herd. On
the outskirts of the town, we halted. "I'm going back to that dance
hall," said Forrest, "and have one round at least with that whore-
herder. No man who walks this old earth can insult me, as he did,
not if he has a hundred stars on him. If any of you don't want to go
along, ride right on to camp, but I'd like to have you all go. And
when I take his measure, it will be the signal to the rest of you to
put out the lights. All that's going, come on."

There were no dissenters to the programme. I saw at a glance
that my bunkie was heart and soul in the play, and took my cue
and kept my mouth shut. We circled round the town to a vacant
lot within a block of the rear of the dance hall. Honeyman was left
to hold the horses; then, taking off our belts and hanging them on
the pommels of our saddles, we secreted our six-shooters inside the
waistbands of our trousers. The hall was still crowded with the
revelers when we entered, a few at a time, Forrest and Priest being
the last to arrive. Forrest had changed hats with The Rebel, who
always wore a black one, and as the bouncer circulated around,
Quince stepped squarely in front of him. There was no waste of
words, but a gun-barrel flashed in the lamplight, and the bouncer,
struck with the six-shooter, fell like a beef. Before the bewildered

spectators could raise a hand, five six-shooters were turned into the ceiling. The lights went out at the first fire, and amidst the rush of men and the screaming of women, we reached the outside, and within a minute were in our saddles. All would have gone well had we returned by the same route and avoided the town; but after crossing the railroad track, anger and pride having not been properly satisfied, we must ride through the town.

On entering the main street, leading north and opposite the bridge on the river, somebody of our party in the rear turned his gun loose into the air. The Rebel and I were riding in the lead, and at the clattering of hoofs and shooting behind us, our horses started on the run, the shooting by this time having become general. At the second street crossing, I noticed a rope of fire belching from a Winchester in the doorway of a store building. There was no doubt in my mind but we were the object of the manipulator of that carbine, and as we reached the next cross street, a man kneeling in the shadow of a building opened fire on us with a six-shooter. Priest reined in his horse, and not having wasted cartridges in the open air shooting, returned the compliment until he emptied his gun. By this time every officer in the town was throwing lead after us, some of which cried a little too close for comfort. When there was no longer any shooting on our flanks, we turned into a cross street and soon left the lead behind us. At the outskirts of the town we slowed up our horses and took it leisurely.

MOONLIGHT CATTLE DRIVE, South Dakota, c. 1868

Andy Adams

The two herds were held together a second night, but after they had grazed a few hours the next morning, the cattle were thrown together, and the work of cutting out ours commenced. With a double outfit of men available, about twenty men were turned into the herd to do the cutting, the remainder holding the main herd and looking after the cut. The morning was cool, every one worked with a vim, and in about two hours the herds were again separated and ready for the final trimming. Campbell did not expect to move out until he could communicate with the head office of the company, and would go-up to Fort Laramie for that purpose during the day, hoping to be able to get a message over the military wire. When his outfit had finished retrimming our herd, and we had looked over his cattle for the last time, the two outfits bade each other farewell, and our herd started on its journey.

The unfortunate accident at the ford had depressed our feelings to such an extent that there was an entire absence of hilarity by the way. This morning the farewell songs generally used in parting with a river which had defied us were omitted. The herd trailed out like an immense serpent, and was guided and controlled by our men as if by mutes. Long before the noon hour, we passed out of sight of Forty Islands, and in the next few days, with the change of scene, the gloom gradually lifted. We were bearing almost due north, and passing through a delightful country. To our left ran a range of mountains, while on the other hand sloped off the apparently limitless plain. The scarcity of water was beginning to be felt, for the streams which had not a source in the mountains on our left had dried up weeks before our arrival. There was a gradual change of air noticeable too, for we were rapidly gaining altitude, the heat of summer being now confined to a few hours at noonday, while the nights were almost too cool for our comfort.

When about three days out from the North Platte, the mountains disappeared on our left while on the other hand appeared a rugged-looking country, which we knew must be the approaches of the Black Hills. Another day's drive brought us into the main stage road connecting the railroad on the south with the mining camps which nestled somewhere in those rocky hills to our right. The stage road followed the trail some ten or fifteen miles before we parted company with it on a dry fork of the Big Cheyenne River. There was a road house and stage stand where these two thoroughfares separated, the one to the mining camp of Deadwood, while ours of the Montana cattle trail bore off for the Powder River to the northwest. At this stage stand we learned that some twenty herds had already passed by to the northern ranges, and that after passing the next fork of the Big Cheyenne we should find no water until we struck the Powder River – a stretch of eighty miles. The keeper of the road house, a genial host, informed us that this drouthy stretch in our front was something unusual, this being one of the dryest summers that he had experienced since the discovery of gold in the Black Hills.

Here was a new situation to be met, an eighty-mile dry drive; and with our experience of a few months before at Indian Lakes fresh in our memories, we set our house in order for the undertaking before us. It was yet fifteen miles to the next and last water from the stage stand. There were several dry forks of the Cheyenne beyond, but as they had their source in the tablelands of Wyoming, we could not hope for water in their dry bottoms. The situation was serious, with only this encouragement: other herds had crossed this arid belt since the streams had dried up, and our Circle Dots could walk with any herd that ever left Texas. The wisdom of mounting us well for just such an emergency reflected the good cow sense of our employer; and we felt easy in regard to our mounts, though there was not a horse or a man too many. In summing up the situation, Flood said, "We've got this advantage over the Indian Lake drive: there is a good moon, and the days are cool. We'll make twenty-five miles a day covering this stretch, as this herd has never been put to a test yet to see how far they could walk in a day. They'll have to do their sleeping at noon; at least cut it into two shifts, and if we get any sleep we'll have to do the same. Let her come as she will; every day's drive is a day nearer the Blackfoot Agency."

We made a dry camp that night on the divide between the road house and the last water, and the next forenoon reached the South Fork of the Big Cheyenne. The water was not even running in it, but there were several long pools, and we held the cattle around them for over an hour, until every hoof had been thoroughly watered. McCann had filled every keg and canteen in advance of the arrival of the herd, and Flood had exercised sufficient caution, in view of what lay before us, to buy an extra keg and a bull's-eye lantern at the road house. After watering, we trailed out some four or five miles and camped for noon, but the herd were allowed to graze forward until they lay down for their noonday rest. As the herd passed opposite the wagon, we cut a fat two-year-old stray heifer and killed her for beef, for the inner man must be fortified for the journey before us. After a two hours' siesta, we threw the herd on the trail and started on our way. The wagon and saddle horses were held in our immediate rear, for there was no telling when or where we would make our next halt of any consequence. We trailed and grazed the herd alternately until near evening, when the wagon was sent on ahead about three miles to get supper, while half the outfit went along to change mounts and catch up horses for those remaining behind with the herd. A half hour before the usual bedding time, the relieved men returned and took the grazing herd, and the others rode in to the wagon for supper and a change of mounts. While we shifted our saddles, we smelled the savory odor of fresh beef frying.

"Listen to that good old beef talking, will you?" said Joe Stallings, as he was bridling his horse. "McCann, I'll take my *carne fresco* a trifle rare to-night, garnished with a sprig of parsley and a wee bit of lemon."

Before we had finished supper, Honeyman had rehooked the mules to the wagon, while the *remuda* was at hand to follow. Before we left the wagon, a full moon was rising on the eastern horizon, and as we were starting out Flood gave us these general directions: "I'm going to take the lead with the cook's lantern, and one of you rear men take the new bull's-eye. We'll throw the herd on the trail; and between the lead and rear light, you swing men want to ride well outside, and you point men want to hold the lead cattle so the rear will never be more than a half a mile behind. I'll admit that this is somewhat of an experiment with me, but I don't see any good reason why she won't work. After the moon gets another hour high we can see a quarter of a mile, and the cattle are so well trail broke they'll never try to scatter. If it works all right, we'll never bed them short of midnight, and that will put us ten miles farther. Let's ride, lads."

By the time the herd was eased back on the trail, our evening camp-fire had been passed, while the cattle led out as if walking on a wager. After the first mile on the trail the men on the point were compelled to ride in the lead if we were to hold them within the desired half mile. The men on the other side, or the swing, were gradually widening, until the herd must have reached fully a mile in length; yet we swing riders were never out of sight of each other, and it would have been impossible for any cattle to leave the herd unnoticed. In that moonlight the trail was as plain as day, and after an hour, Flood turned his lantern over to one of the point men, and rode back around the herd to the rear. From my position that first night near the middle of the swing, the lanterns both rear and forward being always in sight, I was as much at sea as any one as to the length of the herd, knowing the deceitfulness of distance of camp-fires and other lights by night. The foreman appealed to me as he rode down the column, to know the length of the herd, but I could give him no more than a simple guess. I could assure him, however, that the cattle had made no effort to drop out and leave the trail. But a short time after he passed me I noticed a horseman galloping up the column on the opposite side of the herd, and knew it must be the foreman. Within a short time, some one in the lead wig-wagged his lantern; it was answered by the light in the rear, and the next minute the old rear song.

> "Ip-e-la-ago, go 'long little doggie,
> You'll make a beef-steer by-and-by,"

reached us riders in the swing, and we knew the rear guard of cattle was being pushed forward. The distance between the swing men gradually narrowed in our lead, from which we could tell the leaders were being held in, until several times cattle grazed out from the herd, due to the checking in front. At this juncture Flood galloped around the herd a second time, and as he passed us riding along our side, I appealed to him to let them go in front, as it now required constant riding to keep the cattle from leaving the trail to graze. When he passed up the opposite side, I could distinctly hear the men on that flank making a similar appeal, and shortly afterwards the herd loosened out and we struck our old gait for several hours.

Trailing by moonlight was a novelty to all of us, and in the stillness of those splendid July nights we could hear the point men chatting across the lead in front, while well in the rear, the rattling of our heavily loaded wagon and the whistling of the horse wrangler to his charges reached our ears. The swing men were scattered so far apart there was no chance for conversation amongst us, but every once in a while a song would be started, and as it surged up and down the line, every voice, good, bad, and indifferent, joined in. Singing is supposed to have a soothing effect on cattle, though I will vouch for the fact that none of our Circle Dots stopped that night to listen to our vocal efforts. The herd was traveling so nicely that our foreman hardly noticed the passing hours, but along about midnight the singing ceased, and we were nodding in our saddles and wondering if they in the lead were never going to throw off the trail, when a great wigwagging occurred in front, and presently we overtook. The Rebel, holding the lantern and turning the herd out of the trail. It was then after midnight, and within another half hour we had the cattle bedded down within a few hundred yards of the trail. One-hour guards was the order of the night, and as soon as our wagon and saddle horses came up, we stretched ropes and caught out our night horses. These we either tied to the wagon wheels or picketed near at hand, and then we sought our blankets for a few hours' sleep. It was half past three in the morning when our guard was called, and before the hour passed, the first signs of day were visible in the last. But even before our watch had ended, Flood and the last guard came to our relief, and we pushed the sleeping cattle off the bed ground and started them grazing forward.

Cattle will not graze freely in a heavy dew or too early in the morning, and before the sun was high enough to dry the grass, we had put several miles behind us. When the sun was about an hour high, the remainder of the outfit overtook us, and shortly afterward the wagon and saddle horses passed on up the trail, from which it was evident that "breakfast would be served in the dining car ahead," as the traveled Priest aptly put it. After the sun was well up, the cattle grazed freely for several hours; but when we sighted the *remuda* and our commissary some two miles in our lead, Flood ordered the herd lined up for a count. The Rebel was always a reliable counter, and he and the foreman now rode forward and selected the crossing of a dry wash for the counting. On receiving their signal to come on, we allowed the herd to graze slowly forward, but gradually pointed them into an immense "V," and as the point of the herd crossed the dry arroyo, we compelled them to pass in a narrow file between the two counters, when they again spread out fan-like and continued their feeding.

The count confirmed the success of our driving by night, and on its completion all but two men rode to the wagon for breakfast. By the time the morning meal was disposed of, the herd had come up parallel with the wagon but a mile to the westward, and as fast as fresh mounts could be saddled, we rode away in small squads to relieve the herders and to turn the cattle into the trail. It was but a little after eight o'clock in the morning when the herd was again trailing out on the Powder River trail, and we had already put over thirty miles of the dry drive behind us, while so far neither horses nor cattle had been put to any extra exertion. The wagon followed as usual, and for over three hours we held the trail without a break, when sighting a divide in our front, the foreman went back and sent the wagon around the herd with instructions to make the noon camp well up on the divide. We threw the herd off the trail, within a mile of this stopping place and allowed them to graze, while two thirds of the outfit galloped away to the wagon.

We allowed the cattle to lie down and rest to their complete satisfaction until the middle of the afternoon; meanwhile all hands, with the exception of two men on herd, also lay down and slept in the shade of the wagon. When the cattle had had several hours sleep, the want of water made them restless, and they began to rise and graze away. Then all hands were aroused and we threw them upon the trail. The heat of the day was already over, and until the twilight of the evening, we trailed a three-mile clip, and again threw the herd off to graze. By our traveling and grazing gaits, we could form an approximate idea as to the distance we had covered, and the consensus of opinion of all was that we had already killed over half the distance. The herd was beginning to show the want of water by evening, but amongst our saddle horses the lack of water was more noticeable, as a horse subsisting on grass alone weakens easily; and riding them made them all the more gaunt. When we caught up our mounts that evening, we had used eight horses to the man since we had left the South Fork, and another one would be required at midnight, or whenever we halted.

We made our drive the second night with more confidence than the one before, but there were times when the train of cattle must have been nearly two miles in length, yet there was never a halt as long as the man with the lead light could see the one in the rear. We bedded the herd about midnight; and at the first break of day, the fourth guard with the foreman joined us on our watch and we started the cattle again. There was a light dew the second night, and the cattle, hungered by their night walk, went to grazing at once on the damp grass, which would allay their thirst slightly. We allowed them to scatter over several thousand acres, for we were anxious to graze them well before the sun absorbed the moisture, but at the same time every step they took was one less to the coveted Powder River.

When we had grazed the herd forward several miles, and the sun was nearly an hour high, the wagon failed to come up, which caused our foreman some slight uneasiness. Nearly another hour passed, and still the wagon did not come up nor did the outfit put in an appearance. Soon afterwards, however, Moss Strayhorn overtook us, and reported that over forty of our saddle horses were missing, while the work mules had been overtaken nearly five miles back on the trail. On account of my ability as a trailer, Flood at once dispatched me to assist Honeyman in recovering the missing horses, instructing some one else to take the *remuda*, and the wagon and horses to follow up the herd. By the time I arrived, most of the boys at camp had secured a change of horses, and I caught up my *grulla*, that I was saving for the last hard ride, for the horse hunt which confronted us. McCann, having no fire built, gave Honeyman and myself an impromptu breakfast and two canteens of water; but before we let the wagon get away, we rustled a couple of cans of tomatoes and buried them in a cache near the camp-ground, where we would have no trouble in finding them on our return. As the wagon pulled out, we mounted our horses and rode back down the trail.

Billy Honeyman understood horses, and at once volunteered the belief that we would have a long ride overtaking the missing saddle stock. The absent horses, he said, were principally the ones which had been under saddle the day before, and as we both knew, a tired, thirsty horse will go miles for water. He recalled, also, that while we were asleep at noon the day before, twenty miles back on the trail, the horses had found quite a patch of wild sorrel plant, and were foolish over leaving it. Both of us being satisfied that this would hold them for several hours at least, we struck a free gait for it. After we passed the point where the mules had been overtaken, the trail of the horses was distinct enough for us to follow in an easy canter. We saw frequent signs that they left the trail, no doubt to graze, but only for short distances, when they would enter it again, and keep it for miles. Shortly before noon, as we gained the divide above our noon camp of the day before, there about two miles distant we saw our missing horses, feeding over an alkali flat on which grew wild sorrel and other species of sour plants. We rounded them up, and finding none missing, we first secured a change of mounts. The only two horses of my mount in this portion of the *remuda* had both been under the saddle the afternoon and night before, and were as gaunt as rails, and Honeyman had one unused horse of his mount in the band. So when, taking down our ropes, we halted the horses and began riding slowly around them, forcing them into a compact body, I had my eye on a brown horse of Flood's that had not had a saddle on in a week, and told Billy to fasten to him if he got a chance. This was in violation of all custom, but if the foreman kicked, I had a good excuse to offer.

Honeyman was left-handed and threw a rope splendidly; and as we circled around the horses on opposite sides, on a signal from him we whirled our lariats and made casts simultaneously. The wrangler fastened to the brown I wanted, and my loop settled around the neck of his unridden horse. As the band broke away from our swinging ropes, a number of them ran afoul of my rope;

but I gave the rowel to my *grulla*, and we shook them off. When I returned to Honeyman, and we had exchanged horses and were shifting our saddles, I complimented him on the long throw he had made in catching the brown, and incidentally mentioned that I had read of vaqueros in California who used a sixty-five foot lariat. "Thunder," said Billy, in ridicule of the idea, "there wasn't a man ever born who would throw a sixty-five foot rope its full length — without he threw it down a well."

The sun was straight overhead when we started back to overtake the herd. We struck into a little better than a five-mile gait on the return trip, and about two o'clock sighted a band of saddle horses and a wagon camped perhaps a mile forward and to the side of the trail. On coming near enough, we saw at a glance it was a cow outfit, and after driving our loose horses a good push beyond their camp, turned and rode back to their wagon.

"We'll give them a chance to ask us to eat," said Billy to me, "and if they don't, why, they'll miss a good chance to entertain hungry men."

But the foreman with the stranger wagon proved to be a Bee County Texan, and our doubts did him an injustice, for, although dinner was over, he invited us to dismount and ordered his cook to set out something to eat. They had met our wagon, and McCann had insisted on their taking a quarter of our beef, so we fared well. The outfit was from a ranch near Miles City, Montana, and were going down to receive a herd of cattle at Cheyenne, Wyoming. The cattle had been bought at Ogalalla for delivery at the former point, and this wagon was going down with their ranch outfit to take the herd on its arrival. They had brought along about seventy-five saddle horses from the ranch, though in buying the herd they had taken its *remuda* of over a hundred saddle horses. The foreman informed us that they had met our cattle about the middle of the forenoon, nearly twenty-five miles out from Powder River. After we had satisfied the inner man, we lost no time getting off, as we could see a long ride ahead of us; but we had occasion as we rode away to go through their *remuda* to cut out a few of our horses which had mixed, and I found I knew over a dozen of their horses by the ranch brands, while Honeyman also recognized quite a few. Though we felt a pride in our mounts, we had to admit that theirs were better; for the effect of climate had transformed horses that we had once ridden on ranches in southern Texas. It does seem incredible, but it is a fact nevertheless, that a horse, having reached

the years of maturity in a southern climate, will grow half a hand
taller and carry two hundred pounds more flesh, when he has
undergone the rigors of several northern winters.

We halted at our night camp to change horses and to unearth
our cached tomatoes, and again set out. By then it was so late in the
day that the sun had lost its force, and on this last leg in overtaking
the herd we increased our gait steadily until the sun was scarcely
an hour high, and yet we never sighted a dust-cloud in our front.
About sundown we called a few minutes' halt, and after eating our
tomatoes and drinking the last of our water, again pushed on.
Twilight had faded into dusk before we reached a divide which we
had had in sight for several hours, and which we had hoped to gain
in time to sight the timber on Powder River before dark. But as we
put mile after mile behind us, that divide seemed to move away
like a mirage, and the evening star had been shining for an hour
before we finally reached it, and sighted, instead of Powder's
timber, the campfire of our outfit about five miles ahead. We
fired several shots on seeing the light, in the hope that they might
hear us in camp and wait; otherwise we knew they would start the
herd with the rising of the moon.

When we finally reached camp, about nine o'clock at night,
everything was in readiness to start, the moon having risen
sufficiently. Our shooting, however, had been heard, and horses
for a change were tied to the wagon wheels, while the remainder of
the *remuda* was under herd in charge of Rod Wheat. The runaways
were thrown into the horse herd while we bolted our suppers.
Meantime McCann informed us that Flood had ridden that
afternoon to the Powder River, in order to get the lay of the land.
He had found it to be ten or twelve miles distant from the present
camp, and the water in the river barely knee deep to a saddle
horse. Beyond it was a fine valley. Before we started, Flood rode in
from the herd, and said to Honeyman, "I'm going to send the
horses and wagon ahead to-night, and you and McCann want to
camp on this side of the river, under the hill and just a few hundred
yards below the ford. Throw your saddle horses across the river,
and build a fire before you go to sleep, so we will have a beacon
light to pilot us in, in case the cattle break into a run on scenting
the water. The herd will get in a little after midnight, and after
crossing, we'll turn her loose just for luck."

It did me good to hear the foreman say the herd was to be turned
loose, for I had been in the saddle since three that morning, had

ridden over eighty miles, and had now ten more in sight, while
Honeyman would complete the day with over a hundred to his
credit. We let the *remuda* take the lead in pulling out, so that the
wagon mules could be spurred to their utmost in keeping up with
the loose horses. Once they were clear of the herd, we let the cattle
into the trail. They had refused to bed down, for they were uneasy
with thirst, but the cool weather had saved them any serious
suffering. We all felt gala as the herd strung out on the trail. Before
we halted again there would be water for our dumb brutes and rest
for ourselves. There was lots of singing that night. "There's One
more River to cross," and "Roll, Powder, roll," were wafted out on
the night air to the coyotes that howled on our flanks, or to the
prairie dogs as they peeped from their burrows at this weird
caravan of the night, and the lights which flickered in our front
and rear must have been real Jack-o'-lanterns or Will-o'-the-wisps
to these occupants of the plain. Before we had covered half the
distance, the herd was strung out over two miles, and as Flood rode
back to the rear every half hour or so, he showed no inclination to
check the lead and give the sore-footed rear guard a chance to close
up the column; but about an hour before midnight we saw a light
low down in our front, which gradually increased until the treetops
were distinctly visible, and we knew that our wagon had reached
the river. On sighting this beacon, the long yell went up and down
the column, and the herd walked as only long-legged, thirsty Texas
cattle can walk when they scent water. Flood called all the swing
men to the rear, and we threw out a half-circle skirmish line
covering a mile in width, so far back that only an occasional
glimmer of the lead light could be seen. The trail struck the
Powder on an angle, and when within a mile of the river, the
swing cattle left the deep-trodden paths and started for the nearest
water.

The left flank of our skirmish line encountered the cattle as they
reached the river, and prevented them from drifting up the stream.
The point men abandoned the leaders when within a few hundred
yards of the river. Then the rear guard of cripples and sore-footed
cattle came up, and the two flanks of horsemen pushed them all
across the river until they met, when we turned and galloped into
camp, making the night hideous with our yelling. The longest dry
drive of the trip had been successfully made, and we all felt
jubilant. We stripped bridles and saddles from our tired horses,
and unrolling our beds, were soon lost in well-earned sleep.

The stars may have twinkled overhead, and sundry voices of the
night may have whispered to us as we lay down to sleep, but we
were too tired for poetry or sentiment that night.

BUFFALO BILL CODY ENTERTAINS GRAND
DUKE ALEXIS OF RUSSIA, Wyoming, January 1872

Buffalo Bill Cody

William F. Cody was a Pony Express and buffalo hunter (hence the
nickname). He eventually turned his natural talent for showmanship into
a world famous Wild West circus.

At last, on the morning of the 12th of January, 1872, the Grand
Duke and party arrived at North Platte by special train; in charge of
a Mr Francis Thompson. Captain Hays and myself, with five or six
ambulances, fifteen or twenty extra saddle-horses and a company of
cavalry under Captain Egan, were at the dépôt in time to receive
them. Presently General Sheridan and a large, fine-looking young
man, whom we at once concluded to be the Grand Duke came out
of the cars and approached us. General Sheridan at once introduced
me to the Grand Duke as Buffalo Bill, for he it was, and said that I
was to take charge of him and show him how to kill buffalo.

In less than half an hour the whole party were dashing away
towards the south, across the South Platte and towards the
Medicine; upon reaching which point we halted for a change of
horses and a lunch. Resuming our ride we reached Camp Alexis in
the afternoon. General Sheridan was well pleased with the arrangements that had been made and was delighted to find that
Spotted Tail and his Indians had arrived on time. They were
objects of great curiosity to the Grand Duke, who spent considerable time in looking at them, and watching their exhibitions of
horsemanship, sham fights, etc. That evening the Indians gave the
grand war dance, which I had arranged for.

General Custer, who was one of the hunting party, carried on a
mild flirtation with one of Spotted Tail's daughters, who had
accompanied her father thither, and it was noticed also that the
Duke Alexis paid considerable attention to another handsome
redskin maiden. The night passed pleasantly, and all retired with
great expectations of having a most enjoyable and successful
buffalo hunt. The Duke Alexis asked me a great many questions
as to how we shot buffaloes, and what kind of a gun or pistol we

used, and if he was going to have a good horse. I told him that he was to have my celebrated buffalo horse Buckskin Joe, and when we went into a buffalo herd all he would have to do was to sit on the horse's back and fire away.

At nine o'clock next morning we were all in our saddles, and in a few minutes were galloping over the prairies in search of a buffalo herd. We had not gone far before we observed a herd some distance ahead of us crossing our way; after that we proceeded cautiously, so as to keep out of sight until we were ready to make a charge.

Of course the main thing was to give Alexis the first chance and the best shot at the buffaloes, and when all was in readiness we dashed over a little knoll that had hidden us from view, and in a few minutes we were among them. Alexis at first preferred to use his pistol instead of a gun. He fired six shots from this weapon at buffaloes only twenty feet away from him, but as he shot wildly, not one of his bullets took effect. Riding up to his side and seeing that his weapon was empty, I exchanged pistols with him. He again fired six shots, without dropping a buffalo.

Seeing that the animals were bound to make their escape without his killing one of them, unless he had a better weapon, I rode up to him, gave him my old reliable "Lucretia," and told him to urge his horse close to the buffaloes, and I would then give him the word when to shoot. At the same time I gave old Buckskin Joe a blow with my whip, and with a few jumps the horse carried the Grand Duke to within about ten feet of a big buffalo bull.

"Now is your time," said I. He fired, and down went the buffalo. The Grand Duke stopped his horse, dropped his gun on the ground, and commenced waving his hat. When his *suite* came galloping up, he began talking to them in a tongue which I could not understand. Presently General Sheridan joined the group, and the ambulances were brought up. Very soon the corks began to fly from the champagne bottles, in honor of the Grand Duke Alexis, who had killed the first buffalo.

It was reported in a great many of the newspapers that I shot the first buffalo for Alexis, while in some it was stated that I held the buffalo while His Royal Highness killed it. But the way I have related the affair is the correct version.

It was thought that we had had about sport enough for one day, and accordingly I was directed by General Sheridan to guide the party back to camp, and we were soon on our way thither. Several of the party, however, concluded to have a little hunt on their own account, and presently we saw them galloping over the prairie in different directions in pursuit of buffaloes.

While we were crossing a deep ravine, on our way to camp, we ran into a small band of buffaloes that had been frightened by some of the hunters. As they rushed past us, not more than thirty yards distant, Alexis raised his pistol, fired and killed a buffalo cow. It was either an extraordinarly good shot or a "scratch" – probably the latter for it surprised the Grand Duke as well as everybody else. We gave him three cheers, and when the ambulance came up we took a pull at the champagne in honor of the Grand Duke's success. I was in hopes that he would kill five or six more buffaloes before we reached camp, especially if a basket of champagne was to be opened every time he dropped one.

General Sheridan directed me to take care of the hides and heads of the buffaloes which Alexis had killed, as the Duke wished to keep them as souvenirs of the hunt. I also cut out the choice meat from the cow and brought it into camp, and that night at supper Alexis had the pleasure of dining on broiled buffalo steak obtained from the animal which he had shot himself.

We remained at this camp two or three days, during which we hunted most of the time, the Grand Duke himself killing eight buffaloes.

One day Alexis desired to see how the Indians hunted buffaloes and killed them with bow and arrow; so Spotted Tail, selecting some of his best hunters, had them surround a herd, and bring the animals down, not only with arrows, but with lances. The Grand Duke was told to follow upon the heels of one celebrated Indian hunter, whose name was "Two Lance," and watch him bring down the game; for this chief had the reputation of being able to send an arrow through and through the body of a buffalo. Upon this occasion he did not belie his reputation, for he sent an arrow *through* a buffalo, which fell dead at the shot, and the arrow was given to Alexis as a souvenir of his hunt on the American Plains.

When the Grand Duke was satisfied with the sport, orders were given for the return to the railroad. The conveyance provided for the Grand Duke and General Sheridan was a heavy double-seated open carriage, or rather an Irish dog-cart, and it was drawn by four spirited cavalry horses which were not much used to the harness. The driver was Bill Reed, an old overland stage driver and wagon master; on our way in, the Grand Duke frequently expressed his admiration of the skillful manner in which Reed handled the reins.

General Sheridan informed the Duke that I also had been a stage-driver in the Rocky Mountains, and thereupon His Royal Highness expressed a desire to see me drive. I was in advance at the time, and General Sheridan sang out to me:

"Cody, get in here and show the Duke how you can drive. Mr. Reed will exchange places with you and ride your horse."

"All right, General," said I, and in a few moments I had the reins and we were rattling away over the prairie. When we were approaching Medicine Creek, General Sheridan said: "Shake 'em up a little, Bill, and give us some old-time stage-driving."

I gave the horses a crack or two of the whip, and they started off at a very rapid gait. They had a light load to pull, and kept increasing their speed at every jump, and I found it difficult to hold them. They fairly flew over the ground, and at last we reached a steep hill, or divide, which led down into the valley of the Medicine. There was no brake on the wagon, and the horses were not much on the hold-back. I saw that it would be impossible to stop them. All I could do was to keep them straight in the track and let them go it down the hill, for three miles; which distance, I believe, was made in about six minutes. Every once in a while the hind wheels would strike a rut and take a bound, and not touch the ground again for fifteen or twenty feet. The Duke and the General were kept rather busy in holding their positions on the seats, and when they saw that I was keeping the horses straight in the road, they seemed to enjoy the dash which we were making. I was unable to stop the team until they ran into the camp where we were to obtain a fresh relay, and there I succeeded in checking them. The Grand Duke said he didn't want any more of that kind of driving, as he preferred to go a little slower.

INDIAN WARS: SKIRMISH WITH TETON SIOUX WAR PARTY, Yellowstone, August 1873

Lieutenant Charles Larned, Seventh Cavalry

The Seventh Cavalry under General George Armstrong Custer had been sent into the Yellowstone – land of the Teton Sioux – as guard to surveyors of the Northern Pacific railroad.

Camp on the Musselshell River August 19, 1873
Dr John Hensinger, veterinary surgeon, Seventh Cavalry, and Mr Balaran, sutler, were [on August 4] the two victims to a want of

caution that our long immunity from attack had engendered. They had left the train during the halt for the purpose of watering their horses, and on their way back skirting the foot of the bluffs in order to meet the column in its descent, quite unconscious of danger and the horrible fate awaiting them, were suddenly surprised by a party of three Sioux, who had secreted themselves in a ravine, and shot from behind with arrows.

General Custer in the morning had taken a squadron, A and B troops of the Seventh Cavalry, and moved rapidly ahead of the main body about four miles beyond the point at which this tragedy occurred. There, in a belt of woods, his escort had unsaddled, picketed their horses and were lying under the trees awaiting the arrival of the main body, when a shot from the pickets and their sudden appearance brought everyone to his feet. Quickly and quietly the horses were brought in and saddled, a dismounted detachment thrown out as skirmishers, while the remainder of the command moved in the direction of the attack. But three or four Indians were to be seen, galloping and gesticulating wildly in front of the column, which moved quickly forward at a trot. Hardly, however, had the flank arrived opposite a second belt of dense woods before a long line of Indians suddenly moved in regular orders from their midst straight to the attack. They were all in full war costume, mounted on stalwart little ponies, and armed, as are all we have seen, with the best of Henry rifles. As rapidly as possible the command was dismounted and formed in skirmish line in front of the horses, but not a moment too soon, as the enemy came whooping and screeching down upon it. A square volley in their teeth cooled their ardor, and sent them flying back to a respectful distance. For three hours the fight was kept up, the Indians maintaining a perfect skirmish line throughout, and evincing for them a very extraordinary control and discipline. After this desultory fighting had become tiresome, the cavalry mounted suddenly and dashed forward at a charge, scattering their wary antagonists, who were not prepared for such a demonstration, in every direction. Our casualties were one man and three horses wounded. The loss of the enemy, estimated from those seen to fall, must have been something in the vicinity of ten in all, and five ponies.

For the next three days nothing was seen of our friendly neighbors in person, but abundant evidence of their camps, and the heavy trail of a retreating village, numbering, as our Indian scouts told us, in the neighborhood of eighty lodges. Each day General Custer, with two squadrons of cavalry, pushed on in advance, following rapidly on the trail.

It was not, however, until the evening of August 8 that he received orders from General Stanley to push on with the whole of the available cavalry force, make forced night marches, and overtake the village, if possible . . .

At early dawn on the 10th our efforts to cross [the Tongue River] commenced, and it was not until 4 in the afternoon that they were reluctantly relinquished, after every expedient had been resorted to in vain. The current was too swift and fierce for our heavy cavalry. We therefore went into bivouac close to the river bank to await the arrival of the main body, and slept that night as only men in such condition can sleep. We hardly anticipated the lively awakening that awaited us. Just at daylight our slumbers were broken by a sharp volley of musketry from the opposite bank, accompanied by shouts and yells that brought us all to our feet in an instant. As far up the river as we could see, clouds of dust announced the approach of our slippery foes, while the rattling volleys from the opposite woods, and the "zip," "zip" of the balls about our ears told us that there were a few evil disposed persons close by.

For half an hour, while the balls flew high, we lay still without replying, but when the occasional quiver of a wounded horse told that the range was being acquired by them, the horses and men were moved back from the river edge to the foot of the bluffs, and there drawn up in line of battle to await developments. A detachment of sharpshooters was concealed in the woods, and soon sent back a sharp reply to the thickening compliments from the other side. Our scouts and the Indians were soon exchanging chaste complimentary remarks in choice Sioux – such as: "We're coming over to give you h – l;" "You'll see more Indians than you ever saw before in your life," and "Shoot, you son of a dog" from ours. Sure enough, over they came, as good as their word, above and below us, and in twenty minutes our scouts came tumbling down the bluffs head overheels, screeching; "Heap Indian come." Just at this moment General Custer rode up to the line, followed by a bright guidon, and made rapid disposition for the defense. Glad were we that the moment of action had arrived, and that we were to stand no longer quietly and grimly in line of battle to be shot at. One platoon of the first squadron on the left was moved rapidly up the bluffs, and thrown out in skirmish line on the summit, to hold the extreme left. The remainder of the squadron followed as quickly as it could be deployed, together with one troop of the Fourth Squadron.

On they came as before, 500 or 600 in number, screaming and yelling as usual, right onto the line before they saw it. At the same moment the regimental band, which had been stationed in a ravine just in rear, struck up "Garry Owen." The men set up a responsive shout, and a rattling volley swept the whole line.

The fight was short and sharp just here, the Indians rolling back after the first fire and shooting from a safer distance. In twenty minutes the squadrons were mounted and ordered to charge. Our evil-disposed friends tarried no longer, but fled incontinently before the pursuing squadrons. We chased them eight miles and over the river, only returning when the last Indian had gotten beyond our reach.

No less than a thousand warriors had surrounded us, and we could see on the opposite bluffs the scattered remnants galloping wildly to and fro. Just at the conclusion of the fight the infantry came up, and two shells from the Rodman guns completed the discomfiture of our demoralized foes. Our loss was one killed, Private Tuttle, E Troop, Seventh Cavalry, and three wounded. Among the latter, Lieutenant [Charles] Braden, Seventh Cavalry, while gallantly holding the extreme left, the hottest portion of the line, was shot through the thigh, crushing the bone badly. Four horses were killed and eight or ten wounded, and deserve honorable mention, although noncombatants. Official estimates place the Indian loss at forty killed and wounded, and a large number of ponies.

CUSTER'S LAST STAND, Montana, 25 June 1876

Two Moon

A little after 2 o'clock on the afternoon of 25 June, General Custer led his 7th US Cavalry battalion in an attack on a hostile Sioux–Cheyenne camp on the Little Bighorn River. His force numbered 255. The Indians sent around 3000 warriors into the field. The battle lasted an hour, perhaps less. Two Moon was a Cheyenne chief.

Then the Sioux rode up the ridge on all sides, riding very fast. The Cheyenne went up the left way. Then the shooting was quick. Pop-

pop-pop very fast. Some of the soldiers were down on their knees, some standing. Officers all in front. The smoke was like a great cloud, and everywhere the Sioux went the dust rose like smoke. We circled all round him – swirling like water round a stone. We shoot, we ride fast, we shoot again. Soldiers drop, and horses fall on them. Soldiers in line drop, but one man rides up and down the line – all the time shouting. He rode a sorrel horse with white face and white fore-legs. I don't know who he was. He was a brave man.

Indians keep swirling round and round, and the soldiers killed only a few. Many soldiers fell. At last all horses killed but five. Once in a while some man would break out and run towards the river, but he would fall. At last about a hundred men and five horsemen stood on the hill all bunched together. All along the bugler kept blowing his commands. He was very brave too. Then a chief was killed. I hear it was Long Hair [Custer], I don't know; and then the five horsemen and the bunch of men, may be forty, started toward the river. The man on the sorrel horse led them, shouting all the time. He wore a buckskin shirt, and had long black hair and mustache. He fought hard with a big knife. His men were all covered with white dust. I couldn't tell whether they were officers or not. One man all alone ran far down toward the river, then round up over the hill. I thought he was going to escape, but a Sioux fired and hit him in the head. He was the last man. He wore braid on his arms [sergeant].

All the soldiers were now killed, and the bodies were stripped. After that no one could tell which were officers. The bodies were left where they fell. We had no dance that night. We were sorrowful.

Next day four Sioux chiefs and two Cheyennes and I, Two Moon, went upon the battlefield to count the dead. One man carried a little bundle of sticks. When we came to dead men we took a little stick and gave it to another man, so we counted the dead. There were 388. There were thirty-nine Sioux and seven Cheyennes killed and about a hundred wounded.

Some white soldiers were cut with knives, to make sure they were dead; and the war women had mangled some. Most of them were left just where they fell. We came to the man with the big mustache; he lay down the hills towards the river. The Indians did not take his buckskin shirt. The Sioux said "That is a big chief. That is Long Hair." I don't know. I had never seen him. The man on the white-faced horse was the bravest man.

THE KILLING OF BILLY THE KID, Fort Sumner, New Mexico, 14 July 1881

Pat Garrett

According to legend, outlaw Billy the Kid (aka William Bonney, aka Henry McCarty) shot 21 men "not including Indians and Mexicans". In truth the Kid's total was a more modest four solo kills, though he had a hand in the murder of more during the Lincoln County War. On the night of 14 July 1881 Pat Garrett, the sheriff of Lincoln and the sometime card-playing friend of the Kid's, tracked the Kid down to Fort Sumner, a former Navajo reservation then owned by the Maxwell family. Billy the Kid was 22 when he died.

I then concluded to go and have a talk with Peter Maxwell, Esq., in whom I felt sure I could rely. We had ridden to within a short distance of Maxwell's grounds when we found a man in camp and stopped. To Poe's great surprise, he recognized in the camper an old friend and former partner, in Texas, named Jacobs. We unsaddled here, got some coffee, and, on foot, entered an orchard which runs from this point down to a row of old buildings, some of them occupied by Mexicans, not more than sixty yards from Maxwell's house. We approached these houses cautiously, and when within earshot, heard the sound of voices conversing in Spanish. We concealed ourselves quickly and listened; but the distance was too great to hear words, or even distinguish voices. Soon a man arose from the ground, in full view, but too far away to recognize. He wore a broad-brimmed hat, a dark vest and pants, and was in his shirtsleeves. With a few words, which fell like a murmur on our ears, he went to the fence, jumped it, and walked down towards Maxwell's house.

Little as we then suspected it, this man was the Kid. We learned, subsequently, that, when he left his companions that night, he went to the house of a Mexican friend, pulled off his hat and boots, threw himself on a bed, and commenced reading a newspaper. He soon, however, hailed his friend, who was sleeping in the room, told him to get up and make some coffee, adding: "Give me a butcher knife and I will go over to Pete's and get some beef; I'm hungry." The Mexican arose, handed him the knife, and the Kid, hatless and in his stocking-feet, started to Maxwell's, which was but a few steps distant.

When the Kid, by me unrecognized, left the orchard, I

motioned to my companions, and we cautiously retreated a short distance, and, to avoid the persons whom we had heard at the houses, took another route, approaching Maxwell's house from the opposite direction. When we reached the porch in front of the building, I left Poe and McKinney at the end of the porch, about twenty feet from the door of Pete's room, and went in. It was near midnight and Pete was in bed. I walked to the head of the bed and sat down on it, beside him, near the pillow. I asked him as to the whereabouts of the Kid. He said that the Kid had certainly been about, but he did not know whether he had left or not. At that moment a man sprang quickly into the door, looking back, and called twice in Spanish, "Who comes there?" No one replied and he came on in. He was barcheaded. From his step I could perceive he was either barefooted or in his stocking-feet, and held a revolver in his right hand and a butcher knife in his left.

He came directly towards me. Before he reached the bed, I whispered: "Who is it, Pete?" but received no reply for a moment. It struck me that it might be Pete's brother-in-law, Manuel Abreu, who had seen Poe and McKinney, and wanted to know their business. The intruder came close to me, leaned both hands on the bed, his right hand almost touching my knee, and asked, in a low tone: – "Who are they Pete?" – at the same instant Maxwell whispered to me. "That's him!" Simultaneously the Kid must have seen, or felt, the presence of a third person at the head of the bed. He raised quickly his pistol, a self-cocker, within a foot of my breast. Retreating rapidly across the room he cried: "Quien es? Quien es?" "Who's that? Who's that?" All this occurred in a moment. Quickly as possible I drew my revolver and fired, threw my body aside, and fired again. The second shot was useless; the Kid fell dead. He never spoke. A struggle or two, a little strangling sound as he gasped for breath, and the Kid was with his many victims.

RAIDING WITH GERONIMO, 1882

Jason Betzinez

Tired of life on the reservation, the Apache warrior Geronimo (1829–1909) absconded in 1881 to resume life as a raider on white and Mexican settlements. To subdue Geronimo and his 36 Chiricahua Apache followers took five years and 5000 soldiers. On being returned to the reservation, the chief spent his last years cannily selling his autograph to inquisitive whites.

The raiding life of Geronimo's band was later recounted by Jason Betzinez, a young Chiricahua, in his autobiography, *I Fought with Geronimo*.

Preparations for the raid deep into Sonora consisted of making extra pairs of moccasins, cleaning our hair, sharpening knives, and cleaning and greasing guns. We had no tomahawks, arrows or spears. The Apaches never did have tomahawks and by 1882 arrows and spears were rarely used.

We established most of the young boys, women, and children on top of the mountain where they could keep a good lookout and take care of themselves. Mother and I went with the men at least part of the way. Our job was to bring back stolen beeves to our camp so that the women and children would have plenty to eat while the men were away.

After crossing a mountain range we bivouacked for the night. The next morning our leaders told us to travel close together because of the dense timbers, briars, and cactus. The trip was to be dangerous and difficult; it would be almost impossible to travel at night. We were nearly among the enemy now but kept on going to the vicinity of the nearest town. Then our men began scouting around for horses and mules while mother and I together with five young boys, waited on a hill top where we could see the surrounding country and watch out for signs of the enemy.

After a long and anxious wait, toward evening we were relieved to see our men coming, driving some horses. It had been a risky adventure for us. Even one Mexican cowboy spotting us would have meant serious trouble, we being without weapons.

The next day the men killed several head of cattle, which we cut up and loaded on horses. Late in the afternoon mother and I, together with five boys, started back toward the rest of our band. We traveled part of the night through the thick timber. In the morning we resumed our journey, our horses heavily laden with meat, arriving late in the afternoon within sight of camp. Some of the women came out to help us carry in the beef. As we climbed up the mountainside we were very careful not to leave tracks that would show. After we got to camp and unloaded the animals some of the boys drove the horses down to the river away from camp. We now had enough dried beef to last us for at least a month.

Meantime our men went on west to where a main road passed

between several towns, south towards Ures, the then capital of Sonora. Where the road ran along the river through the timber was the locality in which the Apaches were accustomed to lie in wait for travelers especially pack trains laden with drygoods.

Our men were gone about fifteen days. Meanwhile we lived very quietly at camp. One day a woman standing in front of her tepee saw a white object approaching us in the distance. The women and children immediately became very excited and fearful, thinking that the enemy were coming. Two of us boys going out to investigate found that it was our warriors coming home with great quantities of dry goods, bolts of cloth and wearing apparel. When they arrived at the foot of the mountain they called up to us whereupon all the people in camp hurried down to meet them. We surely were glad to see them and they to see us. One thing we *didn't* see was scalps. The Apaches did not practice the custom of scalping a fallen enemy. There may have been exceptions to this but they were very, very rare. Concerning Geronimo I never knew him to bring in a scalp. Much nonsense has been written about this.

After our warriors returned, we hiked farther up the Yaqui River, camped for awhile, then again moved upstream. Here we had plenty of food and nothing to worry about. Nevertheless we were very careful not to disclose our presence because we were quite near a number of Mexican towns. Every day our men stationed lookouts on the hills. Our camp at this time was at the junction of the Bavispe and Yaqui Rivers.

The leaders decided to raid toward the northwest. This time we started off on foot leaving all the animals in the valley near the Bavispe River where there was plenty of good grass. We concealed in caves our saddles and the loot which the men had brought back from the earlier raid, as well as all our camp gear which we could not carry on our backs. We took only one mule, my big mule, on which Geronimo's wife and baby rode.

Our band moved straight west toward a Mexican town. Just when it appeared that we were going right on into the village the leaders stopped a few miles to the east. The plan was to avoid stealing any horses or mules while we were sneaking around in between these towns, two of which lay to the west and one to the east of our route.

From the last campsite the band turned northwest toward the mountains. Since we were about to cross the main road we were especially careful not to be seen or leave any sign that would put the soldiers on our trail. Our men knew that each town contained a garrison of troops. So we carefully covered our tracks.

We camped at the foot of a mountain a few miles from the road running between Buenavista and Moctezuma. Early next morning Geronimo told the men that they could now go out to look for horses and mules. They should drive in all that they could find, as we needed them for the expected move north into the mountains. About noon our men drove in quite a number of animals stolen from the Mexicans. We had a great time roping them and breaking them for the women and children to ride. My cousin roped a mule but it broke away from him. I chased it out into the prairie for nearly two miles. I nearly went too far. Suddenly I saw Mexican soldiers only a short distance away.

As I galloped back to the group of Apaches I heard my cousin shouting to me to hurry up, the enemy were coming along behind me. Meanwhile the Indians were taking up a position from which to attack the soldiers. As I sped over a low ridge I heard the shooting start. The Indians charged so fast toward the enemy that they failed to notice one soldier who was hiding in the bushes. This man shot and killed the last Apache to ride by him. The warriors, hearing the shot, came dashing back just in time to shoot the Mexican.

The band felt dreadfully sad over losing a warrior. He was a Warm Springs Apache who had no near relatives in the band with us.

Late that afternoon we started off to the west then camped at the foot of the mountains for supper. While we were thus engaged, a sentinel ran in to report that the enemy were at the skirmish ground of that afternoon, not far behind us. We moved out hastily into the foothills where we remained in concealment during the night. In the morning we saw the soldiers following our tracks and approaching our hill. At once the warriors took up positions ready for a fight. But the Mexicans didn't attempt to follow our trail up the mountainside.

Finally our men got tired of waiting, so we moved on, traveling very fast right on into the night. We came to a short steep canyon where we made camp and enjoyed a good night's rest.

In the morning we set a course across the wide valley of the Bavispe. Although our horses and mules were in good shape we traveled slowly, enjoying the trip and the pleasant surroundings. That night we camped beside the Bavispe River. The chiefs told the men not to shoot any deer because the Mexicans might hear the firing.

This country looked as though it belonged to us. For some days owing to the wise leadership of Geronimo we had not been disturbed by an enemy. We crossed the river and moved through the woods discussing the fact that the country seemed to be full of deer and other game. In fact the deer just stood and watched us pass. It seemed that they had never been disturbed by anyone hunting them. A person living in this favored spot would never have to go hungry. There were plenty of wild animals and other food, easily obtainable. But at this time the men all obeyed Geronimo and didn't fire a shot. Besides, we still had plenty of dried beef.

Arriving at our next objective we again settled down for an indefinite stay. It was just like peacetime. We had plenty to eat, good clothing taken from the stolen stocks, and no enemies nearby. We were about thirty miles southeast of Fronteras.

During this period the women, assisted by some of the boys, were gathering and drying the fruit of the yucca, preparing for a winter to be spent in the Sierras. It was in the late summer or early fall of 1882.

MASSACRE AT WOUNDED KNEE, Pine Ridge Reservation, South Dakota, 29 December 1890

Black Elk

The endplay in the long conflict between Native Americans and white settlers. 153 Sioux were killed.

That evening before it happened, I went in to Pine Ridge and heard these things, and while I was there, soldiers started for where the Big Foots were. These made about five hundred soldiers that were there next morning. When I saw them starting I felt that something terrible was going to happen. That night I could hardly sleep at all. I walked around most of the night.

In the morning I went out after my horses, and while I was out I heard shooting off toward the east, and I knew from the sound that it must be wagon-guns (cannon) going off. The sounds went right through my body, and I felt that something terrible would happen.

When I reached camp with the horses, a man rode up to me and said: "Hey-hey-hey! The people that are coming are fired on! I know it!"

I saddled up my buckskin and put on my sacred shirt. It was one I had made to be worn by no one but myself. It had a spotted eagle outstretched on the back of it, and the daybreak star was on the left shoulder, because when facing south that shoulder is toward the east. Across the breast, from the left shoulder to the right hip, was the flaming rainbow, and there was another rainbow around the neck, like a necklace, with a star at the bottom. At each shoulder, elbow, and wrist was an eagle feather; and over the whole shirt were red streaks of lightning. You will see that this was from my great vision, and you will know how it protected me that day.

I painted my face all red, and in my hair I put one eagle feather for the One Above.

It did not take me long to get ready, for I could still hear the shooting over there.

I started out alone on the old road that ran across the hills to Wounded Knee. I had no gun. I carried only the sacred bow of the west that I had seen in my great vision. I had gone only a little way when a band of young men came galloping after me. The first two who came up were Loves War and Iron Wasichu. I asked what they were going to do, and they said they were just going to see where the shooting was. Then others were coming up, and some older men.

We rode fast, and there were about twenty of us now. The shooting was getting louder. A horseback from over there came galloping very fast toward us, and he said: "Hey-hey-hey! They have murdered them!" Then he whipped his horse and rode away faster toward Pine Ridge.

In a little while we had come to the top of the ridge where, looking to the east, you can see for the first time the monument and the burying ground on the little hill where the church is. That is where the terrible thing started. Just south of the burying ground on the little hill a deep dry gulch runs about east and west, very crooked, and it rises westward to nearly the top of the ridge where we were. It had no name, but the Wasichus [white men], sometimes call it Battle Creek now. We stopped on the ridge not far from the head of the dry gulch. Wagon-guns were still going off over there on the little hill, and they were going off again where they hit along the gulch. There was much shooting down yonder, and there were many cries, and we could see cavalrymen scattered over the hills ahead of us. Cavalrymen were riding along the gulch and shooting into it, where the women and children were running away and trying to hide in the gullies and the stunted pines.

A little way ahead of us, just below the head of the dry gulch, there were some women and children who were huddled under a clay bank, and some cavalrymen were there pointing guns at them.

We stopped back behind the ridge, and I said to the others: "Take courage. These are our relatives. We will try to get them back." Then we all sang a song which went like this:

> A thunder being nation I am, I have said.
> A thunder being nation I am, I have said.
> You shall live.
> You shall live.
> You shall live.
> You shall live.

Then I rode over the ridge and the others after me, and we were crying: "Take courage! It is time to fight!" The soldiers who were guarding our relatives shot at us and then ran away fast, and some more cavalrymen on the other side of the gulch did too. We got our relatives and sent them across the ridge to the northwest where they would be safe.

I had no gun, and when we were charging, I just held the sacred bow out in front of me with my right hand. The bullets did not hit us at all.

We found a little baby lying all alone near the head of the gulch. I could not pick her up just then, but I got her later and some of my people adopted her. I just wrapped her up tighter in a shawl that was around her and left her there. It was a safe place, and I had other work to do.

The soldiers had run eastward over the hills where there were some more soldiers, and they were off their horses and lying down. I told the others to stay back, and I charged upon them holding the sacred bow out toward them with my right hand. They all shot at me, and I could hear bullets all around me, but I ran my horse right close to them, and then swung around. Some soldiers across the gulch began shooting at me too, but I got back to the others and was not hurt at all.

By now many other Lakotas, who had heard the shooting, were coming up from Pine Ridge, and we all charged on the soldiers. They ran eastward toward where the trouble began. We followed down along the dry gulch, and what we saw was terrible. Dead and wounded women and children and little babies were scattered all along there where they had been trying to run away. The soldiers had followed along the gulch, as they ran, and murdered them in there. Sometimes they were in heaps because they had huddled together, and some were scattered all along. Sometimes bunches of them had been killed and torn to pieces where the wagon-guns hit them. I saw a little baby trying to suck its mother, but she was bloody and dead.

There were two little boys at one place in this gulch. They had guns and they had been killing soldiers all by themselves. We could see the soldiers they had killed. The boys were all alone there, and they were not hurt. These were very brave little boys.

When we drove the soldiers back, they dug themselves in, and we were not enough people to drive them out from there. In the evening they marched off up Wounded Knee Creek, and then we saw all that they had done there.

Men and women and children were heaped and scattered all over the flat at the bottom of the little hill where the soldiers had their wagon-guns, and westward up the dry gulch all the way to the high ridge, the dead women and children and babies were scattered.

When I saw this I wished that I had died too, but I was not sorry for the women and children. It was better for them to be happy in the other world, and I wanted to be there too. But before I went there I wanted to have revenge. I thought there might be a day, and we should have revenge.

After the soldiers marched away, I heard from my friend, Dog Chief, how the trouble started, and he was right there by Yellow Bird when it happened. This is the way it was:

In the morning the soldiers began to take all the guns away from the Big Foots, who were camped in the flat below the little hill where the monument and burying ground are now. The people had stacked most of their guns, and even their knives, by the tepee where Big Foot was lying sick. Soldiers were on the little hill and all around, and there were soldiers across the dry gulch to the south and over east along Wounded Knee Creek too. The people were nearly surrounded, and the wagon-guns were pointing at them.

Some had not yet given up their guns, and so the soldiers were searching all the tepees, throwing things around and poking into everything. There was a man called Yellow Bird, and he and another man were standing in front of the tepee where Big Foot was lying sick. They had white sheets around and over them, with eyeholes to look through, and they had guns under these. An officer came to search them. He took the other man's gun, and then started to take Yellow Bird's. But Yellow Bird would not let go. He wrestled with the officer, and while they were wrestling, the gun went off and killed the officer. Wasichus and some others have said he meant to do this, but Dog Chief was standing right there, and he told me it was not so. As soon as the gun went off, Dog Chief told me, an officer shot and killed Big Foot who was lying sick inside the tepee.

Then suddenly nobody knew what was happening, except that the soldiers were all shooting and the wagon-guns began going off right in among the people.

Many were shot down right there. The women and children ran into the gulch and up west, dropping all the time, for the soldiers shot them as they ran. There were only about a hundred warriors and there were nearly five hundred soldiers. The warriors rushed to where they had piled their guns and knives. They fought soldiers with only their hands until they got their guns.

Dog Chief saw Yellow Bird run into a tepee with his gun, and from there he killed soldiers until the tepee caught fire. Then he died full of bullets.

It was a good winter day when all this happened. The sun was shining. But after the soldiers marched away from their dirty work, a heavy snow began to fall. The wind came up in the night. There was a big blizzard, and it grew very cold. The snow drifted deep in the crooked gulch, and it was one long grave of butchered women and children and babies, who had never done any harm and were only trying to run away.

MANILA BAY, Philippines, 1 May 1898
Admiral George Dewey

Dewey's rout of the Spanish fleet at Manila Bay was complete, and opened the door to America's seizure of the Philippines as its own colonial possession. America's imperial age began at Manila Bay.

When we were ten miles from Boca Grande we judged, as we saw signal lights flash, that we had already been sighted either by small vessels acting as scouts or by land lookouts. El Fraile was passed by the flag-ship at a distance of half a mile and was utilized as a point of departure for the course up the bay clear of the San Nicolas

Shoals. When El Fraile bore due south (magnetic) the course was changed to northeast by north. We were not surprised to find the usual lights on Corregidor and Caballo Islands and the San Nicolas Shoals extinguished, as this was only a natural precaution on the part of the Spaniards.

There were no vessels, so far as we could see, cruising off the entrance, no dash of torpedo-launches which might have been expected, no sign of life beyond the signalling on shore until the rear of the column, steaming at full speed, was between Corregidor and El Fraile.

As we watched the walls of darkness for the first gun-flash, every moment of our progress brought its relief, and now we began to hope that we should get by without being fired on at all. But about ten minutes after midnight, when all except our rear ships had cleared it, the El Fraile battery opened with a shot that passed between the *Petrel* and the *Raleigh*. The *Boston, Concord, Raleigh*, and *McCulloch* returned the fire with a few shots. One 8-inch shell from the *Boston* seemed to be effective. After firing three times El Fraile was silent. There was no demonstration whatever from the Caballo battery, with its three 6-inch modern rifles, no explosion of mines, and no other resistance. We were safely within the bay. The next step was to locate the Spanish squadron and engage it.

Afterward we heard various explanations of why we were not given a warmer reception as we passed through. Some of the officers in the El Fraile battery said that their dilatoriness in opening fire was due to the fact that their men were ashore at Punta Lasisi and could not get off to their guns in time after they heard of the squadron's approach. An eye-witness on Corregidor informed me that our squadron was perfectly visible as it was passing through the entrance, but for some extraordinary reason the commanding officer gave no orders to the batteries to open fire.

Perhaps the enemy thought that he had done all that was necessary by cutting off the usual lights on Corregidor and Caballo Islands and San Nicolas Shoals for guiding mariners, and he expected that without pilots and without any knowledge of the waters we would not be guilty of such a foolhardy attempt as entering an unlighted channel at midnight.

Once through the entrance, as I deemed it wise to keep moving in order not to be taken by surprise when the ships had no headway, and as, at the same time, I did not wish to reach our destination before we had sufficient daylight to show us the position of the Spanish ships, the speed of the squadron was reduced to four knots, while we headed toward the city of Manila. In the meantime the men were allowed to snatch a little sleep at their guns; but at four o'clock coffee was served to them, and so eager were they that there was no need of any orders to insure readiness for the work to come.

Signal lights, rockets, and beacon lights along the shore, now that we were sure of grappling with the enemy, no longer concerned us. We waited for dawn and the first sight of the Spanish squadron, which I had rather expected would be at the anchorage off the city of Manila. This seemed naturally the strong position for Admiral Montojo to take up, as he would then have the powerful Manila battery, mounting the guns which have already been enumerated, to support him. But the admiral stated in his report that he had avoided this position on account of the resultant injury which the city might have received if the battle had been fought in close proximity to it.

The *Nanshan* and *Zafiro*, as there was no reserve ammunition for either to carry, had been sent, with the *McCulloch*, into an unfrequented part of the bay in order that they should sustain no injury and that they might not hamper the movements of the fighting-ships. When we saw that there were only merchantmen at the Manila anchorage, the squadron, led by the flag-ship, gradually changed its course, swinging around on the arc of a large circle leading toward the city and making a kind of countermarch, as it were, until headed in the direction of Cavite. This brought the ships within two or three miles of shore, with a distance of four hundred yards between ships, in the following order: *Olympia* (flag), *Baltimore, Raleigh, Petrel, Concord,* and *Boston.*

About 5.05 the Luneta and two other Manila batteries opened fire. Their shots passed well over the vessels. It was estimated that some had a range of seven miles. Only the *Boston* and *Concord* replied. Each sent two shells at the Luneta battery. The other vessels reserved their fire, having in mind my caution that, in the absence of a full supply of ammunition, the amount we had was too precious to be wasted when we were seven thousand miles from our base. My captains understood that the Spanish ships were our objective and not the shore fortifications of a city that would be virtually ours as soon as our squadron had control of Manila Bay.

With the coming of broad daylight we finally sighted the

Spanish vessels formed in an irregular crescent in front of Cavite. The *Olympia* headed toward them, and in answer to her signal to close up, the distance between our ships was reduced to two hundred yards. The western flank of the Spanish squadron was protected by Cavite Peninsula and the Sangley Point battery, while its eastern flank rested in the shoal water off Las Pinas.

The Spanish line of battle was formed by the *Reina Cristina* (flag), *Castilla, Don Juan de Austria, Don Antonio de Ulloa, Isla de Luzón, Isla de Cuba*, and *Marqués del Deuro*

The *Velasco* and *Lezo* were on the other (southern) side of Cavite Point, and it is claimed by the Spaniards that they took no part in the action. Some of the vessels in the Spanish battle-line were under way, and others were moored so as to bring their broadside batteries to bear to the best advantage. The *Castilla* was protected by heavy iron lighters filled with stone.

Before me now was the object for which we had made our arduous preparations, and which, indeed, must ever be the supreme test of a naval officer's career. I felt confident of the outcome, though I had no thought that victory would be won at so slight a cost to our own side. Confidence was expressed in the very precision with which the dun, war-colored hulls of the squadron followed in column behind the flag-ship, keeping their distance excellently. All the guns were pointed constantly at the enemy, while the men were at their stations waiting the word. There was no break in the monotone of the engines save the mechanical voice of the leadsman or an occasional low-toned command by the quartermaster at the conn, or the roar of a Spanish shell. The Manila batteries continued their inaccurate fire, to which we paid no attention.

The misty haze of the tropical dawn had hardly risen when at 5.15, at long range, the Cavite forts and Spanish squadron opened fire. Our course was not one leading directly toward the enemy, but a converging one, keeping him on our starboard bow. Our speed was eight knots and our converging course and ever-varying position must have confused the Spanish gunners. My assumption that the Spanish fire would be hasty and inaccurate proved correct.

So far as I could see, none of our ships was suffering any damage, while, in view of my limited ammunition supply, it was my plan not to open fire until we were within effective range, and then to fire as rapidly as possible with all of our guns.

At 5.40, when we were within a distance of 5,000 yards (two and one-half miles), I turned to Captain Gridley and said:

"You may fire when you are ready, Gridley."

While I remained on the bridge with Lamberton, Brumby, and Stickney, Gridley took his station in the conning-tower and gave the order to the battery. The very first gun to speak was an 8-inch from the forward turret of the *Olympia*, and this was the signal for all the other ships to join the action.

At about the time that the Spanish ships were first sighted, 5.06, two submarine mines were exploded between our squadron and Cavite, some two miles ahead of our column. On account of the distance, I remarked to Lamberton:

"Evidently the Spaniards are already rattled."

However, they explained afterward that the premature explosions were due to a desire to clear a space in which their ships might manœuvre.

At one time a torpedo-launch made an attempt to reach the *Olympia*, but she was sunk by the guns of the secondary battery and went down bow first, and another yellow-colored launch flying the Spanish colors ran out, heading for the *Olympia*, but after being disabled she was beached to prevent her sinking.

When the flag-ship neared the five-fathom curve off Cavite she turned to the westward, bringing her port batteries to bear on the enemy, and, followed by the squadron, passed along the Spanish line until north of and only some fifteen hundred yards distant from the Sangley Point battery, when she again turned and headed back to the eastward, thus giving the squadron an opportunity to use their port and starboard batteries alternately and to cover with their fire all the Spanish ships, as well as the Cavite and Sangley Point batteries. While I was regulating the course of the squadron, Lieutenant Calkins was verifying our position by cross-bearings and by the lead.

Three runs were thus made from the eastward and two from the westward, the length of each run averaging two miles and the ships being turned each time with port helm. Calkins found that there was in reality deeper water than shown on the chart, and when he reported the fact to me, inasmuch as my object was to get as near as possible to the enemy without grounding our own vessels, the fifth run past the Spaniards was farther inshore than any preceding run. At the nearest point to the enemy our range was only two thousand yards.

There had been no cessation in the rapidity of fire maintained by our whole squadron, and the effect of its concentration, owing to the fact that our ships were kept so close together, was smothering, particularly upon the two largest ships, the *Reina Cristina* and *Castilla*. The *Don Juan de Austria* first and then the *Reina Cristina* made brave and desperate attempts to charge the *Olympia*, but becoming the target for all our batteries they turned and ran back. In this sortie the *Reina Cristina* was raked by an 8-inch shell, which is said to have put out of action some twenty men and to have completely destroyed her steering-gear. Another shell in her forecastle killed or wounded all the members of the crews of four rapid-fire guns; another set fire to her after orlop; another killed or disabled nine men on her poop; another carried away her mizzen-mast, bringing down the ensign and the admiral's flag, both of which were replaced; another exploded in the after ammunition-room; and still another exploded in the sick-bay, which was already filled with wounded.

When she was raised from her muddy bed, five years later, eighty skeletons were found in the sick-bay and fifteen shot holes in the hull; while the many hits mentioned in Admiral Montojo's report, and his harrowing description of the shambles that his flag-ship had become when he was finally obliged to leave her, shows what execution was done to her upper works. Her loss was one hundred and fifty killed and ninety wounded, seven of these being officers. Among the killed was her valiant captain, Don Luis Cadarso, who, already wounded, finally met his death while bravely directing the rescue of his men from the burning and sinking vessel.

Though in the early part of the action our firing was not what I should have liked it to be, it soon steadied down, and by the time the *Reina Cristina* steamed toward us it was satisfactorily accurate. The *Castilla* fared little better than the *Reina Cristina*. All except one of her guns was disabled, she was set on fire by our shells, and finally abandoned by her crew after they had sustained a loss of twenty-three killed and eighty wounded. The *Don Juan de Austria* was badly damaged and on fire, the *Isla de Luzón* had three guns dismounted, and the *Marqués del Duero* was also in a bad way. Admiral Montojo, finding his flag-ship no longer manageable, half her people dead or wounded, her guns useless and the ship on fire, gave the order to abandon and sink her, and transferred his flag to the *Isla de Cuba* shortly after seven o'clock.

Victory was already ours, though we did not know it. Owing to the smoke over the Spanish squadron there were no visible signs of the execution wrought by our guns when we started upon our fifth run past the enemy. We were keeping up our rapid fire, and the flag-ship was opposite the centre of the Spanish line, when, at 7.35, the captain of the *Olympia* made a report to me which was as startling as it was unexpected. This was to the effect that on board the *Olympia* there remained only fifteen rounds per gun for the 5-inch battery.

It was a most anxious moment for me. So far as I could see, the Spanish squadron was as intact as ours. I had reason to believe that their supply of ammunition was as ample as ours was limited.

Therefore, I decided to withdraw temporarily from action for a redistribution of ammunition if necessary. For I knew that fifteen rounds of 5-inch ammunition could be shot away in five minutes. But even as we were steaming out of range the distress of the Spanish ships became evident. Some of them were perceived to be on fire and others were seeking protection behind Cavite Point. The *Don Antonio de Ulloa*, however, still retained her position at Sangley Point, where she had been moored. Moreover, the Spanish fire, with the exception of the Manila batteries, to which we had paid little attention, had ceased entirely. It was clear that we did not need a very large supply of ammunition to finish our morning's task; and happily it was found that the report about the *Olympia*'s 5-inch ammunition had been incorrectly transmitted. It was that fifteen rounds had been fired per gun, not that only fifteen rounds remained.

Feeling confident of the outcome, I now signalled that the crews, who had had only a cup of coffee at 4 A. M., should have their breakfast. The public at home, on account of this signal, to which was attributed a nonchalance that had never occurred to me, reasoned that breakfast was the real reason for our withdrawing from action. Meanwhile, I improved the opportunity to have the commanding officers report on board the flag-ship.

There had been such a heavy flight of shells over us that each captain, when he arrived, was convinced that no other ship had had such good luck as his own in being missed by the enemy's fire, and expected the others to have both casualties and damages to their ships to report. But fortune was as pronouncedly in our favor at Manila as it was later at Santiago. To my gratification not a single life had been lost, and considering that we would rather measure the importance of an action by the scale of its conduct than by the number of casualties we were immensely happy. The concentration of our fire immediately we were within telling range had given us an early advantage in demoralizing the enemy, which has ever been the prime factor in naval battles. In the War of 1812 the losses of the *Constitution* were slight when she overwhelmed the *Guerrière* and in the Civil War the losses of the *Kearsarge* were slight when she made a shambles of the *Alabama*. On the *Baltimore* two officers (Lieutenant F. W. Kellogg and Ensign N. E. Irwin) and six men were slightly wounded. None of our ships had been seriously hit, and every one was still ready for immediate action.

In detail the injuries which we had received from the Spanish fire were as follows:

The *Olympia* was hulled five times and her rigging was cut in several places. One six-pound projectile struck immediately under the position where I was standing. The *Baltimore* was hit five times. The projectile which wounded two officers and six men pursued a most erratic course. It entered the ship's side forward of the starboard gangway, and just above the line of the main deck, passed through the hammock-netting, down through the deck planks and steel deck, bending the deck beam in a wardroom state-room, thence upward through the after engine-room coaming, over against the cylinder of a 6-inch gun, disabling the gun, struck and exploded a box of three-pounder ammunition, hit an iron ladder, and finally, spent, dropped on deck. The *Boston* had four unimportant hits, one causing a fire which was soon extinguished, and the *Petrel* was struck once.

At 11.16 A. M. we stood in to complete our work. There remained to oppose us, however, only the batteries and the gallant little *Ulloa*. Both opened fire as we advanced. But the contest was too unequal to last more than a few minutes. Soon the *Ulloa*, under our concentrated fire, went down valiantly with her colors flying.

The battery at Sangley Point was well served, and several times reopened fire before being finally silenced. Had this battery possessed its four other 6-inch guns which Admiral Montojo had found uselessly lying on the beach at Subig, our ships would have had many more casualties to report. Happily for us, the guns of this battery had been so mounted that they could be laid only for objects beyond the range of two thousand yards. As the course of our ships led each time within this range, the shots passed over and beyond them. Evidently the artillerists, who had so constructed their carriages that the muzzles of the guns took against the sill of the embrasure for any range under two thousand yards, thought it out of the question that an enemy would venture within this distance.

The *Concord* was sent to destroy a large transport, the *Mindanao*, which had been beached near Bacoor, and the *Petrel*, whose light draught would permit her to move in shallower water than the other vessels of the squadron, was sent into the harbor of Cavite to destroy any ships that had taken refuge there. The *Mindanao* was set on fire and her valuable cargo destroyed. Meanwhile, the *Petrel* gallantly performed her duty, and after a few shots from her 6-inch guns the Spanish flag on the government building was hauled down and a white flag hoisted. Admiral Montojo had been wounded, and had taken refuge on shore with his remaining officers and men; his loss was three hundred and eighty-one of his officers and crew, and there was no possibility of further resistance.

At 12.30 the *Petrel* signalled the fact of the surrender, and the firing ceased. But the Spanish vessels were not yet fully destroyed. Therefore, the executive officer of the *Petrel*, Lieutenant E. M. Hughes, with a whale-boat and a crew of only seven men, boarded and set fire to the *Don Juan de Austria, Isla de Cuba, Isla de Luzón, General Lezo, Coreo,* and *Marqués del Duero,* all of which had been abandoned in shallow water and left scuttled by their deserting crews. This was a courageous undertaking, as these vessels were supposed to have been left with trains to their magazines and were not far from the shore, where there were hundreds of Spanish soldiers and sailors, all armed and greatly excited. The *Manila,* an armed transport, which was found uninjured after having been beached by the Spaniards, was therefore spared. Two days later she was easily floated, and for many years did good service as a gunboat. The little *Petrel* continued her work until 5.20 P. M., when she rejoined the squadron, towing a long string of tugs and launches, to be greeted by volleys of cheers from every ship.

The order to capture or destroy the Spanish squadron had been executed to the letter. Not one of its fighting-vessels remained afloat.

SPANISH-AMERICAN WAR: A JOURNALIST ON THE FRONTLINE, June 1898

Stephen Crane

Although Crane had written his great war novel *The Red Badge of Courage* (1895) without any personal experience of combat, he made good his education by reporting the Spanish-American War for the New York *World* and *McClure's* in 1898. Crane died two years later, of tuberculosis, aged twenty-eight.

SIBONEY, June 24

And this is the end of the third day since the landing of the troops. Yesterday was a day of insurgent fighting. The Cubans were supposed to be fighting somewhere in the hills with the regiment of Santiago de Cuba, which had been quite cut off from its native city. No American soldiery were implicated in any way in the battle. But to-day is different. The mounted infantry – the First Volunteer Cavalry – Teddie's Terrors – Wood's Weary Walkers – have had their first engagement. It was a bitter hard first fight for new troops, but no man can ever question the bravery of this regiment.

As we landed from a despatch boat we saw the last troop of the mounted infantry wending slowly over the top of a huge hill. Three of us promptly posted after them upon hearing the statement that they had gone out with the avowed intention of finding the Spaniards and mixing it up with them.

Through the thickets

They were far ahead of us by the time we reached the top of the mountain, but we swung rapidly on the path through the dense Cuban thickets and in time met and passed the hospital corps, a vacant, unloaded hospital corps, going ahead on mules. Then there was another long lonely march through the dry woods, which seemed almost upon the point or crackling into a blaze under the rays of the furious Cuban sun. We met nothing but blankets, shelter-tents, coats and other impediments, which the panting Rough Riders had flung behind them on their swift march.

In time we came in touch with a few stragglers, men down with the heat, prone and breathing heavily, and then we struck the rear of the column. We were now about four miles out, with no troops nearer than that by the road.

I know nothing about war, of course, and pretend nothing, but I have been enabled from time to time to see brush fighting, and I want to say here plainly that the behavior of these Rough Riders while marching through the woods shook me with terror as I have never before been shaken.

Superb courage

It must now be perfectly understood throughout the length and breadth of the United States that the Spaniards have learned a great deal from the Cubans, and they are now going to use against us the tactics which the Cubans have used so successfully against them. The marines at Guantanamo have learned it. The Indian-fighting regulars know it anyhow, but this regiment of volunteers knew nothing but their own superb courage. They wound along this narrow winding path, babbling joyously, arguing, recounting, laughing; making more noise than a train going through a tunnel.

Any one could tell from the conformation of the country when we were liable to strike the enemy's outposts, but the clatter of tongues did not then cease. Also, those of us who knew heard going from hillock to hillock the beautiful coo of the Cuban wood-dove – ah, the wood-dove! the Spanish guerilla wood-dove which had presaged the death of gallant marines.

For my part, I declare that I was frightened almost into convulsions. Incidentally I mentioned the cooing of the doves to some of the men, but they said decisively that the Spaniards did not use this signal. I don't know how they knew.

Silence – action

Well, after we had advanced well into the zone of the enemy's firemark that – well into the zone of Spanish fire – a loud order came along the line: "There's a Spanish outpost just ahead and the men must stop talking."

"Stop talkin', can't ye, – it," bawled a sergeant.

"Ah, say, can't ye stop talkin'?" howled another.

I was frightened before a shot was fired; frightened because I thought this silly brave force was wandering placidly into a great deal of trouble. They did. The firing began. Four little volleys were fired by members of a troop deployed to the rights. Then the Mauser began to pop – the familiar Mauser pop. A captain announce that this distinct Mauser sound was our own Krag-Jorgensen. O misery!

Then the woods became aglow with fighting. Our people advanced, deployed, reinforced, fought, fell – in the bushes, in the tall grass, under the lone palms – before a foe not even half seen. Mauser bullets came from three sides. Mauser bullets – not Krag-Jorgensen – although men began to cry that they were being fired into by their own people – whined in almost all directions. Three troops went forward in skirmish order and in five minutes they called for reinforcements. They were under a cruel fire; half of the men hardly knew whence it came; but their conduct, by any soldierly standard, was magnificent.

Green heroes

Most persons with a fancy for military things suspect the value of an announcedly picked regiment. Better gather a simple collection of clerks from anywhere. But in this case the usual view changes. This regiment is as fine a body of men as were ever accumulated for war.

There was nothing to be seen but men straggling through the underbrush and firing at some part of the landscape. This was the scenic effect. Of course men said that they saw five hundred, one thousand, three thousand, fifteen thousand Spaniards, but – poof – in bush country of this kind it is almost impossible for one to see more than fifty men at a time. According to my opinion there were never more than five hundred men in the Spanish firing line. There might have been aplenty in touch with their center and flanks, but as to the firing there were never more than five hundred engaged. This is certain.

The Rough Riders advanced steadily and confidently under the Mauser bullets. They spread across some open ground – tall grass and palms – and there they began to fall, smothering and threshing down in the grass, marking man-shaped places among those luxurious blades. The action lasted about one-half hour. Then the Spaniards fled. They had never seen men fight them in this manner and they fled. The business was too serious.

Then the heroic rumor arose, soared, and screamed above the bush. Everybody was wounded. Everybody was dead. There was nobody. Gradually there was somebody. There was the wounded, the important wounded. And the dead.

Marshall's courage

Meanwhile a soldier passing near me said: "There's a correspondent all shot to hell."

He guided me to where Edward Marshall lay, shot through the body. The following conversation ensued:

"Hello, Crane!"

"Hello, Marshall! In hard luck, old man?"

"Yes, I'm done for."

"Nonsense! You're all right, old boy. What can I do for you?"

"Well, you might file my despatches. I don't mean file 'em ahead of your own, old man – but just file 'em if you find it handy."

I immediately decided that he was doomed. No man could be so sublime in detail concerning the trade of journalism and not die. There was the solemnity of a funeral song in these absurd and fine sentences about despatches. Six soldiers gathered him up on a tent and moved slowly off.

"Hello!" shouted a stern and menacing person, "who are you? And what are you doing here? Quick!"

"I am a correspondent, and we are merely carrying back another correspondent who we think is mortally wounded. Do you care?"

The Rough Rider, somewhat abashed, announced that he did not care.

New york to the fore

And now the wounded soldiers began to crawl, walk and be carried back to where, in the middle of the path, the surgeons had established a little field hospital.

"Say, doctor, this ain't much of a wound. I reckon I can go now back to my troop," said Arizona.

"Thanks, awfully, doctor. Awfully kind of you. I dare say I shall be all right in a moment," said New York.

This hospital was a spectacle of heroism. The doctor, gentle and calm, moved among the men without the commonsenseless bullying of the ordinary ward. It was a sort of fraternal game. They were all in it, and of it, helping each other.

In the mean time three troops of the Ninth Cavalry were swinging the woods, and a mile behind them the Seventy-first New York was moving forward eagerly to the rescue. But the day was done. The Rough Riders had bitten it off and chewed it up – chewed it up splendidly.

HOLD-UP: THE WILD BUNCH ROB THE OVERLAND FLYER, Wyoming, 2 June 1899

Robert Lawson

"The Wild Bunch" were the last of the old-style robber gangs of the West. Here Union Pacific mail clerk Robert Lawson recounts their robbery of the Overland Flyer at Wilcox Siding, Wyoming, in summer 1899. The gang was led by Robert "Butch Cassidy" Parker and Harry "Sundance Kid" Longbaugh, whose lives (and deaths) were immortalized in the Redford–Newman movie *Butch Cassidy and the Sundance Kid*.

As soon as we came to a standstill, Conductor Storey went forward to see what was the matter and saw several men with guns, one of whom shouted that they were going to blow up the train with dynamite. The conductor understood the situation at once and, before meeting the bandits, turned and started back to warn the second section. The robbers mounted the engine and at the point of their guns forced the engineer and fireman to dismount, after beating the engineer over the head with their guns, claiming that he didn't move fast enough, and marched them back over to our car.

In a few moments we heard voices outside our car calling for Sherman and looking out saw Engineer Jones and his fireman accompanied by three masked men with guns.

They evidently thought Clerk Sherman was aboard and were calling him to come out with the crew. Burt Bruce, clerk in charge, refused to open the door, and ordered all lights extinguished. There was much loud talk and threats to blow up the car were made, but the doors were kept shut. In about 15 minutes two shots were fired into the car, one of the balls passing through the water tank and on through the stanchions.

Following close behind the shooting came a terrific explosion, and one of the doors was completely wrecked and most of the car windows broken. The bandits then threatened to blow up the whole car if we didn't get out, so Bruce gave the word and we jumped down, and were immediately lined up and searched for weapons. They said it would not do us no good to make trouble, that they didn't want the mail – that they wanted what was in the express car and was going to have it, and that they had powder enough to blow the whole train off the track.

After searching us they started us back and we saw up the track the headlight of the second section. They asked what was on the train, and somebody said there were two cars of soldiers on the train. This scared them and they hastened back to the engine, driving us ahead. They forced us on the engine, and as Dietrick moved too slowly they assisted him with a few kicks. While on the engine, Dietrick, in the act of closing the furnace door, brushed a mask off one of the men, endeavoring to catch a glimpse of his face. The man quickly grasped his mask and threatened to "plug" Dietrick.

They then ran the train ahead across a gully and stopped. There were two extra cars on the train. They were uncoupled. Others of the gang went to the bridge, attempting to destroy it with their giant powder, or dynamite, which they placed on the timbers. After the explosion at the bridge they boarded the engine with the baggage, express, and mail cars, went for about 2 miles, leaving the extra cars.

Upon arriving at the stopping place they proceeded to business again and went to the express car and ordered the messenger, E. C. Woodcock, to open. He refused, and the outlaws proceeded to batter down the doors and blew a big hole in the side of the car. The explosion was so terrific that the messenger was stunned and had to be taken from the car. They then proceeded to the other mail car, occupied by Clerks O'Brian and Skidmore and threatened to blow it up, but the boys were advised to come out which they did.

The robbers then went after the safes in the express car with dynamite and soon succeeded in getting into them, but not before the car was torn to pieces by the force of the charges. They took everything from the safes and what they didn't carry away they destroyed. After finishing their work they started out in a northerly direction on foot.

The men all wore masks reaching below their necks and of the three I observed, one looked to be 6 foot tall, the others being about ordinary sized men. The leader appeared to be about 50 years old and spoke with a squeaky voice, pitched very high.

Part Four

CENTURY
America 1901–2001

Introduction

If the 19th century belonged to Britain, the 20th century was America's. To astute observers this was clear at the outset. Aside from the big matter of the dynamism of the American economy, America's success in whipping up trouble in Panama in 1903 to create a new pro-US republic (one which kindly let the US build and control the Canal) stood in marked contrast to Britain's inability to defeat some uppity Dutch settlers in South Africa.

The Panama venture was largely the work of Theodore Roosevelt, the youngest ever (at 42) President of the USA, who dramatized in human form the new American imperialism. Roosevelt was as diplomatically aggressive as he was astute – he won the Nobel prize for mediation in the Russo-Japanese War – and oversaw a rapid buildup of the US's naval strength; between 1900 and 1910 the warship tonnage of the USA burgeoned from 333,000 to 824,000. Just to make certain the whole world knew that the USA had arrived as a Great Power, Roosevelt dispatched "the great white fleet" on a showboating trip around the world in 1907.

On the domestic front, Roosevelt was much influenced by Progressivism and sought a "square deal" for labour by restricting the power of the industrial monopolies. When his handpicked successor, Taft, turned pro big business, Roosevelt stood against him in the election of 1913, which let the Democrat Woodrow Wilson slip through the middle to the White House. Wilson, even more so than Roosevelt, was a child of Progressivism, and "New Freedom" ideas in education, labor relations, welfare and electoral processes did much to modernize and make equitable.

The First World War proved a rude interruption to Wilson's New Freedom at home. As zealous in waving the "Big Stick" as his predecessors in backyard territories (he sent troops into Mexico and Nicaragua, after all), he was traditionally "isolationist" with regard to spats in Europe. This suited the electorate well, and in 1916 Wilson was re-elected on a peace ticket. Germany's unrestricted U-boat campaign, however, provoked the USA into the First World War in April 1917, where her sheer output of war *material* and men (a million troops) finished off Germany in 1918.

Germany defeated. France, Great Britain and Russia exhausted. The Old Order was gone. By 1918 all the world knew that America was *the* Great Power.

Not that she chose to play the part. Within a year America had retreated into collective isolationism and refused to ratify the Treaty of Versailles (which established the League of Nations). America's withdrawal from the wider diplomatic world was only confirmed by Republican Warren G. Harding's election to the presidency in 1920 on a return to "normalcy" ticket.

It was business as usual in '20s America. Her standard of living aroused the envy of the world, and more and more people – especially from impoverished Europe – fled to her shores. There seemed no limits to American acumen and entrepreneurship – witnessed, above all, by Henry Ford's introduction of mass production methods for the Model T automobile. Meanwhile, the stock market boomed, real estate went wild, and the immoderate whooped it up on bootleg liquour in speakeasies (prohibition had outlawed the manufacture and sale of alcohol in 1919). Some called it the Golden Age.

But all that glitters is not gold. American agriculture had long been depressed and the consumption of consumer goods dependent on thin credit. On 24 October Wall Street crashed as 13 million shares changed hands. Over the ensuing three weeks shares lost $30,000 million in paper value. Factories closed, farms were repossessed by banks. The Great Depression was on. Within three years 15 million Americans were out of work.

Against this grim background, the nation put its faith in the "New Deal" of Democratic candidate Franklin D. Roosevelt, who was elevated to the White House on 8 November. Loans to businesses, price supports for farmers and public works – notably the Tennessee Valley electrification scheme – slowly began to promote recovery. But it was war in Europe that really got the wheels of industry and agriculture whirling again, due to increased armament orders from Britain from 1939 onwards.

Although Roosevelt's personal predilection was for American involvement in World War II, the mood of the country was against him. In the event, Roosevelt had his way, for the war came to America. On 7 December 1941 the Japanese made a surprise attack on Pearl Harbor. Showing the same rashness as the Kaiser, Hitler then declared war on the USA. This totally changed the balance of forces in the conflict. As Churchill said, after 1941, the war henceforth was merely "the proper application of overwhelming force". The US, aside from provisioning its Allies (she was producing an aircraft every five minutes by 1944), led both the Second Front in Europe and the campaign in the Pacific. Only a technological miracle could have saved the Axis against US money and manpower. In fact, the technological miracle, the Atom bomb, was saved for America.

Unlike 1918, the US determined not to retreat into post-war isolationism. Aside from being a founder member of the United Nations, America also took a lead hand in establishing NATO and SEATO, the purposes of which – in accordance with the Truman Doctrine – was the curtailment of Communist expansion. The "Cold War" with the USSR also shaped politics at home, with Senator Joe McCarthy leading a witch-hunt from 1952–4 of Communists and "fellow travelers". There was a less obvious effect of the Cold War on the US domestic scene: it was military spending and the space race with the USSR which provided the long boom of Eisenhower's '50s.

Eisenhower's tenure of the White House came to an end in 1960, with the election of Democrat John F. Kennedy to the presidency. Something changed in America in that year, some of the pall of Cold War suspicion and oppression lifted. Kennedy caught the mood perfectly in his inaugural speech which called for a New Frontier in social legislation, particularly in civil rights. Abroad, Kennedy promoted humanitarianism (the Peace Corps) alongside traditional anti-communism: even conservatives admired his refusal to blink in the confrontation with the USSR over the latter's installing of missiles in Cuba in 1962.

The life of "JFK" was cut short on 22 November 1963 when Kennedy was assassinated at Dallas, but his successor Lyndon Baines Johnson continued Kennedyism without Kennedy. Yet as the '60s rolled on the problems on Johnson's desk mounted;

America's embroilment in the Vietnam war split the nation (radicalized youth chanted "Hey, hey LBJ/How many kids you killed today") and there was widespread racial unrest in Los Angeles (Watts), Detroit and New York. In 1968 both Martin Luther King and Robert Kennedy (JFK's brother) were assassinated. That same year, Johnson decided not to seek re-election and Richard Nixon won the presidency for the Republicans on a platform of withdrawal from Vietnam and increased law and order in America's cities (then enduring a drug and crime wave). Enjoying the afterglow of the 1969 Apollo mission, which placed Armstrong and Aldrin on the moon, and detentes with Russia and China, Nixon was re-elected in 1972. That election, which came with a landslide of votes, was his undoing, for during its course White House operatives had burgled the Democrat HQ at the Watergate complex, Washington. Nixon resigned the presidency (the only man to have done so) on 9 August 1974 under threat of impeachment. His VP, Gerald Ford, took the seat in the Oval office but irreparably destroyed his reputation by granting his old boss a pardon.

To an electorate dismayed by the chicanery of "Tricky Dickey", Democrat Jimmy Carter's populist down-home politics seemed the ideal antidote and he was duly elected in 1976.

Already the fingers of economic downturn were gripping the US economy, as high oil prices and cheap foreign competition decimated the traditional industries of the rust belt. Inflation reached a 30 year high in 1979. Carter's attempt to control inflation by raising interest rates only produced a fully fledged recession. Any goodwill Carter enjoyed disappeared on 4 November 1979 when fanatics took 66 hostages at the US embassy in Iran. The bungled attempt to rescue them sealed Carter's electoral fate in the election of 1980.

At the age of 70, former B-movie actor and governor of California, Ronald Reagan was the oldest man to be elected president of the USA, but any doubt about his durability was ended when he survived an assassination attempt in 1981. Elected on a Republican promise to restore American supremacy, Reagan proved politically durable also and sat tight through the worsening recession. By late 1983 the economy had picked up – due to Reagan's supplyside economics claimed his supporters, due to the drop in oil price claimed his detractors – and Reagan won a record 525 electoral votes in the 1984 election.

Unlike his presidential forbears, Reagan pursued a vigorous anti-communist stance abroad (calling the Soviet Union the "evil empire"). Accordingly, Reagan supplied arms to "Contras" in Marxist-dominated Nicaragua and illegally but effectively invaded Grenada and toppled its pro-Cuban leader. All this plus air attacks on Libya and the creation of the Strategic Defense Initiative ("Star Wars") took defence spending to World War II levels. Eventually, Reagan was obliged to produce before Congress the first trillion-dollar budget. Meanwhile the economy was badly shaken by the 1987 stock market crash.

Reagan's heir, George Bush, was similarly unable to conjure a sustained domestic recovery. If this was partly due to the paucity of his economic agenda, it was also due to forces beyond mere presidential control. In retrospect, it can be seen that the '80s and early '90s were years of deep structural change in the US economy and society, as the traditional industries passed away and new hi-tec industries arose in the "Sun Belt". Demographic shifts were fantastic: internal migration caused the population of some Sun Belt states to rise by 50%.

Thus it was that George Bush – despite huge approval for his quick and easy win over Saddam Hussein in the 1991 Persian Gulf War – lost the 1992 election to Democratic Nominee Bill Clinton. A consummate politician, Clinton accurately assessed the hopes and fears of the American people as "the economy, stupid", and it was Clinton's luck that during the '90s the US economy went into big boom. Like Kennedy, however, Clinton found that his more radical social measures (notably health-care reform) were blocked by Republicans in the legislature, the situation worsening after 1994 when the GOP controlled both the Senate and Congress. There were also repeated clashes over the federal budget. Adroitly, Clinton worked his way out of the impasse – and a low standing in the polls – by facing down the Republicans over the budget whilst borrowing some of their conservative welfare policies. He was re-elected in 1996, but his second term was dominated by the Monica Lewinsky sex scandal (dubbed, probably inevitably, "zippergate") which saw Clinton threatened with impeachment. Most of the American public, who were pretty much enjoying the affluent ride in USS *America*, had no great desire to rock the boat. The stock markets were reaching record highs, the budget was improving, unemployment was low (although some Cassandras pointed out that the gap the between the rich and poor was at an

historic worst). "It was the economy, stupid." Clinton was acquitted in February 1999.

On the international stage, Clinton enjoyed almost unsurpassed
standing. The collapse of the Soviet Union in the early '90s had left
the US as the only super-power, and Clinton used US prestige to
broker a peace agreement in Northern Ireland and a Yugoslavian
withdrawal from Kosovo. A Middle East settlement between
Palestine and Israel proved more elusive.

The 2000 presidential election between Clinton's VP, Al Gore,
and Republican Texan governor George W. Bush ended in chaos
due to the closeness of the vote in Florida. After weeks of recounting, the matter was settled by the Supreme Court which voted (on
party political lines) to declare Bush the winner of the state.
Despite garnering less of the national popular vote than Gore,
the securing of Florida gave Bush more electoral college votes and
the White House.

Eight months into his presidency, George W. Bush was faced
with one of the gravest crises to ever befall an incumbent of the
White House. On the 11th of September 2001 Islamic terrorists
from the Al Qaeda group hijacked four passenger airliners, flying
two of them into the World Trade Center in New York, one into
the Pentagon; the last crashed harmlessly, probably after an
onboard struggle with passengers, into fields in Pennsylvania.
Three thousand people were killed or posted missing. The War
on Terror ensued.

MAN FLIES, North Carolina, 17 December 1903

Orville Wright

The feat of powered flight was finally achieved on a blustery winter's day
at Kitty Hawk, North Carolina, by the brothers Orville and Wilbur
Wright. In a telegram to their father Orville wrote: SUCCESS FOUR FLIGHTS
THURSDAY MORNING ALL AGAINST TWENTY-ONE MILE WIND STARTED FROM LEVEL
WITH ENGINE POWER ALONE AVERAGE SPEED THROUGH AIR THIRTY-ONE MILES
LONGEST 59 SECONDS INFORM PRESS HOME CHRISTMAS. The longest flight was
the last of the day, with Wilbur flying the 600-pound biplane. Orville later
recorded in his diary:

At just twelve o'clock Will started on the fourth and last trip. The
machine started with its up and downs as it had before, but by the

time he had gone 300 or 400 feet he had it under much better control, and was travelling on a fairly even course. It proceeded in this manner till it reached a small hummock out about 800 feet from the starting ways, when it began pitching again and suddenly darted to the ground. The front rudder frame was badly broken up, but the main frame suffered none at all. The distance over the ground was 852 feet in 59 seconds. The engine turns was 1,071, but this included several seconds while on the starting ways and probably about half a second after landing. The jar of the landing had set the watch on the machine back, so we have no exact record for the 1,071 turns.

THE SAN FRANCISCO EARTHQUAKE, 17 April 1906

Jack London

As recorded by London for *Collier's Weekly*.

THE earthquake shook down in San Francisco hundreds of thousands of dollars worth of walls and chimneys. But the conflagration that followed burned up hundreds of millions of dollars worth of property There is no estimating within hundreds of millions the actual damage wrought. Not in history has a modern imperial city been so completely destroyed. San Francisco is gone. Nothing remains of it but memories and a fringe of dwelling-houses on its outskirts. Its industrial section is wiped out. Its business section is wiped out. Its social and residential section is wiped out. The factories and warehouses, the great stores and newspaper buildings, the hotels and the palaces of the nabobs, are all gone. Remains only the fringe of dwelling houses on the outskirts of what was once San Francisco.

Within an hour after the earthquake shock the smoke of San Francisco's burning was a lurid tower visible a hundred miles away. And for three days and nights this lurid tower swayed in the sky, reddening the sun, darkening the day, and filling the land with smoke.

On Wednesday morning at a quarter past five came the earthquake. A minute later the flames were leaping upward. In a dozen different quarters south of Market Street, in the working-class ghetto, and in the factories, fires started. There was no opposing the flames. There was no organization, no communication. All the cunning adjustments of a twentieth century city had been smashed by the earthquake. The streets were humped into ridges and depressions, and piled with the debris of fallen walls. The steel rails were twisted into perpendicular and horizontal angles. The telephone and telegraph systems were disrupted. And the great water-mains had burst. All the shrewd contrivances and safe-guards of man had been thrown out of gear by thirty seconds' twitching of the earth-crust.

The Fire Made its Own Draft

By Wednesday afternoon, inside of twelve hours, half the heart of the city was gone. At that time I watched the vast conflagration from out on the bay. It was dead calm. Not a flicker of wind stirred. Yet from every side wind was pouring in upon the city. East, west, north, and south, strong winds were blowing upon the doomed city. The heated air rising made an enormous suck. Thus did the fire of itself build its own colossal chimney through the atmosphere. Day and night this dead calm continued, and yet, near to the flames, the wind was often half a gale, so mighty was the suck.

Wednesday night saw the destruction of the very heart of the city. Dynamite was lavishly used, and many of San Francisco's proudest structures were crumbled by man himself into ruins, but there was no withstanding the onrush of the flames. Time and again successful stands were made by the fire-fighters, and every time the flames flanked around on either side or came up from the rear, and turned to defeat the hard-won victory.

An enumeration of the buildings destroyed would be a directory of San Francisco. An enumeration of the buildings undestroyed would be a line and several addresses. An enumeration of the deeds of heroism would stock a library and bankrupt the Carnegie medal fund. An enumeration of the dead will never be made. All vestiges of them were destroyed by the flames. The number of the victims of the earthquake will never be known. South of Market Street, where the loss of life was particularly heavy, was the first to catch fire.

Remarkable as it may seem, Wednesday night while the whole city crashed and roared into ruin, was a quiet night. There were no crowds. There was no shouting and yelling. There was no hysteria, no disorder. I passed Wednesday night in the path of the advancing flames, and in all those terrible hours I saw not one woman who wept, not one man who was excited, not one person who was in the slightest degree panic stricken.

Before the flames, throughout the night, fled tens of thousands of homeless ones. Some were wrapped in blankets. Others carried bundles of bedding and dear household treasures. Sometimes a whole family was harnessed to a carriage or delivery wagon that was weighted down with their possessions. Baby buggies, toy wagons, and go-carts were used as trucks, while every other person was dragging a trunk. Yet everybody was gracious. The most perfect courtesy obtained. Never in all San Francisco's history, were her people so kind and courteous as on this night of terror.

A Caravan of Trunks

All night these tens of thousands fled before the flames. Many of them, the poor people from the labor ghetto, had fled all day as well. They had left their homes burdened with possessions. Now and again they lightened up, flinging out upon the street clothing and treasures they had dragged for miles.

They held on longest to their trunks, and over these trunks many a strong man broke his heart that night. The hills of San Francisco are steep, and up these hills, mile after mile, were the trunks dragged. Everywhere were trunks with across them lying their exhausted owners, men and women. Before the march of the flames were flung picket lines of soldiers. And a block at a time, as the flames advanced, these pickets retreated. One of their tasks was to keep the trunk-pullers moving. The exhausted creatures, stirred on by the menace of bayonets, would arise and struggle up the steep pavements, pausing from weakness every five or ten feet.

Often, after surmounting a heart-breaking hill they would find another wall of flame advancing upon them at right angles and be compelled to change anew the line of their retreat. In the end, completely played out, after toiling for a dozen hours like giants, thousands of them were compelled to abandon their trunks. Here the shopkeepers and soft members of the middle class were at a disadvantage. But the working-men dug holes in vacant lots and backyards and buried their trunks.

The Doomed City

At nine o'clock Wednesday evening I walked down through the very heart of the city. I walked through miles and miles of magnificent buildings and towering skyscrapers. Here was no fire.

All was in perfect order. The police patrolled the streets. Every building had its watchman at the door. And yet it was doomed, all of it. There was no water. The dynamite was giving out. And at right angles two different conflagrations were sweeping down upon it.

At one o'clock in the morning I walked down through the same section. Everything still stood intact. There was no fire. And yet there was a change. A rain of ashes was falling. The watchmen at the doors were gone. The police had been withdrawn. There were no firemen, no fire-engines, no men fighting with dynamite. The district had been absolutely abandoned. I stood at the corner of Kearney and Market, in the very innermost heart of San Francisco. Kearny Street was deserted. Half a dozen blocks away it was burning on both sides. The street was a wall of flame. And against this wall of flame, silhouetted sharply, were two United States cavalrymen sitting their horses, calming watching. That was all. Not another person was in sight. In the intact heart of the city two troopers sat their horses and watched.

Spread of the Conflagration

Surrender was complete. There was no water. The sewers had long since been pumped dry. There was no dynamite. Another fire had broken out further uptown, and now from three sides conflagrations were sweeping down. The fourth side had been burned earlier in the day. In that direction stood the tottering walls of the Examiner building, the burned-out Call building, the smoldering ruins of the Grand Hotel, and the gutted, devastated, dynamited Palace Hotel.

The following will illustrate the sweep of the flames and the inability of men to calculate their spread. At eight o'clock Wednesday evening I passed through Union Square. It was packed with refugees. Thousands of them had gone to bed on the grass. Government tents had been set up, supper was being cooked, and the refugees were lining up for free meals.

At half past one in the morning three sides of Union Square were in flames. The fourth side, where stood the great St Francis Hotel was still holding out. An hour later, ignited from top and sides the St Francis was flaming heavenward. Union Square, heaped high with mountains of trunks, was deserted. Troops, refugees, and all had retreated.

A Fortune for a Horse!

It was at Union Square that I saw a man offering a thousand dollars for a team of horses. He was in charge of a truck piled high with trunks from some hotel. It had been hauled here into what was considered safety, and the horses had been taken out. The flames were on three sides of the Square and there were no horses.

Also, at this time, standing beside the truck, I urged a man to seek safety in flight. He was all but hemmed in by several conflagrations. He was an old man and he was on crutches. Said he: "Today is my birthday. Last night I was worth thirty thousand dollars. I bought five bottles of wine, some delicate fish and other things for my birthday dinner. I have had no dinner, and all I own are these crutches."

I convinced him of his danger and started him limping on his way. An hour later, from a distance, I saw the truck-load of trunks burning merrily in the middle of the street.

On Thursday morning at a quarter past five, just twenty-four hours after the earthquake, I sat on the steps of a small residence on Nob Hill. With me sat Japanese, Italians, Chinese, and negroes – a bit of the cosmopolitan flotsam of the wreck of the city. All about were the palaces of the nabob pioneers of Forty-nine. To the east and south at right angles, were advancing two mighty walls of flame.

I went inside with the owner of the house on the steps of which I sat. He was cool and cheerful and hospitable. "Yesterday morning," he said, "I was worth six hundred thousand dollars. This morning this house is all I have left. It will go in fifteen minutes." He pointed to a large cabinet. "That is my wife's collection of china. This rug upon which we stand is a present. It cost fifteen hundred dollars. Try that piano. Listen to its tone. There are few like it. There are no horses. The flames will be here in fifteen minutes."

Outside the old Mark Hopkins residence a palace was just catching fire. The troops were falling back and driving the refugees before them. From every side came the roaring of flames, the crashing of walls, and the detonations of dynamite.

The Dawn of the Second Day

I passed out of the house. Day was trying to dawn through the smoke-pall. A sickly light was creeping over the face of things. Once only the sun broke through the smoke-pall, blood-red, and showing quarter its usual size. The smoke-pall itself, viewed from beneath, was a rose color that pulsed and fluttered with lavender shades Then it turned to mauve and yellow and dun. There was no sun. And so dawned the second day on stricken San Francisco.

An hour later I was creeping past the shattered dome of the City Hall. Than it there was no better exhibit of the destructive force of the earthquake. Most of the stone had been shaken from the great dome, leaving standing the naked framework of steel. Market Street was piled high with the wreckage, and across the wreckage lay the overthrown pillars of the City Hall shattered into short crosswise sections.

This section of the city with the exception of the Mint and the Post-Office, was already a waste of smoking ruins. Here and there through the smoke, creeping warily under the shadows of tottering walls, emerged occasional men and women. It was like the meeting of the handful of survivors after the day of the end of the world.

Beeves Slaughtered and Roasted

On Mission Street lay a dozen steers, in a neat row stretching across the street just as they had been struck down by the flying ruins of the earthquake. The fire had passed through afterward and roasted them. The human dead had been carried away before the fire came. At another place on Mission Street I saw a milk wagon. A steel telegraph pole had smashed down sheer through the driver's seat and crushed the front wheels. The milk cans lay scattered around.

All day Thursday and all Thursday night, all day Friday and Friday night, the flames still raged on.

Friday night saw the flames finally conquered though not until Russian Hill and Telegraph Hill had been swept and three-quarters of a mile of wharves and docks had been licked up.

The Last Stand

The great stand of the fire-fighters was made Thursday night on Van Ness Avenue. Had they failed here, the comparatively few remaining houses of the city would have been swept. Here were the magnificent residences of the second generation of San Francisco nabobs, and these, in a solid zone, were dynamited down across the path of the fire. Here and there the flames leaped the zone, but these fires were beaten out, principally by the use of wet blankets and rugs.

San Francisco, at the present time, is like the crater of a volcano, around which are camped tens of thousands of refugees. At the Presidio alone are at least twenty thousand. All the surrounding cities and towns are jammed with the homeless ones, where they are being cared for by the relief committees. The refugees were carried free by the railroads to any point they wished to go, and it is estimated that over one hundred thousand people have left the peninsula on which San Francisco stood. The Government has the situation in hand, and, thanks to the immediate relief given by the whole United States, there is not the slightest possibility of a famine. The bankers and business men have already set about making preparations to rebuild San Francisco.

CHICAGO: A NIGHT AT THE FIRST WARD BALL, 1908

Will Irwin

"The First Ward Ball" was a political fund raiser run by the Chicago crooks-cum-politicians Michael Kenna and John Coughlin for half a century.

"Bathhouse John" Coughlin stood on the center floor of the great Coliseum, swept his eye over the outpouring of the moral sewers of Chicago, and waved his hand to the two bands, one in either gallery, as a signal that the Grand March of the First Ward Ball was to begin.

"Bathhouse John" is a large, bull necked Irishman of the John L. Sullivan type, the kind of Celt whose spirit responds, as a flower in rain, to polite public ceremonial. Over the white shirt-front, which clothed his well-provisioned torso, he wore a red sash, with the inscription: "Grand Marshal". Eight and forty floor managers, selected either from the powers which rule in Chicago or the powers which rob Chicago – one does not know in which division to place many of them – scattered through the dancing floor, arranging the couples into line. The band masters flourished their staves, and brass and wind struck into the key tune of the evening:

> Hail, Hail, the Gang's all right –
> What the hell do we care;
> What the hell do we care –

A movement surged through the tawdry masters on the floor – they were singing. From end to end of the great hall ran the refrain – women of the half-world and of no world, all the cheapest, dirtiest and most abbreviated costumes, hired, for two dollars and deposit from professional costumiers; scrubby little boys of the slums, patching out their Sunday clothes with five cent masks that they might obey the rules of the floor; pickpockets, refraining, by the truce of the devil which reigned that night, from plying their trade; scarlet women and yellow men who live from and by them; bartenders; professional repeaters; small politicians; prosperous beggars; saloon bouncers; prize-fight promoters; liquor salesmen; police captains; runners for gambling houses – all united in this hymn to the power that is in the First Ward of Chicago:

> Hail, Hail, the gang's all right –
> What the hell do we care now?

It was just striking midnight when "Bathhouse John" strode out before the assembled couples to lead the grand march. For two hours the sweepings and scourings had crowded into the Coliseum, the largest assembly hall in the United States. At that very moment the police were raiding the crowd without and closing the doors, for the hall was packed to danger point. That overflow crowd, shoving and rioting to express their disappointment, filled the streets for a block either way. Within, floor, gallery, passage-ways and boxes were choked. Those boxes ran all the way about the dancing floor and only a step above it, like the boxes at the horse show. They were reserved, mainly, either for rich slummers or for the aristocracy of the ministers of dissipation. The galleries held those who came not to revel but to look on. Along the passage way, behind the boxes, moved a crowd which jammed into knots at intervals, and untied itself with much mauling of women and many fights. A policeman skated across the floor just as "Bath-house John" set off the grand march. He was shoving before him a young man who lagged back and who threw out his knees very far in front as he walked. The first serious fight of the evening was being bounced. As "Bathhouse John" pranced down the floor at the head of the march, beating time to the music with his out-stretched hands, the tables in the boxes began to blossom with the white and bronze seals of the brands of champagne whose agents were the most liberal buyers that night. One, it appeared, had anticipated the blossoming of the tables. From an end box resounded a feminine shriek which rose above the bands, the singings, and the shuffling feet. The woman who shrieked had risen and was pouring Tenderloin billingsgate at some enemy on the floor. Her man hauled her back and carried her away. The first drunk of the evening had passed out.

They are not here strictly for the joy of it, these greasy revellers; let me make that plain before I go further. Strictly, "Bathhouse John" Coughlin and "Hinky-Dink" Kenna, aldermen of the First Ward, need money to pay repeaters, colonisers, district leaders, and hellers – money for all the expenses of keeping in line this, the richest graft district in the United States. The annual ball is their way of collecting that money.

A month before, certain collectors, known for their works in the Tenderloin, have visited every saloon, every brothel, every opium joint, every dance hall, and certain favoured business houses. They carry sheaves of tickets – and lists. "A hundred and fifty tickets for yours this year," says the collector to the saloonkeeper. "What are youse giving us?" says the saloonkeeper. "It was only a hundred last year." "Yes, but look at all the business you done last year – things is coming the way of this corner." And a hundred and fifty it is – unless the saloonkeeper wishes to add a fourth fifty as a token of his esteem. "Mercy, a hundred tickets!" says the fat, marcelled woman in the mirrored room. "Why, it was only seventy-five last year – and my girls don't go anymore, it is getting that common!" "You've got two more girls here than you had last winter, ain't you? Well, then." And a hundred it is. "Seventy-five tickets?" says the man at the roll-top desk. "Your ball is getting pretty tough and the newspapers –" "You got a permit for a sign last year, didn't you? Huh?" And seventy-five it is. Lower and higher elements than these pay their tribute of fifty, a hundred, two hundred tickets – the dens from which footpads for their periodical raids on Chicago, the legitimate business houses which furnish supplies or service to the dark end of the First Ward. This bit of business conversation floated into my box from the door: "Say, the – Carriage Company only took thirty tickets. Think of all the business they get hauling souses out of Twenty-second Street!" "Oh, well, they're a new concern – and the Bathhouse knows his business." Still other ways there are of making the First Ward profitable.

Let us push the hands of the clock ahead for an hour, during which times the piles of empty champagne bottles in the boxes have grown and grown, during which the great Annex, where the common herd is served, has become a dump of empty beer bottles. In a box over by the Northeast corner sits a little man, swaying gently under his load of champagne. Everything about him is slight – his legs, his shoulders, the lines of his drawn face. His skin is as white as his hair, and that is the colour of fresh paper. He appears like a man who is struggling with a great hidden grief. You look a second time before you perceive that the mere mechanics of his face produce this effect. For his eyebrows are set slantwise, so that they rise at the inner corner above the nose, giving what actors call the "grief forehead". His large violet eyes are never still, even when the champagne has clouded them a little. One bejewelled hand rests on the edge of the box. Slender as it is, the soft, white flesh conceals every knuckle – it is a hand that has never been clenched.

The maskers on the floor, promenading between the crowded dancers, nudge each other as they pass, and halt to stare. The ribboned committeemen, as police captains, police-court lawyers, popular saloonkeepers and ward heelers, all stop to exchange the time of night. He answers them in a flat voice, devoid of inflection, and in flat words devoid of individual turns of expression: "Sure. More here than there ever was before. Those damn reformers tried to blow the place up, and look what they got for it. Every big business house is represented here; all my friends are out." Where he sits is the royal box, for this is Hinky-Dink Kenna; and it is his ball. He will run for re-election next Spring; so that the profits tonight – the guesses at these profits run from $60,000 up – all go to his campaign fund. Next year, "Bathhouse John", on the eve of his own re-election, will get the profits.

Drinking is in full swing now; the effects of it show not in any special joyousness, but in a sodden and dirty aspect of the whole place – floor, boxes and Annex, and especially that cellar cafe, where one drunk has already tried to undress a woman in a scarlet costume, and succeeded to the point of attracting police attention. No Latin verve and gaiety about it; not Mardi Gras, but Gin Lane. In passing, these public debaucheries with the English-speaking peoples seem always to accompany a bad conscience . . . Ten thousand "revellers" in floor and boxes and cafes getting joylessly drunk on champagne; five thousand spectators, come to see how the other half thinks that it lives, looking joylessly on! . . .

So it goes on, more and more noisy, more and more unsteady, more and more noisome, until half-past two. The early comers have left, but there is no diminution of the crowd. The people whose business keeps them until midnight in the Tenderloin have finished their work. They are sweeping in to take the vacant places, and to increase the sales of the white foil and the bronze. This year the reformers have threatened to make arrests if the sale of drinks does not stop promptly at three o'clock, according to law and licence. The waiters pass from box to box with the admonition: "Order all the wine you want now; bar closes at three!" Later, they come back with sheaves of bottles for the grand, final alcoholic burst of the evening. By half-past three, even the provident are drinking their last glasses; and "Bathhouse John", waving to the musicians in the gallery, shouts: "Give 'em 'Home, Sweet Home.'" There is a flurry about the royal box. Hinky-Dink is going away. He steadies himself as he rises by the little hand without knuckles which moves all these dirty puppets of First Ward politics. Five thousand drunken people at this hour of half-past three doing everything that a drunk does! In the box next to that of the most popular wine agent a woman has gone clean mad with liquor, as women do. She wears an extreme Directoire costume, with a large hat. The hat has fallen back on her shoulders, and her hair has tumbled down over it. As she stands on the table with outstretched arms, shouting loud obscenities to the crowd which collects to watch her, she bears a fearful resemblance to one of those furies of the French Revolution. Before her box lies a little flashily dressed man, dead drunk, grovelling in the lees of the floor. No one pays more than passing attention to him. A telegraph messenger boy sways in the corner, very sick from free champagne. A woman in a bedraggled white evening dress hangs draped head down over the edge of her box, like clothes on a line. The two men and the other woman in her box are drinking a standing toast, oblivious of her. A woman in a page's costume passes another similarly dressed. She hurls a vivid insult as she passes; the other turns, spitting like a cat, and lays hold on her hair. The drunkards in the vicinity gather about them and cheer until the police break through and "bounce" them to the ladies' dressing room. An old-time wrestler, now a saloon bouncer, lolls over the edge of a box talking to a woman who sprawls across the table, regarding him with fishy eyes. A little scrubby boy, a pick-pocket from the look of him, comes along in the blazing, nervous stage of drunkenness. He lurches against the rail and begins to address the woman. The bouncer wheels and hits him just once in the middle of the body. The scrubby boy shoots back like a cannon ball and brings up sprawling on the floor, where he lies kicking. The bouncer, taking no further look at him, goes on with the conversation. Four fat women sit in a corner box, drinking stupidly. Dressed gaudily in evening clothes, their laces, their white gloves, even their powdered complexions, are becoming grimy with the soot of drunkenness which falls over the great hall. Between them, on the table, stand seven empty champagne bottles and a monumental bouquet of wilting pink roses. They have been taking their pleasures very, very sadly. One nods drowsily; the others watch with eyes as hard and dead as pebbles the crowd which pays tribute to notoriety by stopping to stare. The pickpocket has recovered now; he picks himself up, reviles the bouncer at a safe distance, and staggers over to his box. Worming his way through the crowd, he halts at the rail and lays hold of the lace sleeve of the nearest woman. Expertly, she gets the lace out of his clutch; calmly, she puts her white-gloved hand in his face, sends him spinning back by a motion like the straight-arm in football, and goes on talking with her neighbour. An old man, blind drunk, comes down the hall brandishing a champagne bottle. A woman gets in his way; he hurls the bottle and strikes her on the shoulder. One spectator, more sober than the rest, complains to a policeman who stands grinning at the spectacle. "Oh, that's all right," says the policeman. "Can't you see he's drunk?"

At four o'clock some merry drunkard, on his way out, smashes the box at the door and rings in a fire alarm. The engines and the hook and ladder, ploughing through the cabs and automobiles parked on the street, finish off the First Ward Ball for the year 1908.

I who had watched this for five hours, jostled to the door over drunken men, past drunken women, got clear of the crowd which still swayed and fought outside, clear of the parasites upon parasites who waited beyond, clear of the shouting newsboys with their early editions, clear of the soliciting nighthawk cabmen. The first breath of clean air struck me; I raised my face to it.

And suddenly, I realised there were stars.

PEARY CONQUERS THE NORTH POLE, 6 April 1909

Commander Robert E. Peary

A former commander in the USN, Peary (1856–1920) achieved the North Pole after a catalogue of failed attempts.

The last march northward ended at ten o'clock of the forenoon of April 6. I had now made the five marches planned from the point at which Bartlett turned back, and my reckoning showed that we were in the immediate neighbourhood of the goal of all our striving. After the usual arrangements for going into camp, at approximate local noon, on the Columbia meridian, I made the first observation at our polar camp. It indicated our position as 89° 57′.

We were now at the end of the last long march of the upward journey. Yet with the Pole actually in sight I was too weary to take the last few steps. The accumulated weariness of all those days and nights of forced marches and insufficient sleep, constant peril and anxiety, seemed to roll across me all at once. I was actually too exhausted to realize at the moment that my life's purpose had been achieved. As soon as our igloos had been completed, and we had eaten our dinner and double-rationed the dogs, I turned in for a few hours of absolutely necessary sleep, Henson and the Eskimos having unloaded the sledges and got them in readiness for such repairs as were necessary. But, weary though I was, I could not sleep long. It was, therefore, only a few hours later when I woke. The first thing I did after awaking was to write these words in my diary: "The Pole at last. The prize of three centuries. My dream and goal for twenty years. Mine at last! I cannot bring myself to realize it. It seems all so simple and commonplace."

Everything was in readiness for an observation at 6 p.m., Columbia meridian time, in case the sky should be clear, but at that hour it was, unfortunately, still overcast. But as there were indications that it would clear before long, two of the Eskimos and myself made ready a light sledge carrying only the instruments, a tin of pemmican, and one or two skins; and drawn by a double team of dogs, we pushed on an estimated distance of ten miles. While we travelled, the sky cleared, and at the end of the journey, I was able to get a satisfactory series of observations at Columbia meridian midnight. These observations indicated that our position was then beyond the Pole.

Nearly everything in the circumstances which then surrounded us seemed too strange to be thoroughly realized, but one of the strangest of those circumstances seemed to me to be the fact that, in a march of only a few hours, I had passed from the western to the eastern hemisphere and had verified my position at the summit of the world. It was hard to realize that, on the first miles of this brief march, we had been travelling due north, while, on the last few miles of the same march, we had been travelling south, although we had all the time been travelling precisely in the same direction. It would be difficult to imagine a better illustration of the fact that most things are relative. Again, please consider the uncommon circumstance that, in order to return to our camp, it now became necessary to turn and go north again for a few miles and then to go directly south, all the time travelling in the same direction.

As we passed back along that trail which none had ever seen before or would ever see again, certain reflections intruded themselves which, I think, may fairly be called unique. East, west, and north had disappeared for us. Only one direction remained and that was south. Every breeze which could possibly blow upon us, no matter from what point of the horizon, must be a south wind. Where we were, one day and one night constituted a year, a hundred such days and nights constituted a century. Had we stood in that spot during the six months of the Arctic winter night, we should have seen every star of the northern hemisphere circling the sky at the same distance from the horizon, with Polaris (the North Star) practically in the zenith.

All during our march back to camp the sun was swinging around in its ever-moving circle. At six o'clock on the morning of April 7, having again arrived at Camp Jesup, I took another series of observations. These indicated our position as being four or five miles from the Pole, towards Behring Strait. Therefore, with a double team of dogs and a light sledge, I travelled directly towards the sun an estimated distance of eight miles. Again I returned to the camp in time for a final and completely satisfactory series of observations on April 7 at noon, Columbia meridian time. These observations gave results essentially the same as those made at the same spot twenty-four hours before.

I had now taken in all thirteen single, or six and one-half double, altitudes of the sun, at two different stations, in three different directions, at four different times. All were under satisfactory conditions, except for the first single altitude on the sixth. The temperature during these observations, had been from minus 11% Farhrenheit to minus 30° Fahrenheit, with clear sky and calm weather (except as already noted for the single observation on the sixth).

In traversing the ice in these various directions as I had done, I had allowed approximately ten miles for possible errors in my observations, and at some moment during these marches and counter-marches, I had passed over or very near the point where north and south and east and west blend into one.

Of course there were some more or less informal ceremonies connected with our arrival at our difficult destination, but they were not of a very elaborate character. We planted five flags at the top of the world. The first one was a silk American flag which Mrs Peary gave me fifteen years ago. That flag has done more travelling in high latitudes than any other ever made. I carried it wrapped about my body on every one of my expeditions northward after it came into my possession, and I left a fragment of it at each of my successive "farthest norths": Cape Morris K. Jesup, the northernmost point of land in the known point of Jesup Land, west of Grant land; Cape Columbia, the northernmost point of North American lands; and my farthest north in 1906, latitude 87° 6' in the ice of the polar sea. By the time it actually reached the Pole, therefore, it was somewhat worn and discoloured.

A broad diagonal section of this ensign would now mark the farthest goal of earth – the place where I and my dusky companions stood.

It was also considered appropriate to raise the colours of the Delta Kappa Epsilon fraternity, in which I was initiated a member while an undergraduate student at Bowdoin College, the "World's Ensign of Liberty and Peace," with its red, white, and blue, in a field of white, the Navy League flag, and the Red Cross flag.

After I had planted the American flag in the ice, I told Henson to time the Eskimos for three rousing cheers, which they gave with the greatest enthusiasm. Thereupon, I shook hands with each member of the party – surely a sufficiently unceremonious affair to meet with the approval of the most democratic. The Eskimos were childishly delighted with our success. While, of course, they did not realize its importance fully, or its world-wide significance, they did understand that it meant the final achievement of a task upon which they had seen me engaged for many years.

Then, in a space between the ice blocks of a pressure ridge, I deposited a glass bottle containing a diagonal strip of my flag and records of which the following is a copy:

> 90 N. Lat., North Pole,
> April, 6, 1909.

Arrived here to-day, 27 marches from C. Columbia.

I have with me 5 men, Matthew Henson, coloured, Oo-tah, E-ging-wah, See-gloo, and Oo-ke-ah, Eskimos; 5 sledges and 38 dogs. My ship, the S. S. *Roosevelt*, is in winter quarters at C. Sheridan, 90 miles east of Columbia.

The expedition under my command which has succeeded in reaching the Pole, is under the auspices of the Peary Arctic Club of New York City, and has been fitted out and sent north by the members and friends of the club for the purpose of securing this geographical prize, if possible, for the honour and prestige of the United States of America.

The officers of the club are Thomas H. Hubbard, of New York, President; Zenas Crane, of Mass., Vice-president; Herbert L. Bridgman, of New York, Secretary and Treasurer.

I start back for Cape Columbia to-morrow.

> ROBERT E. PEARY,
> *United States Navy.*

> 90 N. Lat., North Pole,
> April 6, 1909.

I have to-day hoisted the national ensign of the United States of America at this place, which my observations indicate to be the North Polar axis of the earth, and have formally taken possession of the entire region, and adjacent, for and in the name of the President of the United States of America.

I leave this record and United States flag in possession.

> ROBERT E. PEARY,
> *United States Navy.*

If it were possible for a man to arrive at 90° north latitude without being utterly exhausted, body and brain, he would doubtless enjoy a series of unique sensations and reflections. But the attainment of the Pole was the culmination of days and weeks of forced marches, physical discomfort, insufficient sleep, and racking anxiety. It is a wise provision of nature that the human consciousness can grasp only such degree of intense feeling as the brain can endure, and the grim guardians of earth's remotest spot will accept no man as guest until he has been tried and tested by the severest ordeal.

Perhaps it ought not to have been so, but when I knew for a certainty that we had reached the goal, there was not a thing in the world I wanted but sleep. But after I had a few hours of it, there succeeded a condition of mental exaltation which made further rest impossible. For more than a score of years that point on the earth's surface had been the object of my every effort. To attain it my whole being, physical, mental, and moral, had been dedicated. Many times my own life and the lives of those with me had been risked. My own material and forces and those of my friends had been devoted to this object. This journey was my eighth into the Arctic wilderness. In that wilderness I had spent nearly twelve years out of the twenty-three between my thirtieth and my fifty-third year, and the intervening time spent in civilized communities during that period had been mainly occupied with preparations for returning to the wilderness. The determination to reach the Pole had become so much a part of my being that, strange as it may seem, I long ago ceased to think of myself save as an instrument for the attainment of that end. To the layman this may seem strange, but an inventor can understand it, or an artist, or any one who has devoted himself for years upon years to the service of an idea.

But though my mind was busy at intervals during those thirty hours spent at the Pole with the exhilarating thought that my dream had come true, there was one recollection of other times that, now and then, intruded itself with startling distinctness. It was the recollection of a day three years before, April 21, 1906, when after making a fight with ice, open water, and storms, the expedition which I commanded had been forced to turn back from 87° 6′ north latitude because our supply of food would carry us no further. And the contrast between the terrible depression of that day and the exaltation of the present moment was not the least pleasant feature of our brief stay at the Pole. During the dark moments of that return journey in 1906, I had told myself that I was only one in a long list of Arctic explorers, dating back through the centuries, all the way from Henry Hudson to the Duke of the Abruzzi, and including Franklin, Kane, and Melville – a long list

of valiant men who had striven and failed. I told myself that I had
only succeeded at the price of the best years of my life in adding a
few links to the chain that led from the parallels of civilization
towards the polar centre, but that, after all, at the end the only
word I had to write was failure.

But now, while quartering the ice in various directions from our
camp, I tried to realize that, after twenty-three years of struggles
and discouragement, I had at last succeeded in placing the flag of
my country at the goal of the world's desire. It is not easy to write
about such a thing, but I knew that we were going back to
civilization with the last of the great adventure stories – a story
the world had been waiting to hear for nearly four hundred years,
a story which was to be told at last under the folds of the Stars and
Stripes, the flag that during a lonely and isolated life had come to
be for me the symbol of home and everything I loved – and might
never see again.

The thirty hours at the Pole, what with my marchings and
counter-marchings, together with the observations and records,
were pretty well crowded. I found time, however, to write to Mrs.
Peary on a United States postal card which I had found on the ship
during the winter. It had been my custom at various important
stages of the journey northward to write such a note in order that,
if anything serious happened to me, these brief communications
might ultimately reach her at the hands of survivors. This was the
card, which later reached Mrs. Peary at Sydney:

                              90 North Latitude, April 7th.
    My dear Jo,
    I have won out at last. Have been here a day. I start for home
and you in an hour. Love to the "kidsies."

                                                      BERT.

In the afternoon of the 7th, after flying our flags and taking our
photographs, we went into our igloos and tried to sleep a little,
before starting south again.

I could not sleep and my two Eskimos, Seegloo and Egingwah,
who occupied the igloo with me, seemed equally restless. They
turned from side to side, and when they were quiet I could tell from
their uneven breathing that they were not asleep. Though they
had not been specially excited the day before when I told them
that we had reached the goal, yet they also seemed to be under the
same exhilarating influence which made sleep impossible for me.

Finally I rose, and telling my men and the three men in the other igloo, who were equally wakeful, that we would try to make our last camp, some thirty miles to the south, before we slept, I gave orders to hitch up the dogs and be off. It seemed unwise to waste such perfect travelling weather in tossing about on the sleeping platforms of our igloos.

Neither Henson nor the Eskimos required any urging to take to the trail again. They were naturally anxious to get back to the land as soon as possible – now that our work was done. And about four o'clock on the afternoon of the 7th of April we turned our backs upon the camp at the North Pole.

Though intensely conscious of what I was leaving, I did not wait for any lingering farewell of my life's goal. The event of human beings standing at the hitherto inaccessible summit of the earth was accomplished, and my work now lay to the south, where four hundred and thirteen nautical miles of ice floes and possibly open leads still lay between us and the north coast of Grand Land. One backward glance I gave – then turned my face toward the south and toward the future.

THE *LUSITANIA* IS TORPEDOED, 7 May 1915

McMillan Adams

The sinking of the British cruise liner *Lusitania* off the coast of Ireland by a German U-boat caused the drowning of over 1,000 people, including 100 Americans. It provoked outrage in the USA, and paved the way for America to enter the First World War. McMillan Adams was an American passenger aboard the liner.

I was in the lounge on A Deck . . . when suddenly the ship shook from stem to stern, and immediately started to list to starboard . . . I rushed out into the companionway . . . While standing there, a second, and much greater explosion occurred. At first I thought the mast had fallen down. This was followed by the falling on the deck of the water spout that had been made by the impact of the torpedo with the ship . . . My father came up and took me by the arm . . . We went to the port side . . . and started to help in the launching of the lifeboats. Owing to the list of the ship, the lifeboats . . . had a tendency to swing inwards across the deck and before they could be launched, it was necessary to push them over the side of the ship. While working there, the staff Captain told us that the boat was not going to sink, and ordered the lifeboats not to be lowered. He also asked the gentlemen to help in clearing the passengers from the boat deck (A Deck) . . . it was impossible to lower the lifeboats safely at the speed at which the *Lusitania* was still going . . . I saw only two boats launched from this side. The first boat to be launched for the most part full of women fell sixty or seventy feet into the water, all the occupants being drowned. This was owing to the fact that the crew could not work the davits and falls properly, so let them slip out of their hands, and sent the lifeboats to destruction . . . I said to my father "We shall have to swim for it. We had better go below and get our lifebelts."

When we got down to Deck D, our cabin deck, we found it was impossible to leave the stairs, as the water was pouring in at all the port holes . . . Finally, we reached the boat deck again, this time on the starboard side, and after filling a lifeboat with women and children, we jumped into it. The lifeboat [No. 19] was successfully lowered until we were about twelve feet from the water, when the man at the bow davit lost his nerve, and let the rope go. Most of the occupants were thrown into the water, but we, being in the stern, managed to stay in. The lifeboat was full of water, but the sailors said it would float if only we could get it away from the *Lusitania* which was now not far from sinking. My Father threw off his overcoat, and worked like a slave trying to help loose the falls from the boat. This, however, was impossible. B. Deck was then level with the water, and I suggested to my Father we should climb up and get into another lifeboat. He, however, looked up, saw the *Lusitania* was very near its end, and was likely to come over on us, and pin us beneath. He shouted to me to jump, which I did. We were both swimming together in the water, a few yards from the ship, when something separated us. That was the last I saw of him. . . . After about an hour I was helped on to a collapsible boat which was upside down. It was at this time that we saw smoke coming towards us on the horizon out to sea, but as soon as the funnel was just in sight, it went away again from us. This must have been one of the boats that the German submarine stopped from coming to our rescue.

Later, another collapsible boat, full of water but right side up and with oars, came and picked us off our upturned boat. We rowed several miles in this sinking condition to [a] fishing boat.

WORLD WAR I: THE WAR THE INFANTRY KNEW, September 1918

Lieutenant Phelps Harding and Rudolph Bowman

Lieutenant Phelps Harding, 306th Infantry Regiment, 77th Division, American Expeditionary Force

10 September 1918

Dear Christine,

The last time I wrote you I was in Paris, having received my Commission and about ready to start for my new Division. Since then I have covered a lot of territory, both in lorries and on foot, and I have passed over a battlefield that has but recently been the scene of some mighty hard fighting – some that my new Division and people of New York will long remember.

My orders took me first to Château Thierry. You have probably read about the fighting in that city. The place is pretty badly banged up from shell fire, but not as badly as most of the smaller villages beyond it. The Huns tore things up in great shape – statues, ornaments and pictures in homes were broken and cut up as if by a band of plundering outlaws. From Château Thierry my trail led toward the Ourcq River, which our men had to cross under heavy machine-gun fire and artillery shelling. Beyond was open country. You will see what a tough proposition it was when you read the casualty list for the few days when the Boche were retreating. They retreated, but they put up a stiff resistance with machine-guns, artillery and planes – and taking machine-gun nests is a real man's job.

I found my Division by the Ourcq, having been relieved, and spent three days in camp with it. The men were pretty tired, and of course they felt the loss of their comrades. I realized this latter point best when censoring their letters. It is mighty hard for a boy to write home to his mother and tell her that his brother has been killed. I read two such letters in the first batch I censored. Each writer tried to tell how painless the death was, and how bravely the brother met it – but in each case I imagine the mother will think only of her loss, and not of the fact that her boy died a true American.

22 September, 1918

Dear Christine,

My last letter was written just before we commenced the St Mihiel offensive, which began September 12th. I am writing this letter in what was then German occupied territory, sixteen kilometers from our original front line.

When the Division left the Chateau Thierry front we thought we were bound for a rest camp, for the organisation was badly in need of both rest and replacements. Then the order came to move. We marched by night and slept in the daytime, arriving at our position back of the front line after several nights of pretty hard going – hard because the rain fell almost continuously, the roads were bad, the traffic heavy. Our stopping places at the end of each march were thick woods. It is no fun moving into thick, wet woods in the dark, and trying to find places to sleep.

The last night the rain and wind were fierce – I had to be careful not to lose my platoon, the night was so dark and the marching conditions so bad. We moved to within about a kilometre of our line, my battalion being in support of the regiment, and took cover in an old drainage ditch. Wet? Rather!

At exactly 1 a.m., the artillery cut loose. It seemed as if all the artillery in France had suddenly opened up. The sky was red with big flashes, the air seemed full of Empire State Expresses, and the explosion of the heavier shells made the ground tremble. It was a wonderful and awe-inspiring sight.

At 5 a.m., the assault troops went over the top. We followed in the third wave. First we passed batteries that had been shoved right up to our lines – 75s firing like six-shooters. Ahead of us French tanks were ploughing along like big bugs, standing on their beam ends at times as they crossed the trenches or unusually bad ground. Our first line went too fast for them, but they did a lot of good work in breaking up machine-gun nests and in taking villages. Our boys in front just couldn't wait for them, even to smash the wire.

Before we had gone far prisoners began to come in first by twos and threes, then by platoons and companies. We took 13,000 Boche that day. We passed dead men of both armies, but many more Boche than Americans. I was surprised at the indifference I felt toward dead Americans – they seemed a perfectly natural thing to come across, and I felt absolutely no shudder go down my back as I would have had I seen the same thing a year ago.

We kept on going forward until we reached the crest of a hill, and here the shelling became so heavy that we made ourselves as small as possible in ditches and holes. Shells were striking all around us, and too close for comfort. A big "dud" – a shell that failed to explode – landed in the middle of my platoon and hit a man from the Engineers on the thigh, practically taking his leg off and tearing him up pretty badly. He died in a short time. The company at our right had sixteen casualties from this shell fire, but we, apparently being better duckers, came out without a scratch except for the Engineer who had happened to take cover with us.

After taking the shelling for possibly twenty minutes our artillery spotted the Boche batteries, which were either destroyed or withdrew, permitting us to move forward again. After this the Boche did not make much of a stand. His artillery was apparently too busy moving homeward to bother about fighting.

The first day we covered nearly sixteen kilometres, reaching our objective on scheduled time. It was pretty hard work, for the going was often bad, even after leaving the front line area. It was up and down hill, and at a fairly fast pace. That night we slept on a hillside, and since then we have been moving around slightly, digging in each time, and acting as a reserve for the troops ahead who, with Engineers, are making a line of trenches and putting up wire, placing machine-guns and doing everything necessary to give the Boche a warm reception if he attempts a counter-attack.

In this recent drive, our artillery moved almost as rapidly as our Infantry – sometimes faster than our kitchens and wagon trains – and a Boche battery would hardly open up before a plane would go over it, signal the battery location, and presto! American shells would drop on it. The Boche may not have had much respect for the American Army a few months ago, but from what prisoners say now, we are about as welcome as the proverbial skunk at a lawn party!

Just one more item before I end this letter and go to inspect my platoon. We had expected to be relieved before now, but yesterday news arrived that changed all our plans. Probably my battalion will go into the new line in a day or so, possibly to stay there for a fairly long period. We may even move forward again – no one knows definitely. Anyway, you may not hear from me for a couple of weeks or so – longer, if we push on toward Berlin.

Rudolph Bowman, Headquarters Troop, 89th Division, American Expeditionary Force
Bowman writes to his wife, Gertrude, and children.

[In German envelope]
France, September 20th 1918

My Darling Wife and Loved Ones:
Has it been ten years since I wrote? Ten years have passed for me. This letter will sound like I am drunk, but I'm not – just tired. This is the synopsis of a long long story.

On Sept 10th I was sent to a village ½ Kilometre behind the front line, for final instructions in enemy observation. Our O.P. (observation post) was shelled that night because an ammunition truck had gotten stuck near it. (Now, all thru this everything seemed natural and I thought nothing of it.) Shrapnel struck our building (the only one with a roof on it in town) but we got no direct hit. The next day we (three other observers & I) went up to the front line trench to take over an advance O.P. Rain-Rain-Rain-Mud-Mud-Mud-Wet to the skin. Well – two of us were on our post at 1:00 A.M. Thurs. Sept 12th when all our big guns broke loose at once.

I can't describe it – it was awful – and wonderful – glorious – hideous – hellish, to think what one shell will do – then to think what 6000 to 8000 guns will do all firing as fast as they can, all sizes – well we stayed on till 3:00 and our relief came – went back to dug out for a last rest, for we had decided to go "Over the Top" with the doughboys ("God Bless Them") on the big drive.

Well we went over in the second wave, its all confused to me – I saw many dead men (mostly Boche) many of our boys wounded, men fell all around us, we were shot at by snipers, machine guns, Boche avions, and went thru our own barrage twice – those guns kept up that fire till about 9:30, then the light artillery tried to move up with us but could not keep up, all I could shoot at was mach. gun nests (I can only hope I got *one* Boche for I got no fair shot) but I saw boys throw grenades in dugouts full of Huns, and was glad, – we advanced all day, first with one company & another, everybody was lost; late in the afternoon we reached our objective, but we could not find where we were to stay, we kept going till 4:30 A.M. Fri, then we came back to this village – and I dropped on the floor with my saddle pockets (I hung on to them) over my shoulder and slept – and my pal could not wake me to make me eat. We'd had no sleep since Sun. night, except an hour at a time.

So we established an O.P. about a Kilometre behind the present line, we can see all the action for six Kilometres, there's not much doing except artillery fire, constantly from both sides, I've been under shell fire almost constantly for ten days – the closest one came within twenty feet, I wouldn't tell this now, but I'm going to send a wire home as soon as we are relieved, which will be soon. I got enough souvinirs too. Expect to get a chance to go to Paris for a week now. I want to come home, but this will be over soon I think. I got six letters from you sweetheart and about six from home yesterday. I'll answer them all when I can. Phone Mother when you get this. I can only write one letter now. I'll have some tales to tell Dear, but the one I want to tell most is the story of my love for my wonderful little wife. You & Mother and the rest must not worry about me, I'll be relieved long before you get this. Now I can come home satisfied to *stay* and *love*. Your Own Loving

Soldier Boy X X

R.M. Bowman

Hq. Troop, 89th Division

American E.F., A.P.O. 761

(I pray always before I sleep, for my wonderful Mother & Wife and the rest, and for our early reunion.)

Heard from Johnnie

DOGFIGHTS, AMBUSHES & PEACE: RICKENBACKER ON THE WESTERN FRONT, October–November 1918

Eddie V. Rickenbacker

With 26 kills Rickenbacker was the "ace of aces" of the US Air Service in France in World War I.

Those were hectic days. I put in six or seven hours of flying time each day. I would come down, gulp a couple of cups of coffee while the mechanics refueled the plane and patched the bullet holes and take off again. I caught an unguarded balloon while returning from a night mission, and Reed Chambers and I together brought down a Hanover. With the dead pilot at the controls, it glided to a perfect landing two miles within our own lines. We hurried to claim it and had it hauled back to our own field. Then Reed and I each dropped a Fokker in the same dogfight. I shot down a German plane so far behind the lines that the victory was never confirmed. Our 94th squadron pulled out well ahead of the 27th, and after that our lead was never threatened.

In my 134 air battles, my narrowest escape came at a time when I was fretting over the lack of action. I was out alone one afternoon, looking for anything to shoot at. There was a thick haze over the valley of the Meuse, however, and the Germans had pulled down their balloons. To the south the weather seemed a little better; the American balloons were still up. German planes rarely came over late in the afternoon, and everyone had relaxed his vigilance. As I was flying toward the nearest Allied balloon, I saw it burst into flames. A German plane had obviously made a successful attack. Because of the bend in the lines of the front at that point, I saw that I could cut off the Boche on his return to his own territory. I had the altitude on him and, consequently, a superior position. I headed confidently to our rendezvous.

Guns began barking behind me, and sizzling tracers zipped by my head. I was taken completely by surprise. At least two planes were on my tail. They had me cold. They had probably been watching me for several minutes and planning this whole thing.

They would expect me to dive. Instead I twisted upward in a corkscrew path called a "chandelle". I guessed right. As I went up, my two attackers came down, near enough for me to see their faces. I also saw the red noses on those Fokkers. I was up against the Flying Circus again.

I had outwitted them. Two more red noses were sitting above me on the chance that I might just do the unexpected.

Any time one plane is up against four and the four are flown by pilots of such caliber, the smart thing to do is to get away from there. There is an old saying that it's no disgrace to run if you are scared.

I zigzagged and sideslipped, but the two planes on top of me hung on, and the two underneath remained there. They were daring me to attack, in which case the two above would be on my tail in seconds. They were blocking me from making a dash for home. I was easy meat sandwiched between two pairs of experts. Sooner or later one would spot an opening and close in.

For a split second one of the Fokkers beneath me became vulnerable. I instantly tipped over, pulled back the throttle and dived on him. As my nose came down I fired a burst ahead of him. Perhaps he did not see the string of bullets. At any rate, he flew right into them. Several must have passed through his body. An incendiary hit his gas tank, and in seconds a flaming Fokker was earthbound.

If I had been either of the two Fokkers above me in such a situation, I would have been on my tail at that very moment. I pulled the stick back in a loop and came over in a renversement, and there they were. Before I could come close enough to shoot, they turned and fled. I suppose that the sight of that blazing plane took some of the fight out of them.

It did not take any fight out of me. I started chasing all three of them back into Germany. We were already three miles behind the lines, but I was annoyed – with them and with myself.

My Spad was faster. One Fokker began to fall behind. He tried a shallow dive to gain speed, but I continued to close in. We were only about a thousand feet up. He began stunting, but I stuck with him and fired a burst of about two hundred shots. He nosed over and crashed. I watched him hit.

All around the crashed plane, I saw flashes of fire and smoke. I was only about five hundred feet above the deck, and the Germans on the ground were shooting at me with all the weapons they had. I could see their white faces above the flashes. The air around me must have been full of flying objects. I got out of there fast and went home to report that I had blundered into a trap and had come out of it with two victories. I now had nineteen.

During the month of October the fortunes of war shifted both on the ground and in the air. From the air we could see the German ground forces retreating, sometimes in complete disorganization. Our bombers were carrying the fight into Germany, and large numbers of German fighters were pulled back from the front in an effort to protect the civilian population.

All along the lines the feeling was growing that the war was coming to an end. I took a three-day leave in Paris and, for the first time, found the streets illuminated at night and unrestrained gaiety.

During the month of October, I shot down fourteen enemy aircraft. On the 30th I got my twenty-fifth and twenty-sixth victories, my last of the war. My title "American Ace of Aces" was undisputed. The last victory for the 94th Squadron came on November 10. The Hat-in-the-Ring Squadron downed sixty-nine Boche planes, more than any other American unit.

On the night of the 10th a group of us was discussing the next day's mission when the phone rang. An almost hysterical voice shouted the news in my ear: at 11:00 the following morning, the war would end. Our mission was called off. For us the war ended at that moment.

I dropped the phone and turned to face my pilots. Everyone sensed the importance of that phone call. There was total silence in the room.

"The war is over!" I shouted. At that moment the anti-aircraft battalion that ringed our field fired off a salvo that rocked the building. We all went a little mad. Shouting and screaming like crazy men, we ran to get whatever firearms we had, including flare pistols, and began blasting up into the sky. It was already bright up there. As far as we could see the sky was filled with exploding shells and rockets, star shells, parachute flares, streams of Very lights and searchlights tracing crazy patterns. Machine guns hammered; big guns boomed. What a night!

A group of men came out of the hangar, rolling barrels of gasoline in front of them. Perhaps I should have made an effort to stop them, but instead I ran over and helped. We dumped them in an open place, and I struck the match myself. Up roared a bonfire that could be seen for miles. We danced around that blazing pyre screaming, shouting and beating one another on the back. One pilot kept shouting over and over and over. "I've lived through the war, I've lived through the war!"

Somebody emptied every bottle of liquor he could find into a huge kettle, and the orderlies served it in coffee cups, including themselves in. For months these twenty combat pilots had been living at the peak of nervous energy, the total meaning of their lives to kill or be killed. Now this tension exploded like the guns blasting around us.

We all ran over to the 95th Squadron. They had a piano, and somebody sat down and began banging the keys. We began dancing or simply jumping up and down. Somebody slipped and fell, and everyone else fell on him, piling up in a pyramid. A volunteer band started playing in the area outside. We ran outside again to continue our dancing and jumping and shrieking under the canopy of bursting rockets. Again somebody went down, and again we all piled on and made a human pyramid, this time bigger and better and muddier, a monument to the incredible fact that we had lived until now and were going to live again tomorrow.

In the morning orders came down that all pilots should stay on the ground. It was a muggy, foggy day. About 10:00 I sauntered out to the hanger and casually told my mechanics to take the plane out on the line and warm it up to test the engines. Without announcing my plans to anyone, I climbed into the plane and took off. Under the low ceiling I hedgchopped towards the front. I arrived over Verdun at 10:45 and proceeded on toward Conflans, flying over no-man's-land. I was at less than five hundred feet. I could see both Germans and Americans crouching in their trenches, peering over with every intention of killing any man who revealed himself on the other side. From time to time ahead of me on the German side I saw a burst of flame, and I knew that they were firing at me. Back at the field later I found bullet holes in my ship.

I glanced at my watch. One minute to 11:00, thirty seconds, fifteen. And then it was 11:00 a.m., the eleventh hour of the eleventh day of the eleventh month. I was the only audience for the greatest show ever presented. On both sides of no-man's-land, the trenches erupted. Brown-uniformed men poured out of the American trenches, gray-green uniforms out of the German. From my observer's seat overhead, I watched them throw their helmets in the air, discard their guns, wave their hands. Then all up and down the front, the two groups of men began edging toward each other across no-man's-land. Seconds before they had been willing to shoot each other; now they came forward. Hesitantly at first, then more quickly, each group approached the other.

Suddenly gray uniforms mixed with brown. I could see them hugging each other, dancing, jumping. Americans were passing out cigarettes and chocolate. I flew up to the French sector. There it was even more incredible. After four years of slaughter and hatred, they were not only hugging each other but kissing each other on both cheeks as well.

Star shells, rockets and flares began to go up, and I turned my ship toward the field. The war was over.

A PORTRAIT OF HENRY FORD, Detroit, 1923

Robert Littell

Henry Ford pioneered "assembly-line" mass production for his Model T automobile, of which 15 million were produced between 1908–28. Ford was sixty at the time of Littell's interview.

I became one of the two hundred people who arrive daily in Detroit to see Henry Ford, usually on a something-for-nothing errand, or in furtherance of some cause which seems to them good and which they think Ford would like too. Since my errand was publicity, I had no trouble in getting an interview, to which, be it said to his credit, he was only forty minutes late.

He came into the office almost surreptitiously, and before I knew it we had shaken hands, and Ford was tilting back in a chair in the corner, with his feet on the radiator. He seemed absent-minded, and as I launched a series of questions he kept looking out of the window. Perhaps he had heard people say that in his factory there was no skill left, but that the men underwent a deadening repetitive grind of work? "There's nothing to it. If the men don't like their particular job, they can ask to be transferred. We shift men from job to job all the time." I tried to make him argue the point, whether the deadly monotony of labour necessary to efficient production wouldn't, in the long run, be an extremely bad thing for a society which he, notably, was anxious to improve. It was a point he would not or could not meet. He didn't want to argue, his first answer was clear, and he returned to it. The question stuck fast on the reef of his mind, where it was followed by all the others. Doubts as to the durability of the V-shape eight-cylinder motor he dismissed in a few words. "There's nothing to it." He was still looking out of the window, and every now and then rubbed his face with both hands, a nervous gesture of weariness and indifference.

We drifted on to the war, which brought from him a wonderfully complete, rapid and rather violent explanation of the whole business in two sentences, laying it all on the "international bankers" and the "diplomatists". "Europe had too many diplomatists. That's all there was to it". So much for the war. The Jews? An equally final and sweeping judgment. "The Jews are the scavengers of the world. They are necessary where there's something to be cleaned up. Wherever there's anything wrong with a country, you'll find the Jews on the job there." This statement quite satisfied him, and he could not be induced to add to it. Try the Negroes. How shall we settle the Negro problem? "We have several thousand in our plant, and no trouble. Whenever there's trouble, it's to somebody's advantage. There's always somebody making money out of it." Wherever I turned, I met this sudden, baffling tendency to pass complete and instantaneous judgment in a brief phrase. If Henry Ford's mind is an oyster, I failed utterly to open it, and I incline to believe that it is not so much an oyster as a stone. When an old farmer on a fence talks so dogmatically, one is not surprised, and one knows no harm will come of it. In Henry Ford, so attractively like the farmer in his unassuming simplicity, his directness, his plain American speech, this hardness of mind is peculiarly sinister, and when one remembers his vast power to put his beliefs into effect, it inspires something like fear.

It is almost the only thing about him that, when one sees him, inspires fear. His low, matter-of-fact voice, accurate and positive, his unaffected bearing, his almost graceful figure, his freedom from all the deadly marks of greatness, make one feel he could never do harm to anybody, and maybe a great deal of good. The face is more difficult to read. It is several faces all at once – ascetic, gentle, shrewd, humorous, sensitive, obstinate, delicate, invulnerable and unprotected, melancholy and serene, old and young, the face of a hardheaded Yankee horse-swapper, of a boy, of a minor saint. In it can be ready by turns eagerness and age-old indifference, childlike content and profound restlessness.

The restlessness, the nervous rubbing, of his face, the gazing out of the window continued as long as we were on general topics. So did the pat elusive answers to all questions. Sometimes they verged on epigram, sometimes they were condensations of prejudice. We were speaking of D—, a man who had once been associated with him, and quit in a huff, and later had criticized him publicly. "The trouble with D—", Ford burst out, "was that he wanted to get rich too quick and couldn't stop smoking." The war was mentioned again. "The Germans," said Ford, "would have been better off if they had had eyes like the woodcock. The woodcock has eyes so near the back of his head that he can see behind. Did you ever see a young woodcock?" Ford is no longer bored, and he turns away from the window. He starts to describe the young woodcock and asks if there are any pictures of the bird in the office. In a few minutes a book is brought in. Not the right book.

Somehow Ford has disappeared. Later his alert head is seen through the glass door of the next office, examining some sort of gum. When the biggest and best bird book arrives, he is gone. By gradual degrees he has slipped away, for good.

Ford slips away. "You can't pin him down", people who know him often say. You go to see him, maybe he does not meet the appointment – maybe he does, and in the end gets away from you. The very definiteness of his brief statements is an evasion. He hates to be tied down. Nobody has any strings on him. He has bought railroads, forests, factories, coal and iron mines because he hates not to be free. He gets rid of men when they threaten to invade his own power or his own mind. He resists compromise with things or men, and he is right, for his power lies in keeping his mind to himself. A president is powerful only by making other men share their minds with his, which means giving large pieces of his mind to theirs, and abandoning much purpose for sake of little result. This is absolutely contrary to Henry Ford's nature. He has always had his way, and he knows no other way but his to get things done. He is aware of this, and at one time he realized what troubles would meet him in the White House, where he would not be boss, but a political chief who could accomplish things only by endless talks and compromise with other men. It was then that he said he "wouldn't walk across the street" for the Presidency. Nearer to his present feelings is the later statement to a friend as they were walking by the White House: "That's where I'll be some day." When asked about it publicly, his eyes twinkle, but that's all. Undoubtedly he wants to be President, against his own better judgment, and that of those nearest him, who say, "If you're a friend of Henry Ford don't work for him", but quite according to the desires of his assistants. At one time they formed a group of hardheaded, capable, fearless men whose independence finally caused them to leave him. The men now around him are of distinctly inferior calibre, but perhaps just as useful and efficient wheels in the Ford system. They know how to keep well within his favour, and how to influence him at the same time; they under-stand what he wants done, and carry it through mercilessly, without question; they do not let him forget that he is one of the greatest men in the world. The former pioneer atmosphere of the Ford personnel is gone, and the give and take among self-made men who were opening up a new country together has been replaced by something much more like the court of an Oriental monarch in its combination of sycophancy and ruthlessness. Perhaps these men know what possibilities of terrible disaster to Ford as President he has within himself, but since the reflected glory they would reap is immeasurable, they help to suppress his doubts, they fan his desire to be a candidate, and it is from their midst that are pulled the skilful and invisible wires which are helping to spread the Ford boom.

LINDBERGH FLIES THE ATLANTIC, May 1927

Charles A. Lindbergh

Flying a Ryan monoplane named *Spirit of St. Louis*, Lindbergh achieved the first solo non-stop flight across the Atlantic. It took 33.5 hours.

The Twenty-sixth Hour

. . . It's twenty-six and a half hours since I took off. That's almost twice as long as the flight between San Diego and St Louis; and that was much the longest flight I ever made. It's asking a lot of an engine to run twenty-six hours without attention. Back on the mail, we check our Liberties at the end of every trip. Are the rocker-arms on my Whirlwind still getting grease? And how long will it keep on going if one of them should freeze?

I shift arms on the stick. My left hand – being free, and apparently disconnected from my mind's control – begins aimlessly exploring the pockets of the chart bag. It pulls the maps of Europe halfway out to reassure my eyes they're there, tucks my helmet and goggles in more neatly, and fingers the shiny little first aid kit and the dark glasses given me by that doctor on Long Island. Why have I let my eyes burn through the morning? Why have I been squinting for hours and not thought of these glasses before? I hook the wires over my ears and look out on a shaded ocean. It's as though the sky were overcast again. I don't dare use them. They're too comfortable, too pleasant. They make it seem like evening – make me want to sleep.

I slip the glasses back into their pocket, pull out the first-aid kit, and idly snap it open. It contains adhesive tape, compact bandages, and a little pair of scissors. Not enough to do much patching after a crash. Tucked into one corner are several silkcovered, glass capsules of aromatic ammonia. "For use as Smelling Salts," the labels state. What did the doctor think I could do with smelling salts over the ocean? This kit is made for a child's cut finger, or for

some debutante fainting at a ball! I might as well have saved its
weight on the take-off, for all the good it will be to me. I put it back
in the chart bag – and then pull it out again. If smelling salts revive
people who are about to faint, why won't they revive people who
are about to fall asleep? Here's a weapon against sleep lying at my
side unused, a weapon which has been there all through the
morning's deadly hours. A whiff of one of these capsules should
sharpen the dullest mind. And no eyes could sleep stinging with the
vapor of ammonia.

I'll try one now. The fumes ought to clear my head and keep the
compass centered. I crush a capsule between thumb and fingers. A
fluid runs out, discoloring the white silk cover. I hold it cautiously,
several inches from my nose. There's no odor. I move it closer,
slowly, until finally it touches my nostrils. I smell nothing! My eyes
don't feel the slightest sting, and no tears come to moisten their dry
edges. I inhale again with no effect, and throw the capsule through
the window. My mind now begins to realize how deadened my
senses have become, how close I must be to the end of my reserves.
And yet there may be another sleepless night ahead.

The Twenty-seventh Hour

I'm flying along dreamily when it catches my eyes, that black
speck on the water two or three miles southeast. I realize it's there
with the same jerk to awareness that comes when the altimeter
needle drops too low in flying blind. I squeeze my lids together and
look again. A boat! A small boat! Several small boats, scattered
over the surface of the ocean!

Seconds pass before my mind takes in the full importance of
what my eyes are seeing. Then, all feeling of drowsiness departs. I
bank the *Spirit of St Louis* toward the nearest boat and nose down
toward the water. I couldn't be wider awake or more keenly aware
if the engine had stopped.

Fishing boats! *The coast, the European coast, can't be far away!* The
ocean is behind, the flight completed. Those little vessels, those
chips on the sea, are Europe. What nationality? Are they Irish,
English, Scotch, or French? Can they be from Norway, or from
Spain? What fishing bank are they anchored on? How far from the
coast do fishing banks extend? It's too early to reach Europe unless
a gale blew behind me through the night. Thoughts press forward
in confused succession. After fifteen hours of solitude, here's human
life and help and safety.

The ocean is no longer a dangerous wilderness. I feel as secure as though I were circling Lambert Field back home. I could land alongside any one of those boats, and someone would throw me a rope and take me on board where there'd be a bunk I could sleep on, and warm food when I woke up.

The first boat is less than a mile ahead – I can see its masts and cabin. I can see it rocking on the water. I close the mixture control and dive down fifty feet above its bow, dropping my wing to get a better view.

But where is the crew? There's no sign of life on deck. Can all the men be out in dories? I climb higher as I circle. No, there aren't any dories. I can see for miles, and the ocean's not rough enough to hide one. Are the fishermen frightened by my plane, swooping down suddenly from the sky? Possibly they never saw a plane before. *Of course* they never saw one out so far over the ocean. Maybe they all hid below the decks when they heard the roar of my engine. Maybe they think I'm some demon from the sky, like those dragons that decorate ancient mariners' charts. But if the crews are so out of contact with the modern world that they hide from the sound of an airplane, they must come from some isolated coastal village above which airplanes never pass. And the boats look too small to have ventured far from home. I have visions of riding the top of a hurricane during the night, with a hundred-mile-an-hour wind drift. Possibly these vessels are anchored north of Ireland, or somewhere in the Bay of Biscay. Then shall I keep on going straight, or turn north, or south?

I fly over to the next boat bobbing up and down on the swells. Its deck is empty too. But as I drop my wing to circle, a man's head appears, thrust out through a cabin porthole, motionless, staring up at me. In the excitement and joy of the moment, in the rush of ideas passing through my reawakened mind, I decide to make that head withdraw from the porthole, come out of the cabin, body and all, and to point toward the Irish coast. No sooner have I made the decision than I realize its futility. Probably that fisherman can't speak English. Even if he can, he'll be too startled to understand my message, and reply. But I'm already turning into position to dive down past the boat. It won't do any harm to try. Why deprive myself of that easy satisfaction? Probably if I fly over it again, the entire crew will come on deck. I've talked to people before from a plane, flying low with throttled engine, and received the answer through some simple gesture – a nod or an outstretched arm.

I glide down within fifty feet of the cabin, close the throttle, and shout as loudly as I can "WHICH WAY IS IRELAND?"

How extraordinary the silence is with the engine idling! I look back under the tail, watch the fisherman's face for some sign of understanding. But an instant later, all my attention is concentrated on the plane. For I realize that I've lost the "feel" of flying. I shove the throttle open, and watch the air-speed indicator while I climb and circle. As long as I keep the needle above sixty miles an hour, there's no danger of stalling. Always before, I've known instinctively just what condition my plane was in – whether it had flying speed or whether it was stalling, and how close to the edge it was riding in between. I didn't have to look at the instruments. Now, the pressure of the stick no longer imparts its message clearly to my hand. I can't tell whether air is soft or solid.

When I pass over the boat a third time, the head is still at the porthole. It hasn't moved or changed expression since it first appeared. It came as suddenly as the boats themselves. It seems as lifeless. I didn't notice before how pale it is – or am I now imagining its paleness? It looks like a severed head in that porthole, as though a guillotine had dropped behind it. I feel baffled. After all, a man who dares to show his face would hardly fear to show his body. There's something unreal about these boats. They're as weird as the night's temples, as those misty islands of Atlantis, as the fuselage's phantoms that rode behind my back.

Why don't sailors gather on the decks to watch my plane? Why don't they pay attention to my circling and shouting? What's the matter with this strange flight, where dreams become reality, and reality returns to dreams? But these aren't vessels of cloud and mist. They're tangible, made of real substance like my plane – sails furled, ropes coiled neatly on the decks, masts swaying back and forth with each new swell. Yet the only sign of crew is that single head, hanging motionless through the cabin porthole. It's like "The Rime of the Ancient Mariner" my mother used to read aloud. These boats remind me of the "painted ship upon a painted ocean."

I want to stay, to circle again and again, until that head removes itself from the porthole and the crews come out on deck. I want to see them standing and waving like normal, living people. I've passed through worlds and ages since my last contact with other men. I've been away, far away, planets and heavens away, until only a thread was left to lead me back to earth and life. I've followed that thread with swinging compasses, through lonely canyons, over pitfalls of sleep, past the lure of enchanted islands, fearing that at any moment it would break. And now I've returned to earth, returned to these boats bobbing on the ocean. I want an earthly greeting. I deserve a warmer welcome back to the fellowship of men.

Shall I fly over to another boat and try again to raise the crew? No, I'm wasting minutes of daylight and miles of fuel. There's nothing but frustration to be had by staying longer. It's best to leave. There's something about this fleet that tries my mind and spirit, and lowers confidence with every circle I make. Islands that turn to fog, I understand. Ships without crews, I do not. And that motionless head at the porthole – it's no phantom, and yet it shows no sign of life. I straighten out the *Spirit of St Louis* and fly on eastward.

The Twenty-eighth Hour
Is that a cloud on the northeastern horizon, or a strip of low fog – or – *can it possibly be land*? It looks like land, but I don't intend to be tricked by another mirage. Framed between two gray curtains of rain, not more than ten or fifteen miles away, a purplish blue band has hardened from the haze – flat below, like a water-line – curving on top, as though composed of hills or aged mountains.

I'm only sixteen hours out from Newfoundland. I allowed eighteen and a half hours to strike the Irish coast. If that's Ireland, I'm two and a half hours ahead of schedule. Can this be another, clearer image, like the islands of the morning? Is there something strange about it too, like the fishing fleet and that haunting head? Is each new illusion to become more real until reality itself is meaningless? But my mind is clear. I'm no longer half asleep. I'm awake – alert – aware. The temptation is too great. I can't hold my course any longer. The *Spirit of St Louis* banks over toward the nearest point of land.

I stare at it intently, not daring to believe my eyes, keeping hope in check to avoid another disappointment, watching the shades and contours unfold into a coast line – a coastline coming down from the north – a coast line bending toward the east – a coast line with rugged shores and rolling mountains. It's much too early to strike England, France, or Scotland. It's early to be striking Ireland; but that's the nearest land.

A fjorded coast stands out as I approach. Barren islands guard it.

Inland, green fields slope up the sides of warted mountains. This *must* be Ireland. It can be no other place than Ireland. The fields are too green for Scotland; the mountains too high for Brittany or Cornwall.

Now, I'm flying above the foam-lined coast, searching for prominent features to fit the chart on my knees. I've climbed to two thousand feet so I can see the contours of the country better. The mountains are old and rounded; the farms small and stony. Rain-glistened dirt roads wind narrowly through hills and fields. Below me lies a great tapering bay; a long, bouldered island; a village. Yes, there's a place on the chart where it all fits – line of ink on line of shore – Valentia and Dingle Bay, *on the south-western coast of Ireland!*

I can hardly believe it's true. I'm almost exactly on my route, closer than I hoped to come in my wildest dreams back in San Diego. What happened to all those detours of the night around the thunderheads? Where has the swinging compass error gone? The wind above the storm clouds must have blown fiercely on my tail. In edging northward, intuition must have been more accurate than reasoned navigation.

The southern tip of Ireland! On course; over two hours ahead of schedule; the sun still well up in the sky; the weather clearing! I circle again, fearful that I'll wake to find this too a phantom, a mirage fading into mid-Atlantic mist. But there's no question about it; every detail on the chart has its counterpart below; each major feature on the ground has its symbol on the chart. The lines correspond exactly. Nothing in that world of dreams and phantoms was like this. I spiral lower, looking down on the little village. There are boats in the harbor, wagons on the stonefenced roads. People are running out into the streets, looking up and waving. This is earth again, the earth where I've lived and now will live once more. Here are human beings. Here's a human welcome. Not a single detail is wrong. I've never seen such beauty before – fields so green, people so human, a village so attractive, mountains and rocks so mountainous and rocklike.

I bank steeply around and set my course southeastward, cutting across the bouldered fjords, flying low over the hilltop farms, the rock fences and the small, green fields of Kerry. Now, I can check the engine – All cylinders hitting on the left switch – All cylinders hitting on the right – And all instrument readings are normal.

Sheep and cattle graze on their sloping pastures. Horse-drawn carts crawl along their shiny roads. People move across walled-in barnyards, through doorways of the primitive stone buildings. It must be a hard place to gain a living from the soil. And it would be worse than New England for a forced landing.

Even the wish to sleep has left, and with it the phantoms and voices. I didn't notice their absence before; but now, as I settle down for the last six hundred miles to Paris, I realize that they remained behind with the fishing fleet. They vanished with that first strange touch of Europe and of man. Since I sighted those specks on the water, I've been as wide awake as though I started the flight this morning after a warm breakfast and a full night's sleep. The thought of floating off in a bed of feathers has lost its attractiveness.

Time is no longer endless, or the horizon destitute of hope. The strain of take-off, storm, and ocean, lies behind. There'll be no second night above the clouds, no more grappling with misty walls of ice. There's only one more island to cross – only the narrow tip of an island. I look at England's outline on my map. And then, within an hour, I'll see the coast of France; and beyond that, Paris and Le Bourget. As Nova Scotia and Newfoundland were stepping-stones from America, Ireland and England are stepping-stones to Europe. Yesterday, each strip of sea I crossed was an advance messenger of the ocean. Today, these islands down below are heralds to a continent.

It's as though a curtain has fallen behind me, shutting off the stagelike unreality of this transatlantic flight. It's been like a theater where the play carries you along in time and place until you forget you're only a spectator. You grow unaware of the walls around you, of the program clasped in your hand, even of your body, its breath, pulse, and being. You live with the actors and the setting, in a different age and place. It's not until the curtain drops that consciousness and body reunite. Then, you turn your back on the stage, step out into the cool night, under the lights of streets, between the displays of store windows. You feel life surging in the crowd around you, life as it was when you entered the theater, hours before. Life is real. It always was real. The stage, of course, was the dream. All that transpired there is now a memory, shut off by the curtain, by the doors of the theater, by the passing minutes of time.

Striking Ireland was like leaving the doors of a theater –

phantoms for actors; cloud islands and temples for settings; the ocean behind me, an empty stage. The flight across is already like a dream. I'm over villages and fields, back to land and wakefulness and a type of flying that I know. I'm myself again, in earthly skies and over earthly ground. My hands and feet and eyelids move, and I can think as I desire. That third, controlling element has retired to the background. I'm no longer three existences in one. My mind is able to command, and my body follows out its orders with precision.

Ireland, England, France, Paris! The night at Paris! *This* night at Paris – less than six hours from Now – *France and Paris!* It's like a fairy tale. Yesterday I walked on Roosevelt Field; today I'll walk on Le Bourget.

THE END FOR SACCO AND VANZETTI, BOSTON, 23 August 1927

Louis Stark

Nicolò Sacco and Bartolomeo Vanzetti were Italian anarchist emigrants to America convicted of double murder during a 1920 payroll robbery. Their conviction was dubious, and the case became a *cause célèbre* around the world. After six years of appeals and stays of execution, the two Italian workmen (one was a fishmonger and the other a shoemaker) were electrocuted on 23 August 1927. In 1977 Sacco and Vanzetti were posthumously pardoned by the Governor of Massachusetts.

Police charged a crowd near the Bunker Hill Monument. The prison area was an armed camp. Searchlights swept glaring fingers over rooftops, revealing whole families gazing at the prison. All streets leading to the prison were roped off, and the public was banned from entering the prison zone. Police horses stamped restlessly in the yellow glare of street lamps.

Mrs Sacco and Miss Vanzetti paid three visits to the prison on the last day and made their final appeal to the Governor in the evening.

Reporters were given special passes to the prison. Those of us who were to do the execution story were asked to present ourselves at the prison by ten o'clock if possible. Eddy remained on the streets observing the police and the crowds, and Gordon covered the last hours at the State House.

When I arrived at the prison, I found that telegraph wires had again been strung into the Prison Officers' Club. From ten o'clock we filed details of the preparations for the execution. The windows had been nailed down by a nervous policeman "because somebody might throw something in". The shades were drawn. The room was stuffy, and in an hour the heat was unbearable. We took off our coats, rolled up our shirt sleeves, and tried to be comfortable. The Morse operators were the coolest of the fifty men and women in the room. The noise of the typewriters and telegraph instruments made an awful din. Our nerves were stretched to the breaking-point. Had there not been a last minute reprieve on August 10? Might there not be one now? We knew of the personal appeal then being made by Mrs Sacco and Miss Vanzetti to the Governor.

W. G. Thompson, counsel for the two men, saw them for the last time. In an extraordinarily moving account of his final talks, later published in *The Atlantic Monthly*, Thompson described the attitude of the two Italians, their calmness in the face of death, their sincerity, their firm belief in their ideals:

"I told Vanzetti that although my belief in his innocence had all the time been strengthened both by my study of the evidence and by my increasing knowledge of his personality, yet there was a chance, however remote, that I might be mistaken; and that I thought he ought for my sake, in the closing hour of his life when nothing could save him, to give me his most solemn reassurance, both with respect to himself and with respect to Sacco. Vanzetti then told me quietly and calmly, and with a sincerity which I could not doubt, that I need have no anxiety about this matter; that both he and Sacco were absolutely innocent of the South Braintree crime and that he [Vanzetti] was equally innocent of the Bridgewater crime; that while, looking back, he now realized more clearly than he ever had the grounds of the suspicion against him and Sacco, he felt that no allowance had been made for his ignorance of American points of view and habits of thought, or for his fear as a radical and almost as an outlaw, and that in reality he was convicted on evidence which would not have convicted him had he not been an anarchist, so that he was in a very real sense dying for his cause. He said it was a cause for which he was prepared to die. He said it was the cause of the upward progress of humanity and the elimination of force from the world. He spoke with calmness, knowledge, and deep feeling.

"I was impressed by the strength of Vanzetti's mind, and by the extent of his reading and knowledge. He did not talk like a fanatic. Although intensely convinced of the truth of his own views, he was still able to listen with calmness and with understanding to the expression of views with which he did not agree. In this closing scene the impression of him which had been gaining ground in my mind for three years was deepened and confirmed – that he was a man of powerful mind, of unselfish disposition, of seasoned character and of devotion to high ideals. There was no sign of breaking down or of terror at approaching death. At parting he gave me a firm clasp of the hand and a steady glance, which revealed unmistakably the depth of his feeling and the firmness of his self-control . . .

"My conversation with Sacco was very brief. He showed no sign of fear, shook hands with me firmly and bade me good-bye. His manner also was one of absolute sincerity."

At quarter past eleven, Musmanno burst into Warden Hendry's office with a plea for a last talk with Vanzetti. The Warden, whose heart was touched by the young lawyer, had to refuse. It was too close to the hour set for the three executions.

Musmanno was on the verge of collapse.

"I want to tell them there is more mercy in their hearts than in the hearts of many who profess orthodox religion," he said. "I want to tell them I know they are innocent and all the gallows and electric chairs cannot change that knowledge. I want to tell them they are two of the kindest and tenderest men I have ever known."

At the State House in the meantime, Governor Fuller talked with Mrs Sacco, Miss Vanzetti, Dr Edith B. Jackson and her brother Gardner, and Aldino Felicani of the Defense Committee.

The Governor was sorry. Everything had been done, the evidence had been carefully sifted. To prove it he called in State Attorney General Arthur K. Reading, whose legal explanations were lost on the three women. Reluctantly they left the Governor. Hope vanished.

Shortly after midnight, Warden Hendry rapped on the door leading to the interior of the prison and the death house. Musmanno, still in the Warden's office, laid a hand on Hendry's arm. "Please, one last request."

"No, no."

Hendry, followed by the official witnesses, solemnly filed into the death chamber. The only reporter present at the execution was W. E. Playfair of the Associated Press. The rules limited the press to one representative, and Mr Playfair had been handed the assignment when the men were convicted in 1921.

Madeiros was the first to go. His cell was the nearest the chair. A messenger hurried to us with a bulletin.

Sacco walked the seventeen steps from his cell to the execution chamber slowly between two guards. He was calm.

"Long live anarchy," he cried in Italian as he was strapped in the chair.

In English: "Farewell my wife and child and all my friends."

This was a slip probably due to his imperfect command of English. He had two children: Dante, fourteen, and Inez, six.

"Good evening, gentlemen," he said.

Then his last words.

"Farewell, Mother."

Vanzetti was the last to die. He shook hands with the two guards.

To Warden Hendry, he said, speaking slowly and distinctly: "I want to thank you for everything you have done for me, Warden. I wish to tell you that I am innocent and that I have never committed any crime but sometimes some sin. [Almost the same words he had used when sentenced by Judge Thayer the previous April.] I thank you for everything you have done for me. I am innocent of all crime not only of this, but all. I am an innocent man."

A pause.

"I wish to forgive some people for what they are now doing to me."

The Warden was overcome. The current was turned on, and when Vanzetti was pronounced dead Hendry could scarcely whisper the formula required by law – "Under the law I now pronounce you dead, the sentence of the court having been carried out."

Mr Playfair lived up to his name. He dashed into our room with all the details of the last Sacco–Vanzetti story most of us were to write.

Governor Fuller remained at the State House until 12.12, a minute after Executioner Elliott had thrown the switch that ended the earthly existence of Sacco. Until a few minutes before midnight, Francis Fisher Kane had begged Governor Fuller for a respite. Thompson, former attorney in the case, remained with the Governor until 11.45, making his final heart-rending plea for mercy.

When the Governor left the State House he knew that the Supreme Court had, on 22 August, docketed two appeals for writs of certiorari. He had a request pending before him that alienists be permitted to examine Sacco and Vanzetti, that execution be delayed until the matter of the Department of Justice's files had been cleared up. He had before him five new affidavits made by new witnesses found by the defense in the closing days. He had, or was presumed to have received from his secretary, the receipt for the eels which Vanzetti had purchased.

So that when the two men died in the electric chair the legal battle to save them was still under way and there was, in the opinion of many of the best minds in America, more than a "reasonable doubt". In the last hour a three- or four-hour reprieve was asked by Defense Attorney Hill so that he could fly to Williamstown in a chartered plane to consult Circuit Court Judge Anderson again.

At the naval airport Hill tried to get in touch with the Governor or the Attorney General, but without success. When a naval officer found out who Hill and his companions were, he ordered them off the grounds and told William Schuyler Jackson, a former New York Attorney General, that "it would give me pleasure to shoot you". Finally a reporter at the State House told them over the telephone that Sacco was in the death chamber. The long battle had ended.

BABE RUTH HITS 60 HOME RUNS, New York, 1927

Mrs Ruth

George Herman "Babe" Ruth (1895–1948) was the greatest all-rounder in the history of baseball. In 1927, while playing for the New York Yankees, he hit a record 60 home runs.

The pennant race was over by 1 September, but Babe was fighting to break his 59 home-run record. He needed 17 to do it in the last month, or better than one every two days. He did it, of course. The 60th was made in Yankee Stadium against Washington. Tom Zachary, a left-hander, was the pitcher, and the homer came in the final game.

Babe had smashed out two home runs the day before to bring his total to 59 for the season, or the exact equal of his 1921 record. He had only this last game to set a new record. Zachary, a left-hander, was by the nature of his delivery a hard man for the Babe to hit. In fact Babe got only two homers in all his life against Tom.

Babe came up in the eighth and it was quite probable that this would be his very last chance to break his own record. My mother and I were at the game and I can still see that lovely, lovely home run. It was a tremendous poke, deep into the stands. There was never any doubt that it was going over the fence. But the question was, would it be fair? It was fair by only six glorious inches!

The Babe later professed himself to be unimpressed and un-excited and certainly not surprised by the blow. "I knew I was going to hit it," he insisted. I didn't, although I was now used to his rising to occasions.

What delighted him as much, more than the homer, was the spectacle of his pal, Charlie O'Leary, jumping and screaming on the coaching lines, his bald head glinting in the failing sun. Charlie had thrown away his cap in jubilation when the umps signalled the ball fair.

Babe knew the extent of Charlie's joy because he knew his little friend was almost psychopathic about his bald dome. They didn't play "The Star-Spangled Banner" before every game then, only on festive occasions. On these occasions Charlie would hide. The baring of Charlie's gleaming head was an appreciated tribute to the popularity of that historic homer.

WALL STREET CRASHES, 24 October 1929

Elliott V. Bell

Throughout the '20s the USA enjoyed unparalleled prosperity; with the stock market crash of October 1929 the bubble burst.

The day was overcast and cool. A light north-west wind blew down the canyons of Wall Street, and the temperature, in the low fifties, made bankers and brokers on their way to work button their topcoats around them. The crowds of market traders in the brokers' board rooms were nervous but hopeful as the ten o'clock hour for the start of trading approached. The general feeling was that the worst was over and a good many speculators who had prudently sold out earlier in the decline were congratulating themselves at having bought back their stocks a good deal cheaper.

Seldom had the small trader had better or more uniform advice to go by.

The market opened steady with prices little changed from the previous day, though some rather large blocks, of 20,000 to 25,000 shares, came out at the start. It sagged easily for the first half-hour, and then around eleven o'clock the deluge broke.

It came with a speed and ferocity that left men dazed. The bottom simply fell out of the market. From all over the country a torrent of selling orders poured onto the floor of the Stock Exchange and there were no buying orders to meet it. Quotations of representative active issues, like Steel, Telephone, and Anaconda, began to fall two, three, five, and even ten points between sales. Less active stocks became unmarketable. Within a few moments the ticker service was hopelessly swamped and from then on no one knew what was really happening. By one-thirty the ticker tape was nearly two hours late; by two-thirty it was 147 minutes late. The last quotation was not printed on the tape until 7.08½ p.m., four hours, eight and one-half minutes after the close. In the meantime, Wall Street had lived through an incredible nightmare.

In the strange way that news of a disaster spreads, the word of the market collapse flashed through the city. By noon great crowds had gathered at the corner of Broad and Wall Streets where the Stock Exchange on one corner faces Morgan's across the way. On the steps of the Sub-Treasury Building, opposite Morgan's, a crowd of press photographers and newsreel men took up their stand. Traffic was pushed from the streets of the financial district by the crush.

It was in this wild setting that the leading bankers scurried into conference at Morgan's in a belated effort to save the day. Shortly after noon Mr Mitchell left the National City Bank and pushed his way west on Wall Street to Morgan's. No sooner had he entered than Albert H. Wiggin was seen to hurry down from the Chase National Bank, one block north. Hard on his heels came William C. Potter, head of the Guaranty Trust, followed by Seward Prosser of the Bankers Trust. Later George F. Baker, Jr, of the First National, joined the group.

The news of the bankers' meeting flashed through the streets and over the news tickers – stocks began to rally – but for many it was already too late. Thousands of traders, little and big, had gone "overboard" in that incredible hour between eleven and twelve. Confidence in the financial and political leaders of the country, faith in the "soundness" of economic conditions had received a shattering blow. The panic was on.

At Morgan's the heads of six banks formed a consortium – since known as the bankers' pool of October, 1929 – pledging a total of $240,000,000, or $40,000,000 each, to provide a "cushion" of buying power beneath the falling market. In addition, other financial institutions, including James Speyer and Company and Guggenheim Brothers, sent over to Morgan's unsolicited offers of funds aggregating $100,000,000. It was not only the first authenticated instance of a bankers' pool in stocks but by far the largest concentration of pool buying power ever brought to bear on the stock market – but in the face of the panic it was pitifully inadequate.

After the bankers had met, Thomas W. Lamont, Morgan partner, came out to the crowd of newspaper reporters who had gathered in the lobby of his bank. In an understatement that has since become a Wall Street classic, he remarked:

"It seems there has been some disturbed selling in the market."

It was at the same meeting that "T.W." gave to the financial community a new phrase – "air pockets" – to describe the condition in stocks for which there were no bids, but only frantic offers. (Mr Lamont said he had it from his partner, George Whitney, and the latter said he had it from some broker.)

After the meeting, Mr Lamont walked across Broad Street to the Stock Exchange to meet with the governors of the Exchange. They had been called together quietly during trading hours and they held their meeting in the rooms of the Stock Clearing Corporation so as to avoid attracting attention. Mr Lamont sat on the corner of a desk and told them about the pool. Then he said:

"Gentlemen, there is no man nor group of men who can buy all the stocks that the American public can sell."

It seems a pretty obvious statement now, but it had a horrid sound to the assembled governors of the Exchange. It meant that the shrewdest member of the most powerful banking house in the country was telling them plainly that the assembled resources of Wall Street, mobilized on a scale never before attempted, could not stop this panic.

The bankers' pool, in fact, turned out a sorry fiasco. Without it, no doubt, the Exchange would have been forced to close, for it did supply bids at some price for the so-called pivotal stocks when, because of the panic and confusion in the market, there were no other bids available. It made a small profit, but it did not have a ghost of a chance of stemming the avalanche of selling that poured in from all over the country. The stock market had become too big. The days that followed are blurred in retrospect. Wall Street became a nightmarish spectacle.

The animal roar that rises from the floor of the Stock Exchange and which on active days is plainly audible in the Street outside, became louder, anguished, terrifying. The streets were crammed with a mixed crowd – agonized little speculators, walking aimlessly outdoors because they feared to face the ticker and the margin clerk; sold-out traders, morbidly impelled to visit the scene of their ruin; inquisitive individuals and tourists, seeking by gazing at the exteriors of the Exchange and the big banks to get a closer view of the national catastrophe; runners, frantically pushing their way through the throng of idle and curious in their effort to make deliveries of the unprecedented volume of securities which was being traded on the floor of the Exchange.

The ticker, hopelessly swamped, fell hours behind the actual trading and became completely meaningless. Far into the night, and often all night long, the lights blazed in the windows of the tall office buildings where margin clerks and bookkeepers struggled with the desperate task of trying to clear one day's business before the next began. They fainted at their desks; the weary runners fell exhausted on the marble floors of banks and slept. But within a few months they were to have ample time to rest up. By then thousands of them had been fired.

Agonizing scenes were enacted in the customers' rooms of the various brokers. There traders who a few short days before had luxuriated in delusions of wealth saw all their hopes smashed in a collapse so devastating, so far beyond their wildest fears, as to seem unreal. Seeking to save a little from the wreckage, they would order their stocks sold "at the market", in many cases to discover that they had not merely lost everything but were, in addition, in debt to the broker. And then, ironic twist, as like as not the next few hours' wild churning of the market would lift prices to levels where they might have sold out and had a substantial cash balance left over. Every move was wrong, in those days. The market seemed like an insensate thing that was wreaking a wild and pitiless revenge upon those who had thought to master it.

The excitement and sense of danger which imbued Wall Street was like that which grips men on a sinking ship. A camaraderie, a kind of gaiety of despair, sprang up. The Wall Street reporter found all doors open and everyone snatched at him for the latest news, for shreds of rumour. Who was in trouble? Who had gone under last? Where was it going to end?

AN INTERVIEW WITH AL CAPONE, Chicago, 1930

Claud Cockburn

The Prohibition-era gangster Alphonse Capone was born in Brooklyn, but achieved his notoriety as a Mafia boss in Chicago.

The Lexington Hotel had once, I think, been a rather grand family hotel, but now its large and gloomy lobby was deserted except for a couple of bulging Sicilians and a reception clerk who looked at one across the counter with the expression of a speakeasy proprietor looking through the grille at a potential detective. He checked on my appointment with some superior upstairs, and as I stepped into the elevator I felt my hips and sides being gently frisked by the tapping hands of one of the lounging Sicilians. There were a couple of ante-rooms to be passed before you got to Capone's office and in the first of them I had to wait for a quarter of an hour or so, drinking whisky poured by a man who used his left hand for the bottle and kept the other in his pocket.

Except that there was a sub-machine-gun, operated by a man called MacGurn – whom I later got to know and somewhat esteem – poking through the transom of a door behind the big desk, Capone's own room was nearly indistinguishable from that of, say, a "newly arrived" Texan oil millionaire. Apart from the jowly young murderer on the far side of the desk, what took the eye were a number of large, flattish, solid silver bowls upon the desk, each filled with roses. They were nice to look at, and they had another purpose too, for Capone when agitated stood up and dipped the tips of his fingers in the waters in which floated the roses.

I had been a little embarrassed as to how the interview was to be launched. Naturally the nub of all such interviews is somehow to get around to the question "What makes you tick?" but in the case of this millionaire killer the approach to this central question seemed mined with dangerous impediments. However, on the way down to the Lexington Hotel I had had the good fortune to see, in I think the *Chicago Daily News*, some statistics offered by an insurance company which dealt with the average expectation of life of gangsters in Chicago. I forget exactly what the average expectation was, and also what the exact age of Capone at that time was – I think he was in his early thirties. The point was, however, that in any case he was four years older than the upper limit considered by the insurance company to be the proper average expectation of life for a Chicago gangster. This seemed to offer a more or less neutral and academic line of approach, and after the ordinary greetings I asked Capone whether he had read this piece of statistics in the paper. He said that he had. I asked him whether he considered the estimate reasonably accurate. He said that he thought that the insurance companies and the newspaper boys probably knew their stuff. "In that case," I asked him, "how does it feel to be, say, four years over the age?"

He took the question quite seriously and spoke of the matter with neither more nor less excitement or agitation than a man would who, let us say, had been asked whether he, as the rear machine-gunner of a bomber, was aware of the average incidence of casualties in that occupation. He apparently assumed that sooner or later he would be shot despite the elaborate precautions which he regularly took. The idea that – as afterwards turned out to be the case – he would be arrested by the Federal authorities for income-tax evasion had not, I think, at that time so much as crossed his mind. And, after all, he said with a little bit of corn-and-ham somewhere at the back of his throat, supposing he had not gone into this racket? What would he have been doing? He would, he said, "have been selling newspapers barefoot on the street in Brooklyn".

He stood up as he spoke, cooling his finger-tips in the rose bowl in front of him. He sat down again, brooding and sighing. Despite the ham-and-corn, what he said was quite probably true and I said so, sympathetically. A little bit too sympathetically, as immediately emerged, for as I spoke I saw him looking at me suspiciously, not to say censoriously. My remarks about the harsh way the world treats barefoot boys in Brooklyn were interrupted by an urgent angry waggle of his podgy hand. "Listen," he said, "don't get the idea I'm one of these goddam radicals. Don't get the idea I'm knocking the American system. The American system . . ." As though an invisible chairman had called upon him for a few words, he broke into an oration upon the theme. He praised freedom, enterprise and the pioneers. He spoke of "our heritage". He referred with contemptuous disgust to Socialism and Anarchism.

"My rackets," he repeated several times, "are run on strictly American lines and they're going to stay that way." This turned out to be a reference to the fact that he had recently been elected the President of the Unione Siciliano, a slightly mysterious, partially criminal society which certainly had its roots in the Mafia. Its power and importance varied sharply from year to year. Sometimes there did seem to be evidence that it was a secret society of real power, and at other times it seemed more in the nature of a mutual benefit association not essentially much more menacing than, say, the Elks. Capone's complaint just now was that the Unione was what he called "lousy with blackhand stuff". "Can you imagine," he said, "people going in for what they call these blood feuds – some guy's grandfather was killed by some other guy's grandfather, and this guy thinks that's good enough reason to kill the other." It was, he said, entirely unbusinesslike. His vision of the American system began to excite him profoundly and now he was on his feet again, leaning across the desk like the chairman of a board meeting, his fingers plunged in the rose bowls.

"This American system of ours," he shouted, "call it American-ism, call it Capitalism, call it what you like, gives to each and every one of us a great opportunity if we only seize it with both hands and make the most of it." He held out his hand towards me, the fingers dripping a little, and stared at me sternly for a few seconds before reseating himself.

HUNGER MARCHERS, Washington D.C., December 1931

John Dos Passos

Ushered in by the Wall Street Crash, the Great Depression was the worst economic downturn of the 20th century. By the early '30s more than a quarter of the US workforce – 12 million people – were unemployed. The novelist Dos Passos wrote this account of hunger marchers for the radical *The New Republic* magazine.

Washington has a drowsy look in the early December sunlight. The Greco-Roman porticoes loom among the bare trees, as vaguely portentous as phrases about democracy in the mouth of a Southern Senator. The Monument, a finger of light cut against a lavender sky, punctuates the antiquated rhetoric of the Treasury and the White House. On the hill, above its tall foundation banked

with magnolia trees, the dome of the Capitol bulges smugly. At
nine o'clock groups of sleepy-looking cops in well-brushed uniforms and shiny-visored caps are straggling up the hill. At the
corner of Pennsylvania Avenue and John Marshall Place a few
hunger marchers stand around the trucks they came in. They
looked tired and frowzy from the long ride. Some of them are
strolling up and down the avenue. That end of the avenue, with its
gimcrack stores, boarded-up burlesque shows, Chinese restaurants
and flophouses, still has a little of the jerkwater, out-in-the-sticks
look it must have had when Lincoln drove up it in a barouche
through the deep mud or Jefferson rode to his inauguration on his
own quiet nag.

Two elderly labouring men are looking out of a cigar-store door
at a bunch of Reds, young Jewish boys from New York or Chicago,
with the white armbands of the hunger marchers. "Won't get
nutten that a-way," one of them says. "Whose payin' for it
anyway, hirin' them trucks and gasoline . . . Somebody's payin'
for it," barks the clerk indignantly from behind the cash register.
"Better'd spent it on grub or to buy 'emselves overcoats," says the
older man. The man who first spoke shakes his head sadly. "Never
won't get nutten that a-way." Out along the avenue a few
Washingtonians look at the trucks and old moving vans with
Daily Worker cartoons pasted on their sides. They stand a good
way off, as if they were afraid the trucks would explode; they are
obviously swallowing their unfavourable comments for fear some
of the marchers might hear them. Tough eggs, these Reds.

At ten o'clock the leaders start calling to their men to fall in.
Some tall cops appear and bawl out drivers of cars that get into the
streets reserved for the marchers to form up in. The marchers form
in a column of fours. They don't look as if they'd had much of a
night's rest. They look quiet and serious and anxious to do the
right thing. Leaders, mostly bareheaded youngsters, run up and
down, hoarse and nervous, keeping everybody in line. Most of
them look like city dwellers, men and women from the needle
trades, restaurant workers, bakery or laundry employees. There's a
good sprinkling of Negroes among them. Here and there the thick
shoulders and light hair of a truck driver or farm hand stand out.
Motorcycle cops begin to cluster around the edges. The marchers
are receiving as much attention as distinguished foreign officials.

Up on the hill, cordons of cops are everywhere, making a fine
showing in the late-fall sunshine. There's a considerable crowd

standing around; it's years since Washington has been interested in the opening of Congress. They are roping off the route for the hunger marchers. They stop a taxicab that is discovered to contain a small white-haired Senator. He curses the cops out roundly and is hurriedly escorted under the portals.

Inside the Capitol things are very different. The light is amber and greenish, as in an aquarium. Elderly clerks white as termites move sluggishly along the corridors, as if beginning to stir after a long hibernation. The elevator boy is very pale. "Here comes the army of the unfed," he says, pointing spitefully out of the window. "And they're carrying banners, though Charlie Curtis said they couldn't." A sound of music comes faintly in. Led by a band with silvery instruments like Christmas-tree ornaments that look cheerful in the bright sunlight, the hunger marchers have started up Capitol Hill. Just time to peep down into the Senate Chamber where elderly parties and pasty-faced pages are beginning to gather. Ever seen a section of a termite nest under glass?

There's a big crowd in the square between the Capitol and the Congressional Library. On the huge ramps of the steps that lead to the central portico the metropolitan police have placed some additional statuary; tastefully arranged groups of cops with rifles, riot guns and brand-new tear-gas pistols that look as if they'd just come from Sears, Roebuck. People whisper "machine-gun nests", but nobody seems to know where they are. There's a crowd on the roof around the base of the dome, faces are packed in all the windows. Everybody looks cheerful, as if a circus had come to town, anxious to be shown. The marchers fill the broad semicircle in front of the Capitol, each group taking up its position in perfect order, as if the show had been rehearsed. The band, playing "Solidarity Forever" (which a newspaper woman beside me recognizes as "Onward Christian Soldiers"), steps out in front. It's a curious little band, made up of martini-horns, drums, cymbals and a lyre that goes tinkle, tinkle. It plays cheerfully and well, led by a drum major with a red tasselled banner on the end of his staff, and repeats again and again "The Red Flag", "Solidarity", and other tunes variously identified by people in the crowd. Above the heads of the marchers are banners with slogans printed out: *IN THE LAST WAR WE FOUGHT FOR THE BOSSES: IN THE NEXT WAR WE'LL FIGHT FOR THE WORKERS . . . $150 CASH . . . FULL PAY FOR UNEMPLOY-MENT RELIEF*. The squad commanders stand out in front like cheerleaders at a football game and direct the chanting: "We Demand – Unemployed Insurance, We Demand – Unemployed Insurance, *WE DEMAND – UNEMPLOYED INSURANCE.*"

A deep-throated echo comes back from the Capitol façade a few beats later than each shout. It's as if the statues and the classical-revival republican ornaments in the pediment were shouting too.

A small group leaves the ranks and advances across the open space towards the Senate side. All the tall cops drawn up in such fine order opposite the hunger marchers stick out their chests. Now it's coming. A tremor goes over the groups of statuary so tastefully arranged on the steps. The tear-gas pistols glint in the sun. The marchers stand in absolute silence.

Under the portal at the Senate entrance the swinging doors are protected by two solid walls of blue serge. Cameramen and reporters converge with a run. Three men are advancing with the demands of the hunger marchers written out. They are the centre of a big group of inspectors, sergeants, gold and silver braid of the Capitol and metropolitan police. A young fellow with a camera is hanging from the wall by the door. "Move the officer out of the way," he yells. "Thank you . . . A little back, please lady, I can't see his face . . . Now hand him the petition."

"We're not handing petitions, we're making demands," says the leader of the hunger marchers. Considerable waiting around. The Sergeant at Arms sends word they can't be let in. Somebody starts to jostle, the cops get tough, cop voices snarl. The committee goes back to report while the band plays the "Internationale" on marinihorns and lyre . . .

THE WORLD PREMIÈRE OF CHAPLIN'S *MODERN TIMES*, New York, 6 February 1936

"Our Correspondent", *London* Daily Telegraph

There was pandemonium on Broadway last night when 1,800 people paid thirty shillings each to see the world première of Charlie Chaplin's new film, *Modern Times*.

Five thousand autograph-hunters collected outside the Rivoli Theatre and mobbed the celebrities – including Evelyn Laye, Tilly Losche, Gloria Swanson, Ginger Rogers, and Eddie Cantor – who attended the performance.

A riot call was issued, but the crowd stoutly resisted the violent attempts of hundreds of policemen to drive them from the entrance of the theatre.

Many celebrities, endeavouring to run the gauntlet from their cars through the crowd, were badly manhandled as college students enthusiastically thrust autograph books under their noses and curious women fingered and clutched the dresses worn by famous actresses and screen stars.

Traffic was halted for more than a quarter of an hour. Many persons slipped on the icy pavements and received minor injuries.

People had come from all over the world to see the first Chaplin picture for nearly five years, and to hear Chaplin's voice on the screen for the first time.

The film was given an enthusiastic reception, and there was tremendous applause when Chaplin uttered his first words. This solitary breach of his silent tradition comes when Charlie sings a song in a night club and reveals that he possesses an unusually pleasant voice.

Losing the detachable linen cuff, on which he had carefully written the words of his song, he has to improvise, with the result that the song deteriorates into extraordinary gibberish reminiscent of the Jabberwock in *Alice in Wonderland*.

We see the same old lovable clown, with the same cane, hat and oversize shoes, again cast as a brow-beaten tramp who, unable to find a niche for himself in modern society, is comforted by the companionship of an irrepressible girl waif, and pursued by the police as a vagrant. The same old "gags" that Chaplin has used for the last twenty years are brought out and surprisingly enough, they stand the test of time. Last night's audience showed their whole-hearted amusement by practically unceasing and vociferous mirth.

The picture ends, as do all Chaplin pictures, with a long shot showing the comedian walking down the highway. On this occasion, however, he is accompanied for the first time by a girl, his little gamin friend, attractively played by Paulette Goddard.

Neither Chaplin nor his leading lady was at the première.

THE GREAT DEPRESSION: "OKIE" MIGRANT CAMPS IN CALIFORNIA, October 1936

John Steinbeck

Steinbeck's report for *San Francisco News*. *The Grapes of Wrath* appeared three years later.

The squatters' camps are located all over California. Let us see what a typical one is like. It is located on the banks of a river, near an irrigation ditch or on a side road where a spring of water is available. From a distance it looks like a city dump, and well it may, for the city dumps are the sources for the material of which it is built. You can see a litter of dirty rags and scrap iron, of houses built of weeds, of flattened cans or of paper. It is only on close approach that it can be seen that these are homes.

Here is a house built by a family who have tried to maintain a neatness. The house is about 10 feet by 10 feet, and it is built completely of corrugated paper. The roof is peaked, the walls are tacked to a wooden frame. The dirt floor is swept clean, and along the irrigation ditch or in the muddy river the wife of the family scrubs clothes without soap and tries to rinse out the mud in muddy water.

The spirit of this family is not quite broken, for the children, three of them, still have clothes, and the family possesses three old quilts and a soggy, lumpy mattress. But the money so needed for food cannot be used for soap nor for clothes.

With the first rain the carefully built house will slop down into a brown, pulpy mush; in a few months the clothes will fray off the children's bodies, while the lack of nourishing food will subject the whole family to pneumonia when the first cold comes. Five years ago this family had 50 acres of land and $1,000 in the bank. The wife belonged to a sewing circle and the man was a member of the Grange. They raised chickens, pigs, pigeons and vegetables and fruit for their own use; and their land produced the tall corn of the middle west. Now they have nothing.

If the husband hits every harvest without delay and works the maximum time, he may make $400 this year. But if anything happens, if his old car breaks down, if he is late and misses a harvest or two, he will have to feed his whole family on as little as $150. But there is still pride in this family. Wherever they stop they try to put the children in school. It may be that the children will be in a school for as much as a month before they are moved to another locality.

There is more filth here. The tent is full of flies clinging to the apple box that is the dinner table, buzzing about the foul clothes of the children, particularly the baby, who has not been bathed nor cleaned for several days. This family has been on the road longer than the builder of the paper house.

There is no toilet here, but there is a clump of willows nearby where human faeces lie exposed to the flies – the same flies that are in the tent.

Two weeks ago there was another child, a four-year-old boy. For a few weeks they had noticed that he was kind of lackadaisical, that his eyes had been feverish. They had given him the best place in the bed, between father and mother. But one night he went into convulsions and died, and the next morning the coroner's wagon took him away. It was one step down.

They knew pretty well that it was a diet of fresh fruit, beans and little else that caused his death. He had had no milk for months. With this death there came a change of mind in this family. The father and mother now feel that paralysed dullness with which the mind protects itself against too much sorrow and too much pain.

Here, in the faces of the husband and his wife, you begin to see an expression you will notice on every face; not worry, but absolute terror of the starvation that crowds in against the borders of the camp. This man has tried to make a toilet by digging a hole in the ground near his house and surrounding it with an old piece of burlap. But he will only do things like that this year. He is a newcomer and his spirit and his decency and his sense of his own dignity have not been quite wiped out. Next year he will be like his next-door neighbour.

This is a family of six; a man, his wife and four children. They live in a tent the colour of the ground. Rot has set in on the canvas so that the flaps and the sides hang in tatters and are held together with bits of rusty bailing wire. There is one bed in the family and that is a big tick lying on the ground inside the tent. They have one quilt and a piece of canvas for bedding. The sleeping arrangement is clever. Mother and father lie down together and two children lie between them. Then, heading the other way, the other two children lie, the littler ones.

If the mother and father sleep with their legs spread wide, there is room for the legs of the children. And this father will not be able to make a maximum of $400 a year anymore because he is no longer alert; he isn't quick at piecework, and he is not able to fight clear of the dullness that has settled on him.

The dullness shows in the faces of this family, and in addition there is a sullenness that makes them taciturn. Sometimes they still start the older children off to school, but the ragged little things will not go; they hide themselves in ditches or wander off by themselves until it is time to go back to the tent, because they are scorned in the school. The better-dressed children shout and jeer, the teachers are quite often impatient with these additions to their duties, and the parents of the "nice" children do not want to have disease carriers in the schools.

The father of this family once had a little grocery store and his family lived in back of it so that even the children could wait on the counter. When the drought set in there was no trade for the store anymore. This is the middle class of the squatters' camp. In a few months this family will slip down to the lower class. Dignity is all gone, and spirit has turned to sullen anger before it dies.

The next-door-neighbour family, of man, wife and three children of from three to nine years of age, have built a house by driving willow branches into the ground and wattling weeds, tin, old paper and strips of carpet against them. A few branches are placed over the top to keep out the noonday sun. It would not turn water at all. There is no bed.

Somewhere the family has found a big piece of old carpet. It is on the ground. To go to bed the members of the family lie on the ground and fold the carpet up over them.

The three-year-old child has a gunny sack tied about his middle for clothing. He has the swollen belly caused by malnutrition. He sits on the ground in the sun in front of the house, and the little black fruit flies buzz in circles and land on his closed eyes and crawl up his nose until he weakly brushes them away. They try to get at the mucus in the eye corners. This child seems to have the reactions of a baby much younger. The first year he had a little milk, but he has had none since. He will die in a very short time.

The older children may survive. Four nights ago the mother had a baby in the tent, on the dirt carpet. It was born dead, which was just as well because she could not have fed it at the breast; her own diet will not produce milk. After it was born and she had seen that it was dead, the mother rolled over and lay still for two days. She is up today, tottering around. The last baby, born less than a year ago, lived a week.

This woman's eyes have the glazed, faraway look of a sleepwalker's eyes. She does not wash clothes anymore. The drive that makes for cleanliness has been drained out of her and she hasn't the energy. The husband was a sharecropper once, but he couldn't make it go. Now he has lost even the desire to talk. He will not look directly at you, for that requires will, and will needs strength. He is a bad field worker for the same reason.

It takes him a long time to make up his mind, so he is always late in moving, and late in arriving in the fields. His top wage, when he can find work now, which isn't often, is $1 a day. The children do not even go to the willow clump anymore. They squat where they are and kick a little dirt. The father is vaguely aware that there is a culture of hookworm, in the mud along the riverbank. He knows the children will get it on their bare feet. But he hasn't the will nor the energy to resist. Too many things have happened to him.

This is the lower class of the camp. This is what the man in the tent will be in six months; what the man in the paper house with its peaked roof will be in a year, after his house has washed down and his children have sickened or died, after the loss of dignity and spirit have cut him down to a kind of subhumanity.

Helpful strangers are not well received in this camp. The local sheriff makes a raid now and then for a wanted man, and if there is labour trouble the vigilantes may burn the poor houses. Social workers have taken case histories. They are filed and open for inspection. These families have been questioned over and over about their origins, number of children living and dead.

The information is taken down and filed. That is that. It has been done so often, and so little has come of it. And there is another way for them to get attention. Let an epidemic break out, say typhoid or scarlet fever, and the county doctor will come to the camp and hurry the infected cases to the pesthouse. But malnutrition is not infectious, nor is dysentery, which is almost the rule among the children.

The county hospital has no room for measles, mumps, whooping cough; and yet these are often deadly to hunger-weakened children. And although we hear much about the free clinics for the poor, these people do not know how to get the aid and they do not get it. Also, since most of their dealings with authority are painful to them, they prefer not to take the chance. This is the squatters' camp. Some are a little better, some much worse. I have described some typical families. In some of the camps there are as many as 300 families like these. Some are so far from water that it must be bought at five cents a bucket. And if these men steal, if there is developing among them a suspicion and hatred of well-dressed, satisfied people, the reason is not to be sought in their origin nor in any tendency to weakness in their character.

THE LOUIS v. SCHMELING FIGHT, New York, 22 June 1938

Bob Considine

This was the return bout; Schmeling, the German champion, had ko-ed the "Brown Bomber" in the 12th round in 1936. By the time of the re-match in 1938, Louis had picked up the World Championship by defeating James J. Braddock.

Listen to this, buddy, for it comes from a guy whose palms are still wet, whose throat is still dry, and whose jaw is still agape from the utter shock of watching Joe Louis knock out Max Schmeling.

It was a shocking thing, that knockout – short, sharp, merciless, complete. Louis was like this:

He was a big lean copper spring, tightened and retightened through weeks of training until he was one pregnant package of coiled venom.

Schmeling hit that spring. He hit it with a whistling right-hand punch in the first minute of the fight – and the spring, tormented with tension, suddenly burst with one brazen spring of activity. Hard brown arms, propelling two unerring fists, blurred beneath the hot white candelabra of the ring lights. And Schmeling was in the path of them, a man caught and mangled in the whirring claws of a mad and feverish machine.

The mob, biggest and most prosperous ever to see a fight in a ball yard, knew that here was the end before the thing had really started. It knew, so it stood up and howled one long shriek. People who had paid as much as $100 for their chairs didn't use them – except perhaps to stand on, the better to let the sight burn forever in their memories.

There were four steps to Schmeling's knockout. A few seconds after he landed his only punch of the fight, Louis caught him with a lethal little left hook that drove him into the ropes so that his right arm was hooked over the top strand, like a drunk hanging to a fence. Louis swarmed over him and hit with everything he had – until Referee Donovan pushed him away and counted one.

Schmeling staggered away from the ropes, dazed and sick. He looked drunkenly toward his corner, and before he had turned his head back Louis was on him again, first with a left and then that awe-provoking right that made a crunching sound when it hit the German's jaw. Max fell down, hurt and giddy, for a count of three.

He clawed his way up as if the night air were as thick as black water, and Louis – his nostrils like the mouth of a double-barrelled shotgun – took a quiet lead and let him have both barrels.

Max fell almost lightly, bereft of his senses, his fingers touching the canvas like a comical stew-bum doing his morning exercises, knees bent and the tongue lolling in his head.

He got up long enough to be knocked down again, this time with his dark unshaven face pushed in the sharp gravel of the resin.

Louis jumped away lightly, a bright and pleased look in his eyes, and as he did the white towel of surrender which Louis' handlers had refused to use two years ago tonight came sailing into the ring in a soggy mess. It was thrown by Max Machon, oblivious to the fact that fights cannot end this way in New York.

The referee snatched it off the floor and flung it backwards. It hit the ropes and hung there, limp as Schmeling. Donovan counted up to five over Max, sensed the futility of it all, and stopped the fight.

The big crowd began to rustle restlessly toward the exists, many only now accepting Louis as champion of the world. There were no eyes for Schmeling, sprawled on his stool in his corner.

He got up eventually, his dirty grey-and-black robe over his shoulders, and wormed through the happy little crowd that hovered around Louis. And he put his arm around the Negro and smiled. They both smiled and could afford to – for Louis had made around $200,000 a minute and Schmeling $100,000 a minute.

But once he crawled down in the belly of the big stadium, Schmeling realized the implications of his defeat. He, who won the title on a partly phony foul, and beat Louis two years ago with the aid of a crushing punch after the bell had sounded, now said Louis had fouled him. That would read better in Germany, whence earlier in the day had come a cable from Hitler, calling on him to win.

It was a low, sneaking trick, but a rather typical last word from Schmeling.

PEARL HARBOR: THE VIEW FROM THE JAPANESE COCKPIT, 7 December 1941

Taisa Mitsuo Fuchida, Imperial Japanese Naval Air Service

Fuchida led the strike force of 353 Japanese fighters and bombers that struck at Pearl Harbor at 7.49 a.m. on the sleepy Sunday morning of 7 December. The attack was launched from carriers 200 miles north of Oahu.

On the flight deck a green lamp was waved in a circle to signal "Take off!" The engine of the foremost fighter plane began to roar. With the ship still pitching and rolling, the plane started its run, slowly at first but with steadily increasing speed. Men lining the flight deck held their breath as the first plane took off successfully just before the ship took a downward pitch. The next plane was already moving forward. There were loud cheers as each plane rose into the air.

Thus did the first wave of 183 fighters, bombers, and torpedo planes take off from the six carriers. Within fifteen minutes they had all been launched and were forming up in the still-dark sky, guided only by signal lights of the lead planes. After one great circling over the fleet formation, the planes set course due south for Oahu Island and Pearl Harbor. It was 0615.

Under my direct command were 49 level bombers. About 500 meters to my right and slightly below me were 40 torpedo planes. The same distance to my left, but about 200 meters above me, were 51 dive bombers, and flying cover for the formation there were 43 fighters. These other three groups were led by Lieutenant Commanders Murata, Takahashi, and Itaya, respectively.

We flew through and over the thick clouds which were at 2000 meters, up to where day was ready to dawn. And the clouds began gradually to brighten below us after the brilliant sun burst into the eastern sky. I opened the cockpit canopy and looked back at the large formation of planes. The wings glittered in the bright morning sunlight.

The speedometer indicated 125 knots and we were favored by a tail wind. At 0700 I figured that we should reach Oahu in less than an hour. But flying over the clouds we could not see the surface of the water, and, consequently, had no check on our drift. I switched on the radio-direction finder to tune in the Honolulu radio station and soon picked up some light music. By turning the antenna I found the exact direction from which the broadcast was coming and corrected our course, which had been five degrees off.

Continuing to listen to the program, I was wondering how to get below the clouds after reaching Oahu. If the island was covered by thick clouds like those below us, the level bombing would be difficult; and we had not yet had reports from the reconnaissance planes.

In tuning the radio a little finer I heard, along with the music, what seemed to be a weather report. Holding my breath, I adjusted the dial and listened intently. Then I heard it come through a second time, slowly and distinctly: "Averaging partly cloudy, with clouds mostly over the mountains. Cloud base at 3500 feet. Visibility good. Wind north, 10 knots."

What a windfall for us! No matter how careful the planning, a more favorable situation could not have been imagined. Weather conditions over Pearl Harbor had been worrying me greatly, but now with this information I could turn my attention to other problems. Since Honolulu was only partly cloudy, there must be breaks in the clouds over the island. But since the clouds over the mountains were at 1000 meters altitude, it would not be wise to attack from the northeast, flying over the eastern mountains, as previously planned. The wind was north and visibility good. It would be better to pass to the west of the island and make our approach from the south.

. . . we had been in the air for about an hour and a half. It was time that we were seeing land, but there was only a solid layer of clouds below. All of a sudden the clouds broke, and a long white line of coast appeared. We were over Kahuku Point, the northern tip of the island, and now it was time for our deployment.

There were alternate plans for the attack: If we had surprise, the torpedo planes were to strike first, followed by the level bombers and then the dive bombers, which were to attack the air bases including Hickam and Ford Island near the anchorage. If these bases were first hit by the dive bombers, it was feared that the resultant smoke might hinder torpedo and level-bombing attacks on the ships.

On the other hand, if enemy resistance was expected, the dive bombers would attack first to cause confusion and attract enemy fire. Level bombers, coming next, were to bomb and destroy enemy anti-aircraft guns, followed by the torpedo planes which would attack the ships.

The selection of attack method was for my decision, to be indicated by signal pistol: one "black dragon" for a surprise attack, two "black dragons" if it appeared that surprise was lost. Upon either order the fighters were immediately to dash in as cover.

There was still no news from the reconnaissance planes, but I had made up my mind that we could make a surprise attack, and thereupon ordered the deployment by raising my signal pistol outside the canopy and firing one "black dragon." The time was 0740.

With this order dive bombers rose to 4000 meters, torpedo bombers went down almost to sea level, and level bombers came down just under the clouds. The only group that failed to deploy was the fighters. Flying above the rest of the formation, they seemed to have missed the signal because of the clouds. Realizing this I fired another shot toward the fighter group. This time they noticed the signal immediately and sped toward Oahu.

This second shot, however, was taken by the commander of the dive bomber group as the second of two "black dragons," signifying a non-surprise attack which would mean that his group should attack first, and this error served to confuse some of the pilots who had understood the original signal.

Meanwhile a reconnaissance report came in from *Chikuma*'s plane giving the locations of ten battleships, one heavy cruiser, and ten light cruisers in the harbor. It also reported a 14-meter wind from bearing 080, and clouds over the U.S. Fleet at 1700 meters with a scale 7 density. The *Tone* plane also reported that "the enemy fleet is not in Lahaina Anchorage." Now I knew for sure that there were no carriers in the harbor. The sky cleared as we moved in on the target and Pearl Harbor was plainly visible from the northwest valley of the island. I studied our objective through binoculars. They were there all right, all eight of them. "Notify all planes to launch attacks," I ordered my radio man who immediately began tapping the key. The order went in plain code: "*To, to, to, to. . . .*" The time was 0749.

When Lieutenant Commander Takahashi and his dive-bombing group mistook my signal, and thought we were making a non-surprise attack, his 53 planes lost no time in dashing forward. His command was divided into two groups: one led by himself which headed for Ford Island and Hickam Field, the other, led by Lieutenant Sakamoto, headed for Wheeler Field.

The dive bombers over Hickam Field saw heavy bombers lined up on the apron. Takahashi rolled his plane sharply and went into a dive, followed immediately by the rest of his planes, and the first bombs fell at Hickam. The next places hit were Ford Island and Wheeler Field. In a very short time huge billows of black smoke were rising from these bases. The lead torpedo planes were to have started their run to the Navy Yard from over Hickam, coming from south of the bay entrance. But the sudden burst of bombs at Hickam surprised Lieutenant Commander Murata who had understood that his torpedo planes were to have attacked first. Hence he took a short cut lest the smoke from those bases cover up his targets. Thus the first torpedo was actually launched some five minutes ahead of the scheduled 0800. The time of each attack was as follows:

> 0755 Dive bombers at Hickam and Wheeler
> 0757 Torpedo planes at battleships
> 0800 Fighters strafing air bases
> 0805 Level bombers at battleships

After issuance of the attack order, my level bomber group kept east of Oahu going past the southern tip of the island. On our left was the Barbers Point airfield, but, as we had been informed, there were no planes. Our information indicated that a powerful anti-aircraft battery was stationed there, but we saw no evidence of it.

I continued to watch the sky over the harbor and activities on the ground. None but Japanese planes were in the air, and there were no indications of air combat. Ships in the harbor still appeared to be asleep, and the Honolulu radio broadcast continued normally. I felt that surprise was now assured, and that my men would succeed in their missions.

Knowing that Admirals Nagumo, Yamamoto, and the General Staff were anxious about the attack, I decided that they should be informed. I ordered the following message sent to the fleet: "We have succeeded in making a surprise attack. Request you relay this report to Tokyo." The radio man reported shortly that the message had been received by *Akagi*.

The code for a successful surprise attack was "*Tora, tora, tora* . . ." Before *Akagi*'s relay of this message reached Japan, it was received by *Nagato* in Hiroshima Bay and the General Staff in Tokyo, directly from my plane! This was surely a long-distance record for such a low-powered transmission from an airplane, and might be attributed to the use of the word. "*Tora*" as our code. There is a Japanese saying, "A tiger (*tora*) goes out 1000 *ri* (2000 miles) and returns without fail."

I saw clouds of black smoke rising from Hickam and soon thereafter from Ford Island. This bothered me and I wondered what had happened. It was not long before I saw waterspouts rising alongside the battleships, followed by more and more waterspouts. It was time to launch our level bombing attacks so I ordered my pilot to bank sharply, which was the attack signal for the planes following us. All ten of my squadrons then formed into a single column with intervals of 200 meters. It was indeed a gorgeous formation.

The lead plane in each squadron was manned by a specially trained pilot and bombardier. The pilot and bombardier of my squadron had won numerous fleet contests and were considered the best in the Japanese Navy. I approved when Lieutenant Matsuzaki asked if the lead plane should trade positions with us, and he lifted our plane a little as a signal. The new leader came forward quickly, and I could see the smiling round face of the bombardier when he saluted. In returning the salute I entrusted the command to them for the bombing mission.

As my group made its bomb run, enemy anti-aircraft suddenly came to life. Dark gray bursts blossomed here and there until the sky was clouded with shattering near misses which made our plane tremble. Shipboard guns seemed to open fire before the shore batteries. I was startled by the rapidity of the counter-attack which came less than five minutes after the first bomb had fallen. Were it the Japanese Fleet, the reaction would not have been so quick, because although the Japanese character is suitable for offensives, it does not readily adjust to the defensive.

Suddenly the plane bounced as if struck by a huge club. "The fuselage is holed to port," reported the radio man behind me, "and a steering-control wire is damaged." I asked hurriedly if the plane was under control, and the pilot assured me that it was.

No sooner were we feeling relieved than another burst shook the plane. My squadron was headed for *Nevada*'s mooring at the northern end of battleship row on the east side of Ford Island. We were just passing over the bay entrance and it was almost time to release our bombs. It was not easy to pass through the concentrated anti-aircraft fire. Flying at only 3000 meters, it seemed that this might well be a date with eternity.

I further saw that it was not wise to have deployed in this long single-column formation. The whole level bomber group could be destroyed like ducks in a shooting gallery. It would also have been better if we had approached the targets from the direction of Diamond Head. But here we were at our targets and there was a job to be done.

It was now a matter of utmost importance to stay on course, and the lead plane kept to its line of flight like a homing pigeon. Ignoring the barrage of shells bursting around us, I concentrated on the bomb loaded under the lead plane, pulled the safety bolt from the bomb release lever and grasped the handle. It seemed as if time was standing still.

Again we were shaken terrifically and our planes were buffeted about. When I looked out the third plane of my group was abeam of us and I saw its bomb fall! That pilot had a reputation for being careless. In training his bomb releases were poorly timed, and he had often been cautioned.

I thought, "That damn fellow has done it again!" and shook my fist in his direction. But I soon realized that there was something wrong with his plane and he was losing gasoline. I wrote on a small blackboard, "What happened?" and held it toward his plane. He explained, "Underside of fuselage hit."

Now I saw his bomb cinch lines fluttering wildly, and sorry for having scolded him, I ordered that he return to the carrier. He answered, "Fuel tank destroyed, will follow you," asking permission to stay with the group. Knowing the feelings of the pilot and crew, I gave the permission, although I knew it was useless to try taking that crippled and bombless plane through the enemy fire. It was nearly time for bomb release when we ran into clouds which obscured the target, and I made out the round face of the lead bombardier who was waving his hands back and forth to indicate that we had passed the release point. Banking slightly we turned right toward Honolulu, and I studied the anti-aircraft fire, knowing that we would have to run through it again. It was now concentrated on the second squadron.

While circling for another try, I looked toward the area in which the bomb from the third plane had fallen. Just outside the bay entrance I saw a large water ring close by what looked like a destroyer. The ship seemed to be standing in a floating dock, attached to both sides of the entrance like a gate boat. I was suddenly reminded of the midget submarines which were to have entered the bay for a special attack.

At the time of our sortie I was aware of these midget submarines, but knew nothing of their characteristics, operational objectives, force organization, or the reason for their participation in the attack. In *Akagi,* Commander Shibuya, a staff officer in charge of submarine operations, had explained that they were to penetrate the harbor the night before our attack; but, no matter how good an opportunity might arise, they were not to strike until after the planes had done so.

Even now the submarines were probably concealed in the bay, awaiting the air attack. Had the entrance been left open, there would have been some opportunity for them to get out of the harbor. But in light of what I had just seen there seemed little chance of that, and, feeling now the bitterness of war, I vowed to do my best in the assigned mission.

While my group was circling over Honolulu for another bombing attempt, other groups made their runs, some making three tries before succeeding. Suddenly a colossal explosion occurred in battleship row. A huge column of dark red smoke rose to 1000 feet and a stiff shock wave reached our plane. I called the pilot's attention to the spectacle, and he observed, "Yes, Commander, the powder magazine must have exploded. Terrible indeed!" The attack was in full swing, and smoke from fires and explosions filled most of the sky over Pearl Harbor.

My group now entered on a bombing course again. Studying battleship row through binoculars, I saw that the big explosion had been on *Arizona.* She was still flaming fiercely and her smoke was covering *Nevada,* the target of my group. Since the heavy smoke would hinder our bomber accuracy, I looked for some other ship to attack. *Tennessee,* third in the left row, was already on fire; but next in row was *Maryland,* which had not yet been attacked. I gave an order changing our target to this ship, and once again we headed into the anti-aircraft fire. Then came the "ready" signal and I took a firm grip on the bomb release handle, holding my breath and staring at the bomb of the lead plane.

Pilots, observers, and radio men all shouted, "Release!" on seeing the bomb drop from the lead plane, and all the others let go their bombs. I immediately lay flat on the floor to watch the

fall of bombs through a peephole. Four bombs in perfect pattern
plummeted like devils of doom. The target was so far away that I
wondered for a moment if they would reach it. The bombs grew
smaller and smaller until I was holding my breath for fear of losing
them. I forgot everything in the thrill of watching the fall toward
the target. They become small as poppy seeds and finally disappeared just as tiny white flashes of smoke appeared on and near
the ship.

PEARL HARBOR: THE VIEW FROM THE GROUND, 7 December 1941

John Garcia, harbor worker

I was sixteen years old, employed as a pipe fitter apprentice at
Pearl Harbor Navy Yard. On 7 December 1941, oh, around 8.00
a.m., my grandmother woke me. She informed me that the
Japanese were bombing Pearl Harbor. I said, "They're just
practising." She said, no, it was real and the announcer is
requesting that all Pearl Harbor workers report to work. I went
out on the porch and I could see the anti-aircraft fire up in the sky.
I just said, "Oh boy."

I was four miles away. I got out on my motor-cycle and it took
me five, ten minutes to get there. It was a mess.

I was working on the USS *Shaw*. It was on a floating dry dock. It
was in flames. I started to go down into the pipe fitter's shop to get
my toolbox when another wave of Japanese came in. I got under a
set of concrete steps at the dry dock where the battleship *Pennsylvania* was. An officer came by and asked me to go into the
Pennsylvania and try to get the fires out. A bomb had penetrated
the marine deck, and that was three decks below. Under that was
the magazines: ammunition, powder, shells. I said, "There ain't no
way I'm gonna go down there." It could blow up any minute. I
was young and sixteen, not stupid, not at sixty-two cents an hour.
(Laughs.)

A week later, they brought me before a navy court. It was
determined that I was not service personnel and could not be
ordered. There was no martial law at the time. Because I was
sixteen and had gone into the water, the whole thing was dropped.

I was asked by some other officer to go into the water and get
sailors out that had been blown off the ships. Some were uncon-

scious, some were dead. So I spent the rest of the day swimming inside the harbour, along with some other Hawaiians. I brought out I don't know how many bodies and how many were alive and how many dead. Another man would put them into ambulances and they'd be gone. We worked all day at that . . .

The following morning, I went with my tools to the *West Virginia*. It had turned turtle, totally upside down. We found a number of men inside. The *Arizona* was a total washout. Also the *Utah*. There were men in there, too. We spent about a month cutting the superstructure of the *West Virginia*, tilting it back on its hull. About 300 men we cut out of there were still alive by the eighteenth day. It took two weeks to get all the fires out. We worked around the clock for three days. There was so much excitement and confusion. Some of our sailors were shooting five-inch guns at the Japanese planes. You just cannot down a plane with a five-inch shell. They were landing in Honolulu, the unexploded naval shells. They have a ten-mile range. They hurt and killed a lot of people in the city.

When I came back after the third day, they told me that a shell had hit the house of my girl. We had been going together for, oh, about three years. Her house was a few blocks from my place. At the time, they said it was a Japanese bomb. Later we learned it was an American shell. She was killed. She was preparing for church at the time.

Nearly 3,700 American soldiers, sailors, marines and civilians were lost at Pearl Harbor. Eighteen warships were sunk or damaged.

DEATH MARCH ON BATAAN: THE FIRST DAY, 10 April 1942

Lieutenant Colonel William Dyess, 21st Pursuit Squadron, USAAF

Despite the condition of the surrendered US troops at Bataan, their captors – led by General Homma – made them march 65 miles north to Camp O'Donnell. About 40,000 Americans and Filipinos died in the infamous "Death March on Bataan" and in the first two months of imprisonment at O'Donnell. It was one of the worst Japanese atrocities of World War II.

Ordinarily, the trip from Mariveles to Cabcaben field is a beautiful one with the grandeur of high greenclad mountains on the north and a view of the sea on the right. The white of the road contrasts pleasantly with the deep green of the tropical growth on either side.

But on this day there was no beauty. Coming toward us were seemingly interminable columns of Jap infantry, truck trains, and horse-drawn artillery, all moving into Bataan for a concentrated assault on Corregidor. They stirred up clouds of blinding dust in which all shape and form were lost.

Every few yards Jap noncoms materialized like gargoyles from the grayish white pall and snatched Americans out of line to be searched and beaten. Before we had gone two miles we had been stripped of practically all our personal possessions.

The Japs made no move to feed us. Few of us had had anything to eat since the morning of April 9. Many had tasted no food in four days. We had a little tepid water in our canteens, but nothing else.

The ditches on either side of the road were filled with overturned and wrecked American army trucks, fire-gutted tanks, and artillery our forces had rendered unusable. At intervals we saw mounds of captured food, bearing familiar trademarks. These had fallen almost undamaged into Jap hands.

As we marched along I rounded up the 110 officers and men of the 21st Pursuit. I didn't know yet what the score was, but I felt we would be in a better position to help one another and keep up morale if we were together.

We hadn't walked far when the rumor factory opened up. In a few minutes it was in mass production. There were all kinds of reports: We were going to Manila and Old Bilibid prison. We were going to San Fernando and entrain for a distant concentration camp. Trucks were waiting just ahead to pick us up. We doubted the last rumor, but hoped it was true.

The sun was nearing the zenith now. The penetrating heat seemed to search out and dissipate the small stores of strength remaining within us. The road, which until this moment had been fairly level, rose sharply in a zigzag grade. We were nearing Little Baguio.

I was marching with head down and eyes squinted for the dual purpose of protecting myself as much as possible from the dust and glare and keeping watch on the Jap guards who walked beside and among us. Halfway up the hill we reached a level stretch where a

Japanese senior officer and his staff were seated at a camp table upon which were spread maps and dispatches.

As I came abreast he saw me and shouted something that sounded like, "Yoy!" He extended his hand, palm downward, and opened and closed the fingers rapidly. This meant I was to approach him. I pretended I didn't see him. He shouted again as I kept on walking. His third "Yoy!" vibrated with anger. The next I knew a soldier snatched me out of line and shoved me toward the table.

"Name!" shouted the officer. He was staring at the wings and my uniform. "You fly?"

I told him my name without mentioning my rank and said I had been a pilot.

"Where you planes?"

"All shot down." I made a downward, spinning motion with my hand.

"No at Cebu? No at Mindanao?"

"No Cebu. No Mindanao."

"Yaah. Lie! We know you got planes. We see. Sometimes one . . . two . . . sometimes three, four, five. Where you airfields?"

I shook my head again and made the spinning motion with my hand. But I located the airfields for him on his map. I pointed to Cabcaben, Bataan, and Mariveles. He knew about these, of course. He made an impatient gesture.

"One more. Secret field!"

"Nope. No secret field."

"True?"

"Yes. True."

"Where are tunnel? Where are underwater tunnel from Mariveles to Corregidor? Where are tunnels on Corregidor Rock?" He held the map toward me.

"I don't know of any tunnels. No tunnels; no place. I never was on Corregidor. I was only at Nichols field and Bataan."

"You flying officer and you never at Corregidor Rock!" His eyes were slits. His staff officers were angry, too. "LIE!" he shrieked and jumped up.

He was powerfully built, as are most Jap officers. He seized my shoulder and whirled me around with a quick twist that almost dislocated my arm. Then came a violent shove that sent me staggering toward the line. I expected a bullet to follow the push, but I didn't dare look back. This would have been inviting them to shoot. As I reached the marching line, the officer shouted something else. The guards shoved me and motioned that I should catch up with my group.

I wanted to be with them, but the double quick up the hill in the scalding heat and dust almost finished me. I had the thought, too, that the guards I passed might get the idea I was trying to escape. My bullet expectancy was so high it made my backside tingle from scalp to heels. I caught up as we were passing through Little Baguio. In a short time we were abreast the blackened ruins of Hospital No. 1, which had been bombed heavily a couple of days before.

Among the charred debris, sick and wounded American soldiers were walking dazedly about. There was no place for them to go.

Their only clothes were hospital pajama suits and kimonos. Here and there a man was stumping about on one leg and a crutch. Some had lost one or both arms. All were in need of fresh dressings. And all obviously were suffering from the shock of the bombing.

They looked wonderingly at the column of prisoners. When the Jap officers saw them, these shattered Americans were rounded up and shoved into the marching line. All of them tried to walk, but only a few were able to keep it up. Those who fell were kicked aside by the Japs.

The Japs forbade us to help these men. Those who tried it were kicked, slugged, or jabbed with bayonet points by the guards who stalked with us in twos and threes.

For more than a mile these bomb-shocked cripples stumbled along with us. Their shoulders were bent and the sweat streamed from their faces. I can never forget the hopelessness in their eyes.

Eventually their strength ebbed and they began falling back through the marching ranks. I don't know what became of them.

About a mile east of the hospital we encountered a major traffic jam. On either side of the congested road hundreds of Jap soldiers were unloading ammunition and equipment.

Our contingent of more than 600 American and Filipino prisoners filtered through, giving the Japs as wide a berth as the limited space permitted. This was to avoid being searched, slugged, or pressed into duty as cargadores [burden carriers].

Through the swirling dust we could see a long line of trucks, standing bumper to bumper. There were hundreds of them. And every last one was an American make. I saw Fords – which predominated – Chevrolets, GMCs, and others.

These were not captured trucks. They bore Jap army insignia and had been landed from the ships of the invasion fleet. It is hard to describe what we felt at seeing these familiar American machines, filled with jeering, snarling Japs. It was a sort of super-sinking feeling. We had become accustomed to having American iron thrown at us by the Japs, but this was a little too much.

Eventually the road became so crowded we were marched into a clearing. Here, for two hours, we had our first taste of the oriental sun treatment, which drains the stamina and weakens the spirit.

The Japs seated us on the scorching ground, exposed to the full glare of the sun. Many of the Americans and Filipinos had no covering to protect their heads. I was beside a small bush, but it cast no shade because the sun was almost directly above us. Many of the men around me were ill.

When I thought I could stand the penetrating heat no longer, I was determined to have a sip of the tepid water in my canteen. I had no more than unscrewed the top when the aluminum flask was snatched from my hands. The Jap who had crept up behind me poured the water into a horse's nosebag, then threw down the canteen. He walked on among the prisoners, taking away their water and pouring it into the bag. When he had enough he gave it to his horse.

Whether by accident or design we had been put just across the road from a pile of canned and boxed food. We were famished, but it seemed worse than useless to ask the Japs for anything. An elderly American colonel did, however. He crossed the road and after pointing to the food and to the drooping prisoners, he went through the motions of eating.

A squat Jap officer grinned at him and picked up a can of salmon. Then he smashed it against the colonel's head, opening the American's cheek from eye to jawbone. The officer staggered and turned back toward us, wiping the blood off.

It seemed as though the Japs had been waiting for just such a brutal display to end the scene. They ordered us to our feet and herded us back into the road.

We knew now the Japs would respect neither age nor rank. Their ferocity grew as we marched on into the afternoon. They no longer were content with mauling stragglers or pricking them with bayonet points. The thrusts were intended to kill.

We had marched about a mile after the sun treatment when I stumbled over a man writhing in the hot dust of the road. He was a

Filipino soldier who had been bayoneted through the stomach. Within a quarter of a mile I walked past another. This soldier prisoner had been rolled into the path of the trucks and crushed beneath the heavy wheels.

The huddled and smashed figures beside the road eventually became commonplace to us. The human mind has an amazing faculty of adjusting itself to shock. In this case it may have been that heat and misery had numbed our senses. We remained keenly aware, however, that these murders might well be precursors of our own, if we should falter or lag.

As we straggled past Hospital No. 2 the Japs were setting up artillery and training it on Corregidor. The thick jungle hid the hospital itself, but we could see that guns were all around it. The Japs regarded this as master strategy; the Rock would not dare return their fire. I wondered what the concussion of the heavy guns would do to the stricken men in the hospital wards. The cannonade began after we had passed by.

A few minutes later a violent blow on the head almost sent me to my knees. I thought one of the Jap guns had made a direct hit on me. My steel helmet jammed down over my eyes with a clang that made my ears ring. I pulled it clear and staggered around to see a non-commissioned Jap brandishing a club the size of a child's baseball bat. He was squealing and pointing to the dented helmet. He lifted the club again. I threw the helmet into the ditch and he motioned me to march on. Like many of my comrades, I now was without protection against the merciless sun.

BABE RUTH HITS 47 (YEARS OLD), New York, 7 February 1942

Al Laney

It was Babe Ruth's birthday yesterday, and the great man got out of bed to receive his guests and submit to the photographs they still want to take of him. He has been ill with grippe for nearly three weeks and he was not really up to the usual birthday interviews, but he went through it in the same old way.

There were not so many reporters and photographers present in the rather luxurious apartment on Riverside Drive as there were a year ago. Every year there are fewer and no doubt one day the great man will sit alone in his splendor on February 7 and wait in vain for them to come. That day, however, has not come yet. There was quite a respectable turnout and they put the ailing Babe through a long workout.

He came into the tastefully furnished living room along the Drive in red silk lounging pajamas and minced along in that same ridiculous little walk of his that used to carry him up to the plate. He stopped in the middle of the room and rattled the windows with a Gargantuan cough that racked the barrel chest and caused him to collapse in an armchair. He took out the handkerchief that had been carefully folded into his jacket pocket and blew a blast through his broad blob of a nose. His eyes were glassy and feverish and anyone could see he felt terrible.

"I got the damnedest cold," he said in a squeaky voice. "Any you fellows want a drink or something? Nora! Bring me some orange juice. Big one. Can't shake it off. Usually takes me only a few days. It sure gets you, don't it? Well, I suppose I got to think up ideas for you guys as usual."

The Babe took a long swig of orange juice and began to brighten up a bit. Before long his voice came back to him and he talked in the same boyish direct way he has always talked. He told the photographers to go on in the bar and see if they could think up something new for a change. Then he just talked along.

He didn't say anything much. The Babe no longer gives out statements about re-entering baseball. He said he hadn't any plans. He was leaving last night with Mrs Ruth for North Conway, New Hampshire, where their daughter and her husband run an inn for skiers, and then in a couple of weeks he would go to Florida to bake out in the sun and play a little golf. He would get back to New York about the time the golf courses open up.

The Babe gave the impression that he has no great enthusiasm for this round of things that fill his life. He is really a simple man and it does not occur to him to try to conceal what he is thinking or feeling. He is a man of substance. His future is secure. But it appears that he is not a happy man. It appears that he thinks quite a lot about not having a job of work to do and worries some too, although he does not speak of these things any more.

"Both girls are married now," he said. "Sure miss those kids round here. We got fourteen rooms. It's too big."

The Babe got up and said to come on in the bar and see what those picture guys were up to. He was a little shaky on his legs and his face was flushed, but he posed for nearly an hour while they shot him from every conceivable angle. He had the maid bring in a huge birthday cake someone had sent him and fifty times without complaining he went through the act of cutting it.

The bar is a little room filled with the Babe's trophies and pictures and you could see that he loves it in there. It reminds him of the great days and he lives a lot in the past now. Pointing to a big frame on the wall inclosing sixty baseballs with a name and date on each one and a picture of the Babe in the middle, he said:

"I want to introduce you to some of my relatives. All cousins of mine."

The names on the baseballs were those of the pitchers off whom the Babe hit the sixty home runs in 1927.

The Babe is forty-seven years old and out of the limelight a long time as such things go. But he is still an altogether engaging fellow and a good deal of the old magic still clings to him. He has not changed much. His moon of a face is still ugly and maybe a little coarse, and when he grins he still seems like an impish but lovable child.

If he were still out there where they could see him the millions would still adore him. It is sad to think they are forgetting the Babe. He is still a great man. He came to the door and stood there in his red pajamas while the elevator was coming up to the fifteenth floor. Just before the door closed he said:

"See you fellows next year." And, after a pause, "I hope so."

"SEVENTH HEAVEN": A PORTRAIT OF HARLEM IN THE 1940s

Malcolm X

Malcolm X (born Malcolm Little), 1925–65.

I went along with the railroad job for my own reasons. For a long time I'd wanted to visit New York City. Since I had been in Roxbury, I had heard a lot about "the Big Apple", as it was called by the well-traveled musicians, merchant mariners, salesmen, chauffeurs for white families, and various kinds of hustlers I ran into. Even as far back as Lansing, I had been hearing about how fabulous New York was, and especially Harlem. In fact, my father had described Harlem with pride, and showed us pictures of the huge parades by the Harlem followers of Marcus Garvey. And every time Joe Louis won a fight against a white opponent, big front-page pictures in the Negro newspapers such as the *Chicago Defender*, the *Pittsburgh Courier* and the *Afro-American* showed a sea of Harlem Negroes cheering and waving and the Brown Bomber waving back at them from the balcony of Harlem's Theresa Hotel. Everything I'd ever heard about New York City was exciting – things like Broadway's bright lights and the Savoy Ballroom and Apollo Theater in Harlem, where great bands played and famous songs and dance steps and Negro stars originated. After a few of the Washington runs, I snatched the chance when one day personnel said I could temporarily replace a sandwich man on the "Yankee Clipper" to New York. I was into my zoot suit before the first passenger got off.

The cooks took me up to Harlem in a cab. White New York passed by like a movie set, then abruptly, when we left Central Park at the upper end, at 110th Street, the people's complexion began to change.

Busy Seventh Avenue ran along in front of a place called Small's Paradise. The crew had told me before we left Boston that it was their favorite night spot in Harlem, and not to miss it. No Negro place of business had ever impressed me so much. Around the big, luxurious-looking, circular bar were thirty or forty Negroes, mostly men, drinking and talking.

I was hit first, I think, by their conservative clothes and manners. Wherever I'd seen as many as ten Boston Negroes – let alone Lansing Negroes – drinking, there had been a big noise. But with all of these Harlemites drinking and talking, there was just a low murmur of sound. Customers came and went. The bartenders knew what most of them drank and automatically fixed it. A bottle was set on the bar before some.

Every Negro I'd ever known had made a point of flashing whatever money he had. But these Harlem Negroes quietly laid a bill on the bar. They drank. They nonchalantly nodded to the bartender to pour a drink, for some friend, while the bartenders, smooth as any of the customers, kept making change from the money on the bar.

Their manners seemed natural; they were not putting on any airs. I was awed. Within the first five minutes in Small's, I had left Boston and Roxbury forever.

I didn't yet know that these weren't what you might call everyday or average Harlem Negroes. Later on, even later that night, I would find out that Harlem contained hundreds of

thousands of my people who were just as loud and gaudy as
Negroes anywhere else. But these were the cream of the older,
more mature operators in Harlem. The day's "numbers" business
was done. The night's gambling and other forms of hustling hadn't
yet begun. The usual night-life crowd, who worked on regular jobs
all day, were at home eating their dinners. The hustlers at this time
were in the daily six o'clock congregation, their favorite bars all
over Harlem largely to themselves.

From Small's, I taxied over to the Apollo Theater. (I remember
so well that Jay McShann's band was playing, because his vocalist
was later my close friend, Walter Brown, the one who used to sing
"Hooty Hooty Blues".) From there, on the other side of 125th
Street, at Seventh Avenue, I saw the big, tall, gray Theresa Hotel.
It was the finest in New York City where Negroes could then stay,
years before the downtown hotels would accept the black man.
(The Theresa is now best known as the place where Fidel Castro
went during his UN visit, and achieved a psychological coup over
the US State Department when it confined him to Manhattan,
never dreaming that he'd stay uptown in Harlem and make such
an impression among the Negroes.)

The Braddock Hotel was just up 126th Street, near the Apollo's
backstage entrance. I knew its bar was famous as a Negro celebrity
hang-out. I walked in and saw, along that jam-packed bar, such
famous stars as Dizzy Gillespie, Billy Eckstine, Billie Holiday, Ella
Fitzgerald, and Dinah Washington.

As Dinah Washington was leaving with some friends, I overheard someone say she was on her way to the Savoy Ballroom
where Lionel Hampton was appearing that night – she was then
Hamp's vocalist. The ballroom made the Roseland in Boston look
small and shabby by comparison. And the lindy-hopping there
matched the size and elegance of the place. Hampton's hard-
driving outfit kept a red-hot pace with his greats such as Arnett
Cobb, Illinois Jacquet, Dexter Gordon, Alvin Hayse, Joe Newman, and George Jenkins. I went a couple of rounds on the floor
with girls from the sidelines.

Probably a third of the sideline booths were filled with white
people, mostly just watching the Negroes dance; but some of them
danced together, and, as in Boston, a few white women were with
Negroes. The people kept shouting for Hamp's "Flyin' Home",
and finally he did it. (I could believe the story I'd heard in Boston
about this number – that once in the Apollo, Hamp's "Flyin'

Home" had made some reefer-smoking Negro in the second
balcony believe he could fly, so he tried – and jumped – and
broke his leg, an event later immortalized in song when Earl Hines
wrote a hit tune called "Second Balcony Jump".) I had never seen
such fever-heat dancing. After a couple of slow numbers cooled the
place off, they brought on Dinah Washington. When she did her
"Salty Papa Blues", those people just about tore the Savoy roof off.
(Poor Dinah's funeral was held not long ago in Chicago. I read
that over 20,000 people viewed her body, and I should have been
there myself. Poor Dinah! We became great friends, back in those
days.)

But this night of my first visit was Kitchen Mechanics' Night at
the Savoy, the traditional Thursday night off for domestics. I'd say
there were twice as many women as men in there, not only kitchen
workers and maids, but also war wives and defense-worker women,
lonely and looking. Out in the street, when I left the ballroom, I
heard a prostitute cursing bitterly that the professionals couldn't
do any business because of the amateurs.

Up and down along and between Lenox and Seventh and
Eighth Avenues, Harlem was like some technicolor bazaar. Hundreds of Negro soldiers and sailors, gawking and young like me,
passed by. Harlem by now was officially off limits to white servicemen. There had already been some muggings and robberies, and
several white servicemen had been found murdered. The police
were also trying to discourage white civilians from coming uptown,
but those who wanted to still did. Every man without a woman on
his arm was being "worked" by the prostitutes. "Baby, wanna
have some fun?" The pimps would sidle up close, stage-whispering,
"All kinds of women, Jack – want a white woman?" And the
hustlers were merchandising: "Hundred dollar ring, man, diamond; ninety-dollar watch, too – look at'em. Take 'em both for
twenty-five."

In another two years, I could have given them all lessons. But
that night, I was mesmerized. This world was where I belonged.
On that night I had started on my way to becoming a Harlemite. I
was going to become one of the most depraved parasitical hustlers
among New York's eight million people – four million of whom
work, and the other four million of whom live off them. Every
layover night in Harlem, I ran and explored new places. I first got
a room at the Harlem YMCA, because it was less than a block
from Small's Paradise. Then, I got a cheaper room at Mrs Fisher's

rooming house which was close to the YMCA. Most of the railroad men stayed at Mrs Fisher's. I combed not only the bright-light areas, but Harlem's residential areas from best to worst, from Sugar Hill up near the Polo Grounds, where many famous celebrities lived, down to the slum blocks of old rat-trap apartment houses, just crawling with everything you could mention that was illegal and immoral. Dirt, garbage cans overflowing or kicked over; drunks, dope addicts, beggars. Sleazy bars, storefront churches with gospels being shouted inside, "bargain" stores, hockshops, undertaking parlours. Greasy "home-cooking" restaurants, beauty shops smoky inside from Negro women's hair getting fried, barbershops advertising conk experts. Cadillacs, secondhand and new, conspicuous among the cars on the streets.

All of it was Lansing's West Side or Roxbury's South End magnified a thousand times. Little basement dance halls with "For Rent" signs on them. People offering you little cards advertising "rent-raising parties". I went to one of these – thirty or forty Negroes sweating, eating, drinking, dancing, and gambling in a jammed, beat-up apartment, the record player going full blast, the fried chicken or chitlins with potato salad and collard greens for a dollar a plate, and cans of beer or shots of liquor for fifty cents. Negro and white canvassers sidled up alongside you, talking fast as they tried to get you to buy a copy of the *Daily Worker:* "This paper's trying to keep your rent controlled . . . Make that greedy landlord kill them rats in your apartment . . . This paper represents the only political party that ever ran a black man for the Vice Presidency of the United States . . . Just want you to read, won't take but a little of your time . . . Who do you think fought the hardest to help free those Scottsboro boys?" Things I overheard among Negroes when the salesmen were around let me know that the paper somehow was tied in with the Russians, but to my sterile mind in those early days, it didn't mean much; the radio broadcasts and the newspapers were then full of our-ally-Russia, a strong, muscular people, peasants, with their backs to the wall helping America to fight Hitler and Mussolini.

But New York was heaven to me. And Harlem was Seventh Heaven!

TALES OF THE SOUTH PACIFIC: A GI WRITES HOME, March 1942–January 1943

Sergeant B. J. Kazazkow, US Army

March 21, 1942

Dear Mom:

We just enjoyed a very mild hurricane – the only damage done being the countryside made ideal for the growth of hordes of mosquitoes. I hate them so that when I manage to get one alive. I torture and maim him – then bury him alive. The war has made me hard and cruel!

Now for the local news – the sun beats down – as usual – and when it gets hot enough – a nice cool shower comes along. Between the incessant combination everything I own, either rusts, or turns greenmoldy. Constant cleaning of equipment is, therefore, in order.

Sept. 22, 1942

Dear Mom:

Today a big vicious sea bass, mouth agape, sped like a bullet upon his prey, a small mallett. As he sped into range, I held my breath, squeezed, and then let fly. Stunned, he turned to go – and crash! I let him have another charge – and lo and behold we had fish steak – baked, garnished, and savory, for dinner. I tell you, this place is a fisherman's paradise. So what? It isn't the first fish dinner we blasted out of the sea, but never before a sea bass, the size and taste of that one.

Some days ago I spent a solid day up in the nearby hills, trying to chase a deer or two – being anxious for a taste of venison again. All day, mind you, and got not a scent. Yesterday morning, with breakfast on the fire, two of the elusive creatures popped up in a nearby pasture – grazing to their hearts content – so-o we sneaked up on them, and fell upon them, blazing away, and got not a hit – they led us a merry chase, finally we lost them, and went back to our French toast, cereal and coffee. No vension. Deah, Deah!

Sounds more like a rich man's holiday than a war – no? Feeling top-hole, hope you are too.

Love and kisses,
Benny

Jan. 8, 1943

Dear Mom:

So its come – 1943, imagine being overseas for nearly a whole year – or at least it will be on January 23rd. On that day last winter we left New York – for parts unknown. We could have ended up in a much worse place, believe me. And time has flown, more rapidly than I ever thought possible, it seems like several weeks, instead of twelve months, since we landed.

And we landed looking for trouble, and we're still looking – and I don't think we'll ever find any here.

The past few nights I haven't been sleeping well, and I keep having dreams about you and home, and it's no good for my morale. I get very homesick, poor boy that I am.

. . . I suppose I'll visit you again, in my dreams tonight, and you might leave some milk and cake on the table for me

Goodnight . . .

> Your loving son,
> Benny

RAID ON TOKYO, 18 April 1942

Colonel James Doolittle, USAAF

The bombing of Tokyo was an act of American defiance in the face of relentless Japanese advance in the Pacific. It was also a feat of airmanship, since it involved flying B-25 bombers off an aircraft carrier (the USS *Hornet*), something widely considered to be impossible. The raid was led by Colonel Doolittle, whose personal report is below.

Took off at 8:18 AM ship time.

Take-off was easy. Night take-off would have been possible and practicable.

Circled carrier to get exact heading and check compass. Wind was from 300° plus-minus.

About a half hour later joined by AC 40–2292, Lt. Hoover, pilot, the second plane to take off.

About an hour out passed a Japanese camouflaged naval surface vessel of about 6,000 tons. Took it to be a light cruiser.

About two hours out passed a multi-motored land plane headed directly for our flotilla and flying at about 3,000 ft.-2 miles away – multi-motored bomber-gunner.

Passed and endeavored to avoid various civil and naval craft until land fall was made north of Grubo Shama(?).

Was somewhat north of desired course but decided to take advantage of error and approach from a northerly direction, thus avoiding anticipated strong opposition to the west.

Many flying fields and the air full of planes north of Tokyo. Mostly small biplanes apparently primary or basic trainers.

Encountered nine fighters in three flights of three. This was about ten miles north of the outskirts of Tokyo proper.

All this time had been flying as low as the terrain would permit.

Continued low flying due south over the outskirts of and toward the east center of Tokyo.

Pulled up to 1,200 ft., changed course to the southwest and incendiary-bombed highly inflammable section. Dropped first bomb at 1:30.

Anti-aircraft very active but only one near hit.

Lowered away to housetops and slid over western outskirts into low haze and smoke.

Turned south and out to sea.

Fewer airports on west side but many army posts.

Passed over small aircraft factory with a dozen or more newly completed planes on the line. No bombs left. Decided not to machine gun for reasons of personal security.

Had seen five barrage balloons over east central Tokyo and more in distance.

Passed on out to sea flying low.

Was soon joined again by Hoover who followed us to the Chinese coast.

Navigator plotted perfect course to pass north of Yoki Shima.

Saw three large naval vessels just before passing west end of Japan. One was flatter than the others and may have been a converted carrier.

Passed innumerable fishing and small patrol boats.

Made land fall somewhat north of course on China coast.

Tried to reach Chuchow on 4495 but couldn't raise.

It had been clear over Tokyo but became overcast before reaching Yoki Shima.

Ceiling lowered on coast until low islands and hills were in it. Just getting dark and couldn't live under overcast so pulled up to 6,000 and then 8,000 ft. in it. On instruments from then on though occasionally saw dim lights on ground through almost solid overcast. These lights seemed more often on our right and pulled us still farther off course.

Directed rear gunner to go aft and secure films from camera (unfortunately they were jerked out of his shirt front where he had put them, when his chute opened).

Decided to abandon ship. Sgt. Braemer, Lt. Potter, Sgt. Leonard and Lt. Cole in order. Left ship on A.F.C.E., shut off both gas cocks and I left. *Should have put flaps down*. This would have slowed down landing speed, reduced impact and shortened glide.

All hands collected and ship located by late afternoon of 19th.

Requested General Ho Yang Ling, Director of the Branch Government of Western Chekiang Province to have a lookout kept along the seacoast from Hang Chow bay to Wen Chow bay and also have all sampans and junks along the coast keep a lookout for planes that went down at sea, or just reached shore.

Early morning of 20th four planes and crews, in addition to ours, had been located and I wired General Arnold, through the Embassy at Chungking, "Tokyo successfully bombed. Due bad weather on China Coast believe all airplanes wrecked. Five crews found safe in China so far."

Wired again on the 27th giving more details.

Discussed possibility of purchasing three prisoners on the seacoast from Puppet Government and endeavoring to take out the three in the lake area by force. Believe this desire was made clear to General Ku Cho-tung (who spoke little English) and know it was made clear to English-speaking members of his staff. This was at Shangjao. They agreed to try purchase of three but recommended against force due to large Japanese concentration.

Left airplane about 9:20 (ship time) after about 13 hours in the air. Still had enough gas for half hour flight but right front tank was showing empty. Had transferred once as right engine used more fuel. Had covered about 2,250 miles. Mostly at low speed, cruising but about an hour at moderate high speed which more than doubled the consumption for this time.

Bad luck:
(1) Early take-off due to naval contact with surface and air craft.
(2) Clear over Tokyo.
(3) Foul over China.

Good luck:
(1) A 25 m/h tail wind over most of the last 1,200 miles.

Take-off should have been made three hours before daylight, but we didn't know how easy it would be and the Navy didn't want to light up.

Dawn take-off, closer in, would have been better as things turned out. However, due to the bad weather it is questionable if even daylight landing could have been made at Chuchow without radio aid.

Still feel that original plan of having one plane take off three hours before dusk and others just at dusk was best all-round plan for average conditions.

Other ideas and impressions were discussed personally with Col. Cooper.

Should have kept accurate chronological record.

Should have all crew members instructed in *exact* method of leaving ship under various conditions.

JAMES H. DOOLITTLE
Airplane AC 40-2344-B-25-B

HOME FRONT: "JIM CROW" IN THE ARMY, 13 May 1942

Private Milton Adams, 240 Quarter Master's Battalion

Adams writes to Warren Hastie, the US Government's adviser on "Colored Affairs".

Pvt. Milton, Adams
Post Stockade
Camp Livingston, La.
May 13, 1942

Dear Mr. W. H. Hastie:

I am private Milton Adams of Co. B. 240th Q. M. Bn of Camp Livingston, La. I inlisted in the army Oct 17, 1942, in Chicago, Ill. And since I been in the Army, I never had any Trouble in the Army in or out of it in my life, until I came to Camp Livingston. I am asking for the help of the N.A.A.C.P. And the Crisis. I am not writing anything against the United States Army. But I am going to tell you what the White officers are doing to us races Soldiers down her in camp Livingston, La. Since they can't very well hang us, they take the next steps, which is court martial, and that is better know as rail-roading. Now you don't stand a chance, before them. They are just like a lynch mob with a neggro to hang. Well they do not want you down hear in the Army, and I did not ask to come down hear I was sent down hear. Well my trouble starter when they found out that I was from Chicago, and I have had a bad deal every since I been hear, I have tried to get away from hear, But it was the same old story. When we finde some places for you to go, we will let you go. Well my Commanding Officer did not like me because, I ask him not to use the word niggers, and he saide I was one of those smart nigger from up north. I was tried once for a offince, and given 30 days and a $12.00 fine. Now after I had finish my sentences, they saide they are going to try me over again. I wish you would look into my case. I thought they could not try any person a second time for the same offince. I really taken all the punishment I can take I could not get a three day pass or a furlo since I been in the army, until my mother pass away in April. They have just about rob me out of very pay day, for things I have never had. There are so many more case like this, a unfair chance. I don't know what to do now. I don't want do the wrong thing, so I am asking for help. But I am not going to take any more of these unfair trials, because I did three months in the stockade once for something I did not have any thing to do with. It was because I was from Chicago, and thats way every trial I ever had is base on the fact that I come from Chicago. So I whish you look into this case, because I can prove everything I am telling you. I will look forward to a answer from you in few days.

Respectfully yours,
Pvt. Milton Adams
Post Stockade
Camp Livingston, La.

BATTLE OF MIDWAY: ONE MAN'S DIARY, 4 June 1942

Robert J. Casey, war correspondent

The naval struggle between Japan and the USA for the Pacific waves culminated at Midway in the Hawaiian archipelago. It was the first sea battle in which the opposing fleets never saw each other: the fighting was done by carrier-based aircraft.

JUNE 4, *Thursday*. North of Midway Islands.

1:00. Just learned that the Army planes from Midway located another part of the Jap invasion force late Wednesday afternoon.

6:00. I got up for reveille and looked out at a clotted sky, a black sea and odd gray moonlight.

8:45. I'm beginning to have a great deal of respect for Admiral Spruance who is conducting this expedition. It is getting more and more apparent as we steam toward the west that we haven't been detected . . . It's a miracle but that seems to be the way of it.

We have an inferior force. It's probably one of the largest the United States ever sent anywhere in a gesture of anger but what of it. About half the Jap navy – and not the worst end of it – is out there ahead.

9:10. We make a right-angle turn. The wind stiffens, if that were possible, and the SBD's and STB's go off.

It's much too windy for me to hear what's being said in sky control so I don't know whether or not any contact has been made with the Japs. Anyway the haul isn't too far for these planes if they have to go all the way to Midway. It's comforting to see them up and something of a relief, too. It won't be long now one way or the other and if anything's coming to us we'll soon know it. If we don't get the Jap he'll certainly get us.

From the signal yards the flags come down and the flags go up – red, yellow, blue, white, crossed, striped, checkered. Lads are running up and down the ladders of the foremast with dispatch blanks in their hands. It's all spectacular and beginning to be thrilling.

10:30. We go into a terrific lateral-pass maneuver and the ships start running across each other's bows. Donald Duck raises his voice: "Antiaircraft stations stand by to repel attack."

I go back to my place on the foremast. Then comes the usual wait and study of the sky. You can't help but think that this fine day which you were finding so useful to our bombers is going to be just as helpful to Hirohito's bombers.

10:35. Usual reports of approaching aircraft . . . "Unidentified plane, bearing three-three-eight – forty-eight thousand." "Unidentified plane bearing two-seven-oh – fifty-two thousand . . ." Everybody is tense of course because sometimes these hysterical shouts turn out to make sense.

We are now leading the procession abreast of the cans. A cruiser

– a floating arsenal of ack-ack – has come over alongside our old carrier.

10:45 Ten planes show up off the starboard bow. They may be the *Yorktown*'s SBD's. As we glower at them we get the answer – the step pyramid of the *Yorktown*'s bridge structure comes up over the horizon. More planes are reported but the *Yorktown* claims them for her own and we withdraw from the contest.

We are still plowing along at top speed. On the lower decks the roar of the engines is so great that you have to shout to be heard a few feet. The cans, if we keep on at this rate, will have to refuel tonight. One lone gooney is sailing along with us easily and hopefully.

At the moment the carrier nearest us has sent out fighters, dive bombers, and torpedo planes. If the *Yorktown* has contributed as many as our old carrier, there ought to be about 180 planes on the way to the attack, 105 of them bombers or torpedo carriers.

11:15. A report has come in that one of our fortresses has attacked and damaged a carrier, presumably in the reserve group. The attack on Midway has been driven off – eight planes shot down over the island, the Marines claiming a bag of thirty off shore.

It's odd how the battle is shaping up to fit the specifications of the story the medical colonel told me when we went into Honolulu after the Coral Sea. The colonel said that the fight had already occurred. I said it hadn't. Nature as usual is imitating art.

11:35. We head now into the wind and it's very chilly. Some fighter planes are coming in, presumably part of our protective patrol. Against the sky they tumble along like a cloud of May flies. We're making crochet patterns all over the sea again.

11:40. There is some contact off the starboard quarter. Maybe that's why the fighters came in. They shoot over the rim of the sea and we continue our cotillion.

I'm getting sleepy. A gray half-moon hanging belatedly in the thin blue sky reminds me so much of myself.

11:45. Fighters come back to land on our carrier. Apparently a false alarm.

12:00. Mickey Reeves signaled me to come down to the bridge for a sandwich. So I was right at headquarters when first reports began to come in from our planes. The first message was brief. The Jap carriers had been located, a little belatedly, and they were virtually without air cover . . . Apparently all their planes had been sent out to make the conquest of Midway quick and easy. However, the squadron commander of the TBD unit reporting, said that his planes were virtually out of fuel.

"Request permission," he called, "to withdraw from action and refuel." The admiral's answer was terse.

"Attack at once."

So as I sat down in the chartroom to bite into a ham sandwich, the planes had begun to move in on the carriers. Whatever might be the result, we'd never be able to criticize the quality of our opportunity . . .

I sat there thinking. The Jap air admiral undoubtedly had figured us as permanent fixtures in the southwest Pacific where last he had had word of us. So just about now he'd be looking up at the sky suddenly clouded with SBD's and asking himself the Japanese equivalent of "Where the hell did those things come from?"

12:45. Enemy planes reported off port at twelve miles. New alert sounds. The kids drop their food and sidle off to their guns. The Grummans once more leap off our carrier.

1:00. Still no sign of the visitors. I guess the contact was another of those phonies that breed so rapidly in times like this.

1:15. Fifteen of the —'s bombers come over. The squadron is intact and in tight formation, its work, whatever it was, finished.

1:20. The carriers swing around, apparently getting ready to take on returning planes which are now showing up in two's and three's. Everything is set to repel an attack, and with good reason. If these planes have failed in their mission or fought a draw or left the Jap carriers usable we may expect a quick and vicious attack in return. If by some remote juju we have put all four carriers out of commission we have just about gained mastery of the Pacific including the Japanese side of the international date line, or so the more educated of my spies tell me.

I went back to the wardroom and contemplated this phenomenon. Presently the word filtered back to us that the attack had been a complete success. All the carriers had been hit and severely damaged. At least three of them were burning. One, apparently, had been sunk in the first two or three minutes of the engagement.

One battleship of the north group of the force that we had attacked was afire. A second battleship had been hit. Reports from the Army told of hits on two more battleships and another carrier, Discounting these messages to the fullest extent and recognizing how easy it is for one observer to duplicate the report of another, it was still obvious that we had had something of a field day, still obvious that the bulk of Japan's attacking planes must presently be going into the drink for want of any other place to land.

June 6, Saturday. At sea west of Midway. Sunny. Calm. Warmer.

It is estimated on the basis of today's reports that between 18,000 and 20,000 men were killed in this brief battle. While we aren't wasting too much sympathy on our enemy at the moment, we are awed by the catastrophe that overtook him. There is chill in the thought that there, but for the Grace of God, go we. Had we been seen . . . Had the Japs attacked us before making the try for Midway . . .

MIDWAY: THE DECISIVE FIVE MINUTES, 4 June 1942

Taisa Mitsuo Fuchida, Imperial Japanese Naval Air Service

As our fighters ran out of ammunition during the fierce battle they returned to the carriers for replenishment, but few ran low on fuel. Service crews cheered the returning pilots, patted them on the shoulder, and shouted words of encouragement. As soon as a plane was ready again the pilot nodded, pushed forward the throttle, and roared back into the sky. This scene was repeated time and again as the desperate air struggle continued.

Preparations for a counter-strike against the enemy had continued on board our four carriers throughout the enemy torpedo attacks. One after another, planes were hoisted from the hangar and quickly arranged on the flight deck. There was no time to lose. At 10:20 Admiral Nagumo gave the order to launch when ready. On *Akagi's* flight deck all planes were in position with engines warming up. The big ship began turning into the wind. Within five minutes all her planes would be launched.

Five minutes! Who would have dreamed that the tide of battle would shift completely in that brief interval of time?

Visibility was good. Clouds were gathering at about 3,000 metres, however, and though there were occasional breaks, they afforded good concealment for approaching enemy planes. At 10.24 the order to start launching came from the bridge by voice-tube. The Air Officer flapped a white flag, and the first

Zero fighter gathered speed and whizzed off the deck. At that instant a look-out screamed: "Hell-Divers!" I looked up to see three black enemy planes plummeting towards our ship. Some of our machine-guns managed to fire a few frantic bursts at them, but it was too late. The plump silhouettes of the American Dauntless dive-bombers quickly grew larger, and then a number of black objects suddenly floated eerily from their wings. Bombs! Down they came straight towards me! I fell intuitively to the deck and crawled behind a command post mantelet.

The terrifying scream of the dive-bombers reached me first, followed by the crashing explosion of a direct hit. There was a blinding flash and then a second explosion, much louder than the first. I was shaken by a weird blast of warm air. There was still another shock, but less severe, apparently a near-miss. Then followed a startling quiet as the barking of guns suddenly ceased. I got up and looked at the sky. The enemy planes were already gone from sight.

The attackers had got in unimpeded because our fighters, which had engaged the preceding wave of torpedo planes only a few moments earlier, had not yet had time to regain altitude. Consequently, it may be said that the American dive-bombers' success was made possible by the earlier martyrdom of their torpedo planes. Also, our carriers had no time to evade because clouds hid the enemy's approach until he dived down to the attack. We had been caught flat-footed in the most vulnerable condition possible – decks loaded with planes armed and fuelled for an attack.

Looking about, I was horrified at the destruction that had been wrought in a matter of seconds. There was a huge hole in the flight deck just behind the amidship elevator. The elevator itself, twisted like molten glass, was dropping into the hangar. Deck plates reeled upwards in grotesque configurations, planes stood tail up, belching livid flame and jet-black smoke. Reluctant tears streamed down my cheeks as I watched the fires spread, and I was terrified at the prospect of induced explosions which would surely doom the ship. I heard Masuda yelling, "Inside! Get inside! Everybody who isn't working! Get inside!"

Unable to help, I staggered down a ladder and into the ready room. It was already jammed with badly burned victims from the hangar deck. A new explosion was followed quickly by several more, each causing the bridge structure to tremble. Smoke from the burning hangar gushed through passageways and into the bridge and ready room, forcing us to seek other refuge. Climbing back to the bridge, I could see that *Kaga* and *Soryu* had also been hit and were giving off heavy columns of black smoke. The scene was horrible to behold.

Akagi had taken two direct hits, one on the after rim of the amidship elevator, the other on the rear guard on the port side of the flight deck. Normally, neither would have been fatal to the giant carrier, but induced explosions of fuel and munitions devastated whole sections of the ship, shaking the bridge and filling the air with deadly splinters. As fire spread among the planes lined up wing to wing on the after flight deck, their torpedoes began to explode, making it impossible to bring the fires under control. The entire hangar area was a blazing inferno, and the flames moved swiftly towards the bridge.

Midway cost the Americans the carrier *Yorktown* and 147 planes; the Japanese lost four carriers and a similar number of aircraft. The tide of war in the Pacific was now against the Japanese.

HOME FRONT: INTERNMENT OF JAPANESE AMERICANS, 1943

Iwao Matsushita

Fort Missoula, Montana
Jan. 2, 1943

The Honorable Francis Biddle,
Attorney General,
Washington, D.C.
Dear Mr Biddle,
I, Iwao Matsushita, an alien Japanese, have been detained in Fort Missoula, since Dec. 28, 1941, and I was recently notified about my internment order, despite the fact the Hearing Board made a recommendation for my release.

Since I read your article in a magazine last spring, regarding your policy of treating "alien enemies" – the words, you mentioned, you even didn't like to use – you have been occupying the innermost shrine of my heart as my only refuge and savior. So when I received your internment order, I was naturally greatly disappointed, because according to your interpretation in the magazine, you intern only those aliens whom you consider to be potentially dangerous to the public safety.

Now, my conscience urges me to make a personal heart-to-heart appeal to you. Kindly allow me to make a brief statement about myself.

I was born a Christian in a Methodist minister's family, educated in an American Mission School, came to this country in 1919 from sheer admiration of the American way of life. I have always been living, almost half and best part of my life, in Seattle, Wash . . . and never went to Japan for the last twenty-four years, despite the fact there were many such opportunities, simply because I liked this country, and the principles on which it stands.

I have never broken any Federal, State, Municipal, or even traffic laws, and paid taxes regularly. I believe myself one of the most upright persons. I have never been, am not, and will never be potentially dangerous to the safety of the United States. There isn't an iota of dangerous elements in me, nor should there be any such evidence against me.

On the contrary I have done much good to the American public. For instance, several years ago, I taught Japanese Language in the University of Washington, Seattle, without any compensation to help out the institution, which couldn't get appropriation for that purpose from the State. I might prove to be of some service in this capacity.

I am quite sure that my life history and my statement regarding loyalty in the hearing record will certainly convince you that I am a bona fide loyal resident.

My wife, with whom I have never been separated even for a short time during the last twenty-five years, and who has the same loyalty and admiration for this country, is living helplessly and sorrowfully in Idaho Relocation Center. You are the only person who can make us join in happiness and let us continue to enjoy the American life.

Therefore, please give my case your special reconsideration and let me anticipate your favorable answer.

Yours respectfully,
Iwao Matsushita

HOME FRONT: RACHEL THE RIVETER,
San Diego, 1943

Rachel Wray, hand riveter, Consolidated Aircraft

I grew up on a farm in northeastern Oklahoma, knowing nothing
but the Depression. My father lost the farm, and we moved to town
just when I was starting junior high school. I lived there until the
eleventh grade, when I was forced to quit school to go to work.

When I was nineteen I fell in love with a boy from Oklahoma.
George was also from a depressed area and joined the Navy to get
ahead. He was stationed in California, and I decided to come and
join him. I felt there would be more opportunity in California, and
I was determined that I was going to have a different life.

I had twenty-five dollars when I left Oklahoma. I answered an
ad in the paper looking for riders to California and paid twelve
dollars for the trip. I arrived here with twelve dollars to my name
and lived with friends until I could get work.

I got a job as a pastry cook at a restaurant in Whittier, a very
exclusive place. I was making fifteen dollars (and board) a week
and was very proud of myself. George and I were planning to
marry. Then Pearl Harbor was attacked, and his ship was sent out
to fight in the Pacific.

After he left I knew I had to make it on my own. I saw an ad in
the paper announcing the opening of a school for vocational
training in aircraft. I was looking for the opportunity to learn
something else, and I wanted to earn more money. I worked
during the day cooking and went to school at night studying bench
mechanics and riveting, how to read blueprints and use different
aircraft tools.

After about three months the instructor said, "There's no use in
you spending any more time here. You can go out and get a job."
He gave me my graduation slip, and I went down to San Diego to
look around, because George's mother lived there. I went to
Convair, which was Consolidated Aircraft then, and they hired
me.

I was one of the first women hired at Convair and I was
determined that I wasn't going to lose the job and be sent back
to working as a pastry cook. Convair had a motto on their plant
which said that anything short of right is wrong, and that stuck
with me. I went to work in the riveting group in metal-bench

assembly. The mechanics would bring us the job they had put together, and we would take the blueprints and rivet what they brought us.

They would always put the new people with another person, a "leadman." The man I went to work for was really great. He saw my determination and would give me hard jobs to do. The other girls would say, "Joplin, don't give her that, I'll do it." But he would say, "I'm going to break her in right, I'm going to do it the hard way." He told me later that he had made a mistake and been too easy with the other girls.

I tackled everything. I had a daring mother who was afraid of nothing: horses, farm implements, anything, so maybe I inherited a little bit of that from her. I remember my brother, who was in the Air Corps at the time, and his friends laughed at me one day thinking I couldn't learn this mechanical stuff. I can still see them, but it only made me more determined. I think it probably hurt their pride a little bit that I was capable of doing this.

Pretty soon I was promoted to bench-mechanic work, which was detailed hand-riveting. Then I was given a bench with nothing to do but repair what other people had ruined. I visited a man recently who's seventy-four years old, and he said to my daughter, "All we had to do was foul up a job and take it to her and she'd fix it."

I loved working at Convair. I loved the challenge of getting dirty and getting into the work. I did one special riveting job, hand riveting that could not be done by machine. I worked on that job for three months, ten hours a day, six days a week, and slapped three-eighth-or three-quarter-inch rivets by hand that no one else would do. I didn't have that kind of confidence as a kid growing up, because I didn't have that opportunity. Convair was the first time in my life that I had the chance to prove that I could do something, and I did. They finally made me a group leader, although they didn't pay me the wage that went with the job, because I was a woman.

Our department was a majority of women. Many of the women had no training at all, particularly the older women. We had women in our department who were ex-schoolteachers, artists, housewives, so when we could give them a job from the production line, the job would have to be set up for them. I'd sit them down and show them how to use the drill press, the size drill to use, the size of screws, the kind of rivets, whether it was an Army rivet or a

Navy rivet – a Navy rivet was an icebox rivet, the Army rivet was not – and so on. Then I would go back and check to see if the riveting was okay, and if there were any bad rivets, they had to take them out. Most of the time I had to take them out myself. As a group leader that's what I did, and I did it at the same time I was doing my job as a bench mechanic. There were four male group leaders and myself. Theoretically we should have been classified as group leaders and paid for that type of work, but we were not. I felt that was discrimination and that we were being used by the company and fought against it.

Shortly after I went to work at Convair I was chosen by the people in our work group to sit on the wage-review board. The company had automatic wage reviews, and when I first started, those were the only raises that we received. The women were lucky, though, if we got a five-cent-an-hour increase on a review. Some of the women got three cents, some of the women even got two cents, and some of the women were passed over. To us it seemed that the men's pay automatically went up, and ours didn't. I was fortunate enough to get raises later, even a ten-cent raise, and I actually had an assistant foreman come up to me and say, "Don't say anything to the other girls about getting a raise." I told him, "I don't discuss my personal wages, but how about the other women who are deserving too?" So on the wage board I fought for the other women as much as I fought for myself. The highest-paid women at that time were making around $.80 an hour, but the men were probably making $1.15 to $1.50 an hour for identically the same work. In fact, there was a lot of feeling that the women were producing more work than the men on final assembly and on the bench because of their agility with their hands.

Some of the things we did change. For example, they were forced to classify you because of your work. And somewhere in the back of their minds they had the idea that they were not going to make a woman anything but a B-mechanic. As a B-mechanic you could only go to $1.00 an hour, and they were determined that no woman would ever become an A-mechanic or an A-riveter. But we really fought that and we proved to them by bringing them on the job that we were doing A-mechanic work and producing more than the men. So I got my A-mechanic classification and a raise to $1.15 an hour.

I also sat on the safety board the whole time I was at Convair, for the safety requirements they demanded of women were more unreasonable than what they demanded of men. In the beginning we had caps and uniforms we were supposed to wear, but the women rebelled at that. We felt that we could be safe and wear the clothes we wanted. Eventually the company did become a little more relaxed about dress, so we won some victories there too.

US BOMBERS RAID PLOESTI, Rumania, 1 August 1943

Captain John S. Young, USAAF

The refineries at Ploesti were one of the main sources of fuel for the Nazi war machine. The raid was carried out by 177 B-24s flying from bases in North Africa.

Weather conditions were perfect when we took off at 0710. We crossed the Mediterranean at 2,000 feet. At our initial point we ran into thick cumulus clouds at 10,000 feet and lowering. Over Yugoslavia, the clouds started settling in, and we had only about 1,000 feet of visibility over the 9,500-foot mountains. As we came into the Danube Valley, we dropped down to 2,500 feet and followed the Danube River to our target.

All the way across the Mediterranean and over part of Occupied Europe, we didn't even see an enemy plane. It was like a practice mission but, naturally, we maintained radio silence. In that long ride, I don't think anybody said a word.

About thirty-five minutes from our target, we lowered to twenty feet off the ground. And I mean twenty feet. We were coming in so low our plane actually had to pull up to avoid hitting a man on a horse. That horse probably is still running.

The fun started when we spotted a freight train sided at a railroad junction. There must have been fifty cars full of oil just inviting our personal attention. T/Sgt. Fred Leard, our right-waist gunner, and Sergeant Weckessler, top-turret gunner, were mighty eager boys. They called Colonel Kane on the interphone and asked if they could "test" their guns. They had gone through a routine test just after we left the field, and everything was in proper working order. But they wanted to make sure, and if a German oil train was sitting beneath them – well, that was just coincidental. The colonel, never a man to object to a "routine" check, gave his approval and the "test" began.

All the other gunners decided that their guns needed a check, too. It probably marked the first time in history that a routine gun inspection resulted in a Nazi train being blown right off its tracks.

About two miles from the target, the flak guns bellowed out a reception comparable to none I had seen in 330 combat hours against some heavily defended targets. Most of it was 20-mm stuff, with some 40-mm and a lot of machine guns. The fire was plenty accurate.

A mile and a half from the refineries, we opened up with our .50s aiming at the oil tanks which held about 55,000 gallons of oil. They started to explode, throwing smoke and flames about 500 feet into the air. There we were, buzzing in at twenty feet, doing 200 miles per hour, flying through intensive flak and bouncing around between oil fires. Play that on your harmonica sometime.

Our particular targets were the Orion and Astra Romana refineries. They had smokestacks about 210 feet high, so we had to climb to about 250 feet to drop our bombs. Flames were biting in through the bomb-bay doors, the heavy smoke fires made visibility difficult, and the flak fire was beating a hellish tattoo all over our ship, but with all the practice under our belt we had no difficulty picking out our targets. We laid our bombs down the middle.

Forty of the forty-eight planes in our element got over the target. One cracked up on the takeoff, and seven others turned back with mechanical troubles. The rest of us didn't miss.

After the bombs were away, we dropped back to twenty feet, and about fifty ME-109s and '110s jumped on us from the right. We were flying so low they couldn't dive on us, but they did lazy eights all over our formation and caused us plenty of trouble.

The housing around the propeller and three cylinders of our number-four engine were shot out. Two feet of the prop on the number-one engine was smashed, tearing a foot-and-a-half hole in the left aileron. The motor was vibrating like a bucking bronco. And we had a wing-cell leak in number three. We (I say "we" because Colonel Kane and I were both flying that airplane) put on ten degrees of flaps – no more. Ten degrees gives you the best lift without creating too much drag. We kept our wings straight by using the rudder, not the ailerons. Use of ailerons under those conditions is liable to drag a wing down.

We were still at twenty feet – maybe less. As a matter of fact, Lt.

R. B. Hubbard, our radio operator, called Colonel Kane and
suggested that we get some altitude because we were collecting a
mess of branches, leaves, and cornstalks. The colonel investigated,
and I'll be damned if Hubbard didn't hand him a cornstalk!

The fighters kept coming in, and we accounted for three. They
attacked for about twenty minutes, and we just put the ship on the
ground and ran like hell.

We muddled through the fighter attack and staggered away
from the target on two and a half engines. About 200 miles south of
the refineries, we realized that we couldn't return over the Mediterranean with our battered ship. We decided to hug a land route
going back. The chief topic of conversation was picking a good
place to set her down. Everybody was pestering our navigator, Lt.
Norman Whalen. For my money he's the best in the business. He
finally had to tell the colonel, "Look, if you guys will just leave me
alone for a while, maybe I'll find a field." We left him alone.
Whalen was navigating for two other damaged planes which were
following, and the three of us were being covered by Lt. Royden
LeBrecht. Nothing had happened to his ship.

We crossed an enemy airfield at 1,500 feet, and the flak batteries
opened up. I don't know who was more surprised. But we got away
without trouble.

In order to gain altitude to cross a mountain range, we threw
out everything that was movable. We released the extra gasoline
tank and tossed out oxygen bottles, gas masks, ammunition, radio
equipment, and anything that a screwdriver could dismantle. I
haven't yet seen the humor in LeBrecht's remark but he called and
inquired: "What the hell are you doing? Redecorating?"

We finally got up to 6,600 feet, but we needed 7,000 feet to cross
the mountains. By picking our way through canyons and ravines,
and with some lucky updrafts, we managed to get over.

The plane was hobbling along now at 130 miles per hour, and
we knew that it might stall at around 125 mph. It was still flying,
however, and we kept plugging along. We had a choice of putting
her down on land or flying across open water to the nearest Allied
landing field. The colonel and I realized that there was a good
chance the ship would flop into the water, but we had come too far
to worry about that. As we crossed the coast, Whalen gave us an
ETA of 2150 for the selected airfield.

Whalen was on the nose to within a minute. Exactly fourteen
hours and forty minutes after we left Africa, we let her down.

We had to crash-land the plane, but nobody was hurt and the first thing I did after we got away from the ship was to kiss the navigator. Yes, I really kissed him.

A MARINE CORPS PILOT IS SHOT DOWN, Bougainville, 3 January 1944
Gregory Boyington, VMF-214 Squadron, USMC

"Pappy" Boyington was the leader of the "Black Sheep" squadron.

It was before dawn on January 3, 1944, on Bougainville. I was having baked beans for breakfast at the edge of the airstrip the Seabees had built, after the Marines had taken a small chunk of land on the beach. As I ate the beans, I glanced over at row after row of white crosses, too far away and too dark to read the names. But I didn't have to. I knew that each cross marked the final resting place of some Marine who had gone as far as he was able in this mortal world of ours.

Before taking off everything seemed to be wrong that morning. My plane wasn't ready and I had to switch to another. At the last minute the ground crew got my original plane in order and I scampered back into that. I was to lead a fighter sweep over Rabaul, meaning two hundred miles over enemy waters and territory again.

We coasted over at about twenty thousand feet to Rabaul. A few hazy clouds and cloud banks were hanging around – not much different from a lot of other days.

The fellow flying my wing was Captain George Ashmun, New York City. He had told me before the mission: "You go ahead and shoot all you want, Gramps. All I'll do is keep them off your tail."

This boy was another who wanted me to beat that record, and was offering to stick his neck way out in the bargain.

I spotted a few planes coming up through the loosely scattered clouds and signaled to the pilots in back of me: "Go down and get to work."

George and I dove first. I poured a long burst into the first enemy plane that approached, and a fraction of a second later saw the Nip pilot catapult out and the plane itself break out into fire.

George screamed over the radio: "Gramps, you got a flamer!"

Then he and I went down lower into the fight after the rest of the enemy planes. We figured that the whole pack of our planes was going to follow us down, but the clouds must have obscured us from their view. Anyway, George and I were not paying too much attention, just figuring that the rest of the boys would be with us in a few seconds, as usually was the case.

Finding approximately ten enemy planes, George and I commenced firing. What we saw coming from above we thought were our own planes – but they were not. We were being jumped by about twenty planes.

George and I scissored in the conventional Thatch-weave way, protecting each other's blank spots, the rear ends of our fighters. In doing this I saw George shoot a burst into a plane and it turned away from us, plunging downward, all on fire. A second later I did the same to another plane. But it was then that I saw George's plane start to throw smoke, and down he went in a half glide. I sensed something was horribly wrong with him. I screamed at him: "For God's sake. George, dive!"

Our planes could dive away from practically anything the Nips had out there at the time, except perhaps a Tony. But apparently George never heard me or could do nothing about it if he had. He just kept going down in a half glide.

Time and time again I screamed at him: "For God's sake, George, dive straight down!" But he didn't even flutter an aileron in answer to me.

I climbed in behind the Nip planes that were plugging at him on the way down to the water. There were so many of them I wasn't even bothering to use my electric gun sight consciously, but continued to seesaw back and forth on my rudder pedals, trying to spray them all in general, trying to get them off George to give him a chance to bail out or dive – or do something at least.

But the same thing that was happening to him was now happening to me. I could feel the impact of the enemy fire against my armor plate, behind my back, like hail on a tin roof. I could see enemy shots progressing along my wing tips, making patterns.

George's plane burst into flames and a moment later crashed into the water. At that point there was nothing left for me to do. I had done everything I could. I decided to get the hell away from the Nips. I threw everything in the cockpit all the way forward – this means full speed ahead – and nosed my plane over to pick up extra speed until I was forced by the water to level off. I had gone practically a half mile at a speed of about four hundred knots, when all of a sudden my main gas tank went up in flames in front of my very eyes. The sensation was much the same as opening the door of a furnace and sticking one's head into the thing.

Though I was about a hundred feet off the water, I didn't have a chance of trying to gain altitude. I was fully aware that if I tried to gain altitude for a bail-out I would be fried in a few more seconds.

At first, being kind of stunned, I thought: "Well, you finally got it, didn't you, wise guy?" and then I thought: "Oh, no you didn't!" There was only one thing left to do. I reached for the rip cord with my right hand and released the safety belt with my left, putting both feet on the stick and kicking it all the way forward with all my strength. My body was given centrifugal force when I kicked the stick in this manner. My body for an instant weighed well over a ton, I imagine. If I had had a third hand I could have opened the canopy. But all I could do was to give myself this propulsion. It either jettisoned me right up through the canopy or tore the canopy off. I don't know which.

There was a jerk that snapped my head and I knew my chute had caught – what a relief. Then I felt an awful slam on my side – no time to pendulum – just boom-boom and I was in the water.

IKE'S DAY BEFORE D-DAY, SHAEF ADVANCE (Near Portsmouth), 5 June 1944
Captain Harry C. Butcher

The Allied invasion of Normandy, 6 June 1944, was the greatest seaborne invasion in history. Some 160,000 troops – British, American, French, Polish and Canadian – embarked in 5,000 craft from southern England to make the journey to Hitler's "Fortress Europe". Butcher was the naval aide to Eisenhower, the Supreme Allied Commander of the Allied Expeditionary Force in Europe.

D-Day is now almost irrevocably set for to-morrow morning, about 6.40, the time varying with tides at different beaches, the idea being to strike before high tide submerges obstacles which have to be cleared away.

"Irrevocable" becomes practically absolute around dusk, Ike said this afternoon while talking to the press and radio men, who heard him explain for more than an hour the "greatest operation we have ever attempted".

This morning Ike went to South Parade Pier in Portsmouth to see the loading of some British soldiers aboard LCILs 600, 601, and 602. He always gets a lift from talking with soldiers. He got one this morning, which partially offset the impatience with which he viewed the cloudy weather which had been predicted clear. While talking to the press he noticed through the tent door a quick flash of sunshine and said: "By George, there *is* some sun."

This evening Ike and a party, including press, are driving to the Newbury area to see the paratroopers of the American 101st Division load for the great flight – one which Leigh-Mallory said would cost so heavily in lives and planes.

About midnight he will have returned and will stop at the Naval Headquarters for a last-minute check on news, and then return to the camp and bed. He expects to return to the Naval Headquarters around 6.30 to get actual news.

The actual decision was confirmed and made final this morning at 4.15 after all the weather dope had been assembled. During yesterday the weather looked as if we might have to postpone for at least two days, until Thursday, with possibility of two weeks. Pockets of "lows" existed all the way from western Canada across the United States and the Atlantic, and were coming our way. What was needed was a benevolent "high" to counteract or divert at least one of the parading lows. During the night, that actually occurred. During the day, Force U, the U.S. task force which started from Falmouth at the western end of the Channel at 6 a.m. Sunday, had become scattered, owing to the gale-like wind sweeping southern England and the Channel. But Admiral Kirk had heard some encouraging news that the scattering was not as bad as feared. It was enough better by the early-morning session to warrant the gamble, which only Ike could take, and he did, but with the chance of decent weather in his favour for possibly only two days. After that we hope to be ashore, and while weather will still be vitally important, we will have gotten over the historic hump.

Air Chief Marshal Tedder told me that at the Sunday-night meeting when the decision was made to launch OVERLORD, subject to final review at the 4 a.m. meeting, Monday morning, the weatherman who had spoken for all the weather services, after having given a rather doleful report, was asked, "What will the weather be on D-Day in the Channel and over the French coast?" He hesitated, Tedder said, for two dramatic minutes and finally said, conscientiously and soberly, "To answer that question would make me a guesser, not a meteorologist."

Despite the refusal of the weather man to be a "guesser", Ike had to take the responsibility of making the decision without satisfactory assurance from the meteorologist – responsibility which Tedder said Ike took without hesitation.

What does the Supreme Commander do just now? Before lunch he played this aide "Hounds and Fox", he being the hounds, and he won consistently, there being a trick in being a hound. We played a game of crackerbox checkers, and just as I had him cornered with my two kings and his one remaining king, damned if he didn't jump one of my kings and get a draw.

At lunch we talked of old political yarns, he having known my old friend Pat Harrison when he was coming up as a young Congressman. I told the story of the Harrison–Bilbo campaign in which the latter supported Governor Conner for Senator against Pat. One of Pat's supporters told a rally the trouble with Pat was that he was too damned honourable and should use Bilbo's tactics. These he illustrated by the famous yarn of Mamma and Papa Skunk and their nine children, which ends with Papa alluding to a new and terrible odour wafting into their nostrils, and adding, "I don't know what it is, Mamma Skunk and children dear, but whatever it is, we must get some of it."

So we talked, during the lunch, on Senators and skunks and civet cats.

After lunch I shepherded the press and radio men to our little camp, introducing them all round, especially to Mickey, Hunt, Williams, and the rest. Ike took over in his tent, and as usual held them on the edge of their chairs. The nonchalance with which he announced that we were attacking in the morning and the feigned nonchalance with which the reporters absorbed it was a study in suppressed emotion which would interest any psychologist.

The names, as I recall them, are: Robert Barr, for BBC; Stanley Burch, for Reuter's; Ned Roberts, of UP, and Red Mueller, of NBC, who had been with us before. In the order named, they are covering colour and personalities of the high command for British radio, British press agencies, American associations, and American networks. In a word, world-wide coverage for the public. Also two lads from the Army Pictorial Service.

Ike has just had a phone call from Beetle at SHAEF Main that de Gaulle, whose visit here yesterday is a story in itself, now says he will not broadcast to-morrow, D-Day, as agreed yesterday. Objects to one paragraph of Ike's broadcast already recorded. De Gaulle's objection has to do with his recognition as the exclusive French authority with which we are to deal in France. Ike said that if he doesn't come through, we'll deal with someone else, another of those last-minute things that worry the devil out of the SC. General "Red" Bull said yesterday that no one in the world could carry the political and military problems as well as Ike. Got to run to dinner.

D-DAY: COMBAT JUMP OVER NORMANDY, 00.07 Hours 6 June 1944

Lieutenant Guy Remington

Remington reported the war for the *New Yorker*.

The parachute infantry regiment to which I was attached spent the eight days before D Day confined in a marshalling area in England, where we stored up food and sleep and so much knowledge of Normandy that we began to feel as though we knew the country at first hand. On Monday, June 5th, D Day-minus-one, after several hours spent in sharpening knives, cleaning guns, being issued grenades, and adjusting our equipment, we had an early supper and heard a final lecture. Then we blackened our faces, collected our gear, and marched off to our planes. As we passed a railroad crossing, the watchwoman on duty caught my arm and squeezed it impulsively. "Give it to them, Lieutenant," she said. There were tears in her eyes, and, for all I know, in mine.

At the airfield, we were directed to the planes that were to carry us over the Channel. I had seen some action before, so I had at least an idea of what to expect. Not many of the other men were so fortunate. The only thing that worried me, as we sat in the dark waiting for the takeoff, was the thought that I might break a leg in my jump. I tried not to think about that. We took off at ten thirty, just as the moon was coming up. There appeared to be very little ground wind, and the weather seemed ideal for a night jump. Through the open door of my plane, I watched the other transports lifting heavily off the ground. They looked like huge, black bats as they skimmed slowly over the treetops and fell into formation. Before long, we took off too. Presently, near the coast of England, a squadron of fighters appeared below us. They flashed their lights on and off, and then wheeled away. That was *adiós*.

We had a two-hour run ahead of us, so I settled down in my seat. A major, sitting directly across from me, smiled, his teeth startlingly white in the dark. I smiled back. The noise of the plane made it impossible to talk. Suddenly the jump master shouted, "Stand up and hook up!" I realized that I had been asleep, hard as it was to believe. The plane was rocking and bucking, trying to dodge the occasional bursts of flak from the dark, anonymous countryside below. A small red light gleamed in the panel by the door. We hooked up our parachutes, lined up close together, and waited. Then we stood there, waiting, for twelve and a half minutes. It seemed a long and terrible time.

The green light flashed on at seven minutes past midnight. The jump master shouted, "Go!" I was the second man out. The black Normandy pastures tilted and turned far beneath me. The first German flare came arching up, and instantly machine guns and forty-millimeter guns began firing from the corners of the fields, striping the night with yellow, green, blue, and red tracers. I pitched down through a wild Fourth of July. Fire licked through the sky and blazed around the transports heaving high overhead. I saw some of them go plunging down in flames. One of them came down with a trooper, whose parachute had become caught on the tailpiece, streaming out behind. I heard a loud gush of air: a man went hurtling past, only a few yards away, his parachute collapsed and burning. Other parachutes, with men whose legs had been shot off slumped in the harness, floated gently toward the earth.

I was caught in a machine-gun crossfire as I approached the ground. It seemed impossible that they could miss me. One of the guns, hidden in a building, was firing at my parachute, which was already badly torn; the other aimed at my body. I reached up, caught the left risers of my parachute, and pulled on them. I went into a fast slip, but the tracers followed me down. I held the slip until I was about twenty-five feet from the ground and then let go the risers. I landed up against a hedge in a little garden at the rear of a German barracks. There were four tracer holes through one of my pants legs, two through the other, and another bullet had ripped off both my breast pockets, but I hadn't a scratch.

I fought behind the German lines for eight days before I was relieved by our seaborne troops.

D-DAY: THE VIEW FROM THE LANDING CRAFT, 6 June 1944

Ernest Hemingway

Hemingway was aboard an LCV (P) as a newspaper reporter.

Out a way, rolling in the sea, was a Landing Craft Infantry, and as we came alongside of her I saw a ragged shell hole through the steel plates forward of her pilot-house where an 88-mm. German shell had punched through. Blood was dripping from the shiny edges of the hole into the sea with each roll of the LCI. Her rails and hull had been befouled by seasick men, and her dead were laid forward of her pilot-house. Out lieutenant had some conversation with another officer while we rose and fell in the surge alongside the black iron hull, and then we pulled away.

Andy* went forward and talked to him, then came aft again, and we sat up on the stern and watched two destroyers coming along toward us from the eastern beaches, their guns pounding away at targets on the headlands and sloping fields behind the beaches.

"He says they don't want him to go in yet; to wait," Andy said.

"Let's get out of the way of this destroyer."

"How long is he going to wait?"

"He says they have no business in there now. People that should have been ahead of them haven't gone in yet. They told him to wait."

"Let's get in where we can keep track of it," I said. "Take the glasses and look at that beach, but don't tell them forward what you see."

Andy looked. He handed the glasses back to me and shook his head.

"Let's cruise along it to the right and see how it is up at that end," I said. "I'm pretty sure we can get in there when he wants to get in. You're sure they told him he shouldn't go in?"

"That's what he says."

"Talk to him and get it straight."

Andy came back. "He says they shouldn't go in now. They're supposed to clear the mines away, so the tanks can go, and he says nothing is in there to go yet awhile."

* Lieutenant (jg) Robert "Andy" Anderson, the officer in charge of Hemingway's landing craft.

The destroyer was firing point blank at the concrete pillbox that had fired at us on the first trip into the beach, and as the guns fired you heard the bursts and saw the earth jump almost at the same time as the empty brass cases clanged back on to the steel deck. The five-inch guns of the destroyer were smashing at the ruined house at the edge of the little valley where the other machine gun had fired from.

"Let's move in now that the can has gone by and see if we can't find a good place," Andy said.

"That can punched out what was holding them up there, and you can see some infantry working up that draw now," I said to Andy. "Here, take the glasses."

Slowly, laboriously, as though they were Atlas carrying the world on their shoulders, men were working up the valley on our right. They were not firing. They were just moving slowly up the valley like a tired pack train at the end of the day, going the other way from home.

"The infantry has pushed up to the top of the ridge at the end of that valley," I shouted to the lieutenant.

"They don't want us yet," he said. "They told me clear they didn't want us yet."

"Let me take the glasses – or Hemingway," Andy said. Then he handed them back. "In there, there's somebody signalling with a yellow flag, and there's a boat in there in trouble, it looks like. Coxswain, take her straight in."

We moved in toward the beach at full speed, and Ed Banker looked around and said, "Mr Anderson, the other boats are coming, too."

"Get them back!" Andy said. "*Get them back!*"

Banker turned around and waved the boats away. He had difficulty making them understand, but finally the wide waves they were throwing subsided and they dropped astern.

"Did you get them back?" Andy asked, without looking away from the beach where we could see a half-sunken LCV(P) foundered in the mined stakes.

"Yes, sir," Ed Banker said.

An LCI was headed straight towards us, pulling away from the beach after having circled to go in. As it passed, a man shouted with a megaphone, "There are wounded on that boat and she is sinking."

"Can you get in to her?"

The only words we heard clearly from the megaphone as the wind snatched the voice away were "machine-gun nest".

"Did they say there was or there wasn't a machine-gun nest?" Andy said.

"I couldn't hear."

"Run alongside of her again, coxswain," he said. "Run close alongside."

"*Did you say there was a machine-gun nest?*" he shouted.

An officer leaned over with the megaphone. "A machine-gun nest has been firing on them. They are sinking."

"Take her straight in, coxswain," Andy said.

It was difficult to make our way through the stakes that had been sunk as obstructions, because there were contact mines fastened to them that looked like large double pie plates fastened face to face. They looked as though they had been spiked to the pilings and then assembled. They were the ugly, neutral grey-yellow colour that almost everything is in war.

We did not know what other stakes with mines were under us, but the ones that we could see we fended off by hand and worked our way to the sinking boat.

It was not easy to bring on board the man who had been shot through the lower abdomen, because there was no room to let the ramp down the way we were jammed in the stakes with the cross sea.

I do not know why the Germans did not fire on us unless the destroyer had knocked the machine-gun pillbox out. Or maybe they were waiting for us to blow up with the mines. Certainly the mines had been a great amount of trouble to lay and the Germans might well have wanted to see them work. We were in the range of the antitank gun that had fired on us before, and all the time we were manoeuvring and working in the stakes I was waiting for it to fire.

As we lowered the ramp the first time, while we were crowded in against the other LCV (P), but before she sank, I saw three tanks coming along the beach, barely moving, they were advancing so slowly. The Germans let them cross the open space where the valley opened on to the beach, and it was absolutely flat with a perfect field of fire. Then I saw a little fountain of water jut up, just over and beyond the lead tank. Then smoke broke out of the leading tank on the side away from us, and I saw two men dive out of the turret and land on their hands and knees on the stones of the beach. They were close enough so that I could see their faces, but no more men came out as the tank started to blaze up and burn fiercely.

By then, we had the wounded man and the survivors on board, the ramp back up, and were feeling our way out through the stakes. As we cleared the last of the stakes, and Currier opened up the engine wide as we pulled out to sea, another tank was beginning to burn.

We took the wounded boy out to the destroyer. They hoisted him aboard it in one of those metal baskets and took on the survivors. Meantime, the destroyers had run in almost to the beach and were blowing every pillbox out of the ground with their five-inch guns. I saw a piece of German about three feet long with an arm on it sail high up into the air in the fountaining of one shellburst. It reminded me of a scene in Petrouchka.

The infantry had now worked up the valley on our left and had gone on over that ridge. There was no reason for anyone to stay out now. We ran in to a good spot we had picked on the beach and put our troops and their TNT and their bazookas and their lieutenant ashore, and that was that.

The Germans were still shooting with their anti-tank guns, shifting them around in the valley, holding their fire until they had a target they wanted. Their mortars were still laying a plunging fire along the beaches. They had left people behind to snipe at the beaches, and when we left, finally, all these people who were firing were evidently going to stay until dark at least.

The heavily loaded ducks that had formerly sunk in the waves on their way in were now making the beach steadily. The famous thirty-minute clearing of the channels through the mined obstacles was still a myth, and now, with the high tide, it was a tough trip in with the stakes submerged.

We had six craft missing, finally, out of the twenty-four LCV(P)s that went in from the *Dix*, but many of the crews could have been picked up and might be on other vessels. It had been a frontal assault in broad daylight, against a mined beach defended by all the obstacles military ingenuity could devise. The beach had been defended as stubbornly and as intelligently as any troops could defend it. But every boat from the *Dix* had landed her troops and cargo. No boat was lost through bad seamanship. All that were lost were lost by enemy action. And we had taken the beach.

There is much that I have not written. You could write for a week and not give everyone credit for what he did on a front of 1135 yards. Real war is never like paper war, nor do accounts of it read much the way it looks. But if you want to know how it was in an LCV(P) on D-Day when we took Fox Green beach and Easy Red beach on the sixth of June, 1944, then this is as near as I can come to it.

D-DAY: OMAHA BEACH, 07.00 6 June 1944
Captain Joseph T. Dawson, 1st Infantry Division

We landed at H + 30 minutes and found . . . both the assault units rendered ineffective because of the enormous casualties they suffered. Fortunately, when we landed there was some let-up in the defensive fire from the Germans. Even so the boat containing assault unit Company G, which I commanded, took a direct hit from the artillery of the Germans, and I suffered major casualties. I lost about twenty men out of a total complement of 250 from that hit on my boat, and this included my naval officer who was communications link with the Navy, who were to support us with their fire from the battleships and cruisers some 8000 yards out in the water.

As soon as we were able to assemble we proceeded off of the beach through a minefield which had been identified by some of the soldiers who had landed earlier. We knew this because two of them were lying there in the path I selected. Both men had been destroyed by the mines. From their position, however, we were able to identify the path and get through the minefield without casualties and proceed up to the crest of the ridge which overlooked the beach. We got about halfway up when we met the remnants of a platoon of E Company, commanded by Lieutenant Spalding. This was the only group – somewhere less than twenty men – we encountered who had gotten off of the beach. They had secured some German prisoners, and these were sent to the beach under escort. Above me, right on top of the ridge, the Germans had a line of defences with an excellent field of fire. I kept the men behind and, along with my communications sergeant and his assistant, worked our way slowly up to the crest of the ridge. Just before the crest was a sharp perpendicular drop, and we were able to get up to the crest without being seen by the enemy. I could now hear the Germans talking in the machine-gun nest immediately above me. I then threw two grenades, which were successful in eliminating the enemy and silencing the machine gun which had been holding up our approach. Fortunately for me this action was done without them having any awareness of my being there, so it was no hero . . . it was an act of God, I guess.

MARINES STORM A PILLBOX, Ngesebus, 28 September 1944

Eugene B. Sledge, 1st Marine Division, USMC

Ngesebus is a small island off Peleliu.

After we moved farther inland, we received orders to set up the mortars on the inland side of a Japanese pillbox and prepare to fire on the enemy to our company's front. We asked Company K's gunnery sergeant, Gy. Sgt. W. R. Saunders, if he knew of any enemy troops in the bunker. It appeared undamaged. He said some of the men had thrown grenades through the ventilators, and he was sure there were no live enemy inside.

Snafu and I began to set up our mortar about five feet from the bunker. Number One mortar was about five yards to our left. Cpl. R. V. Burgin was getting the sound-powered phone hooked up to receive fire orders from Sgt. Johnny Marmet, who was observing.

I heard something behind me in the pillbox. Japanese were talking in low, excited voices. Metal rattled against an iron grating. I grabbed my carbine and yelled, "Burgin, there're Nips in that pillbox."

All the men readied their weapons as Burgin came over to have a look, kidding me with, "Shucks, Sledgehammer, you're crackin' up." He looked into the ventilator port directly behind me. It was rather small, approximately six inches by eight inches, and covered with iron bars about a half inch apart. What he saw brought forth a stream of curses in his best Texas style against all Nippon. He stuck his carbine muzzle through the bars, fired two quick shots, and yelled, "I got 'em right in the face."

The Japanese inside the pillbox began jabbering loudly. Burgin was gritting his teeth and calling the enemy SOBs while he fired more shots through the opening.

Every man in the mortar section was ready for trouble as soon as Burgin fired the first shot. It came in the form of a grenade tossed out of the end entrance to my left. It looked as big as a football to me. I yelled "Grenade!" and dove behind the sand breastwork protecting the entrance at the end of the pillbox. The sand bank was about four feet high and L-shaped to protect the entrance from fire from the front and flanks. The grenade exploded, but no one was hit.

The Japanese tossed out several more grenades without causing us injury, because we were hugging the deck. Most of the men crawled around to the front of the pillbox and crouched close to it between the firing ports, so the enemy inside couldn't fire at them. John Redifer and Vincent Santos jumped on top. Things got quiet.

I was nearest the door, and Burgin yelled to me, "Look in and see what's in there, Sledgehammer."

Being trained to take orders without question, I raised my head above the sand bank and peered into the door of the bunker. It nearly cost me my life. Not more than six feet from me crouched a Japanese machine gunner. His eyes were black dots in a tan, impassive face topped with the familiar mushroom helmet. The muzzle of his light machine gun stared at me like a gigantic third eye.

Fortunately for me, I reacted first. Not having time to get my carbine into firing position, I jerked my head down so fast my helmet almost flew off. A split second later he fired a burst of six or eight rounds. The bullets tore a furrow through the bank just above my head and showered sand on me. My ears rang from the muzzle blast and my heart seemed to be in my throat choking me. I knew damned well I had to be dead! He just couldn't have missed me at that range.

A million thoughts raced through my terrified mind: of how my folks had nearly lost their youngest, of what a stupid thing I had done to look directly into a pillbox full of Japanese without even having my carbine at the ready, and of just how much I hated the enemy anyway. Many a Marine veteran had already lost his life on Peleliu for making less of a mistake than I had just made.

Burgin yelled and asked if I were all right. A hoarse squawk was all the answer I could muster, but his voice brought me to my senses. I crawled around to the front, then up on top of the bunker before the enemy machine gunner could have another try at me.

Redifer yelled, "They've got an automatic weapon in there." Snafu disagreed, and a spirited argument ensued. Redifer pointed out that there surely was an automatic weapon in there and that I should know, because it came close to blowing off my head. But

Snafu was adamant. Like much of what I experienced in combat, this exchange was unreal. Here we were: twelve Marines with a bull by the tail in the form of a well-built concrete pillbox containing an unknown number of Japanese with no friendly troops near us and Snafu and Redifer – veterans – in a violent argument.

Burgin shouted, "Knock it off," and they shut up.

Redifer and I lay prone on top of the bunker, just above the door. We knew we had to get the Japanese while they were bottled up, or they would come out at us with knives and bayonets, a thought none of us relished. Redifer and I were close enough to the door to place grenades down the opening and move back before they exploded. But the Japanese invariably tossed them back at us before the explosion. I had an irrepressible urge to do just that. Brief as our face-to-face meeting had been, I had quickly developed a feeling of strong personal hate for that machine gunner who had nearly blasted my head off my shoulders. My terror subsided into a cold, homicidal rage and a vengeful desire to get even.

Redifer and I gingerly peeped down over the door. The machine gunner wasn't visible, but we looked at three long Arisaka rifle barrels with bayonets fixed. Those bayonets seemed ten feet long to me. Their owners were jabbering excitedly, apparently planning to rush out. Redifer acted quickly. He held his carbine by the barrel and used the butt to knock down the rifles. The Japanese jerked their weapons back into the bunker with much chattering.

Behind us, Santos yelled that he had located a ventilator pipe without a cover. He began dropping grenades into it. Each one exploded in the pillbox beneath us with a muffled *bam*. When he had used all of his, Redifer and I handed him our grenades while we kept watch at the door.

After Santos had dropped in several, we stood up and began to discuss with Burgin and the others the possibility that anyone could still be alive inside. (We didn't know at the time that the inside was subdivided by concrete baffles for extra protection.) We got our answer when two grenades were tossed out. Luckily for the men with Burgin, the grenades were thrown out the back. Santos and I shouted a warning and hit the deck on the sand on top of the pillbox, but Redifer merely raised his arm over his face. He took several fragments in the forearm but wasn't wounded seriously.

Burgin yelled, "Let's get the hell outa here and get a tank to help us knock this damn thing out." He ordered us to pull back to some craters about forty yards from the pillbox. We sent a runner to the beach to bring up a flamethrower and an amtrac armed with a 75 mm gun.

As we jumped into the crater, three Japanese soldiers ran out of the pillbox door past the sand bank and headed for a thicket. Each carried his bayoneted rifle in his right hand and held up his pants with his left hand. This action so amazed me that I stared in disbelief and didn't fire my carbine. I wasn't afraid, as I had been under shell fire, just filled with wild excitement. My buddies were more effective than I and cut down the enemy with a hail of bullets. They congratulated each other while I chided myself for being more curious about strange Japanese customs than with being combat effective.

The amtrac rattling toward us by this time was certainly a welcome sight. As it pulled into position, several more Japanese raced from the pillbox in a tight group. Some held their bayoneted rifles in both hands, but some of them carried their rifles in one hand and held up their pants with the other. I had overcome my initial surprise and joined the others and the amtrac machine gun in firing away at them. They tumbled onto the hot coral in a forlorn tangle of bare legs, falling rifles, and rolling helmets. We felt no pity for them but exulted over their fate. We had been shot at and shelled too much and had lost too many friends to have compassion for the enemy when we had him cornered.

The amtrac took up a position on a line even with us. Its commander, a sergeant, consulted Burgin. Then the turret gunner fired three armor-piercing 75 mm shells at the side of the pillbox. Each time our ears rang with the familiar *wham-bam* as the report of the gun was followed quickly by the explosion of the shell on a target at close range. The third shell tore a hole entirely through the pillbox. Fragments kicked up dust around our abandoned packs and mortars on the other side. On the side nearest us, the hole was about four feet in diameter. Burgin yelled to the tankers to cease firing lest our equipment be damaged.

Someone remarked that if fragments hadn't killed those inside, the concussion surely had. But even before the dust settled, I saw a Japanese soldier appear at the blasted opening. He was grim determination personified as he drew back his arm to throw a grenade at us.

My carbine was already up. When he appeared, I lined up my sights on his chest and began squeezing off shots. As the first bullet hit him, his face contorted in agony. His knees buckled. The grenade slipped from his grasp. All the men near me, including the amtrac machine gunner, had seen him and began firing. The soldier collapsed in the fusilade, and the grenade went off at his feet.

Even in the midst of these fast-moving events, I looked down at my carbine with sober reflection. I had just killed a man at close range. That I had seen clearly the pain on his face when my bullets hit him came as a jolt. It suddenly made the war a very personal affair. The expression on that man's face filled me with shame and then disgust for the war and all the misery it was causing.

My combat experience thus far made me realize that such sentiments for an enemy soldier were the maudlin meditations of a fool. Look at me, a member of the 5th Marine Regiment – one of the oldest, finest, and toughest regiments in the Marine Corps – feeling ashamed because I had shot a damned foe before he could throw a grenade at me! I felt like a fool and was thankful my buddies couldn't read my thoughts.

Burgin's order to us to continue firing into the opening interrupted my musings. We kept up a steady fire into the pillbox to keep the Japanese pinned down while the flame-thrower came up, carried by Corporal Womack from Mississippi. He was a brave, good-natured guy and popular with the troops, but he was one of the fiercest looking Marines I ever saw. He was big and husky with a fiery red beard well powdered with white coral dust. He reminded me of some wild Viking. I was glad we were on the same side.

Stooped under the heavy tanks on his back, Womack approached the pillbox with his assistant just out of the line of our fire. When they got about fifteen yards from the target, we ceased firing. The assistant reached up and turned a valve on the flamethrower. Womack then aimed the nozzle at the opening made by the 75 mm gun. He pressed the trigger. With a *whooooooooosh* the flame leaped at the opening. Some muffled screams, then all quiet.

IWO JIMA: THE MARINE CORPS IN ACTION, Pacific Ocean, March 1945

US Marine Corps correspondent

Iwo Jima is a small volcanic island at the end of an archipelago which stretches into Tokyo Bay. In early 1945 USAAF determined to build an airbase on the island – then Japanese controlled and heavily fortified – to enable fighters to support B29s in raids over Japan. The invasion of Iwo Jima was launched on 19 February 1945. The fighting was expected to take eight days; it lasted five weeks.

When the 24th Marine Regiment's, 2nd Battalion reached the scene, they called it "the Wilderness", and there they spent four days on the line, with no respite from the song of death sung by mortars among those desolate crevices and gouged shell holes. The Wilderness covered about a square mile inland from Blue Beach 2, on the approaches to Airfield no. 2, and there was no cover. Here and there stood a blasted dwarf tree; here and there a stubby rock ledge in a maze of volcanic crevices.

The 2nd Battalion attacked with flame throwers, demolition charges, 37-millimetre guns, riflemen. A tank advancing in support was knocked out by a mortar shell. After every Japanese volley, Corsair fighter planes streamed down on the mortar positions, ripping their charges of bombs into the Wilderness. But after every dive was ended, the mortars started their ghastly song again.

Cracks in the earth run along the open field to the left of the Wilderness, and hot smoke seeped up through the cracks. Gains were counted in terms of 100 or 200 yards for a day, in terms of three or four bunkers knocked out. Losses were counted in terms of three or four men suddenly turned to bloody rags after the howl of a mortar shell, in terms of a flame-thrower man hit by a grenade as he poured his flame into a bunker. The assault platoon of flame throwers and demolitionists, spearheading the regiment's push through the Wilderness, lost two assistant squad leaders killed.

The Japs were hard to kill. Cube-shaped concrete block-houses had to be blasted again and again before the men inside were silenced. Often the stunned and wounded Japs continued to struggle among the ruins, still trying to fire back. A sergeant fired twenty-one shots at a semi-concealed Jap before the latter was killed. Another Marine assaulting a pillbox found a seriously wounded Jap trying to get a heavy machine gun into action. He emptied his clip at him but the Jap kept reaching. Finally, out of ammunition, the Marine used his knife to kill him.

Forty-eight hours after the attack began, one element of the Third Division moved into the line under orders to advance at all costs.

Behind a rolling artillery barrage and with fixed bayonets, the unit leaped forward in an old-fashioned hell-bent-for-leather charge and advanced to the very mouths of the fixed Jap defences. Before scores of pillboxes the men flung themselves at the tiny flaming holes, throwing grenades and jabbing with bayonets. Comrades went past, hurdled the defences and rushed across Airfield no. 2. In three minutes one unit lost four officers. Men died at every step. That was how we broke their line.

Across the field we attacked a ridge. The enemy rose up out of holes to hurl our assault back. The squads re-formed and went up again. At the crest they plunged on the Japs with bayonets. One of our men, slashing his way from side to side, fell dead from a pistol shot. His comrade drove his bayonet into the Jap who had killed him. The Japs on the ridge were annihilated.

And now behind those proud and weary men, our whole previously stalled attack poured through. Tanks, bazookas and demolition men smashed and burned the by-passed fortifications. In an area 1,000 yards long and 200 deep, more than 800 enemy pillboxes were counted.

The survivors of this bold charge covered 800 yards in an hour and a half. Brave men had done what naval shelling, aerial bombardment, artillery and tanks had not been able to do in two days of constant pounding. What was perhaps the most intensively fortified small area ever encountered in battle had been broken.

Six thousand Americans died on Iwo Jima. Another 12,500 died in April in the seizure of Okinawa, an island in the Ryukyu chain in the Pacific, also designated as a USAAF fighter base. The Japanese dead numbered 21,000 on Iwo Jima, and around 100,000 on Okinawa.

THE FUNERAL OF PRESIDENT ROOSEVELT, Georgia, 20 April 1945

Douglas B. Cornell

Franklin Delano Roosevelt, US President, had died on the morning of 12 April. He was buried at his family home in Georgia. He was succeeded as US President by Harry S. Truman, the Vice-President.

As President Truman looked on with a face frozen in grief, Franklin D. Roosevelt was committed today to the warm brown earth of his native soil.

Under a cloudless, spring sky, the body of the late Chief

Executive was lowered solemnly into a grave in the flower garden of his family estate.

Watching with strained faces were members of the family, dignitaries of government and little sad-faced groups of plain people – the employees on the place and neighbours from the countryside.

A detail of grey-clad cadets from the US Military Academy at West Point fired a volley of three farewell salutes. A bugler played "Taps", its sweet but still sad notes echoing through the wooded estate.

Soldiers, sailors and marines, who had held an American flag over the casket, folded it and handed it to Mrs Roosevelt.

The garden where Mr Roosevelt rests lies between the family home where he was born sixty-three years ago and the library which houses his state papers and the gifts of a world which recognized him as one of its pre-eminent leaders.

It was exactly ten a.m. when the first gun of a presidential salute was fired from a battery in the library grounds to the east of the quarter-acre garden. They boomed at solemnly spaced intervals.

An honour guard lining the hemlock hedge around the garden stood at attention.

A few moments later, the distant melody of a bugle came to those within the garden. A flight of bombers and another of training planes droned overhead.

The beat of muffled drums in slow cadence rolled through the wooded hills above the Hudson. In the distance, gradually drawing nearer, a band played a funeral dirge.

Promptly at ten-thirty a.m., the National Anthem sounded and, as the wheels of the caisson noisily ground the gravel of the roadway, the notes of "Nearer, My God, to Thee", were played softly. Through a passageway at one corner, the elderly, grey-bearded rector of the President's Episcopal Church at Hyde Park walked across the newly clipped grass toward the grave.

The Rev. George W. Anthony was wearing the black and white surplice and stole of the clergy. He removed a black velvet skull-cap and took his position at the head of the grave, toward the west.

"All that the father giveth me shall come to me," the Rev. Mr Anthony said.

A lone plane circling above almost drowned his words as he declared that unto Almighty God "we commit his body to the ground; earth to earth, ashes to ashes, dust to dust."

There was a stirring in the crowd.

"Blessed are the dead who die in the Lord," the rector intoned. "Lord, have mercy upon us. Christ, have mercy upon us. Lord, have mercy upon us."

The pastor repeated the words of the Lord's Prayer. Elliott's lips moved with him.

The services followed the ordinary Episcopal burial rites for the dead. There were no words of eulogy, only the word of God.

Near its conclusion the Rev. Mr Anthony recited the poem written by John Ellerton in 1870: "Now the labourer's task is o'er; now the battle-day is past."

"Father, in Thy gracious keeping we now leave Thy servant sleeping," the rector continued.

The services were brief. They were over by ten-forty-five. The flag which Mrs Roosevelt clutched tightly was handed to Elliott, and the family filed out.

THE WORLD'S FIRST ATOM BOMB TEST, Los Alamos, New Mexico, 17 July 1945

Sir Geoffrey Taylor

If the war in Europe had ended, the war in the Far East was still being fought. The Allies, however, had developed a secret and deadly weapon. Code-named "The Manhattan Project", the world's first atomic bomb was built by the Allies and detonated at a test in the New Mexico desert. The world had entered the nuclear age.

I was one of the group of British scientific men who worked at Los Alamos in New Mexico, where most of the recent experimental work on atomic bombs was carried out, and I saw the first bomb explode. Before I tell you about this, I ought to say that I have witnessed many ordinary bomb trials. In such trials the kind of result to be expected are always known beforehand, and the trial is designed to find out just how much damage the bomb will do. The first atomic bomb test had to be approached with a totally different outlook because it was not possible to make any previous experiment on a smaller scale. None of us knew whether we were going to witness an epoch-making experiment or a complete failure. The physicists had predicted that a self-propagating reaction involving neutrons was possible and that this would lead to an explosion. The mathematicians had calculated what mechanical results were to be expected. Engineers and physicists had set up an apparatus rather like that used in testing ordinary bombs, to measure the efficiency of the explosion. But no one knew whether this apparatus would be needed, simply because nobody knew whether the bomb would go off.

Our uncertainty was reflected in the bets which were made at Los Alamos on the amount of energy to be released. These ranged from zero to the equivalent of 80,000 tons of TNT. Those of us who were to witness the test assembled during a late afternoon in July at Los Alamos for the 230-mile drive to the uninhabited and desolate region where the test was to be made. We arrived about three o'clock in the morning at a spot twenty miles from the hundred-foot tower on which the bomb was mounted. Here we were met by a car containing a radio receiver. Round this we assembled, listening for the signal from the firing point which would tell us when to expect the explosion. We were provided with a strip of very dark glass to protect our eyes. This glass is so dark that at midday it makes the sun look like a little undeveloped dull green potato. Through this glass I was unable to see the light which was set on the tower to show us where to look. Remember, it was still dark. I therefore fixed my eyes on this light ten seconds before the explosion was due to occur. Then I raised the dark glass to my eyes two seconds before, keeping them fixed on the spot where I had last seen the light. At exactly the expected moment, I saw through the dark glass a brilliant ball of fire which was far brighter than the sun. In a second or two it died down to a brightness which seemed to be about that of the sun, so, realizing that it must be lighting up the countryside, I looked behind me and saw the scrub-covered hills, twenty-two miles from the bomb, lighted up as though by a midday sun. Then I turned round and looked directly at the ball of fire. I saw it expand slowly, and begin to rise, growing fainter as it rose. Later it developed into a huge mushroom-shaped cloud, and soon reached a height of 40,000 feet.

Though the sequence of events was exactly what we had calculated beforehand in our more optimistic moments, the whole effect was so staggering that I found it difficult to believe my eyes, and judging by the strong ejaculations from my fellow-watchers other people felt the same reaction. So far we had heard no noise. Sound takes over one and a half minutes to travel twenty miles, so we next had to prepare to receive the blast wave. We had been advised to lie on the ground to receive the shock of the wave, but few people did so, perhaps owing to the fact that it was still dark, and rattle-snakes and tarantulas were fairly common in the district. When it came it was not very loud, and sounded like the crack of a shell passing overhead rather than a distant high-explosive bomb. Rumbling followed and continued for some time. On returning to Los Alamos, I found that one of my friends there had been lying awake in bed and had seen the light of the explosion reflected on the ceiling of his bedroom, though the source of it was over 160 miles away in a straight line.

THE ALLIES DECIDE TO DROP THE ATOMIC BOMB ON JAPAN, Potsdam, 25 July 1945

President Harry S. Truman

Diary: Potsdam 25 July 1945

We met at eleven today. That is Stalin, Churchill, and the US President. But I had a most important session with Lord Mountbatten and General Marshall before that. We have discovered the most terrible bomb in the history of the world. It may be the fire destruction prophesied in the Euphrates Valley Era, after Noah and his fabulous Ark.

Anyway we "think" we have found the way to cause a disintegration of the atom. An experiment in the New Mexican desert was startling – to put it mildly. Thirteen pounds of the explosive caused the complete disintegration of a steel tower 60 feet high, created a crater 6 feet deep and 1,200 feet in diameter, knocked over a steel tower 1/2 mile away and knocked men down 10,000 yards away. The explosion was visible for more than 200 miles and audible for 40 miles and more.

This weapon is to be used against Japan between now and August 10th. I have told the Sec. of War, Mr Stimson, to use it so that military objectives and soldiers and sailors are the target and not women and children. Even if the Japs are savages, ruthless, merciless and fanatic, we as the leader of the world for the common welfare cannot drop this terrible bomb on the old capital or the new.

He and I are in accord. The target will be a purely military one and we will issue a warning statement asking the Japs to surrender and save lives. I'm sure they will not do that, but we will have given them the chance. It is certainly a good thing for the world that Hitler's crowd or Stalin's did not discover this atomic bomb. It seems to be the most terrible thing ever discovered, but it can be made the most useful.

The following day, 26 July, the Allies called upon Japan to surrender. The alternative they said was "prompt and utter destruction". Japan did not surrender.

HIROSHIMA, Japan, 6 August 1945

Colonel Tibbets, USAAF

The destruction promised by the Allies came on 6 August, when three B29s of the US air force took off from Tinian and flew to Hiroshima, the eighth largest city in Japan. One of the planes, the *Enola Gay*, carried an atomic bomb. The commander of the mission was Colonel Tibbets.

We started our take-off on time which was somewhere about two-forty-five I think, and the aeroplane went on down the runway. It was loaded quite heavily but it responded exactly like I had anticipated it would. I had flown this aeroplane the same way before and there was no problem and there was nothing different this night in the way we went. We arrived over the initial point and started in on the bomb run which had about eleven minutes to go, rather a long type of run for a bomb but on the other hand we felt we needed this extra time in straight and level flight to stabilize the air speed of the aeroplane, to get everything right down to the last-minute detail. As I indicated earlier the problem after the release of the bomb is not to proceed forward but to turn away. As soon as the weight had left the aeroplane I immediately went into this steep turn and we tried then to place distance between ourselves and the point of impact. In this particular case that bomb took fifty-three seconds from the time it left the aeroplane until it exploded and this gave us adequate time of course to make the turn. We had just made the turn and rolled out on level flight when it seemed like somebody had grabbed a hold of my aeroplane and gave it a real hard shaking because this was the shock wave that had come up. Now after we had been hit by a second shock wave not quite so strong as the first one I decided we'll turn around and go back and take a look. The day was clear when we dropped that bomb, it was a clear sunshiny day and the visibility was unrestricted. As we came back around again facing the direction of Hiroshima we saw this cloud coming up. The cloud by this time, now two minutes old, was up at our altitude. We were 33,000 feet at this time and the cloud was up there and continuing to go right on up in a boiling fashion, as if it was rolling and boiling. The surface was nothing but a black boiling, like a barrel of tar. Where before there had been a city with distinctive houses, buildings and everything that you could see from our altitude, now you couldn't see anything except a black boiling debris down below.

The first atomic bomb to be dropped in warfare killed 80,000 people – a quarter of Hiroshima's inhabitants.

ANNOUNCING THE END OF THE SECOND WORLD WAR, 10 August 1945

Maxine Andrews

Maxine Andrews was one of the Andrews Sisters, a popular singing group during the 1940s. The Sisters entertained troops all over the world, including in August 1945 a glum group of GIs in Italy who were about to be shipped out to fight in the Far East.

Our last date was in Naples. We were billeted in Caserta, eighteen miles away. We did all our shows at repo depots, where all the guys were being shipped out. We had one more show to do. It was loaded with about eight thousand of the most unhappy-looking audience you'd ever seen. They were hanging from the rafters. All these fellas were being shipped out to the South Pacific. They hadn't been home for four years, and it was just their bad luck. We were trying to get them into good spirits.

We were pretty well through with the show when I heard someone offstage calling me: "Pssst. Pssst." Patty was doing a little scene with Arthur Treacher. The soldier said to me, "I have a very important message for Patty to tell the audience." I started to laugh, because they were always playing tricks on us. He said, "I'm not kidding. It's from the CO." I said, "I can't do it in the middle of the show." He said, "You're gonna get me in trouble." So I took the piece of paper. I didn't read it. I walked out on the stage, saying to myself I'm gonna get in trouble with Patty, with Arthur, with the CO. I waited until the skit was over. Patty said, "Stop your kidding. We can't read that here. We've got to finish the show." I shoved the note at her. She finally said, "All right, I'll go along with the gag."

So she said to the fellas, "Look, it's a big joke up here. I have a note supposedly from the CO." Without reading it first, she read it out loud. It announced the end of the war with Japan. There wasn't a sound in the whole auditorium. She looked at it again. She looked at me. It was serious. So she said, "No, fellas, this is from the CO. This is an announcement that the war is over, so you don't have to go." With that, she started to cry. Laverne and I were crying. Still there was no reaction from the guys. So she said it again: "This is the end, this is the end."

All of a sudden, all hell broke loose. They yelled and screamed. We saw a pair of pants and a shirt come down from above. Following it was a body. He came down and fell on the guys sitting downstairs. Patty said, "You want to go out and get drunk? Or you want to see the show?" "No, no, no, we want to see the rest of the show." We made it very short.

We got into the jeep, and all of a sudden it hit us. Oh heavens, if this is a joke, they're gonna tar and feather us. We'll have to swim all the way back to the States. We suffered until we got to Caserta. They reassured us that the announcement was true.

A few years ago, Patty was working someplace in Cleveland. She checked into the hotel and was in the elevator. This elevator man said, "Don't you remember me?" He was a short, bald-headed guy. She said, "Should I?" He said, "Yeah, remember Naples? Remember the guy that fell off the rafter? That was me."

MARILYN MONROE IN HOLLYWOOD, 1950
Arthur Miller

The playwright – and future husband of Marilyn Monroe – describes his first meeting with the movie icon of the century.

A few days earlier I had gone to the Twentieth Century Fox studio with Kazan, who was under contract there and had many friends working on the sound stages. One of them, his former film editor, was now directing *As Young As You Feel*, a comedy with my father's *bête noire* Monty Woolley and, in a bit part, Marilyn. Moviemaking was still an exotic and fantastic affair for me, and full of mysteries. We had just arrived on a nightclub set when Marilyn, in a black open-work lace dress, was directed to walk across the floor, attracting the worn gaze of the bearded Woolley. She was being shot from the rear to set off the swivelling of her hips, a motion fluid enough to seem comic. It was, in fact, her natural walk: her footprints on a beach would be in a straight line, the heel descending exactly before the last toeprint, throwing her pelvis into motion.

When the shot was finished she came over to Kazan, who had met her with Hyde on another visit some time before. From where I stood, yards away, I saw her in profile against a white light, with her hair coiled atop her head; she was weeping under a veil of black lace that she lifted now and then to dab her eyes. When we shook hands the shock of her body's motion sped through me, a sensation at odds with her sadness amid all this glamour and technology and the busy confusion of a new shot being set up. She had been weeping, she would explain later, while telling Kazan that Hyde had died calling her name in a hospital room she had been forbidden by his family to enter. She had heard him from the corridor, and had left, as always, alone.

KOREAN WAR: RETREAT FROM CHONGCHON RIVER, 27–28 November 1950

Reginald Thompson

Following MacArthur's amphibious landing at Inchon, UN troops moved northwards, crossing into North Korea on 1 October. This caused China to enter the war (on the side of N Korea); the deployment of 180,000 Chinese "volunteers" on 25 November forced Allied troops to retreat. By 15 December the UN army was back at the 38th Parallel.

It was a game of blind man's buff in these wild rugged irregular hills in which the enemy moved freely, easily eluding the groping arms of the Americans by day, and swooping down upon them, blind in the night, with devastating fury and magnificent discipline. Not a shot was fired by the Chinese until they were within thirty yards of the target.

Meanwhile the Americans were road-bound with their immense weight of useless weapons. The guns were rolling back. The great columns had gone into reverse. For a hundred miles the huge vehicles crammed the narrowing road lanes nose to tail. Back across the Chongchon the 25th Division were coming over the fordings while Colonel Stevens threw his rearguard round the Pakchon bridgehead and the road through to Sinanju. But there were few enemy hampering him; only the sense of terrific urgency before the torrent might burst these slender human dams and envelop the whole Eighth Army.

The smoke rising from ten thousand fires blotted out the moon and threw the stricken figures of the toiling refugees into silhouette, like some ancient frieze, an endless repetition of characters, the human story, plodding on.

There was no rest or sleep by night. Within five seconds of wild bugle calls the attacks came in, seven men out of each ten literally draped with percussion grenades on sticks, and the remaining three with automatic weapons. The lead battalion across the river was hit on the night of the 27th, and as it tried to withdraw across the Chongchon the Chinese were already waiting on the banks with machine-guns sited in the American rear. A bazooka brewed up an American tank, and in the lurid glare of the blazing tank the battalion struggled through, the remaining tanks carrying men across the frozen river. The jeeps had frozen solid to the ground, the men struggled in the shallows at the fording point with their unwieldy shoe paks freezing in great blocks to their feet. And all the time the enemy machine-guns rasped their leaden terror through the night.

The second in command was no sooner across the river than he turned back with a tank to rescue more of his men under a hail of fire. A grenade exploded on his tin hat, but by a miracle the dazed man struggled to his feet, collected ten of his comrades, regained the tank and got back. Others bore wounded on their backs.

From a military point of view it was a disaster. There was never any question of staying and meeting these attacks, of regaining the lost ground by day – for it was deserted – and even pushing forward. Only trained and disciplined troops could do that. These men acted and behaved as heroically as men may hope to behave, but their attitude when attacked was always, quite openly: "Let's get the hell out of here!" And they did. Often it would have paid them to stay, but this would have meant hard training, good officers and NCOs, a fire plan, strict discipline, and these things they had not got.

It was curious that in the day we could move back over the eerie wilderness of the night. It was like moving in a land of shadows and ghosts and dead. It was a terrible prospect to stand in the midst of the burning hills which rise in cones and ridges from the bleak banks of the Chongchon in a desolate grandeur, and it is as though an ocean had been frozen, petrified suddenly, in the midst of storm, a wild riot of hills.

"We're like the meat in a sandwich," said a young GI, "and the

Chinks are the bread." There was a quietness and humour in the Americans I had not known before. You could see here quite clearly the great gash in the middle of the whole race where the middle class would have been. At the top there were these first-class colonels, and at the bottom these first-class people. But all the people from whom officers, civil servants, and all the rest of the educated men of background and integrity are drawn just were not there.

"Seems like the Chinese don't want us on that Yalu River," remarked a sergeant, as he led a weary section back to find some transport. He said it without a trace of bitterness. It was "OK with him". They could have it. And they all knew that the Korean war was ended.

APPEARING BEFORE THE HOUSE UN-AMERICAN ACTIVITIES COMMITTEE, Washington, 21 May 1952

Lillian Hellman

The internal politics of the USA in the early 1950s were conditioned by fears of the Cold War with the USSR. A witch-hunt led by Senator McCarthy attacked citizens suspected of left-wing views, many of whom were "blacklisted" – prevented from working. A particular target for the attentions of McCarthyism was the entertainment industry; playwright Lillian Hellman was only one of many writers and artists to be asked to appear before Congress's House Un-American Activities Committee to admit their political belief and "name names" of other suspected Communists.

The Committee room was almost empty except for a few elderly, small-faced ladies sitting in the rear. They looked as if they were permanent residents and, since they occasionally spoke to each other, it was not too long a guess that they came as an organized group or club. Clerks came in and out, put papers on the rostrum, and disappeared. I said maybe we had come too early, but Joe [Rauh, Hellman's lawyer] said no, it was better that I get used to the room.

Then, I think to make the wait better for me, he said, "Well, I can tell you now that in the early days of seeing you, I was scared that what happened to my friend might happen to me."

He stopped to tell Pollitt [Rauh's assistant] that he didn't understand about the press – not one newspaperman had appeared.

I said; "What happened to your friend?"

"He represented a Hollywood writer who told him that he would under no circumstances be a friendly witness. That was why my friend took the case. So they get here, in the same seats we are, sure of his client, and within ten minutes the writer is one of the friendliest witnesses the Committee has had the pleasure of. He throws in every name he can think of, including his college roommate, childhood friend."

I said, "No, that won't happen and for more solid reasons than your honour or even mine. I told you I can't make quick changes."

Joe told Pollitt that he thought he understood about no press and the half-empty room: the Committee had kept our appearance as quiet as they could. Joe said, "That means they're frightened of us. I don't know whether that's good or bad, but we want the press here and I don't know how to get them."

He didn't have to know. The room suddenly began to fill up behind me and the press people began to push toward their section and were still piling in when Representative Wood began to pound his gavel. I hadn't seen the Committee come in, don't think I had realized that they were to sit on a raised platform, the government having learned from the stage, or maybe the other way around. I was glad I hadn't seen them come in – they made a gloomy picture. Through the noise of the gavel I heard one of the ladies in the rear cough very loudly. She was to cough all through the hearing. Later I heard one of her friends say loudly, "Irma, take your good cough drops."

The opening questions were standard: what was my name, where was I born, what was my occupation, what were the titles of my plays. It didn't take long to get to what really interested them: my time in Hollywood, which studios had I worked for, what periods of what years, with some mysterious emphasis on 1937. (My time in Spain, I thought, but I was wrong.)

Had I met a writer called Martin Berkeley? (I had never, still have never, met Martin Berkeley, although Hammett* told me later that I had once sat at a lunch table of sixteen or seventeen people with him in the old Metro-Goldwyn-Mayer commissary.) I said I must refuse to answer that question. Mr Tavenner said he'd

---

* Dashiell Hammett. The detective-story writer, author of such private eye classics as *The Maltese Falcon*, was Hellman's long-time partner.

like to ask me again whether I had stated I was abroad in the summer of 1937. I said yes, explained that I had been in New York for several weeks before going to Europe, and got myself ready for what I knew was coming: Martin Berkeley, one of the Committee's most lavish witnesses on the subject of Hollywood, was now going to be put to work. Mr Tavenner read Berkeley's testimony. Perhaps he is worth quoting, the small details are nicely formed, even about his "old friend Hammett", who had no more than a bowing acquaintance with him.

MR TAVENNER: . . . I would like you to tell the committee when and where the Hollywood section of the Communist Party was first organized.
MR BERKELEY: Well, sir, by a very strange coincidence the section was organized in my house . . . In June of 1937 the middle of June, the meeting was held in my house. My house was picked because I had a large living room and ample parking facilities . . . And it was a pretty good meeting. We were honoured by the presence of many functionaries from downtown, and the spirit was swell . . . Well, in addition to Jerome and the others I have mentioned before, and there is no sense in me going over the list again and again . . . Also present was Harry Carlisle, who is now in the process of being deported, for which I am very grateful. He was an English subject. After Stanley Lawrence had stolen what funds there were from the party out here, and to make amends had gone to Spain and gotten himself killed, they sent Harry Carlisle here to conduct Marxist classes . . . Also at the meeting was Donald Ogden Stewart. His name is spelled Donald Ogden S-t-e-w-a-r-t. Dorothy Parker, also a writer. Her husband Allen Campbell, C-a-m-p-b-e-l-l; my old friend Dashiell Hammett, who is now in jail in New York for his activities; that very excellent playwright, Lillian Hellman . . .

And so on.
When this nonsense was finished, Mr Tavenner asked me if it was true. I said that I wanted to refer to the letter I had sent, I would like the Committee to reconsider my offer in the letter.

MR TAVENNER: In other words, you are asking the committee not to ask you any questions regarding the participation of other persons in the Communist Party activities?
I said I hadn't said that.

Mr Wood said that in order to clarify the record Mr Tavenner should put into the record the correspondence between me and the Committee. Mr Tavenner did just that, and when he had finished Rauh sprang to his feet, picked up a stack of mimeographed copies of my letter, and handed them out to the press section. I was puzzled by this – I hadn't noticed he had the copies – but I did notice that Rauh was looking happy.

Mr Tavenner was upset, far more than the printed words of my hearing show. Rauh said that Tavenner himself had put the letters in the record, and thus he thought passing out copies was proper. The polite words of each as they read on the page were not polite as spoken. I am convinced that in this section of the testimony, as in several other sections – certainly in Hammett's later testimony before the Senate Internal Security Subcommittee – either the court stenographer missed some of what was said and filled it in later, or the documents were, in part, edited. Having read many examples of the work of court stenographers, I have never once seen a completely accurate report.

Mr Wood told Mr Tavenner that the Committee could not be "placed in the attitude of trading with the witnesses as to what they will testify to" and that thus he thought both letters should be read aloud.

Mr Tavenner did just this, and there was talk I couldn't hear, a kind of rustle, from the press section. Then Mr Tavenner asked me if I had attended the meeting described by Berkeley, and one of the hardest things I ever did in my life was to swallow the words, "I don't know him, and a little investigation into the time and place would have proved to you that I could not have been at the meeting he talks about." Instead, I said that I must refuse to answer the question. The "must" in that sentence annoyed Mr Wood – it was to annoy him again and again – and he corrected me: "You might refuse to answer, the question is asked, do you refuse?"

But Wood's correction of me, the irritation in his voice, was making me nervous, and I began to move my right hand as if I had a tic, unexpected, and couldn't stop it. I told myself that if a word irritated him, the insults would begin to come very soon. So I sat up straight, made my left hand hold my right hand, and hoped it would work. But I felt the sweat on my face and arms and knew that something was going to happen to me, something out of control, and I turned to Joe, remembering the suggested toilet intermission. But the clock said we had only been there sixteen minutes, and if it was going to come, the bad time, I had better hang on for a while.

Was I a member of the Communist Party, had I been, what year had I stopped being? How could I harm such people as Martin Berkeley by admitting I had known them, and so on. At times I couldn't follow the reasoning, at times I understood full well that in refusing to answer questions about membership in the Party I had, of course, trapped myself into a seeming admission that I once had been.

But in the middle of one of the questions about my past, something so remarkable happened that I am to this day convinced that the unknown gentleman who spoke had a great deal to do with the rest of my life. A voice from the press gallery had been for at least three or four minutes louder than the other voices. (By this time, I think, the press had finished reading my letter to the Committee and were discussing it.) The loud voice had been answered by a less loud voice, but no words could be distinguished. Suddenly a clear voice said, "Thank God somebody finally had the guts to do it."

It is never wise to say that something is the best minute of your life, you must be forgetting, but I still think that unknown voice made the words that helped to save me. (I had been sure that not only did the elderly ladies in the room disapprove of me, but the press would be antagonistic.) Wood rapped his gavel and said angrily, "If that occurs again, I will clear the press from these chambers."

"You do that, sir," said the same voice.

Mr Wood spoke to somebody over his shoulder and the somebody moved around to the press section, but that is all that happened. To this day I don't know the name of the man who spoke, but for months later, almost every day I would say to myself, I wish I could tell him that I had really wanted to say to Mr Wood: "There is no Communist menace in this country and you know it. You have made cowards into liars, an ugly business, and you made me write a letter in which I acknowledged you power. I should have gone into your Committee room, given my name and address, and walked out." Many people have said they liked what I did, but I don't much, and if I hadn't worried about rats in jail, and such . . . Ah, the bravery you tell yourself was possible when it's all over, the bravery of the staircase.

In the Committee room I heard Mr Wood say, "Mr Walter does

not desire to ask the witness any further questions. Is there any reason why this witness should not be excused from further attendance before the Committee?"

Mr Tavenner said, "No, sir."

My hearing was over an hour and seven minutes after it began. I don't think I understood that it was over, but Joe was whispering so loudly and so happily that I jumped from the noise in my ear.

He said, "*Get up. Get up*. Get out of here immediately. Pollitt will take you. Don't stop for any reason, to answer any questions from anybody. Don't run, but walk as fast as you can and just shake your head and keep moving if anybody comes near you."

Some years later Hellman asked Rauh why she was not prosecuted by the Committee:

He said, "There were three things they wanted. One, names which you wouldn't give. Two, a smear by accusing you of being a 'Fifth Amendment Communist'. They couldn't do that because in your letter you offered to testify about yourself. And three, a prosecution which they couldn't do because they forced us into taking the Fifth Amendment. They had sense enough to see that they were in a bad spot. We beat them, that's all."

LITTLE ROCK: VIOLENCE AT CENTRAL HIGH, 3 September 1957

Relman Morrin, Associated Press

Passions erupted throughout the American south in the 1950s as black Americans sought equal educational opportunities. The most famous of the clashes between segregationists and anti-segregationists came at Little Rock, where Governor Orval E. Faubus used National Guard troops at Central High School to prevent integration. The troops were withdrawn after a federal court ruling, but replaced by a large crowd which declared its intention of keeping black children out. Relman Morrin won a Pulitzer prize for his reporting of the school integration crisis at Little Rock.

It was exactly like an explosion, a human explosion.

At 8.35 a.m., the people standing in front of the high school looked like the ones you see every day in a shopping centre.

A pretty, sweet-faced woman with auburn hair and a jewel-green jacket. Another holding a white portable radio to her ear.

"I'm getting the news of what's going on at the high school," she said. People laughed. A grey-haired man, tall and spare, leaned over the wooden barricade. "If they're coming," he said, quietly, "they'll be here soon." "They better," said another, "I got to get to work."

Ordinary people – mostly curious, you would have said – watching a high school on a bright blue-and-gold morning.

Five minutes later, at 8.40, they were a mob.

The terrifying spectacle of 200-odd individuals, suddenly welded together into a single body, took place in the barest fraction of a second. It was an explosion, savagery chain-reacting from person to person, fusing them into a white-hot mass.

There are three glass windowed telephone booths across the street from the south end of the high school.

At 8.35, I was inside one of them, dictating.

I saw four Negroes coming down the centre of the street, in twos. One was tall and big shouldered. One was tall and thin. The other two were short. The big man had a card in his hat and was carrying a Speed Graphic, a camera for taking news pictures.

A strange, animal growl rose from the crowd.

"Here come the Negroes."

Instantly, people turned their backs on the high school and ran toward the four men. They hesitated. Then they turned to run.

I saw the white men catch them on the sidewalk and the lawn of a home, a quarter-block away. There was a furious, struggling knot. You could see a man kicking at the big Negro. Then another jumped on his back and rode him to the ground, forearms deep in the Negro's throat.

They kicked him and beat him on the ground and they smashed his camera to splinters. The other three ran down the street with one white man chasing them. When the white man saw he was alone, he turned and fled back toward the crowd.

Meanwhile, five policemen had rescued the big man.

I had just finished saying, "Police escorted the big man away –"

At that instant, a man shouted, "Look, the niggers are going in."

Directly across from me, three Negro boys and five girls were walking toward the side door at the south end of the school.

It was an unforgettable tableau.

They were carrying books. White bobby-sox, part of the high school uniform, glinted on the girls' ankles. They were all neatly dressed. The boys wore open-throat shirts and the girls ordinary frocks.

They weren't hurrying. They simply strolled across perhaps fifteen yards from the sidewalk to the school steps. They glanced at the people and the police as though none of this concerned them.

You can never forget a scene like that.

Nor the one that followed.

Like a wave, the people who had run toward the four Negro men, now swept back toward the police and the barricades.

"Oh, God, the niggers are in the school," a man yelled.

A woman – the one with the auburn hair and green jacket – rushed up to him. Her face was working with fury now.

Her lips drew back in a snarl and she was screaming, "Did they go in?"

"The niggers are in the school," the man said.

"Oh, God," she said. She covered her face with her hands. Then she tore her hair, still screaming.

She looked exactly like the women who cluster around a mine head when there has been an explosion and men are trapped below.

The tall, lean man jumped up on one of the barricades. He was holding on to the shoulders of others nearby.

"Who's going through?" he roared.

"We all are," the people shrieked.

They surged over and around the barricades, breaking for the police.

About a dozen policemen, in short-sleeved blue shirts, swinging billy clubs, were in front of them.

Men and women raced toward them and the policemen raised their clubs, moving this way and that as people tried to dodge around them.

A man went down, pole-axed when a policeman clubbed him.

Another, with crisp curly black hair, was quick as a rat. He dodged between two policemen and got as far as the schoolyard. There the others caught him.

With swift, professional skill, they pulled his coat half-way down his back, pinning his arms. In a flash they were hustling him back toward the barricades.

A burly, thick-bodied man wearing a construction worker's "hard hat" charged a policeman. Suddenly, he stopped and held both hands high above his head.

I couldn't see it, but I assume the officer jammed a pistol in his ribs.

Meanwhile, the women – the auburn-haired one, the woman with the radio, and others – were swirling around the police commanding officers.

Tears were streaming down their faces. They acted completely distraught.

It was pure hysteria.

And they kept crying, "The niggers are in our school. Oh, God, are you going to stand here and let the niggers stay in school?"

Then, swiftly, a line of cars filled with state troopers rolled toward the school from two directions. The flasher-signals on the tops of the cars were spurting red warnings.

A VISIT TO CAMELOT, Washington, 25 January 1961

J.K. Galbraith

Recently appointed US ambassador to India by JFK, Galbraith writes in his diary:

After the meeting, Mac Bundy told me "The Boss" (a new term) had been asking for me. I went into Ken O'Donnell's office and presently the President came through, grabbed me by the arm, and we had an hour-and-a-half chat which included a tour of the upstairs of the White House. We saw where Ike's golf shoes had poked innumerable holes in his office floor. When we left the office in the West Wing for the house proper, we went headlong into a closet. The President turned over furniture to see where it was made, dismissed some as Sears, Roebuck and expressed shock that so little – the Lincoln bed apart – consisted of good pieces. Only expensive reproductions. The effect is indeed undistinguished although today the house was flooded with sunlight and quite filled with flowers.

CUBAN MISSILE CRISIS: JFK ORDERS NAVAL BLOCKADE, 22–28 October 1962

Robert F. Kennedy

After aerial reconnaissance showed that Russia was siting ballistic missiles on Cuba, President John F. Kennedy determined to remove this threat to the USA's eastern seaboard. Hawks in his administration urged a preemptive strike on Cuba, but as Kennedy's brother, the Attorney General, relates here the President calmly decided on a naval blockade of the island. Even so, the blockade caused the USA and the USSR to stand eye-to-eye, fingers on nuclear buttons, until on 28 October Kruschchev blinked and agreed to remove the missiles.

We met all day Friday and Friday night. Then again early Saturday morning we were back at the State Department. I talked to the President several times on Friday. He was hoping to be able to meet with us early enough to decide on a course of action and then broadcast it to the nation Sunday night. Saturday morning at 10 o'clock I called him at the Blackstone Hotel in Chicago and told him we were ready to meet with him. It was now up to one single man. No committee was going to make this decision. He canceled his trip and returned to Washington.

As he was returning to Washington, our Armed Forces across the world were put on alert. Telephoning from our meeting in the State Department, Secretary McNamara ordered four tactical air squadrons placed at readiness for an air strike, in case the President decided to accept that recommendation.

The President arrived back at the White House at 1:40 p.m. and went for a swim. I sat on the side of the pool, and we talked. At 2:30 we walked up to the Oval Room.

The meeting went on until ten minutes after five. Convened as a formal meeting of the National Security Council, it was a larger group of people who met, some of whom had not participated in the deliberations up to that time. Bob McNamara presented the arguments for the blockade; others presented the arguments for the military attack.

The President made his decision that afternoon in favor of the blockade. There was one final meeting the next morning, with General Walter C. Sweeney, Jr. Commander in Chief of the Tactical Air Command, who told the President that even a major surprise air attack could not be certain of destroying all the missile sites and nuclear weapons in Cuba. That ended the small, lingering doubt that might still have remained in his mind. It had worried him that a blockade would not remove the missiles – now it was clear that an attack could not accomplish that task completely, either.

CIVIL RIGHTS MARCH ON WASHINGTON DC, 29 August 1963

Vincent Ryder and David Shears

The Great Negro March on Washington yesterday turned out to be an orderly, good-humoured stroll around the Lincoln Memorial by the 200,000 Civil Rights demonstrators.

Only two arrests were made. One was of a follower of George Rockwell, the United States Nazi leader. Police hustled him away when he tried to make a speech.

Before the 200,000-strong Civil Rights march in Washington today was half over, Mr Bayard Rustin, deputy organizer and the real moving spirit, spoke of the next move.

He said: "Already one of our objectives has been met. We said we would awaken the conscience of the nation and we have done it."

The next move would be a "counter-filibuster" if opponents in the Senate tried to talk the proposed Civil Rights Bill to death. On every day of this "filibuster" 1,000 Negroes would be brought into Washington to stage a demonstration.

A great roar of approval met the warning by the Rev. Martin Luther King, the integrationist leader, that America was in for "a rude awakening" if she thought she could go back to business as usual.

"Let us not seek to satisfy our thirst for freedom by drinking from the cup of hatred and bitterness," said Mr King. Negroes would go on with the struggle until "justice flows like water and righteousness like a stream".

The cheers rolled over the crowd, jammed in front of the Lincoln Memorial and along the shallow reflecting pool.

It was a day of quiet triumph, a mingling of fervent demands with a show of orderly, relaxed calm. Earlier fears of disorder seemed almost laughably out of place.

Personalities in the march included Marlon Brando, Burt Lancaster, Lena Horne, Judy Garland, Sammy Davis, Sidney Poitier and Josephine Baker, who flew from Paris.

For two hours the marchers' numbers swelled around the monument within sight of the White House and the Capitol, which houses Congress.

They were entertained by singers and by brief speeches from

their heroes, Jackie Robinson, the baseball player, and a man who roller-skated all the way from Chicago, and admitted his legs were tired.

The organizers expected that this sort of distraction would be necessary to keep tempers under control. They need not have worried. The crowd seemed almost as determined to be respectable as to demand civil rights.

Black suits and dresses predominated. A group of poor Negroes from Parksville, Mississippi, were in well-pressed overalls.

There were clerical collars by the dozen. Clergymen of every denomination joined the demonstration.

THE ASSASSINATION OF PRESIDENT JOHN F. KENNEDY, Dallas, 23 November 1963

Merriman Smith

Lee Harvey Oswald, the alleged assassin, was himself shot and killed days later. Disquiet over the assassination and rumours of Mafia, even US secret service, involvement eventually led to a US senate inquiry. In 1979 the House Assassination's Committee found that Kennedy was "probably assassinated as a result of a conspiracy". Merriman Smith, a UPI reporter, won a Pulitzer Prize for this record of JFK's assassination.

It was a balmy, sunny noon as we motored through downtown Dallas behind President Kennedy. The procession cleared the centre of the business district and turned into a handsome highway that wound through what appeared to be a park.

I was riding in the so-called White House press "pool" car, a telephone company vehicle equipped with a mobile radio-telephone. I was in the front seat between a driver from the telephone company and Malcom Kilduff, acting White House press secretary for the President's Texas tour. Three other pool reporters were wedged in the back seat.

Suddenly we heard three loud, almost painfully loud cracks. The first sounded as if it might have been a large firecracker. But the second and the third blasts were unmistakable. Gunfire.

The President's car, possibly as much as 150 or 200 yards ahead, seemed to falter briefly. We saw a flurry of activity in the secret service follow-up car behind the chief executive's bubble-top limousine.

Next in line was the car bearing Vice-President Lyndon B. Johnson. Behind that, another follow-up car bearing agents assigned to the vice-president's protection. We were behind that car.

Our car stood still for probably only a few seconds, but it seemed like a lifetime. One sees history explode before one's eyes and for even the most trained observer, there is a limit to what one can comprehend.

I looked ahead at the President's car but could not see him or his companion, Gov. John Connally. Both had been riding on the right side of the limousine. I thought I saw a flash of pink that would have been Mrs Jacqueline Kennedy.

Everybody in our car began shouting at the driver to pull up closer to the President's car. But at this moment, we saw the big bubbletop and a motorcycle escort roar away at high speed.

We screamed at our driver, "get going, get going". We careened around the Johnson car and its escort and set out down the highway, barely able to keep in sight of the President's car and the accompanying secret service car.

They vanished around a curve. When we cleared the same curve we could see where we were heading – Parkland Hospital. We spilled out of the pool car as it entered the hospital driveway.

I ran to the side of the bubbletop.

The President was face down on the back seat. Mrs Kennedy made a cradle of her arms around the President's head and bent over him as if she were whispering to him.

Gov. Connally was on his back on the floor of the car, his head and shoulders resting in the arms of his wife, Nellie, who shook with dry sobs. Blood oozed from the front of the governor's suit. I could not see the President's wound. But I could see blood spattered around the interior of the rear seat and a dark stain spreading down the right side of the President's dark grey suit.

From the telephone car, I had radioed the Dallas UPI Bureau that three shots had been fired at the Kennedy motorcade.

Clint Hill, the secret service agent in charge of the detail assigned to Mrs Kennedy, was leaning over into the rear of the car.

"How badly was he hit, Clint?" I asked.

"He's dead," Hill replied curtly.

WATTS: THE BROTHERS CELEBRATE, Folsom Prison, 16 August 1965

Eldridge Cleaver

In August 1965 the black ghetto of Watts in South Central Los Angeles exploded into the worst urban riots in the USA since the Civil War. Racism and poverty were prime incendiaries. Watts was the scene of disturbances again in 1992 (see pp 485–6). Eldridge Cleaver was a follower of Malcolm X, and later "minister of information" for the Black Panther Party.

Folsom Prison
August 16, 1965

As we left the Mess Hall Sunday morning and milled around in the prison yard, after four days of abortive uprising in Watts, a group of low riders from Watts assembled on the basketball court. They were wearing jubilant, triumphant smiles, animated by a vicarious spirit by which they, too, were in the thick of the uprising taking place hundreds of miles away to the south in the Watts ghetto.

"Man," said one, "what they doing out there? Break it down for me, Baby."

They slapped each other's outstretched palms in a cool salute and burst out laughing with joy.

"Home boy, them Brothers is taking care of Business!" shrieked another ecstatically.

Then one low rider, stepping into the center of the circle formed by the others, rared back on his legs and swaggered, hunching his belt up with his forearms as he'd seen James Cagney and George Raft do in too many gangster movies. I joined the circle. Sensing a creative moment in the offing, we all got very quiet, very still, and others passing by joined the circle and did likewise.

"Baby," he said, "they walking in fours and kicking in doors; dropping Reds* and busting heads; drinking wine and committing crime, shooting and looting; high-siding and low-riding, setting fires and slashing tires; turning over cars and burning down bars; making Parker mad and making me glad; putting an end to that 'go slow' crap and putting sweet Watts on the map – my black ass is in Folsom this morning but my black heart is in Watts!" Tears of joy were rolling from his eyes.

* barbiturates

It was a cleansing, revolutionary laugh we all shared, something we have not often had occasion for.

Watts was a place of shame. We used to use Watts as an epithet in much the same way as city boys used "country" as a term of derision. To deride one as a "lame", who did not know what was happening (a rustic bumpkin), the "in-crowd" of the time from L.A. would bring a cat down by saying that he had just left Watts, that he ought to go back to Watts until he had learned what was happening, or that he had just stolen enough money to move out of Watts and was already trying to play a cool part. But now, blacks are seen in Folsom saying, "I'm from Watts, Baby!" – whether true or no, but I think their meaning is clear. Confession: I, too, have participated in this game, saying, I'm from Watts. In fact, I did live there for a time, and I'm *proud* of it, the tired lamentations of Whitney Young, Roy Wilkins, and The Preacher [M. L. King] notwithstanding.

VIETNAM WAR: THE CITADEL OF HUÉ, Vietnam, February 1968

Michael Herr

On 30 January 1968, the North Vietnamese marked the beginning of the Tet (lunar new year) by launching an offensive against 125 locations held by the South Vietnamese and US troops, including Khe Sahn, Saigon and Hué. This account of Hué during the fighting of February 1968 is from Michael Herr's classic of war journalism, *Dispatches*.

Going in, there were sixty of us packed into a deuce-and-a-half, one of eight trucks moving in convoy from Phu Bai, bringing in over 300 replacements for the casualties taken in the earliest fighting south of the Perfume River. There had been a harsh, dark storm going on for days, and it turned the convoy route into a mudbed. It was terribly cold in the trucks, and the road was covered with leaves that had either been blown off the trees by the storm or torn away by our artillery, which had been heavy all along the road. Many of the houses had been completely collapsed, and not one had been left without pitting from shell fragments. Hundreds of refugees held to the side of the road as we passed, many of them wounded. The kids would laugh and shout, the old would look on with that silent tolerance for misery that made so many Americans uneasy, which was usually misread as indifference. But the younger men and women would often look at us with unmistakable contempt, pulling their cheering children back from the trucks.

We sat there trying to keep it up for each other, grinning at the bad weather and the discomfort, sharing the first fear, glad that we weren't riding point or closing the rear. They had been hitting our trucks regularly, and a lot of the convoys had been turned back. The houses that we passed so slowly made good cover for snipers, and one B-40 rocket could have made casualties out of a whole truckload of us. All the grunts were whistling, and no two were whistling the same tune, it sounded like a locker room before a game that nobody wanted to play. Or almost nobody. There was a black Marine called Philly Dog who'd been a gang lord in Philadelphia and who was looking forward to some street fighting after six months in the jungle, he could show the kickers what he could do with some city ground. (In Hué he turned out to be incredibly valuable. I saw him pouring out about a hundred rounds of .30-calibre fire into a breach in the wall, laughing, "You got to bring some to get some"; he seemed to be about the only man in Delta Company who hadn't been hurt yet.) And there was a Marine correspondent, Sergeant Dale Dye, who sat with a tall yellow flower sticking out of his helmet cover, a really outstanding target. He was rolling his eyes around and saying, "Oh, yes, oh yes, Charlie's got his shit together here, this will be *bad*," and smiling happily. It was the same smile I saw a week later when a sniper's bullet tore up a wall two inches above his head, odd cause for amusement in anyone but a grunt.

Everyone else in the truck had that wild haunted going-West look that said it was perfectly correct to be here where the fighting would be the worst, where you wouldn't have half of what you needed, where it was colder than Nam ever got. On their helmets and flak jackets they'd written the names of old operations, of girlfriends, their war names (FAR FROM FEARLESS, MICKEY'S MONKEY, AVENGER V, SHORT TIME SAFETY MOE), their fantasies (BORN TO LOSE, BORN TO RAISE HELL, BORN TO KILL, BORN TO DIE), their ongoing information (HELL SUCKS, TIME IS ON MY SIDE, JUST YOU AND ME GOD RIGHT?). One kid called to me, "Hey man! You want a story, man? Here man, write this: I'm up there on 881, this was May, I'm just up there walkin' the ridgeline like a movie star and this Zip jumps up smack into me, lays his AK-47 fucking right *into* me, only he's so *amazed* at my *cool* I got my whole clip off 'fore he knew how to thank me for it. Grease one." After twenty kilometers of this, in spite of the black roiling sky ahead, we could see smoke coming up from the far side of the river, from the Citadel of Hué.

The bridge was down that spanned the canal dividing the village of An Cuu and the southern sector of Hué, blown the night before by the Viet Cong, and the forward area beyond the far bank wasn't thought to be secure, so we bivouacked in the village for the night. It had been completely deserted, and we set ourselves up in empty hootches, laying our poncho liners out over broken glass and shattered brick. At dusk, while we all stretched out along the canal bank eating dinner, two Marine gunships came down on us and began strafing us, sending burning tracers up along the canal, and we ran for cover, more surprised than scared. "Way to go, motherfucker, way to pinpoint the fuckin' enemy," one of the grunts said, and he set up his M-60 machine-gun in case they came back. "I don't guess we got to take *that* shit," he said. Patrols were sent out, guards posted, and we went into the hootches to sleep. For some reason, we weren't even mortared that night.

In the morning we crossed the canal on a two-by-four and started walking in until we came across the first of the hundreds of civilian dead that we were to see in the next weeks: an old man arched over his straw hat and a little girl who'd been hit while riding her bicycle, lying there with her arm up like a reproach. They'd been lying out like that for a week; for the first time we were grateful for the cold.

Along the Perfume River's south bank there is a long, graceful park that separates Hué's most pleasant avenue, Le Loi, from the river-front. People will talk about how they'd sit out there in the sun and watch the sampans moving down the river, or watch the girls bicycling up Le Loi, past the villas of officials and the French-architected University buildings. Many of those villas had been destroyed and much of the University permanently damaged. In the middle of the street a couple of ambulances from the German Mission had been blown up, and the Cercle Sportif was covered with bullet holes and shrapnel. The rain had brought up the green, it stretched out cased in thick white fog. In the park itself, four fat green dead lay sprawled around a tall, ornate cage, inside of which sat a small, shivering monkey. One of the correspondents along stepped over the corpses to feed it some fruit. (Days later, I came back to the spot. The corpses were gone, but so was the monkey.

There had been so many refugees and so little food then, and someone must have eaten him.) The Marines of 2/5 had secured almost all of the central south bank and were now fanning out to the west, fighting and clearing one of the major canals. We were waiting for some decision on whether or not US Marines would be going into the Citadel itself, but no one had any doubts about what that decision would be. We sat there taking in the dread by watching the columns of smoke across the river, receiving occasional sniper rounds, infrequent bursts of .50-calibre, watching the Navy LCUs on the river getting shelled from the wall. One Marine next to me was saying that it was just a damned shame, all them poor people, all them nice-looking houses, they even had a Shell station there. He was looking at the black napalm blasts and the wreckage along the wall. "Looks like the Imperial City's had the schnitz," he said.

THE VIETNAM WAR: THE PACIFICATION OF MY LAI, 16 March 1968

Time *magazine correspondent*

The My Lai massacre, committed by C Company of the US 11th Infantry Brigade, resulted in the court martial of Lieutenant William Calley for the murder of 109 Vietnamese citizens.

West, a squad leader in a platoon commanded by Lieutenant Jeffrey La Cross, followed Calley's platoon into My Lai. "Everyone was shooting," he said. "Some of the huts were torched. Some of the *yanigans* [young soldiers] were shooting kids." In the confusion, he claims, it was hard to tell "mama-sans from papa-sans", since both wore black pyjamas and conical hats. He and his squad helped round up the women and children. When one of his men protested that "I can't shoot these people", West told him to turn a group over to Captain Medina. On the way out of the village, West recalls seeing a ditch filled with dead and dying civilians. His platoon also passed a crying Vietnamese boy, wounded in both a leg and an arm. West heard a GI ask, "What about him?" Then he heard a shot and the boy fell. "The kid didn't do anything," said West, "He didn't have a weapon" . . .

Another soldier in the group following Calley's was SP4 Varnado Simpson, twenty-two. "Everyone who went into the village had in mind to kill," he says. "We had lost a lot of buddies and it was a VC stronghold. We considered them either VC or helping the VC." His platoon approached from the left flank. "As I came up on the village there was a woman, a man and a child running away from it towards some huts. So I told them in their language to stop, and they didn't, and I had orders to shoot them down and I did this. This is what I did. I shot them, the lady and the little boy. He was about two years old."

A detailed account came from Paul David Meadlo, twenty-two, a member of Calley's platoon . . . Meadlo says his group ran through My Lai, herding men, women, children and babies into the centre of the village – "like a little island".

"Lieutenant Calley came over and said, 'You know what to do with them, don't you?' And I said, 'Yes.' And he left and came back about ten minutes later, and said, 'How come you ain't killed them yet?' And I told him that I didn't think he wanted us to kill them, that he just wanted us to guard them. He said, 'No, I want them dead.' So he started shooting them. And he told me to start shooting. I poured about four clips [68 shots] into them. I might have killed ten or fifteen of them.

"So we started to gather more people, and we had about seven or eight, and we put them in the hootch [hut] and then we dropped a hand grenade in there with them. And then they had about seventy to seventy-five people all gathered up by a ravine, so we threw ours in with them and Lieutenant Calley told me, 'Meadlo, we got another job to do.' And so he walked over to the people, and he started pushing them off and started shooting. We just pushed them all off and just started using automatics on them."

According to SP5 Jay Roberts, the rampaging GIs were not interested solely in killing, although that seemed foremost in their minds. Roberts told *Life*, "Just outside the village there was this big pile of bodies. This really tiny kid – he had only a shirt on, nothing else – he came over to the pile and held the hand of one of the dead. One of the GIs behind me dropped into a kneeling position thirty metres from this kid and killed him with a single shot." Roberts also watched while troops accosted a group of women, including a teenage girl. The girl was about thirteen, wearing black pyjamas: "A GI grabbed the girl and with the help of others started stripping her," Roberts related. "Let's see what she's made of," a soldier said. "VC boom-boom," another said, telling the thir-

teen-year-old girl that she was a whore for the Vietcong. "I'm
horny," said a third. As they were stripping the girl, with bodies
and burning huts all around them, the girl's mother tried to help
her, scratching and clawing at the soldiers.

Continued Roberts: "Another Vietnamese woman, afraid for
her own safety, tried to stop the woman from objecting. One
soldier kicked the mother, and another slapped her up a bit.
Haeberle [the photographer] jumped in to take a picture of the
group of women. The picture shows the thirteen-year-old girl
hiding behind her mother, trying to button the top of her pyjamas.
When they noticed Ron, they left off and turned away as if
everything was normal. Then a soldier asked, 'Well, what'll we
do with 'em?' 'Kill 'em,' another answered. I heard an M60 go off,
a light machine-gun, and when we turned all of them and the kids
with them were dead."

CIVIL RIGHTS: THE FUNERAL OF MARTIN LUTHER KING, 9 April 1968

Alistair Cooke

Dr King was assassinated in Memphis, Tennessee, on 4 April.

Once before, the ninth of April was memorial day throughout
the South. One hundred and three years ago today Robert E.
Lee tendered his sword to General Grant and was granted in
return the release of your men and their mules to assist in the
spring ploughing. Today, on a flaming spring day, with the
magnolias blooming and the white dogwood and the red sprinkling the land, they brought a farm wagon and its mules to stand
outside the church on the street where Martin Luther King was
born and after the funeral service to carry his body four miles to
his college and lay it to rest. The mule train is the oldest and still
most dependable form of transport of the rural poor in the
Southland. And somebody had the graceful idea that a mule
train would be the aptest cortege for the man who was the
apostle of the poor.

From the warm dawn into the blazing noon, the black bodies
wearing more suits and ties than they would put on for a corona-
tion, moved through the Negro sections of the town towards the
street of comfortable, two-storey frame houses where the coloured
business and professional men live and where, across from Cox's

Funeral Home, the Rev. Martin Luther King lived and preached, in the Ebenezer Baptist Church, a red-bricked nondescript tabernacle.

Thousands of college students had volunteered to act as marshals to hold the crowds; but though there was a tremendous push and jostle of people before the service began, there were enough police on hand to stem the crush and hand the visiting celebrities through like very pregnant women.

The bell tolled out the tune of "We Shall Overcome" and big cars slid up to the entrance, and out of them climbed the Attorney General, Ramsey Clark, and Mrs John H Kennedy, and Richard Nixon and Senator Eugene McCarthy, Governor and Mrs Romney of Michigan, and Governor Rockefeller and John Lindsay of New York, the new Roman Catholic Archbishop Terence Cooke, Sidney Poitier, the Metropolitan Opera's Leontyne Price, Eartha Kitt, Sammy Davis Jr. Bobby and Ethel Kennedy and brother Edward, and Dr Ralph Bunche, U. Thant's man and Dr. King's friend.

Over the breaking waves of street noise and the tolling bell, the strong baritone of the Rev. Ralph Abernathy, Dr King's heir, chanted from time to time: "We will please be orderly now . . . let us have dignity . . . please . . . there are no more seats in the church." Somebody lifted a squalling baby and passed it out over the tossing heads to safety.

It is a small church, and shortly after 10.30 the last cars and the last mourners were slotted in their places. First, Mrs King and her four children and the dead man's brother, and Harry Belafonte. Then at last an alert squad of aides and Secret Service men surrounding Vice-President Humphrey. The conspicuous absentee was Lester Maddox, the Governor of Georgia, a segregationist whose presence could upset a coloured funeral any place North or South.

The inside of the church impressively belies its outside. It is a pleasantly modern room with a single oriel window, above a white cross over the choir and the pulpit. The flanking walls have two simple Gothic windows decorated alike with a single shield bearing a cross and surmounted with the crown of Christ. Tiny spotlights embedded in the ceiling threw little pools of light on the famous and the obscure equally. The warm shadows these shafts encouraged gave an extraordinary chiaroscuro to the congregation, making Bobby Kennedy at one point look like the captain of

Rembrandt's "Night Guard" amid his lieutenants slumbering in the shade.

It was a normal Baptist service with Southern overtones of gospel singing and solos, by black girls in white surplices, of Dr King's favourite hymns sung with impassioned locking of the hands and closed eyes. Through it all, Mrs King sat back at a sideways angle with the carved, sad fixity of an African idol. Dr King's brother covered his face with a handkerchief once and others dabbed at their eyes: and the youngest King daughter sagged over in deep sleep like a rag doll. But Mrs King was as impassive as Buddha behind her thin veil while the prayers were given, the hymns, the eulogy by a New York dean as white as Siegfried, who had taught theology to Dr King. Once there was a suspicion of a glitter in her eyes when the Rev. Abernathy told of the last meal he had with Dr King, an anecdote as simple as a parable.

On that Thursday noon in the Lorraine Motel, in Memphis, Tennessee, the maid served up only one salad, and Martin took a small portion of it and left the rest. Then someone reminded the girl that she had brought up one order of fish instead of two. And Martin said, "Don't worry about it. Ralph and I can eat from the same plate", and I ate my last meal that Thursday noon. And I will not eat bread or meat or anything until I am thoroughly satisfied that I am ready for the task at hand."

There was one innovation that was nearly forgotten at the end. Both the casket and the family were ready to go, but there was a quick whisper in the Rev. Abernathy's ear and he announced that Mrs King had requested a playback of one of Dr King's last sermons.

It was the premonitory vision of his inevitable end, and his voice resounded through the hushed church: "I think about my own death, and I think about my own funeral . . . and every now and then I ask myself what it is that I would want said and I leave the word to this morning . . . I don't want a long funeral, and if you get somebody to deliver the eulogy, tell him not to talk too long . . . tell him not to mention that I have a Nobel peace prize – that isn't important. Tell him not to mention that I have 300 or 400 awards – that's not important . . . I'd like somebody to mention that day that Martin Luther King tried to give his life serving others. I want you to say that day that I tried to be right and to walk with them. I want you to be able to say that day that I did try to feed the hungry. I want you to be able to say that day that I did try in my life to clothe the naked . . . I want you to say that I tried to love and serve humanity."

Then the doors were opened and the family went out and all the parsons, and the mule team bore its flowered casket and moved towards the many, many thousands that had gone on before to Morehouse College.

VIETNAM WAR: LETTERS HOME, 1968–1970

Second-Lieutenant Robert ("Mike") Ransom Jnr., 4th Battalion, 3rd Infantry

April 1968

Dear Mom and Dad,

Well, I've had my baptism by fire, and it's changed me I think. Two days ago my platoon was on a mission to clear three suspected minefields. We were working with a mechanized platoon with four tracks, and our tactic was to put the tracks on line and just roar through the minefields, hoping to blow them. Since the majority of the VC mines are antipersonnel, the tracks could absorb the explosions with no damage done to them or the people inside. My platoon rode along just as security in case we were attacked. We spent the whole day clearing the three fields and came up with a big zero.

The tracks were then returning us to where we would stay overnight. When we reached our spot we jumped off the tracks, and one of my men jumped right onto a mine. Both his feet were blown off, both legs were torn to shreds – his entire groin area was completely blown away. It was the most horrible sight I've ever seen. Fortunately he never knew what hit him. I tried to revive him with mouth-to-mouth resuscitation, but it was hopeless to begin with.

In addition, the explosion wounded seven other people (four seriously) who were dusted off by medevac, and three others lightly, who were not dusted off. Of the four seriously wounded, one received a piece of shrapnel in the heart and may not survive. The other three were almost completely riddled with shrapnel, and while they will be completely all right, it will be a slow and painful recovery.

I was one of the slightly wounded. I got three pieces in my left arm, one in my right knee, and about twenty in both legs. I am completely all right. In fact I thought I had only gotten one in the arm and one in the knee. It was not until last night when I took off my clothes to take a shower that I noticed the other spots where I had been hit.

I came back to Chu Lai yesterday because my knee is now quite stiff and swollen, and will probably be here a couple of days, what with x-rays and what not. Believe it or not, I am extremely anxious to get back to platoon. Having been through this, I am now a bonafide member of the platoon. They have always followed my orders, but I was an outsider. Now I'm a member of the team, and it feels good.

I want to assure you that I am perfectly all right. You will probably get some sort of notification that I was lightly wounded, and I just don't want you to worry about it at all. I will receive a Purple Heart for it. People over here talk about the Million-Dollar Wound. It is one which is serious enough to warrant evacuation to the States but which will heal entirely. Therefore, you might call mine a Half-Million-Dollar Wound. My RTO, who was on my track sitting right next to me, caught a piece of shrapnel in his tail, and since he had caught a piece in his arm about two months ago, he'll get out of the field with wounds about as serious as a couple of mosquito bites.

I said earlier that the incident changed me. I am now filled with both respect and hate for the VC and the Vietnamese. Respect because the enemy knows that he can't stand up to us in a fire fight due to our superior training, equipment and our vast arsenal of weapons. Yet he is able. Via his mines and booby traps, he can whittle our ranks down piecemeal until we cannot muster an effective fighting force.

In the month that I have been with the company, we have lost 4 killed and about 30 wounded. We have not seen a single verified dink the whole time, nor have we even shot a single round at anything. I've developed hate for the Vietnamese because they come around selling Cokes and beer to us and then run back and tell the VC how many we are, where our positions are, and where the leaders position themselves. In the place where we got hit, we discovered four other mines, all of them placed in the spots where I, my platoon sergeant, and two squad leaders had been sitting. I talked to the mechanized platoon leader who is with us and he said that as he left the area to return to his fire base, the people in the village he went through were laughing at him because they knew we had been hit. I felt like turning my machine guns on the village to kill every man, woman and child in it.

Sorry this has been an unpleasant letter, but I'm in a rather unpleasant mood.

All love,
Mike

Ransom died of wounds on 11 May 1968.

PFC David Bowman, 1st Battalion, 8th Cavalry
n.d. [1968]

Dear Civilians, Friends, Draft Dodgers, etc:

In the very near future, the undersigned will once more be in your midst, dehydrated and demoralized, to take his place again as a human being with the well-known forms of freedom and justice for all; engage in life, liberty and the somewhat delayed pursuit of happiness. In making your joyous preparations to welcome him back into organized society you might take certain steps to make allowances for the past twelve months. In other words, he might be a little Asiatic from Vietnamesitis and Overseasitis, and should be handled with care. Don't be alarmed if he is infected with all forms of rare tropical disease. A little time in the "Land of the Big PX" will cure this malady.

Therefore, show no alarm if he insists on carrying a weapon to the dinner table, looks around for his steel pot when offered a chair, or wakes you up in the middle of the night for guard duty. Keep cool when he pours gravy on his dessert at dinner of mixed peaches with his Seagrams VO. Pretend not to notice if he acts dazed, eats with his fingers instead of silverware and prefers C-rations to steak. Take it with a smile when he insists on digging up the garden to fill sandbags for the bunker he is building. Be tolerant when he takes his blanket and sheet off the bed and puts them on the floor to sleep on.

Abstain from saying anything about powdered eggs, dehydrated potatoes, fried rice, fresh milk or ice cream. Do not be alarmed if he should jump up from the dinner table and rush to the garbage can to wash his dish with a toilet brush. After all, this has been his standard. Also, if it should start raining, pay no attention to him if he pulls off his clothes, grabs a bar of soap and a towel and runs outdoors for a shower.

When in his daily conversation he utters such things as "Xin loi" and "Choi oi" just be patient, and simply leave quickly and calmly if by some chance he utters "didi" with an irritated look on his face because it means no less than "Get the h – out of here." Do not let it shake you up if he picks up the phone and yells "Sky King forward, Sir" or says "Roger out" for good-by or simply shouts "Working."

Never ask why the Jones' son held a higher rank than he did, and by no means mention the word "extend." Pretend not to notice if at a restaurant he calls the waitress "Numbuh I girl" and uses his hat as an ashtray. He will probably keep listening for "Homeward Bound" to sound off over AFRS. If he does, comfort him, for he is still reminiscing. Be especially watchful when he is in the presence of women – *especially* a beautiful woman.

Above all, keep in mind that beneath that tanned and rugged exterior there is a heart of gold (the only thing of value he has left). Treat him with kindness, tolerance, and an occasional fifth of good liquor and you will be able to rehabilitate that which was once (and now a hollow shell) the happy-go-lucky guy you once knew and loved.

Last, but not least, send no more mail to the APO, fill the ice box with beer, get the civvies out of mothballs, fill the car with gas, and get the women and children off the streets – BECAUSE THE KID IS COMING HOME!!!!!

Love,
Dave

Sergeant Stanley Homiski, 3/4 Cavalry, 25th Infantry Division

Homiski writes to his wife.

Vietnam, 25 May, 1968

Dear Roberta,
Today is probably the worst day I have ever lived in my entire, short life. Once again we were in contact with Charlie, and once again we suffered losses. The losses we had today hit home, as my best friend in this shit hole was killed. He was only 22 years old and was going on R&R on the first of June to meet his wife in Hawaii. I feel that if I was only a half second sooner in pulling the trigger, he would still be alive.

Strange how short a time a half of a second is – the difference between life and death. This morning we were talking about how we were only two years different in age and how we both had gotten married before coming to this place. You know, I can still feel his presence as I write this letter and hope that I am able to survive and leave this far behind me.

If there is a place called Hell this surely must be it, and we must be the Devil's disciples doing all his dirty work. I keep asking myself if there is a God, then how the hell come young men with so much to live for have to die. I just hope that his death is not in vain.

I look forward to the day when I will take my R&R. If I play my cards right, I should be able to get it for Hawaii so our anniversary will be in that time frame. The reason I say this is by Sept., I will have more than enough time in country to get my pick of places and dates. I promise I will do everything necessary to insure that I make that date, and I hope that tomorrow is quiet.

We will be going into base camp soon for our three-day stand down. I will try to write you a longer letter at that time. Please don't worry too much about me, as if you won't, for I will take care of myself and look forward to the day I am able to be with you again.

Love,
Stan

Sergeant Joseph Morrissey, 1st Battalion, 12th Cavalry
Feb. 9, 1970

Hello Brother,
How is America acting these days? Are the youth still planning new ways to change our world? I think the 70s will see a lot of things changed for the better.

I'm still trying to survive over here but the NVA aren't making it too easy lately. We've just been in contact with them for three days and things aren't looking too bright. When you have bullets cracking right over your head for a couple days in a row, your nerves begin to fizzle. When you're getting shot at, all you can think about is – try to stay alive, keep your head down and keep shooting back.

When the shooting stops, though, you sort of sit back and ask yourself, Why? What the hell is this going to prove? And man, I'm still looking for the answer. It's a real bitch.

Thanks for that *Playboy* you sent me. I sort of forgot what girls looked like. I think the real personality of Jesus has been sort of hidden from us. Either that or no one's wanted to look for it before. If he were alive today he'd probably be living in Haight-Ashbury and getting followed by the FBI who'd have him labeled as a communist revolutionary. He'd definitely be shaking some people up . . .

Well, it's time to make my delicious C-ration lunch. Stay loose and stay young . . .

The beat goes on,
Joe

THE SHOOTING OF ROBERT KENNEDY, Los Angeles, 5 June 1968

Alistair Cooke

At the time of his assassination by Sirhan Sirhan, Senator Robert Kennedy was running for the Democratic Party presidential nomination.

It was just after midnight. A surge of cheers and a great swivelling of lights heralded him, and soon he was up on the rostrum with his eager, button-eyed wife and Jesse Unruh, his massive campaign manager. It took minutes to get the feedback boom out of the mikes but at last there was a kind of subdued uproar and he said he first wanted to express "my high regard to Don Drysdale for his six great shut-outs". (Drysdale is a baseball pitcher whose Tuesday night feat of holding his sixth successive opposing teams to no runs has made him a legend.)

It was the right, the wry Kennedy note. He thanked a list of helpers by name. He thanked "all those loyal Mexican Americans" and "all my friends in the black community". Then he stiffened his gestures and his style and said it only went to show that "all those promises and all those party caucuses have indicated that the people of the United States want a change".

He congratulated McCarthy on fighting for his principles. He hoped that now there might be "a debate between the Vice-President and perhaps myself." He flashed his teeth again in his chuckling, rabbity smile and ended, "My thanks to all of you – and now it's on to Chicago and let's win there."

A delirium of cheers and lights and tears and a rising throb of "We want Bobby! We want Bobby! We want Bobby!"

He tumbled down from the rostrum with his aides and bodyguards about him. He would be with us in twenty seconds, half a minute at most. We watched the swinging doors of the kitchen. Over the gabble of the television there was suddenly from the direction of the kitchen a crackle of sharp sounds. Like a balloon popping.

An exploded flash bulb maybe, more like a man banging a tray several times against a wall. A half-dozen or so of us trotted to the kitchen door and at that moment time and life collapsed. Kennedy and his aides had been coming on through the pantry. It was now seen to be not a kitchen but a regular serving pantry with great long tables and racks of plates against the wall.

He was smiling and shaking hands with a waiter, then a chef in a high white hat. Lots of Negroes, naturally, and they were glowing with pride for he was their man. Then those sounds from somewhere, from a press of people on or near a steam table. And before you could synchronize your sight and thought, Kennedy was a prone bundle on the greasy floor, and two or three others had gone down with him. There was an explosion of shouts and screams and the high moaning cries of mini-skirted girls.

The doors of the pantry swung back and forth and we would peek in on the obscene disorder and reel back again to sit down, then to glare in a stupefied way at the nearest friend, to steady one boozy woman with black-rimmed eyes who was pounding a table and screaming, "Goddam stinking country!" The fat girl was babbling faintly like a baby, like someone in a motor accident.

Out of the chaos of the ballroom, Kennedy's brother-in-law was begging for doctors. And back in the pantry they were howling for doctors. It was hard to see who had been badly hit. One face was streaming with blood. It was that of Paul Schrade, a high union official, and it came out that he got off lightly.

A woman had a purple bruise on her forehead. Another man was down. Kennedy was looking up like a stunned choirboy from an open shirt and a limp huddle of limbs. Somehow, in the dependable fashion of the faith, a priest had appeared.

We were shoved back and the cameramen were darting and screaming and flashing their bulbs. We fell back again from the howling pantry into the haven of the press room.

Suddenly, the doors opened again and six or eight police had a curly black head and a blue-jeaned body in their grip. He was a swarthy, thick-featured unshaven little man with a tiny rump and a head fallen over, as if he had been clubbed or had fainted perhaps.

He was lifted out into the big lobby and was soon off in some mysterious place "in custody". On the television Huntley and Brinkley were going on in their urbane way about the "trends" in Los Angeles and the fading McCarthy lead in Northern California.

A large woman went over and beat on the screen, as if to batter these home-screen experts out of their self-possession. We had to take her and say, "Steady" and "Don't do that". And suddenly the screen went berserk, like a home movie projector on the blink. And the blurred, whirling scene we had watched in the flesh came wobbling in as a movie.

Then all the "facts" were fired or intoned from the screen. Roosevelt Grier, a 300 lb. coloured football player and a Kennedy man, had grabbed the man with the gun and overwhelmed him. A Kennedy bodyguard had taken the gun, a .22 calibre. The maniac had fired straight at Kennedy and sprayed the other bullets around the narrow pantry.

Kennedy was now at the receiving hospital and soon transferred to the Good Samaritan. Three neurologists were on their way. He had been hit in the hip, perhaps, but surely in the shoulder and "the mastoid area". There was the first sinister note about a bullet in the brain.

In the timelessness of nausea and dumb disbelief we stood and sat and stood again and sighed at each other and went into the pantry again and looked at the rack of plates and the smears of blood on the floor and the furious guards and the jumping-jack photographers.

It was too much to take. The only thing to do was to touch the shoulder of the Kennedy man who had let you in and get out on to the street and drive home to the top of the silent Santa Monica Hills, where pandemonium is rebroadcast in tranquillity and where a little unshaven guy amuck in a pantry is slowly brought into focus as a bleak and shoddy villain of history.

MAN LANDS ON THE MOON, 20 July 1969

Neil Armstrong, Buzz Aldrin

At 10.56 p.m., EDT, on 20 July 1969, Neil A. Armstrong stepped down from the bottom rung of *Apollo* 11's landing craft and became the first person to walk on the moon. Seconds later he was followed by his crewmate, Edwin (Buzz) Aldrin. Through the miracle of modern communications, hundreds of millions of people witnessed the event via TV.

Below is Armstrong and Aldrin's commentary on the landing, as spoken to mission control at Houston.

ARMSTRONG: I'm at the foot of the ladder. The LM [lunar module] foot beds are only depressed in the surface about one or two inches, although the surface appears to be very, very fine grained as you get close to it. It's almost like a powder. It's very fine. I'm going to step off the LM now.

That's one small step for man, one giant leap for mankind.

The surface is fine and powdery. I can pick it up loosely with my toe. It does adhere in fine layers like powdered charcoal to the sole and the sides of my boots. I only go in a small fraction of an inch, maybe an eighth of an inch but I can see the footprints of my boots and the treads in the fine sandy particles.

There seems to be no difficulty in moving around this and we suspect that it's even perhaps easier than the simulations of 1/6 G that we performed in various simulations on the ground. Actually no trouble to walk around. The descent engine did not leave a crater of any size. It has about one-foot clearance on the ground. We're essentially on a very level place here. I can see some evidence of rays emanating from the descent engine, but a very insignificant amount.

HOUSTON: Neil, this is Houston did you copy about the contingency sample? Over.

ARMSTRONG: Roger. Going to get to that just as soon as I finish these picture series.

ALDRIN: Are you going to get the contingency sample? Okay. That's good.

ARMSTRONG: The contingency sample is down and it's up. Like it's a little difficult to dig through the crust. It's very interesting. It's a very soft surface but here and there where I plug with the contingency sample collector I run into very hard surface but it appears to be very cohesive material of the same sort. I'll try to get a rock in here.

HOUSTON: Oh, that looks beautiful from here, Neil.

ARMSTRONG: It has a stark beauty all its own. It's like much of the high desert of the United States. It's different but it's very pretty out here. Be advised that a lot of the rock-samples out here, the hard rock samples have what appear to be vesicles in the surface. Also, as I look at one now that appears to have some sort of feenacres [spelled phonetically].

HOUSTON: Roger. Out.

ARMSTRONG: This has been about six or eight inches into the surface. It's easy to push on in. I'm sure I could push it in further, but it's hard for me to bend down further than that.

ALDRIN: I didn't know you could throw so far, Neil.

ARMSTRONG: See me throw things? Is my pocket open?

ALDRIN: Yes it is. It's not up against your suit, though. Hit it back once more. More toward the inside. Okay that's good.

ARMSTRONG: Put it in the pocket.

ALDRIN: Yes. Push down. Got it? No it's not all the way in. Push. There you go.

ARMSTRONG: The sample is in the pocket. My oxygen is 81 per cent. I have no flags and I'm in minimum flow.

HOUSTON: Roger, Neil.

ALDRIN: How far are my feet from the . . .

ARMSTRONG: Okay, you're right at the edge of the porch.

ALDRIN: Now I want to back up and partially close the hatch – making sure not to lock it on my way out.

ARMSTRONG: . . . Good thought.

ALDRIN: That's our home for the next couple hours; we want to take good care of it. Okay, I'm on the top step and I can look down over the ICU and landing-gear pad. It's a very simple matter to hop down from one step to the next.

ARMSTRONG: Yes, I found that to be very comfortable, and walking is also very comfortable, Houston.

ARMSTRONG: You've got three more steps and then a long one.

ALDRIN: Okay. I'm going to leave that one foot up there and both hands down to about the fourth rung up.

ARMSTRONG: Now I think I'll do the same.

A little more. About another inch. There you got it. That's a good step.

About a three footer.

Beautiful view.

Ain't that somethin'?

ALTAMONT, December 1969

Paul Cox

At the Rolling Stones free concert at Altamont Speedway, California, the Hell's Angel security force ran amok, beating and stabbing – and killing a black fan, Meredith Hunter. The hopes of the 1960s, the decade of peace and love, were dashed in that moment. Paul Cox was standing near Meredith Hunter in the crowd at Altamont.

An Angel kept looking over at me and I tried to keep ignoring him and I didn't want to look at him at all, because I was very scared of them and seeing what they were doing all day and because he kept trying to cause a fight or something and kept staring at us. He kept on looking over, and the next thing I know he's hassling this Negro boy on the side of me. And I was trying not to look at him, and then he reached over and shook this boy by the side of the head, thinking it was fun, laughing, and I noticed something was going to happen so I kind of backed off.

The boy yanked away, and when he yanked away, next thing I know he was flying in the air, right on the ground, just like all the other people it happened to. He scrambled to his feet, and he's backing up and he's trying to run from the Angels, and all these Angels are – a couple jumped off the stage and a couple was running alongside the stage, and his girlfriend was screaming to him not to shoot, because he pulled out his gun. And when he pulled it out, he held it in the air and his girlfriend is like climbing on him and pushing him back and he's trying to get away and these Angels are coming at him and he turns around and starts running. And then some Angel snuck up from right out of the crowd and leaped up and brought this knife down in his back. And then I saw him stab him again, and while he's stabbing him, he's running. This Negro boy is running into the crowd, and you could see him stiffen up when he's being stabbed.

He came running toward me. I grabbed on to the scaffold, and he came running kind of toward me and fell down on his knees, and the Hell's Angel grabbed onto both of his shoulders and started kicking him in the face about five times or so and then he fell down on his face. He let go and he fell down on his face. And then one of them kicked him on the side and he rolled over, and he muttered some words. He said, "I wasn't going to shoot you." That was the last words he muttered.

If some other people would have jumped in I would have jumped in. But nobody jumped in and after he said, "I wasn't going to shoot you," one of the Hell's Angels said, "Why did you have a gun?" He didn't give him time to say anything. He grabbed one of those garbage cans, the cardboard ones with the metal rimming, and he smashed him over the head with it, and then he kicked the garbage can out of the way and started kicking his head in. Five of them started kicking his head in. Kicked him all over the place. And then the guy that started the whole thing stood on his head for a minute or so and then walked off. And then the one I was talking about, he wouldn't let us touch him for about two or three minutes. Like, "Don't touch him, he's going to die anyway, let him die, he's going to die."

Chicks were just screaming. It was all confusion. I jumped down anyway to grab him and some other dude jumped down and grabbed him, and then the Hell's Angel just stood over him for a little bit and then walked away. We turned him over and ripped off his shirt. We rubbed his back up and down to get the blood off so we could see, and there was a big hole in his spine and a big hole on the side and there was a big hole in his temple. A big open slice. You could see all the way in. You could see inside. You could see at least an inch down. And then there was a big hole right where there's no ribs on his back − and then the side of his head was just sliced open − you couldn't see so far in − it was bleeding quite heavily − but his back wasn't bleeding too heavy after that − there − all of us were drenched in blood.

WATERGATE: NIXON RESIGNS, 8 August 1974

Richard Nixon

Richard Milhous Nixon, 37th President of the USA, resigned office under the threat of impeachment, when several leading members of his government were found guilty of organizing a break into the Democratic National Committee's headquarters in the Watergate Hotel, Washington.

Two minutes before nine o'clock I went into the Oval Office. I sat in my chair behind the desk while the technicians adjusted the lighting and made their voice check.

At forty-five seconds after nine, the red light on the camera facing my desk went on − it was time to speak to America and the world.

I began by saying how difficult it was for me to leave the battle unfinished, but my lack of congressional support would paralyse the nation's business if I decided to fight on.

In the past few days . . . it has become evident to me that I no longer have a strong enough political base in the Congress to justify continuing that effort. As long as there was such a base, I felt strongly that it was necessary to see the constitutional process through to its conclusion, that to do otherwise would be unfaithful to the spirit of that deliberately difficult process, and a dangerously destabilizing precedent for the future.

But with the disappearance of that base, I now believe that the constitutional purpose has been served, and there is no longer a need for the process to be prolonged.

Then I came to the most difficult sentence I shall ever have to speak. Looking directly into the camera, I said,

Therefore, I shall resign the presidency effective at noon tomorrow.

I continued:

By taking this action, I hope that I will have hastened the start of that process of healing which is so desperately needed in America.

I regret deeply any injuries that may have been done in the course of the events that led to this decision. I would say only that if some of my judgements were wrong – and some were wrong – they were made in what I believed at the time to be in the best interest of the nation.

I talked briefly about America and about the world. I talked about my own attempts in twenty-five years of public life to fight for what I believed in. I recalled that in my first inaugural address I had pledged to consecrate myself and my energies to the cause of peace among nations. I went on:

I have done my very best in all the days since to be true to that pledge. As a result of these efforts, I am confident that the world is a safer place today, not only for the people of America, but for the people of all nations, and that all of our children have a better chance than before of living in peace rather than dying in war.

This, more than anything, is what I hoped to achieve when I sought the presidency. This, more than anything, is what I hope will be my legacy to you, to our country, as I leave the presidency.

Throughout the speech I looked down at the pages of the text, but I did not really read it. That speech was truly in my heart. At the end, I said: "To have served in this office is to have felt a very personal sense of kinship with each and every American. In leaving it, I do so with this prayer: May God's grace be with you in all the days ahead."

The red light blinked off. One by one the blinding television lights were switched off. I looked up and saw the technicians respectfully standing along the wall, pretending that they were not waiting for me to leave so that they could dismantle their equipment. I thanked them and left the Oval Office.

Kissinger was waiting for me in the corridor. He said, "Mr President, after most of your major speeches in this office we have walked together back to your house. I would be honoured to walk with you again tonight."

As we walked past the dark Rose Garden, Kissinger's voice was low and sad. He said that he thought that historically this would rank as one of the great speeches and that history would judge me one of the great Presidents. I turned to him and said, "That depends, Henry, on who writes the history." At the door of the Residence I thanked him and we parted.

I quickly headed for the elevator that would take me to the Family Quarters. The long hall was dark and the police and Secret Service had mercifully been removed or were keeping out of sight. When the doors opened on the second floor, the family was all waiting there to meet me. I walked over to them. Pat put her arms around me. Tricia. Julie. Ed. David. Slowly, instinctively, we embraced in a tender huddle, drawn together by love and faith.

We sat talking for a few minutes about the day and the speech. Suddenly I began to shake violently, and Tricia reached over to hold me. "Daddy!" she exclaimed, "the perspiration is coming clear through your coat!" I told them not to worry. I had perspired heavily during the speech, and I must have caught a chill walking over from the office. In a minute it had passed.

THE RUMBLE IN THE JUNGLE: MUHAMMAD ALI KNOCKS OUT GEORGE FOREMAN IN EIGHT, Kinshasa, Zaïre, 30 October 1974

Norman Mailer

Well, George came off the ropes and pursued Ali like a man chasing a cat. The wild punch seemed to have refreshed him by its promise that some of his power was back. If his biggest punches were missing, at least they were big. Once again he might be his own prodigy of strength. Now there were flurries on the ropes which had an echo of the great bombardment in the fifth round. And still Ali taunted him, still the dialogue went on. "Fight hard," said Ali, "I thought you had some punches. You're a weak man. You're all used up." After a while, Foreman's punches were whistling less than his breath. For the eighteenth time Ali's corner was screaming, "Get off the ropes. Knock him out. Take him home!" Foreman had used up the store of force he transported from the seventh to the eighth. He pawed at Ali like an infant six feet tall waving its uncoordinated battle arm.

With twenty seconds left to the round, Ali attacked. By his own measure, by that measure of twenty years of boxing, with the knowledge of all he had learned of what could and could not be done at any instant in the ring, he chose this as the occasion and lying on the ropes, he hit Foreman with a right and left, then came off the ropes to hit him with a left and a right. Into this last right hand he put his glove and his forearm again, a head-stupefying punch that sent Foreman reeling forward. As he went by, Ali hit him on the side of the jaw with a right, and darted away from the ropes in such a way as to put Foreman next to them. For the first time in the entire fight he had cut off the ring on Foreman. Now Ali struck him a combination of punches fast as the punches of the first round, but harder and more consecutive, three capital rights in a row struck Foreman, then a left, and for an instant on Foreman's face appeared the knowledge that he was in danger and must start to look to his last protection. His opponent was attacking, and there were no ropes behind the opponent. What a dislocation: the axes of his existence were reversed! He was the man on the ropes! Then a big projectile exactly the size of a fist in a glove drove into the middle of Foreman's mind, the best punch of the startled night, the blow Ali saved for a career. Foreman's arms flew out to the side like a man with a parachute jumping out of a plane, and in this doubled-over position he tried to wander out to the center of the ring. All the while his eyes were on Ali and he looked up with no anger as if Ali, indeed, was the man he knew best in the world and would see him on his dying day. Vertigo took George Foreman and revolved him. Still bowing from the waist in this uncomprehending position, eyes on Muhammad Ali all the way, he started to tumble and topple and fall even as he did not wish to go down. His mind was held with magnets high as his championship and his body was seeking the ground. He went over like a six-foot sixty-year-old butler who has just heard tragic news, yes, fell over all of a long collapsing two seconds, down came the Champion in sections and Ali revolved with him in a close circle, hand primed to hit him one more time, and never the need, a wholly intimate escort to the floor.

The referee took Ali to a corner. He stood there, he seemed lost in thought. Now he raced his feet in a quick but restrained shuffle as if to apologize for never asking his legs to dance, and looked on while Foreman tried to rouse himself.

Like a drunk hoping to get out of bed to go to work, Foreman rolled over, Foreman started the slow head-agonizing lift of all that foundered bulk God somehow gave him and whether he heard the count or no, was on his feet a fraction after the count of ten and whipped, for when Zack Clayton guided him with a hand at his back, he walked in docile steps to his corner and did not resist. Moore received him. Sadler received him. Later, one learned the conversation.

"Feel all right?"

"Yeah," said Foreman.

"Well, don't worry. It's history now."

"Yeah."

"You're all right," said Sadler, "the rest will take care of itself."

SAIGON: THE FINAL DAY, 29 April 1975

John Pilger

As the victorious Communist forces closed in on Saigon, the last Americans were being evacuated from the compound of the US embassy. Also awaiting a helicopter out was Australian journalist John Pilger.

People were now beginning to come over the wall. The Marines, who had orders not to use their guns, had been up all night and were doped with "speed" – methedrine – which provides a "high" for twenty-four hours before the body craves sleep. But methedrine also whittles the nerve ends, and some of the young Marines were beginning to show the effects. As the first Chinook helicopter made its precarious landing, its rotors slashed into a tree, and the snapping branches sounded like gunfire. "*Down! Down!*" screamed a corporal to the line of people crouched against the wall, waiting their turn to be evacuated, until an officer came and calmed him.

The helicopter's capacity was fifty, but it lifted off with seventy. The pilot's skill was breathtaking as he climbed vertically to two hundred feet, with bullets pinging against the rotors and shredded embassy documents playing in the downdraft. However, not all the embassy's documents were shredded and some were left in the compound in open plastic bags. One of these I have. It is dated 25 May, 1969 and reads, "Top Secret . . . memo from John Paul Vann, counter insurgency":

. . . 900 houses in Chau Doc province were destroyed by American air strikes without evidence of a single enemy being killed . . . the destruction of this hamlet by friendly American firepower is an event that will always be remembered and never forgiven by the surviving population . . .

From the billowing incinerator on the embassy roof rained twenty, fifty and one hundred dollar bills. Most were charred; some were not. The Vietnamese waiting around the pool could not believe their eyes; former ministers and generals and torturers scrambled for their bonus from the sky or sent their children to retrieve the notes. An embassy official said that more than five million dollars were being burned. "Every safe in the embassy has been emptied and locked again," said the official, "so as to fool the gooks when we've gone."

The swishing of rotors now drowned the sounds of the dusk: the crump of artillery, the cries of women attempting to push young children over the wall. Two Marines watched a teenage girl struggle through the barbed wire. At first they did nothing, then as her hands clawed the last few inches one of them brought his rifle butt down on one hand, while the other brought his boot down on the other. The girl fell, crying, back into the mob. Somehow, most of one family had managed to get over the wall: a man, his wife, and her father. Their sons and his grandmother were next, but the barrel of an M-16 spun them back to the other side. The wife pleaded with a Marine to let the rest of her family over, but he did not hear her.

At least a thousand people were still inside the embassy, waiting to be evacuated, although most of the celebrities, like "Giggles" Quang, had seen themselves on to the first helicopters; the rest waited passively, as if stunned. Inside the embassy itself there was champagne foaming on to polished desks, as several of the embassy staff tried systematically to wreck their own offices: smashing water coolers, pouring bottles of Scotch into the carpets, sweeping pictures from the wall. In a third-floor office a picture of the late President Johnson was delivered into a wastepaper basket, while a framed quotation from Lawrence of Arabia was left on the wall. The quotation read:

> Better to let them do it imperfectly, than to do it perfectly yourself, for it is their country, their war, and your time is short.

From the third floor I could see the British embassy across the road. It was being quietly ransacked now. The Union Jack, which had been spread across the main entrance, perhaps to ward off evil spirits, had been torn away and looters were at work with little interference from the police. I derived some small satisfaction from the sight of this. It was there, a few days earlier, that the British Ambassador, a spiffy chap called John Bushell, had shredded his own papers and mounted his own little evacuation without taking with him a dozen very frightened British passport holders. Before he drove away, Mr Bushell gave an impromptu press conference.

"We are pulling out for reasons of safety," he said. "Our main responsibility is the safety of the British community in Saigon."

I asked him about people who were waving their British passports outside the gates of the British embassy. Why were they not even allowed into the compound?

"Look here," he replied, "we gave ample warning. We put advertisements in the local papers. The trouble with these people, as I understand it, was that they didn't have tax clearance, which takes ten days, as well as exit visas from the Vietnamese government."

Exit visas? Tax clearances? But wasn't this an emergency evacuation for reasons, as he had just said, of protecting life?

"Well, yes," he replied, "but we really can't break the rules laid down by government, can we?"

But surely this government had ceased to exist and there might be anarchy and a great deal of danger, which was why he was getting out?

"That may be true," said the Ambassador, "but we gave these people a reasonable time to get the paperwork done, and you really can't expect us to help them at such short notice . . . look here, the Americans surely will pick up any stray palefaces."

But "these people" were Indians and Chinese. The Ambassador looked confused.

"Oh, you mean Hong Kongers," he said. "They should have heeded our warnings . . . they'll have just to work hard at it, won't they?" At this, he turned to another British official and said, "How many coolies . . . Vietnamese . . . are we leaving, do you know?"

The official replied, "Coolies? Oh, about thirty-six in all."

At six-fifteen p.m. it was my turn for the Jolly Green Giant as it descended through the dark into the compound. The loadmaster stopped counting at sixty; people were in each other's arms. The helicopter tilted, rose, dropped sharply, then climbed as if laden with rocks; off to the starboard there were shots. We flew low over the centre of the city, over the presidential palace where "Big" Minh awaited his fate, and the Caravelle Hotel, where I owed for two days, then out along the Saigon River, over the Rung Sat, the "swamp of death" which lay between the city and the sea. The two gunners scanned the ground, as they always used to, looking for "Charlie". Some of us had on our minds the heat-seeking missile which had brought a helicopter down as we watched in the early hours. There was small arms fire around us, but they were letting us go; and when the South China Sea lay beneath us, the pilot, who was red-eyed with fatigue and so young he had acne, lit up a cigarette and handed the packet around. In the back of the helicopter there was a reminder of what we had left: a woman, who had left her daughter on the other side of the wall, cried softly.

PERSIAN GULF WAR: SCUD-HUNTING, 23 February 1991

Eric Schmitt, New York Times

Operation Desert Storm to drive Sadam Hussein from his illegal occupation of Kuwait saw the largest deployment of American military personnel since Vietnam.

In Saudi Arabia, Feb. 23 – Preparations for an allied ground offensive have brought no respite for the men who fly the Air Force's F-15E Strike Eagle jets. For them, the air war remains a deadly race of dodging spitting anti-aircraft guns and streaking rockets over targets they have christened Scudville, Samstown, AAA Alley and Rat a Tat Tat.

In the crater-pocked landscape they stalk their quarry: tanks, bridges and the main targets, long-range Scud missiles.

The search is carried out in a cramped cockpit for up to eight hours, with fliers peering into the darkness and then down to the surreal glow of an infrared radar screen that turns night into day on the ground below.

The two-man F-15E crews on Scud patrol do not talk openly about death or fatigue, their two greatest worries. They busy themselves with routine tasks to crowd out fears of exploding surface-to-air missiles. They speak of "spanking" a 60-ton Iraqi tank they blast into a burning metal carcass with a laser-guided 2,000-pound bomb.

"You're trained to hit targets, not people, so you never have to see anyone eye to eye," said First Lieut. Glenn G. Watson, a 24-year-old weapons officer from Austin, Tex. "But at night, you sit alone in bed knowing there are people out there and you're bombing them."

At a sprawling air base in central Saudi Arabia, two squadrons of the pointy-nosed, twin-tailed Strike Eagles from North Carolina roar off every night to the north, usually in pairs, to run carefully planned raids. Some nights the jets bomb tanks; on others they seek out Scud missiles and launchers and whatever else lies in their "kill box", an area defined by grid coordinates.

Bristling with precision-guided bombs, air-to-air missiles and a 20-millimeter cannon, the dark-gray, all-weather F-15E is designed to use its heavy firepower and night-fighting sensors to attack targets that are more easily defended in daylight.

The F-15E pilots and back-seat weapons officers, who aim the bombs, have been flying one mission a night – usually three to five hours – six nights a week since the war began. That tempo far surpasses normal peacetime training, and the fliers have had to cope with much higher stress and fatigue.

"There are so many things going on around you in the pitch dark," said Capt. John Hoff Jr, 28, of Boonville, Mo., the pilot who flies with Lieut Watson. "You're watching where other aircraft are, where people are shooting from, where your target is, and all the while the plane is moving at 500 miles an hour."

Flight surgeons assigned to the F-15E units, the 335th and the 336th Tactical Fighter Squadrons, prescribed amphetamines with the kick of 20 cups of coffee to keep crews awake during the hectic first week of the war. Sedatives were distributed to help them sleep.

Even when fliers adjust their internal clocks to working at night and sleeping in the day, night flying has other burdens. The crews have few outside visual references once they turn out their running lights when they cross the border into Kuwait or Iraq. They face the danger of losing their bearings, even judging which way is up and down.

In recent weeks, the flight schedule for the night fighters has eased a bit and drugs are rarely used anymore.

Fliers have also adapted to the missions and know better the type of enemy fire to expect.

Physicians who monitor the crews daily for signs of fatigue nonetheless worry that a prolonged war, with continued bombing, could push fliers to their physical and psychological limits.

"I'm extremely concerned about them," said Capt. Jack Ingari, a flight surgeon with the F-15E squadrons, who flies periodic missions to understand the strains of night flying. "These are untested waters. We've never been in such a high-technology, prolonged air war."

For Capt. Hoff and Lieut Watson, and most of the F-15E crews here, work begins around 4 p.m. after eight hours' rest in tents segregated from the rest of this base.

In a tent along the flight line that serves as squadron head-quarters, the two young fliers meet Lieut. Col. Mike DeCuir, 40, and Maj. Larry Coleman, 37, an experienced pilot and weapons officer team who make up the other half of the two-plane patrol.

Working side-by-side for weeks, even months, the partners come to know each other's tiniest habits and idiosyncrasies – crucial nuances during combat missions when radio chatter is limited and decisions are made in split seconds.

The two teams pore over their assigned target, a communications complex, assessing the route, the attack strategy, the appropriate bombs to drop and the enemy antiaircraft fire anticipated.

Like batters scouting a new pitcher, the partners have already discussed weather, ground artillery threats and targets with counterparts who flew earlier missions.

More than a month into the war, the two teams, with 25 to 30 missions each, plan carefully, but an air of quiet confidence has replaced the tense anxiety that filled the squadron room in the war's early days.

"You slowly work your way up to the mission, whereas 30 days ago, emotionally, we were up immediately," said Col. DeCuir. "We've learned to pace ourselves a bit."

What took five or six hours to plan when the Iraqi Air Force was still a threat and ground-fire batteries were unknown, is now finished in about 60 minutes.

The first few days of war were the roughest, mentally and physically, the fliers said. The strain from the sudden surge in the frequency and duration of missions was intense.

"You would think, 'How am I going to perform? Am I going to screw up?' " said Maj. Coleman, who lives in the Cumberland Gap area of eastern Tennessee.

The fliers wear one-piece olive-green flight suits made of flame-retardant fabric. They strap on a parachute harness and a G-suit, which, when it is plugged to a hose in the cockpit, inflates during combat maneuvers to keep the blood from rushing from a flier's head, causing blackouts. Finally, there are lucky charms.

"There's no fighter pilot who's superstitious, but everyone carries a charm," said Lieutenant Watson, grinning, but declining to reveal his talisman.

Slung over a flier's shoulder are dark-green survival bags holding a steel-gray fiberglass helmet, checklists, radios, flight manuals and a handgun, either .38 caliber or 9 millimeter.

For the younger men, there have been many long, private talks to prepare for the likelihood of killing and the possibility of dying.

"You get into little groups and talk about everything: being scared about getting shot at, watching someone else go down and working together," Lieut Watson said.

The patrol's mission tonight was quick and uneventful, meaning no antiaircraft fire. The two jets dropped their laser-guided, 500-pound bombs in 18 minutes, destroying several buildings and vehicles, and quickly headed home.

Even on the best-scouted missions, though, there is always the fear of SAMs, surface-to-air missiles: a sudden white flash on the ground and then a "red ball of fire" rocketing toward you, Capt. Hoff said.

"It's a completely new experience having someone on the ground trying to kill you as hard as they can," Capt. Ingari said.

For the crews, survival depends on split-second midair gyrations – "shucking and jiving" in fighter-pilot lingo – to shake a missile.

"You hear a lot of chatter on the radio," Maj. Coleman said. "You shouldn't hear any explosions. If you hear an explosion, it's too close."

In the first three days of the mission, however, the F-15E

squadrons had two planes shot down. Two crew members were captured; two are still listed as missing.

"It's a bad feeling talking to someone on the radio and suddenly they're not there," Maj. Coleman said.

The fliers say they are containing their grief, but flight surgeons said the bottled-up emotions will be reckoned with.

RIOT IN L.A. 30 April–1 May 1992

"West Coast Correspondent", Economist

The acquittal of four policemen who beat black motorist Rodney King torched off the most lethal urban riot in American history, leaving 50 dead and over $1 billion worth of damage in the South Central area of Los Angeles.

In front of the smoking electronics store, the small black boy had a problem. He had looted six items, but he could carry only five. For around fifteen minutes he hesitated, shielding them from other, older pillagers, while he tried to arrange them. Then flames spouted from the shop, driving out the remaining looters. A scuffle broke out across the street and the boy loped off down an alley, leaving a radio-alarm clock behind. It was probably his most valuable booty and it would have made a good present for a friend. A bearded (white) hippie, muttering an apology, picked it up instead.

Barely twenty-four hours before, Los Angeles had seemed its usual smoggy, complacent self. The first news of the acquittals in the Rodney King beatings arrived in the late afternoon. When asked for their reaction, two policemen parked opposite *The Economist* office at the *Los Angeles Times* gave a non-committal grunt. At first, the most distraught people seemed to be guilty liberals (some journalists burst into tears). Then a young mob appeared downtown. They smashed the windows and doors of the *Times* building and burnt the local coffee shop. But the television pictures from South Central were much more frightening.

After that first angry night, what followed in most parts of Los Angeles was more pillage than riot. The fires were started by thugs (supposedly gang members who had pledged to add ten new fires every hour), but the looting was done by petty thieves. The atmosphere was usually like a disorganized rock concert: at its worst, it resembled an angry English soccer crowd – with guns.

One Hispanic man scurried away carrying several cartons of tampons. Television coverage, with its maps and pictures of defenceless stores, provide a looter's guide to the best local bargains.

Gradually the fires spread northwards and westwards towards the prosperous "Westside" that tourists visit. There a different type of riot was taking place. A supermarket on the border of West Hollywood and Beverly Hills was packed with queues 30-deep. Each shopper seemed to be carrying enough provisions to last a month. There was a screaming match at the kosher food counter. Gossip spread that a British billionaire's daughter had said the riots were boring, "but if they ever heave a brick through Tiffany's window, I might join them."

She never got her chance: West Los Angeles survived largely untouched. Even in heavily looted areas like Korea-town and Mid-Wilshire, many of the rioters like the small black boy, seemed almost innocently childlike. However, in South Central, the atmosphere changed. The shops – particularly those owned by Asians – were stripped bare. The crowds hanging on street corners seemed to be looking for victims rather than bargains. Women screamed about their neighbourhood being destroyed; onlookers were no more welcome than at a funeral.

The most enduring memory from the riots was the signs in shop windows. In South Central, they pleaded pathetically. "Black owned business". Some stooped lower, putting "blak owned business" in an attempt to mollify one gang, the Bloods, who dislike the letter "c" because it reminds them of their arch-enemies, the Crips. On Rodeo Drive, where there are fewer black-owned businesses, shops at first bravely sported signs saying "No Justice" to show that their sympathies lay with Mr King. When the riots died down the signs disappeared.

TYSON DISQUALIFIED FOR BITING HOLYFIELD'S EAR, Las Vegas, 29 June 1997

Ken Jones

Born in 1966, Afro-American boxer "Iron" Mike Tyson became the undisputed heavyweight champion of the world at the unprecedented age of 21, unifying the WBA, WBC and IBF titles. After serving a prison sentence for rape, Tyson late tried to restart his career with bouts against, amongst others, Evander Holyfield.

There can be no escape for Mike Tyson now. His ill-starred career in jeopardy, his behaviour so savagely bizarre that all sympathy for him has gone. Who but that squalid crew of associates and hangers-on can defend him now?

When it once more became the sort of fight Tyson simply could not handle, one so rough that both men received stern warnings in the first two rounds, he lost all control and was disqualified on his stool at the end of the third for biting Evander Holyfield's ears.

Tyson's $30 m (£18.75 m) purse was immediately frozen by the Nevada State Athletic Commission and at a meeting called for Wednesday he could be fined $10 m and suspended from the ring.

Still in a rage, roaring obscenities, hurling his corner men aside, Tyson twice tried to break through the cordon that stood between him and Holyfield. Fury filled Tyson's face as he left the ring under a bombardment of abuse and debris that resulted in arrests and a scuffle in the corridor leading to his dressing-room.

Explaining his decision shortly afterwards, Mills Lane, the circuit judge from Reno who took over as referee when Mitch Halpern withdrew following a protest by the Tyson camp, said: "I deducted two points from Tyson in the third round, first for biting Holyfield's right ear, then for pushing him in the back. At the end of the round I could see that Tyson had bitten Holyfield's other ear and I had no option but to disqualify him. The second bite was the end of the stretch. Boxing is a business that happens to get on the sports pages but fighters must have discipline."

Holyfield was bitten so badly the first time that he needed plastic surgery to reattach the inch-long slice of flesh Tyson actually spat on to the canvas. It was recovered by an assistant in Holyfield's corner who took it to the dressing-room. "I saw Tyson spit something into the centre of the ring," he said. "Then there was a lot of hassle and I hoped that nobody stepped on it. When the ring cleared I put on surgical gloves and went into the middle. Seeing that it was flesh I picked it up and took it to them – they were surprised."

Tyson was still wild-eyed and ranting when fulfilling an obligation to Showtime, the cable television network linked to his promoter, Don King, that put out the contest. Pointing to a wide gash in the lid of his right eye caused by a head butt in the second round, accidental in Lane's view, he snarled: "Look at this. How much was I expected to put up with. He [Holyfield] was butting me all the time. He butted me in the first fight. I was left with only one eye. My career was on the line. I've got kids to bring up. Who cares about me and my children?

"The referee didn't listen to my protests. When Richie [Tyson's trainer, Richie Giachetti] complained about the butt he was told it was accidental. That was ridiculous, an insult. I had one eye, Holyfield had two ears. What else was I supposed to do? I had to retaliate. He's not tough. I'll fight him now, here, even with only one good eye."

Before leaving for hospital Holyfield said: "When he bit me the first time, I couldn't believe it. They have rules and regulations for this. After he bit me, I went back to my corner and they told me to take a deep breath and concentrate. He caught me with a good shot, bit my ear and spat it out. Look at the bite. I'm missing part of my ear. I heard Mills Lane tell him one more time and he's gone. He continued to foul and that was it.

"I'm not thinking about a rematch. I just want to concentrate on what happened. I can't understand the biting and he was trying to break my arm. He fouled in every way. He had no real courage. I think what he did was caused by fear."

Not so much by fear as, surprisingly, Tyson's obvious concern when he has to deal with rough-house tactics. It is not just the aura of invincibility that has slipped from him but the notion of a street fighter's grim purpose.

Evidence of a serious flaw came eight years ago in the first of two contests against Frank Bruno: Battered into submission after being penalised for fouling, Bruno, a limited heavyweight, nevertheless troubled Tyson with the hard approach advised by his trainer, George Francis.

With his warrior instinct, superior boxing skills and vast experience Holyfield was far better equipped to exploit Tyson's fallibility under fire, the confusion caused in him by violent transgressions. This was obvious last November when Tyson, unable to cope with Holyfield's persistent, unpunished fouling, was stopped in the 11th round.

Infringements run the risk of retribution, but Holyfield was again prepared to take the risk, using his head so dangerously that Tyson was stunned by a butt and felt blood seeping from his right eyelid early in the second round. Tyson waved angrily at Holyfield and was given time to recover but the damage had been done.

If the impression then was that Tyson would have gone for Holyfield with an iron bar had one been available in his corner, subsequent events suggested an emotional collapse. Having lost the first two sessions Tyson made Holyfield look anxious for the first time, at last getting to the champion with heavy head blows.

Then, just when it looked as though Tyson was getting on top he bit Holyfield's right ear. Holyfield jumped and twisted in pain and was facing his corner when Tyson charged in and pushed him violently in the back. Lane halted the contest and signalled that Tyson had been deducted two points, making it impossible for him to even share the round unless Holyfield took a count.

Before they were called back to the centre of the ring, Holyfield, who had been passed fit to continue by the ringside doctor, turned to his trainer, Don Turner and said, "Put my mouthpiece in, I'm going to knock him out." But before Holyfield could attempt it Tyson closed in and bit him again.

At the bell Lane examined Holyfield before crossing to tell Tyson that he had been disqualified. In the pandemonium that followed, security guards and police wrestled with Tyson and his entourage and then plunged into the audience to make arrests. Shortly afterwards the MGM casino was sealed off after the firing of a shot.

For once Don King was conspicuous by his silence, making only a brief appearance on television. "Mike was ready to fight. I don't know why they stopped it," he said lamely. "I want to see the replays before I comment further. I will find out the facts and see what we will do."

The sadly predictable thing is that King and his television associates will attempt to profit from scandal, perhaps even believing that it adds to Tyson's market value. The truth is that the bully has been found out. He was only at his best when the going was good.

"ZIPPERGATE": FELLATIO IN THE OVAL OFFICE

Report of the Office of the Independent Counsel to Congress, Washington DC, 11 September 1998

After a lengthy investigation into the affair between President Clinton and White House intern Monica Lewinsky, Kenneth Starr, Independent Counsel, reported to Congress in September 1998, citing eleven grounds for impeaching the President. These included perjury and obstruction of justice by concealing his sexual relationship with Lewinsky. Evidence against Clinton included Lewinsky's own testimony and a DNA test on semen stains found on Lewinsky's Gap dress. According to the FBI's DNA test, the odds of the semen not coming from President Clinton were 1 in 7.87 trillion white males.

According to Ms Lewinsky, she and the President had a sexual encounter on Thursday, February 28 – their first in nearly 11 months. White House records show that Ms Lewinsky attended the taping of the President's weekly radio address on February 28. She was at the White House from 5:48 to 7:07 p.m. The President was in the Roosevelt Room (where the radio address was taped) from 6:29 to 6:36 p.m., then moved to the Oval Office, where he remained until 7:24 p.m. He had no telephone calls while Ms Lewinsky was in the White House.

Wearing a navy blue dress from the Gap, Ms Lewinsky attended the radio address at the President's invitation (relayed by Ms Currie), then had her photo taken with the President. Ms Lewinsky had not been alone with the President since she had worked at the White House, and, she testified, "I was really nervous." President Clinton told her to see Ms Currie after the photo was taken because he wanted to give her something. "So I waited a little while for him and then Betty and the President and I went into the back office," Ms Lewinsky testified. (She later learned that the reason Ms Currie accompanied them was that Stephen Goodin did not want the President to be alone with Ms Lewinsky, a view that Mr Goodin expressed to the President and Ms Currie). Once they had passed from the Oval Office toward the private study, Ms Currie said, "I'll be right back," and walked on to the back pantry or the dining room, where, according to Ms Currie, she waited for 15 to 20 minutes while the President and Ms Lewinsky were in the study. Ms Currie (who said she acted on her own initiative) testified that she accompanied the President and Ms Lewinsky out of the Oval Office because "I didn't want any perceptions, him being alone with someone."

In the study, according to Ms Lewinsky, the President "started to say something to me and I was pestering him to kiss me, because . . . it had been a long time since we had been alone." The President told her to wait a moment, as he had presents for her. As belated Christmas gifts, he gave her a hat pin and a special edition of Walt Whitman's *Leaves of Grass*.

Ms Lewinsky described the Whitman book as "the most sentimental gift he had given me . . . it's beautiful and it meant a lot to me." During this visit, according to Ms Lewinsky, the President said he had seen her Valentine's Day message in the Washington Post, and he talked about his fondness for "Romeo and Juliet".

Ms Lewinsky testified that after the President gave her the gifts, they had a sexual encounter:

"[W]e went back over by the bathroom in the hallway, and we kissed. We were kissing and he unbuttoned my dress and fondled my breast with my bra on, and then took them out of my bra and was kissing them and touching them with his hands and with his mouth.

"And then I think I was touching him in his genital area through his pants, and I think I unbuttoned his shirt and was kissing his chest. And then . . . I wanted to perform oral sex on him . . . and so I did. And then . . . I think he heard something, or he heard someone in the office. So, we moved into the bathroom.

"And I continued to perform oral sex and then he pushed me away, kind of as he always did before he came, and then I stood up and I said . . . I care about you so much; . . . I don't understand why you won't let me . . . make you come; it's important to me; I mean, it just doesn't feel complete, it doesn't seem right."

Ms Lewinsky testified that she and the President hugged, and "he said he didn't want to get addicted to me, and he didn't want me to get addicted to him." They looked at each other for a moment. Then, saying that "I don't want to disappoint you," the President consented. For the first time, she performed oral sex through completion . . . When Ms Lewinsky next took the navy blue Gap dress from her closet to wear it, she noticed stains near one hip and on the chest. FBI Laboratory tests revealed that the stains are the President's semen.

HAVE/HAVE NOT @ SILICON VALLEY,
California, December 1998

Martha Mendoza, Associated Press

An urban belt running south-east from San Francisco, Silicon Valley was the technological epicentre of the world at the end of the 20th century.

Connie Tort, a 25-year-old single mother of four, spends $400 a month for an unheated room in a sour-smelling house with cracked walls and blankets on the windows.

Just outside looms Adobe Systems Inc., a software company with annual revenue close to $1 billion.

"*Silicon* Valley? No, I never heard that term," said Ms Tort, who gets a $500 disability check each month. "Not everyone out here is involved in this technological stuff. A lot of us are barely making it with our kids."

The high-tech prosperity that has transformed Silicon Valley over the past decade has bypassed the poor and is even pushing out the middle class, forcing teachers and police officers into long commutes.

For every five jobs created this year in Silicon Valley, only one new home was built. The average rent for new tenants seeking unsubsidized apartments soared 29 per cent over the past two years, from $935 to $1,208.

At the end of 1997, only 37 per cent of Santa Clara County's homes were within the reach of families earning the average household income, $70,200. During the first half of 1998, housing prices soared from $288,000 to $317,000 in the county, which forms the heart of Silicon Valley, according to the National Association of Home Builders.

Silicon Valley is the world's leading high-tech region, home to 20 per cent of the biggest software and electronics companies. At Intel Corp., Hewlett-Packard Co. and Apple Computer Inc., annual revenues are counted by the billions.

"It's shameful that anyone is in need in the Silicon Valley," said Millard Fuller, founder of Habitat for Humanity International in Americus, Ga., an organization that builds homes for the poor. "If that brainpower could be focused on making sure that everyone's needs are met, you would have no substandard housing, you would have no food lines, you would have no homeless people."

To try to ease the pressure, the San Jose City Council adopted the nation's highest minimum wage last month. City contractors now have to pay at least $9.50 an hour with health benefits and $10.75 if benefits aren't provided.

"I don't mean to sound like I'm not grateful, because I know that's a lot of money," said Larry Contreras, 32, who scrubs vomit off the commuter rail tracks and picks gum off benches. "But I run out of money every pay period. In this town, it's really barely enough."

Contreras supports three children. More than half of his wages go to the room he rents in a relative's home.

"This has become a major problem in the Silicon Valley," said

Andy Grove, founder and chief executive of Intel, the world's largest maker of computer chips. "It's starting to remind me of a tourist resort where the hotels have driven prices so high that the people who work there have to live out of town."

The Second Harvest Food Bank serves 108,000 people a month in Silicon Valley. Only 11 per cent are homeless, said executive director David Sandretto, a former IBM manager.

"The rent prices are causing this. They have only so much money to spend and the rent prices are so expensive in Silicon Valley that they have to devote a huge amount of money to housing," Sandretto said:

The average salary in the high-tech sector – about one out of every four workers in Silicon Valley – was more than $72,000 last year. But overall, the 1 million workers in the geographical area known as Silicon Valley averaged only $46,000. And after taxes, a low-skilled worker earning minimum wage brings home less than $10,000 a year.

Some say the gap between the haves and the have-nots might not be so huge if Silicon Valley's high-tech executives and companies spread more of the wealth around.

The family of David and Lucile Salter Packard – of computer giant Hewlett-Packard Co. fame – is leading the charge, pledging $400 million in the coming year for environmental, social and educational organizations and projects, giving special consideration to Silicon Valley applicants.

But the Packards are an exception, said Tim Lenoir, who teaches the history of science and technology at Stanford University. "It is notoriously difficult to get people in the high-tech world to contribute," he said.

A survey by Community Foundation Silicon Valley found that giving as a percentage of pre-tax profits remained constant from 1994 to 1997 at just over 1 per cent.

Last week, retired lithographer Paul Savage donated a sleeping bag to the Sacred Heart Community Service center for a giveaway of clothes, food and medical care. The free child care center was filled. So were the computer classes.

"The rich just don't share," Savage said as people lined up for free groceries. "There are people making $100,000 to $200,000 a year in this town and they don't share anything."

Ms Tort picked up the sleeping bag and showed it to her 2-year-old son, Anthony.

"You like it, son?" she asked.

He nodded.

"OK," she said. "This can be your bed."

THE EXECUTION OF KARLA FAYE TUCKER,
Huntsville, Texas, 3 February 1999

Michael Graczyk, Associated Press

A former prostitute and drug-addict, who began using heroin at the age of ten, Karla Faye Tucker was sentenced to death for her part in the pickax murders of two people during a 1983 house break-in. During her fourteen years on death row, she became a Born Again Christian and drugs counsellor, and there were appeals for commutation of her sentence from figures as diverse as Pope John Paul II and TV evangelist Pat Robertson. These went unheeded and Tucker was executed by lethal injection on 3 February 1999 – the first woman to be executed in Texas since Chipita Rodriguez in 1863, and only the second in the USA since 1984.

Karla Tucker was calm, composed and contrite.

Wearing a prison issue white shirt and pants and wearing white running shoes, the 38-year-old pickax murderer expressed love to her family, sought forgiveness from the survivors of her victims and said she hoped she would see them later in heaven.

Those of us who were witnesses entered the Huntsville Unit of the Texas Department of Justice just after 6.40 pm, CST, were frisked by correction officers and then were quickly led outside to a small courtyard and through a steel door into the death house.

Five people selected by the inmate entered first and crowded to the double-pane of plastic glass. I was the lone media witness accompanying them.

She already had been strapped to the gurney, leather belts pulled snug across her chest, body, legs and arms. Her long curly hair trailed behind her on the white sheets. And the two needles – one in each arm just inside the elbow – were carrying a saline solution.

Several of the witnesses used sign language to express their sentiments.

Warren Morris Jones, standing near her head, asked if she had a final statement. A prison chaplain, Jim Brazzil, stood at her feet.

She turned to another window where the survivors of murder victim Deborah Thornton waited.

"Yes sir. I would like to say to all of you – the Thornton family and Jerry Dean's family – that I am so sorry. I hope God will give you peace with this."

She turned toward the window we were looking through. The nearest person was her husband, Dana Brown.

"Baby, I love you," she said.

Then she addressed Ron Carlson, Mrs Thornton's brother. He is philosophically opposed to the death penalty and befriended Ms Tucker.

"Ron, give Peggy a hug for me. Everybody has been so good to me.

"I love all of you very much. I am going to be face to face with Jesus now. Warden Baggett, thank all of you so much. You have been so good to me. I love all of you very much. I will see you all when you get there. I will wait for you."

She closed her eyes briefly, licked her lips, then began a silent prayer, her lips forming words.

Some of her witnesses cried softly. Several stood with their arms around each other.

As the drugs began taking effect, she gasped slightly twice, then let out a five- to ten-second wheeze as the air emptied from her lungs.

Her eyes remained nearly wide open. Her mouth remained slightly open.

"I love you, Karla," her sister, Kari Weeks, cried out.

"She loves you, too", Brown replied.

Then another friend, Jacki Oncken, turned to Carlson.

"She told me to tell you she loved you, Ron", Mrs Oncken said.

About four minutes after we arrived in the death house, a Huntsville physician, Daryl Wells, entered the chamber through a steel door. He shined a light in each of her eyes, used his fingers to check her neck for pulse, then repeated his examination for a pulse and heartbeat using a stethoscope.

He looked at his watch.

"6.45," he said.

The warden repeated. "6.45".

The steel door behind us opened. A prison guard said: "Family first."

I followed them.

"ZIPPERGATE": PRESIDENT CLINTON IS ACQUITTED BY THE SENATE, Washington D.C., 12 February 1999

Doyle McManus, Los Angeles Times

Some stood at attention, like military men, and called their votes out loud and clear. Others rose to their feet with what looked like reluctance and delivered their verdicts – "guilty," or "not guilty" – in hoarse, almost pleading tones.

It took a little more than eight minutes both times, all 100 senators rising in practiced alphabetical order.

But once the two solemn roll calls were over and the chief justice declared the result – "William Jefferson Clinton, president of the United States . . . hereby is acquitted of the charges in the said articles" – the Senate dissolved into bipartisan relief like a high school class at graduation.

Party leaders Trent Lott (R-Miss.) and Tom Daschle (D-S.D.) got a standing ovation and clasped each other's hands in mutual congratulation. "We did it!" Daschle said with a grin. "We sure did," Lott said, grinning back.

U.S. Chief Justice William H. Rehnquist got a plaque, like a Rotary Club honoree, and gamely hoisted it for the cameras. And after 13 months of scandal, five weeks of trial proceedings and three days of closed-door deliberations, both Democrats and Republicans declared that they were better for the experience.

"It was emotional," said Sen. Dianne Feinstein (D-Calif.). "In a way, it was profound."

"It's like boot camp," said Sen. Larry E. Craig (R-Idaho), one of the Senate's most conservative members. "It brought us closer in a way that I doubt would have otherwise happened."

Even Republicans who had sought to convict Clinton – and for whom the president's acquittal might thus seem something of a failure – pronounced the trial a splendid success.

"There was a tremendous feeling of bipartisan cooperation and good will," said Sen Rick Santorum (R-Pa). "We showed that just because you disagree, you don't have to be disagreeable."

Old arguments – in some cases, only hours old – were determinedly forgotten. Sen. Patrick J. Leahy (D-Vt.), one of Clinton's most fervent defenders, gave House Judiciary Chairman Henry J. Hyde (R-Ill.) a high-five. Rep. Asa Hutchinson (R-Ark.), one of the president's most relentless accusers, crossed the well to pump the hand of every White House lawyer. Rep. Maxine Waters (D-Los Angeles), who came to show support for Clinton, roamed the Senate floor collecting autographs on her tally sheet, a souvenir of the vote.

And everyone, Democrat and Republican alike, agreed that it was time to move on – literally. An hour after the last vote was cast, the Capitol was virtually empty. Most senators were on their way out of town, and the impeachment of Clinton was a waning memory.

"Why in the world would we want to keep the issue of President Clinton and Monica Lewinsky before us?" asked Sen. Wayne Allard (R-Colo.), who until Friday was a dogged proponent of the president's impeachment.

The final day of the Senate trial began at 6:30 a.m. PST Friday, with a last, two-hour session behind closed doors for a handful of senators who had not spoken in the chamber's deliberations.

One was Robert C. Byrd (D-W. Va.), the self-appointed guardian of Senate rules and constitutional order, whose votes were still in doubt. Byrd said that he felt Clinton had "abused the powers vested in him by the people" and that the president's offenses did add up to "high crimes and misdemeanors."

"This is, without question, the most difficult, wrenching, soul-searching vote that I have ever cast," Byrd said.

Then, just as he was about to announce his decision, Byrd ran out of time, other senators said. Rehnquist gaveled his speech to an end.

"We didn't know what he was going to do," said Sen. John B. Breaux (D-La.). "Everybody was holding their breath."

When the roll call came on Article I, which accused Clinton of perjury, Byrd stood stiffly even before his name was called. When his turn came, he looked down for a moment, then said quietly: "Not guilty."

When Sen. John W. Warner (R-Va.) voted "not guilty," there were gasps in the packed galleries, but not on the floor. Warner had told his GOP colleagues that he would vote to acquit on Article I.

Article I failed by 22 votes, 45 to 55.

Article II, which accused Clinton of obstruction of justice, was closer. Five Republicans joined all 45 Democrats in voting "not guilty." But neither vote even approached the two-thirds majority needed to throw Clinton out of the White House.

Sen. John H. Chafee (R-R.I.) pronounced the verdict crisply; Sen. Susan Collins (R-Maine) almost inaudibly; Sen. James M. Jeffords (R-Vt.) slowly and solemnly; Sen. Olympia J. Snowe (R-Maine) in a firm New England twang. The last Republican to vote for acquittal, Sen. Arlen Specter (R-Pa.), gave the verdict a personal twist: "Not proven, therefore not guilty."

After the vote and the back-slapping congratulations, the Senate returned abruptly to its normal muddle. Feinstein sought a vote on her proposal to censure Clinton. Sen. Phil Gramm (R-Texas) objected and the Senate voted to keep it off the floor. Other senators, including many Democrats, said that they had no desire to restart the debate over Clinton's sins.

Instead, they had other business to do. Allard headed for Colorado and a series of town meetings on Social Security. Sen. Carl Levin (D-Mich.) headed for a television interview, then a flight to Detroit. Sen. John McCain (R-Ariz.) dashed for the airport to fly to Miami, where he was due at a fund-raiser for his nascent 2000 presidential campaign.

On the Capitol's east lawn, a tiny band of anti-Clinton protesters – numbering exactly 12 on Friday morning – waved signs from a distance, held back by a flimsy temporary fence.

Even they acknowledged that the country had moved on.

"It's not Clinton. It's not Congress. It's the people of this nation who are dropping the ball," said Paul Mitchell, a retired firefighter-turned-evangelist from Norco, Calif., who came to Washington for the trial.

Besides, noted demonstrator Kristinn Taylor, 36, of Washington, it's hard to turn out protesters these days. "People have jobs," he said. "We're in a full-employment economy."

THE MERCHANDIZING OF *STAR WARS: THE PHANTOM MENACE*, Atlanta, 3 May 1999

Bob Longino, The Atlanta Journal-Constitution

Call it the Darth Mauling of America. George Lucas's fourth *Star Wars* film, with new evil character Darth Maul, isn't due in theaters until May 19, but it's already coming at fans from all directions. Today, John Williams' soundtrack to *Star Wars: Episode*

1 – The Phantom Menace goes on sale at record stores across the country. On Monday, fans flocked to Toys "R" Us, Target, Kmart and Wal-Mart locations nationwide to buy Anakin Skywalker and Darth Maul action figures, electronic QuiGon Jinn light sabers and other items from the new line of *Star Wars* merchandise, the largest and most-hyped in the history of toys.

Also on Monday, writer Terry Brooks' 352-page *Phantom Menace* novel from Ballatinc Books, which relates the story of the dawn of *Star Wars*, was being sold on the Internet (www.amazon.com) for $15. MTV revealed a new "Menace" video for the soundtrack's first single, "Duel of the Fates". And Pepsi USA, launched its commemorative *Episode I* can collection, including special gold Yoda cans worth $20 each in prize money.

It's all serious business.

The Toys "R" Us in Buckhead, for instance, sold $12,000 worth of *Star Wars* merchandise in 90 minutes on Monday, surpassing total sales for Sunday.

In Cobb County, William Horowitz, 17, of Avondale Estates, pushed a wheelbarrow into the Toys "R" Us on Cobb Parkway for that store's early opening Monday so his friends could load up on the new *Star Wars* toys.

As theme music from the upcoming film blared over the store's in-store system, more than 100 early-bird customers swarmed the *Phantom Menace* section, grabbing up armloads of talking action figures, Darth Maul 3-D Painter sets and Anakin Skywalker Pod Racers.

"I'm here to get as much as I can get," Tally Shafizadeh, 14, of Atlanta said moments before he and his brother Jeffrey, 12, began loading a shopping cart with box after box of toys to add to their already sizable collection of 244 *Star Wars* action figures at home. They planned to spend $453 – all in cash they'd been saving for months from allowances, yardwork and odd jobs.

"This is the biggest single release of toys I've ever seen," said Dan Sierra, district manager of K-Bee Toys in metro Atlanta. "We're having a lot of fun."

K-Bee Toys at North DeKalb Mall did half of its projected day's business by 8 a.m., Sierra said, adding that the hottest-selling items included Samuel L. Jackson's Mace Windu action figure and Sebulo Pod Racer.

By 9:30 a.m. Monday, some stores found their merchandise,

especially items portraying the menacing Darth Maul, significantly depleted.

"Pretty much all the action figures are gone," said Nancy Gilber, assistant manager of the Toys "R" Us on Cobb Parkway. A fresh shipment of *Star Wars* toys is expected Wednesday.

MTV's premiere of the four-minute, 14-second "Duel of the Fates" video was enveloped in Monday afternoon's special 90-minute edition of "Total Request Live".

The video includes a few fresh snippets from the movie, several shots of Darth Maul snarling with rotten teeth and ample footage of stars Liam Neeson, Natalie Portman and Ewan McGregor (including a shot of his hair being trimmed for the movie). Mixed in with the film's scenes are shots of John Williams conducting the London Symphony, of director George Lucas exclaiming, "Cut!" and a few behind-the-scenes movie-making moments.

Expect both MTV and VH1 to air the new video repeatedly for the next couple of weeks.

9/11: COLLAPSE OF THE NORTH TOWER OF THE WORLD TRADE CENTER, New York, 11th September 2001

FDNY Battalion Commander Pitch Picciotto

On the humdrum morning of 11 September 2001 fanatics from the Al-Qaeda terror group hijacked four American airliners. Of these, two were flown into the Twin Towers of the World Trade Center in New York, while another crashed into the Pentagon – all symbolic targets, all full of human life. The fourth plane, after a struggle between passengers and terrorists, crashed into Pennsylvania farmland.

Fireman Pitch Picciotto was in the second tower of the World Trade Center when it was attacked.

I was on the landing between the seventh and sixth floor when it hit. At least, that's where I place myself in recollection. I could have made it all the way down to the sixth, but I seem to recall pulling up on the return landing, about to zag back down the next half-flight. All along the building had been shaking, rocking like crazy, and here it was shaking so hard it was an effort to keep my balance. Beams started falling. Big chunks of concrete. All kinds of shit, just raining down on me, like a friggin' plague. Raining down on *us*, I should say, because I wasn't the only one on those stairs. Even now, at the very end, I didn't stop running, hurtling down those stairs with everything I had left, making the turn on the landing. I pressed on, until finally a beam or a plank or some blunt object hit me on the head and sent me reeling. Knocked my helmet off, too. Whatever it was had whacked me pretty good, and I was down and thinking that would be it.

But that wasn't it. The noise kept coming. The debris kept falling. The building kept shaking. And I was still breathing, and conscious, and alert to the whole damn thing.

I tried to stand, but stumbled before I could right myself, and in the stumbling I cursed the fact that I was still alive. Really, I was pissed. And afraid. I should have been dead by now. I'd hoped I'd be dead by now. So much for praying it would be quick. I'd thought it would be instantaneous, however it was gonna happen, but this was taking way too much time. This was torture.

All of this unfolded in a blip. The south tower had taken ten seconds to come down, and this one would take only eight seconds, according to published reports after the attack. Once again, eight seconds doesn't seem to cut it, in my estimation. It had to have been longer. Three or four times longer. How else to explain these runaway thoughts, these stops and starts as I made to escape, these twists and turns? But I suppose there's no explaining it, this stretching out of time.

I did manage to stand, finally, only as soon as I got to my feet the landing fell away. Like a trap door. It was there, and then it wasn't there, and as it fell I moved with it. The weird thing is, I don't really recall hearing any noise at this point. Either it was so deeply ingrained and so much a part of this harrowing scene it had quickly become like background music, to where I no longer noticed it, or it had become quieter. This last makes sense, when I think about it, because by this point much of the wreckage had settled into the sub-basement and surrounding area; by the time it reached my little landing between seven and six there was hardly any noise left to be made. And you know how it is at the silent end of a great racket. There's this eerie hollow, this audible emptiness. This giant nothing-at-all where there had only recently been everything, and too, too much, and it was into this space that I fell as well.

Please, God, make it quick.

Actually, it was more ride than fall, more slide than drop,

because as the landing gave way, the rubble it became kinda cascaded and skated along, bumping up against walls and stairs and railings and beams and whatever the hell else was in its path. I was a big piece of debris, hurtling through the shell of that stairwell. There was a brief stomach-dropping falling sensation, mixed with all kinds of banging and tumbling, and then a descent in slow motion, and the reason it felt like slow motion, I later figured, was because it wasn't a sheer drop. It *was* slow motion – sort of. Anyway, it was slower than I would have thought. It was like being on the rough end of a relentless rockslide. Someone suggested to me later it was probably like getting caught in unbelievably rough surf, like when you're body surfing and a wave sneaks up and knocks you silly and over and forward, to where you no longer know which way is up or how to arrest your fall. But that wasn't it. Close, but not quite. It was more like a short free fall, where you never fully leave the ground, because the ground is free-falling with you. Tumbling, as if down a flight of stairs, but as if I was taking the stairs with me. Hard to explain, and equally hard to understand when it's happening to you.

At some point during this wild ride, the lights went out. I didn't notice them going, and it's possible I had my eyes closed to what was happening, but when I opened them there was nothing to see. Just blackness, all around. Nothing more. The kind of blackness you need to raise your arms against, to cover yourself, for protection, because you've got no idea what's coming, or from what direction. But there was nothing coming, nothing still falling. There was no more noise. It's like those stupid rides they've got in shopping malls, where you put a quarter in the slot and sit your kid on top and the thing shakes and shakes for a half-minute or so and then the quarter runs out.

And here's another weird piece: I didn't land. There was no big trauma, or impact, when the falling stopped. It just stopped. I had my bunker gear on, which offered some degree of padding and protection, but no way was I impact-proof; I was getting whacked and paddled and smacked around pretty good, and then all of a sudden the whacking and paddling and smacking sort of stopped. It slowed, then it stopped. It lasted for a good few seconds, and at the other end there was nothing. I didn't really have a single clear thought, as I tumbled. I was just waiting on the end. Disorientated, and waiting on the end. My end. It hadn't claimed me before, that first whack that had knocked me to the ground, but surely I couldn't survive such as this. Here again, as before, my head was filled with every possible thought, every conceivable outcome, every unfolding detail, and somewhere in there too were the stuffings of my life, the small moments I couldn't shake, the *what if?* scenarios we all carry. As I fell, I expected my thoughts to slam shut on me with some final impact. There'd be thinking, and feeling, and then there'd be no thinking, no feeling.

Please, God, make it quick.

But nothing happened. I stopped moving, that's all. I stopped thinking in any forward-thinking kind of way. I stopped *being*, if that makes any sense, for a beat or two anyway. I didn't black out or anything, never lost consciousness, but I did momentarily lose a full grasp on where I was and what had happened and what I was doing. There had to have been a couple of ticks of the clock in there where I was merely still, and not thinking, and unaware of any single thing. Understand, I couldn't see. I couldn't grasp my situation. I couldn't move, once again for fear of making the wrong move. Plus, as I began to assess the scene, I didn't think I had any ability to move, or any right. Or even anything to move. I thought I was dead. I actually wondered if this was what it felt like to be dead. Think about it: it was pitch dark. There was no sound, no movement, no nothing. My mind was still working, but to someone who'd been raised Catholic, to someone who believed in the concept of Heaven and Hell, this didn't strike me as too surprising. Out of my experience, perhaps, but not out of the realm of possibility.

Okay, I determined, so I could think. For a second, I even allowed myself a secret sigh of relief that the memories I'd made up until just that moment wouldn't die with me. I could still think and feel . . . and *remember*. This wasn't so bad, I thought, this being dead. I'd thought I'd be above the clouds, floating and flitting about with angels, looking down from above, but maybe this is what my afterlife would look like. In the beginning, anyway, this was how it would be. The clouds and the angels and the somersaults would come later. So, no, this wasn't too bad. Wasn't how I'd pictured it, but it wasn't too bad. And I hadn't really suffered, beyond the unbearable fear of suffering. It was over, and yet it wasn't over.

Gradually, though, I began to notice my body, and as I did I took time to realize that if I had been dead I wouldn't be noticing my body. There'd be no body, right? There'd be no arms to move, no head to turn. But here it was, my body, very much intact. I could *feel*. *I* could squeeze my fingers into a fist. I was lying on my back, not quite flat, splayed across an uneven surface of rubble and cement and uncertain debris. My head was resting on a cement boulder, which appeared to be about the size of a softball. There were no beams crushing me, no piles of concrete. I had no idea what sort of space I'd been dropped into, but nothing was confining, or constricting me, not that I could tell anyway. I could feel with my hands that I was lying among a mess of building materials that had been reduced to pebbles, stones. And, mostly, a very fine, fine powder. I reached around, to get a feel for where I was, and my hands noticed that I was pretty much covered with the stuff. Ash, dust, powder . . . whatever it was. It was in my mouth, in my nose, in my eyes, in my ears. Everywhere there was an opening, there it was. It was beneath my clothes, even. It was all around. I was buried beneath a coating of about six inches of the stuff. Buried alive. It's a stupid phrase to use in this particular instance, because even a coating of six inches of the stuff can be shaken off without too much trouble, but it's what popped into my head at the time. No, I wasn't buried to the point where I couldn't claw my way out, but I was covered. Completely covered. And I was alive!

Appendix: Presidents of the U.S.

President	Party	Served
George Washington	Federalist	1789–97

George Washington became the first President of the United States with a unanimous vote and it was his decision that he and future holders of the office should be addressed simply as "Mr President."

John Adams	Federalist	1797–1801

John Adams had 5 children and his eldest son John Qunicy Adams became the 6th President of the United States. In an incredible coincidence John Adams and Thomas Jefferson passed away on the same day, July 4, 1826, exactly 50 years after the Declaration of Independence was signed.

Thomas Jefferson	Republican	1801–09

Thomas Jefferson's greatest triumph was the Louisiana Purchase which doubled the size of the United States. Rumours still persist that he had an affair with an African American nursemaid Sally Hemmings but little evidence exists as to the validity of this.

James Madison	Republican	1809–17

In later years, James Madison was active in the American Colonization Society, whose mission was the resettlement of slaves. This was despite the fact that he had been a slaveholder all his life.

James Monroe	Republican	1817–25

With James Madison and Thomas Jefferson, James Monroe co-founded the Democratic-Republican party. Monroe's administration was a time of peaceful prosperity for America and it became known as the "era of good feeling."

John Quincy Adams   Republican   1825–9
John Quincy Adams became President after a very close battle with
Andrew Jackson. This caused a split in the Democratic-Republican party
and Adams's group became the National Republicans.

Andrew Jackson   Democrat   1829–37
Andrew Jackson was a man who fiercely believed in honour and in a duel
in 1806 killed a man who made derogatory comments about his wife.

Martin Van Buren   Democrat   1837–41
Martin Van Buren was the son of a tavern keeper who began to study
law aged 14 and was admitted to the bar at the incredibly young age
of 21.

William H. Harrison (died in office)   Whig   1841
William H. Harrison was the first President to die in office of a cold that
developed into pneumonia, after only a month.

John Tyler   Whig   1841–5
John Tyler was the first Vice-President to become President by the death
of his predecessor and the first to be faced with impeachment.

James K. Polk   Democrat   1845–9
James K. Polk became Speaker of the House in 1835 and remains the only
Speaker to have also become President.

Zachary Taylor (died in office)   Whig   1849–50
Zachary Taylor, nicknamed "Old Rough and Ready" was a renowned
Indian fighter and hero of the Mexican War (1846-8).

Millard Fillmore   Whig   1850–3
Millard Fillmore's wife, Abigail, was a former schoolteacher who on
entering the White House found that there were no books and subsequently appealed for a grant from Congress to establish the White House
Library.

Franklin Pierce   Democrat   1853–7
In 1853 Franklin Pierce and his family were in a train crash in which their
only surviving child, 11-year-old Benjamin was killed. Mrs Pierce, already
unhappy in Washington withdrew completely from public life after this
tragedy.

James Buchanan   Democrat   1857–61
After the (possible) suicide of his fiancée James Buchanan never married
and became the only bachelor President.

Abraham Lincoln (assassinated)   Republican   1861–5

Abraham Lincoln was the author of the Gettysburg Address and victor in the Civil War, but he was plagued by his wife's obsessive behaviour. He was assassinated by Southern sympathizer John Wilkes Booth while at the theatre.

Andrew Johnson   Democrat   1865–9

Andrew Johnson had no formal schooling and while apprenticed to a tailor managed to teach himself to read, he went on to take over the Presidential office following the assassination of Abraham Lincoln.

Ulysses S. Grant   Republican   1869–77

On the death of Ulysses S. Grant, the New York Tribune said that "the greatest mistake of his life was the acceptance of the Presidency."

Rutherford B. Hayes   Republican   1877–81

Rutherford B. Hayes was a religious man who did not smoke or drink, he and his wife supported the temperance movement and banned all alcohol from the White House. She was the first President's wife to be termed the "First Lady" in a magazine article, which has been used for the wife of the President ever since.

James A. Garfield (assassinated)   Republican   1881

James A. Garfield was successfully nominated as Republican candidate in 1880 on the 36th ballot. After only 4 months in office he was fatally shot by a disgruntled office-seeker Charles Jules Guiteau because Garfield had given preferential treatment to radical Republicans.

Chester A. Arthur   Republican   1881–5

Chester A. Arthur, generally remembered as the best-dressed President, being nicknamed "Elegant Arthur." There is the possibility that he was born in Canada where his parents lived for some time which would mean he was the only President not to have been born in America and therefore not eligible for the Presidential office.

Grover Cleveland   Democrat   1885–9

Grover Cleveland was seen as a honest man but earlier in his life he had paid a substitute to take his place in the army (which was legal), this was used against him later by his political enemies. His is also the only presidential marriage, to date, to have taken place at the White House.

Benjamin Harrison   Republican   1889–93

Benjamin Harrison considered becoming a Presbyterian minister but decided to study law instead. Inaugurated 100 years after George Washington he is often known as the "Centennial President."

Grover Cleveland (second term)   Democrat   1893–7
Grover Cleveland was re-elected in 1892, the only President elected to two non-consecutive terms. In 1895 he electrified the world by applying the anti-colonial "Monroe Doctrine" to Britain because of her dispute with Venezuela.

William McKinley (assassinated)   Republican   1897–1901
William McKinley has historically been seen as a rather weak President but looking at his achievements it is difficult to accept this. During his presidency America built up a strong marine and merchant navy, became a colonial power, adopted the monetary gold standard and became a significant player in world trade.

Theodore Roosevelt   Republican   1901–09
Aside from his political career Theodore Roosevelt will be remembered for two things, his immense literary output, (he was the author of 26 books and over 1000 magazine articles) and most important of all as the namesake of the "Teddy Bear."

William Howard Taft   Republican   1909–13
William Howard Taft had a love of law that was to last him all his life. After a disastrous presidency he became the Chief Justice of the Supreme Court, the only person in history to have held both posts.

Woodrow Wilson   Democrat   1913–21
Woodrow Wilson broke with previous presidential practice by appearing in Congress in person. He was also awarded the 1919 Nobel Peace Prize.

Warren G. Harding (died in office)   Republican   1921–3
Warren G. Harding's government was accused of corruption and to increase his popularity and dispel rumours he undertook a strenuous speaking tour of America. He suffered an attack of food poisoning and four days later died. His death was so unexpected it was rumoured that his wife had orchestrated it to avoid him facing possible impeachment.

Calvin Coolidge   Republican   1923–9
On the death of Warren G. Harding, Calvin Coolidge's father, who was a Justice of the Peace, administered the oath of office before Coolidge going back to bed! When Coolidge was re-elected for a second term it was the first inauguration to be broadcast over the radio.

Herbert C. Hoover   Republican   1929–3
Herbert C. Hoover's term as President coincided with the stock market crash of October 1929 heralding the beginning of the Great Depression.

Faced with the biggest economic crisis in US history Hoover lost to Franklin D. Roosevelt when he stood for re-election.

Franklin D. Roosevelt (died in office)   Democrat   1933–45
Franklin D. Roosevelt contracted severe polio myelitis in 1921. He lost the use of his legs and hands and it seemed that his political career was over, but with the help of his wife Eleanor he fought the disease to become President. His radio broadcasts were dubbed "fireside chats" and became a bond of trust between Roosevelt and the America people.

Harry S. Truman   Democrat   1945–53
Harry S. Truman was the President who ordered the dropping of the H-bomb on Japan in 1945 which brought about the end of World War II and ushered in the developing "Cold War" against Communism.

Dwight D. Eisenhower   Republican   1953–61
Dwight D. Eisenhower was appointed Supreme Commander of the combined land forces for NATO and urged the world to harness nuclear power for peaceful means, setting up a program called "Atoms for Peace" with the UN, he also financed America's first foray into the "space race" with Explorer 1 which was launched into orbit 31 January 1958.

John F. Kennedy (assassinated)   Democrat   1961–3
John F. Kennedy was the first Roman Catholic and the youngest person to enter the White House. Criticized for the Bay of Pigs fiasco in Cuba he was largely overshadowed by his wife Jacqueline Kennedy who was with him in Dallas in an assassination that still abounds with conspiracy theories.

Lyndon B. Johnson   Democrat   1963–9
Lyndon B. Johnson was elected for a second term with the widest popular margin in American political history. In his first years in office he initiated changes in housing, education, crime prevention and urban renewal in one of the most comprehensive legislative programs ever seen.

Richard M. Nixon (resigned)   Republican   1969–74
Richard M. Nixon resigned over the "Watergate" scandal when it was proved that he had known of attempts to cover up the burglary of the Democratic party headquarters. He was given a full pardon just one month later by President Gerald Ford.

Gerald R. Ford   Republican   1974–7
At Gerald R. Ford's inauguration it was the first time in American history that the President had not been elected as either President or Vice-President. His decision to pardon Nixon made him very unpopular

and he voluntarily appeared before a sub-committee of the House of Representatives, the first time that a serving President had formally testified before such a committee.

James Carter   Democrat   1977–81

James Carter was practically unknown when he stood for President. Bringing honesty and decency to the office following in the footsteps of Nixon and the Vietnam War persuaded the American people to elect him. When it came to re-election it was very different, he polled the lowest presidential popularity rating in history and was swept away by Reagan and Bush.

Ronald Reagan   Republican   1981–9

Before becoming President Ronald Reagan had a career as a film star where he made his film debut in *Love is on the Air* (1937). He was shot in the chest in 1981 but managed to make a full recovery. He was implicated in the sale of US weapons to Iran during his administration but after denying all knowledge emerged relatively unscathed.

George Bush   Republican   1989–93

George Bush had most of his successes in foreign policy, having come on the heels on the popular Reagan. Bush sent troops into Panama to arrest General Noriega who was subsequently tried and convicted in a US court. He also handled the unexpected fall of Soviet power in Eastern Europe well and used his diplomatic skills to liberate Kuwait in 1990.

Bill Clinton   Democrat   1993–2001

Bill Clinton's record as President includes substantial intervention in trouble spots such as the Middle East and Northern Ireland as well as committing peacekeeping troops to Bosnia and Herzegovina. Back home he managed to turn the greatest deficit in American history into a period of economic prosperity. Dogged by scandal including a sexual relationship with White House intern Monica Lewinsky and the Whitewater real estate investigation Clinton still managed to remain a popular political figure.

George W. Bush   Republican   2001–

George W. Bush started his presidential term under a wave of controversy with a close result in Florida that triggered an automatic recount. Law suits followed and unofficial recounts point to Al Gore being the true winner. Regardless of these controversies George W. Bush is the 43rd President of the United States of America.

Acknowledgments & Sources

The editor has made every effort to locate all persons having rights in the selections which appear in this anthology, and to secure permission from the holders of such rights to reprint material. The editor apologizes in advance for any errors or omissions inadvertently made. Queries regarding the use of material should be addressed to the editor c/o the publisher.

Part I

Columbus, Christopher, *The Voyages of Christopher Columbus*, ed Cecil Janes, 1930

De Leon, Ponce, 'History of Juan Ponce de Leon's Voyages to Florida', trans T.F. Davis, *Florida Historical Quarterly*, 14, 1935

De Coronado, Francisco, *Narratives of the Coronado Expedition*, 1940

De Soto, Hernando, *True relation of the hardship suffered by Governor Don Fernando de Soto and certain Portuguese Gentlemen in the Discovery of the Province of Florida. Now newly set forth by a Gentlemen of Elvas*, trans JA Robertson, 1933

Drake, Sir Francis, *The World Encompassed by Sir Francis Drake*, 1854

Barlowe, Arthur, quoted in *The Principall Voyages, Traffiques and Discourses of the English Nation*, Richard Hakluyt, reprinted in *American History Told by Contemporaries*, ed. A Bushnell Hart, 1898

Hariot, Thomas, quoted in *The Principall Voyages, Traffiques and Discourses of the English Nation*, Richard Hakluyt, ibid

Smith, John, *The True Travels & Adventures of Captain of John Smith*, ed Alex Philip, 1907

De Champlain, Samuel, *Voyages of Samuel de Champlain*, ed WL Grant, 1907

Bradford, William, *History of Plimouth Plantation*, 1898

Chester, Anthony, *Voyage of Anthony Chester to Virginia*, 1707

Thacher, Anthony, *Original Letters of Eminent Men of the Sixteenth, Seventeenth and Eighteenth Centuries*, ed Henry Ellis, 1843

Morton, Thomas, *The Library of Original Sources*, ed Oliver J Thatcher, 1907

Berkeley, Sir William, quoted *Virtual Jamestown* website

Lawson, Deodat, *A Real & True Narative of Some Remarkable Passages relating to Sundry Persons Afflicted by Witchcraft at Salem Village*, 1692

Mather, Cotton, *Selected Letters of Cotton Mather*, ed Kenneth Silverman, 1971. Copyright (c) 1971 Louisiana State University Press

Winthrop, Wait, quoted *Fathers to Sons*, ed Alan Valentine, 1963

Smith, Venture, *A Narrative of the Life and Adventures of Venture, A Native of Africa*, 1896.

Mittelberger, Gottlieb, *Gottlieb Mittelberger's Journey to Pennsylvania in the Year 1750 and Return to Germany in 1754*, 1898

Washington, George, *The Life of George Washington*, Jared Sparks, 1839.

Part II

Daniel Boon, *Life and Adventures of Colonel Daniel Boon*, 1823

Jefferson, Thomas, The Letters of Thomas Jefferson, ed HR Macilwaine,

Preston, Thomas, *English Historical Documents ix*, 1955

British Customs, quoted *North Carolina Historical Review*, 11, 1934

Andrews, John, *Letters of John Andrews Esq*, ed Winthrop Sargeant, 1866

Smith, F, quoted *They Saw It Happen 1689-1897*, ed T Charles Edwards and B Richardson, 1958

Potter, Israel R, *The Magazine of History*, 1911

Adams, John, *The Works of John Adams*, ed Charles Francis Adams, Vol II, 1850

Waldo, Albigence, *Pennsylvania Magazine of History and Biography*, 1896

Tanner, John, *Occasional Papers of the Sutro Branch of California State Library*, Reprint Series No 20, ed Paul Radin, 1940

Pendleton, Nathaniel and W.P. Van Ness, *A Collection of Facts and*

Documents, relating to the Death of Alexander Hamilton, ed William Coleman, 1804

Hosack, Dr, *A Collection of Facts and Documents, relating to the Death of Alexander Hamilton*, ibid

Lewis, Meriwether and William Clark, *The Journals of Lewis and Clark*, ed Frank Bergon, 1989

Hull, Isaac, *Official letters of the Military and Naval Officers of the United States During the War with Great Britain in the Years 1812, 13, 14, 15*, ed John Brannan, 1823

Stubbs, Samuel, *The Magazine of History*, USA, 1929

Madison, Dolley, quoted *The Book of Virtues*, ed William J Bennett, 1993

Part III

Smith, Jedediah Strong, *Missouri Republican*, October 11 1827

Downe, John, quoted *Letters of a Nation*, ed. Andrew Carroll, 1997

Ingraham, Joseph, *The South-West by a Yankee*, 1835

Travis, William Barrett, quoted *The Mammoth Book of the West*, Jon E. Lewis, 1996

Catlin, George, (Mandan chief excerpt) *Letters & Notes on the Manners, Customs, Conditions of the North American Indians*, 1841

Douglass, Frederick, *The Life and Times of Frederick Douglass*, 1882

Fremont, John Charles, *The Life of Col. John Charles Fremont and his Narrative of Explorations and Adventures, in Kansas, Nebraska, Oregon and California*, 1856

Russell, Osborne, *Journal of a Trapper*, Oregon Historical Society Proceedings, 1951

Catlin, George (Sun dance), *Illustrations of the Manners, Customs, and Condition of the North American Indians*, 1848

Taylor, William E., *Overland in 1846*, ed Dale Morgan, 1963

Twain, Mark, (steamboats on the Mississippi) *Life on the Mississippi*, 1883

Parkman, Francis

Howe, Samuel Gridley, Letter to Charles Sumner, quoted in *A Key to Uncle Tom's Cabin*, Harriet Beecher Stowe, 1853

Fellun, Captain, quoted *Overland in 1846*, ibid

Strother, David Hunter, *Harper's Weekly*, 5 November 1859

Burton, Richard F., *The City of the Saints*, 1861

Mark Twain, *Roughing It*, 1872

Osbon, B.S., New York *World*, April 13 1861

Chesnut, Mary Boykin, *A Diary from Dixie 1861-65*, ed Ben Ames Williams, 1949

Trollope, Anthony, *North America*, 1862

Ballou, Sullivan, quoted *Letters of a Nation*, ed. Andrew Carroll, 1997

Green, Dana, quoted US Postal Services website

Anon, (Shiloh), quoted *The Mammoth Book of War Diaries & Letters*, Jon E. Lewis, 1998

Ford, Dennis, quoted Life in the 28th Massachusetts: Letters by the Soldiers website

Cleveland Herald Special Correspondent, *The North Reports the Civil War*, ed J. Cutler Andrews, 1955

Twain, Mark, *Innocents Abroad*, 1869

Buerstatte, Frederick C., *Manitowoc County Historical Society Newsletter*, March 1975, vol 9, no. 2. Translation copyright (c) 1974 George Ermne

Porter, Horace, quoted in *Battles and Leaders of the Civil War*, Vol IV, ed Clarence Buel & Robert U. Johnson, 1888

Beekman, Daniel Dean, *We Saw Lincoln Shot - one hundred eyewitness accounts*, Timothy S. Good, 1995

Doherty, Edward, *Century Magazine*, January 1890

Browne, J. Ross, *Harper's Monthly Magazine*, June 1865

Godfrey, Edward S., *Cavalry Journal*, October 1928

Adams, Andy, *The Log of a Cowboy*, 1969

Cody, Buffalo Bill, *The Life of Buffalo Bill*, 1977

Larned, Charles, extracted from 'Expedition to the Yellowstone River in 1873: Letters of a Young Cavalry Officer', ed George Frederick Howe, *Mississippi Valley Historical Review* 39, December 1952

Two Moon, *The Penguin Book of Interviews*, ed Christopher Silvester, 1993

Garrett, Pat, *The Authentic Life of Billy the Kid*, 1882

Betzinez, Jason, *I Fought with Geronimo*, 1959

Black Elk, *Black Elk Speaks*, (with John G. Neihardt), 1932. Copyright (C) 1961 John G. Neihardt Trust

Dewey, George, *Autobiography of George Dewey*, 1913

Crane, Stephen, *McClure's*, July 1898

Lawson, Robert, *The Buffalo Bulletin*, 8 June 1859

Part IV

Wright, Orville, quoted in *Miracle at Kitty Hawk*, Fred C. Kelly

London, Jack, *Collier's Weekly*, 5 May 1906

Irwin, Will, quoted in *The Book of Modern Scandal*, ed Bruce Palling, 1996

Peary, Robert E., *The North Pole*, 1910

Adams, McMillan, quoted www.spartacus.sschoolnet.co.uk/ FWWlusitania

Bowman, Rudolph, file 180920, World War I Documents Archives website

Rickenbacker, Eddie V., *Fighting the Flying Circus*, 1919

Littell, Robert, *The New Republic*, 14 November 1923

Lindbergh, Charles A., *The Spirit of St. Louis*, 1953

Stark, Louis, *We Saw It Happen*, 1938

Bell, Elliott, *We Saw It Happen*, 1938

Cockburn, Claud, *I, Claud*, 1967. Copyright (c) Claud Cockburn 1967

Dos Passos, John, *The New Republic* 23 December 1931

Our Correspondent, *Daily Telegraph*, 7 February 1936

Steinbeck, John, *San Francisco News* October 1936. Reprinted from *Harvest Gypsies*, 2002

Considine, Bob, *International News Service*, 22 June 1938

Fuchida, Taisa Mitsuo, quoted in *Bombs Away*!, ed Stanley M. Ulanoff, 1971.

Garcia, John, *The Good War: An Oral History of World War II*, Studs Terkel, 1984

Dyess, William, *The Dyess Story*, 1944. Copyright (c) 1944 Marajen Stevick Dyess

Laney, Al, New York *Herald Tribune*, 8 February 1942. Copyright (c) 1942 New York Herald Tribune Inc

X, Malcolm (with Alex Haley), *The Autobiography of Malcolm X*, 2001. Copyright (c) 1965 Malcolm X

Kazazkow, B.J., *Jewish Youth: Letters from American Soldiers*, 1945

Doolittle, James, quoted in *Bombs Away*!, ed Stanley M. Ulanoff, 1971

Adams, Milton, *Taps for Jim Crow Army*, ed Phillip McGuire, 1983

Casey, Robert J., *The Story of World War II*, ed Curt Riess, 1945

Fuchida, Mitsuo, *Midway: The Battle That Doomed Japan*, 1955. Copyright (c) 1955 US Naval Institute, Annapolis, Maryland, USA

Matsushita, Iwao, quoted in *Letters of a Nation*, ed Andrew Carroll, 197

Wray, Rachel, *The Home Front: America During World War II*, Mark Harris, 1984. Copyright (c) 1984 Mark J. Harris. Reprinted by permission of Penguin Putnam Inc

Young, John S., quoted in *Bombs Away!*, ed Stanley M. Ulanoff, 1971

Boyington, Gregory, *Baa Baa Black Sheep*, 1958. Copyright (c) 1958 Gregory Boyington

Butcher, Harry C., *Three Years with Eisenhower*, 1946

Remington, Guy, *New Yorker*, 19 August 1944

Hemingway, Ernest, *Collier's*, 22 July 1944. Reprinted from *By-Line Ernest Hemingway*, ed William White, 1968.

Dawson, Joseph, quoted in *Eye-witness D-Day*, Jon E. Lewis, 1994

Sledge, Eugene B., *With the Old Breed*, 1981. Copyright (c) 1981 E.B. Sledge

USMC Correspondent, *US Marines on Iwo Jima*, 1945. Copyright (c) The Dial Press Inc. and Infantry Journal

Cornell, Douglas B., Associated Press, 20 April 1945. Copyright (c) AP 1945

Taylor, Geoffrey, *Voices from Britain*, ed Henning Krabbe, 1947

Truman, Harry S., *Off the Record: The Private Papers of Harry S. Truman*, 1986. Copyright (c) the estate of Harry S. Truman

Tibbets, Colonel, quoted in *The World at War*, Mark Arnold-Forster, 1989. Copyright (c) 1973, 1981 Thames TV Ltd

Andrews, Maxine, *The Good War: An Oral History of World War II*, Studs Terkel, 1984

Miller, Arthur, *Timebends*, 1987. Copyright (c) 1987 Arthur Miller

Thompson, Reginald, *Cry Korea*, 1951

Hellman, Lillian, *Scoundrel Time*, 1976

Morrin, Relman, Associated Press, 3 September 1957. Copyright (c) AP 1957

Galbraith, J.K.

Kennedy, Robert F., *13 Days: the Cuban Missile Crisis October 1962*, 1969

Ryder, Vincent & David Shears, *Daily Telegraph* 30 August 1963

Smith, Merriman, UPI 23 November 1963. Copyright (c) UPI 1963

Cleaver, Eldridge, *Soul on Ice*, 1968. Copyright (c) 1968 Eldridge Cleaver

Herr, Michael, *Dispatches*, 1977. Copyright (c) 1977 Michael Herr. Reprinted by permission of Macmillan

Time, 5 December 1969. Copyright (c) Time Inc. 1969

Cooke, Alistair, *Guardian* 9 April 1968. Copyright (c) the Guardian 1968

Ransom Jnr, Robert, *Dear America: Letters Home from Vietnam*, ed Bernard Edelman, 1985. Copyright (c) 1985 The New York Vietnam Veterans Memorial Commission

Bowman, David, *Dear America* ibid

Homiski, Stanley, *Letters from Vietnam*, grunt.space.swri.edul/letters. Copyright (c) 1997 Stanley Homiski

Morrisey, James, *Dear America*, op cit

Cooke, Alistair

Armstrong, Neil, and Buzz Aldrin, quoted in the *New York Times*, 21 July 1969

Nixon, Richard, *The Memoirs of Richard Nixon*, 1978

Mailer, Norman, *The Fight*, 1974. Copyright (c) Norman Mailer 1974

Pilger, John, *The Last Day*, 1975. Copyright (c) 1975 John Pilger. Reprinted by permission of MSI

Schmitt, Eric, *New York Times*, 24 February 1991

West Coast Correspondent, *Economist*, 5 May 1992

Jones, Ken, *The Independent*, 30 June 1997. Copyright The Independent (UK) Ltd 1997

Mendoza, Martha, Associated Press December 1998. Copyright (c) 1988 AP

Graczyk, Michael, Associated Press 3 February 1999. Copyright (c) 1999 AP

McManus, Doyle, *Los Angeles Times*, 13 February 1999. Copyright (c) 1999 Times Mirror Inc

Longino, Bob, *The Atlanta-Journal Constitution*, 3 May 1999. Copyright (c) The Atlanta-Journal Constitution

Picciotto, Richard 'Pitch' (with Daniel Paisner), *Last Man Down*, 2002. Copyright (c) 2002 Richard Picciotto